BY THE PEOPLE

DEBATING AMERICAN GOVERNMENT

:S A. MORONE
Brown University

ROGAN KERSH
Wake Forest University

THIRD EDITION

BY THE PEOPLE

DEBATING AMERICAN GOVERNMENT

NEW YORK   OXFORD
OXFORD UNIVERSITY PRESS

Oxford University Press is a department of the University of Oxford.
It furthers the University's objective of excellence in research,
scholarship, and education by publishing worldwide. Oxford is a
registered trademark of Oxford University Press in the UK and
certain other countries.

Published in the United States of America by Oxford University Press
198 Madison Avenue, New York, NY 10016, United States of America.

Cataloging-in-Publication Data is on file at the Library of Congress
ISBN 978-0-19-029841-8

9 8 7 6 5 4 3 2 1

Printed by LSC Communications, United States of America

Many teachers and colleagues inspired us. We dedicate this book to four who changed our lives. Their passion for learning and teaching set the standard we aim for every day—and on every page that follows.

Richard O'Donnell

Murray Dry

Jim Barefield

Rogers Smith

By the People comes from the Gettysburg Address. Standing on the battlefield at Gettysburg, President Abraham Lincoln delivered what may be the most memorable presidential address in American history—defining American government as a government "of the people, by the people, for the people." Here is the full address.

Four score and seven years ago our fathers brought forth on this continent, a new nation, conceived in liberty, and dedicated to the proposition that all men are created equal.

Now we are engaged in a great civil war, testing whether that nation, or any nation so conceived and so dedicated, can long endure. We are met on a great battle-field of that war. We have come to dedicate a portion of that field, as a final resting place for those who here gave their lives that that nation might live. It is altogether fitting and proper that we should do this.

But, in a larger sense, we can not dedicate—we can not consecrate—we can not hallow—this ground. The brave men, living and dead, who struggled here, have consecrated it, far above our poor power to add or detract. The world will little note, nor long remember what we say here, but it can never forget what they did here. It is for us the living, rather, to be dedicated here to the unfinished work which they who fought here have thus far so nobly advanced. It is rather for us to be here dedicated to the great task remaining before us—that from these honored dead we take increased devotion to that cause for which they gave the last full measure of devotion—that we here highly resolve that these dead shall not have died in vain—that this nation, under God, shall have a new birth of freedom—and that government of the people, by the people, for the people, shall not perish from the earth.

About the Authors

JAMES MORONE (BA, Middlebury College, MA and PhD, University of Chicago) is the John Hazen White Professor of Political Science and Public Policy at Brown University and five-time winner of the Hazeltine Citation for outstanding teacher of the year. Dr. Morone, an award-winning author, has published ten books, including *The Heart of Power* (2009, a "*New York Times* Notable Book"), *Hellfire Nation* (2003, nominated for a Pulitzer Prize), and *The Democratic Wish* (1990, winner of the American Political Science Association's Kammerer Award for the best book on American politics). He has written over 150 articles and essays, and has commented on politics in the *New York Times*, the *London Review of Books*, and the *American Prospect*. Dr. Morone has been elected to the National Academy of Medicine and the National Academy of Social Insurance. He has served as president of the politics and history section of the American Political Science Association and the New England Political Science Association. He also has served on the board of editors for eight scholarly journals.

ROGAN KERSH (BA, Wake Forest University, MA and PhD, Yale University) is provost and professor of political science at Wake Forest University. A leading scholar in American political science, Dr. Kersh is best known for his work on health reform, obesity politics, and interest groups/lobbying. As a political science faculty member at Syracuse from 1996 to 2006, he won three different teaching awards; from 2006 to 2012, as associate dean of New York University's Wagner School of Public Service, he won both the Wagner and NYU's teaching awards, as well as the Martin Luther King Jr. Award for scholarship, teaching, and university service. Dr. Kersh has published two books and more than fifty academic articles and has provided commentary on U.S. politics for dozens of different media outlets including CNN, *Newsweek*, and the *New York Times*. He was president of the American Political Science Association's organized section on health politics and policy in 2011–2012 and is an elected fellow of the National Academy of Public Administration.

Preface

At first, they came in small numbers: one child, two children, a few huddled together. Then a surge: In the spring and summer of 2014, more than 63,000 unaccompanied minors crossed the Mexican border into the United States. The exhausted children—mostly from Honduras, Guatemala, and El Salvador—faced poverty and violence at home. Their exodus was a humanitarian tragedy. But it was also a political problem.

Conservative critics of the Barack Obama administration slammed the White House for not acting sooner to stem the tide and for being "soft on immigration." Donald Trump launched his long-shot presidential bid, a year later, with a tough attack on undocumented migrants. From the left, another set of voices condemned the president for not providing services to children whose families were so desperate they would send them alone across dangerous ground to an uncertain destiny. Whatever course the administration took, it faced angry rebukes.

As partisans traded insults and pundits criticized the government's mistakes, something remarkable happened: Americans of all backgrounds—urban and rural, churched and secular, liberal and conservative—came together to help the children. College students and local residents joined to hand out medical kits and food packets. Lawyers flew in to offer free legal assistance in securing asylum. Church leaders created makeshift shelters and organized short-term housing among the congregants. One bishop in San Antonio, Texas, said the crisis had deepened his prayer life. This is a classic story that runs right through American history: People pull together in the face of troubled times.

Help or Clash?

That's the United States in a nutshell. People pitch in. This is a nation of joiners and helpers and activists. It always has been. Visitors in the nineteenth century were astonished by the nation's civic spirit. To this day Americans form book groups, organize car washes to raise money for good causes, stack sandbags during floods, send checks to the Red Cross, support the military, and insist that the government help those who need help. "We are inevitably our brother's keeper because we are our brother's brother," wrote Martin Luther King. "Whatever affects one directly affects all indirectly."[1]

But that's only one side of the story. Stream a news show and what do you see? Fights! A few years ago, one of us (Jim) was about to go on a news show to discuss the fallout after singer Janet Jackson inadvertently (and very briefly) went X-rated during the Super Bowl halftime show. Jim was scheduled alongside another commentator who was very agitated about Jackson's behavior and believed that it signaled the decline of America. Jim told the producer that, after exploring our different views, it would be great if we could find some common ground. No way, retorted the producer, who explained her ideal closing shot: You'll be shouting over each other on a split screen while the host coolly ends the segment by saying, "We'll have to leave it there for now, but feelings run high and we'll be hearing a lot more on this topic." Unfortunately, searching for common ground does not draw an audience like people screaming onscreen.

The producer was demonstrating another side of America: rugged individualists who push their own views and self-interests. Individualism is also an all-American story. Its origins lie in a frontier culture that expected everyone to watch out for themselves. This is the America that resents anyone—especially the government—telling people what to do.

Which is the real America? They both are. Sometimes this is a land of cooperation, sometimes a nation of competition. American politics, as you will see, reflects both views.

By the People?

We picked the book's title—*By the People*—because Lincoln's phrase raises the deepest question in American politics: Who has the power? Or to put it more pointedly, do the people rule in this day and age? Democracy is a constant struggle; it is an aspiration, a wish, a quest. In every chapter we'll ask how well Americans are living up to Lincoln's ideal. Does the new media (Chapter 9) or the contemporary Congress (Chapter 13) or the bureaucracy (Chapter 15) or state government (Chapter 4) support or subvert government by the people? We'll present the details—and let you decide whether we should press for reform or leave things alone.

We'll be straight with you: We won't pretend there was a golden age in some imaginary past. After all, the United States has been home to political machines that enthusiastically stole votes, maintains an Electoral College designed to distort the people's vote for president, and governs through an elaborate system of checks and balances that blunts the popular will. (Again, you'll soon see two sides to each of these features of American government.) At the same time, you'll read about bold popular movements and unexpected electoral surges that changed the face of the nation. In many ways, these are the most exciting moments in American history. They spring up at unexpected times, inspiring ordinary people to achieve great things. Does Donald Trump's election signify such a surge? Or are the protest movements that have sprung up the larger agent of change? Read on and you'll be able to answer those questions—and many more.

---

[1] *Where Do We Go from Here: Chaos or Community?* (New York: Harper & Row, 1967) 181.

Who Are We?

Here's Jim's very first political memory: My parents were watching TV, and as soon as I walked into the room I could see that my mother was trying hard not to cry. "What's going on?" I asked my parents nervously. My dad—a proud Republican who had fought in World War II—said, "Well, the U.S. had a racial problem, but that man there, he's going to get us past it." "That man there" was Martin Luther King Jr., giving one of the most famous speeches in American history: "I have a dream," said King, that "my four little children will one day live in a country where they will not be judged by the color of their skin but by the content of their character." My mother had been born in Poland and her near tears reflected pride in her new nation—and the uplifting aspirations of that August day.

Both of us grew up thinking about the dream—and about the nation that dreams it. America is constantly changing, constantly new. In every chapter we'll ask the same question: Who are we? We'll explore a lot of different answers.

Four themes are especially important in this book. **Race** touches everything in the United States, from the Constitution (Chapter 3) to our political parties (Chapter 11). The nation rose up out of both freedom and slavery; race quickly became one of the great crucibles of American liberty. Likewise, **immigration** includes some of history's saddest passages involving the mistreatment of recent arrivals. And yet we are a nation of immigrants that continues to welcome the world's "huddled masses yearning to breathe free"—the famous words long associated with the Statue of Liberty. More than a fifth of all the emigrants around the globe come to the United States every year. Race and immigration are tied up in another powerful topic: **gender and sexuality**. From women in Congress to same-sex marriage, from teen pregnancy to abortion, we'll show how negotiating an answer to "Who are we?" always puts an emphasis on questions of gender and sexuality. Finally, we're especially interested in **American generations**, and more specifically the attitudes and contributions of today's young people, the millennial generation. If you're one of them, the future belongs to you. This book is an owner's manual for the government that you're going to inherit. We'll have much to say about you as we go along.

The most important thing about all these categories is not their history, or the ways they've influenced voting behavior, or how the courts treat them—although we'll cover all those topics. Rather, what matters most about American politics are the opportunities to get involved. As you'll see, groups and individuals can and do make a difference in a nation that is always evolving. We hope our book inspires you to actively participate in making the American future.

How Government Works

We won't oversell the role of individuals. People's ability to advance political change is always shaped by the way the government is organized and operates. From the very start, this book emphasizes the unusual structure of American government.

Begin with a Constitution full of checks and balances, add a multilayered federalism, develop a chaotic public administration (President Franklin Roosevelt cheerfully called the uproar a three-ring circus), spin off functions to the private sector (especially during wars), complexify Congress (thirty-one different committees and subcommittees tried to claim jurisdiction over just one national health insurance proposal), and inject state and federal courts into every cranny of the system. Then throw the entire apparatus open to any interest group that shows up.

The twenty-first century adds a 24/7 news cycle with commentary all the time and from every angle.

Turn to foreign policy, where high principles contend with tough-minded realism in a fractious world. When the most formidable military in human history is mustered into action, watch presidential power expand so rapidly that it sets off international debates about whether the great republic is morphing into an empire.

In Short

As you read this book, you'll repeatedly encounter four questions:

- *Who governs?* This is the question of democracy and power—or, as we phrased it earlier: Is this government by the people? And if and where it falls short, how might we refresh our democracy?

- *How does American politics work?* Our job is to make you think like a political scientist. What does that involve? You'll learn in the next chapter—and throughout the book.

- *What does government do?* You can't answer the first two questions if you don't know what the courts or the White House or Congress or interest groups actually do—and how they do it.

- *Who are we?* Americans endlessly debate America's identity. We are students, businesspeople, Hispanics, seniors, Texans, environmentalists, gays, Republicans, Democrats, Christians, Muslims, military families—and the list goes on. Sometimes it adds up to one united people; at other times we're left to wonder how to get along. Either way, American politics rises up from—and shapes—a cacophony of identities and interests.

Changes to the Third Edition

In this new edition, we have,

- Analyzed recent seismic events that have shaken up our institutions, ideas, and interests alongside new and updated statistics and figures in each chapter to track slower moving, but influential, trends.

- Analyzed the raucous 2016 primary and general election season.

- Explored the Black Lives Matter movement that reached into campuses where students engaged in an active questioning of First Amendment rights.

- Assessed the Tea Party's breaching of the Republican Party and changes within both parties.

- Considered the ramifications of the unexpected death of a justice that left the fate of a deeply divided Supreme Court in the hands of the first Republican majority in eight years.

- Examined the dissolution of nation–states in the Middle East with the outbreak of a Sunni–Shia regional war.

- Added an entirely new section on how federalism evolved during the Obama administration, using the term *progressive federalism* to indicate the increased tendency to set goals at the national level but rely on states to implement these goals, whether related to education, healthcare, or other policy areas.

- Provided updated and new statistics on the growing income gap and its political ramifications including a new graph showing that the middle class is losing ground relative to upper and lower classes, an analysis of current views of the American Dream, and assessment of the NAFTA and TTIP debates.

- Incorporated new data on millennial trends regarding party affiliation, attitudes, and involvement in the types of participation.

- Added coverage of government-sponsored cyberwarfare.

- Revised terrorism coverage extensively alongside new discussions of the role of the media and the handling of recent terrorist attacks in light of bureaucratic pathologies and updated discussions on contact with forbidden groups, the reauthorization of the Patriot Act, and the ending of the NSA's collection of telecommunication data.

- Added new section on in-depth analysis of how far we have come in granting civil rights by examining voting rights, income, poverty rates, health, life expectancy, and incarceration rates. This highlights the Supreme Court ruling on the Voting Rights Act and voter turnout.

- Switched the order of Chapters 7 and 8 to better integrate concepts of political socialization and public opinion shifts into our understanding of trends in political participation.

Getting Involved

By the People is a new approach to courses in American government. The book displays U.S. politics and government in all its glory, messiness, and power. Like every textbook, this one informs our readers. But, as we hope you can already see, we don't describe government (or ideas about government) as inert and fixed. What's exciting about American politics, like the nation itself, is how fast it changes. And the constant, endless arguments about what it is and what it should be next. Our aim is to get you engaged—whether you already love politics, are a complete newcomer to government, or whether you are a newcomer to the United States itself. In the pages that follow, we'll bring American government to life. Get ready to start a great debate . . . about your future.

One final word: We've been working out the story line for this book throughout our teaching careers. We've taught everything from very large lectures to small seminars. Like all teachers, we've learned through trial and error. We've worked hard to pack this book with the stories, questions, and features that all our students have found effective. That spirit—the lessons we've learned in the classroom—animates everything that follows.

Ensuring Student Success

Oxford University Press offers instructors and students a comprehensive ancillary package for qualified adopters of *By the People*.

- **Dashboard with LeaP (www.oup.com/us/dashboard)** is Oxford University Press's nationally hosted learning management system. Designed to offer students and instructors maximum flexibility, numerous assessment options, a variety of interactive content organized by chapter, and adaptive learning tools, this learning management system offers best in-class, cutting-edge functionality

- **Maximum Flexibility:** Dashboard with LeaP offers a variety of ways for students to interact with their course material so they can spend more time learning by studying smarter.
  - **Read and Learn:** Students can read our new **enhanced eBook,** work on interactive media activities, review concept tutorials, and watch videos—helping them to learn and retain key concepts, **OR . . .**
  - Students can complete a **Learning Path Pretest**, follow their **customized learning path**, and prioritize their time on mastering challenging content and concepts, **OR . . .**
  - Students can take **multiple quizzes** with five different quiz options, **OR . . .**
  - **Students can choose what works for them** and simply complete chapter-level media exercises and quizzes.
- **Numerous Assessment Options:** Every chapter has at least five chapter-level tests to help your students learn—and not memorize—important concepts.
  - **Check My Learning**
  - **Key Concepts Quiz**
  - **Chapter Quiz**
  - **Chapter Exam**
  - **LeaP Learning Path Pretest**
- **Available anytime/anywhere:** Everything is in one place, and is accessible from any device, anywhere students can get connected.
- **Interactive Content:** Students have access to 70 videos, 12 Interactive Media Activities, 10 "A Closer Look" Media Tutorials, adaptive quizzing, and Key Terms Flashcards.

For more information about Dashboard with LeaP, and ordering information, contact your Oxford University Press Representative or call 800.280.0280

Interactive Media Activities, available on Dashboard and on Morone/Kersh's Free and Open Companion Website (www.oup.com/us/morone), are designed to reinforce key concepts with real-world situations. Each activity:

- Takes 15 to 20 minutes to complete, and produces unique results for each student
- Enables students to experience how politics works, seeing the trade-offs required to produce meaningful policies and outcomes
- Is optimized to work on any mobile device or computer
- Ends with Assessments to connect the activity to classroom discussions

Interactive Media Activities include:

- NEW—Individualism vs. Solidarity
- Passing Immigration Reform
- Electing Cheryl Martin
- Building the USS *Relief*
- Intervening in Bhutan
- The Fight Against Warrantless Wiretapping
- Balancing the Budget

- NEW—Redistricting in "Texachusetts"
- NEW—Saving the Electric Car
- Election Reform
- NEW—Fact-checking the Media
- NEW-Passing the Thirteenth Amendment
- NEW—Negotiating with China

NEW—A Closer Look **Media Tutorials:** Available on Dashboard and on the *By the People*, Third Edition, Free and Open Companion Website (**www.oup.com/us/morone**), these activities are designed to teach key concepts and help students master important, High-interest class material. Each tutorial runs 3–5 minutes and ends with assessment opportunities students to test what they know. Topics include:

- The Constitution: A Brief Tour
- Civil Rights: How does the Fourteenth Amendment ensure equal rights for all Citizens?
- Federalism: What does it mean to Incorporate the Bill of Rights?
- Political Participation: What affects voter turnout?
- Media: How is the news shaped by agenda setting, framing, and profit bias?
- Interest Groups: What is a Political Action Committee (PAC), and what makes some PACs Super PACs?
- Congress: Why do we hate Congress but keep electing the same representatives?
- The Judiciary: How do judges interpret the Constitution?
- Polling: How do we know what people know?
- Campaigns and Elections: How does gerrymandering work?

Companion website at www.oup.com/us/morone: This open-access companion website includes a number of learning tools to help students study and review key concepts presented in the text, including learning objectives, key-concept summaries, quizzes, essay questions, web activities, and web links.

Ancillary Resource Center (ARC): This convenient, instructor-focused website provides access to all of the up-to-date teaching resources for this text while guaranteeing the security of grade-significant resources. In addition, it allows Oxford University Press to keep instructors informed when new content becomes available. Register for access and create your individual user account by visiting **www.oup.com/us/morone**.

The following items are available on the ARC:

- **Instructor's Manual and Test Bank:** includes chapter objectives, detailed chapter outlines, lecture, suggestions and activities, discussion questions, and video and web resources. The test bank includes multiple-choice, short answer, and essay questions.
- **Computerized Test Bank:** utilizes Diploma, a test-authoring and management tool. Diploma is designed for both novice and advanced users and enables instructors to create and edit questions, compose randomized quizzes and tests with an intuitive drag-and-drop tool, post quizzes and tests to online courses, and print quizzes and tests for paper-based assessments.

- **Downloadable and customizable PowerPoint slides:** includes one set for in-class presentations and the other for text images
- **Access to thirty CNN videos** correlated to the chapter topics of the text. Each clip is approximately five to ten minutes long, offering a great way to launch your lecture
- **Clicker questions** to be used in conjunction with any classroom response system

Course Cartridges containing student and instructor resources are available through Angel, Blackboard, Canvas, D2L, Moodle, Respondus, or whatever course management system you prefer.

Now Playing: Learning American Government Through Film: Through documentaries, feature films, and YouTube videos, *Now Playing: Learning American Government Through Film* provides a variety of suggested video examples that illustrate concepts covered in the text. Each video is accompanied by a brief summary and discussion questions. It is available in both a student and an instructor version and can be packaged with *By the People*, Third Edition, for free.

Format Choices: Oxford University Press offers cost-saving alternatives to meet the needs of all students. This text is offered in a Loose-leaf format at a 30% discount off the list price of the text; and in an eBook format, through CourseSmart, for a 50% discount. You can also customize our textbooks to create the course material you want for your class. For more information, please contact your Oxford University Press sale representative, call 800.280.0280, or visit us online at www .oup.com/us/morone.

Packaging Options

Adopters of *By the People* can package *any* Oxford University Press book with the text for a twenty percent savings off the total package price. See our many trade and scholarly offerings at www.oup.com, then contact your local OUP sales representative to request a package ISBN. In addition, the following items can be packaged with the text for free:

- *Now Playing: Learning American Government Through Film*: ISBN 9780190233358
- Williams, *Research and Writing Guide for Political Science*: ISBN 9780190243548
- Dashboard: ISBN 9780190237677

We also encourage the following texts for packaging:

- Very Short Introduction Series:
  - Valelly, *American Politics*
  - Crick, *Democracy*
  - Boyer, *American History*
- Lindsay, *Investigating American Democracy: Readings on Core Questions*
- Niven, *Barack Obama: A Pocket Biography of Our 44th President*
- Wilkins, *Questioning Numbers: How to Read and Critique Research*

Acknowledgments

When he signed us up to write this book, publisher John Challice looked us each in the eye and said, "You know, this is going to be so much work—you're going to be married to us." He was right. Yes, it was a lot of work. And yes, the Oxford team has been like a family that carried us through the process.

There would be no book without Jennifer Carpenter, our extraordinary editor. She guided us through the process with enormous skill. Along the way, Jen earned the highest praise authors can give their editor: She cared about the book as much as we did. Our development editor, Naomi Friedman, helped us so much she ought to be considered a coauthor—she suggested, edited, cut, and cheered. Ryan Emenaker, a political scientist at the College of the Redwoods, was a remarkable partner for the third edition—Ryan helped us organize, research, and write. Development manager Thom Holmes gracefully turned our messy manuscript into a tight narrative bursting with special features. Assistant editor Matt Rohal guided the art program and tracked down every picture in the following pages. Production manager Roxanne Klaas coordinated an amazing production process; we broke the publishing record for the number of times two authors wrote, "Good point!" in the margins of an edited manuscript. Judy Ann Levine did a fine copyedit on an impossible schedule. Art director Michele Laseau did the beautiful design. We are especially grateful to marketing manager Tony Mathias for getting this book into your hands. To all of you in our immediate Oxford family: Thank you! Thank you!

We had an even more important team at our side—our families and our friends. Over the course of this book's initial conception and subsequent writing, Rogan moved from Syracuse University's Maxwell School to New York University's Wagner School, with a sabbatical leave at Yale along the way—and then, just as we were finishing the first edition, to Wake Forest University. Colleagues in all four places were unfailingly generous with ideas and comments; thanks especially to Suzanne Mettler, Jeff Stonecash, David Mayhew, Ellen Schall, Shanna Rose, and Shankar Prasad. Because we strive throughout to get both the political science and the practical politics right, a group of experienced and reflective inside-the-Beltway friends cheerfully and patiently provided insight into their world: Bill Antholis, Matt Bennett, Laura Schiller, Erik Fatemi, Tom Dobbins, Dan Maffei, Bob Shrum, Marylouise Oates, and Don and Darrel Jodrey. Grateful thanks to them as well as a wonderful set of current and former students, many now working in government and politics.

By the People's long journey to completion grew infinitely more enjoyable once Sara Pesek joined me for the trip—through this book and everywhere else, from Australia to Ze Café in midtown New York City. Sara's insights into public policy made for the liveliest newlyweds' conversations (if you're a politics junkie) imaginable; my biggest bouquet of thanks to her for that rarest of gifts: loving, fully joined partnership.

Jim offers warm thanks to my colleagues at Brown who form a wonderful community of scholars and teachers—always ready for coffee, lunch, or wine and a conversation about political science. Extra thanks to Peter Andreas, Mark Blyth, Corey Brettschneider, Ross Cheit, Elisabeth Fauquert, Alex Gourevitch, Rebecca Henderson, Bonnie Honig, Sharon Krause, Rick Locke, Susan Moffitt, Rich Snyder, Wendy Schiller, and Ashu Varshney. And my wonderful students sampled every idea in this book. They are my constant teachers. Grateful thanks to Ryan Emenaker, Dan Carrigg, Kevin McGravey, Ferris Lupino, Rachel Meade, Meghan Wilson, Aaron Weinstein, Brandon Welch, and Cadence Willse.

My brothers, Joe and Peter Morone—and their families—are lifelong companions always ready with a cheerful take on the state of politics and the world. Special thanks to Lindsay, Ann, Joe, James (now a rising political scientist at Penn), Noreen, and Maegan Morone. My mother, Stasia, kept reminding me to enjoy the journey—and that there might be more to life than *By the People*. And the memory of my dad was a constant visitor as I read, and thought, and wrote. The revisions for this edition were joyfully interrupted by Jim's wedding. If you detect a smile between the lines, it's because we were celebrating my new family. Rebecca Henderson leapt into my life filling it with talk and ideas and dreams (and much more). And Harry, my wonderful son, takes me hiking and talks me through high ridges that I couldn't imagine trying without him. If this edition reads happier than the last—it's the spirit of Harry and Rebecca on the pages.

Manuscript Reviewers

We have greatly benefited from the perceptive comments and suggestions of the many talented scholars and instructors who reviewed the manuscript of *By the People*. They went far beyond the call of duty in sharing thoughts and making corrections. Their insight and suggestions contributed immensely to the work.

Third Edition

Bryan T. Calvin
Tarrant County College, Northwest

John Carnes
Lone Star College–Kingwood

Rosalind Blanco Cook
Tulane University

Paul B. Davis
Truckee Meadows Community College

Michael Dichio
Fort Lewis College

Dawn Eaton
San Jacinto College South

Kathleen Ferraiolo
James Madison University

Ingrid Haas
University of Nebraska–Lincoln

James Hite
Portland State University

Jeneen Hobby
Cleveland State University

Michael Hoover
Seminole State College

Daniel Hummel
Idaho State University

Nina Kasniunas
Goucher College

Nicholas LaRowe
University of Southern Indiana

Brad Lockerbie
East Carolina University

A. Lanethea Mathews-Schultz
Muhlenberg College

Don Mirjanian
College of Southern Nevada

Carolyn Myers
Southwestern Illinois College

Hong Min Park
University of Wisconsin–Milwaukee

Marjorie K. Nanian
Schoolcraft College

Coyle Neal
Southwest Baptist University

Paul Parker
Truman State University

Jane Rainey
Eastern Kentucky University

Joseph Romance
Fort Hays State University

Michael Romano
Georgia Southern University

Jennifer Sacco
Quinnipiac University

Eric Schwartz
Hagerstown Community College

Daniel Lavon Spinks
Stephen F. Austin State University

Jeffrey M. Stonecash
Syracuse University

Kathleen Tipler
University of Oklahoma

Carl Wege
Social Sciences College of Coastal Georgia

Geoffrey Willbanks
Tyler Junior College

Second Edition

Nathan Blank
Casper College, University of Wyoming, Kentucky Community & Technical College System

Nichole Boutte-Heiniluoma
Jarvis Christian College

Blake Farrar
Texas State University

Jennifer Felmley
Santa Fe Community College

Paul Foote
Eastern Kentucky University

Jeneen Hobby
Cleveland State University

Gary Johnson
Weber State University

Steven Nawara
Valdosta State University

Geoffrey Peterson
University of Wisconsin–Eau Claire

Ronald C. Schurin
University of Connecticut

John Shively
Longview Community College

Toni-Michelle C. Travis
George Mason University

First Edition

Brian A. Bearry
University of Texas at Dallas

Emily Bentley
Savannah State University

R. M. Bittick
Sam Houston State University

Wendell S. Broadwell Jr.
Georgia Perimeter College

Allison Bunnell
Fitchburg State University

Frank P. Cannatelli
Southern Connecticut State University

Jason P. Casellas
University of Texas at Austin

Stefanie Chambers
Trinity College, Hartford, Connecticut

Suzanne Chod
Pennsylvania State University

Michael Cobb
North Carolina State University

McKinzie Craig
Texas A&M University

Michael Crespin
University of Georgia

Amanda DiPaolo
Middle Tennessee State University

Stewart Dippel
University of the Ozarks

Jasmine Farrier
University of Louisville

Michaela Fazecas
University of Central Florida

Joseph J. Foy
University of Wisconsin–Parkside

Megan Francis
Pepperdine University

Rodd Freitag
University of Wisconsin–Eau Claire

Joseph Gardner
Northern Arizona University

David Goldberg
College of DuPage

Frederick Gordon
Columbus State University

Jeff Harmon
University of Texas at San Antonio

Jeneen Hobby
Cleveland State University

Mark S. Jendrysik
University of North Dakota

Brian Kessel
Columbia College

Christopher L. Kukk
Western Connecticut State University

Sujith Kumar
University of Central Arkansas

Lisa Langenbach
Middle Tennessee State University

William W. Laverty
University of Michigan–Flint

Jeffrey Lazarus
Georgia State University

Angela K. Lewis
University of Alabama
at Birmingham

Gregg Lindskog
Temple University

Brent A. Lucas
North Carolina State University

Thomas R. Marshall
University of Texas at Arlington

A. Lanethea Mathews
Muhlenberg College

Vaughn May
Belmont University

Lauri McNown
University of Colorado at Boulder

Christina A. Medina
New Mexico State University

Patrick R. Miller
University of Cincinnati

Michael K. Moore
University of Texas at Arlington

Roger Morton
California State University,
Long Beach

Yamini Munipalli
Florida State College at Jacksonville

Gary Mucciaroni
Temple University

Jason Mycoff
University of Delaware

Steven Nawara
Valdosta State University

Anthony Neal
Buffalo State College

Mark Nicol
Saginaw Valley State University

Stephen A. Nuño
Northern Arizona University

Michael Parkin
Oberlin College

Richard Pious
Barnard College

Elizabeth A. Prough
Eastern Michigan University

Wesley B. Renfro
St. John Fisher College

John F. Roche, III
Palomar College

Amanda M. Rosen
Webster University

Anjali Sahay
Gannon University

Joanna Vecchiarelli Scott
Eastern Michigan University

Samuel Shelton
Troy University

Majid Shirali
University of Nevada, Las Vegas

Joyce Stickney Smith
Hillsborough Community College,
Ybor Campus

Mitchel A. Sollenberger
University of Michigan–Dearborn

Chris Soper
Pepperdine University

Barry L. Tadlock
Ohio University

Edwin A. Taylor, III
Missouri Western State University

Delaina Toothman
Texas State University

Jan P. Vermeer
Nebraska Wesleyan University

Jennifer E. Walsh
Azusa Pacific University

Donn Worgs
Towson University

Larry L. Wright
Florida A&M University

Shoua Yang
St. Cloud State University

Mike Yawn
Sam Houston State University

Melanie C. Young
University of Nevada, Las Vegas

Khodr M. Zaarour
Shaw University

Marketing Reviewers

Oxford University Press would also like to acknowledge the contribution of additional scholars and instructors who class tested and provided their assessment of the completed manuscript, using this work with hundreds of students in classrooms across the nation.

Second Edition

Ted Anagnoson
University of California, Santa Barbara

Steven Bayne
Century College

Joshua Berkenpas
Western Michigan University

Jeff Bloodworth
Gannon University

Theodore C. Brown
Virginia State University

Kim Casey
Northwest Missouri State University

Jay Cerrato
Bronx Community College

Ericka Christensen
Washington State University

Kevin Davis
North Central Texas College—Corinth

Dennis Driggers
California State University, Fresno

Paul Gottemoller
Del Mar College

Sara Gubala
Lamar University

Dan Guerrant
Middle Georgia College

Timothy Kersey
Kennesaw State University

Michael Latner
California Polytechnic State University

Maruice Mangum
Texas Southern University

Donna Merrell
Kennesaw State University

Patrick Moore
Richland College

Martha Musgrove
Tarrant County College—Southeast Campus

Michael Petersen
Utah State University

Mikhail Rybalko
Texas Tech University

Joanna Sabo
Monroe County Community College

Hayden Smith
Washington State University

First Edition

Gayle Alberda
Owens Community College

Herrick Arnold
Orange Coast College

Alex L. Avila
Mesa Community College

John Barnes
University of Southern California

Charles Barrilleaux
Florida State University

Ronald Bee
Cuyamaca College

Michael Berkman
Pennsylvania State University

Angelina M. Cavallo
San Jacinto College

Adam Chamberlain
Coastal Carolina University

Matt Childers
University of Georgia

Benjamin Christ
Harrisburg Area Community College

Diana Cohen
Central Connecticut State University

Paul M. Collins
University of North Texas

William Corbett
New Mexico State University

Mark Ellickson
Missouri State University

Deborah Ferrell-Lynn
University of Central Oklahoma

Paul Foote
Eastern Kentucky University

Peter L. Francia
East Carolina University

Rodd Freitag
University of Wisconsin–Eau Claire

Fred Gordon
Columbus State University

John I. Hanley
Syracuse University

Jeff Hilmer
Northern Arizona University

Jeneen Hobby
Cleveland State University

Ronald J. Hrebenar
University of Utah

Mark Jendrysik
University of North Dakota

Aubrey Jewett
University of Central Florida

Gary Johnson
Weber State University

Michelle Keck
The University of Texas at Brownsville

William Kelly
Auburn University

John Klemanski
Oakland University

Richard Krupa
Harper College

Christine Lipsmeyer
Texas A&M University

Brent Lucas
North Carolina State University

Margaret MacKenzie
San Jacinto College

Jason McDaniel
San Francisco State University

John Mercurio
San Diego State University

Melissa Merry
University of Louisville

Roger Morton
California State University, Long Beach

Gary Mucciaroni
Temple University

Adam J. Newmark
Appalachian State University

Randall Newnham
Pennsylvania State University

Roger Nichols
Southwestern College

Anthony J. Nownes
University of Tennessee, Knoxville

Anthony O'Regan
Los Angeles Valley College

Kenneth O'Reilly
Milwaukee Area Technical College

Sunday P. Obazuaye
Cerritos College

Amanda M. Olejarski
Shippensburg University

Kevin Parsneau
Minnesota State University

Michelle Pautz
University of Dayton

Martin J. Plax
Cleveland State University

Sherri Replogle
Illinois State University

Kim Rice
Western Illinois University

Ray Sandoval
Dallas County Community College
District

Laura Schneider
Grand Valley State University

Scot Schraufnagel
Northern Illinois University

Ronnee Schreiber
San Diego State University

Ronald Schurin
University of Connecticut

Jeffrey M. Stonecash
Syracuse University

Katrina Taylor
Northern Arizona University

Ryan Lee Teten
University of Louisiana

John P. Todsen
Drake University

Delaina Toothman
University of Maine

Dan Urman
Northeastern University

Ronald W. Vardy
University of Houston

Adam L. Warber
Clemson University

Gerald Watkins
Kentucky Community & Technical
College System

Patrick Wohlfarth
University of Maryland, College Park

Wayne L. Wolf
South Suburban College

Jeff Worsham
West Virginia University

Finally, thanks to you for picking up this book. We hope you enjoy reading it as much as we did writing.

Jim Morone and Rogan Kersh

BY THE PEOPLE

DEBATING AMERICAN GOVERNMENT

Brief Contents

Contents

MOST RECENT CHANGES
1. Replaces the Adding and Dropping Classes Policy, Auditing Classes Policy and Incomplete Grade Policy.
2. Implements 'no late' registration.
3. Eliminates the instructor-initiated 'W'.

I. POLICY PURPOSE

The purpose of this policy is to set deadlines for class registration and withdrawal. It also sets the criteria for late-registration, the grade of "Incomplete", and for auditing classes.

II. POLICY STATEMENT

A. Course Registration

1. Registration in a class must be completed by 11:59 p.m. on the day before the session (as defined in Attachment B-Glossary) begins.
2. Exceptions to registration deadline:
   a. Exceptions are limited to:
      i. Restricted courses requiring permission of instructor
      ii. Courses requiring auditions or try-outs
      iii. Courses for Special Populations or Cohorts, including but not limited to Jump Start and courses designated in a Memorandum of Understanding
      iv. Students dropped due to human or system errors made by the institution including a delay in financial aid awards caused by the institution
      v. Courses that were cancelled within 6 days of the start of the session
   b. Exceptions require permission of appropriate instructor(s) and the department chair. The communications can be done via email or official form. The student must be enrolled in the class by the end of the first week of the session.

B. Course Withdrawal

PLEASE NOTE: Before withdrawing from a course, students are strongly encouraged to discuss their decisions with an academic counselor, academic adviser or success coach AND Student Financial Services since these decisions may affect a student's financial aid and Satisfactory Academic Progress. Any such students receiving financial aid may find their awards reduced.

1. Instructors do not have the option of withdrawing students. The student must receive a grade of "A" through "D-", "F", "Pass", "I" or "AU" if still on the roster after the 60% point in the session (as defined in Attachment B-Glossary).
2. CSN administration may withdraw a student at any time during the session for just cause including, but not limited to, failure to pay for the course and violations of the Student Conduct Code.
3. Students with documented exceptional circumstances may follow the grade change process to request a grade change to W.
4. Students may withdraw from a course with a grade of W during the first 60% of a session (as defined in Attachment B-Glossary), measured by time, not assignments. If the withdrawal occurs during the refund period, the class will not appear on the student's transcript. When withdrawing from the class, the official withdrawal date is the date processed by the Office of the Registrar, not the date last attended, unless the two dates coincide.
5. In order to adhere to financial aid guidelines, at the end of the second week of the semester or summer session, the instructor submits to the Registrar's Office the names of students who have not

participated at all in the course. Participation is defined in Attachment B.

C. Grading Policy (as it pertains to Audit, Incomplete and Withdrawal)

1. A student enrolled in the course through the withdrawal date but unable to continue for legitimate reasons can apply to the instructor and provide supporting documentation for an Incomplete ("I") grade. The instructor will determine if the student qualifies for the incomplete process, and if so, the instructor will determine and document the outstanding requirements for the student to finish the course and convert the "I" grade as well as the time frame to complete those requirements, not to exceed one year. If the work is not completed during that time frame, the "I" converts to an "F" unless a different grade is indicated by a grade change form. If the instructor is no longer available to submit a grade change form, it is the responsibility of the department chair to do so, if applicable. The "I" grade is not included in the student's grade point average and therefore is worth 0 points. If a student wishes to retake the entire course, he or she must re-register and pay for the class. Unless approved by the dean in the student's major or the VPAA or VPAA's designee, a student with 3 current "I" grades may not register for additional coursework. If the student is not enrolled at CSN at the time he or she needs to complete the coursework and he or she needs to use CSN facilities not open to the public (such as labs), the student must receive permission from the department chair or program director to use those facilities, sign a waiver of liability to CSN, and, if applicable, receive permission from the clinic site.
2. If the withdrawal happens after the refund period, the student will receive a grade of "W" for the class as long as withdrawal occurs before the course is 60% complete as defined in Attachment B. Lack of attendance does not constitute withdrawal; failure to properly withdraw will result in the assignment of an "F" grade on the student's transcript in accordance with NSHE Grading Policy.
3. A grade of "AU" is posted on the student's transcript for audited courses.

D. Auditing Classes

PLEASE NOTE: Before taking steps to audit (as defined in Attachment B-GLOSSARY) a course, students should be AWARE that:

i. Federal financial aid will not pay for audited courses, and students should not include aid for audited courses in their financial planning.
ii. Satisfactory Academic Progress related to federal financial aid takes attempted credits into consideration when assessing a student's ongoing eligibility for federal financial aid. Credit-to-Audit conversions are counted among "Attempted" credits but not as "Completed" credits for financial aid purposes.

Students are strongly advised to consult with an Academic Counselor or Advisor and Student Financial Services, if the student receives financial aid, prior to making any course registration changes.

1. Except for programs with applicable limitations (such as limited entry or specialized accreditation), a student may elect to audit a course.
2. A student must pay the normal registration fees for audited courses.
3. Audited courses will NOT be counted as part of the academic load when full-time or part-time status is reported, for any reason, to any internal or external office or agency; this includes, by way of example only, the financial aid office, Social Security Administration, an employer, and others.

III. PROCEDURE

A. Course Auditing Procedures

1. To audit a course, a student must register for the course and pay the regular fees (and tuition, if applicable).
2. Credit to audit: To change the status of a course from credit to audit, a student must complete the change on or before the last day to withdraw. Students must sign a statement acknowledging the consequences of their decision.
3. Students cannot change their status from audit to credit.
4. All enrollment changes are processed through the Office of the Registrar.

IV. AUTHORITY AND CROSS REFERENCE LINKS

A. Board of Regents Handbook, Grading Policy, Title 4, Chapter 16, Section 38
B. Board of Regents Handbook, Registration Policy, Title 4, Chapter 16, Sections 22 and 24
C. Financial Aid-Satisfactory Academic Progress requirements (http://www.csn.edu/pages/627.asp)
D. Mandatory Pell Recalculation requirement (http://www.csn.edu/pages/627.asp)
E. Return to Title IV requirement (http://www.csn.edu/pages/627.asp)
F. CSN's Financial Aid Census Date:
   http://www.csn.edu/PDFFiles/StuFinAid/Census%20Date%20%20Disbursement%20announcement%20s pring%202012.pdf)

V. DISCLAIMER

The President has the discretion to suspend or rescind all or any part of this policy or related procedure(s). The President shall notify appropriate CSN personnel, including the Administrative Code Officer and Faculty Senate Chair, of the suspension or rescission.

Questions about this policy should be referred to the CSN Administrative Code Officer (general.counsel@csn.edu, 702.651.7488) and/or the Faculty Senate Chair (office.facultysenate@csn.edu, 702.651.7330).

VI. SIGNATURES

Recommended by:

/s/ Darin Dockstader   12/09/2013

Faculty Senate Chair   Date

Reviewed for Legal Sufficiency:

/s/ Richard Hinckley   12/17/2013

General Counsel   Date

Approved by:

/s/ Michael D. Richards   12/17/2013

CSN President   Date

VII. ATTACHMENTS

A. History
B. Glossary

ATTACHMENT A
History

1. First adopted by Faculty Senate: December 6, 2013

2. Approved by CSN President: December 17, 2013

3. **"Audit"** means the student will enroll in the course but receive no credit or grade.

4. **"60% of a session"** refers to the length of the session in days, not to the number of assignments or percentage of points earned. Refer to the academic calendar for the appropriate date.

5. **"Session"** refers to semester or a period less than 16 weeks. Refer to the academic calendar for the appropriate date.

6. **"Participation"** as defined by the U.S. Department of Education means physically attending a class with direct interaction between the instructor and students and/or submitting an academic assignment and/or taking an exam, interactive tutorial or computer-assisted instruction and/or attending a study group assigned by the institution and/or participating in an on-line discussion about academic matters and/or initiating contact with the faculty member to ask a question about the academic subject studied in the course.

The Spirit
of American Politics

1

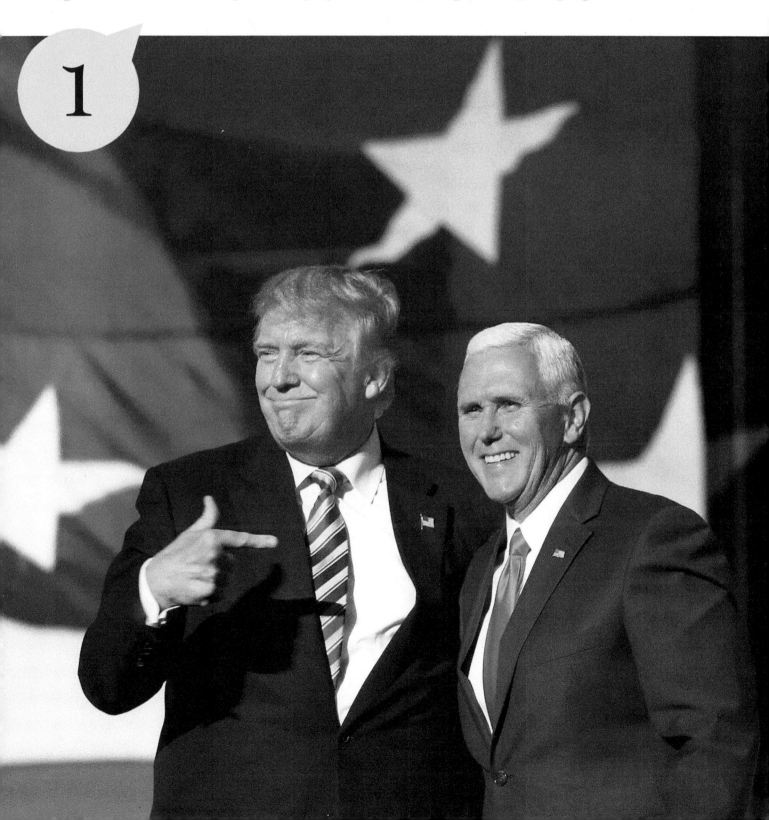

INAUGURATION DAY, 2017 . . . 2021 . . . 2025 . . .

Every four years, the president stands in front of the U.S. Capitol and repeats the oath of office. The ceremony represents an American legacy that stretches all the way back to President George Washington, who first used in 1789 the same words we hear today. The inaugural oath remains a highlight in the world's oldest **democracy**. It is a solemn moment: Even George Washington was visibly nervous when he spoke the oath.

Members of Congress surround the president on the inaugural stage. Chief Justice John Roberts of the U.S. Supreme Court leads the president through the oath of office. The Supreme Court serves as a check on Congress and the executive branch. It decides whether government actions (both national and state) violate the U.S. Constitution. For example, the Court recently ruled that laws forbidding same-sex marriage violated the Fourteenth Amendment.

What you cannot see on Inauguration Day is the sheer depth of this democracy. Americans elect five hundred thousand public officials—from the governors of their states to the mayors of their cities, from soil and water commissioners in Iowa City, Iowa, to cemetery trustees in Lempster, New Hampshire. No other country in the world comes close to voting on so many offices.

Yet this proud democracy is full of paradoxes. On five occasions, Americans have inaugurated presidential candidates who received fewer popular votes than their opponents. Think about that: Nearly one in ten presidents was not the people's choice. Congress adds another peculiar twist to the notion of popular rule. Its approval rating averaged a dismal 16 percent in 2016. In one typical poll, nearly 80 percent agreed that Congress was "out of touch with average Americans."[1] Yet that same year nearly 97 percent of House incumbents won reelection, most of them by large majorities. The public expressed sharp disapproval—then voted to return nearly all of them to Washington for another term.

The Supreme Court's nine members represent still another limit to American democracy. Justices are not elected but are appointed for life. At times, the Court has looked more like a bastion of privilege than a protector of rights. Back in 1857, the Court ruled that, according to the Constitution,

Democracy: A form of government involving power held by the people, who may rule directly or through elected representatives.

● *President Trump and Vice President Pence greet supporters after winning the 2016 election.*

3

The first inauguration: George Washington takes the oath of office in New York in 1789 while a crowd cheers from the street . . . compared to . . . President Obama's inauguration in Washington, DC, 223 years later. Though the faces of America change, each new generation embraces this time-honored democratic tradition.

black people "were so far inferior" that they had "no rights which the white man was bound to respect."[2] More recently the Court has struck down legislation banning partial-birth abortion, introducing prayer into schools, limiting campaign donations, and many other Congressional and state legislative actions that were popular with a majority of Americans.

As you can see, democracy is complicated. Yes, the United States is the world's oldest democratic country. Yet a candidate who loses the popular vote can win the White House, most members of a terribly unpopular Congress are reelected in landslides, and unelected judges, appointed for life, can strike down the will of the people's representatives. Over the course of this book, you will see why these limits to democracy were introduced; and we will ask you to think about whether they are still important—or out of date.

We address four questions throughout this book to help make sense of American politics and government. By the time you finish reading, you will understand the debates sparked by each question—and you will be able to participate knowledgeably yourself.

1. **Who governs?** Do the people rule? Some of us would answer, "Yes, and today more than ever." Others are not so sure. What if the people are *not* really in charge—then who is?

2. **How does American politics work?** This may be the most confusing, messy, and fascinating government on earth. We will guide you through the political maze, helping you understand what makes American politics and government tick.

3. **What does government do?** Many people view politics as dirty and see government as a problem, or irrelevant to their lives. We will show you how politics can be honorable, and why government is often important, even essential. By the time you finish this book, you will have the tools to make informed judgments about what public officials actually do and whether government is a problem, a solution . . . or perhaps a bit of both.

4. **Who are we?** In a rapidly changing, diverse, immigrant nation, this may be the deepest question of all. American politics helps define who we are—as a community, a people, and a nation.

Before we examine these four questions, we want to share our bias: We love politics. We think there is nothing more interesting—not Kanye West, not *Game of Thrones*, not the Super Bowl. Actually, all those involve politics too. We aim to project the excitement of politics and power and democracy. We will brief you on basic facts, then ask you to ponder some key questions and join in the debates. And we will suggest many ways that you can get involved in the pageant of American politics.

Who Governs?

As Benjamin Franklin left the Constitutional Convention in 1787, a woman stopped him. "What kind of government have you given us?" she asked. According to legend, the wise old Franklin responded, "A republic, madam—if you can keep it." The United States organized itself around a ringing declaration of popular rule: Governments derive "their just powers from the consent of the governed," as the Declaration of Independence declares. In a **republic**, the people are in charge. The Constitution drives home this point in its first three words: "We the People." Franklin knew, however, that popular governments were extremely difficult to "keep." All previous republics—such as Athens, Rome, and Florence—had collapsed. His point was that the people have to be vigilant and active if they are to maintain control.

Popular rule in the United States was a bold breakthrough by eighteenth-century standards, but it certainly did not empower everyone. The Constitution protected slavery and gave slaveholders three-fifths of a vote for every person they kept in chains. Women could not vote, nor could most poor men, white or black. American Indians were considered foreigners in their native land. At the heart of American history lies the long, hard struggle to actually live up to the republic's founding ideals, to genuinely empower "We the People."

Now that most adults finally have the right to vote (eighteen-year-olds won the vote in 1971, though many states still deny felons the right), does the public really rule? Or do the rich and powerful make most of the decisions? Americans have always worried that ordinary people will lose control. In 1961, for example, President Dwight Eisenhower, a Republican concerned about the size of government, warned that the military, its corporate suppliers, and those groups' political friends were coming together to form a military–industrial complex. These insiders wielded too much power, he warned, creating a juggernaut of big government, big business, and big contracts. Eisenhower's background gave him special credibility: He was a five-star general who had commanded U.S. forces during World War II.

Today, critics still charge that the very wealthy—the top 1 percent—have stripped the people of money and influence. Comedian and political commentator Stephen Colbert held rallies in which he mocked the Supreme Court for striking down laws that limited contributions to political campaigns. Colbert shouted, his voice edged with sarcasm, that the Court had ended "the tragic lack of influence" that "corporations and billionaires and unions (but mostly corporations)" exercise in our government.[3] At the same time, many conservative Americans felt that it was government bureaucrats and the mainstream media elites who had grabbed the power; in response, they flocked to the Tea Party, designed to return control to the people. In 2015, sparked by police shootings of African Americans, the Black

Republic: A government in which citizens rule indirectly and make government decisions through their elected representatives.

see for yourself 1.1

Go online to see President Eisenhower's warning against the creation of a military–industrial complex. We discuss the context in Chapter 18.

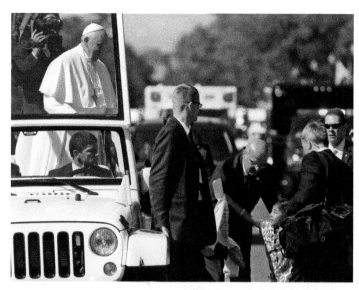

Five-year-old Sophie Cruz climbed over the security barrier and chased after the Pope's vehicle during his tour of Washington DC. As millions of people watched, she handed the Pope a letter asking that her foreign-born parents be allowed to stay in the United States. Individuals can make a difference.

see for yourself 1.2

Go online to see Colbert mocking the Supreme Court's controversial decision to strike down election-financing laws.

Lives Matter movement called for equality, inclusion, and empowerment. Notice how many different types of voices have been raised in protest: a conservative president, a liberal talk show host, a very conservative movement, and civil rights campaigners. What do they all have in common? Each believes the people's voice is not being properly heard.

Alongside these fears, we see many examples where ordinary American people have made enormous differences. Sometimes they have done so simply by voting for change, sometimes by organizing a political movement, and sometimes by taking a courageous stand.

Over the years, political scientists have developed different theories to answer the question of where power really lies in American politics. The following four theories (summarized in Table 1.1) are especially important:

- *Pluralist theory* suggests that people can influence government through the many interest groups that spring up to champion everything from fighting global warming to banning abortions. Pluralists suggest that interest groups give most people a voice. Competing and bargaining, interest groups are a prime mover in many government decisions.

- *Elite theory* counters that power actually rests in the hands of a small number of wealthy and powerful individuals—especially corporate executives and top government officials. The Tea Party, Black Lives Matter, and many other movements all charged that elites were not sharing power with common people.

- *Bureaucratic theory* argues that real control lies with the millions of men and women who carry out the day-to-day operations of modern government. Here the power of most Americans to weigh in on policymaking is sidelined, as bureaucratic experts establish policy.

- *Social movement theory* emphasizes the power citizens can wield when they organize and rise up in protest—regardless of who is in control of day-to-day politics.

TABLE 1.1 Theories of Power

THEORY	LOCATION OF POLITICAL POWER	SOURCE OF INFLUENCE
Pluralist theory	Interest groups	A group's organization, resources, and connections
Elite theory	"Power elite" in government, corporations, and the military	Status based on economic influence and leadership positions
Bureaucratic theory	Government organizations	Organizational rules and day-to-day decisions
Social movement theory	Protest movements	The ability to persuade the rest of the country to support their cause

Who Governs?

Political scientists' two most popular theories of power are pluralism and elite theory. If you had to choose between them, which would you pick?	Pluralism! Power is spread out in America. Any group can have its say.	Elitism! A small circle of wealthy and powerful people hold most of the control in America.	Perhaps you would like to speak up for one of the other theories. Do you prefer social movement theory, which places power in the hands of an active, engaged group of citizens? If you're not sure, don't worry: We're just getting started.

These theories represent very different answers to the vital question: Who rules in America? Have we remained a republic, governed by the people? We will often return to this question—and ask you to consider which of these theories best describes power in the United States today. (And, yes, you'll be able to mix, match, and create your own.)

THE BOTTOM LINE

» In a republic, power rests with the people. However, this is a difficult form of government to maintain. The first question of American politics—raised in every generation—is whether the people hold the power. Is the United States a government by the people?

» Scholars have developed four approaches to political power in America: pluralism, elite theory, bureaucratic theory, and social movement theory.

» We return to this issue in every chapter of this book.

How Does American Politics Work?

Consider a classic definition of politics: *Who gets what, when, and how.*[4] Every society has limited amounts of desirable goods such as money, prestige, and power. Politics helps determine how those resources are distributed—to which people, in what amounts, under which rules. A second definition is even simpler: Politics is how a society makes its collective decisions. Every nation has its own way of deciding. This book explains how collective decisions are made in the United States. The key to understanding our political decision making lies in the four "Is": ideas, institutions, interests, and individuals.

Ideas

Powerful ideas shape American politics. The nation began by declaring what at the time was a stunning idea: "All men are created equal" and "are endowed by their Creator with certain unalienable rights." In Chapter 2, we explore seven essential ideas: liberty, democracy (or self-rule), individualism, limited government, the American dream, equality, and faith in God. At first glance, these ideas may all look simple, but as you will quickly learn, each has at least two very different sides. Each idea provokes long, loud controversies about what values and policies Americans should pursue.

Take democracy as an example. It may sound simple—government by the people—but defining and achieving democracy in America has been a constant struggle. The United States has seen a Constitution that limited the people's influence, an elaborate system of **checks and balances** that blunts the popular will, political machines that enthusiastically stole votes, and many other limits to democracy. As one anxious delegate put it on the first day of the Constitutional Convention in 1787, "the people should have as little to do as may be about the government. They lack information and are constantly liable to be misled."[5] Can checking the people's influence elevate popular rule? Americans still debate this question.

Instead of embracing popular sovereignty, generation after generation of American leaders has preferred the rule of a few—the elite founders of the nation, expert bureaucrats trying to solve technical problems, or judges appointed for life who are removed from the public's influence. All have aimed to protect government from the tumult of the masses.

At the same time, bold popular movements and unforeseen electoral surges have changed the nation. In many ways, these are the most exciting moments in American history. They attract widespread attention, inspiring ordinary citizens to achieve great things. The chapters that follow highlight moments when the United States has reflected populist democracy, as well as periods when it has turned away from the people. We also explore the great contested zone between democracy and elitism, one that is often up for grabs. Ultimately, the struggle for power between the elite few and the democratic many goes back to our first question: Who governs?

The United States bursts with entrepreneurial energy. New ideas bubble up all the time. Many of these notions concern specific policy issues, but occasionally a major reform shakes the entire political system. Ideas alone do not drive government decisions, but it is impossible to make sense of American politics without understanding ideas, big and small.

> **Checks and balances:** The principle that each branch of government has the authority to block the other branches, making it more difficult for any one branch or individual to exercise too much power. This system makes passing legislation far more difficult in the United States than in most other democracies.

> **Institutions:** The organizations, norms, and rules that structure government and public action.

Institutions

When most people talk about politics, they think about individuals: President Donald Trump, senators such as Marco Rubio (R-FL), governors like Jerry Brown (D-CA) and Nikki Haley (R-SC), or commentators such as Rush Limbaugh and Rachel Maddow. Political scientists, on the other hand, stress **institutions**—*the organizations, norms, and rules that structure political action.*

Congress, the Texas legislature, the Missoula (Montana) City Council, the Supreme Court, and the Department of Homeland Security are all institutions. Why did the nation hold its breath in 2015, as the Supreme Court reviewed the Obama administration's healthcare reform law five years after the president signed it? Study the rules that govern institutions such as Congress, the presidency, and the Supreme Court and you will understand.

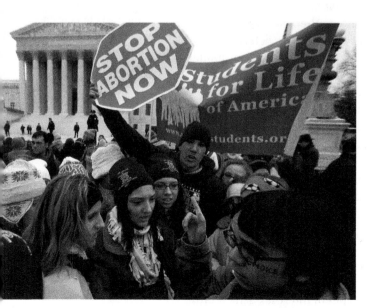
Students take to the streets of the capital to express their pro-life values.

The media represents another institution that shapes politics. Just think about how media outlets are organized. Have you ever "liked" a candidate on Facebook? Have you checked out a YouTube or Vine video of a candidate making a fool of him or herself? Facebook, Twitter, Instagram, Vine, and YouTube organize political discourse very differently from the way your grandparents' morning newspaper did.

The U.S. Capitol, Washington, DC. Tourists see an impressive monument to democracy. Political scientists see an institution with complicated rules that give advantage to some individuals and groups.

Or think about how institutions influence your own behavior. You may compete in a classroom by making arguments. If the debate gets heated and you shove someone, however, you are in trouble. But if you play basketball after class, things are quite the opposite. There, a little shoving is fine, but no one wants to play hoops with someone who is always arguing. Different institutions—the classroom, the gym—have different rules, and most people adopt them without a second thought. Notice how shifting institutional rules give some people advantages over others. Smart students who think quickly have an advantage in one institution (the classroom), while fast, athletic students with good post moves have an advantage in another (the gym). Political institutions work in the same way. The U.S. Senate, the Chicago City Council, the Nevada legislature, the state courts in Florida, the governor's office in Wisconsin, the Marine Corps, the Department of Agriculture, and thousands of other institutions all have their own rules and procedures. Each institution organizes behavior. Each gives an advantage to some interests over others.

Once you finish this book, you will routinely know to ask every time you encounter a political issue: Which institutions are involved? How do they influence the politics?

Interests

For many social scientists, interests are the center of the story. Political action often flows from individuals, groups, and nations pursuing their own self-interest.

Individuals promote their interests in politics, just as they do in economic markets. Many political scientists rely on **rational-choice theory**: Members of the public, in this view, calculate the costs and benefits of any action to determine what will maximize their own self-interest. At an extreme, these "rat-choice" models hold that all political outcomes—elections, the passage of a law, even mass rallies— are an aggregate of the public's individual interests.

Rational-choice theory: An approach to political behavior that views individuals as rational, decisive actors who know their political interests and seek to act on them.

A more traditional view of interests focuses not on individuals but on groups. Arthur Bentley recognized back in 1908 that interest groups had become a powerful force in U.S. politics. Whether they use their influence for good or for ill, they are a permanent feature of free societies. (Remember that pluralists believe interest groups are the central actors in American government.)

Finally, political theorists and politicians alike often seek (or claim to seek) the public interest, the shared good of the whole society. Idealists have argued against pandering to the interests of individuals or groups. Instead, they suggest that government ought to pursue "the greatest good for the greatest number." But who decides what is the "greatest good?" This returns us to our first question: Who governs? The answer lies in who can most effectively get his or her voice heard.

In the chapters that follow, we explore all three types of interests: self-interest, group interest, and public interest. Behavioral scientists add one more twist.

Although we may think of our own interests, including our political views, as perfectly rational, most people exhibit a large degree of self-deception and nonrational behavior. Experiments repeatedly show, for example, that many people tend to vote for the name that appears first on a list of candidates, especially in elections for obscure offices. Other experiments show that people do not change their views when confronted with evidence that they are wrong—it only makes them cling more strongly to their position. Experts are no more rational than anyone else. Even experienced analysts are overconfident about their ability to predict political events and outcomes—and, despite their certainty, they are often wrong.[6]

Individuals

Finally, individuals influence political outcomes. This book puts special emphasis on how ordinary people change the world. Our hope is simple: We want to inspire you, the reader, to get involved. Here we share one example.

Marla Ruzicka was one of the first American civilians to arrive in Iraq after the United States toppled Saddam Hussein in 2003. A self-described "civics junkie" since high school, Marla had visited Afghanistan and seen the terrible toll that wars could take on civilian populations. With no particular foreign policy experience, the twenty-five-year-old established a public service organization in Iraq that she called the Campaign for Innocent Victims in Conflict, or CIVIC. Along with providing first aid, food, clothing, and comfort to ordinary Iraqis injured during the war, Marla formed survey teams of volunteers that kept a count of Iraqi civilians killed, whether by insurgents, the remnants of Saddam's army, or U.S. forces.

Marla's efforts attracted attention back in Washington, where Pentagon officials initially sought to dissuade her from publicizing her count. Eventually she received substantial support from Congress for her CIVIC efforts to aid civilian victims in both Iraq and Afghanistan.

Marla described herself as "an ordinary American girl." She grew up in California, attended Long Island University, and relied on friends and well-wishers to sponsor her initial CIVIC work.

There is a tragic note to Marla's story: In April 2005, as she traveled to an injured Iraqi's home, her car was targeted by an explosive device, and she was killed. We highlight Marla's example both to honor her memory (one of your authors was her friend) and to emphasize the importance of individual initiative in every operation of American government. Today, the organization she founded has programs not only in Iraq and Afghanistan, but also in Syria, Somalia, Mali, and other war-torn countries. She is an example of how individuals with a passion for political change can make a difference in politics—and in people's lives.

History

As the four "Is" reappear throughout this book, you will see that we pay special attention to the history of each. Why is an idea like freedom powerful? Why does an institution such as Congress look like it does? To understand you have

Individuals can make a difference. Marla Ruzicka in Kabul, Afghanistan.

to know how they developed over time. While we hope you share our passion for the drama and excitement of American history, we tell historical stories for a more important reason. You cannot understand where the nation is, or where it might be going, without knowing where it has been.

<table>
<tr><td>

THE BOTTOM LINE

</td><td>

» American political decisions are shaped by four "I" factors: ideas, institutions, interests, and individuals.

» Mastering how the four "Is" shaped politics also requires an understanding of history.

</td></tr>
</table>

What Does Government Do?

Americans are suspicious of government, especially national government. Patrick Henry, a Virginia politician, is famous for declaring, "Give me liberty or give me death!" at the start of the Revolutionary War.[7]

When he heard about the new Constitution in 1787, he made another famous statement: "I smell a rat." Henry spoke for many Americans, down through the years, when he charged that the federal government would be too strong. And yet that government has grown—and continues to grow. To understand why, we need to recognize what government is and what it actually does.

Context: Government in Society

There are three sectors of society. *Private life* involves individuals, their families, and their closest friends, connecting primarily (or exclusively) with one another. *Civil society* refers to people joining with others to achieve

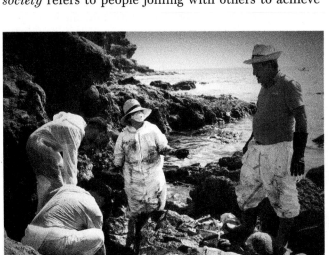

● *The three sectors of society. Individuals engage in all three sectors: personal life when they pray, play, and raise a family; civil society when they volunteer to clean up an oil spill; and government in all its forms—as when they help a police officer master hop scotch.*

some goal. Examples include a student government, a Bible study circle, a group of recycling volunteers, or a business association. Finally, *government* involves formal and informal institutions that make decisions for the whole society.

The lines separating these different sectors are blurry. Successful democracy requires a vibrant civic spirit. When people join groups—even if it's just a soccer club or knitting circle, they get used to interacting with others and solving problems together. They develop what Alexis de Tocqueville, a French visitor to America in 1831–1832, called the "habits of the heart"—the interchanges and projects that build the foundation of robust democracies. Private groups foster the skills and attitudes that make people effective citizens.[8]

In addition, the different sectors come together to undertake public projects. **Public–private partnerships** bring private actors such as businesses together with government officials to renovate parks, construct sports arenas, or launch innovative schools.

Public–private partnership:
A government program or service provided through the joint efforts of private sector actors (usually businesses) and public officials.

No Big Government!

Americans have a very active civil society. In the abstract, at least, they prefer voluntary groups to government action. Polls consistently reflect public disapproval for all aspects of government: bureaucrats, the mainstream media, lobbyists, and Congress. Today, only 24 percent of Americans trust the national government "to do the right thing most of the time"[9] (see Figure 1.1).

If Americans dislike "Big Government," then how did we get such a thicket of over thirteen hundred federal agencies and fifteen Cabinet departments, populated by more than 2.2 million civilian employees? Include another nearly 2.5 million members of the active and reserve armed forces, and you get a sprawling national government. Add state (4.4 million) and local (12.2 million) workers alongside the 500,000 elected officials, and you get an idea of the sheer size of the U.S. government— almost 22 million men and women who touch every aspect of our lives.

Americans have long told admiring stories about individual heroes who won greatness on their own—free of government meddling. But the details are often

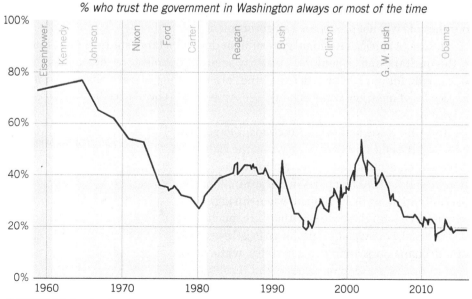

% who trust the government in Washington always or most of the time

FIGURE 1.1 *American trust in government remains at historic lows. (Pew Research Center)*

more nuanced. Take those famous inventors, the Wright brothers. Working out of their bicycle shop, Orville and Wilbur created the first viable airplanes, opening the path to air travel. What you may not have heard is that the Wrights were able to develop their invention because of timely investments from their first client: the U.S. military.[10] Yes, government support was essential to launching the aviation industry—just as it was to exploring space, creating the Internet, and building the infrastructure we drive, walk, fly, run, and otherwise move around on every day. And, in reality, despite the low trust in government generally, Americans give the government high marks for specific tasks—for example, for responding to natural disasters (79% approval), keeping the country safe from terrorism (72%), and ensuring safe food and medicine (72%).[11]

Could we—and should we—shift some of the national government's functions to civil society and let volunteers do the work? To answer such questions, you first have to know what government does.

What Government Does

Back in 1787, the Constitution's creators set out the basic functions of government, as they imagined them: "Establish justice, ensure domestic tranquility, provide for the common defense, promote the general welfare, and secure the blessings of liberty." Their list—which we detail in Chapter 3—is still remarkably accurate, even as the size of our government has expanded dramatically. Today you also can get a good idea of the federal government's priorities by looking at its major budget categories. Figure 1.2 shows you how the federal government spends its $4.1 trillion annual budget.

Many people are surprised when they examine the federal budget for the first time. More than 61 percent of all federal government spending goes to just four programs: the military, Social Security (which provides a steady income for people over sixty-five, as well as for those with disabilities), Medicare (which provides healthcare for people over sixty-five), and Medicaid (which provides healthcare for some poor people; about half of Medicaid spending also goes to those over sixty-five). These four programs total over $2.4 trillion—that qualifies as "Big Government," regardless of anything else we spend public funds on. These programs' strong popularity means that politicians meddle with them at their peril. Public officials often talk about cutting the budget. But unless they are cutting one of the big four the cuts will not produce a lean government.

In sum, America's national government devotes a large share of its resources to the military and to seniors. This may seem to uphold the Constitution's call to "provide for our common defense" and "promote the general welfare." But it also raises a lot of questions: only one in seven Americans is over sixty-five—what about the rest of us?

To fulfill these and other functions, the government sets the rules for society. Drive on the right side of the street. Stop at red lights. No tobacco for children. No rat hairs or bug parts in restaurant food. No discrimination against women when hiring. Most people agree with these rules. Others are much more controversial. Some 750,000 people go to jail every year for marijuana possession in some states, while pot is legal in others. In Oregon people with terminal illnesses can choose to end their lives with the assistance of a physician; but anyone who assisted euthanasia

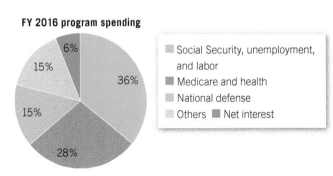

FIGURE 1.2 *The U.S. federal budget. (Christopher Chantrill)*

FY 2016 program spending

- Social Security, unemployment, and labor
- Medicare and health
- National defense
- Others
- Net interest

36%
28%
15%
15%
6%

Medicare and Social Security create a safety net, and make up the bulk of the federal government's annual mandatory spending. These programs have deep roots that make it hard to cut the budget and reduce our deficit.

in Georgia or Florida would face murder charges. Abortions are much easier to obtain in New York than in North Dakota. Guns are easier to get in Texas than California. Government—national, state, and local—constantly sets the rules for society. Sometimes the rules make sense to most people; other times, they trigger fierce debates. In either case, governments affect what we do almost every minute of every day. As you read this book, think about what government should do, what it should stay out of, and why.

A Chronic Problem

Although Americans dislike government in the abstract, by and large they support many of the things that government actually does. This paradox creates a chronic problem: How should we pay for government spending? Americans pay lower taxes compared to citizens of most other advanced industrial nations. Yes, you read that right. The U.S. tax burden ranks thirty-first—near the bottom—among the thirty-four wealthiest nations[12] (see Comparing Nations 1.1). Even so, many Americans think they are taxed too much. Americans like their federal programs but oppose paying taxes to support them.

Partly as a result of our antitax spirit, the federal government usually spends more than it takes in. You can see one consequence in Figure 1.2. Notice the fifth-largest spending category: interest on the national debt. The United States borrows money to cover the difference between government spending and tax revenues. The resulting debt reflects a serious political problem. It is hard to raise taxes (people hate them), but it is also hard to cut programs (people like them), so the United States keeps borrowing to make up the difference.

The Hidden Government

Another peculiar aspect of modern American government is that it can be hard to see. Scholars identify a "hidden" or "submerged" central government, with many functions deliberately tucked out of sight. Why is it people do not see their government at work?[13]

Because of Americans' antipathy to "big government," many federal programs work *indirectly*: they operate through the private sector. Take healthcare as an example. Rather than administering a national health insurance program as in Canada or France, the American government provides employers a major tax deduction if they offer employees health insurance. Today, the tax deduction for employers amounts to $250 billion a year.[14] That makes it one of the largest government-funded healthcare programs in the world. The national government offers similar tax deductions that help people buy homes, save for retirement, pay for schooling, or receive support if their income is low. However, the people who benefit do not see the government's hand at work.[15]

Political scientist Suzanne Mettler asked American citizens whether they receive federal benefits; more than half of the respondents incorrectly answered "no." They did not stop to think that the government had helped set up their

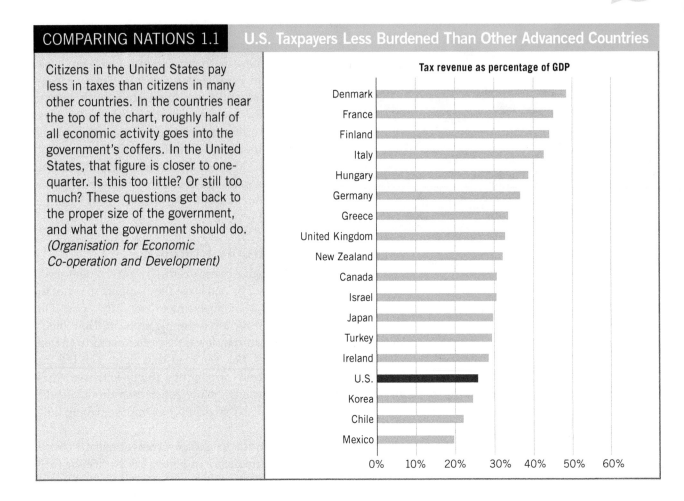

COMPARING NATIONS 1.1 U.S. Taxpayers Less Burdened Than Other Advanced Countries

Citizens in the United States pay less in taxes than citizens in many other countries. In the countries near the top of the chart, roughly half of all economic activity goes into the government's coffers. In the United States, that figure is closer to one-quarter. Is this too little? Or still too much? These questions get back to the proper size of the government, and what the government should do. *(Organisation for Economic Co-operation and Development)*

retirement savings or their student loans by organizing the tax code to encourage their behavior. About a quarter of the people getting healthcare coverage through Medicaid or groceries through food stamps did not realize they were involved in government programs (see Figure 1.3).

Liberal scholars conclude that the government does not get enough credit for helping people and creating a stronger nation. Conservatives, on the other hand, are more likely to worry that a hidden government is more difficult to control and cut back. Our job is to make sure you see all the ways that government operates—then you can decide whether it should grow, shrink, or stay about the same size.

The Best of Government

Despite powerful antigovernment sentiment—or perhaps inspired by it to promote change—millions of Americans cheer what is best in our national government and seek to improve it. In this book, you will meet dozens of people who, like Marla Ruzicka, act to improve government. You will meet policy entrepreneurs who promote innovative new solutions to pressing problems; organizers who engage their neighbors and larger communities in collective action for change; inventive bureaucrats who conceive ways to deliver public services more effectively; and tech wizards who devise faster, better connections between national policymakers and the public.

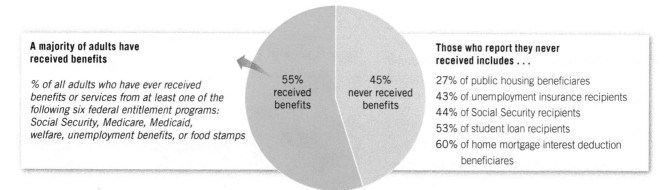

A majority of adults have received benefits

% of all adults who have ever received benefits or services from at least one of the following six federal entitlement programs: Social Security, Medicare, Medicaid, welfare, unemployment benefits, or food stamps

55% received benefits

45% never received benefits

Those who report they never received includes . . .

27% of public housing beneficiares
43% of unemployment insurance recipients
44% of Social Security recipients
53% of student loan recipients
60% of home mortgage interest deduction beneficiares

● **FIGURE 1.3** *A recent poll found that 55 percent of Americans report receiving government benefits, but Suzanne Mettler has calculated that the number is closer to 96 percent. Even beneficiaries of the biggest programs do not realize they are getting benefits from the government. (Pew Research Center and Washington Post)*

Take one small example of how a good idea can make a difference. The Consumer Financial Protection Bureau (CFPB), a federal agency, features on its homepage a crowd-sourcing "IdeaBox" seeking creative ways to help out Americans in debt. In spring 2015, federal student-loan recipients proposed a new online form to track more clearly how much a student owes and a schedule for repayment. The CFPB responded swiftly, and the online form was revised and went live within weeks. Today, students around the country have an easier time navigating the complex realm of federal loan repayment.[16]

Although our government can appear large and remote, individuals can make a real impact on its operations. In this book, we return repeatedly to ways you can get involved, have a say, and enhance the workings of American government. You can engage within our political system: volunteer on a Senate campaign, attend a town meeting, intern at a federal agency, or run for office yourself. You also can get involved from outside: call media attention to a problem, serve in (or start) an advocacy group, or launch an online idea. In addition, you can get involved in the life of your community. You are already enough of a social scientist to know that when you join a group or activity, you are participating in "civil society"—the basic building block of strong democracy.

THE BOTTOM LINE

» Every nation is made up of three primary sectors: private life; civil society, where people interact voluntarily; and government. Those sectors are increasingly blurred in the United States.

» Americans tend to dislike their national government—but like the benefits that government programs provide.

» Democratic government at its best involves popular involvement, either through direct engagement with public officials or through civil society activities that help develop "habits of the heart."

Who Are We?

The United States is a nation of immigrants, a country where individuals come to reinvent themselves. The nation is always changing. American politics constantly addresses the most fundamental question about a people: Who are we?

This question goes back to the earliest European settlers. When the Puritans landed in Massachusetts in 1630, they suddenly had to define their community for themselves. The colonists came up with a remarkable response: We are a collection of saints, a "city on a hill," a model for the whole world to follow. That city on a hill immediately discovered threats: The Puritans defined or imagined enemies that included Indians, witches, and heretics. These settlers learned to answer the question "Who are we?" both by affirming who they were ("us!") and by sharply declaring who they were *not* ("them!"). They defined themselves by celebrating their values, but also by demonizing their foes—promoting their cohesion by opposing dangerous "others."

New York, Ellis Island, reg. No. 3163 E

● *The United States grew as a nation of immigrants. One hundred years ago, immigrants passed through Ellis Island, where they were turned away if immigration officers thought they were unhealthy or unable to support themselves.*

At the same time, different settlers were arriving chained in terrible slave ships. Slave drivers and traders tried to strip Africans of their families, their heritage, their names, and their very identities. Together, American slaves would have to remake their lives and redefine themselves. Through religion, close communities, great myths, secret gatherings, personal narratives, and an enduring struggle for freedom, this community too would help the nation face up to the great question, *Who are we?*

Every generation brings new Americans. They arrive from all corners of the world: Ireland and Germany in the 1840s; Poland and Italy in the 1900s; Mexico, China, India, and Korea (among a great many other places) today. The newcomers, each in their own turn, wrestle with their identity in a new land. Each generation helps remake American society, culture, and politics. Each tells us who we are.

We are also an aging nation. As the baby boomers get older (Figure 1.4) Americans need a different mix of government services. Today, a larger proportion of Americans receive Social Security and Medicare than ever before. Younger generations also introduce new ideas, especially around social issues. Sixty-nine percent of **millennials** (born after 1983) believe marijuana should be legalized, while only 30 percent of the generation born between 1928–1945 agrees.[17] Each generation of Americans embraces different values, engages in civic life to greater/lesser degrees, and accesses some but not other institutions.

Millennials: Americans born between 1983–2001. Though very large (some 80 million people) and diverse, millennials tend to share certain characteristics, including political outlook.

We begin every chapter of this book by showing how the topics in the chapter help explain who we are. All the features of American politics—foundational ideas, the Constitution, presidents, justices, media personalities, bureaucrats, interest groups, and more—are part of the struggle to define and redefine the nation.

Who are we? The most important answer to that question is *you*. If you are part of the so-called millennial generation, defined as including those aged 16 to 34, you are the future of American politics. To us, that is a comforting thought. Studies of millennials show that you are, on average, more responsible, harder working, and more law-abiding than the generations that came before (including

More Old People, Fewer Youngsters
U.S. Population by age group, 1960, 1990, 2020

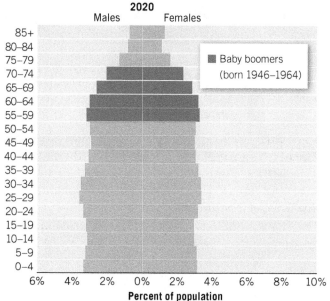

Getting Engaged in Politics—Or Not

In this section we note that public opinion data suggest that the millennial generation is less involved and interested in politics than were previous generations. What is your experience? Do you agree or disagree with this assertion?

Disagree.
Do you think there is more involvement than the polls are picking up? Perhaps there are new types of activities and engagements that more traditional observers have failed to appreciate. If so, describe the types of activities you have seen or engaged in.

Agree.
Do you see a lack of political engagement around you? Do you agree that this is a problem for American democracy? Or are you not convinced that more political activity would be good for the community or the nation? Do you want to argue against getting involved in politics altogether? Do you see more activity in private society than in civil society?

Unsure.
You may be new to the study of politics—or to the United States itself. If so, no worries. We are just beginning. By the end of the book, we think you will have strong opinions on this and many other matters.

INFO/DATA: Changing Face of America: Percentage of Total U.S. Population by Race and Ethnicity, 1960–2060

Answers to the age-old question "Who are we?" have been changing as long as there have been settlers on our shores, dating back to the Native American inhabitants. Looking back fifty years and forward a half-century, we see dramatic changes in the American population: Notice that by 2050, Hispanic, Asian, and black people will add up to a majority of the American population.

1. How do you think American politics and culture might change as the U.S. population becomes increasingly majority–minority?

2. The Hispanic population will grow from around 5 percent of Americans in 1960 to nearly 31 percent by 2060. Should the proportion of members of Congress, or Supreme Court justices, who are Hispanic also grow? Why or why not?

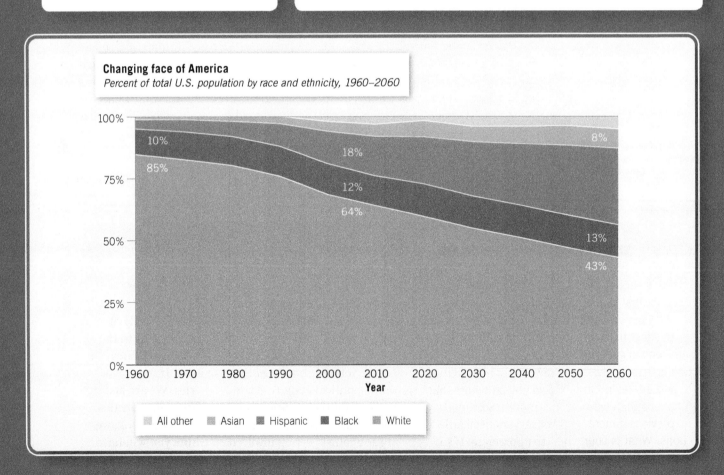

Changing face of America
Percent of total U.S. population by race and ethnicity, 1960–2060

Legend: All other — Asian — Hispanic — Black — White

Source: Pew Research Center

those of your authors). You tend to volunteer more, donate a higher share of your income to charity, and start more entrepreneurial organizations with social impact. You are also a generation at home in a rapidly changing and diverse world.

We do have one concern, however. Compared to previous generations, millennials are less interested in politics, public service, or even news events. Will this generation take up the challenge of "keeping the republic"? If a whole generation is reluctant to get involved, American democracy will suffer.

THE BOTTOM LINE

» American politics constantly addresses the most fundamental question about a people: Who are we?

» Because the nation is so diverse—and so rapidly changing—the answer to this question is constantly being rewritten.

» Each generation of Americans, including newly arriving immigrants, answers this question in its own way. Today we see millennials constructing their own version of a response.

Conclusion: Your Turn

The United States has solved many problems in the last two generations. It also has failed in some dramatic ways. The torch is now passing to you. We do not encourage you to get involved naively. This book details the many problems and frustrations of getting involved in politics. But we also hope our book will inspire you—whatever your age, whatever your background—to join the great debate about how to forge a better society. We invite you to use what you learn about American politics and government to help build a good community around you.

CHAPTER SUMMARY

To understand America's—or any other nation's—government and politics, keep four central questions in mind.

Who governs? This remains a deeply disputed topic, organized around four main theories. *Pluralist* thinkers claim that a wide array of interest groups, both private firms and public interest advocates, shapes government decisions and policy outcomes. *Elite theorists* view a handful of powerful people in prominent roles, and their wealthy supporters, as the central sources of political influence. *Bureaucratic theorists* look to millions of public officials in government organizations as the primary decision makers. Adherents of *social movement theory* argue that members of the public, when they join a protest movement, can have the ultimate say. Note that more than one of these theories can be true at the same time.

How does American politics work? Politics involves collective decisions about American society. To understand the decision-making process we focus on four "I" factors. The first is *ideas*: every day, people rally, debate, and even die on behalf of ideas such as liberty and democracy. *Institutions* like Congress, the Tennessee legislature, Treasury, or regular elections provide the rules and procedures that shape political outcomes. *Interests* motivate people to act politically and come in different forms: individual self-interest, the goals of interest groups, and the overarching public interest we all share. *Individuals* can have surprising amounts of political influence, even in a nation as large as the United States.

What does government do? With many Americans opposed to strong national government, one may imagine ours as a small and limited government. In reality, the United States has a very large one. The majority of the public embraces programs such as Social Security, Medicare, and a strong military. We also depend on vigorous civic engagement by the American public. In addition, government regulates the rules of everyday life, from who can get married to where to place a stoplight.

Who are we? American politics constantly addresses the most fundamental question about a people: Who are we? Because the nation is so diverse—and so rapidly changing—the answer to this question is constantly being rewritten. Every feature of American politics—the foundational ideas, the Constitution, the media, Congress, the courts, and now the millennial generation—engages in this constant debate over defining the nation and its people.

KEY TERMS

Checks and balances, p. 8
Democracy, p. 3
Institutions, p. 8

Millennials, p. 17
Public–private
    partnership, p. 12

Rational-choice
    theory, p. 9
Republic, p. 5

STUDY QUESTIONS

1. Why do we describe American democracy as "paradoxical" at the opening of this chapter?
2. Why did Franklin add "if you can keep it" to his description of the new American nation as a republic?
3. What are some of the ways that ideas are influential in national government and politics?
4. Think of a political issue you care about—cutting taxes, global warming, immigration, healthcare, and so forth. Which government institutions are involved in determining how that issue is addressed and resolved?

5. What are the three types of "interests" that political scientists pay attention to in assessing whether political outcomes are interest based?
6. How might an individual make an impact on the vast U.S. system of government and politics? How might *you* be meaningfully involved?
7. Think of the various groups that you belong to. How would you describe each group? In what ways is each group part of the larger American society?

Go to www.oup.com/us/Morone to find quizzes, flash cards, simulations, tutorials, videos, and other study tools.

The Ideas That Shape America

2

ARMY CAPTAIN RUSSELL BURGOS hunkered down in his bunker as mortars ripped through the night. A year ago he had been a political science professor; now he was fighting in Iraq. Burgos's unit was operating in the Sunni Triangle, where the fighting was fiercest. "A mortar attack in the middle of the night," he mused, "is an odd place to reconsider a course syllabus." But that is exactly what he found himself doing. Experiencing war made him see politics and societies in new ways.

As shells fell on the American base, Burgos thought about something that his classes had been missing: the study of ideas. The United States went to war in Iraq because of what key decision makers believed. All around him, men and women were fighting and dying over ideas—ideas such as freedom, democracy, equality, power, and faith in God.

Strangely enough, Burgos wrote later, ideas had barely come up in his own political science classes. Yet ideas helped explain why the United States launched the war, how it fought the war, and how it explained the war to both friends and enemies.

Who are we? Our ideas tell us—and they tell the world. The United States is a nation built on ideas. You will see ideas at work in every chapter of this book, for they touch every feature of government and politics. They affect the way Americans define their national ideals, their political goals, and their nation itself. As you read about these ideas—and as you continue through this book—think about other important ideas that should be added to the list alongside the seven we discuss in this chapter. If you come up with a compelling example, we may quote you in the next edition.

In this chapter, you will:

- Learn about the seven key American ideas.

- Review the arguments that surround each of them.

- Explore the essential question: How do ideas affect politics?

A Nation of Ideas

On July 4, 1776, American leaders issued a Declaration of Independence explaining their decision to break away from England. Its second paragraph describes the idea that animated them:

> We hold these truths to be self-evident, that all men are created equal, that they are endowed by their Creator with certain unalienable rights, that among these are life, liberty and the pursuit of happiness.

● *Army Captain Russell Burgos hands out supplies to Iraqi children.*

23

American Ideas

Rank of Americans in terms of self-reported happiness compared to more than 100 other nations, according to the latest World Happiness Report: **15**

Rank of Swiss, Mexicans, and Afghans, respectively: **1, 14, 153**

Number of times the word *rights* appears in the Declaration of Independence: **10**

Number of times the word *rights* appears in the original Constitution: **0**

Number of times the word *rights* appears in amendments to the Constitution: **15**

Number of times the word *democracy* appears in the Constitution: **0**

Percentage of Americans who say that the gap between the rich and everyone else has increased in the last 10 years: **65**

Percentage of Americans who say that government should act to reduce economic inequality: **69**

Percentage of Republicans and Democrats, respectively, who say this: **45, 90**

Percentage of Italians, Poles, and Americans, respectively, who agree that "it is the role of the government to take care of people who cannot care for themselves": **66, 56, 23**

Percentage of Americans who say that religion is "very important" to them: **50**

Percentage of Spaniards, British, and French who say the same: **22, 17, 13**

Percentage of Americans who disagree that "All men are created equal": **22**

Percentage of Americans who agreed that "most people who work hard will get ahead" in 2000: **74**

Percentage of Americans who agreed in 2016: **62**

Percentage of millennials (aged 18–29, in a Harvard study) who say "the American dream is dead": **48**

Most people have heard that line so often that it has lost its force, but it is one of the most powerful ideas in history. It explains the role of government—securing each individual's rights to life, liberty, and the pursuit of happiness. The Declaration states that people form governments for one purpose—"*to secure those rights.*" And although the men and women who fought the revolution fell far short of this ideal, they left the nation an inspiring goal. Every American generation argues about how it can best achieve the Declaration's shimmering promise to "secure" the rights of every citizen.

Many people believe that the United States is a unique nation, different from every other. That view is known as **American exceptionalism**. Of course, every nation is distinctive in some way. The United States is exceptional in large part because of seven key ideas that guide our politics. Most of them can be traced back to the Declaration of Independence.

What are the seven big ideas? Liberty, self-rule (which is often called democracy), individualism, limited government, the American dream, equality, and faith in God. These ideas touch almost everything we do as a nation. They are the foundation of American politics and lie at the core of what makes America distinctive.

American exceptionalism:
The view that the United States is uniquely characterized by a distinct set of ideas such as equality, self-rule, and limited government.

JOHN HANCOCK'S DEFIANCE.
JULY 4TH 1776.
The Declaration of Independence being fully adopted, John Hancock, President of the Continental Congress took up the pen and signed his name to it in a large bold hand; then rising he said, "There! John Bull can read my name without spectacles, and may double his reward for my head. That is my defiance!"

Ideas have consequences. John Hancock of Massachusetts defiantly signs the Declaration. According to legend, he signed it in big, bold letters so that King George III could read Hancock's name without his spectacles—and "double the reward for my head."

There is an unusual twist to these ideas. Americans rarely agree on what they mean. Instead, we constantly debate them. The Declaration of Independence declares that all men are created equal, but many of the men who signed it owned slaves. Our stamps and coins say "In God We Trust," but Americans passionately disagree about whether the Constitution permits prayer in schools or menorahs in public parks. All our foundational ideas have (at least) two sides and spark ardent disputes. To reveal the real truth about American politics, we should post signs at all the airports that say: *"Welcome to the great argument that is the USA."*

Now let's consider the first key idea.

Liberty

As the Revolutionary War broke out, the royal governor of Virginia promised freedom to any slave who joined the British. Eighty thousand slaves ran for the British lines. Some of them fought in black units, with their motto—"liberty for the slaves"—sewn onto their uniforms.[1]

The enslaved men and women who fought for the British saw their hopes dashed when their side surrendered at the Battle of Yorktown in 1781—effectively ending the Revolutionary War. After the battle, the Redcoats, as the English soldiers were known, began to withdraw, rowing out to the warships bobbing in the harbor for their long retreat. One desperate group of slaves raced past the sentries on the wharf, dove into the sea, and swam toward the long rowboats that were ferrying the defeated British troops out to their naval vessels.

● During the Revolutionary War, radicals met under trees they called "liberty trees" and erected poles they called "liberty poles." In this painting, Bostonians have dragged the British tax collector to the liberty tree where they have tarred and feathered him. The painting was British propaganda that mocked the liberty tree and the revolutionaries.

As the black men tried to clamber aboard the small boats, British troops pushed them away. Fearful that the swimmers would swamp the craft, the troops pulled out axes and hacked off the slaves' hands and fingers. And *still* they kept coming, trying to surge aboard, thrashing after their fading dream of liberty. The image is unforgettable: These men were so desperate for freedom that even as the Redcoats swung their bloody hatchets, they kept clutching for the boats that might carry them away from bondage.

"The Land of the Free"

No idea comes up more often in American history than *freedom* or *liberty* (we use the words interchangeably in this book). The national anthem declares America "the land of the free." During the civil rights movement of the 1950s and 1960s, high school students spilled out of Baptist churches and marched toward dogs and high-pressure fire hoses, singing, "Everyone shout freedom, freedom, freedom!" The Statue of Liberty is inscribed "Give me your huddled masses . . . yearning to breathe free." President George W. Bush declared in his second inaugural address, "The best hope for peace in our world is the expansion of freedom in all the world." A group of conservative Republicans in Congress established the Freedom Caucus in 2015.

Freedom: The ability to pursue one's own desires without interference from others.

What is **freedom**? *It means that the government will protect your life, your liberty, and your property from the coercion of others (including public officials) in order to permit you to pursue the goals you define for yourself.*

The Two Sides of Liberty

Everyone agrees that freedom is a basic American value. But, in practice, Americans disagree about what it means—and what governments should do to ensure it. There are two different views: negative liberty and positive liberty.[2]

Negative liberty: Freedom from constraints or the interference of others.

The more familiar view is **negative liberty**: *Freedom is the absence of constraints.* Society's responsibility, from this perspective, is to make sure that others (especially government officials) do not interfere with individuals. The government protects your right to believe what you wish, to say what you like, to declare any faith (or none), and to go into whatever profession you want—all without constraints or fear of punishment. Negative liberty firmly limits government action. Public officials violate your freedom when they collect taxes from you to feed the hungry or punish you for smoking tobacco or marijuana. Negative freedom is the right to act as you want.

Positive liberty: The ability—and provision of basic necessities—to pursue one's goals.

The alternative is **positive liberty**: *the freedom to pursue one's goals.* From this perspective, individuals cannot really be free—they cannot pursue their desires—if

What Do You Think?

Negative Versus Positive Liberty

Americans often disagree about the meaning of "freedom." Is freedom the absence of constraints (negative liberty) or the freedom to pursue one's goals with equal opportunity (positive liberty)?	**Do you believe in negative liberty?** Government should not interfere with individuals. Freedom means leaving every person alone to do what he or she wishes—without interference.	**Or do you believe in positive liberty?** Freedom simply is not a meaningful concept if you or your family are chronically hungry. A decent society has to lift everyone to a basic minimum. That's what living in a democracy should be about.	**Or do your beliefs fall somewhere in between?** Think about how you might combine these two concepts. You may find it easier to answer this question after reading about the other major ideas. If you are not ready to choose, read on—and then return to this question.

they lack the basic necessities of life. Protecting liberty means ensuring that every citizen has food, shelter, health care, and educational opportunities. After all, how can people truly be free if they are hungry or homeless? This view justifies government action as a way to help give all people a legitimate chance to achieve their desires.

President Franklin D. Roosevelt forcefully expressed this view in 1941. As the United States prepared for World War II, he proclaimed that the nation was fighting for "four freedoms": freedom of speech, freedom of worship, freedom from want, and freedom from fear. The first two—freedom of speech and religion—were traditional negative liberties: No one could infringe on these individual rights. However, "freedom from want" was something new, a positive liberty that entails helping needy people who have fallen on hard times. Roosevelt was suggesting that social welfare policies such as unemployment insurance and Social Security were part of the all-American idea of freedom. Contemporary ideas of positive freedom include efforts to ensure that all people are well educated or to stop them from smoking. The guiding notion is that a lack of education, or illness or addiction, makes it difficult for individuals to pursue their goals.

see for yourself 2.1

Go online to hear President Roosevelt deliver his speech on the four freedoms.

Which side is a more accurate view of freedom? That depends on your values. Beneath these two visions of liberty lie different accounts of the good society. The negative view emphasizes personal autonomy: Taxing me violates my freedom of property. Strong proponents of negative liberty are known as **libertarians** and oppose most forms of government action. Libertarians call for a small government that simply leaves people alone as long as they are not interfering with the rights of others. The positive view follows Roosevelt: Membership in a free society means sharing enough wealth so that everyone enjoys freedom from want. The two perspectives reflect different values, different visions of society, and different definitions of liberty.

Libertarians: People who believe in minimal government—specifically, that public officials' only role should be defending borders, prosecuting crime, and protecting private property.

The Idea of Freedom Is Always Changing

Once upon a time, Americans permitted slavery and racial segregation. Women lost all their legal rights the day they were married; their possessions—even their very bodies—passed into the custody of their husbands. Immigrants from China, and later from India, were denied any hope of becoming Americans no matter how long they lived in the country. The ideal of freedom moved Americans to reverse each of these prejudices.

Scholars disagree about how to interpret the results. Some see American history as a steady march toward greater liberty. Yes, they admit, American history is full of oppression. However, our faith in freedom leads oppressed groups to fight for their rights. The American promise, wrote Samuel Huntington, is the "promise of disharmony," as a constant parade of groups—African Americans, women, immigrants, and many others—successfully challenge the nation to live up to its ideals.

Other political thinkers, such as Rogers Smith, warn against viewing American history as a steady rise of freedom. The outcome in the fight is never inevitable, they argue. Instead, freedom is won and lost . . . and won and lost again. Americans fought their bloody civil war to end slavery, only to watch new forms of racial segregation and oppression take hold and last for almost another century. Native Americans have never had their place on the land or in society fully restored. Struggles to secure rights are still part of the long battle for freedom. No one can say how those conflicts will end. Nor should we ever take liberty for granted, and indeed fewer Americans are satisfied with the freedom they have today than they were just a few years ago (see Figure 2.1).[3]

● **FIGURE 2.1** *Fewer Americans are satisfied with their freedom to choose what they want to do with their lives. Some conservatives blame too much government interfering with negative liberty; some liberals respond that cuts in government programs have undercut positive freedom. (Gallup)*

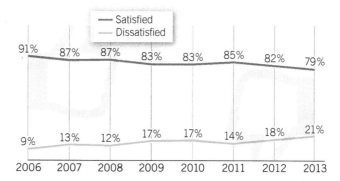

THE BOTTOM LINE

» Liberty—or the freedom to pursue your goals—is the most often-invoked American value.

» There are two different views of what liberty means. *Negative liberty* emphasizes a lack of constraints on individuals, even if those constraints are intended to help others. *Positive liberty* calls on the community to help everyone satisfy their basic needs.

» Guarantees of individual liberty have developed over time. Some scholars see the rise of freedom as inevitable, reflecting American ideals; others see it as a constant battle that can always go either way.

Self-Rule

As the American Revolution began, mobs gathered in the towns and cities. The people, they declared, would seize authority from their royal governors (appointed by the tyrannical king) and exercise power themselves. "The mob has begun to think for itself," complained one wealthy New Yorker. "Poor reptiles, before noon they will bite" (meaning *revolt*).[4]

Patriotic crowds ignored the skeptics. At mass meetings, the people voted for laws, enforced decrees, and even issued wedding licenses. They dispatched boisterous pro-American toughs who used sticks and stones to discourage individuals from acknowledging British institutions. Here is a powerful image of democracy: American people bypassing government officials and running the country themselves from the town commons. The people ruled.

That principle sounds simple. The United States is the world's longest running democracy—of course the people rule. But from the beginning, a great debate arose about how to achieve **self-rule**. The Constitution was meant to settle the issue—but we are still arguing about its meaning over 229 years later.

Self-rule: The idea that legitimate government flows from the people.

How do we achieve self-rule? Americans have long vacillated between two very different paths—a *democracy* and a *republic*.

One Side of Self-Rule: Democracy

Democracy involves citizen participation in making government decisions. Whether directly or through freely elected representatives, they exercise self-rule. (*Demos* is the Greek word for "the people," and *kratia* is the Greek word for "rule/power.") In early New England, citizens governed in town meetings—without relying on elected officials. To this day, some towns are still run this way. How high should taxes be? How much should the town pay its schoolteachers? Eligible voters all can have their say before voting to decide the matter.

Many states still reach for this democratic ideal—let the public make decisions without relying on elected officials. In 2016, voters in voters in 35 states weighed in on 157 ballot questions, including such issues as legalizing marijuana (in four states from Massachusetts to California), gun controls (three states), minimum wage increase (four states), minimum wage *decrease*, for minors (South Dakota), rights to hunt and fish (Indiana and Kansas), and even a measure strengthening

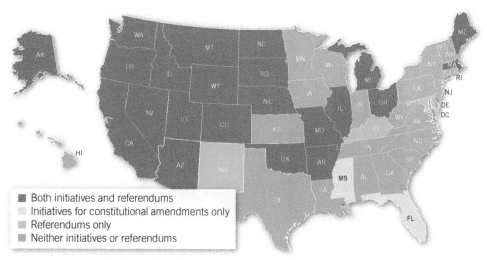

● **FIGURE 2.2** *Most states in the Midwest and Pacific Northwest both have referendums and initiatives. These vehicles of direct democracy are less common along the East Coast. (NY Constitution.org)*

Referendum: An election in which citizens vote directly on an issue.

Initiative: A process in which citizens propose new laws or amendments to the state constitution.

Sunshine laws: Laws that permit the public to watch policymakers in action and to access the records of the proceedings.

state prohibitions against slavery (Colorado). People vote directly on an issue through a **referendum**, allowed by twenty-seven states and the District of Columbia (see Figure 2.2). **Initiatives** permit the public in every state to circulate a petition that would propose a new law or amendment to its Constitution. And most city and state governments have **sunshine laws** that open their meetings to the public.

Thomas Jefferson, who drafted the Declaration of Independence and served as the third U.S. president, was the most vocal proponent of maximizing democracy. "The will of the majority," wrote Jefferson, is a "sacred principle" and "the only sure guardian of the rights of man." If the people cannot govern themselves, asked Jefferson, how can they possibly be trusted with the government of others?[5]

The result is a rich American legacy of taking to the streets to demonstrate, rally, and protest. Examples include the "Occupy Wall Street" demonstrations against income inequality; Tea Party protests against too much government; Black Lives Matter rallies; giant Earth Day demonstrations that launched the modern environmental movement; and the 1963 March on Washington, which was electrified by Martin Luther King's "I Have a Dream" speech.

Thomas Jefferson's dream of direct democracy lives on. Idealists throughout American history have returned to the democrat's first principle: The people should exercise power as much as possible.

Another Side of Self-Rule: A Republic

Most of the men who drafted the Constitution did not agree with Jefferson about democracy. The states had tried to create direct democracy right after the American Revolution. George Washington thought the result was chaos. "We have probably had too good an opinion of human nature," he grumbled. James Madison put it most famously: "Democracies have [always] been spectacles of turbulence and contention . . . as short in their lives as violent in their deaths." The problem, said Madison, was that in direct democracy, the majority often gets carried away. They push their self-interest without paying attention to the rights of the minority. Direct democracy, he concluded, offers no barrier to lynch mobs crying for blood.[6]

The alternative is a **republic**. In this form of government, the people rule indirectly through their elected representatives. The constitutional framers made an important contribution to the theory of self-rule. Classical democratic theory suggested that popular government would only work if the people were virtuous. The founders realized that popular government would have to work with leaders and citizens who were often not very virtuous at all. "If men were angels," wrote James Madison in *Federalist* No. 51, "no government would be necessary." The great challenge, he concluded, was to devise government institutions that would protect individual rights even if a majority of the people were selfish and corrupt. His solution: A republic.

A Mixed System

Which view of self-rule holds in the United States? Both do. We can say that the United States is a democratic republic because it includes elements of a democracy *and* of a republic. There are

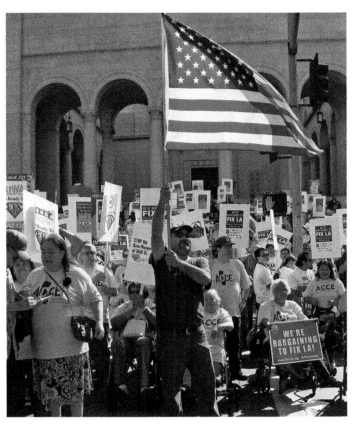

Another form of democracy in action? Americans take to the streets to express their views. California residents rally for a 2016 ballot measure to raise the minimum wage.

plenty of opportunities for direct participation. At the same time, American government is organized to check the majority. The House, the Senate, the president, and the Supreme Court all put the brakes on one another. And all of them face fifty different state governments, each with its own politics, powers, and programs. The American government operates through elected and unelected officials who answer (sometimes indirectly) to the public.

Republic: A government in which citizens rule indirectly and make government decisions through their elected representatives.

The sheer number of U.S. elected officials—more than five hundred thousand—reveals our hybrid form of government. There is one elected government official for every six hundred people in the country. Few other nations come close to this ratio. We elect representatives, reflecting our origins as a republic, but the enormous number of opportunities to serve in elective office moves us closer to a democracy.

Although our government combines elements of both democracy and republic, the debate continues about which way we should tilt. Which stance do you prefer? Jefferson's faith in direct democracy? Or Madison's warning that people are not angels and that government is best pursued indirectly, with the people electing some representatives who in turn select others?

You may have noticed that these two principles—the democratic and the republican—are also the names of America's two major political parties. However, to complicate matters, the party labels do not really correspond to the party principles. Many Republican Party members are committed democrats and vice versa. We always capitalize the names of the parties—Democrats and Republicans—to avoid confusing them with the two pathways to self-rule.

Limited Government

Back in 1691, while America was still part of Great Britain, King William III appointed Benjamin Fletcher to be governor of New York and gave him control over the New England colonies (which had been independent until then). The Connecticut legislature did not want to cede its power to Governor Fletcher and immediately selected a new commander for the local militia—a direct challenge to the new governor's authority. Fletcher could not ignore this intransigence, so on a beautiful October day he sailed to Hartford, the capital of Connecticut, with a small detachment of troops. He assembled the Connecticut militia and had an officer read aloud the royal proclamation declaring his authority over the state—and its militia.

As the officer spoke, the Connecticut militiamen began to beat their drums in defiance. Fletcher tried to restore order by commanding his soldiers to fire their muskets in the air; in the ensuing quiet, he threatened to punish the militia members for their insolence. In response, the commander of the Connecticut militia stepped forward, put his hand on the hilt of his sword, and issued his own warning: "If my drummers are again interrupted, I'll make sunlight shine through you. We deny and defy your authority." Outnumbered and in no mood for bloodshed, Fletcher beat a quick retreat to his vessel and sailed ignominiously back to New York City. Because the king and his ministers were more than three thousand miles away, they never heard about this little rebellion against their authority.[7]

The Origins of Limited Government

The tale of Governor Fletcher illustrates an enduring idea: Americans distrust centralized leadership and have consistently sought to limit its power. Eighty years before the Revolutionary War, Connecticut had grown used to electing its own leaders and going its own way. The people saw the king as a distant figure with no right to interfere in their affairs. The image of central government as a remote, unfeeling, untrustworthy authority that threatens our freedoms runs through American history.

Why did Americans develop this distrust? The answer lies in how the people secured their rights in the first place. In most nations, the central government—made up of kings or aristocrats, or both—grudgingly granted their people rights such as the vote or jury trials. Sometimes the people rebelled (as in France), sometimes they negotiated with kings (England), and sometimes monarchs expanded rights to modernize their nations (Thailand). All these countries share a common experience: kings or the central governments that replaced them were the source of rights and liberties. No wonder citizens in these nations instinctively look to the government for help in solving their problems.

The United States was dramatically different. Americans enjoyed political rights such as voting long before they even had a central government. As Governor Fletcher's humiliation illustrates, for most of colonial history the king was too far away to meddle in colonial affairs. Experience taught Americans to see the central government not as a potential source of rights, but as a threat to their life, liberty, and happiness.

This is one important reason why Americans are slow to trust their national government (see Figure 2.3 and Table 2.1). Proposals such as national health insurance, a cap on carbon emissions to stop global warming, or a nationwide registry of gun sales all run up against a deep suspicion of government. The French aristocrat Alexis de Tocqueville was struck by this lack of trust. Any visitor from Europe, he wrote back in 1831, would be amazed that the American government is so "feeble and restricted." Fifty years later, the English ambassador to the United States summarized the American spirit: "The less of government the better."[8]

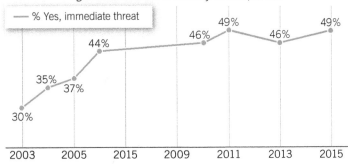

Do you think the federal government poses an immediate threat to the rights and freedoms of ordinary citizens, or not?

— % Yes, immediate threat

30% 35% 37% 44% 46% 49% 46% 49%

2003 2005 2015 2009 2011 2013 2015

FIGURE 2.3 *American distrust of government is growing.*

And Yet . . . the United States Has a Big Government

Here is the paradox lying at the heart of the limited-government idea. People across the political spectrum demand government action. Many **conservatives** seek to use federal authority to crack down on drugs, root out obscenity, limit marriage to heterosexual couples, get tougher on crime, forbid abortions, grow the military, secure the borders, or enhance homeland security. Back in the 1920s, conservatives in both parties banded together with feminists and public health reformers to outlaw all sales of alcohol from coast to coast—a remarkably ambitious government effort to change people's everyday behavior.

Most **liberals** reject the idea that public officials should interfere in people's private lives. But they are all for active government when it comes to economic policy or corporate regulation. They call on the government to sponsor fast trains, bank regulations, environmental protections, and school lunch programs (there's the freedom from want, again).

Libertarians break with both liberals and conservatives and challenge America to live up to our ideals of limited government. Government, libertarians insist, should protect public safety, private property, and national borders—and do little else. No giant army or navy; no public schools; no regulating banks; no telling people which drugs they cannot use; no helping people who are hungry, or homeless, or need healthcare; no laws against discrimination. The popularity of

Conservatives: Americans who believe in reduced government spending, personal responsibility, traditional moral values, and a strong national defense. Also known as *right* or *right-wing*.

Liberals: Americans who value cultural diversity, government programs for the needy, public intervention in the economy, and individuals' right to a lifestyle based on their own social and moral positions. Also known as *left* or *left-wing*.

Senator Rand Paul ran for the Republican nomination in 2016 on a libertarian platform but never gathered much support or attention.

TABLE 2.1 A Large Minority of Americans Express Hostility to Government

Do You See Government as Posing an Immediate Threat to the Rights and Freedoms of Its Citizens? How So?	% MENTIONING
Too many laws/government too big in general	19
Violations of freedoms/civil liberties	15
Gun control/violating Second Amendment	12
Too much involvement in people's private lives	10
Socialist government	6
Taking away freedom of religion	6
Police/law enforcement violence/arrests	4
Government surveillance of citizens/emails/phone records	4
Marriage issue	4
Overregulation/too much involvement in business	3
Overtaxing/taxes too high	3
Healthcare law	3
Failing to secure borders/illegal immigration	3
Too much spending	3
Government unfair/picks winners and losers	3
Not focused on needs of country/puts politics first	3
Too involved in things it shouldn't be	2
Violating separation of power/no accountability	2
Environmental regulations/EPA	1
Education/school system	1

Source: Gallup

this perspective rises and falls over time because every national crisis—from tainted food to bank failures to terrorist attacks—inspires widespread demands for government action. However, libertarians reflect a profound American suspicion of government that goes back to colonial times.

Limits on Government Action

In short, Americans often say they do not like government and then demand government do something about the causes they care about. The calls for action generally face two hurdles: the desire to limit government and the Constitution.

When the framers designed our political system, they built suspicion of government right into the system. The federal Constitution includes an intricate system of checks and balances on power, which we will explore in the next chapter. The Constitution limits what Congress may do—and Americans vigorously debate exactly where those boundaries actually lie.

Although it is difficult for government officials to undertake new tasks, the barriers they face are not insurmountable. During times of crisis, people turn to the government and demand action. Skilled leadership can also negotiate sweeping changes. And once programs go into effect, they often prove popular.

Ironically, the limits on change make it difficult to repeal new programs once they make it past all the hurdles and are up and running. For example, Social Security was passed in 1935 during the economic crisis of the Great Depression; Medicare passed in part because of a great electoral landslide in 1964. Both are now extremely popular; in fact, they are so widely embraced that they are known in Washington as "the third rails" of American politics—touch them and die (politically, of course).

New Jersey governor Chris Christie comforts victims of Hurricane Sandy. During crises such as this one, even many critics of the government set their views aside to demand action.

When Ideas Clash: Self-Rule and Limited Government

When Democrat Bernie Sanders ran for president in 2016, he vowed to raise taxes on wealthy people—those making $250,000 or more. Over on the Republican side, candidates Donald Trump and Ted Cruz insisted that lower taxes for everyone would boost economic performance.

Democrats and Republicans offered very different policies. In the 2016 election, voters made a clear choice: stop illegal immigration, fight crime, and address the consequences of international trade. With majorities in both the House and Senate, President Trump may be able to push through much of his agenda. However, it is normally very hard for winners to put their policies into effect—as a result of all the limits that Americans have placed on their own government.

Note the clash between two leading American ideas: self-rule and limited government. Self-rule says that the winning party should be able to put their policies into place. Jefferson expressed this point plainly: "The will of the majority," he wrote, is a "sacred principle" and "the only sure guardian of the rights of man."[9]

But another value, limited government, responds: Not so fast. We do not like government meddling in our private lives, so we make it very difficult for elected officials to follow through on their promises and actually get things done. Even a president who wins a national election by a large margin must still convince the majority in the House of Representatives and 60 percent of the Senate to vote his way. (Why 60 percent of the Senate? You'll see in Chapter 13.) Even when Congress does pass a law—which is no easy task—the program often faces challenges in the courts for violating constitutional limits on government power.

The result is an important question for political scientists—and for all Americans: How should we balance self-rule and limited government? Erecting too many boundaries means that we undermine government by the majority. But if voters get everything the winning candidates promise them, the result could be a host of expensive new programs and policies.

see for yourself 2.2

Go online and listen to the 2016 Republican National Convention chant: Lock her up!

What Do You Think?

Self-Rule Versus Limited Government

Many observers think we no longer have government by the people because it is too difficult for elected officials to get things done, even with a large popular majority. These reformers seek an easier path to government action. However, that prospect raises fears of a more active government. Which should we emphasize, self-rule or limited government? It's time to make your choice.

I'm with Thomas Jefferson. It should be easier for elected officials to enact the programs they promised. If they cannot do so, elections become less meaningful. When the people vote for something and their representatives fail to deliver, it fosters cynicism about the entire political process. Self-rule requires us to follow the people's mandate. If the majority does not like the results, it can express its displeasure in the next election.

I'm with James Madison. The checks and balances that make large-scale reforms difficult protect the United States from overbearing government and from sudden changes—whether rapidly expanding or cutting programs. The barriers to government action *should* be high. If the public really wants something, it will probably happen over time. Limited government is more important. Don't change the process.

Not sure? This is a formidable question. You may very well change your mind—maybe more than once—as you continue to read this book.

THE BOTTOM LINE

» Americans *distrust their government* far more than people in most other democracies. The Constitution builds that distrust into our governing rules by providing for *limited government*. The result is a very durable status quo.

» In many other countries, politicians can usually deliver the programs they promised on the campaign trail. In the United States, winners confront multiple barriers to fulfilling their pledges. That's the antigovernment strain in American thinking.

» However, once programs do go into effect, they often prove popular and difficult to change.

Individualism

Political scientist John Kingdon was visiting his niece in Norway. She was expecting a baby, and Professor Kingdon asked what she planned to do about her job. Casually, she replied that she would receive a full year's leave at 80 percent of her normal pay, and that her company was required to give her job back after the leave. "Who pays for all this?" asked Professor Kingdon. "The government, of course," his niece replied. She was surprised the question had even come up. "Is it any different in the United States?" she asked innocently.[10]

As Kingdon explained, it is completely different in the United States: Advocates fought for years to win the Family and Medical Leave Act (1993), which requires employers with more than fifty workers to allow up to twelve weeks of *unpaid* leave for pregnancy, adoption, illness, or military service. In 2012, the Supreme Court struck down part of the law by ruling that it could not cover state government employees.

Americans generally value **individualism**: *The idea that individuals, not the society or the community or the government, are responsible for their own well-being.* We, as a society, do not pay for maternity leave. Instead, we expect private individuals and families to handle birth, or adoption, or care giving.

Individualism: The idea that individuals, not the society, are responsible for their own well-being.

Community Versus Individualism

The idea of individualism is a source of controversy in every nation. There are two ways to see any society: as a single *community* or as a collection of *individuals*. Every nation includes both, but government policies can be designed to emphasize the community or to focus on individuals. Let us take a closer look at these two principles.

Countries that emphasize the community are called **social democracies**. Social democrats believe that members of a society are responsible for one another. They view government as a source of mutual assistance. The government provides citizens with the basics: good health insurance, retirement benefits, generous unemployment packages, and—as we saw in the Norwegian case—maternity benefits.

Social democracy: A government in which citizens are responsible for one another's well-being and use government policy to ensure that all are comfortably cared for.

In exchange, people pay high taxes. Almost half of a Norwegian's income goes to taxes. One effect of high taxation is to make it difficult for most citizens to get very rich. At the same time, the extensive welfare state makes it far less likely that people will live in poverty. Communal societies are far more equal—not just in opportunity, but in outcome. Most Western European nations are social democracies.

Social democracies are based on *solidarity*, the idea that people have a tight bond and are responsible for one another. Some societies exhibit a very strong sense of solidarity. In general, this will increase during wars, economic depressions, or other crises that get everyone to pull together. Scholars have found that more homogeneous societies—those in which people look alike, share the same values, and practice the same religion—exhibit higher rates of solidarity than very diverse societies. They point out that even long-established social democracies in Europe (historically populated primarily by Christians) have seen their sense of solidarity falter with the arrival of Muslim immigrants. Growing diversity has challenged national solidarity.

American politics includes a streak of solidarity. Martin Luther King put it eloquently: "I am inevitably my brother's keeper because I am my brother's brother."[11] However, the commitment to solidarity rises and falls in the United States. Perhaps it will strengthen, again, with the rising millennial generation?

Now let us turn to individualism. In this view, people and their families are responsible for their own welfare. The economist Milton Friedman famously wrote that "the world runs on individuals pursuing their separate interests." Leave people free to choose their interests, Friedman continued, and the public interest of the whole society will emerge.[12]

● *Residents and volunteers work together to clear debris after a tornado struck this rural Alabama community—solidarity in action.*

Rather than taxing people and using funds to aid the less well-off, proponents of this perspective opt for low taxes and a green light for private entrepreneurs. People who work hard will get ahead, they believe, and society will grow and prosper.

Individualists value the chance to get ahead more than they value a society in which everyone is equal. In social democracies, government regulations aim to protect workers. In contrast, individualists oppose government controls and believe that private companies should be able to expand or contract their workforce as they see fit (as long as they hire and fire without discriminating). Individualism points toward limited government, faith in economic markets, and a strong emphasis on *negative liberty*.

Opinion polls confirm what political theorists have long suspected: Americans tend to lean more toward individualism than toward social democracy—much more so than citizens of most other nations. In one prominent cross-national study, people were asked which is more important: being free to pursue life goals (individualism) or making sure that nobody in society is in need (community). The American majority (58 percent) chose freedom, whereas most people in nations such as Germany and Spain chose taking care of those in need. Compared to other countries, Americans lean more heavily toward individualism (see Comparing Nations 2.1).[13]

The Roots of American Individualism: Opportunity and Discord

Americans lean toward individualism and away from social democracy. Why? Two famous explanations look to the past. One finds the answer in golden opportunities. A second emphasizes social and racial discord.

Golden Opportunity.   For centuries, most Europeans and Asians lived as serfs or peasants working small plots of land. Powerful rulers kept them firmly in their place—there was little chance for individuals to get ahead by working hard. In early America, by contrast, there appeared to be endless land and opportunity. With hard work and a little luck, anyone (at least any white male) could earn a decent living and perhaps even a fortune. Stories about early settlers clearing their own land were later reinforced by images of rugged individuals on the western frontier. Hard workers relied on themselves—not the government.

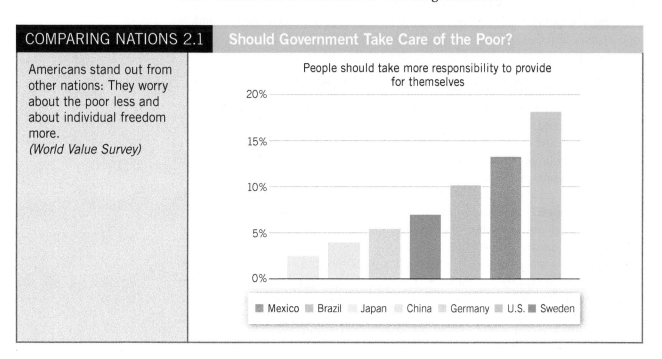

COMPARING NATIONS 2.1   Should Government Take Care of the Poor?

Americans stand out from other nations: They worry about the poor less and about individual freedom more.
(*World Value Survey*)

People should take more responsibility to provide for themselves

Mexico   Brazil   Japan   China   Germany   U.S.   Sweden

There is a lot of myth in these stories. Frontier life was less about brave individualism and more about communities. Settlers could not build a barn, a church, or a meetinghouse without their neighbors' help. But the image of hardy individuals on the frontier remains a powerful ideal in American culture and politics. And there was an important truth at its core: Few societies have ever offered so many individuals as much opportunity to rise and prosper as early America did.[14]

Social Conflict. Another explanation for American individualism emphasizes the enormous differences within our society. The country is too big and the population too diverse to develop a sense of solidarity. What, after all, did Calvinist Yankees in New England have in common with Roman Catholics in Baltimore or Anglican planters in Virginia—much less Spanish speakers in Florida or Texas? Moreover, a nation that included four million black slaves by 1860 had a terrible divide running through its heart.

● *Individualism in historical memory: At high noon on April 22, 1889, bugles sounded and a great mob—lined up impatiently outside the territory—surged across the Oklahoma border and snatched up as much land as they could stake out. Although the government sponsored the land giveaway, the image that has stuck is of people grabbing the land for themselves. Oklahoma still honors the scalawags that snuck in early ("sooner") and staked the best land—which is where the motto "The Sooner State" comes from.*

By the 1830s still another source of division had arisen. Immigrants speaking different languages and practicing what seemed like strange customs were arriving by the tens (and later hundreds) of thousands. Each generation of immigrants added to the American cacophony. For example, Irish Catholics (who arrived in the 1830s and 1840s) seemed strange to the English Protestants who had immigrated a century earlier. Could Catholics, with their allegiance to a foreign pope, really understand or uphold American values? Fifty years later, newly arriving Italians, Poles, and Chinese seemed just as threatening to the Irish, who by then had settled in.[15] All of these divisions made solidarity far more difficult to feel than in more stable, homogeneous populations.

Which explanation is correct? Both are on target. Unprecedented economic opportunity and vast social divisions have reinforced individualism.

Who We Are: Individualism and Solidarity?

Yet Americans are not individualists pure and simple. Rather, the two themes—individualism and solidarity—always compete in American politics. Individualism is more robust and more often in evidence, but a sense of solidarity also unites the American population. We often pull together as a nation. We often take care of our neighbors and pass government programs to improve the lives of people we do not know. The United States may have deep divisions, but it is remarkable how quickly they can disappear. A substantial majority of Americans today are children, grandchildren, or great-grandchildren of immigrants—many of whom were once regarded as strange and different.

All this raises another question to ponder: Where would you draw the line between solidarity and individualism? The answer directly relates to one of this book's central questions: *Who are we?* Take the test in "What Do You Think?" to learn where you stand on the continuum between rugged individualism and strong solidarity.

Individualism Versus Solidarity

Please score yourself on the following ten statements:

0 = Disagree strongly
1 = Disagree
2 = Agree
3 = Agree strongly

1. It is the responsibility of the government to take care of poor people who cannot take care of themselves.		0 1 2 **3**
2. Everyone should have health insurance in case they become ill.		0 1 **2 3**
3. In fact, everyone should have the same health insurance. It doesn't make sense for some people to get better care than others just because they can afford it.		0 **1** 2 3
4. I'd be willing to pay a little more in taxes so that no person in America goes hungry or homeless.		0 **1** 2 3
5. I'd be willing to pay a lot more in taxes so that everyone in America has a pretty decent life.		0 **1** 2 3
6. I agree with Dr. Martin Luther King, Jr.: "I am inevitably my brother's keeper because I am my brother's brother [and my sister's sister]. . . . The betterment of the poor enriches the rich."		0 1 2 **3**
7. I don't believe big companies should be permitted to fire people without providing two months' salary and some retraining.		0 1 2 **3**
8. Most Americans want the same things out of life.		0 1 2 3
9. We should think about others as much as we think about ourselves.		0 1 2 3
10. It is wrong to step over others to get ahead in life.		0 1 2 3

Scoring

0–5 = You are truly a rugged individualist!
6–14 = You are largely an individualist.
15–20 = You are a moderate who sees both sides of the issue.
21–24 = You are a social democrat.
25–30 = You are a true blue believer in solidarity!

Now, speak with someone who scored very differently from you. Try to explain how and why you came to hold your views.

THE BOTTOM LINE

» American politics includes both individualism and solidarity.

» Different leaders, parties, groups, and individuals weigh the two values in different ways. However, compared to other nations, the United States is very much at the individualist end of the spectrum.

The American Dream

Benjamin Franklin perfected a classic American literary form—tips for getting rich. Anyone, he assured his readers, could be successful by following a formula: be frugal ("A penny saved is a penny earned"), hardworking ("No gains without pains"), steady ("Little strokes fell great oaks"), bold ("God helps those who help themselves"), and—most important—morally upright ("Leave your vices, though ever so dear").[16]

Franklin summarized what later became known as the American dream: *If you are talented and work hard, you can achieve personal (and especially financial) success.* A popular historian, James Truslow Adams, was the first to actually call it the American dream. The United States, he wrote, is "a land in which life should be better and richer and fuller for everyone, with opportunity for each according to ability or achievement."[17] The idea scarcely changes across generations. "The American dream that we were all raised on is a simple but powerful one," averred President Bill Clinton more than two centuries after Ben Franklin. "If you work hard and play by the rules, you should be given a chance to go as far as your God-given abilities will take you."[18]

Spreading the Dream

The legacy of the Revolutionary War, according to historian Gordon Wood, was the spread of the American dream to all classes. National leaders originally imagined that they were establishing a classical republic, such as Athens, in which a few outstanding men would govern the people. Instead, the Revolution established the common people as the basis of government and gave them an unprecedented chance to make their fortunes. What did the mass of people care about? "Making money and getting ahead," wrote Wood. Yes, it was vulgar, material, and crass. But such opportunity had never been available on such a broad scale before.[19]

Enabling the dream of success remains an important part of any policy debate. Will a proposal help small business? Will it create jobs? Will it stifle entrepreneurs? Immigrants still come to the United States in large numbers—far more than to any other country—partly to pursue the dream of success.

Challenging the Dream

As with every important idea, the American dream generates conflict. Critics raise two questions: Has the system become rigged to favor some (usually the wealthy) over others? And is the pursuit of wealth an undesirable value, either on its own merits or because it crowds out other important values?

Is the System Tilted Toward the Wealthy? Some critics question whether the American dream is still open to everyone or whether it has grown biased toward the rich and powerful. When Tocqueville wrote *Democracy in America* in the 1830s, the United States offered more opportunities to get ahead than perhaps any nation in history. Vast open lands (open, that is, once Native Americans had been driven away) offered a fresh start for the ambitious and the resourceful.

For much of U.S. history, including the boom years after World War II, middle-class incomes rose faster than incomes at the top. Then, starting around 1979, this trend changed. Money began to flow to the wealthiest more than to the other classes. Figure 2.4A and 2.4B compare the two periods.

Income growth, 1949–1979

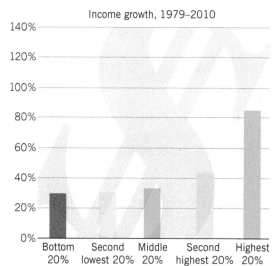

Income growth, 1979–2010

● **FIGURE 2.4A** *Between 1949 and 1979, those on the bottom saw their earnings grow faster than those on the top. (Robert Frank, Falling Behind)*

● **FIGURE 2.4B** *. . . but look how that changed after 1979. Now those on the bottom have very little income growth while the wealthy have very rapid growth. Is this a bad thing? Americans disagree. (Russell Sage Foundation, Chartbook of Inequality)*

Today, the top 1 percent of Americans holds more wealth than the bottom 90 percent combined. Three million people enjoy more wealth than 270 million others taken together. Sixty million Americans at the bottom of the charts own almost nothing—one-tenth of one percent of the national wealth. And inequality continues to rise, as the gap between richest and poorest is widening fastest in U.S. metro areas with high concentrations of well-paying jobs in information, technology, and finance.[20]

Many social scientists now argue that the chance of moving up from poverty to wealth is fading in the United States. Studies suggest that someone in the bottom fifth of the income distribution is twice as likely to move up at least one category (or quintile) in Canada, Denmark, or France as they are in the United States (see Comparing Nations 2.2). Critics—both liberal and conservative—increasingly challenge the system for not offering real equality of opportunity.[21]

Does the American Dream Promote the Wrong Values?   A second critique of the American dream questions the chase for wealth as a human value. Environmentalists criticize the damage caused by big houses, sprawling suburbs, gas-guzzling cars, and opulent lifestyles. Others cite the harm to old-fashioned communal ideals. "These dark days will be worth all they cost us," said President Franklin Roosevelt during the depths of the Great Depression, "if they teach us that our true destiny is . . . to minister . . . to our fellow man." Repeatedly, he urged Americans to rethink their basic values before an upturn in the stock market "dulled our moral sense."[22]

President Lyndon Johnson put civil rights in the same larger context. "Should we double our wealth and conquer the stars, and still not be equal to this issue [racial equity], then we will have failed as a people and as a nation. For with a whole country as with a person, 'What is a man profited, if he should gain the whole world, and lose his own soul?'" Voices like these have questioned the pursuit of economic success to the exclusion of community and social justice.[23]

COMPARING NATIONS 2.2 | Social Mobility Around the World

Many nations—including Japan, New Zealand, and even Pakistan—have developed more social mobility than the United States. In 2015, China's president Xi Jinping began calling the aspirations of upward mobility the "Chinese dream," nudging the American dream aside—though China still has lower mobility rates than most Western democracies, including the United States. The chart at right displays the sharp increase in U.S. inequality over a 30-year period, compared to other countries.

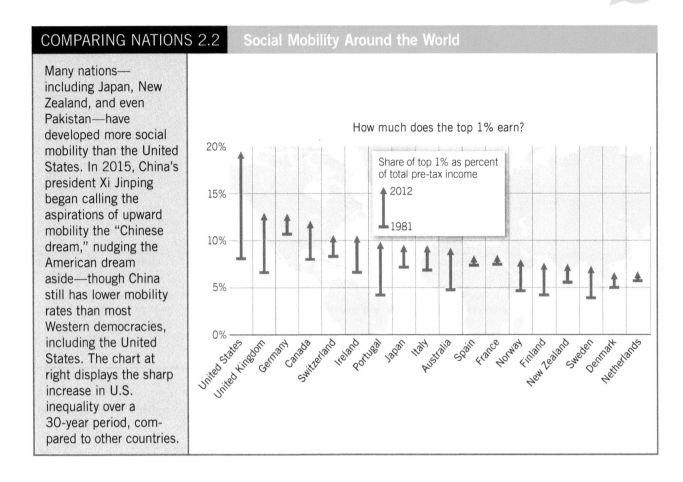

How much does the top 1% earn?

Share of top 1% as percent of total pre-tax income

2012

1981

The criticism, however, rarely sticks for long. Ralph Waldo Emerson, a nineteenth-century essayist and lecturer, summed up the usual view when he questioned the motives of his iconoclastic friend, Henry David Thoreau. "I cannot help counting it a fault in him that he had no ambition," said Emerson at Thoreau's funeral. "Instead of engineering for all America, he was the captain of a huckleberry-party."[24]

Many people would rather go out in the woods like Thoreau and pick huckleberries than join the rat race for greater material benefits. The capitalists who celebrate wealth often have to wrestle with economic populists who would rather share it. During difficult economic times—like those accompanying the "Great Recession" that began in the fall of 2008—faith in the American dream lags.

Despite critics and challenges, Americans usually celebrate the gospel of success. The nation's politics, economics, and culture accommodate dreams of wealth. In comparison with other wealthy nations, our taxes are relatively low, we regulate business less, we take fewer vacations, and we place more emphasis on getting ahead. One group that may be questioning these long-standing truths is the millennial generation, comprising many American college students today. In a recent Harvard University poll, nearly half (48%) of 18–29 year-olds said that the American Dream did not apply to their generation—a trend worth watching closely in coming years.[25]

» The American dream is the belief that anyone who works hard can get ahead and grow wealthy.

» Critics argue that hard work is no longer enough. They offer two criticisms: First, the poor and the middle class are falling farther behind the wealthy because of bias in the political economy; and second, other values are more important than wealth.

» Despite the critics, the dream remains a powerful American idea.

Equality

When Tocqueville arrived in the United States in 1831, he was amazed by the widespread equality. In one of his first letters home, he reported watching servers in a tavern sit down at the next table to eat and drink alongside the guests. Here was a society in which people from all ranks shook hands, discussed politics, and chased money. Everyone seemed to be equals.

Tocqueville distilled this thought into the first sentence of his great book *Democracy in America*: "No novelty in the United States struck me more vividly . . . than the equality of condition." In a world that was still full of aristocrats and inherited privilege, American society embodied the great idea at the heart of the Declaration of Independence: "All men [and women] are created equal."[26]

Equality means that *every citizen enjoys the same privileges, status, and rights before the laws*. There are three different types of equality to consider when analyzing the concept: *social, political*, and *economic*.

> **Equality:** All citizens enjoy the same privileges, status, and rights before the laws.

Three Types of Equality

Social equality means that all individuals enjoy the same status in society. There are no American barons or archdukes who inherit special benefits when they are born. This aspect of American society has not changed since the nation's founding. Except for slavery, there have never been fixed social classes. Few American politicians boast of noble origins or good family lineage. On the contrary, for the past 150 years candidates have flaunted (or invented) their working-class roots. Even very wealthy politicians often claim to have humble origins (for many years, they boasted about the log cabins they supposedly grew up in). An old cliché in American politics, one with a lot of truth to it, is the saying that any little boy or girl could grow up to be the president—or a millionaire.

> **Social equality:** All individuals enjoy the same status in society.

Political equality means that every citizen has the same political rights and opportunities. Americans enjoyed universal white, male *suffrage*—or the right to vote—much earlier than did citizens of most nations. Over time the opportunity to vote spread. Today there are lively debates about whether we still ensure everyone an equal opportunity to affect the political process. Some reformers suggest, for example, that if everyone is to have the same chance to influence the political process, we should remove money from elections. Otherwise, the wealthy will have outsized influence over the outcome. Others counter that individuals who are excited by candidates should be allowed to contribute to them.

> **Political equality:** All citizens have the same political rights and opportunities.

INFO/DATA: In the United States, Fewer Believe There Is "Opportunity to Get Ahead"

Although the American dream remains a shimmering ideal for many, in recent years the public has been less likely to share this vision. A declining number agree that the United States provides "plenty of opportunity" so that "anyone who works hard can go as far as they want." Some attribute this loss of faith to declining economic opportunities available to the middle and working classes.

1. Do you think that you are likely to have a better life than your parents? Polling results show that most Americans thought so until around 2010—then they became more pessimistic. What do you think explains the change?

2. Which goals of the middle-class lifestyle do people feel are hardest for young people to achieve?

% Plenty of opportunity — **% Not much opportunity**

87 — 81 — 57 52
8 — 17 — 41 43

1950   1960   1970   1980   1990   2000   2010   2020

Year

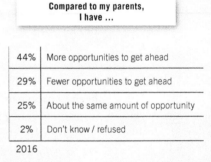

Compared to my parents, I have ...

44%	More opportunities to get ahead
29%	Fewer opportunities to get ahead
25%	About the same amount of opportunity
2%	Don't know / refused

2016

The middle-class lifestyle is increasingly out of reach for millennials
(Compared to 20 or 30 years ago)

I think it is harder for young people today to ...

Save for retirement	Own a home	Have a stable, decent-paying job	Have stable affordable housing	Have health insurance	Obtain education beyond high school
81%	76%	71%	71%	50%	45%

Sources: University of Michigan National Election Survey; Gallup; MacArthur Foundation

45

The quest for political equality raises many other issues: Does everyone enjoy an equal right to a fair trial—or have the costs of going to court elevated this basic value beyond the reach of many people? Does the voting system make it too difficult for some people to register and cast their ballots? Does every citizen have an *equal opportunity* to influence the political process, and are they all treated the same way before the law?

Economic equality focuses on differences in wealth. When President Washington toured the country in 1790 he noticed that in some regions there were few very wealthy people and little poverty. For more than a century and a half, the nation truly was exceptional in its economic equality.[27]

Today the United States has changed dramatically—toward inequality. In 1970, the level of economic inequality in the United States was similar to that in most other wealthy democracies. On one measure of economic inequality, known as the Gini coefficient, the United States ranked between France and Japan on the equality tables. Today, in contrast, America has become far less equal than nations such as Japan, Sweden, and Germany. We are now closer to the most unequal country in the world (Lesotho) than we are to the most equal (Sweden). Should we adopt public policies that aim to limit economic inequality? Let us look more closely at this much-contested issue.

> **Economic equality:** A situation in which there are only small differences in wealth among citizens.

How Much Economic Inequality Is Too Much?

Inequality in America has reached levels not seen in almost a century. One illustration of national differences in economic inequality is the "salary gap." In 1965, the **median** (or typical) American chief executive officer (CEO) made twenty-six times more than a typical worker in his or her company. In Japan today the figure is roughly the same. But in the contemporary United States, the average CEO makes (depending on the study) between three hundred to five hundred times the salary of the average employee. Is this a problem for the idea that "all men are created equal"?

People in many countries would answer "yes." Too much inequality, they say, divides society. In Japan, cultural norms encourage individuals to avoid attracting

> **Median:** A statistical term for the number in the middle or the case that has an equal number of examples above and below it.

Cleveland Cavaliers forward Lebron James.

Should we worry about economic inequality? Lebron James (flying in for a dunk at left) makes more than $70 million a year for playing basketball and endorsing products. Is that too much for a superstar—even one as good as James? Should we change the rules so that the wealthy get less and poor people more?

attention through great wealth or ostentation. In fact, Tocqueville warned Americans that they might be vulnerable to economic inequality: "The friends of democracy should keep their eyes anxiously fixed in [the] direction [of] . . . the manufacturing aristocracy we see rising up."[28]

As discussed in the section on the American dream, our public policies (and public opinions) often endorse the race to wealth. Why not let the winners—hedge-fund managers, basketball stars, successful musicians, CEOs, and breakout entrepreneurs—enjoy fabulous success? Some activists charge that the richest 1 percent take advantage of everyone else; those on the other side criticize such talk for fostering "socialism" and "class warfare." In fact, this is an old debate stretching back through time.

Opportunity or Outcome?

Many Americans accept high levels of economic inequality, contending that these are not fatal to our hopes for an egalitarian society. That is because of an important distinction between *equal opportunity* and *equal outcome*.

Equal opportunity is the idea that every American has a similar chance in life. In politics, this means that each person gets one vote and that the process is transparent and open to all. In economics, it means that every individual gets a fair shot at achieving the American dream. Whether you are white or black, Anglo or Latino, male or female, rich or poor, you have a similar opportunity to influence the political process and to win economic success.

Equal outcome, in contrast, is the idea that a society guarantees not just opportunity but also results. Some nations reserve a minimum number of seats in the national legislature for women or members of specific ethnic groups. And, as we have already seen, others keep their taxes high and offer extensive social benefits, knowing that this arrangement will keep successful people from getting too far ahead of everyone else.

Today, the United States aims for equal opportunity. The winners fly in private jets; the losers may end up with nothing. Questions—and hard political choices—about equal opportunity remain. How do we give people a real chance to affect the governing process? How much education is enough to help ensure that a graduate can make it in the marketplace? Do we need to provide early childhood reading programs? Offer English-language programs for everyone not fluent? And what should we do about past injustices? Does the long legacy of slavery, segregation, and repressive policies toward Native American Indians require our society to offer special forms of compensation to these groups?

These questions return us to the same policy debates we introduced during the discussion of positive and negative liberty. Should we guarantee the basics—or simply protect individual rights and let every person run the great race alone? As you can see, debates about equality lead back to debates about freedom (positive or negative) and individualism.

Might the gap between rich and poor grow so large that it undermines equality of opportunity? Americans have long pointed proudly to our prosperous middle class—and indeed, for most of the nation's history middle-class Americans had the highest average incomes in the world. Yet percentage of Americans who are middle class shrunk from 61 in 1971 to 50 by 2015[29] (see Figure 2.5). As the gap continues to widen, liberals warn that growing disparities are creating a land of a few billionaires and many hungry children with grim prospects. Conservatives respond that the effort to redistribute wealth from rich to poor

Equal opportunity: The idea that every American has the same chance to influence politics and achieve economic success.

Equal outcome: The idea that citizens should have roughly equal economic circumstances.

Middle-income Americans are no longer in the majority ...

Adult population by income tier (millions)

● **FIGURE 2.5** *The middle class is losing ground in the United States. (Pew Social Research)*

discourages entrepreneurs from innovating and generating new wealth. Expanded wealth at the top, they say, will help the many through job creation.

Over time, the United States has gone from the most equal society in the world to one that is considerably less equal than other wealthy nations. The past thirty-five years, in particular, have seen a very sharp spike in inequality. American politics has come to emphasize other ideas—negative liberty, individualism, the American dream of getting ahead—over equality. Still, we live in a dynamic and fluid society. Today, many Americans, both conservatives and liberals, have begun to call for renewed efforts to increase equality of opportunity.

THE BOTTOM LINE

» Equality means that every citizen enjoys the same privileges, status, and rights before the law.

» Equality applies to social status, political rights, and economic conditions.

» Today, America generally aims for *equal opportunity* rather than *equal outcome*, though heated discussions rage over what society must provide to ensure equal opportunity.

Religion

In the 1630s, a large contingent of Puritans escaped European persecution and sailed to New England with an ambitious aim: to establish a biblical commonwealth that would serve as a Christian model for the rest of the world. Governor John Winthrop called their settlement "a city upon a hill" and expected "the eyes of all people on us."[30] How did they fare? If anyone really was watching, they soon saw unexpected complications.

For example, Quakers from Pennsylvania—whom the Puritans despised for lacking discipline—began sailing north to convert the New Englanders. If the Quakers succeeded, they would subvert the whole idea of the model Puritan society. New England's women, the ministers worried, might be especially vulnerable to Quaker heresies. The authorities banned Quakers from Massachusetts under threat of having an ear cut off (one each for the first and second offense), having their tongues pierced by hot pokers (third offense), and finally death. Quaker martyrs piously and joyfully challenged the Puritan authorities. Four were hanged before English authorities ordered an end to the punishment.

This story illustrates the importance of religion, the intense competition between sects, and a missionary fervor to save the world. Even today, politicians of every stripe repeat the idea of a "city on a hill" (although few realize that Winthrop was quoting the Sermon on the Mount from the New Testament).

Percentage that reports being a member of a church or religious organization

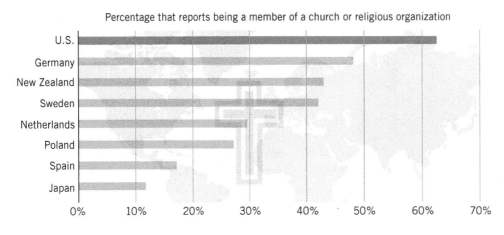

FIGURE 2.6 *Look how American religiosity stands out. As nations grow wealthy, religion nearly always loses its importance. The United States is the great exception. (World Values Survey)*

Still a Religious Country

Religion plays an enduring role in American politics and society. The centrality of religion in U.S. national life may not surprise you. But it is a powerful example of American exceptionalism. As most nations grow wealthier, their religious fervor wanes. Citizens in developed countries, from Britain and France to Japan and South Korea, tell pollsters that God is not very important in their lives. In contrast, Americans maintain high (and by some measures, rising) levels of religiosity. Some 86 percent of Americans say they believe in God, almost 56 percent belong to a church, and nearly 47 percent attend church regularly (see Figure 2.6).[31] To find higher levels you have to go to poorer nations such as India, Egypt, and Indonesia. However, the percentage of Americans who are religiously unaffiliated—who describe themselves as atheist, agnostic, or "nothing in particular"—appears to be growing. A recent survey found a little more than one in five (one in three for millennials) identified with these "nones."[32]

So Many Religions

Americans have a lot of religions to choose from (see Figure 2.7). One recent survey found sixteen different Christian denominations with more than a million members each.[33] That is just the beginning. Jews number over 6.7 million, Muslims some three million, and seven other non-Christian groups over 100,000 adherents each (two of the fastest growing are Wiccans and Pagans).[34] In contrast, many other nations have a single major faith, often supported by the government through tax dollars.

Why does the United States have so many religions? From the start, different colonies began with distinct religious affiliations. By forbidding the federal government from boosting any official faith, the

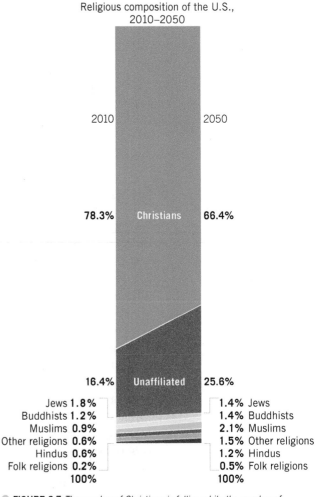

Religious composition of the U.S., 2010–2050

2010   2050

78.3%   Christians   66.4%

16.4%   Unaffiliated   25.6%

Jews **1.8%**
Buddhists **1.2%**
Muslims **0.9%**
Other religions **0.6%**
Hindus **0.6%**
Folk religions **0.2%**
100%

1.4% Jews
1.4% Buddhists
2.1% Muslims
1.5% Other religions
1.2% Hindus
0.5% Folk religions
100%

FIGURE 2.7 *The number of Christians is falling while the number of unaffiliated are rapidly rising. Muslims, Hindus, and folk religions are also rising. Even with these changes the U.S. population remains more churched than most wealthy nations. (Pew Forum)*

TABLE 2.2 **Changing American Religious Landscape**

	SILENT GENERATION (BORN 1928–1945)	BABY BOOMERS (BORN 1946–1964)	GENERATION X (BORN 1965–1980)	OLDER MILLENNIALS (BORN 1981–1989)	YOUNGER MILLENNIALS (BORN 1990–1996)
Christian	85	78	79	57	56
Other faiths	4	5	6	8	8
Unaffiliated	11	17	23	24	36
Source: Pew Forum					

Constitution has kept the field open for any new preacher with a religious idea that might attract a following. Because none can win official recognition, each religious institution is only as strong as the congregation it can muster.

This open market explains why new religions spring up all the time. It does not explain why Americans respond. One of the great mysteries of our political culture is why Americans continue to worship, while citizens in other wealthy nations show a declining interest in religion.

Religious observance is not the same throughout the United States. Texas and Georgia (proud members of the "Bible Belt") have very high religiosity, Florida and Missouri are in the middle, Colorado and Wisconsin are not especially religious, and Maine is the least religious of all.

Generational change is also at work: Although millennials continue to report high rates of religious faith, an unusual number do not affiliate with any denomination (see Table 2.2). Most believe in God but not organized religion.[35] In surveys asking about formal religious affiliation, nearly a quarter of Americans, and more than a third of millennials, responded "none."

Politics of Religion

How is religion relevant to politics? The First Amendment declares, "Congress shall make no law respecting an establishment of religion or prohibiting the free exercise thereof." Thomas Jefferson described "a wall of separation between church and state."[36] And yet America's energetic religious life—marked through our history by great evangelical revivals—injects three different types of political issues into American politics.

First, there is the question of what exactly the Constitution forbids. Even the founders disagreed. Presidents George Washington and John Adams held national days of prayer; President Jefferson thought that this practice violated the First Amendment.

The argument about what is permissible continues to this day. May teachers lead prayers in public schools? May public school students in the bleachers organize prayers before football games? May judges post the Ten Commandments in a courthouse? Questions such as these spark intense debates about where to draw the line between church and state (see Chapter 5 for the answers).

Second, religious faith often inspires people to throw themselves into political issues. The civil rights movement spilled out from Baptist and Methodist churches across the South, with religious rhetoric, religious symbols, and religious zeal. The opponents of racial equality—arguing for slavery and segregation—also framed their response in religious terms. In American politics, both sides often invoke God.

The controversies swirling around the politics of peace, abortion, the environment, equality, same-sex marriage, and many other issues have all, to varying extents, made the same leap from pulpit to politics. Today, conservatives are more likely to take their faith into the political arena, but this has not always been true.

Third, religious fervor sometimes fosters a missionary sense in American politics. As the nation expanded westward, Americans declared their "manifest destiny"—God had given an entire continent to his chosen people. During the Cold War, American leaders constantly invoked God as a way of contrasting the United States with communist nations. Congress added "under God" to the Pledge of Allegiance in 1954 and "In God We Trust" to paper money in 1955. A half-century later, President George W. Bush invoked "God's gift of freedom" to explain America's mission in Iraq. John Winthrop's idea—America as a model for the world—echoes from one generation to the next.

Political scientists often write about liberty, democracy, and equality. Religion usually flies below researchers' radar, but it is a constant element in American politics. Ignoring religion means regularly being surprised as intense religious feelings sweep past the separation between church and state.

What constitutes religious teaching?

THE BOTTOM LINE

» Religion plays an enduring role in American politics and society. This is unusual—almost unique—among wealthy countries.

» Americans have an unusually large number of faiths to choose from, although younger people are less likely than their elders to affiliate with an organized religion.

» Religious politics raise questions about the role and extent of religion in our national public life. They inspire political participation on a host of issues—from civil rights to abortion. And they foster a missionary sense in American foreign policy.

How Do Ideas Affect Politics?

Most political scientists agree that the seven ideas of this chapter are central to American society. But how do these ideas influence our politics? There are two familiar answers. Either ideas influence our culture, or they operate through our institutions. There is still another possibility to bear in mind, however, perhaps they have a life all their own.

Ideas in American Culture

Political culture: The orientation of citizens of a state toward politics.

Each nation has a unique **political culture**, constructed over the years by a people and its leaders. Anthropologist Clifford Geertz described culture as the stories a group tells about itself. Ideas such as liberty, the fear of government, individualism, and the American dream together are the foundation of American political culture. They are the stories we tell about ourselves.[37]

A culture shapes the way people think about politics and government. Culture develops slowly over time, shaped by history and experience. Colonial Americans' shared beliefs, stories, and mental habits—their culture—inspired the founding generation to develop a Constitution that limits the power of government. Why did the framers add a bill of rights to the Constitution? Their abiding faith in individualism. Why are there so many checks and balances in our national government? A fear of too much government dating back to colonial times. Why do we regulate and tax less than other nations? The American dream's gospel of success. This shared culture leads men and women to fight for policies that reflect freedom or democracy; policies that reflect social-democratic solidarity are more difficult to win because they resonate more faintly in American culture. Americans' hopes and fears often seem peculiar to people in other nations—just as their hopes and fears may not make sense to us.

Ideas in Political Institutions

A different perspective suggests that ideas operate through political institutions. The institutions are the key to political action. James Madison explained the *institutional perspective*. Past political theory expected republican citizens to virtuously seek the public interest. But, Madison wrote sardonically in the *Federalist Papers*, "enlightened statesmen will not always be at the helm."[38] The Constitution did not ask people to be virtuous; instead, it envisioned a government that could

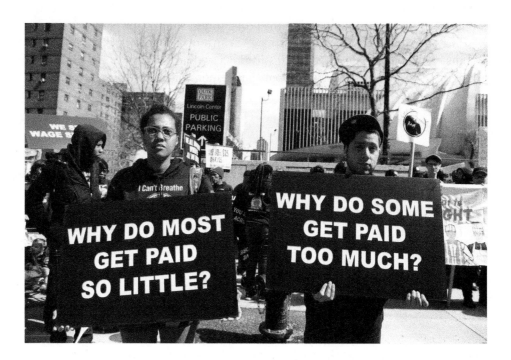

● *Ideas move politics. Young people protest inequality.*

operate smoothly even if its citizens were greedy and their leaders corrupt. The institution—the rules and organizations built into the government—would shape popular behavior.

Many political scientists continue to follow in Madison's footsteps. It is our governing institutions, starting with the Constitution, that shape American political behavior.

From an institutional perspective, the barriers to enacting new programs emerge not from a dislike of government but from the way the government is organized. The U.S. government is slow to act, according to this view, because we have *designed* it to be slow to act by building in multiple checks and balances on every level of government. When Americans criticize their policymakers for inaction, perhaps they miss the point: Gridlock is a consequence of the institutions we have inherited.

Culture or Institutions?

While historians and sociologists tend to emphasize political culture, many political scientists are skeptical about its explanatory power. How, they ask, can something as static as national culture explain the fluid, fast-changing American political scene?

For example, the cultural perspective suggests that the United States has never had national health insurance, supplied and paid for by the federal government, because Americans do not trust government. The institutional perspective counters that this lack of legislation is less a matter of popular belief and more the way we have designed the government. After all, they say, Harry Truman won the presidential election of 1948 in part by promising national health insurance. No deep-seated fear of government reared its head while Americans were voting. If we had been operating with a Canadian or English legislature, we would have put the program in place after Truman won the election. But Congress—using the checks and balances central to our national government's institutions—buried the proposal.

Proponents of culture as the primary driver of politics respond that cultural values are not meant to explain every possible political action. Events, leaders, movements, and government agencies all introduce change. But culture forms the boundary of those changes. It limits the possibilities, shapes our perceptions, and influences our reactions. When terrorists launch an attack, for example, the American response is driven by the types of institutions we have built to provide for the common defense—but the debate about that response is deeply influenced by the values and ideas we share.

THE BOTTOM LINE

» Political scientists point to three different ways in which foundational ideas influence politics.

» First, ideas shape American culture, which in turn affects our politics.

» Second—and the most popular argument among political scientists—ideas operate through political institutions. We have to study those institutions to appreciate how ideas shape politics and policies.

» Third, ideas may have their own independent power.

Conclusion: Culture and Institutions, Together

Do the ideas described in this chapter add up to a political culture that shapes the attitudes of American men and women? That cultural argument seems intuitive to many people. On balance, however, most political scientists underscore the importance of institutions.

As a political science student, you can decide for yourself on the relative power of ideas and institutions as you read this book. But you do not have to choose one or the other. We believe that culture and institutions together play a role in American politics. They reinforce each other. Yes, national institutions make it difficult to pass big national programs like health insurance; and, yes again, opponents invoke powerful cultural norms—such as individualism and liberty—to persuade Americans that such legislation threatens their values. For us, the most interesting question is how ideas, culture, and institutions (along with interests and individuals—the four "Is" in the introductory chapter) all interact to shape American politics.

Finally, ideas have a power of their own—above and beyond the culture and institutions they have helped to shape. Ideas of liberty, democracy, and the American dream can move people to act. That is exactly what Captain (and Professor) Russell Burgos was thinking as the mortars slammed into his post in northern Iraq. As you read this book, you will constantly encounter the seven ideas we described in this chapter. Think about which seem most important and powerful to you. And pay attention to how they appear to operate—through the culture, through institutions, with a life of their own, or (as we believe) in all these ways at different times and in different circumstances.

CHAPTER SUMMARY

● Seven important ideas influence American politics. Each idea has at least two different interpretations—differences that spur intense political debates. The seven key American ideas are freedom, self-rule, limited government, individualism, the American dream, equality, and religion.

● *Freedom* means that the government will protect your life, liberty, and property from the coercion of others (including government) so that you can pursue the goals you define for yourself. In one view, freedom requires *positive government action* to make sure that everyone has the basics to permit them to pursue their goals. In another view, the government guarantees only *negative freedom*—the freedom to pursue your goals. You are free to succeed or to fail on your own, but there are no guarantees about food, or homes, or healthcare.

● *Self-rule* means that people govern themselves through clearly defined procedures such as elections. In a democracy, citizens participate directly in making government decisions. In a republic, the people rule indirectly through their elected representatives. The American system is a combination of the two, a democratic republic.

● Americans value *limited government*: They distrust government and place limits on the authority it can exercise.

● *Individualism* means that individuals—not society or the government—are responsible for their own well-being. For those who favor community or social democracy, the public interest is best served when members of a society use government to take care of one another. Americans take both an individual and a communal view, but in contrast to many other nations, the individualistic view is more powerful.

● The *American dream* holds that if you are talented and work hard, you will succeed and grow wealthy. Critics argue that the system is rigged and that the dream promotes the wrong values. However, the dream remains a powerful force in American politics.

⬤ *Equality* allows each citizen to enjoy the same privileges, status, and rights before the law. Some define equality as a matter of *opportunity*—the idea that every American has an equal chance. Others promote equal *outcome*—a guarantee of results. There are three types of equality to consider: Social equality means that all individuals enjoy the same status in society. Political equality guarantees every citizen the same rights and opportunities to participate in politics. Economic equality minimizes the gap between citizens' wealth and earnings.

⬤ *Religion* plays an enduring role in American politics and society. The great question is how we limit government interference without limiting religion itself.

⬤ These seven ideas mark Americans' beliefs as a people. They shape politics through national culture, through political institutions, and through their direct public influence.

KEY TERMS

American exceptionalism, p. 24	Individualism, p. 37	Positive liberty, p. 26
Conservatives, p. 33	Initiative, p. 30	Referendum, p. 30
Economic equality, p. 46	Liberals, p. 33	Republic, p. 31
Equality, p. 44	Libertarians, p. 27	Self-rule, p. 29
Equal opportunity, p. 47	Median, p. 46	Social democracy, p. 37
Equal outcome, p. 47	Negative liberty, p. 26	Social equality, p. 44
Freedom, p. 26	Political culture, p. 52	Sunshine laws, p. 30
	Political equality, p. 44	

STUDY QUESTIONS

1. The second paragraph of the Declaration of Independence boldly explains why "governments are instituted among men." Why? Why are governments formed? Do you agree with that assertion about government's most basic function?

2. *Liberty* is often described as the most important American idea. Describe the two different views of liberty. Which do you think is more accurate?

3. Review the seven principal "American ideas" we have identified in this chapter. Are *new* foundational ideas bubbling up in American politics today? What examples can you imagine?

4. The Declaration of Independence asserts that all men are endowed by their creator with the inalienable rights to life, liberty, and the pursuit of happiness. Over time, Americans have extended that idea to more and more people, such as former slaves and women. Are there groups in our society today who are *not* getting the full benefits of this ideal? How might that change?

5. What is the difference between a democracy and a republic? Which principle does contemporary American government reflect, or does it reflect both? If you were a founder, which of these principles would you emphasize?

6. George Washington declared national days of prayer during his presidency. Thomas Jefferson rejected this practice, saying that it violated the First Amendment. Who was right, in your view—and what *does* the First Amendment say about this?

7. There are three forms of equality—social, political, and economic. Define each.

8. Describe the two approaches to economic equality: opportunity and outcome.

9. When it comes to religion, the United States is different from most wealthy societies. How? How do young people differ from previous generations in their approach to religion?

10. Ideas shape both culture and institutions. Explain.

 Go to www.oup.com/us/Morone to find quizzes, flash cards, simulations, tutorials, videos, and other study tools.

The Constitution

THE R. R. MOTON HIGH SCHOOL, in Farmville, Virginia, was a mess. The roof leaked, the heat barely worked, the classrooms were over-crowded, and the school bus kept breaking down. When it rained, students sat under umbrellas and shivered in their coats. Moton was a black school; across town, the white students were warm and dry. On April 23, 1951, a Moton junior named Barbara Johns decided to take action. She fooled the principal into leaving the school for the day and forged notes to the teachers calling an assembly. When the students had all filed into the auditorium, the sixteen-year-old stood on stage, called for a strike, and led a student march to the Prince Edward County Courthouse to protest the shabby state of the school.

As you can imagine, Barbara Johns and her fellow student protesters landed in trouble. The students and their families called a leading civil rights group, the National Association for the Advancement of Colored People (NAACP), which dispatched a team of lawyers. The lawyers explained that local governments run American schools, and there was not much the NAACP could do about the conditions at Moton High. However, continued the lawyers, they could challenge the entire policy of racial segregation. The NAACP sued the school district, arguing that forcing African Americans into a separate school violated the United States Constitution. The Supreme Court took the case, *Davis v. School Board of Prince Edward County*, bundled it together with two similar cases, and three years after the student strike delivered one of the most famous court decisions in American history, a ruling known as *Brown v. Board of Education*.

A sixteen-year-old took a bold risk, the Supreme Court unanimously ruled that she was right, and hundreds of laws across many states were struck down for violating the Constitution. The Court ruled that segregated education facilities are inherently unequal and violated the Fourteenth Amendment of the United States Constitution, which declares: "No state shall . . . deny to any person . . . the equal protection of the laws."

Stop and think about the power Americans invest in this document written nearly 230 years ago. The Constitution is the owner's manual and rulebook for American government. It specifies how the government operates. It tells us what the government may do and how it should do it. If you want to learn about any feature of American politics, always check the Constitution first.

In this chapter, you will:

- Discover the roots of the Constitution.

- See why Americans declared independence from England and learn about their first constitution, the Articles of Confederation.

- Follow the arguments that shaped the Constitution.

- Read about the great national debate over whether to adopt the Constitution.

- Learn how Americans have changed the Constitution—and how the Constitution has changed America.

● *Student strikers at Moton High School, led by Barbara Johns. The protestors had an enormous impact because civil rights lawyers found a way to place their grievance in the context of the U.S. Constitution.*

57

Who are we? The answer to that question is always changing, but the Constitution provides the ground rules for those changes. It organizes our political life. The Declaration of Independence sets out the ideas behind America. The Constitution takes those ideas and turns them into laws. It *institutionalizes* American ideas.

This sounds simple: The Constitution guides the government. But there is a wrinkle. It is often unclear how the Constitution applies to modern questions. After all, it is just 4,400 words written on four pages of parchment a long time ago. Many provisions can be read in two (or more) different ways, and the document is silent on many topics. As a result, we always have to *interpret* how the Constitution applies to a case today.

Segregation is a prime example. The Constitution does not say anything about racial segregation. Back in 1896, the Supreme Court ruled that segregation did not violate the "equal protection" clause of the Fourteenth Amendment. In 1954, the Court ruled that it did. Different justices in different eras read the same words in changing ways. We constantly debate how to read the Constitution's words—and how to apply them to the questions we face.

BY THE NUMBERS
The Constitution

Number of articles (or sections) in the U.S. Constitution: **7**

Number of articles in the constitution of India (1950) and the constitution of South Africa (1996), respectively: **395; 244**

Number of words in the U.S. Constitution, including all 27 amendments: **7,591**

Number of words in average state constitution: **36,000**

Number of times the word *power* or *powers* appears in the U.S. Constitution: **16**

Number of times the word *liberty* appears in the U.S. Constitution: **1**

Number of times the word *equality* appears in the U.S. Constitution: **0**

Number of times the word *democracy* appears in the U.S. Constitution: **0**

Years after the U.S. Constitution was written that the Fourteenth Amendment added the idea of equality to the document: **81**

Number of *proposed* amendments to the U.S. Constitution introduced in Congress since 1791: **over 11,600**

Number of *successful* amendments since 1791: **17**

Percentage of the U.S. population that can block a constitutional amendment: **3**

Number of the 13 states that voted for the Constitution within six months: **6**

Number of states that initially voted against the Constitution: **2**

Number of delegates in New York, Virginia, and Massachusetts who could have defeated the entire Constitution by switching their votes: **18 (3% of the delegates in those states)**

Number of words that the Constitution uses to describe and empower Congress: **2,243**

Number of words that the Constitution uses to describe and empower the president: **1,015**

Number of words that the Constitution uses to describe and empower the courts: **364**

The Colonial Roots of the Constitution

No nation in the eighteenth century had anything like the American Constitution. Most nations wrote their governing documents much later; some countries, such as England and Israel, never wrote one at all (see Comparing Nations 3.1). However, the American Constitution did not appear out of nowhere. Many features of colonial politics propelled the new nation toward its constitution.

- First, the colonies were three thousand miles away from the king and his armies. Authorities back in England debated policies and issued orders; the American colonists frequently ignored them and did what they wished.

COMPARING NATIONS 3.1	The U.S. Constitution in Comparative Context	
The United States has the oldest constitution still in use. Of the 18 democratic countries listed here, only Canada and the Netherlands wrote a still-operating constitution within a century of the United States. Many political scientists believe the American document has lasted so long because it works well. Others, however, believe that it has grown out of date and that our form of government is not effective or fair enough for the twenty-first century. Keep this debate in mind as you read about how the American Constitution came into existence.	**NATION**	**YEAR THE CURRENT CONSTITUTION WAS WRITTEN**
	United States	1789
	Argentina	1853 (revised text, 1994)
	Austria	1920
	Brazil	1988
	Canada	1867 (revised text, 1982)
	Costa Rica	1949
	Denmark	1953
	France	1958
	Germany	1949
	Great Britain	No written constitution
	India	1950
	Ireland	1937
	Israel	No written constitution
	Italy	1948
	Japan	1947
	Nepal	2015
	Netherlands	1814
	New Zealand	No written constitution

No one back in London paid much attention. The English policy of ignoring colonies was known as *salutary neglect*; it permitted the colonies to develop their own political institutions. When England started interfering in colonial affairs, the Americans revolted.

- Second, beginning with the Virginia House of Burgesses in 1620, every colony elected its own legislature. As a result, the colonists had a great deal of experience with representation. New settlements demanded seats in the assemblies. New immigrants wanted the right to vote (e.g., Polish men went on strike in Virginia over the issue). In some places, such as New Jersey, women with property could vote. America grew up arguing about representation—and that prepared them for the debate over the Constitution.

- Third, plentiful land created opportunities for ordinary people. Early America was not an equal society by any means: there were aristocratic families and slaves, prosperous merchants and **indentured servants**. However, by the standards of the time, the New World was a land of extraordinary social mobility. When North Carolina tried to set up a system of titles and social classes, the effort collapsed as ordinary people made their fortunes and soon were wealthier than the would-be lords and dukes. Economic conditions helped foster a republic.

- Fourth, some colonies began with mutual agreements between the settlers, known as **compacts** or **covenants**. The Pilgrims, who landed in Massachusetts in 1620, introduced the idea; before they went ashore all forty-one adult males signed a mutual agreement known as the Mayflower Compact (named after their vessel, the *Mayflower*). In most nations, the right to rule stretched back through history and was based on tradition and military force. In contrast, the individuals on the *Mayflower* formed a new society based on their mutual agreement and consent. Many New England communities began with such compacts or covenants—roughly, often religiously inspired forerunners of a constitution. In fact, the preamble to the U.S. Constitution took the same form as that used in the New England covenants.

Indentured servant: A colonial American settler contracted to work for a fixed period (usually three to seven years) in exchange for food, shelter, and transportation to the New World.

Compact: A mutual agreement that provides for joint action to achieve defined goals.

Covenant: A compact invoking religious or moral authority.

The Mayflower Compact. The settlers agreed among themselves to enter into a "civic body politic"—a government. The authority of their government rose from their own agreement, which was signed only by men.

- Fifth, many colonists came to the New World to practice their religion in peace. Across the colonies, different religions flourished: Calvinists in Boston, Quakers in Philadelphia, Catholics in Baltimore, Anglicans in Virginia, and an unusually diverse mix of religions in Savannah, Georgia, which was home to Anglicans, Lutherans, and Jews, among others. All these different faiths did not always live in harmony; the Massachusetts Puritans hanged Quaker missionaries who had sailed there. But beginning in Rhode Island in 1636, a revolutionary idea began to emerge: the individual's freedom to practice religion without government interference. In some colonies, this idea was followed by other rights, such as freedom of speech and freedom of the press. The rights of citizens would become the single greatest issue in the debate over whether to accept (ratify) the new constitution.

- Sixth, border areas in early America were violent and insecure. Brutal wars with the Native Americans marked many of the colonies. The French claimed land to the north and west, the Spanish to the south and west. Colonists also constantly fought one another over their own boundaries. After the break with England, insecure borders helped inspire the colonists to adopt a strong central government.

Each colony governed itself in its own way. However, the six features described here—distance from English authority, representation, social mobility, covenants, individual rights, and violent borders—all propelled Americans toward the Constitution of 1787.

Why the Colonists Revolted

The roots of the American Revolution lie in a great English victory. Centuries of rivalry between England and France burst into war in 1754. Known as the French and Indian War, the conflict spread through the colonies from Virginia all the way to Canada. Colonial American militias fought side by side with the British army and defeated the French in 1763. Thirteen years later the colonists declared independence and turned their muskets on the English.

Why did the Americans suddenly revolt? Because the victory over France introduced two fateful changes. First, ten thousand English troops remained in the colonies to protect the newly won land. The existence of those "Redcoats" meant that England could now enforce its policies: the days of salutary neglect were over. Second, the English had run up a crushing debt during the ten years of war and decided that the colonists should help pay it. The Americans' reaction was explosive.

The Colonial Complaint: Representation

It was not just Britain's demand for money that provoked the colonists. Americans had grown used to making their own decisions through their elected assemblies. When the English imposed new taxes, without the approval of the thirteen colonial assemblies, they violated the idea of self-rule. The result was an unusual revolution. Most revolutionaries rise up against regimes that have long repressed them. In contrast, the Americans fought to preserve rights that they had been exercising during the many years of happy neglect.

Beneath the conflict lay a deep philosophical difference about representative democracy. The colonists considered their assemblies the legitimate voice of the people; if taxes had to be raised, they were the ones to do it. Colonial assemblies were very responsive to the voters and their daily concerns—they worried about things such as building roads and surveying new lands. Political theorists call the colonial view **delegate representation**: Do what the voters want.

The British never understood this view of representation because they operated under an entirely different one. Unlike the colonists, the English did not change their electoral districts every time the population shifted. English elected officials were expected to pursue the good of the whole nation. Your representative is not an "agent" or an "advocate," argued English statesman Edmund Burke, but a member of Parliament who must be guided by "the general good." This view is known as **trustee representation**—do what is best for the voters regardless of what they want you to do.[1] The debate would spur an innovative provision in the U.S. Constitution: The United States would conduct a census every ten years to

Delegate representation:
Representatives follow the expressed wishes of the voters.

Trustee representation:
Representatives do what they regard as being in the best interest of their constituents—even if constituents do not agree.

The colonial borders were the site of considerable fighting, with both the French and the Native Americans.

ensure that congressional districts matched up to the changing population—a direct reaction to Britain's trustee theory of representation.

The Conflict Begins with Blood on the Frontier

After the French and Indian War, settlers poured westward (Figures 3.1 and 3.2). Native Americans fought back; they rallied around Chief Pontiac and overran colonial settlements and English forts in Virginia, Maryland, and Pennsylvania. To end the fighting, England closed the border and prohibited settlers from moving westward past the crests of the lengthy Appalachian Mountain chain. The colonists were stunned. The arbitrary boundary, announced in the Proclamation of 1763, had been drawn amid lobbying by land speculators, who could make or lose fortunes depending on whether their own land was open to settlement. The proclamation threatened the westward thrust that spelled opportunity to the restless colonists. American settlers did not care about Native American rights to the land. As they saw it, a corrupt English monarchy was blocking American pioneers from settling the wide-open spaces that they had helped win from France.

FIGURE 3.1 AND FIGURE 3.2 *The colonies before (left) and after (right) the French and Indian War. Spain lost Florida but gained the land west of the Mississippi in compensation for having supported France. Napoleon would later grab this land back from Spain and then, in 1803, sell it to the United States. Note the line formed by the Proclamation of 1763 on the map on the right. England tried to forbid settlers from crossing that line.*

The colonists responded in their traditional way—they ignored regulations that did not suit them. But now there was a British army in America to enforce the English policies. The Proclamation of 1763 was followed by the Quartering Act (1765), which required colonial assemblies to billet British troops in empty barns and warehouses. Suddenly, the Redcoats seemed like an occupying army.

Britain also began to enforce its **mercantilist** trade policies, which meant American ships had to bypass their traditional (and lucrative) partners and do business only with English colonies at higher prices. Colonists who ignored the decree were charged with smuggling—wealthy merchants now faced imprisonment or large fines for trading with French colonies. To make matters even worse, the English introduced taxes to help support their army of Redcoats. These widely reviled duties culminated in the Stamp Act of 1765.

Mercantilism: An economic theory according to which government controls foreign trade to maintain prosperity and security.

The Stamp Tax and the First Hints of Independence

Stamp taxes were a common way to raise money in England, but the effort to impose one on the colonies set off a firestorm. Parliament ignored the colonial assemblies (violating colonial ideas of representation) and simply announced the new tax. Colonists responded by convening a Stamp Act Congress that met in October 1765. Delegates from nine colonies sent a protest to the king and to Parliament. The English policies were pushing the colonists into working together. In fact, the name *Stamp Act Congress* may have been more alarming to the English authorities than the petition the body drafted. In the eighteenth century, the word *congress* meant a diplomatic assembly of representatives from independent nations. The very name of this meeting intimated independence.

Protests against the stamp tax spread throughout the colonies. Mobs hung, burned, and beheaded tax collectors in effigy. They attacked tax collectors' offices and homes. Across the sea, English authorities were incredulous. All they could see were ungrateful colonists who refused to pay for their own protection.[2]

The Townshend Acts Worsen the Conflict

After Parliament reluctantly lifted the stamp taxes, colonists celebrated the repeal and tensions eased—until Parliament followed up with the Townshend Acts in 1767. These acts instituted another round of new taxes; revenues were earmarked to pay a new colonial authority, the American Board of Customs, which would collect taxes independently of the colonial assemblies. Now an imperial bureaucracy was explicitly denying the colonists self-governance. The Townshend Acts also suspended the New York State Assembly for refusing to house and supply British troops.

Once again, American colonists responded with meetings, petitions, and mobs. New Yorkers and, later, Bostonians seethed with anger over having their legislatures dissolved. Mobs harassed the customs officials, who found it impossible to carry out their duties and called for help. A British warship arrived in Boston, discharging officials who seized a vessel owned by John Hancock, one of the resistance leaders, and charged him with smuggling. That move set off riots, bringing British troops into the city to restore order. Before long, there were almost four thousand Redcoats in a city of fifteen thousand people. The Boston mobs harassed the soldiers with taunts, rocks, and snowballs until, on March 5, 1770, one detachment of Redcoats panicked and fired point-blank on the crowd.

The Boston Massacre, as the event quickly became known, left five civilians dead. The first to fall was a sailor named Crispus Attucks, the son of an African slave and a Natick Indian who had escaped slavery some twenty years earlier.

An engraving of the Boston Massacre done by Paul Revere. This version of the event makes the British look like cold-blooded killers—not historically accurate, but powerful propaganda for independence.

Ironically, the son of two groups who would not be liberated by the Revolution—an African slave and an American Indian—was the first to bleed for the cause. Paul Revere memorialized the massacre in an engraving that transformed the panicky soldiers threatened by a mob into a line of killers firing into a heroic cluster of civilians. Historian Gordon Wood described the engraving as "perhaps the most famous piece of anti-military propaganda in American history."[3]

English policy was in shambles; colonists' anger at a fever pitch. At the start of the crisis, six years earlier, colonial leaders had respectfully petitioned the king to rescind his policies. Now, blood had been shed and the colonists began to talk about rebellion.

The Boston Tea Party

The British repealed all the Townshend duties except a tariff on tea. Tea was a global industry in 1773; think of it as the must-have product of the eighteenth century. But the East India Tea Company, which had a monopoly in England, was on the verge of bankruptcy. In 1773, Parliament tried to rescue the company by granting it a monopoly over the tea trade in the New World. The colonial shippers who had long been trading tea would be shut out by this rival trading network.

When ships with East India tea arrived, mobs in Philadelphia and New York forced them to sail away without unloading their cargo. In Boston, however, Governor Thomas Hutchinson would not permit such nonsense. He insisted that the three ships in Boston Harbor not leave until their tea was safely delivered. On a dark December night, about fifty men, some "dressed in the Indian manner," blackened their faces and boarded one of the ships. They hefted 342 chests of tea onto the deck, bashed them open with hatchets, and dumped the contents—worth about £9,600 (between $1.5 and $2.5 million today)—into Boston Harbor.[4]

Revolution!

British leaders were furious. Past insubordination paled next to this direct economic hit on a struggling British company. They first demanded compensation; when a Boston town meeting voted that down, the English introduced what colonists dubbed the Intolerable Acts. The laws closed Boston Harbor until the tea was paid for, abolished town meetings, authorized the quartering of troops in any home in Massachusetts, and essentially put the state under military control. King George III himself put it bluntly: "The colonists must either triumph or submit."

Americans refused to submit. Instead, twelve colonies sent representatives to the **First Continental Congress** in September 1774. The Congress petitioned for an end to the Intolerable Acts, called for a boycott on British goods, and asserted colonial rights to "life, liberty, and property." They agreed to meet again in May 1775.

Before the Continental Congress reconvened, fighting had begun. In April 1775, the British commander in Boston, General Thomas Gage, sent one thousand troops

First Continental Congress:
A convention of delegates from twelve of the thirteen colonies that met in 1774.

from Boston to seize guns and ammunition stored at Concord, Massachusetts. Armed colonists who called themselves "minutemen" blocked the way and came under British fire at Lexington and Concord. Eight were shot dead. The British found and destroyed the weapons, but their march back to Boston was horrific. Minutemen hid behind rocks and trees and sniped at them all along the way. By the time the English army limped back into the city, they had lost three hundred men.

A Long Legacy

Revolutionary images and slogans still resonate in American politics today. The Tea Party holds rallies around the nation. Civilians anxious about immigration call themselves "minutemen" and patrol the border with Mexico. "Militias" organize and train to defend their personal rights. The Revolution left the new United States with symbols, slogans, and an enduring political concern: arbitrary government that threatens the people's liberties.

THE BOTTOM LINE

» For over a century England ignored its American colonies and elected assemblies governed the colonists. After the French and Indian War, the English bypassed the colonial legislatures and imposed new rules and taxes.

» These actions violated traditional colonial rights and exposed two different ideas of representation—the American concept of *delegate representation* (representatives respond to their constituents' desires) and the English concept of *trustee representation* (representatives do what they consider best for all, regardless of constituent demands).

» English action also harmed colonial economic interests. The conflict very quickly escalated.

» Americans fought an unusual revolution: Rather than demanding new rights, they were trying to preserve rights and economic interests they had long been exercising.

The Declaration of Independence

The **Second Continental Congress**, which met in May 1775, faced the job of declaring independence, mobilizing an army, organizing a government, and rallying thirteen very different colonies around a single cause. A year later, on July 4, 1776, the Congress voted to adopt a Declaration of Independence as a statement to the world of America's purpose. The document has two parts: a statement of principles and a list of grievances. (The full Declaration is reprinted in Appendix I to this book.)

Second Continental Congress: A convention of delegates from the thirteen colonies that became the acting national government for the duration of the Revolutionary War.

The Principle: "We Hold These Truths . . ."

In one elegant paragraph, the Declaration of Independence distills America's political philosophy (see Table 3.1 for how the Declaration reflects the ideas discussed in the last chapter):

- All people are equal.
- Their creator endowed them with rights that cannot be taken away.

- These rights include life, liberty, and the pursuit of happiness.
- People form governments to protect those rights.
- Governments derive their just powers from the consent of the governed.

These ideas were not new. Political philosophers, especially the English thinker John Locke, had used very similar language. In his *Two Treatises on Government*, published more than a century earlier, Locke argued that in nature, there are no rules. Life is ruled by force and violence. To secure safety and freedom, people contract with one another, enter into civil society, and form governments that can protect one another's life, liberty, and property. Locke was enormously influential in revolutionary America. One curious indicator: the elegant furniture of this era, which often featured carved busts of writers, includes more carvings of John Locke than anyone else.[5]

As a statement of governing ideals, the Declaration of Independence was—and to this day, still is—breathtaking. In 1776, it was also a far cry from reality. Thomas Jefferson, who drafted much of the document, was a slave owner. The Declaration

TABLE 3.1 The Declaration of Independence and America's Enduring Ideas

HOW DOES THE DECLARATION REFLECT THE KEY AMERICAN IDEAS DISCUSSED IN CHAPTER 2?
Liberty. The Declaration asserts that liberty is an "unalienable right" (meaning that no one can take it away), endowed to all people by their creator.
Self-rule. The right of representation is one of the Declaration's central themes: It contends that governments derive "their just powers from the consent of the governed." Ten of the twenty-seven grievances charged against the king directly address the issue of self-rule.
Limited government. The idea of limited government had more space than any other in both the Declaration and the Constitution. Most of the Declaration recites the ways King George III overstepped his "just powers." Eleven years later, the Constitution would carefully limit the powers given to the federal government.
Individualism. The Declaration states that "governments are instituted among men . . . to secure [the] rights" with which the creator has endowed each individual. These include "life, liberty, and the pursuit of happiness." Here is the cornerstone of American individualism. At the same time, the Declaration also talks about "one people" and "the people"—collective ideas that have to be balanced with individualism. Recall the great American debate: How do we balance individualism and communalism? The Declaration emphasizes both.
The American dream. The Declaration of Independence promises the pursuit of happiness. What does this mean? The phrase is borrowed from John Locke, who wrote that governments are instituted to protect "life, liberty, and *property.*" Jefferson, in his first draft of the Declaration, changed "property" to "happiness." But right from the start, "the pursuit of happiness"—what we now call the American dream—has often been cast as the pursuit of wealth.
Equality. This idea seems clear enough: Because "all men are created equal," they all have the same rights to life, liberty, and the pursuit of happiness. But do we as a society need to feed the hungry and clothe the poor to ensure that everyone has an equal shot at the pursuit of happiness? This remains a controversial matter.
Faith in God. The words "the Creator" appear right at the start of the Declaration. But religion soon became controversial. Thomas Jefferson, who drafted the Declaration, was not a religious man. (As a deist, he thought that God did not interfere in human affairs.) Jefferson later ignited a controversy during his presidency when he refused to call national days of prayer as George Washington had done. Instead, Jefferson argued that there must be "a wall of separation between church and state." But Jefferson's wall raises as many questions as it resolves, as debates and court cases have attested for generations.

essentially invites future cruelty when it refers to "merciless Indian savages." Its authors did not live up to their noble sentiments. We do not fully live up to them today. Even so, the document stands as the great statement of American idealism—something every generation can fight for.

Grievances

The second part of the Declaration lists twenty-seven grievances against King George III. These tell us what the American colonists cared about as they began the Revolution. Three complaints dominate the list:

- *Violations of the right of representation.* This complaint comes up in ten of the twenty-seven charges against England. It is by far the most intensely felt grievance described in the Declaration.
- *Maintenance of a standing army not under civilian control.* In particular, British soldiers acted in peacetime without the consent of American legislatures. Five complaints are about the British military.
- *Loss of an independent court.* This violation of traditional justice comes up six times.

Today the Revolution is often boiled down to the colonists' slogan "No taxation without representation." The Declaration emphasized *representation* much more than taxation; taxes did not show up until way down the list, as grievance number 17 ("Imposing taxes on us without our consent"). That is not to say that economics did not matter. Many of the British steps that preceded rebellion, from the imposition of taxes to the enforcement of trade rules, were essentially economic challenges. However, those which reverberate most forcefully are the *right of representation* and the *consent of the governed.*

THE BOTTOM LINE

» The Declaration of Independence asserted philosophical ideals as the basis of the new American government.

» The first part of the Declaration features five ideals that sum up the nation's political principles.

» The second part of the Declaration lists twenty-seven grievances that led to the break. They emphasized the right of representation and the consent of the governed.

The First American Government: The Articles of Confederation

When the United States declared its independence, it linked the thirteen former colonies—now states—into a **confederation**, or *alliance of independent states.* Although this first American government lasted only a little more than a decade, it taught the new nation valuable lessons about effective government.

Confederation: A group of independent states or nations that yield some of their powers to a national government, although each state retains a degree of sovereign authority.

Independent States

The states organized their governments to reflect popular desires. They introduced annual elections, extended the right to vote, and opened legislative deliberations to public view. Some states built benches in the assembly halls so that the public could watch their representatives in action. States also enlarged their legislatures so that members would be more responsive to citizens.

Of course, the new rules still left many people out. Women had participated in the Revolutionary War. Some dressed as men and fought, most often in artillery units; others cooked, worked as nurses, and cleared the battlefields after combat. The English estimated that "women and waggoners make up half of their [American] army."[6] Nevertheless, women could not vote in most states. And, despite the Declaration of Independence's ringing statement of "unalienable rights," slavery persisted in every state.

Still, the revolutionary spirit unleashed a powerful egalitarian urge. States from Massachusetts to Virginia pondered the abolition of slavery. In some states, such as New Jersey, women with property were allowed to vote. And across the nation, state legislatures were, as historian Gordon Wood put it, "probably as equally and fairly representative of the people as any legislatures in history."[7]

The National Government

The Continental Congress approved its first constitution, called the Articles of Confederation, in November 1777. The document, which reflected Americans' recent experience with England, kept the national government weak and dependent on the states. The Articles named the new nation the United States of America and described the central government as "a league of friendship" among states: "Each . . . retains its sovereignty, freedom and independence, and every power, jurisdiction and right." In a sign of what was to come, Congress had to wait more than three years to get approval from all thirteen states for the Articles of Confederation.

Central government power was placed in a Congress whose members were selected and paid by the states. There was no chief executive (the states would implement the laws), no central authority to tax (all revenues would come from state governments), and no central power to muster an army (the states supplied the troops). Each state had a single vote in Congress. Important matters required the vote of nine states. Any changes to the Articles of Confederation required the agreement of all thirteen states. Today, we call such extra-large majorities **supermajorities**. The Articles created a very weak central government.[8]

A series of legends have developed concerning Molly Pitcher, whose real name was Mary Ludwig Hays McCauley. The most famous has her stepping in to take the place of her fallen husband at the cannon during the Battle of Monmouth. The stories are most likely a composite of descriptions of many women who fought with the American army.

Supermajority: An amount higher than a simple majority (50 percent plus one)—typically, three-fifths or two-thirds of the voters.

Some Success . . .

Americans had good reason to be proud of their new government. Power remained close to the people. The new government overcame incredible odds and, by April

1783, had defeated the most powerful military force in the world. The population grew rapidly in the 1780s—the fastest rise of any decade in American history. After a brief postwar recession, the economy also expanded. Americans considered themselves both democratic and prosperous.[9]

The Continental Congress also won a major policy success when it stopped the squabbling among states over claims to western land. Instead, the Northwest Ordinance of 1787 established a process by which individuals could buy western lands: When an area attracted a minimum number of settlers, it could apply to be a state with all the same powers and privileges as the existing states. With this act, the United States established its mechanism for western expansion.

. . . And Some Problems

But four major problems plagued the new American government.

First, Congress could not raise taxes and had no money of its own. The states were reluctant to provide funds. The Continental Congress had trouble supplying (much less paying) the army throughout the Revolutionary War. George Washington drew a lesson that would always guide his politics: *The new republic needed a vigorous national government if it was to survive.*[10]

Second, the requirement of unanimity made it impossible to amend the Articles. When Congress tried to fix its financial problems by levying a 5 percent tax on imported goods, twelve of the states agreed. However, Rhode Island's legislature denounced the proposal as "the yoke of tyranny fixed on all the states."[11] When loans from France and Holland came due, there was no way to pay them. Again, many leaders drew a lesson: *A vigorous national government needed a stable source of revenue.*

Third, state governments were dominated by their legislatures, which operated without any checks or balances. The result was often bias and even chaos. Legislatures wrote (and repealed) laws to benefit individuals. They forgave debts. They seized private property. Leaders eventually reached yet another important conclusion: *Different sources of government power should balance one another, governors should balance legislatures, and the central government should balance the states.*

● *Captain Daniel Shays led a rebellion in protest of farm foreclosures in 1786.*

Fourth, the weak national government had a difficult time standing up to foreign powers. Spain closed the Mississippi to American vessels. Britain's trade policy played the states against one another. Pirates brazenly seized American ships in North Africa. National-minded Americans drew an obvious conclusion: *a weak central government left the nation vulnerable.*

One event, Shays' Rebellion, dramatized the problems of government under the Articles. Captain Daniel Shays, a veteran of the Revolutionary War, led a rebellion that broke out in western Massachusetts in August 1786 and spread across the state. Thousands of farmers, protesting high taxes and interest rates, took up their muskets and shut down courthouses to stop foreclosures on their farms. When Governor James Bowdoin summoned the local militia to defend the Worcester courthouse, members refused; some joined the rebellion. The same thing happened in Concord, just forty miles from Boston. By December, the rebels had seized

Your Advice Is Needed

If you could go back and offer advice to American leaders in 1787, what would you tell them? Should they stick with the Articles of Confederation or write a new constitution?

Yes, stick with the Articles of Confederation. It is weak and at times chaotic. But this government is very democratic and reflects popular wishes. It does not rely on a distant national government to make and impose policies.

No, build a new central government. Leaders will be less responsive to the public on day-to-day matters. However, the nation will be less chaotic, more powerful, and more secure. The government will become powerful enough to repel foreign threats.

I am divided about this. Of course, at the time, the colonists voted for a new Constitution—but it was a close call, as you will see. The Constitution would enable the United States to eventually become a powerful nation—but at the expense of more responsive local government.

six courthouses and an armory. Governor Bowdoin appealed to the national government for help, but Congress had no army and no money. Finally, Bowdoin hired an army and broke the rebellion. Shays' sympathizers shifted strategy: They won seats in the legislature the following year and legislated the debt relief that the farmers had been fighting for.[12]

For many national leaders, Shays' Rebellion was the last straw. Under the Articles of Confederation, neither the national government nor an individual state was strong enough to protect public property (e.g., courthouses) or private property (the repayment of loans). Shays' Rebellion pushed the most influential men in the colonies to write a new constitution. Not everyone agreed. Many Americans thought that problems such as Shays' Rebellion were the growing pains of a more democratic government that reflected the people and their desires.

The First Step: Annapolis Convention

Alarmed by spreading chaos, the Continental Congress called for a national meeting in Annapolis to impose order on commerce among the states. Only twelve delegates from five states showed up—not enough to do official business. With Shays' Rebellion raging, the delegates requested each state to appoint representatives to meet in Philadelphia the following May, in 1787, to devise such "provisions as should appear to them necessary to render the constitution of the federal government adequate to the exigencies of the union." That may not sound earthshaking, but the twelve delegates in Annapolis had quietly authorized a convention that would write an entirely new constitution—and permanently transform the United States.

Secrecy

Spring 1787 arrived cold and blustery, delaying many of the delegates on their way to Philadelphia. James Madison from Virginia got there first, with a plan for a new constitution. Madison was short, shy, and balding; today, we recognize him as one of America's greatest political thinkers. The next delegate from Virginia arrived

George Washington sat for this portrait in Philadelphia during the Constitutional Convention. Washington presided over the convention and brought his enormous prestige to the effort. In the background is William Lee, a slave who served as Washington's personal attendant throughout the Revolutionary War and after. When former military officers visited Washington, they often stopped in to see Lee as well.

James Madison was the most diligent delegate. Small, shy, and unimpressive looking, he stood just five feet tall. No one would notice Madison standing next to the tall and muscular Washington or the charismatic Franklin. However, Madison was a brilliant thinker and one of the chief architects of the Constitution and Bill of Rights. He had more influence over the shape of the final text than any other single individual.

with more fanfare. As George Washington approached, church bells pealed, cannons thundered, army officers donned their old uniforms to ride escort, and local citizens lined the streets and cheered. The presence of the great American hero made the convention's success more likely.

On the first day, the delegates unanimously elected George Washington to chair the convention. Then they agreed on a controversial rule: The deliberations would be completely secret. Guards were placed at the doors. Windows were shut and remained closed, even after the Philadelphia summer turned stifling. George Washington made only three comments during the convention—and one was to rebuke an unknown delegate who had carelessly dropped a copy of proposed resolutions. Most of what we know about the convention comes from James Madison himself, who took a seat at the front of the room and kept meticulous notes—though they were not made public until 1837, a year after Madison's death.

Was it a good idea to impose secrecy? The young republic had only recently opened up its political process to the people. Thomas Jefferson called the decision to close the convention "an abominable precedent." In a republic, he argued, the people should always know what their leaders are doing.[13]

However, the delegates wanted to speak their minds freely without worrying about how their words would appear in the newspapers. Many also believed that powerful politicians in their home states would withdraw their delegation as soon as they heard that the convention was debating an entirely new constitution. Without secrecy, they might have to abandon their bold plan and simply amend the Articles of Confederation—which was, after all, what they had been asked to do.

» Under the Articles of Confederation, thirteen independent states bound themselves into a confederation with a weak central government that had to rely on the states to implement its decisions.

» Though feeble, this first U.S. government was, by the standards of the time, a very democratic one.

» Delegates to the Constitutional Convention convened to fix the problems with the Articles of Confederation but chose to go much further and propose a new American government.

The Constitutional Convention

As they thought about reorganizing their new government, American leaders balanced the two political dangers they had recently encountered.

- British officials' behavior warned them that a powerful central government could strip the people of their rights.
- Experience with the Articles of Confederation warned them that a weak government could fail to protect their rights.

The delegates debated from May into September 1787. They touched on almost every aspect of government, ranging from how to elect the legislature to what to do about slavery. Throughout the discussions, six major themes dominated their attention.

1. How Much Power to the People?

Most Constitutional Convention delegates believed the states had gone too far in empowering the voters. Too much democracy, they thought, had led to chaotic government. Several put their views bluntly right at the start of the convention. "The evils we are experiencing flow from an excess of democracy," argued Elbridge Gerry of Massachusetts. "The people . . . are the dupes of pretended patriots." Roger Sherman, a shrewd Yankee from Connecticut, summed up this perspective: "The people . . . should have . . . little to do . . . [with] government. They want [or lack] information and are constantly liable to be misled."[14]

The delegates faced a dilemma. They wanted their government to answer to the public; that was why they had fought the Revolution. Recent experience, however, also made them fear a system that responded too readily to the people (or, more precisely, to white men with property). The delegates wished to represent the public through better educated, wealthier, and more experienced leaders—men like themselves.

Over the course of the convention, the delegates developed a view of representation that Madison called *filtration*, or *indirect elections*: The public would vote for men (and later women) who would in turn vote for public officials. Examples of filtration appear throughout the Constitution. The speeches during the convention's first days are a bit shocking to us today. The delegates wanted to make the public *less* involved in government than they had been in the eleven years since the United States declared its independence. The new Constitution would permit the public to vote for only one federal office—members of the House of Representatives.

The debate about public involvement did not end with the Constitution. Over time, Americans would get a more active role in their governance. Citizens would win more control over presidential elections beginning in the 1820s, when voting reforms were passed on the state level; they started voting directly for senators after passage of the Seventeenth Amendment in 1913. The "public" also would expand over time. Women became voters with passage of the Nineteenth Amendment in 1920; four years later, Congress ensured Native American voting rights. African Americans, who won the right to vote in 1870 (with the Fifteenth Amendment), were later denied suffrage, and finally won the right all over again with the Voting Rights Act of 1965. Younger Americans (eighteen- to twenty-year-olds) became eligible to vote in 1971.

● Over time, common men began voting in American elections. This painting shows the raucous results. Note the heavy drinking—and how this, as with all early American elections, was a completely male event.

The debate that began at the Constitutional Convention continues to this day. It animates one of the key ideas we discussed in Chapter 2: self-rule, balanced between direct democracy and indirect representation. At a still more fundamental level, the debate speaks to one of the great questions of American politics: *Who governs?* Public involvement in government has grown dramatically over the centuries, but Madison's principle of filtration still keeps the people at arm's length from their government in many areas.

2. National Government Versus State Government

The Articles of Confederation left most power with the states. Madison's plan for the new government took that power and vested it in a strong national government. The very first motion that the delegates debated called for "a national government . . . consisting of a *supreme* legislature, executive, and judiciary." In fact, Madison's original plan would have shifted most governing authority to the national level.[15]

Many delegates disagreed with this dramatic change. They believed that state and local governments were closer to the people and could more accurately reflect public sentiments—precisely what Madison was trying to avoid. Some pro–states' rights delegates charged Madison and his allies with trying to "abolish the State Governments altogether." Ultimately, delegates from New York walked out of the convention; and Rhode Island refused to send any delegates in the first place. The convention was soon down to eleven of the thirteen states.[16]

In the end, the delegates compromised on a system that included both national and state power. The federal government took over many functions—but far fewer than Madison had originally proposed. The states kept many duties—but far fewer than the states' rights advocates wanted. This mixed system, with a stronger national government that leaves considerable power with the state governments, is called **federalism** (and we'll discuss it in Chapter 4). The debate about how to balance national government power and state power continues to the present day.

3. Big States Versus Small States

Another intense dispute at the Constitutional Convention revolved around a division we rarely notice today: the large, more populous states (led by Virginia and Pennsylvania) versus the smaller states (led by New Jersey and Delaware). Large states argued that representation should be based on population; small states wanted each state to have an equal voice. That debate led to two different plans, one put forward by Virginia (a big state) and the other by New Jersey (on behalf of the small states).

The Virginia Plan.   Large and small states squared off as soon as Governor Edmund Randolph of Virginia presented Madison's original plan for the Constitution. A powerful speaker, Randolph addressed the delegates for four hours. The plan, which became known as the **Virginia Plan**, had five key points.

1. Congress would have two chambers, a form known as a **bicameral** legislature, with representation in both chambers based on state population.
2. Citizens would vote for members of the House of Representatives; the number of representatives would reflect the size of the state. The House of Representatives would, in turn, vote for senators from a list of candidates provided by the state legislatures. This limited the states' role and is an example of filtration, or indirect elections.
3. Congress would elect the president. Here the Virginia Plan suddenly turned vague and did not specify whether the president would be one man or a committee; nor did it say how long the executive would serve. Madison told George Washington that he had not made up his mind.
4. A national judiciary with one or more supreme courts would be established, and the judges would have life tenure.
5. Congress would have broad powers to legislate in all cases where the states were "incompetent." A "council of revision" made up of the president and the Supreme Court would have the authority to review and nullify any state law.

Delegates who had not already been briefed by Madison were stunned. Randolph was urging them to build a robust national government. The Virginia Plan empowered Congress to "call forth the force of the union" against any state "failing to fulfill its duties" under the new constitution. The federal government could strike down state laws. Early votes indicated that the Virginia Plan enjoyed a small majority at the convention.

Delegates from small states were especially critical of Madison's blueprint. Small states such as New Jersey lamented that they would soon "be swallowed up." Each state had "its peculiar habits, usages, and manners," small-state advocates insisted, and these must be protected. Under Madison's plan, three states (Virginia, Pennsylvania, and Massachusetts) would have enough members in Congress to form a majority all by themselves. Representatives from the smaller states repeatedly threatened to walk out of the convention.[17]

Federalism: Power divided between national and state government. Each has its own sovereignty (independent authority) and its own duties.

Virginia Plan: Madison's plan, embraced by the Constitutional Convention delegates from larger states; this plan strengthened the national government relative to state governments.

Bicameral: Having two legislative houses or chambers—such as the House and the Senate.

The New Jersey Plan. The small states pushed back with their own plan, introduced by William Paterson of New Jersey and known as the **New Jersey Plan**. Rather than construct a new national government, this plan focused on strengthening the Articles of Confederation. It had four key points:

1. Congress would have only one chamber, a form known as a **unicameral** legislature. Each state would have one vote in Congress, regardless of its size—exactly the same as in the Articles. However, congressional acts would be the supreme law of the land, making the new constitution stronger than the Articles of Confederation.

2. Congress would elect a committee to serve as the federal executive for one term only.

3. The executive committee would select a supreme court, which would be responsible for foreign policy, economic policy, and the impeachment of federal officials.

4. The national government could tax the states and would have the exclusive right to tax imports.

The New Jersey Plan left the states at the center of American government but took a step toward union by building a stronger national government, one that could raise its own taxes and exercise more authority over interstate commerce. When the vote was called, only three states supported the New Jersey Plan.

The Connecticut Compromise. Convention delegates decisively approved the Virginia Plan's bicameral Congress with a House and a Senate. They voted for a House of Representatives based on population. Then debate turned to the Senate. If the delegates voted with the Virginia Plan—in which the House of Representatives would vote for senators—the big states would essentially win the debate. Tempers grew short. "I do not, Gentlemen, trust you," declared Gunning Bedford of Delaware.

He hinted darkly that the small states would look for foreign allies if they lost this vote. William Paterson announced that he would rather "submit to a monarch, a despot," than accept the Virginia Plan. Luther Martin, a garrulous delegate from Maryland, wrote home that the convention was on the verge of breaking up over this issue.[18] Big states pushed back: "Will it require 150 voters from my state [Pennsylvania]," asked James Wilson, "to balance 50 from yours [New Jersey]?"[19]

Big states seemed to have the votes to carry seven states and win the Virginia Plan's version of Senate elections. But when the roll was called on July 2, one big-state supporter from Maryland and two from Georgia slipped out of the convention hall. With their exits, both states shifted, and the vote came out a tie: five states for the Virginia Plan, five against, and one evenly split.

To break the deadlock, the delegates formed a committee, which was tilted toward the small

New Jersey Plan: Put forward at the Constitutional Convention by the small states, this plan left most government authority with the state governments.

Unicameral: Having a single legislative house or chamber.

● *Louis Glanzman's recent painting of the Constitutional Convention. Washington towers over everyone at the center in a black frock coat. To his right stands James Madison. Alexander Hamilton is the red-haired man standing sixth from the right. Aged Benjamin Franklin, eighty-one years old, sits at the center of the room, chatting with Hugh Williamson, a delegate from North Carolina.*

states. The committee came up with a compromise, brokered by Roger Sherman of Connecticut and therefore known as the Connecticut Compromise. The House would be based on population; the Senate would have two representatives for each state, chosen by the state legislature. (Americans did not vote directly for their senators in all states until 1913.) Because legislation had to pass through both houses, the public and the states would each have a say. Because the delegates wanted power over taxes and spending to be in the people's hands, they required that all finance-related bills had to be introduced first in the House.

The compromise squeaked through—five states voted "yes," four "no," and one split. The big states won the House of Representatives; the small states got their way in the Senate. The compromise continues to give rural states a great deal of clout in the Senate—and, because all legislation requires approval from both houses, in Congress.

More immediate, the Constitution had its legislature. Two difficult issues, however, remained—the power of the president and the agonizing question of slavery.

4. The President

Even the master planner James Madison arrived at the convention without a clear design for the presidency—also known as the *executive authority* because it *executes* (or puts into effect) the laws. The delegates even wavered about whether executive authority should be placed in one individual or a committee.

Committee or Individual?   Many delegates worried that a single executive would grow powerful and become, as Governor Randolph put it, "the fetus of monarchy." Madison and his allies, however, feared that the Connecticut Compromise opened the Senate door to the same petty state politics that had wrecked the Articles of Confederation. They therefore decided that the president should be one individual, independent of Congress, who could represent the public. After much back-and-forth, they settled on a four-year term and permitted reelections. (In 1951, the Twenty-Second Amendment limited the president to two terms.)

The Electoral College.   How would the United States choose the president? The Constitution's framers saw a problem with every option. They did not think the people had enough information or wisdom. They did not trust state legislators to put aside their own narrow concerns and think about the national interest. Delegates from the big states no longer wanted to give Congress the job now that state legislators were picking the senators. What could they do? In response, they came up with the most complicated rigmarole in the Constitution: the **Electoral College**. Each state would select individuals known as *electors*—the delegates hoped that they would be well-known individuals with sound judgment—and the electors would then choose the president.

How many electors would each state have? Another compromise: Each state would have the same number of electors as it had members of Congress. That meant a state's population would matter (given proportional representation in the House) but also that every state was assured of two more votes (reflecting their representation in the Senate). If no individual received a majority of electoral votes—which

Electoral College:
The system established by the Constitution to elect the president; each state has a group of electors (equal in size to that of its congressional delegation in the House and the Senate); the public in each state votes for electors, who then vote for the president.

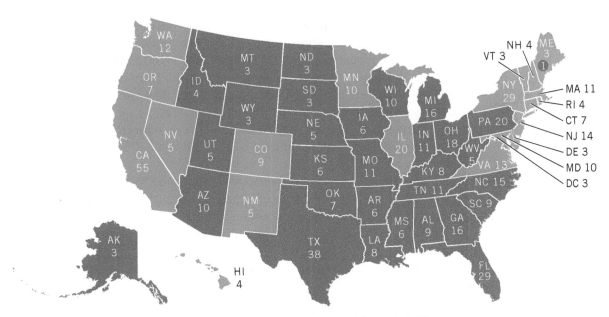

● **FIGURE 3.3** *Electoral College map for the 2016 presidential election. For the second time in the last five elections, the candidate who lost the popular vote became president by winning the Electoral College.*

last happened in 1824—the House of Representatives would choose from among the five candidates with the most votes. They would vote by state, and each state would get just one vote—again, a concession to small states.

Who would elect the electors? The convention simply left this question to the states. At first, the state legislatures got the job of voting for the electors. But in the late 1820s, the states ceded this right to the people (again, white men, although by then they did not need to own any property). The people voted state by state for their electors—as we still do.

Today, all the electors in a state generally cast their votes for the candidate who won the state (although only twenty-six states require them to do so; Figure 3.3). As we saw in Chapter 1, the system has elected four men who lost the popular vote—but won in the Electoral College.

The President: Too Strong or Too Weak?   All these details can obscure a crucial fact about the Constitution and the presidency. The delegates arrived at the Constitutional Convention less certain about this office than any other. Some feared putting too much power in one person's hands. Others recognized the need for a leader who could energetically pursue the nation's interests. Despite all that was at stake, arguments about the presidency never got very heated. Why? Because every delegate in the room knew exactly who the first president was going to be. There sat George Washington, calmly presiding over the convention. Knowing that Washington would almost certainly be thrust into the role of president cooled the tempers in the room. In the end, the delegates built a general framework and left many details to be defined by the presidents themselves.

Sometimes, the presidency has been a very powerful office. At other times, it has seemed perilously weak. We explore this paradox when we examine the presidency in Chapter 14.

5. Separation of Powers

One idea that evolved during the convention was the separation of powers. Each branch of government—the president, Congress, and the Court—has its job to do: The delegates vested "all legislative powers" in Congress, the executive power in the president, and the judicial power (to try cases) in the courts. The Articles of Confederation had created only a national legislature; in Britain, power was also concentrated in Parliament, their national legislature. Now, the United States would have three independent branches.

The framers added a crucial twist: checks and balances. *Each power the Constitution grants to Congress or the presidency or the judiciary is balanced by a "countervailing" power assigned to another branch.* Each branch is involved in the others' business. In this way, as Madison later put it, one branch's ambition for power would always check the other branches' ambitions (see Figure 3.4).

For example, Congress passes legislation but needs the president to sign a bill into law. The president can veto (reject) the bill (checking Congress); Congress can override the veto by a two-thirds vote of both chambers (balancing the president).

The president is commander-in-chief, but the Constitution gives Congress the power to declare war and set the military's budget. The president negotiates treaties, but the Senate must ratify them by a two-thirds vote. The president appoints ministers and Supreme Court justices, but the Senate must approve (or confirm) them. Congress holds the ultimate power over all federal officers. As specified in the last section of Article II, the House can impeach (or formally accuse) the president or any other officer in the executive or judicial branch of "Treason, Bribery or other

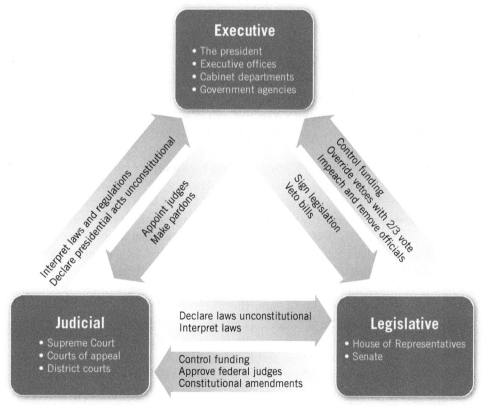

● **FIGURE 3.4** *Separation of powers—the checks on the federal level. Multiply these checks across all three levels and a vital question of American politics arises: Is this chaotic and fragmented state ready to take on the world? We have been posing this question since 1787.*

high Crimes and Misdemeanors"; the Senate looks into the accusation and decides whether to actually remove the person from office. What is a "high crime and misdemeanor"? Well, as they have never been fully defined, Congress must use its judgment.

These checks and balances are among the most distinctive features of the American Constitution. The French political philosopher Montesquieu wrote an influential treatise, *The Spirit of the Laws* (published in 1748), which argued that to avoid tyranny, the executive, legislative, and judicial functions of government must be separated from one another—and never placed in a single individual or body. However, very few governments have ever developed this principle as fully as the U.S. Constitution did.

Checks and balances continue to spark disagreement in the present. Many scholars argue that American-style separated systems are more prone to gridlock—a paralysis of governing institutions—than other democracies. The danger of gridlock is that major issues such as gun violence become harder to address. Has the U.S. government developed too many checks and balances to meet the challenges of the twenty-first century? Or do the Constitution's checks and balances remain in good working order, controlling power and preserving self-rule—just as James Madison planned?

6. "A Principle of Which We Were Ashamed"

The convention rethought almost every aspect of government—except slavery. Why? For some delegates, the answer came down to self-interest. Of the fifty-five delegates, twenty-five were slave owners. George Washington brought three slaves with him to Philadelphia. In three states—Georgia, South Carolina, and Virginia—slaves made up more than one-third of the population. And the men and women in bondage were a source of wealth and power. Each time the subject of slavery came up, delegates from South Carolina and Georgia offered the convention a stark choice—protect slavery or form a union without us.

In the end, the delegates wanted a strong union more than they hated slavery. The Constitution includes three major references to slavery—without ever mentioning the word itself. Each time, the slave-holding states got what they wanted.

The Three-Fifths Compromise.   Slavery was first thrust on the convention's agenda with the question of how to count slaves when allocating seats in the House of Representatives. As Table 3.2 shows, nearly four in ten of Virginia's residents were slaves. If slaves were counted as part of the population, southern states would have as many members in the House of Representatives as the northern states.

As soon as the issue came up, James Wilson of Pennsylvania sprang to his feet and offered a compromise. For the purpose of apportioning representation, Wilson proposed, let the total number of slaves count as three-fifths of the free people of a state. The strange fraction came from the Continental Congress. When it was trying to raise revenue from the states, Congress calculated each state's wealth on the basis of population. It then arbitrarily estimated that slaves would generate three-fifths as much wealth as free people.

This crude calculation now came back to haunt the Constitution. The delegates immediately accepted the Three-Fifths Compromise. Its actual wording is as peculiar as the rule itself.

> *Representatives . . . shall be apportioned among the several states according to their respective numbers, which shall be determined by adding the*

TABLE 3.2 Enslaved Proportion of the U.S. Population in 1790

STATE	TOTAL POPULATION	SLAVES	PERCENTAGE OF POPULATION ENSLAVED
Connecticut	237,655	2,648	1.1
Delaware	59,096	8,887	15.0
Georgia	82,548	29,264	34.5
Maryland	319,728	103,036	32.2
Massachusetts	378,556	0	0.0
New Hampshire	141,899	157	0.1
New Jersey	184,139	11,423	6.2
New York	340,241	21,193	6.2
North Carolina	395,005	100,783	25.5
Pennsylvania	433,611	3,707	0.9
Rhode Island	69,112	958	1.4
South Carolina	249,073	107,094	43.0
Virginia	747,550	292,627	39.1

whole number of free persons, including those bound to service for a term of years [indentured servants] and excluding Indians not taxed, three fifths of all other persons.

The Constitution never says "slave," but simply "three fifths of all other persons." In fact, a reader who did not know that the passage refers to slavery would have a hard time understanding it. Why did the Constitution's framers—who were usually so precise—write such a convoluted sentence? They did not want the word *slavery* to appear in the Constitution. John Dickinson, a thoughtful delegate from Delaware, put it best: The awkward wording was, he said, "an endeavor to conceal a principle of which we were ashamed."[20]

The Slave Trade. A second question involved the slave trade. Could the federal government regulate or abolish it? Many delegates were repulsed by the idea of stealing human beings from Africa, chaining them into the hulls of ships bound for America, and selling the survivors to the highest bidder. George Mason from Virginia rose and gave the most prophetic speech of the convention: "Every master of slaves is born a petty tyrant. They bring the judgment of heaven on a country. As nations cannot be rewarded or punished in the next world they must be in this. Providence punishes national sins, by national calamities." It was a powerful speech. However, Mason himself owned more than three hundred slaves. Their worth would rise if the slave trade were abolished.

No one else at the convention was willing to follow Mason's attack. In the end, backers of a strong Constitution struck a bargain and permitted the slave trade for another twenty years, in exchange for more national power over interstate commerce and the authority to tax imports. Historian William Beeman calculated that by permitting the slave trade for another twenty years they condemned 200,000 Africans to slavery—almost equaling the total (250,000) from the preceding 170 years.[21]

Fugitive Slaves. Finally, in August, as the convention was winding down, delegates from the slave states proposed a fugitive slave clause—requiring the rest of the nation to assist in returning runaway slaves. This time there were no deals and barely any debate. The northern delegates simply accepted the proposal. Northern merchants, after all, benefited from the slave trade right alongside Southern planters. Every region was complicit in the tragic decision.

"The National Calamity." Many Americans revere the document that has guided the nation for more than 225 years. However, George Mason

A vivid example of slavery's brutality. Fifty years after the Constitutional Convention, abolitionists rose up and denounced the Constitution as a "covenant with death and an agreement with hell" because of its slavery compromises. Advertisements for runaway slaves reported identifying marks—such as horrific scars from whipping and even branding.

was right when he predicted a "national calamity." Seventy-two years later, Abraham Lincoln would echo Mason as he reflected on the carnage of the Civil War in his second inaugural address: "God . . . gives to both North and South this terrible war as the woe due to those by whom the offense [of slavery] came."

The Constitution's slavery passages—as with the Civil War that led to their repeal—remind us that the Convention was the beginning of an American journey. Each generation has to face the same challenges that confronted the founders. *Who are we?* Can we try to make the United States more just, more democratic, and more inclusive? The Declaration of Independence gives America its ideals: All people are created equal. The Constitution, in turn, provides the rules. Americans have struggled over the meaning of the ideals and the implementation of the rules ever since these documents were written.

THE BOTTOM LINE

» The constitutional framers balanced two dangers: government that was too strong (the king of England) versus government that was too weak (the Articles of Confederation).

» The debates focused on five central issues:

1. Should the people be directly involved in government? Most delegates believed in filtration, or indirect elections.

2. National versus state power, which came down to a standoff between larger and smaller states. Led by Madison, the big states introduced the Virginia Plan. Small states countered with the New Jersey Plan. The Connecticut Compromise offered a solution: House members were elected on the basis of population, but every state had two Senate seats.

(Continued)

3. The nature of the presidency.

4. How best to separate governing powers, answered through a system of checks and balances. For the most part, these limits on concentrated authority would continue to develop long after ratification.

5. Slavery: Pragmatic compromise in the name of union overcame moral concerns. Delegates took care not to use the word *slavery* in the Constitution, but several clauses enabling the institution to expand would lead to the greatest conflict in the nation's future.

An Overview of the Constitution

By September 17, after four months of deliberation, the Constitutional Convention had done its work. Thirty-nine of the original fifty-five delegates lined up to sign the document. Benjamin Franklin, pointing to a sunburst painted on the back of the president's chair, reflected on how he had gazed at that sun throughout the convention "without being able to tell if it was rising or setting. But now . . . I have the happiness to know that it is a rising and not a setting sun."[22] A more pessimistic observer might have pointed out that sixteen delegates—almost a third—had either left the convention or refused to sign: a portent of the battles ahead.

There are only seven articles in the Constitution, each broken down into multiple sections. (Their full text appears in Appendix II.) These passages remain the institutional foundation of the American political system.

Preamble

The Constitution begins with a preamble, the most elegant sentence in the document:

> *We the people of the United States, in order to form a more perfect union, establish justice, insure domestic tranquility, provide for the common defense, promote the general welfare, and secure the blessings of liberty to ourselves and our posterity, do ordain and establish this Constitution for the United States of America.*

The Constitution's authority rests not on the states, but on "we the people." As we have seen, the Constitutional Convention produced a weak version of the people—one that permitted slavery, excluded women, and permitted "we the people" to vote for exactly one branch of Congress. The next phrase—"in order to form a more perfect union"—addresses these limitations. Americans always struggle toward that more perfect union.

The preamble also offers six goals for a successful government. Ask yourself how you would rate the U.S. government on each of them today (see What Do You Think?).

Article 1: Congress

Article 1, the longest in the Constitution, describes the new Congress. Section 2 of the article establishes a House of Representatives elected every two years. In 1789,

	What Do You Think?	**Have We Achieved the Constitution's Goals Today?**

	Goal:	**Grade Today:**
Think about the goals listed in the preamble. Then give a grade to each: An "A" if you think the United States has lived up to its goals, and a . . . well, we're sure you know all about grades!	Form a strong union	_____
	Establish equal justice for all	_____
	Insure domestic tranquility (that is, peace at home)	_____
	Provide for the common defense (today, we might say homeland security)	_____
	Promote the general welfare	_____
	Secure liberty for ourselves and posterity	_____

the average size of a House district was around 33,000 people—today the size of an average district has grown to nearly 733,000 people. Representatives must be twenty-five years old and have been a citizen for seven years. Section 3 establishes a Senate with two members from every state, elected every six years; they must be at least thirty and have been a citizen for nine years.

Section 8 is the most important passage in Article 1—and perhaps the entire Constitution. Its seventeen short paragraphs tell Congress what it may do, including the "power to lay and collect taxes," declare war, regulate interstate commerce, coin money, and raise an army.

Think about the reach of congressional authority. The largest and most expensive program that Congress oversees is Social Security, which pays monthly pensions to retired people over sixty-six. If you read all of Section 8, you may be puzzled—nothing in it remotely justifies paying for retirement pensions. How, then, could Congress create the Social Security program? Because the very last paragraph of Section 8 empowers Congress "to make all laws which shall be necessary and proper for carrying into execution the foregoing powers, and all other powers vested by this Constitution in the government of the United States." That phrase, known as the *necessary and proper clause*, gives Congress—and the government— a great deal of creative leeway. What are the limits of the power granted to Congress by this clause? This is another point on which the delegates in Philadelphia disagreed. Not surprisingly, scholars argue still about how far the necessary and proper clause stretches congressional authority.

Section 9 of Article 1 lists the things Congress may *not* do. Its second prohibition is especially important today: "The privilege of the writ of habeas corpus shall not be suspended unless when in cases of rebellion or invasion the public safety may require it." *Habeas corpus* means that government cannot hold prisoners without formally charging them with a crime. The U.S. government may not simply throw someone in jail without a charge. What about terrorist suspects held without charges? Again, experts disagree. Both the Bush and Obama administrations argued that "public safety" requires indefinite detention. Others counter that this practice undermines liberty, one of the basic rights that the Constitution was established to protect.

Article 2: The President

The Constitution's second article shifts focus from the legislature to the executive branch. The president, Article 2 specifies, must be a natural-born American at least

COMPARING NATIONS 3.2 The U.S. Government Is Different from Most Democracies

Of these twelve advanced democracies, only two—Argentina and Brazil—mirror the American Constitution on all three dimensions. Most democracies are parliamentary systems, in which the lower house selects the chief executive (a prime minister). Ironically, that was the idea in both the Virginia and New Jersey Plans, the original drafts of the Constitution. None of these other democracies has as many checks and balances as the United States.

NATION	HEAD OF GOVERNMENT ELECTED BY	FEDERALISM	CHECKS/ BALANCES
United States	Public/electors	Yes	Yes
Argentina	Public	Yes	Yes
Australia	Parliament (lower house)	Yes	Some
Brazil	Public	Yes	Yes
Canada	Parliament (lower house)	Yes	No
France	Public	No	Sometimes
Germany	Parliament (lower house)	Yes	Some
Great Britain	Parliament (lower house)	No	No
India	Parliament (lower house)	Yes	No
Israel	Parliament (lower house)	No	No
Japan	Parliament (lower house)	No	No

thirty-five years old and is chosen by electors for a four-year term. As we saw, each state originally decided who elects the electors—today every state has turned the power to choose electors over to the public. Our process for selecting the head of state is still very different from that followed by other nations (see Comparing Nations 3.2).

Whereas Article 1 lists congressional do's and don'ts in detail, Article 2 says very little about presidential powers and duties. The president is commander in chief of the army and the navy.[23] Presidents make treaties if two-thirds of the Senate approve; they appoint ambassadors, Supreme Court justices, and all other officials—again with the advice and consent of the Senate.

Although that seems like a limited set of powers, the Constitution includes another clause that has permitted an enormous expansion of presidential powers: "The executive power shall be vested in a President of the United States." What that "executive power" is, and how far it can stretch, has been debated throughout American history. President Obama, for example, facing a Congress unwilling to act on immigration reform, in 2012 unilaterally declared a "Dreamers" policy that allowed young children brought illegally into the United States to apply for work permits and avoid deportation. How could he do so? The administration claimed he was using his authority to execute the laws that govern immigration.In 2016, the Supreme Court ruled on the president's policy, reaching a split decision that left the original plan in place but enabled states to scale it back in the future. Even the executive-power clause has limits.

Section 4 allows for removing a president "on impeachment for, and conviction of, treason, bribery, or other high crimes and misdemeanors." What constitutes a high crime or misdemeanor? Again, the Constitution does not say, which makes any impeachment effort highly charged on all sides. Three presidents have faced formal impeachment proceedings, although only one, Richard Nixon, has been forced to resign his office.[24]

Article 3: The Courts

Article 3 creates the Supreme Court and authorizes Congress to organize additional courts. Alexander Hamilton called the Supreme Court "the least dangerous" branch of government, and the Constitution describes it only briefly. The justices are selected by the president, approved by the Senate, and have tenure for life—still another buffer against democratic politics. Article 3 grants the Supreme Court power over all cases "arising under this Constitution, the laws of the United States and treaties made."

The Constitution is silent on the Court's most formidable power: May it overrule an act of Congress? Or an executive declaration by the White House? Sixteen years after the Constitutional Convention, Chief Justice John Marshall, in deciding a case called *Marbury v. Madison*, ruled that the Court could strike down an act of Congress. (We review this case in detail in Chapter 16.) In other words, because the Court has authority over all cases "arising under this Constitution," Marshall claimed it also had a responsibility to review the constitutionality of legislation. The delegates debated this power but, in the end, sidestepped the controversy and left the language vague. Ever since Marshall's decision, however, the courts have ruled whether Congress and the President are abiding by the Constitution's rules. In 2016, the Supreme Court ruled that universities could use race as one legitimate factor in admissions decisions, after years of challenges to affirmative action policies. Once again, you see how Americans are constantly challenged to read and interpret precisely what the Constitution requires.

Article 4: Relations Between the States

Article 4 defines the relationship between the states that had so plagued the Articles of Confederation. A state may not discriminate against citizens of other states, and each must give "full faith and credit" to the official acts of other states. Article 4 also describes the process for adding new states to the union and requires the United States to guarantee every state a republican form of government.

The "full faith and credit" clause became a major issue when some states recognized same-sex marriage while others refused. After more than a decade, the Supreme Court took the issue off the table by striking down all state laws that limited marriage to a man and a woman. Now you know where they got the authority to do so: the Supreme Court's authority to judge which laws and regulations violate the rules laid down by the Constitution.

Article 5: Amendments

Article 5 authorizes amendments to the Constitution. Creating an amendment is an extremely difficult process. Two-thirds of both the House and the Senate must approve the amendment. Then three-fourths of the states must ratify it—either through the state legislature or through state conventions. The only amendment to be ratified the second way is the Twenty-First Amendment, which in 1933 repealed the prohibition on alcohol.

Over one hundred thousand amendments have been proposed since 1791 (when the first ten amendments, or Bill of Rights, were ratified); only seventeen have passed. When citizens or companies disagree with a Supreme Court ruling, occasionally they try to push through a constitutional amendment. As you can see, they very rarely succeed.

The Constitution forbids amendments on two matters: No amendment could stop the slave trade before 1808, and no state could be denied equal suffrage in the Senate (two seats) without its approval. In this way, the two fiercest debates at the convention were placed beyond the reach of future generations.

Article 6: The Law of the Land

Article 6 makes the Constitution the supreme law of the land. It also specifies that there must be no religious test for holding any federal office. Some states, however, had religious tests for holding state and local office and even for voting, up until the 1830s.

Article 7: Ratification

Article 7 announced that the Constitution would go into effect after nine states had ratified it—a controversial move, because the United States was still operating under the Articles of Confederation, which could be amended only by all thirteen states.

The Missing Articles

Many Americans thought that the original Constitution was missing something important. Only a handful of individual rights were mentioned in the document. It said nothing about free speech, a free press, freedom of religion, jury trials, or the right to bear arms. The debate over ratifying the Constitution would quickly expose this weakness. As we will see, ratification helped introduce an important addition: the ten amendments known as the Bill of Rights.

THE BOTTOM LINE

» The Constitution is a brief, elegant document with a preamble and seven articles (or major sections).

» The Articles of the Constitution address (1) Congress, (2) the President, (3) the Courts, (4) relations between the states, (5) instruction for amending the Constitution, (6) an assertion that the Constitution is the supreme law of the land, and (7) a process for ratifying the Constitution.

Ratification

The new Constitution now went to the states, where ratifying conventions would vote it up or down. While most states were closely divided, the Constitution had two big advantages. First, it offered a clear plan in a time of trouble; opponents could only say "no" and force the nation to start all over again. Second, the convention had attracted many of the most prestigious men in America, beginning with Washington and Franklin, who were the most widely admired figures in two of the largest states. Supporters of the Constitution were known as *Federalists*—making their opponents the *Anti-Federalists*.

The Anti-Federalists

The Anti-Federalists rooted their argument against ratification in **classical republicanism**. Popular government, in this view, ought to model itself on ancient republics such as Athens and Rome. Republics should be small and local, permitting maximum popular participation in public affairs. When we discussed the idea of self-rule in Chapter 2, we introduced the idea of direct democracy (celebrated by Thomas Jefferson); classical republicanism is the original version of that idea.

The Anti-Federalists were not interested in a centralized nation–state such as the European empires. They had four major criticisms of the new Constitution:

Classical republicanism: A democratic ideal, rooted in ancient Greece and Rome, that calls on citizens to participate in public affairs, seek the public interest, shun private gain, and defer to natural leaders.

- First, it stripped political control from citizens and placed it in a powerful national government over which the people would not have much influence.

- Second, the president looked too much like a king.

- Third, standing armies and navies were a threat to peace and liberty. Republics relied on citizen militias—which could be mustered during wartime—to protect the people.

- Fourth, and most important, the Anti-Federalists hammered away at the Constitution's missing piece, a bill of rights.[25]

Politics also played a role in the Anti-Federalist argument. Many of the men who opposed the Constitution were powerful political figures in their own states. A national government would diminish their influence.

Many of the Anti-Federalist (and civic-republican) arguments remain alive today. Americans often criticize the federal government and cheer the idea of restoring power to state and local officials, who are closer to the people. The Anti-Federalists may have lost the debate in 1788, but their fear of federal power and their yearning to return authority to the people endures—and shapes one answer to our great question, *Who are we?*

The Federalists

The arguments in favor of the new Constitution were summarized by an editorial dream team. James Madison and Alexander Hamilton (with a little help from John Jay, who would become the first chief justice of the United States) wrote eighty-five short essays that appeared in newspapers to explain and defend the Constitution. Known as the *Federalist Papers*, these essays achieved three very different purposes. First, they are pro-Constitution editorials, even propaganda; the authors were fighting to get New York to approve the new Constitution, and they did not pretend to be neutral. Second, they are the single best guide to the thinking that guided the Constitution. However, we have to read them carefully, always weighing the *Papers* as persuasive rhetoric on the one hand and as explanations of constitutional logic on the other. Finally, the *Federalist Papers* are outstanding theoretical essays about politics and government.

The two most famous *Federalist Papers*, no. 10 and no. 51, are reprinted in Appendix III to this book. Their eighteenth-century language sounds strange to our ears, but the argument is brilliant. *Federalist* no. 10 argues, surprisingly, that a

The ratification of the Constitution was a close call. Patrick Henry, a powerful orator, led the opponents (known as Anti-Federalists) in Virginia. Virginia was one of seven states in which the vote was close.

large national government can protect liberty more effectively than small local governments. Madison begins the essay by introducing the "mortal disease" that always destroys popular government. You might think that he was referring to tyrants like George III. Instead, he points to *factions*—groups that pursue their self-interest at the expense of others. And in the United States, said Madison, factions usually reflect economic interests. This issue still haunts American foreign policy today: Removing tyrants will not achieve stable popular government until factions are controlled.

How can we diminish the effects of factions? Not through local governments, argued Madison. In each local area, one economic interest is likely to predominate—farmers, merchants, big manufacturers, or even poor people eager to tax the rich. Because the same local group will always be in the majority, it is difficult to stop that group from taking advantage of the minority.

Madison's realistic assessment was a breakthrough in political theory. The classical view assumed that for popular government to survive, the people—that is, the voters—had to be virtuous and respect one another. Madison introduced a more modern view: expect people to pursue their own self-interest. As he wrote in *Federalist* no. 51, "if men were angels, no government would be necessary." If popular government is to survive, it must be organized to protect minorities from majorities who are going to pursue their own self-interest.

How can we do this? Move the debate to the national level, said Madison. A larger political sphere—a bigger government—will always have a great many diverse interests, arising from all the states. With so many different factions, no one interest will be able to dominate. Each faction will form a small minority of the whole and will therefore need to form alliances. As the issues change, so will the groups that are in the majority and the minority. As a result, no one faction will be able to impose its will on the minority for very long.

Two Strong Arguments

To this day, both sides—Anti-Federalist and Federalist—sound persuasive. The Anti-Federalists tapped into a deep American yearning for local governments that respond directly to popular concerns. The Federalists argued that only a national government could really protect the people's rights and turn the new nation into a great power.

A Very Close Vote

The small states got their way at the Constitutional Convention, and, not surprisingly, they ratified quickly and unanimously—Delaware, New Jersey, and Georgia all signed by January 2, 1788. In Pennsylvania, some members of the assembly hid to slow down the process. Enthusiastic mobs found the reluctant members and marched them to the deliberations. The public crammed into the hall and gathered outside the building. After a month, Pennsylvania ratified the Constitution 46 to 23, and Benjamin Franklin led a cheering throng through the streets to Epple's Tavern for celebratory toasts (see Table 3.3 for a summary of the voting).

In Massachusetts, Governor John Hancock, who had been the first delegate to sign the Declaration of Independence, dramatically switched to the Federalist side—on one crucial condition. He asked that amendments protecting individual rights be introduced to the new Constitution. It was the first prominent insistence on a bill of rights. Even with his switch, the Constitution won ratification in Massachusetts only narrowly, 187 to 168. Once the votes were counted, the Anti-Federalists announced that they would "support the Constitution as cheerfully and as heartily as though [they] had voted on the other side." Other states followed the two Massachusetts precedents: request a bill of rights and unite after the debate.

After Maryland and South Carolina voted for the Constitution, the action moved to Virginia—the largest state and the most intense contest to date. Anti-Federalist opposition was led by Patrick Henry, known as "the son of thunder" for his rhetorical power; at one point he spoke without notes for seven straight hours. Governor William Randolph, who had presented the Virginia Plan at the convention, and George Mason, who had scorched the slave trade, both refused to sign the Constitution and joined Henry on the Anti-Federalist side. Despite the strong opposition, Virginia voted for the Constitution 89 to 79.

TABLE 3.3 **Final Vote for the Constitution**

STATE	DATE OF RATIFICATION	VOTE IN STATE CONVENTION
1. Delaware	December 7, 1787	Unanimous (30–0)
2. Pennsylvania	December 12, 1787	46–23
3. New Jersey	December 18, 1787	Unanimous (38–0)
4. Georgia	January 2, 1788	Unanimous (26–0)
5. Connecticut	January 9, 1788	128–40
6. Massachusetts	February 7, 1788	187–168
7. Maryland	April 28, 1788	63–11
8. South Carolina	May 23, 1788	149–73
9. New Hampshire	June 21, 1788	57–47; required two meetings
10. Virginia	June 25, 1788	89–79
11. New York	July 25, 1788	30–27
12. North Carolina	July 21, 1789 (after the election of Washington)	194–77
13. Rhode Island	May 29, 1790 (first Congress in session)	34–32
Key: Easy Ratification	Tough Fight	Originally Refused

New York was even more contentious than Virginia. New York City supported the Constitution, but the rest of the state opposed it. In the end, the new Constitution squeaked through by 30 to 27.

Not every state voted in favor. Rhode Island town meetings voted against holding a convention to debate the Constitution. Rhode Island would reluctantly join the union after George Washington had been president for two months. North Carolina initially rejected the Constitution by a lopsided vote of 184 to 83. In New Hampshire a convention met, refused to ratify, and adjourned; four months later the delegates reconvened and voted yes, and on June 21, 1788, New Hampshire became the ninth state to ratify. The Constitution would now be the law of the land.

Ratification was a very close contest. If a total of just 3 percent of the delegates across Virginia, Massachusetts, and New York had changed their vote, the Constitution would have gone down to defeat. Americans came within a whisker of rejecting the Constitution that now defines the nation and its government.

New York celebrated ratification by cheering Alexander Hamilton—still remembered as a major intellectual force. Here, Broadway hit Hamilton recalls the most forceful Federalist. From left, Daveed Diggs, Okieriete Onaodowan, Anthony Ramos, and Lin-Manuel Miranda in the musical Hamilton.

A Popular Surge Propels People into Politics

The Federalists ultimately won the constitutional debate and created a strong central government far removed from the people. At first it seemed as if Roger Sherman's comment at the convention had won the day: "The people . . . should have . . . little to do . . . [with] government." But something unexpected happened. The Revolution set off a democratic surge that liberated popular energies. Not everyone was included—not women, not black people, not Native Americans. But the idea that ordinary citizens should be kept at arm's length from government was soon swamped by a great tide of participation that many of the founders neither imagined nor desired.[26] People raced to participate in both economic and political life. However, American history is not a simple story of ever-expanding participation. Rather, the battle for a more perfect union has been long and unpredictable. Over more than two centuries, rights, liberties, and democracy have been gained and lost and gained again.

THE BOTTOM LINE

» The debate over ratifying the Constitution featured two visions of American government.

» The *Federalists* argued that only an energetic national government could protect the nation and secure liberty. The *Anti-Federalists* called instead for a modest government that left power in state and local hands.

» The state-by-state voting on ratification was very close, and it was well over a year before the Constitution was approved.

» More than 225 years later, Americans are still debating the same question—How strong should the federal government be?

Changing the Constitution

Although most Anti-Federalist leaders eventually rallied to the new Constitution, they insisted on a crucial addition to the Constitution: a bill of rights. The state ratification conventions proposed over two hundred amendments. When the first Congress met, in 1789, most members did not want to bother with amendments. The Constitution was ratified, Congress elected, and President George Washington's administration organized. However, one representative insisted on adding liberties to the Constitution. James Madison had been through a tough election campaign and had pledged to support a bill of rights. With his word of honor at stake, Madison took the two hundred proposed amendments, boiled them down to seventeen, and pushed his reluctant colleagues into passing them. The Senate reduced the list to twelve; the states ratified ten.

The Bill of Rights

Today, the first ten amendments to the Constitution, known as the **Bill of Rights**, form a crucial feature of the Constitution and of American government. *These set out the rights—the protections from government—that every citizen is guaranteed.* Freedom of speech, freedom of the press, freedom of religion, the right to bear arms, and the long list of additional rights are an essential part of America's identity. Table 3.4 summarizes the amendments that make up the Bill of Rights.

Originally, the Bill of Rights applied only to the federal government. The First Amendment reads, "Congress shall make no law . . . abridging the freedom of speech." At the time, states that wanted to limit speech or set up an official religion were free to do so.

Bill of Rights: The first ten amendments to the Constitution, listing the rights guaranteed to every citizen.

TABLE 3.4 **Summarizing the Bill of Rights**
1. Congress may not establish a religion or prohibit the free exercise of religion; it may not abridge freedom of speech or of the press or of the people's right to assemble and to petition government.
2. Citizens have the right to bear arms.
3. No soldier may be quartered in any house without the consent of the owner.
4. There must be no unreasonable searches or seizures. Government authorities may not break into your house without a search warrant.
5. No one may be forced to testify against him or herself (declining to do so is now known as "taking the Fifth"), and no one may be deprived of life, liberty, or property without due process of law. The government may not take private property (if, for example, it wants to build a highway) without just compensation.
6. Certain rights are guaranteed in criminal trials.
7. Accused persons are guaranteed the right to trial by jury.
8. The government may not force citizens to pay excessive bails and may not impose cruel and unusual punishments.
9. The enumeration of certain rights does not diminish the other rights retained by the people.
10. Any powers not given to the federal government are reserved for the states and the people.

TABLE 3.5 **Amendments to the U.S. Constitution**

AMENDMENT	DESCRIPTION	YEAR RATIFIED	RESULT
11	Required state consent for individuals suing a state in federal court	1795	Modified government operations
12	Separated votes within the Electoral College for president and vice president	1804	Shifted election rules
13	Prohibited slavery	1865	Expanded individual rights
14	Provided citizenship to former slaves and declared that states could not deny civil rights, civil liberties, or the equal protection of the laws	1868	Expanded individual rights
15	Granted voting rights to members of all races	1870	Expanded individual rights
16	Permitted national income tax	1913	Expanded government powers over individuals
17	Provided direct election of senators	1913	Shifted election rules
18	Prohibited alcohol	1919	Expanded government powers over individuals
19	Extended the vote to women	1920	Expanded individual rights
20	Changed Inauguration Day from March to January	1933	Modified government operations
21	Repealed Prohibition	1933	Adjusted government powers over individuals
22	Limited president to two terms	1951	Shifted election rules
23	Extended the vote for president to citizens in Washington, D.C.	1961	Expanded individual rights
24	Prohibited a poll tax (one way to keep black people from voting)	1964	Expanded individual rights
25	Established a succession plan in case of president's death or disability	1967	Modified government operations
26	Extended the vote to eighteen- to twenty-year-olds	1971	Expanded individual rights
27	Established that congressional pay raises couldn't go into effect until the next election	1992	Modified government operations

Incorporation: The process by which the Supreme Court declares that a right in the Bill of Rights also applies to state governments.

The Fourteenth Amendment, ratified after the Civil War in 1868 to protect the former slaves, commands that no *state* may deny "any person . . . the equal protection of the laws." In theory, this amendment extended the Bill of Rights to the states—meaning state governments must honor each right just as the national government must do. However, the Fourteenth Amendment only kicked off a long process, known as **incorporation**: the Supreme Court applied (or "incorporated") each right to state government, one right at a time. That process continues down to the present day: The Supreme Court "incorporated" the right to bear arms in 2010. As a result, no state or city may violate the second amendment right to bear arms. Where exactly does this leave gun control laws? That debate continues—stay tuned!

Ratifying the Constitution and the Bill of Rights was just the start of a long debate. We will return to the story of the Constitution and individual rights in Chapter 5 and explore how they guide government today.

The Seventeen Amendments

After the Bill of Rights was passed, constitutional amendments became rare events—only seventeen have passed since 1791. Successful amendments all do at least one of four things: They *extend rights*—for example, guaranteeing the right to vote to eighteen-year-olds (seven amendments extend rights). They *adjust election rules*—for example, limiting the president to two terms (eleven amendments focus on elections). They *change government operations*—for example, switching Inauguration Day from March to January (four amendments focus on government rules). Or they *affect governmental powers over individuals*—for example, prohibiting alcohol and then (fourteen years later) permitting alcohol again. Table 3.5 summarizes the seventeen amendments that have been ratified since 1791.

Apart from formal amendments, American government—and how we interpret the Constitution—has changed over time. We constantly debate how to apply the Constitution and its amendments to current issues. May Congress limit the money corporations give political candidates? May a woman have an abortion? May a college campus stop people from carrying guns? May universities consider an applicant's race as part of admissions decisions? May a Christian student group pray before class? The wording of the Constitution permits different interpretations. These questions—and many more—require Americans to read the Constitution and reflect on what it tells us, more than 225 years after it was ratified.

Originalism: A principle of legal interpretation that relies on the original meaning of those who wrote the Constitution.

The Constitution Today

The political life of the American colonies prepared the way for something no nation had done before: The United States organized a new government around a Constitution, written in the people's name and voted on by the people's representatives in every state. The document still guides American politics today. Who are we? Reading the U.S. Constitution is one important way to find out.

But there is a catch. Americans disagree about how to read the Constitution. One view, called **originalism**, or *strict construction*, insists that *Americans are bound to the literal meaning of the Constitution and its amendments, as their original authors and debaters understood them.* From this perspective, the Constitution's meaning does not change with the times.

● *A group of children pray together in their elementary-school class. Does the Constitution permit prayer in public schools? Or would that mean the government was endorsing (or "establishing") a religion—violating the First Amendment? In 2014, North Carolina re-ignited this debate when it loosened restrictions on praying in school.*

What Do
You Think?

How Strictly Should We Interpret the Constitution?

After considering the two approaches to interpreting the Constitution known as originalism and pragmatism, choose a position.

I'm an originalist. Contemporary justices should not try to substitute their judgment for that of the Constitution's framers. We cannot avoid the arbitrary use of power if we permit everyone to read the Constitution as they like. Before long, the Constitution will not mean anything at all.

I'm a pragmatist. Times change and conditions evolve. The modern world imposes challenges (and features new technologies) that the framers could not have imagined. Failing to permit the text to evolve would turn the document into an eighteenth-century straitjacket.

I'm in the middle. I believe the difference between these positions is far less stark than it appears at first glance. Even if we try very hard to get back to the document's original meaning, we always read the Constitution in light of the present. Every effort to interpret the Constitution will be guided by our own ideas and our own times.

see for yourself 3.1

Go online to view The 10-Minute Guide to the Constitution from Cornell University.

Pragmatism: A principle of legal interpretation based on the idea that the Constitution evolves and that interpretations of the Constitution must be put in the context of contemporary realities.

Another view was first articulated by Thomas Jefferson, who warned Americans not to view the Constitution with "sanctimonious reverence," as if it were "too sacred to be touched." The nation's founders should not be worshiped. He knew their limits, he said, because he was one of them. "I know also," concluded Jefferson, "that laws and institutions must go hand in hand with the progress of the human mind."[27] Many scholars and politicians have followed Jefferson's advice. They see a living, breathing, changing Constitution—one that speaks to each generation a little differently. This view of an evolving Constitution is known as **pragmatism**. *We cannot help bringing our own background, ideas, and judgments to bear as we think about the meaning of the document.*

As we will see throughout this book, it is often hard to tell exactly how the Constitution applies to our times. Different people reading the document come to very different conclusions—even if they're searching for the original meaning. In the end, the difference between originalism and pragmatism may not be as large as their proponents think.

THE BOTTOM LINE

» The Bill of Rights comprises the first ten amendments to the Constitution, which define the rights of American citizens.

» Seventeen more amendments (out of more than one hundred thousand proposals) followed over the next 215 years.

» American politics is always changing, but the Constitution still stands as the American political rulebook. However, the Constitution must be interpreted, for it is often unclear what the document means and how it applies to contemporary cases.

INFO/DATA: Limits to Free Speech? Most Americans say "No!"

Most Americans ardently support free speech—even if it means protecting offensive statements against minorities. The only group that is somewhat mixed are millennials: 40 percent would censor offensive statements about minorities. In recent years, the defense of free speech tends to evaporate for one group: anti-American Muslims.

1. How has tolerance for unpopular speech changed over time and across generations?

2. *Where do you stand?* Should we censor offensive statements about minorities? How about speeches made by avowed anti-American groups? Is there a limit to free speech? Or should the Constitution protect all speakers, even if the message is unpopular or anti-American?

U.S. millennials more likely to support censoring offensive statements about minorities?

	Government should be able to prevent people from saying these things	People should be able to say these things publicly
Total	28%	67%
Millennial (ages 18–34)	40%	58%
Gen X (35–50)	27%	70%
Boomer (51–69)	24%	71%
Silent (70–87)	12%	80%
Men	23%	73%
Women	33%	62%
Republican	18%	77%
Democrat	35%	60%
Independent	27%	68%
White non-Hispanic	23%	72%
Non-white	38%	57%
College degree or more	22%	75%
Some college	29%	66%
High school or less	31%	63%

Who should be allowed to give a speech in your community?

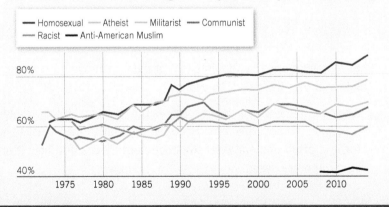

— Homosexual — Atheist — Militarist — Communist — Racist — Anti-American Muslim

Sources: Spring 2015 Global Attitudes survey; General Social Survey; The Washington Post

95

🛈 Conclusion: Does the Constitution Still Work?

Every chapter that follows will focus on a different feature of the Constitution as it operates today—federalism, civil liberties, civil rights, Congress, the presidency, and so on. As you explore these institutions, keep asking yourself: Does the world's oldest constitution still work? Almost all politicians—and most Americans—believe that it does. That is why it has lasted so long. But some disagree. Robert Dahl, a much revered political scientist, argued that the Constitution is just not democratic enough.[28] It does not include modern rights. Checks and balances are sometimes too cumbersome, making it difficult to pass needed laws. Congress no longer checks the president when it comes to war. The general effect, explained Dahl, is to water down American democracy.

The debate takes us back to the very first question we asked in Chapter 1. Who governs? Do "we the people" still rule? Or has real power slipped away to the rich and powerful? These are questions that every chapter will address.

Regardless of whether you are an *originalist*, a *pragmatist*, or somewhere in between, you should check to see what the Constitution says every time you study another feature of American politics. Start with the Constitution and you will know the basic rules of American politics.

CHAPTER SUMMARY

🔵 The Constitution provides the ground rules for American politics. However, it is often unclear exactly how the Constitution applies to contemporary issues. We have to interpret its meaning.

🔵 The colonial experience prepared America for thinking about a constitution. The English practice of *salutary neglect* permitted the colonies to develop their own political institutions, centered on their legislatures. Americans became used to *delegated*, or *actual, representation* (reflecting voter sentiment), which contrasted with the British view of *trustee*, or *virtual, representation* (representing the whole nation regardless of public opinion).

🔵 The Declaration of Independence has two parts. First, it states the American ideal: all people "are created equal" and "endowed by their creator with certain unalienable rights" including "life,

liberty, and the pursuit of happiness." Second, it lists colonial grievances, emphasizing the rights of free people to elect their legislatures.

🔵 The first American government, under the Articles of Confederation, was an alliance of independent states that maximized popular participation. This government had some great successes, but many leaders felt that it was too weak and left the United States vulnerable to foreign powers.

🔵 The Constitutional Convention, convened to fix the problems with the first American government, focused on six broad issues: popular involvement, national versus state power, big versus small states, checks and balances, the presidency, and slavery.

Ratification of the Constitution involved an extremely close battle between Anti-Federalists, who opposed the Constitution, and Federalists, who supported it. The first ten amendments, known as the Bill of Rights, came out of the ratification debates and were approved by the First Congress. Seventeen more amendments followed in the next 215 years. American politics has changed enormously, but the Constitution continues to stand as the basic blueprint for American political life.

KEY TERMS

Bicameral, p. 74
Bill of Rights, p. 91
Classical republicanism, p. 87
Compact, p. 60
Confederation, p. 67
Covenant, p. 60
Delegate representation, p. 61
Electoral College, p. 76

Federalism, p. 74
First Continental
    Congress, p. 64
Incorporation, p. 92
Indentured servant, p. 60
Mercantilism, p. 63
New Jersey Plan, p. 75
Originalism, p. 93

Pragmatism, p. 94
Second Continental
    Congress, p. 65
Supermajority, p. 68
Trustee representation,
    p. 62
Unicameral, p. 75
Virginia Plan, p. 74

STUDY QUESTIONS

1. Describe five ways that the colonial experience prepared the United States for a constitution.
2. Winning the French and Indian War drove two wedges between England and the colonies. What were they?
3. What is the difference between delegate or actual representation and trustee or virtual representation? How did the difference lead to the American Revolution?

> Optional assignment: A colonist from Virginia and a member of the English Parliament get into a furious debate about the true nature of representation. You are lucky enough to overhear them. Describe what each says during the debate. Try to make both sides sound reasonable.

4. What are the five overarching ideas introduced by the Declaration of Independence? In your opinion, how close are we to achieving those aspirations today?
5. Describe the first government that Americans organized after they broke away from England. Where was most of the power located? What problems arose under this government? What was successful about it?
6. When it came to writing the Constitution, the delegates had to balance two fears. One emerged from the battle with England, the other from American experience under the Articles of Confederation. Describe these two fears.
7. What did Madison mean by "filtration of representatives"? List two examples of filtration in the original Constitution.

> *What do you think?* Would you support filtration or the direct election of representatives?

8. Describe the differences between the Virginia Plan and the New Jersey Plan. If you had to choose between them, which would you choose, and why?
9. Describe what the Constitution says about the following:
   How the House of Representatives is elected.
   How the president is elected.
   How the Supreme Court is chosen.
   How amendments can be added to the Constitution.
10. Describe the differences between the Federalists and the Anti-Federalists. Which side would you be on? Why?

> Optional assignment: Choose one of the thirteen original states. Now, write a speech to be presented before its ratifying convention arguing for or against the new constitution.

 Go to www.oup.com/us/Morone to find quizzes, flash cards, simulations, tutorials, videos, and other study tools.

Federalism and Nationalism

DOLORES WAS FRIGHTENED. Her child was seriously ill. Yet she was afraid to drive him to the hospital because she is an undocumented person. She had no driver's license and no legal right to be in the United States. If the police stopped her car or made a sweep through the hospital waiting room, they would ask for proof of her status; when she failed to provide it, they would hold her in a jail cell until federal agents arrived to pick her up and start deportation procedures. Dolores, like many of the 12 million undocumented people in the United States, lives in the shadows—afraid to report a crime, visit a school, or drive a child to a hospital.

In response, cities such as Houston, Texas, have become "sanctuary cities"—the police do not ask about legal status during routine encounters. Immigrant advocacy groups argue that the policy protects the basic human rights of undocumented people.

Many Americans oppose the idea of sanctuary cities. Republican presidential nominee Donald Trump turned up the heat on this issue when he publicized a terrible incident that occurred in San Francisco. Juan Francisco Lopez-Sanchez, an undocumented Mexican who had been convicted of seven felonies (and had been deported five times), shot and killed Kathryn Steinle. Because San Francisco is a sanctuary city, Lopez had avoided police custody after a prior arrest.[1] He has become a symbol for Americans who want to get tougher on illegal immigrants.

Some states have passed laws requiring the local police to check the status of anyone they suspect may be undocumented. In Texas, Senator Charles Perry of Lubbock submitted a bill to end sanctuary practices. Governor Greg Abbot weighed in by declaring that sanctuary cities will "no longer be tolerated in Texas."[2]

Here is the odd thing about the debate in Texas: The Constitution clearly gives the federal government—not the cities or the states—authority over immigration.

However, in the immigration debate, the lines of authority—flowing between federal, state, municipal, and city governments—have gotten all tangled up. The Houston police, responsible for public safety, were operating

● *Protesters against allowing Syrian refugees into Washington State face off on the state capitol steps against advocates for expanded immigration, including of refugees who have passed background checks. Immigration is a classic federalist subject, with national, state, and local governments all involved.*

99

● *Undocumented Mexican Juan Francisco Lopez-Sanchez is escorted into the courtroom after the shooting death of Kathryn Steinle in the sanctuary city of San Francisco.*

under one set of regulations that one observer described as "don't ask; don't tell." The state government had another standard ("ask and hold") and wanted to impose it on the city. And the Supreme Court recently affirmed that immigration is a federal issue. Ultimately, the debate over sanctuary cities in Texas and California comes down to whether state laws require local officials to cooperate with a federal agency, Immigration Control Enforcement (ICE), to enforce a federal law.

Who is in charge? They all are—local, county, state, and federal authorities. Welcome to the politics of federalism. In the United States, most problems and many government programs fall under both national and state jurisdiction. To complicate matters further, counties, towns, and cities also play a vital role. *Who governs?* As you can see, the lines of responsibility between levels of government are often blurred and constantly negotiated and renegotiated.

See for yourself 4.1:

Watch the first few minutes of this U.S. House floor debate about a bill requiring stricter screening of Syrian and Iraqi refugees seeking to enter the United States.

In the last chapter, we traced the constitutional checks and balances between Congress, the executive, and the courts. Now we explore an even more intricate balancing act: federalism. Federalism is the relationship between different levels of government, sharing and squabbling over power. This complex interplay between national and state governments stretches all the way back to the founding-era clash between Federalists (who wanted a strong national government) and Anti-Federalists (who sought more power for the states). The division of power between national, state, and local government reflects longstanding American debates about democracy, equality, and effective government.

Who are we? A nation of divided loyalties and governments. We are from the United States *and* Texas *and* Houston or the United States *and* California *and* the Bay Area. The results are innovation, liberty, and confusion. A flood in the Midwest, an oil spill off Alaska's coast, food poisoning at Chipotle, or a suspected terrorist in Seattle bring out local authorities, state officials, and national agencies, all scrambling to get on the same wavelength. The same goes for legalizing pot, setting the minimum wage, protecting clean water, managing public schools, and—until 2015—the definition of marriage. Federalism is ingrained in our Constitution, our institutions, and our national culture.

This chapter explains how federalism works in the United States. The story in a nutshell: Federalism is a source of creativity and innovation, but it makes effective and efficient governance far more difficult.

❽ Forging Federalism

Early American government began on the state level—although at the time the states were called colonies. Americans' first loyalty was to Virginia or Pennsylvania or New York. When Americans declared independence, leaders had to unite thirteen

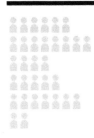

BY THE NUMBERS
Federalism

Estimated number of governments in the United States: **90,056**
Number of national governments: **1**
Number of state governments: **50**
Number of county or parish governments: **3,031**

Number of counties in Texas, each with its own government: **254**
Number of town or city governments or districts: **87,025**
Town and city governments as percentage of all American government: **96.6%**

Number of U.S. states whose capital is located in the state's largest city: **17**

Number of nonmilitary personnel who work for the federal government: **2.7 million**
Number who work for state governments: **5.3 million**
Number who work for local governments: **13.7 million**

Number of Americans who move to a different county each year: **17 million**

Percentage of Americans who say they trust the federal government to do what is right most of the time: **19**
Percentage who said this in 1958: **73**
Percentage who trust their state government to do what is right: **58**
Percentage who trust their local government: **70**
Percentage of Americans over 65 who believe the United States is "the greatest country in the world": **64**
Percentage of Americans under 30 who believe this: **32**

---

very different states under a national government. History gave them two choices about how to organize their union: a unitary government or a confederation. After trying each, the Americans invented a third approach.

Most nations in the 1780s had **unitary governments**. The national government—the king and Parliament in England, for example—made policy for the nation and local governments carried out their decrees. To this day, most nations are organized this way. Local government is an administrative extension of national government. Because Americans rebelled against Britain's unitary government, most did not want to reintroduce the same system all over again.

A second traditional form, **confederation**, leaves most power in the states or provinces while a weak central authority provides common defense or economic benefits. Today, the European Union is struggling to make a confederation work. Americans tried this system under the Articles of Confederation. As we saw in the previous chapter, it proved too weak.

At the Constitutional Convention, the delegates devised an innovative hybrid: a *federal system* in which power is divided and shared between national and state governments. The Constitution gives some decisions to the national government (for example, declaring war, coining money); others reside with the states

Unitary government:
A national polity governed as a single unit, with the central government exercising all or most political authority.

Confederation: A group of independent states or nations that yield some of their powers to a national government, although each state retains a degree of sovereign authority.

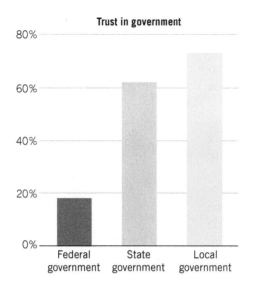

Trust in government

● **FIGURE 4.1** *Trust in government gets stronger as government gets closer to the public. (Gallup)*

(establishing schools); and some are made at both levels (raising taxes, running courts, regulating business). Over time, the shared tasks mushroomed. Because each level is independent and their powers overlap, conflict is built into the system.

To complicate matters, the United States also has independent local governments at the town, city, and county level. These add still more layers of elected officials, government employees, services to provide, taxes to be paid, and seats at the table when decisions are made. However, local governments are *not* sovereign units. The Constitution balances authority between national and state governments; local leaders, in turn, derive their authority from the state government. Some states grant their local governments broad powers, known as *home rule*; others jealously hold onto authority and approve or reject every major action a local government wishes to take. When Detroit mayor Dennis Archer (a Democrat) wanted to take control of the failing Detroit school system, he needed approval from the Michigan governor (a Republican) as well as the state legislature (which originally said no, then relented). Likewise, when Denton, Texas, forbade fracking (an oil-extraction process that raises concerns about environmental damage), the state government stepped in—fearing that Texas would lose its pro-business reputation—and rejected the local regulations. All the overlap and conflict we have described between federal and state governments gets replicated—sometimes with even more intensity—between state and local governments.

On the surface, the state and local governments might seem to have a built-in advantage in any conflict with the national government. As Figure 4.1 shows, the more local the government, the more the people trust it. Yet Americans also express an unusually strong *nationalist* outlook—few people from other countries are quite as patriotic. As we will see, that unusual distrust of national government and strong patriotism directly affects our politics and government.

THE BOTTOM LINE

» The United States rebelled against a *unitary* system and rejected a *federation* after trying one for a decade.

» The Constitutional Convention created a new hybrid form of government: a federal system of shared and overlapping power. Power is divided and shared between national and state governments.

» American federalism is further complicated by local governments, which are reliant on state government for their authority.

Who Holds Government Authority?

A federal system constantly poses the same question: Where should we locate authority? Let us start with two recent cases.

In 2014, Colorado permitted adults to buy up to an ounce of marijuana in licensed stores. Other states followed. There was just one problem: Federal laws outlaw the possession, manufacture, and sale of marijuana. Growing ninety-nine plants, which is now legal in Colorado, can bring lifetime imprisonment in other states. After Colorado legalized marijuana, the Obama administration announced it would not prosecute legal users in the state—essentially setting aside the federal laws. Meanwhile, cities such as Colorado Springs moved to forbid marijuana stores in their areas. Neighboring states that want to uphold the federal prohibition have sued states that legalized the drug. Should we leave marijuana use to the states, or insist on a national standard? What about towns and cities that prefer federal to state law? How about other illegal drugs—should they be controlled by national, state, or local laws?

Environmental regulations differ dramatically across the United States. Here, a worker struggles in freezing temperatures to help clean up an oil spill in the Yellowstone River, in lightly regulated Montana.

Authorities warned three hundred thousand people in West Virginia to stay away from their water faucets. Old liquid storage tanks built in the 1940s and 50s had leaked a toxic chemical into the Elk River and contaminated the region's water supply. People were frightened and angry. Some residents charged that state officials were only concerned with protecting the local coal and chemical industries and called for national regulation and oversight. Others noted that West Virginia was proud of its independence and antiregulatory stance; it would be "political suicide," they concluded, for any politician to call for more federal regulation. Different states have very different attitudes toward regulating industry. Vermont and New York offer strong controls; Texas and West Virginia think more about protecting businesses than regulating them. Should we insist on federal standards that aim to protect all citizens? Or should we leave regulatory policies to the states?

Each of these cases illustrates federalism's most important question: Who holds authority—the federal government or the states? And when responsibility is shared—as it so often is, where do we draw the line between the roles played by different governments? Political scientists generally see advantages to each level of government.[3]

Advantages of State-Level Policy

First, proponents of state-level policy argue that states are *more responsive* to citizen needs and desires. The United States is a vast nation spanning states with very different problems and attitudes. Maine and Minnesota do not need to regulate water in the same way as desert states like Arizona and Nevada. Large cities try to curb gang violence with curfews and gun buy-back programs that would not make much sense in rural areas. Citizens of Massachusetts expect more government services (and pay higher taxes) than people in Montana. In short, state and local government can match policies to local conditions and values without a "one-size-fits-all" national policy.

Second, states sometimes offer more *protection for individual rights*. Same-sex couples found success on the state level long before federal officials were willing to support their right to marry. In the nineteenth century, national officials ridiculed the idea of women voting while feminists were busy winning voting rights in the states. On the other hand, states vehemently denied African Americans the right to vote, forcing supporters of racial equality to take the fight to the national level (we'll explore all these topics in Chapters 5 and 6).

Third, federalism fosters *political innovation*. Different states can experiment with different programs. Supreme Court Justice Louis Brandeis put it famously: "A single courageous State may . . . serve as a laboratory; and try novel social and economic experiments without risk to the rest of the country."[4] Ever since, states in a federal system have been called "laboratories of democracy"—allowing us to test policy options. Throughout American history, innovations have bubbled up from the states before going national. The list includes Social Security pensions for retirees, environmental protection laws, worker safety rules, direct election of senators, welfare reform, child nutrition programs, alcohol prohibition, and marijuana legalization. This process of testing and spreading ideas is known as **diffusion**.

Diffusion: The spreading of policy ideas from one city or state to others; a process typical of U.S. federalism.

Finally, a more controversial point: Some argue that federalism gives people more *choices*. Each state offers a different bundle of costs and services (see Figure 4.2). People who want or need many government services can move to Connecticut or Alaska. Those who want a more limited government can choose the South or the "red states" of the Rocky Mountain West. Likewise, people who care about tough environmental standards can choose places with stringent rules such as California or Oregon.

This last point is disputed. Opponents point out that many Americans are not free to simply move. If a policy is a good one, they argue, all Americans deserve to enjoy it—which brings us to the advantages of national policies.

The Advantages of National Policy

First, national policy is often more *fair*. A single mother working full time for nine dollars an hour can be treated for breast cancer under New York's Medicaid program but is not eligible for any treatment at all in Texas. Health advocates

● **FIGURE 4.2** *Per capita state spending. Some states spend more than others per person. You can think of this as a choice between values: Some states emphasize individualism (less government spending) while others aim to implement positive freedoms (more spending). Can Americans choose a state that reflects their own values? (The Kaiser Family Foundation)*

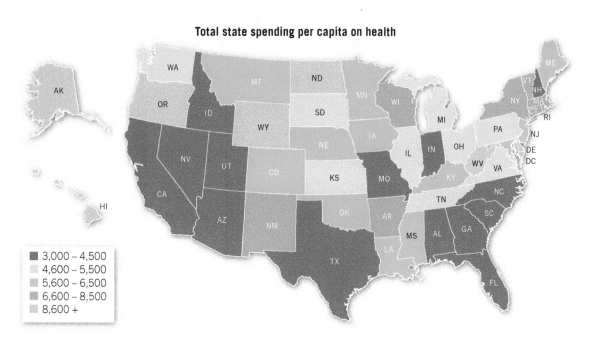

Total state spending per capita on health

- ■ 3,000 – 4,500
- ■ 4,600 – 5,500
- ■ 5,600 – 6,500
- ■ 6,600 – 8,500
- ■ 8,600 +

charge that this is unjust and call for uniform national policies. Likewise, environmentalists argue that every citizen ought to have clean air and clean water regardless of their state's history of supporting regulation (they also note that air and water pollution don't stop at state boundaries). Finally, America's racial experience suggests that, at least sometimes, national decisions are required to overcome local prejudices.

This desire for fairness leads critics to worry that competition between states and localities leads to a *race to the bottom*. Leave social welfare policy to the states, argue defenders of national standards, and the result is a bidding war in which each state tries to cut programs (and taxes) more than neighboring states to attract middle-class people and new business. Although the race to the bottom hypothesis is hard to measure, political scientists have found some evidence that states do follow one another as programs are cut and benefits are reduced.[5]

Second, national policies can *equalize resources across the nation*. Every time there is a crisis—a hurricane, an oil spill, or an earthquake—all eyes turn to the U.S. government, which can bring more resources and expertise to bear on the problem than individual states can. Those resources also can make day-to-day policies work across all fifty states. That way, even poorer states can have the resources they need.

Third, national policies can *standardize best practices* across the nation. After new policies are tested in the state "laboratories of democracy," a national policy can ensure that the lessons are spread to everyone. Minimum standards ensure that no state chooses inadequate health or education policies for its children.

Finally, leaving authority in state hands introduces *problems of coordination* among federal, state, and local agencies. All respond to crises. All address chronic problems such as poverty, pollution, and crime. Simply getting all the first responders onto the same communication frequency has taken many years and millions of dollars. With many different agencies responding to multiple layers of authorities, using different procedures, and trying to achieve slightly different goals, the result can be chaos. A patchwork of rules and regulations across the states can leave citizens and national companies bewildered about which rules apply where.

What Do You Think?

Preserving Local Values or Continuing a Terrible Injustice?

Law and order issues are largely in the hands of local and state governments. One result: Florida has 401 people waiting on death row, while Ohio has 145. Meanwhile, New York, Minnesota, and many other states have no one waiting to be executed because they banned the death penalty altogether. Should we leave the question of executions to the states? What do you think?

Yes. Law enforcement ought to reflect local values. This is just the way it should be, because conditions such as crime rates and public attitudes vary from state to state. Let the local population decide.

No. Executions are too important to leave up to such a patchwork of local laws. This should be a question we decide collectively as a nation so that a death sentence does not depend on the state you live in. We might decide as a nation to *abolish* the death penalty altogether. Or we might choose to permit executions, while seeking to ensure that no innocent person is executed, perhaps by mandating DNA testing of the accused.

Not sure where you stand? In the next chapter we'll explore whether the death penalty violates the Constitution—if so, it would not be permitted anywhere regardless of what the people in a particular locality think.

In sum, the ambiguity in federalism sets up a constant dispute about where to place authority. Do we leave decisions with the states because they are closer to the people? Or do we place them on the national level to try to promote equality and high standards across the country, even if local people resent them? For many Americans, the answer shifts with the issue.

Should federal laws criminalizing marijuana possession trump state efforts to decriminalize it? Liberals generally say no and support local choice. Should stricter national clean air standards override state pollution regulations and expanded national healthcare standards override state insurance regulations? Now most liberals switch sides and say yes, while conservatives disagree. These debates began at the Constitutional Convention and rage around every major problem and policy. They are built into our federal institutions and are an integral part of our federalist system. Recognize one key institutional point: *Federalism gives advocates on both sides many different political venues in which to address problems, challenge policies, and assert rights.*

THE BOTTOM LINE

» The most important question in federalism is where to place responsibility—on the state or national level.

» State-level policy has at least four advantages: it responds to local needs, enables innovation in the laboratories of democracy, protects individual rights, and enhances individual choice.

» National-level policy also has four main advantages: it enhances fairness (avoiding a race to the bottom), equalizes resources, promotes national standards and best practices, and facilitates coordination.

» Understanding the pros and cons of federalism is important as we decide whether to create national standards and programs or whether to leave judgment to local populations. This question is generally decided issue by issue and program by program.

How Federalism Works

So far this chapter's message is clear: federalism offers endless opportunities for confusion and discord, as different layers of government tussle over who has responsibility for what. However, there are well-defined patterns to this contest. Americans have hammered out rules that enable our federalist system to function pretty well—most of the time. These rules evolve with time and are not always clear or straightforward. Even the terminology can be elusive: Americans routinely call the national government the "federal government," a practice we follow in this chapter, even though that term formally refers to the whole system of shared powers stretching across national, state, and local units.

The Constitution Sets the Ground Rules

The Constitution can be read two ways. In some respects, it restricts the national government in favor of the states; in other ways, it empowers it.

The Constitution Empowers National Authority. Article 1, Section 8, lists nineteen powers vested in the national government: Congress has the authority to pay debts, raise an army, punish pirates, establish a post office, handle U.S. foreign policy, and so forth. Because they are set out in black and white, scholars call these **granted powers**—also known as *express* or *enumerated powers* (you can read them in the Constitution in Appendix II). This section of the Constitution is crisp and clear about the limited list of national government powers.

The third enumerated power is especially important. It grants the national government authority over international and interstate commerce. How far does that authority extend? A loose reading gives Congress power over everything touched by goods shipped between states. For example, Congress used the **commerce clause** to forbid racial discrimination in restaurants—after all, their salt and the sugar come from out of state. This broad reading is increasingly controversial. What do you think? Is it appropriate to use the interstate commerce power to outlaw racial discrimination?

The final clause adds another ambiguity by authorizing Congress to make all laws *necessary and proper* for carrying out the enumerated powers—*or any other power the Constitution vests in the national government*. The **necessary and proper clause**, also known as the *elastic clause*, stretches national government authority to include anything implied in the Constitution's text. Over two centuries, the elastic clause—especially when it is combined with the interstate commerce clause—has expanded national authority to include everything from creating banks to regulating airlines to overseeing zoos. These new areas of jurisdiction are known as **inherent powers**—powers that are implied by, but not specifically named in, the Constitution's text.

The **supremacy clause**, found near the end of the Constitution in Article 6, buttresses these granted (or explicit) and inherent (or implicit) powers. The clause declares that the national government's laws and treaties are the "supreme law of the land" and are superior to state laws whenever the two clash—provided the power is granted to the federal government. As you might imagine, fierce debates (and court cases) regularly turn on whether national officials indeed hold the authority to overturn state decisions.

The Constitution Protects State Authority. At the same time, the states have their own authority guaranteed by the Tenth Amendment—the final amendment in the Bill of Rights. This "reserves" to the states all powers not specifically granted to the national branches in Washington. Small-government advocates brandish the Tenth Amendment to bolster their argument. Starting in 2011, the Republican-controlled House, eager to roll back national authority, required all bills to list the specific section(s) of the Constitution that authorized any proposed law.

The states' **reserved powers** include public education, public health, public morality, commerce within the state, and organizing state elections. Police, prisons, and local courts are also in each state's hands. State and local officials carry out most investigations, arrests, trials, and incarcerations—unless a federal law has been violated. The vast majority of American court cases are adjudicated in state courts, and state prisons and local jails hold 89 percent of the inmates in the United States.

The Constitution Authorizes Shared Power. It is a mistake to think of federalism simply as conflict between government levels. State and national authorities share many responsibilities—these are termed **concurrent powers**. Both national and state governments have the power to raise taxes, build roads, construct bridges,

Granted powers: National government powers listed explicitly in the Constitution.

Commerce clause: The Constitutional declaration (in Article 1, Section 8) empowering Congress to regulate commerce with foreign nations, between states, and with Indian tribes.

Necessary and proper clause: The constitutional declaration (in Article 1, Section 8) that defines Congress's constitutional authority to exercise the "necessary and proper" powers to carry out its designated functions.

Inherent powers: National government powers implied by, but not specifically named in, the Constitution.

Supremacy clause: The constitutional declaration (in Article 6, Section 2) that the national government's authority prevails over any conflicting state or local government's claims, provided the power is granted to the federal government.

Reserved powers: The constitutional guarantee (in the Tenth Amendment) that the states retain government authority not explicitly granted to the national government.

Concurrent powers: Governmental authority shared by national and state governments, such as the power to tax residents.

● *The many faces of federalism: after the Boston Marathon bombings, national, state, and local law enforcement agencies—all pictured here—coordinated efforts to find the perpetrators. Later, Massachusetts and U.S. officials clashed over whether the trial would be held in federal or state court.*

Full faith and credit clause: The constitutional requirement (in Article 4, Section 1) that each state recognize and upholds laws passed by any other state.

build railways, update telecommunications networks, borrow money, and regulate business. The next time you are stuck in traffic inching past a sign announcing new transportation construction, look it over carefully: you will usually see a combination of national, state, and local funds listed in support.

Federalism also involves relations among the states. The Constitution directs each state to give **full faith and credit** to the actions of other states. This requirement becomes controversial, however, when states disagree with policies enacted by others. For example, when a same-sex couple adopted three children in Georgia, Alabama refused to legally recognize the adoption. Does this violate full faith and credit? In 2016, the U.S. Supreme Court ruled that it did; Alabama was constitutionally required to honor its neighboring state's adoption laws.

The Constitution also sets up some definite barriers to the states. A state may not launch its own navy, sign treaties with another country, or coin its own money. The Bill of Rights—though it originally applied only to the federal government—imposes a long list of limits on government in the name of individual rights and freedoms. In short, the Constitution empowers and limits both the national and the state governments. Figure 4.3 illustrates powers shared by and reserved to the different levels of government.

Emphasizing some parts of the Constitution—inherent powers, the interstate commerce clause, the necessary and proper clause, the supremacy clause—justifies a robust national government. This reading of the Constitution enables a national government that regulates toxic spills, forbids racial discrimination, enforces airport security, and prosecutes the war on drugs. Emphasizing other clauses—as in

● **FIGURE 4.3** *The Constitution delegates some powers to the federal government, reserves some to the states, and allocates some to both. Those joint (or concurrent powers) have stretched dramatically over the years.*

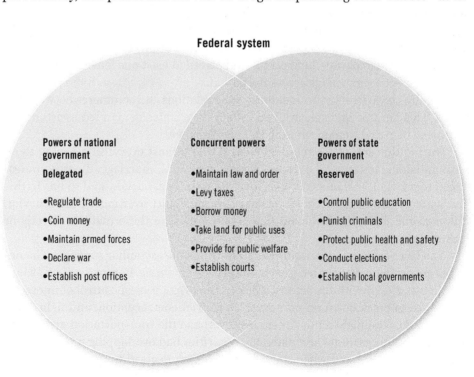

Federal system

Powers of national government

Delegated

- Regulate trade
- Coin money
- Maintain armed forces
- Declare war
- Establish post offices

Concurrent powers

- Maintain law and order
- Levy taxes
- Borrow money
- Take land for public uses
- Provide for public welfare
- Establish courts

Powers of state government

Reserved

- Control public education
- Punish criminals
- Protect public health and safety
- Conduct elections
- Establish local governments

the Tenth Amendment—yields a more modest national government that defers to the people of each state. That is the reading that leaves West Virginia alone to regulate its own water supply, lets states legalize marijuana, and limits federal government efforts to ban discrimination in restaurants or golf clubs.

Again we return to a vital point: American government is a perpetual argument, a work in progress. The Constitution's ground rules for federalism are open to interpretation and reinterpretation. They have guided a long, often creative debate about which level of government should be doing what.

In different eras, Americans have organized the federal system in different ways. The next sections introduce the most important shifts that have occurred over the years.

Dual Federalism (1789–1933)

For its first 150 years or so, the United States practiced a form of **dual federalism**, in which state and national governments had relatively clear responsibilities. The state governments wielded at least as much authority as the federal government. American historians with an eye for metaphor describe this arrangement as "layer cake" federalism: The different levels of government—national, state, and local—fell more or less into separate layers. Each level of government was supreme within its own band of influence.

Dual federalism: Also called layer cake federalism, the clear division of governing authority between national and state governments.

This division of labor left the national government in charge of three major areas. One was international relations—trade, war, diplomacy, and immigration. This was a significant role, as the United States deployed troops overseas 165 times in its first 150 years—and that count does not include the long and bloody series of conflicts with Native American tribes.

Second, the national government was responsible for "internal improvements" such as transportation, a single currency, and overseeing westward expansion. In early America, it was cheaper to ship iron from London to Philadelphia than it was to move it fifty miles inland from Philadelphia. Developing transportation networks—roads, canals, and railroads—solved the problem of moving freight (and people). For eighty years, Americans did not even share a currency. Instead, state-chartered banks each issued their own money, which was only as solid as the (often shaky) banks themselves. The Banking Acts of 1863 and 1864 finally set a uniform currency. And perhaps most important of all, the federal post office united an increasingly far-flung people and placed at least one federal official—the postmaster—in every village across the nation.

Finally, the federal government regulated relations and commerce between the states. This became an explosive issue when slave states demanded assistance in capturing men and women running for their freedom.

During this era, states retained control over almost everything having to do with individual citizens. The states oversaw education, marriage, divorce, professional regulation, business contracts, driving, drinking, burials, and so on. To this day, state governments wield the primary responsibility over individual behavior, although the federal government now touches most of these matters directly or indirectly.

The layer cake was never quite as clear-cut as the metaphor suggests. The national government distributed land in unsettled territories. Before the Civil War, it wrestled endlessly with the slavery issue. In the 1870s, it used control of interstate commerce to crack down on pornography, restrict contraception, and fight abortion. In 1920, the Eighteenth Amendment forbade the transportation and sale of intoxicating liquors. State and national authorities had overlapping jurisdiction in enforcing this act[6]—and when states like New York decided to ignore the ban on

Constructing canals, bridges, roads,—and later, railroads—was a major national government responsibility in the nineteenth century, as was delivering the mail, a task that briefly included the Pony Express (right).

Cooperative federalism:
Also called marble cake federalism, a system of mingled governing authority, with functions overlapping across national and state governments.

Grants-in-aid: National government funding provided to state and local governments, along with specific instructions about how the funds may be used.

liquor, federal officials stepped in to enforce it (a 1920s version of the marijuana debate). Still, despite many exceptions, government activity remained, very roughly, separated into layers.

Cooperative Federalism (1933–1981)

During the New Deal of the 1930s, the dual arrangement collapsed. President Franklin Roosevelt (FDR) and large Democratic majorities in Congress vigorously responded to the Great Depression by passing policies that decisively strengthened the national government's role. Roosevelt presided over a shift toward **cooperative federalism**, characterized by a far more active federal government and blurred lines of authority (Table 4.1). A new bakery metaphor emerged: a *marble cake*, in which the various ingredients—the different government functions—were all swirled together. In one program after another, the responsibilities of federal, state, and local governments were increasingly mingled: funding, rules, administration, implementation, and execution all cut across the different layers of federalism (Figure 4.4).

Officials in Washington provided federal funds through **grants-in-aid**—national funds accompanied by specific instructions to state and local officials about how the money could be spent. Governors and other state leaders, desperate for resources during the Depression, accepted these national grants for roads,

TABLE 4.1 Comparing Dual and Cooperative Federalism

DUAL FEDERALISM	COOPERATIVE FEDERALISM
NATIONAL POWERS	
Enumerated: The national government may only utilize powers specifically listed in the Constitution.	**Elastic:** The national government may wield powers "necessary and proper" to support its function.
LOCATION OF SUPREME AUTHORITY	
Separate sovereignty: National and state governments each have authority within their own spheres.	**National supremacy:** States retain important powers but are subordinate to the national government except where the Constitution strictly forbids it.
KEY PRINCIPLE	
States' rights: Each state is largely free to govern its own affairs.	**Power sharing:** National and state officials work together whenever possible; this principle was later extended to include local officials, who became more prominent after the 1930s.

bridges, hospitals, healthcare clinics, Social Security support for seniors, welfare payments for poor people, and the list goes on. Most of the funds came with Washington rules and oversight.

After the long Depression and World War II, a new era of economic prosperity emerged. Many state and local officials began expressing resentment at the national meddling in their affairs. Federal funds continued to flow, however, and during this era, supported items ranging from school lunches to modern highways and up-to-date hospitals. Even the most ardent states' rights advocates were not going to deny their constituents this national bounty.

Cooperative federalism, and Washington's domination of many policy areas, lasted from the New Deal (starting in 1933) through the 1970s. Senator Everett Dirksen (R-IL) quipped in 1964 that if the trend toward increasing national power continued, only mapmakers would care about the state boundaries.[7]

New Federalism

Ronald Reagan's presidency (1981–1989) ushered in another significant change in American federalism, enthusiastically termed **new federalism** by its advocates. Reagan and fellow conservatives tipped the pendulum of power away from national officials, promoting more authority by state and local officials. In place of grants-in-aid, with national officials carefully specifying the rules and regulations that accompanied the funds, the Reagan administration relied more heavily on **block grants**: federal dollars flow to specific policy areas, such as education or transportation or health, but leave the program's details to state and local officials. Block grants had been developed and expanded throughout the 1970s under presidents Richard Nixon (1969–1974), Gerald Ford (1974–1977), and Jimmy Carter (1977–1981); Reagan used them to rethink federalism.

One feature of block grants has made them controversial. The grants-in-aid that marked cooperative federalism often provided unlimited funding for a specific purpose—for example, everyone who qualifies for Medicaid receives hospital coverage, and anyone eligible for food stamps gets food stamps. In contrast, block grants provided a fixed amount of funds for healthcare or nutrition. State and local officials get to do what they think best with the funds; however, the federal government limits its contribution, forcing state officials to make hard choices about who qualifies for the program and who does not. Shifting grant-in-aid

American federalism
Layer cake or marble cake?

Layer cake federalism
has a clear division of governing authority between national and state governments.

Marble cake federalism
mingles governing authority with functions overlapping across national and state governments.

● **FIGURE 4.4** *Different federalist styles throughout U.S. history.*

> **New federalism:** A version of cooperative federalism, but with stronger emphasis on state and local government activity versus national government.

"In Two Words, Yes And No"

● *Struggles over the extent of cooperative federalism, captured in 1949—and still an issue, nearly seventy years later.*

Block grants: National government funding provided to state and local governments with relatively few restrictions or requirements on spending.

programs to block grants introduced a trade-off for state officials: more authority, fewer funds.

Notice that new federalism does not restore the neat layers of dual federalism—if anything, the lines of authority are even more swirled together than ever. Now, federal, state, and local authorities all compete for influence over programs. Perhaps you can think of this scenario as a many-flavored marble cake.

Progressive Federalism

Progressive Federalism: Approach that gives state officials considerable leeway in achieving national programs and goals.

The Obama administration, building on the George W. Bush administration, introduced **progressive federalism** in 2009: The national government sets program goals and relies on state innovations to achieve them. Note the mix of traditional Democratic approach (national goals) and Republican values (state innovation). The Obama administration deployed this approach across a host of policy areas—education, health care, the environment, and more.

Education. After the Bush administration introduced extensive testing requirements for schools at the national level, the Obama administration granted waivers that permitted 43 states to set aside the national rules and design their own procedures. The administration then devised its own program, Race to the Top, put even more emphasis on state innovation by encouraging states to compete for national dollars by devising creative education policies. Winning proposals included promoting charter schools, basing teacher pay on performance rather than the number of years served, and developing new measures to track student progress. By promoting *competition* among states, the administration sought to nudge states toward desired policy goals without relying on overbearing national regulations.

Healthcare. Perhaps the most controversial program during the Obama Administration, the Affordable Care Act (or ACA) aimed to deliver healthcare to the 50 million Americans going without. Congress mandated that all uninsured people buy coverage. The federal government issued rules and regulations (defining the insurance products); the states were incentivized to build insurance exchanges where individuals could shop among competing health insurance plans. If the states were not up to the task—or simply opposed to the policy—the federal government came in and built the website that sold the insurance plans. Before long, many states were negotiating with the federal government over various aspects of the ACA. The administration, eager to implement the program, waived regulations and made adjustments for individual states. In progressive federalism, the federal and state governments are partners who constantly negotiate the outlines of their joint program. Sometimes the debate is friendly, sometimes adversarial; it sometimes takes place through the courts or in Congress or across the media. The key point is that programs are defined in an intricate back and forth between federal and state negotiators.

Children from public schools in the town of Chatfield, Minnesota, seen with President Barack Obama who was publicizing his education program, Race to the Top.

THE BOTTOM LINE

» The Constitution grants the national government both enumerated (or explicit) powers and inherent (or implicit) powers. You can read it to emphasize broad national powers, using the elastic clause, or state dominance, emphasizing the Tenth Amendment.

» There have been three important eras of federalism: dual federalism included clearly demarcated authority (the layer cake); cooperative federalism, arising with FDR's New Deal, introduced federal dominance and blurred the lines of authority (the marble cake); President Reagan's new federalism relied on federal funds but shifted more decision making about spending those monies back to the states; President Obama's progressive federalism set national goals but relies on state innovations to achieve them.

Issues in Federalism Today

Dual, cooperative, new, and progressive—these successive versions of federalism point to the perpetually shifting nature of government power and accountability. Today, federalism is in unusual flux as national government authority both expands (healthcare) and contracts (marijuana control); as states make more choices in some areas (environmental regulation) and less in others (same-sex marriage); and as the parties take turns calling for more national power in some areas and less in others. Let us take a look at some of the current issues in this debate.

Unfunded Mandates

Some voices in federalism debates accept national government authority in some areas, but argue that when responsibility is passed to state or local officials, there must be resources to match. Otherwise, they claim, Washington saddles states and localities with an **unfunded mandate**—a law or regulation that imposes a duty that must be paid for primarily by state or local officials. For example, when federal regulations impose new safety requirements on commuter trains, state and local governments are left to buy and install the new technology, regardless of what shape their budget is in.

Unfunded mandate: An obligation imposed on state or local government officials by federal legislation without sufficient federal funding support to cover the costs.

The Problems We Face: How Government Grows

Even with the sufficient funding, however, serious problems often lead to a greater national government role. Sometimes local governments face problems that are beyond their capacity to solve. For example, many states' rights advocates have pushed hard to limit federal endangered species regulation. Yet after the national government cut back Environmental Protection Agency and Forest Service supervision of wildlife management, invasive species such as zebra mussels and milfoil (a plant native to Asia that has choked the life out of many American ponds and lakes) overwhelmed local wildlife agencies and caused billions of dollars in damage. Harmful plants and creatures are oblivious to local and state boundaries; many wildlife officials—including in states with conservative leadership—immediately called for a federal government response that could coordinate eradication efforts across multiple jurisdictions.

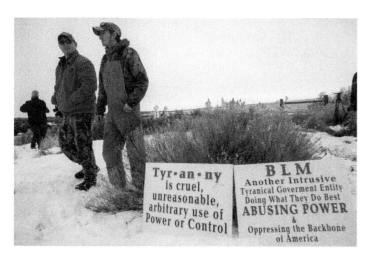

Members of an armed antigovernment militia monitor the entrance to the Malheur National Wildlife Refuge Headquarters near Burns, Oregon, in 2016. The occupation of a wildlife refuge by armed protesters in Oregon reflects a decades-old dispute over land rights in the United States, where local communities have increasingly sought to take back federal land.

Drowned in the Bathtub? Reducing the Federal Government

The debate over federalism often reflects a particular American passion, which is especially strong among conservatives: the desire to reduce the size and scope of government. One pillar of the new and progressive federalism—at least in theory—has been **devolution**, or the transfer of responsibility for government programs from national to state and local authorities and then to the private sector. Devolutionists have fought to reduce the influence of government at every level. "I don't want to abolish government," declared conservative activist Grover Norquist. "I simply want to reduce it down to the size where I can . . . drown it in the bathtub."[8] This attack on big government gets fervent support from the conservative grassroots. Tea Party activists attacked federal programs throughout the Obama years. Ranchers in the West have challenged federal ownership of lands for over forty years.

In theory, Republicans prefer state and local control, while Democrats are more likely to seek Washington-based solutions. The reality is far more complicated: Both parties sometimes press for increased national authority and, at other times, defer to the states.

Devolution: The transfer of authority from the national to the state or local government level.

On Both Sides of the Issue

Why do both Democratic and Republican administrations regularly stray from their parties' images? Partially because elected officials must confront complicated problems, and struggle to make troubled programs more effective. There is also a political dimension. Republicans are often criticized for being hard-hearted budget cutters. In response, every Republican administration introduces new social policies designed to show compassion and energetic management. For the last seventy-five years, for example, every single Republican president has sponsored new, often very innovative, healthcare programs. The two largest expansions of the Medicare program, the health insurance program for people over 65, came under Republicans, Ronald Reagan (who covered high or catastrophic health costs—later repealed) and George W. Bush (who expanded the program to cover prescription drugs).

The Democrats face the opposite criticism: too much federal government spending. As a result, Democratic administrations also regularly go against type and rely on state innovation and initiatives. Bill Clinton's Democratic administration rewrote welfare policy to shift authority and discretion to state and local governments. Clinton ended Aid to Families with Dependent Children (often known simply as "welfare"), a program that provided unlimited funds to support roughly one in six American children. In its place, the administration (working with Republicans in Congress) introduced a block grant program called Temporary Assistance for Needy Families (TANF). TANF makes funds available and leaves most details up to the states. This policy, signed into law by a Democratic president,

● As this cartoon humorously shows, which level of our federalist government a politician supports generally depends on the issue in question (Nick Anderson).

sure looked Republican—an issue that blew up in the 2016 Democratic primaries when liberals who supported the idea came under attack for supporting a policy that doubled the number of Americans in extreme poverty.[9]

What happens when the states want more innovation than the federal government? When states like California legislated strong environmental measures, the Republican Bush administration overruled them through **preemption**. The Obama administration quickly reversed that policy and encouraged states to launch forceful environmental protections. Notice how the old rule of thumb is reversed: Democrats urged strong state action; Republicans overruled it with (weaker) federal regulations.

Preemption: The invalidation of a U.S. state law that conflicts with federal law.

In a Nutshell: Our Three-Dimensional Political Chess

How do these examples add up? They all tell us to put aside the simple idea that conservatives want less federal government and liberals more. A more sophisticated view of federalism is to see it as a kind of three-dimensional political chess. Policy debates take place in Washington and in fifty state capitals; every now and then, thousands of municipalities also weigh in. The different sides act with more or less strength in the different political venues. Each decision about where to locate authority over a program advances some perspectives and limits others. The great debate about where to locate authority is part of the larger debate that shapes American politics and policy.

Today, relations between national, state, and local levels take a dizzying array of forms—sometimes they work in partnership, sometimes they are locked in combat. The one contemporary constant is *connection*: There are almost no issues in which the different levels of government exert separate functions, as in the old dual federalist system. To keep all the tangled relationships clear, intergovernmental liaison officers work across national, state, city, and even town governments.

INFO/DATA: Regulatory Policies Differ by State

What are the chances you will be behind the 'wheel' of a self-driving car in the near future? It depends on the state where you live. Like so many policy matters in the federalist United States, rules may differ dramatically from one state to the next.

1. In your view, are there benefits to the ■ patchwork of regulation? Or would our lives (political and otherwise) be improved if most laws covered the entire nation, as in some other countries? Justify your answer.

2. Suppose you are an opponent of abortion but live in a blue (majority Democratic/liberal) state where restrictions ■ on this procedure are unlikely to pass. Or suppose you support environmental policies aimed at mitigating climate change, but your fellow red-state (majority Republican/conservative) dwellers are enacting laws promoting the use of more fossil fuels. Should your views be represented in policy outcomes? Or is your best option to move out of the state?

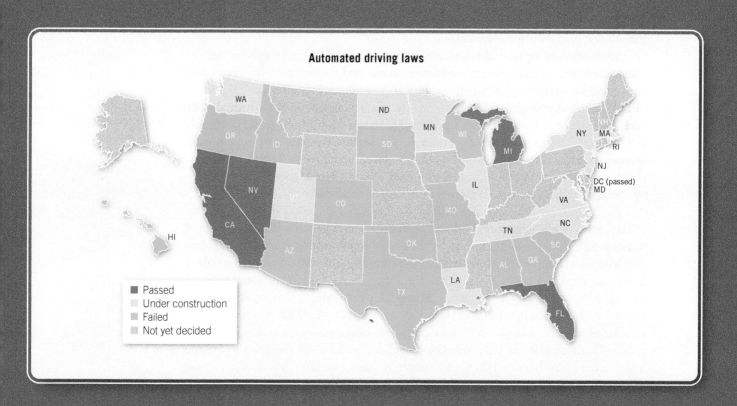

Automated driving laws

- ■ Passed
- ■ Under construction
- ■ Failed
- ▨ Not yet decided

Source: Center for Internet and Society, "Automated Driving" Policy Tracker (2016).

Federalism in the Courts

Most federalism disputes are about drawing a line where national power ends and states' authority begins—and how best to ensure that the division of power is honored in practice. One explanation for the historical shifts in federalism is simple: the party in power changed. The Roosevelt administration initiated a new (Democratic) era in Washington and soon introduced cooperative federalism. The Nixon and Reagan administrations brought Republicans to the center of power and introduced new federalism. Republicans took control of Congress in 1995 and immediately passed limits on unfunded mandates. The Democratic Obama administration introduced progressive federalism.

Another key to the tides of federalism lies in the courts. U.S. courts early on became a key player in allocating powers between the states and the nation. Judges have typically played a balancing role when it comes to federalism. Supreme Court decisions favored national prerogatives during the early republic, when many individual states had more power and prestige than the federal government in Washington. During the country's first decades, it was often unclear whether the national government could sustain its strength compared to the power enjoyed by long-established states. In a series of landmark decisions, the Supreme Court—led by Chief Justice John Marshall—protected national government powers from state incursions.

The first such case was *McCulloch v. Maryland*, decided in 1819.[10] A year before, Maryland's legislature had sought to impose a tax on the Baltimore branch of the first U.S. national bank. The bank refused to pay and was sued by the state. The Maryland Supreme Court ruled that the Constitution is silent about the federal power to establish a bank—and that the bank was therefore unconstitutional. Maryland was perfectly free to tax it. Marshall overruled the Maryland court and struck down the tax. Invoking the necessary and proper (or elastic) clause, he ruled that Congress could draw on "implied powers" required to operate a functional national government and that states blocking such actions—in this case, by levying a tax on the bank—violated the Constitution. In these and later decisions, Marshall and many other officials in the early republic were anxious to keep dual federalism in balance. At the time, doing so meant expanding national power.

As we will see in Chapter 16, in some eras—such as the period between the 1880s and the 1930s—the court tilted away from federal authority to states and private corporations. Conversely, the rise of activist government during the 1930s probably would not have been possible if the Supreme Court had not, quite dramatically, reversed its course and accepted New Deal legislation beginning in 1937. This transition to federal power led later Courts to uphold congressional actions such as the Civil Rights Act (1964) and the Voting Rights Act (1965), which limited

TABLE 4.2 Recent Supreme Court Decisions on Federalism

Gonzales v. Oregon (2006). Ruled that national government power to regulate drugs was limited by a state's right to exercise authority over drug laws within its jurisdiction.

Medellin v. Texas (2008). Permitted states to file a type of legal petition repeatedly, overturning national government rules declaring otherwise.

Bond v. United States (2011). Extended to individuals the right to challenge federal statutes on the grounds that these statutes interfere with powers reserved to the states.

National Federation of Independent Business v. Sebelius (2012). This decision on the Affordable Care Act (ACA) struck down the national government's power to set standards for expanded Medicaid eligibility across the states. But in *King v. Burwell* (2015), the same Supreme Court justices ruled that premium tax credits provided under the ACA applied in every state, though several conservative-led states had argued otherwise.

United States v. Windsor (2013). Struck down a section of the federal Defense of Marriage Act (DOMA) and declared that same-sex couples who are legally married deserve equal rights to all federal benefits that other married couples enjoy.

Arizona v. United States (2012). Struck down key provisions in an Arizona immigration law, upholding federal-government authority to set immigration policy and laws.

Shelby County v. Holder (2013). Reversed a long-standing provision in the Voting Rights Act that required states with a history of voting discrimination to obtain federal permission before making changes to their election laws.

Obergefell v. Hodges (2015). Requires all states to issue marriage licenses to same-sex couples and to recognize same-sex marriages validly performed in other jurisdictions.

United States v. Texas (2016). Invalidated (by a 4–4 vote, returning the case to a lower court) Obama Administration's executive act protecting from deportation certain unauthorized immigrants (parents of U.S. citizens, or legal permanent residents), and granting them work permits. twenty-six states, led by Texas, challenged the White House policy.

the ways that state and private actors could discriminate. It also led the Court to strike down state actions, as when they denied Texas's right to ban abortion (*Roe v. Wade*, 1973), or, in 2015, struck down several states' "three strikes" laws that jailed people for life, often for minor offenses.

In recent years—beginning under Chief Justice Rehnquist in the mid-1990s and gaining strength with a consistently conservative majority under Chief Justice Roberts since 2005—the Supreme Court has emphasized local and state power. In fact the Rehnquist Court (1994–2005) struck down more acts of Congress than any previous Court in U.S. history; many of these decisions were premised on defending state power. A series of prominent cases has shifted power away from the national government toward the states (see Table 4.2). The Roberts Court (2005–current) has continued this trend, for example striking down the Affordable Care Act requirement that states must expand their Medicaid program. If history is a reliable guide, the current judicial trend will fade over time, as the pendulum of state and national power swings yet again.

THE BOTTOM LINE

» The Supreme Court protected the powers of the federal government from state governments in the early years of our nation.

» With some exceptions, the courts have trended toward returning power to state and local government in recent years.

Nationalism, American Style

Federalism trains our focus on the Constitution (the elastic clause vs. the Tenth Amendment), on how institutions evolve (dual federalism vs. cooperative federalism, layer cake vs. marble cake), and on the clash between national versus state (seeking equity vs. "drown it in the bathtub!"). However, something deeper holds the entire complicated apparatus in place. It is the elusive cultural sentiment known as *nationalism*: the American public's sense of identity as Americans. Nationalism helps maintain the federal balance by instilling loyalty to nation, state, and locality. In this section, we explore the development of American nationalism.

The Rise of American Nationalism

In the excitement of the Revolution, former colonists from New Hampshire to Georgia celebrated the defeat of the British army. Yet, after the revolution, the sense of "Americanhood" began to wane. By the mid-1780s, founders such as John Adams worried that "we are finished as a united nation, before we are properly begun."[11]

Restored national sentiment came from an unlikely source—a piece of parchment. The Constitution became a touchstone for Americans' shared sense of belonging. Following ratification in 1789, celebrations broke out across the new nation. In Boston, a three-day festival featured a town feast for twelve thousand and a grand parade with more marchers than today's Macy's Thanksgiving Day Parade—at a time when Boston held barely one-hundredth the population of modern New York City. Despite North Carolina's delay in ratification, its capital, Raleigh, greeted the Constitution with so many twenty-one-gun salutes (using cannons) that elderly residents feared the Revolutionary War had started again. The Marquis de Lafayette, the French general who had fought next to George Washington, wrote back home to Paris that he was astonished to be "in the midst of perpetual fêtes [celebratory parties]."[12] It was the start of the nationalism that lives on to this day.

Powerful nationalism is a double-edged sword. Political scientist Elizabeth Theiss-Morse notes that on the one hand, a strong sense of national identity fosters mutual support and loyalty. On the other hand, the most enthusiastic nationalists are those most likely to draw strict boundaries around who counts as an American. "Help and loyalty are offered only to 'true Americans,' not Americans who do not count and who are pushed to the periphery of the national group," she argues.[13] The Republican Party's national convention in 2016, with speaker after speaker extolling American virtues and sometimes impugning immigrants and other "outsiders," was a prime example of strong nationalism—for good and ill.

America's Weak National Government

In sum, Americans exhibit a passionate sense of nationalism linked to relatively weak governing institutions. Today, we measure the strength of central governments by looking at an updated version of the same principles: size, authority, and independence.

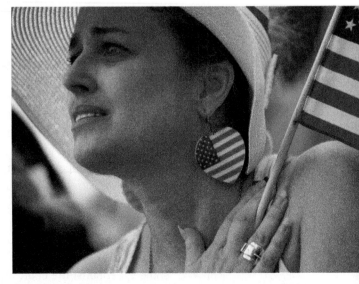

Kimberlee Crawford from Los Angeles listens to a speaker during a Tea Party Patriots rally against the Iran nuclear deal on Capitol Hill in Washington, DC. (Getty Images)

While U.S. levels of government spending are lower, they have held steady for the past decade, while in much of Europe the amount has fallen. (Organisation for Economic Co-operation and Development)

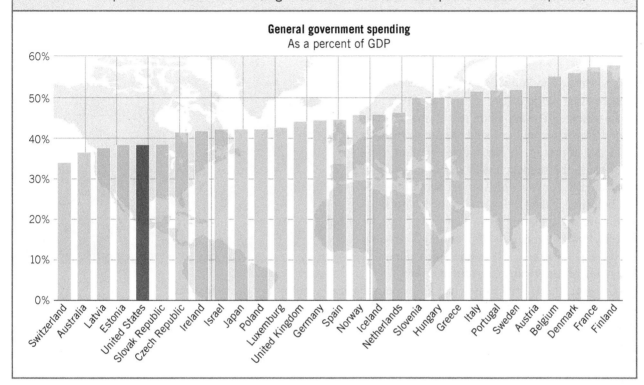

General government spending
As a percent of GDP

Size. For many years, American national government was smaller than those in other nations. It grew in leaps during World War I, the Great Depression, World War II, the Cold War, and the Great Society of the 1960s. Each growth spurt brought protests and efforts to cut the government back to size. In the 1930s, opponents, fearful of the growing New Deal bureaucracy, called President Franklin Roosevelt a communist, a socialist, and worse. Critics have blasted recent presidents for adding thousands more federal employees. Despite all the fears—or perhaps because of them—the U.S. government spends less than the governments of most other wealthy nations—and leaves more to the private sector (see Comparing Nations 4.1).

In areas like education, the U.S. Department of Education spends far, far less per pupil in public schools than its counterparts in democracies like France. Does this mean the American government ignores education? Hardly: Our federalist style shifts much education spending to state and local sources. American public education funding runs over $850 billion a year and involves a huge array of decision makers: the federal government, fifty state governments, and thousands of local school boards across the nation.

Authority. By the mid-nineteenth century, most developed nations—from France and Germany to China and the British colonies in India—had powerful and efficient national bureaucracies, known as the civil service. In sharp contrast, nineteenth-century American government engaged its citizens (that is, its white males) without a strong central administration or bureaucracy. European observers were stunned at the haphazard, chaotic nature of American administration.

Communal activity stretched well beyond the government. American **civic voluntarism** presented a virtually unprecedented spectacle in the nineteenth and early twentieth centuries: robust nationalist feeling stimulating widespread individual effort in cooperation with other community members. The spirit of voluntary

Civic voluntarism: Citizen participation in public life without government incentives or coercion (speaking at a town meeting vs. paying taxes, for example).

participation has lived on for generations, inspiring mass public involvement in everything from bowling leagues to civil rights organizations.[14]

Contemporary administration reflects these roots. In France today, the minister of public instruction sets education policy for the entire nation. He or she knows what the students are doing in every meticulously regulated schoolroom across France at every hour of the day. In the United States, no public official has anything near that kind of power—or knowledge of what happens inside the schools. Local school boards are made up of volunteers. Most must stand for election before they take their turn at overseeing education in their community. They may not be experts, but they generally understand their town or city and its values. The same spirit pervades every area of American government today.

In short, the United States has always emphasized community participation over centralized administration. The same local spirit that helps define federalism limits the authority of national officials.

● *Civic voluntarism in action—a source of wonder for nineteenth-century European visitors such as Tocqueville—and a key feature of American-style federalism and nationalism.*

Independence. In a powerful centralized system, government officials can act forcefully—as long as their superiors approve. In contrast, Americans separate and divide governing power more extensively than any other modern country. Federalism operates along a vertical dimension, with power shared among different levels of government—national, state, and local.

At every level and within every branch and institution there are further internal checks. All but one American state legislature, like Congress, has two chambers (Nebraska is the lone exception); all have multiple committees and subcommittees within each chamber. Each legislature faces an executive and an independent judiciary. In short, checks and balances at every level multiply federalism's horizontal division of power. No public official can act independently. Each needs cooperation from others.

The effort to advance public policies in a weak central government involves more conflict—many participants reflect many different interests. That, in turn, forces public officials to build support for their policies in creative ways: They call out the citizens to show support for an idea. They seek help from lobbyists. They mobilize powerful allies. They raise (and often share) enormous amounts of money to fund future campaigns. We explore all these modes of action in future chapters.

THE BOTTOM LINE

» Americans have long felt a strong sense of nationalism. This helps bind together a large and diverse nation with a fragmented government.

» "Strong nation, weak national government" is a great American paradox. A weak government means that American institutions (and officials) rank relatively low on three dimensions: size, authority, and independence.

» The political results of this paradox include an emphasis on citizen participation, the importance of building alliances, and a reliance on power and money.

🎱 Conclusion: Who Are We?

Federalism seems, on the surface, like a simple matter of government engineering: How do we decide who does what on the federal, state, and local levels? In reality, federalism reflects an intense philosophical debate, carved into institutional stone.

Conflicting views about power and democracy, fairness, and liberty have always marked American politics. Successive eras allocated power differently. Dual federalism (the layer cake) largely kept the state and national spheres separate. The era of cooperative federalism saw the national government expand its role and mix with state and local functions (the marble cake). Today, conservatives and courts promote a new federalism that devolves more decisions to state and local governments. The latest variation of federalism, the Obama era progressive federalism tries to combine state innovation and national goals. These efforts involve more layers of government and make more ambiguous than ever who is responsible for what.

Issue after issue returns us to this question of where to locate government authority: federal, state, or local. Who should decide whether to decriminalize marijuana? Address climate change? Mete out the death penalty? Promote educational standards? Allow—or halt—government collection of cellphone data? Protect the homeland?

Federalism is the mark of a weak national government. However, the paradox of American politics is that weak government is balanced by a powerful nation with a robust, patriotic sense of national identity. That force helps bind together all the centrifugal institutions of a federal system shot through with checks and balances on every level of government.

● Presidential candidate Carly Fiorina speaks at a forum on "practical federalism"; note the battle metaphor. Federalism has been contested since the Constitutional Convention.

Many critics suggest that the weak central government diminishes America's capacity to face the challenges of the twenty-first century. Others fear the opposite: an inexorably growing state marks the decline of American liberty. We will revisit these fears throughout this book. For now, simply recognize that this debate echoes those that engaged Federalists and Anti-Federalists in the 1780s. The conflict involves balancing the most important American values, never an easy task.

CHAPTER SUMMARY

● Americans are a people of multiple loyalties—to their nation, state, and home city or town. These divides are mirrored in our federalist politics. The United States separates power in multiple ways, both horizontally (across branches of government) and vertically (across national, state, and local levels).

● Only two dozen nations worldwide share America's federalist-style political organization; most have more centralized unitary governments.

● The American founders adopted a federalist system, in part to protect against concentrating too much power in one person or branch, but also to expand protections for individual rights, increase government's flexibility, and enable more political innovations to flourish. Federalism has drawbacks, but it has never seriously been questioned as the American governing style.

● Different versions of federalism are evident in U.S. history, from dual federalism (in which the states and the national government perform largely separate functions) to cooperative and new versions that involve closer partnership across government levels. Issues such as devolution and unfunded mandates mark ongoing negotiations over the terms of the elaborate arrangement of local, state, and national governing power.

● Given this divided authority, we might wonder what has held the United States together, especially given regional differences that culminated in civil war. An uncommonly strong sense of national identity is a large part of the answer. Born during the Revolution and powerfully evident after the Constitution's ratification, Americans' devotion to national unity was instrumental in building a robust nation—although nationalism has its ugly, xenophobic sides as well.

● Alongside America's strong nation is its relatively weak national government, an anomaly among most countries with a similarly robust national spirit. This less powerful set of government institutions is found across American history in both the limited size of our federal bureaucracy and Washington's constrained capacity to act.

● An abiding commitment to separated powers, evident in the Constitution and fiercely defended in the *Federalist Papers*, helps explain the persistence of this weak-government phenomenon alongside our strong nation. Debates about how to reform the United States' federalist, separated-powers polity also have persisted over the years. We invite you to join the debate in the months and years to come.

KEY TERMS

Block grants, p. 111
Civic voluntarism, p. 120
Commerce clause, p. 107
Concurrent powers, p. 107
Confederation, p. 101
Cooperative federalism, p. 110
Devolution, p. 114
Diffusion, p. 104

Dual federalism, p. 109
Full faith and credit clause, p. 108
Granted powers, p. 107
Grants-in-aid, p. 110
Inherent powers, p. 107
Necessary and proper clause, p. 107

New federalism, p. 111
Preemption, p. 115
Progressive federalism, p. 112
Reserved powers, p. 107
Supremacy clause, p. 107
Unfunded mandate, p. 113
Unitary government, p. 101

STUDY QUESTIONS

1. Can you imagine the United States without federalism? Suppose that a central national authority ran the country and governors and mayors—and other subnational officials—were entirely subordinate to the national government. Describe some of the changes that would likely result. Would this shift toward a unitary state be an improvement, in your view? Why or why not?

2. The current Supreme Court has tended to side with state and local governments in federalist clashes, limiting the national government's power in case after case. Why has the Court adopted this approach? Do you find it desirable?

3. Define the following: Dual Federalism; Competitive Federalism; New Federalism; Progressive Federalism.

4. You're asked to advise the president's staff. How would you advise them to approach the issue of federalism? Should they give more or less discretion to the states?

5. Think about your own political loyalties. Are they most strongly felt for your hometown or home city, the state where you grew up (or where you live now), or the nation as a whole? What do you think accounts for your outlook? If you are not from the United States, reflect on your own sense of political identity: Is it primarily to a nation, a region, or a local place?

6. If you feel a strong sense of national pride, do you think it comes with any undesirable aspects? If you are not an especially avid American nationalist, why not? What would it be like if most citizens exhibited a skeptical outlook toward the country?

7. A wide range of reforms have been suggested for improving the American system of separated powers. Are there any other changes you would make to the federalist division of power across branches and between national, state, and local governments?

 Go to www.oup.com/us/Morone to find quizzes, flash cards, simulations, tutorials, videos, and other study tools.

Civil Liberties

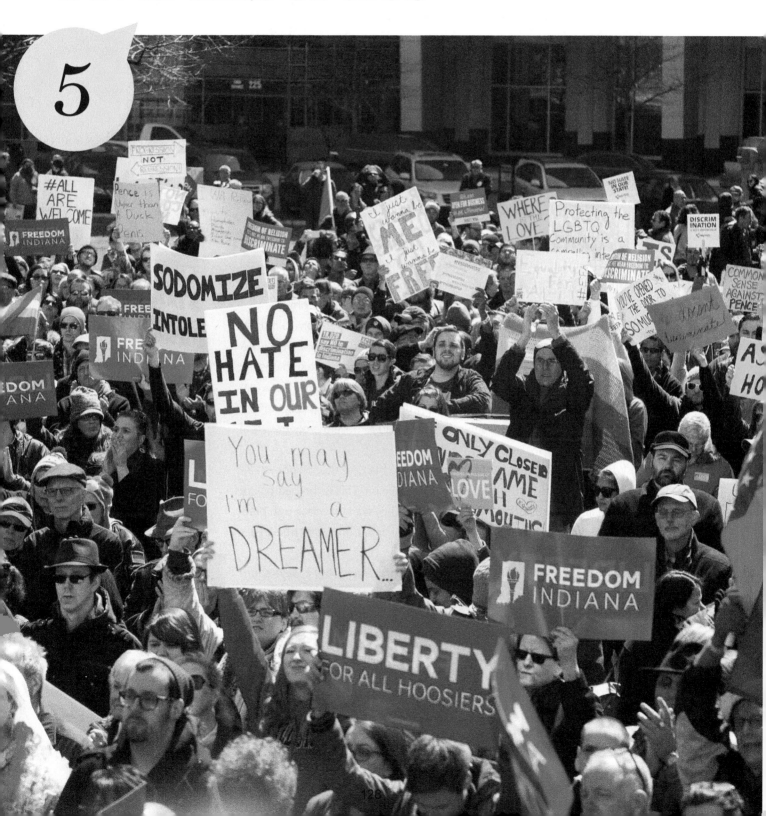

IN MARCH 2015, the Indiana legislature passed the Religious Freedom Restoration Act designed, among other things, to protect businesses which might refuse to serve same-sex couples. In an interview with a local television station, the owner of Memories Pizza in the small town of Walkerton explained that her religious convictions did not permit her to cater same-sex weddings. "We're a Christian establishment," said owner Crystal O'Connor.[1] Her father, Kevin O'Connor, later told reporters that he welcomes gay customers, but serving at a gay marriage is against his religious principles: "It's my belief. It's our belief. It's what we grew up on."[2] Governor (and now Vice President) Mike Pence, the Indiana Legislature, and many Americans all believe that we must respect and protect these religious convictions—even if we disagree with them.

The LGBTQ community, along with many other Americans, believes differently. The O'Connors are practicing discrimination, plain and simple, and fundamentally violating the rights of gay Americans. The law—and statements like O'Connor's—stirred up furious controversy. CEOs from many of Indiana's largest companies, the Indiana Pacers, and Hoosier-born talk show host David Letterman all denounced or mocked the legislation. The NCAA threatened to move its Final Four men's college-basketball championship, scheduled in Indianapolis. A high school golf coach was suspended for tweeting, "Who's going to Walkerton, IN to burn down #memoriespizza w me?"[3] Within a week, the legislature amended the law to remove the controversial religious protections.

Which side is right? The First Amendment to the Constitution *does* guarantee people's right to the "free exercise" of religion. This is the bedrock of American liberty: protecting individuals when they want to speak out, practice their religion, or assemble in peace—even if what they say or believe is very unpopular.

However, every right has limits. Individual protections are always counter-balanced by community needs and by other people's rights. The Indiana case forces us to choose between clashing ideas of rights. One person's right to practice their faith (protected by the First Amendment) clashes with another person's right for equal protection under the laws (secured by the Fourteenth Amendment)—in this case, the right to marry without facing discrimination. Subsequent debates have arisen in other states: a Mississippi

Hoosiers demonstrate against Indiana's Religious Freedom Restoration Act. Americans prize our civil liberties—but when core values are in conflict, who decides?

- Learn about the rise of civil liberties.

- Examine the right to privacy—a controversial liberty that is not mentioned in the Constitution and involves abortion and same-sex marriage.

- Study the freedom of religion.

- Explore the right to free speech—and its special status—and the right to bear arms.

- Consider the rights of suspected criminals.

- Reflect on the difficult balance between fighting terrorism and protecting civil liberties.

125

see for yourself 5.1

Go online to view a lively discussion about Indiana's religious-freedom law. *Requires Flash*

"religious liberty" law also targeting LGBTQ people, passed in April 2016, was struck down by a federal judge just a few weeks later. In North Carolina, a law denying transgender people the right to use public bathrooms corresponding to their gender identity set off a major backlash—the NCAA relocated championship games scheduled for North Carolina, PayPal backed out of constructing headquarters in the state, and a federal court blocked enforcement of the statue.

Context matters. As Supreme Court Justice Oliver Wendell Holmes put it back in 1919, every action "depends upon the circumstances in which it is done. . . . The most stringent protection of free speech would not protect a man from falsely shouting fire in a crowded theater and causing a panic."

Who are we? We are a nation always wrestling with a great trade-off—individual rights versus majority rule. On the one hand, we are the home of rugged individualism, which tilts us toward protecting individual rights. On the other hand, we believe in self-rule, which means the majority should get its way. What we will see in this chapter is that a majority—even a very large majority—cannot violate the right of even a small minority.

The tension is exacerbated because we are (and always have been) a nation of minority groups—black, Latino, Hmong, Muslim, gay, transgender, and the list goes on. When the majority feels threatened or offended it sometimes moves to limit the minority's rights, making civil liberties all the *more* important.

Civil liberties: The limits on government that allow people to freely exercise their rights.

What are **civil liberties**? They are the limits we put on governments (and the majorities that elect them) so that individuals can exercise their rights and freedoms. Americans have long embraced the figure of the brave individual, standing up for their rights: John Hancock signing the Declaration of Independence or Sojourner Truth fighting slavery. In practice, complexity abounds. In the Indiana religious freedom case, both religious conservatives ("I have the right to not cater a wedding that violates my faith") and LGBTQ advocates ("I have the right to live a life free of discrimination") called on the government to protect their constitutional liberties. This brings us to the eternal complication of civil liberties—deciding who deserves which rights.

The Rise of Civil Liberties

May a racist burn a cross as a symbol of white supremacy? May states ban violent video games? May a skinhead stand on a street corner and urge people to attack Latinos, Sikhs, or Jews? The answer to all three questions is "sometimes." We always weigh the rights of individuals against the concerns and safety of the community. Who decides? Usually, the courts do. And there is often more than one reasonable answer when the courts take up a question.

Civil Rights and Civil Liberties

Civil rights and civil liberties demand opposite things from government. Civil rights require government action to help secure individual rights; civil liberties restrict government action to protect individual rights. Until people have won their rights, the idea of protecting them is meaningless. When governments enforce civil rights for some people, they often limit the liberty of others. For example, as we will

BY THE NUMBERS

Civil Liberties

Number of rights listed in the Bill of Rights: **31**
Number of rights protecting freedom of religion: **2**
Number of rights protecting people accused of crimes: **19**

Number of times that the Supreme Court has permitted the government to block publication of sensitive material: **0**
Number of years after the Bill of Rights was ratified before the Supreme Court ruled that state governments could not interfere with freedom of speech: **134**
Number of years before it ruled that states could not interfere with the right to bear arms: **219**

Number of new rights secured by constitutional amendment in the past fifty years: **1** (the Twenty-Sixth Amendment extended the right to vote to eighteen- to twenty-year-olds)
Percentage of Americans who say antiterrorism efforts should not violate civil liberties (according to a 2015 Gallup poll): **65**
Percentage who say we have not gone far enough in antiterrorism efforts to protect the U.S. (according to a 2016 Pew poll): **50**
Percentage who believe their own individual liberty is constrained by government antiterrorism efforts: **41**

Percentage of Americans who supported the death penalty in 1994 and today, respectively: **80, 61**

Percentage of support for death penalty among self-identified Democrats, Independents, and Republicans: **49, 62, 76**
Number of states that have not executed anyone since 1976: **16**
Total number executed in Texas, Virginia, Oklahoma, and Florida since 1976: **844**
Total number executed by the federal government in that period: **3**

see in Chapter 6, the Civil Rights Act of 1964 outlawed segregated restaurants. That legal action freed blacks and Latinos to eat wherever they wished but limited the liberty of racist restaurant owners to serve whomever they wanted to serve.

In practice, the two concepts are not opposites. The long battle for civil rights led to more robust civil liberties for everyone. The fight against slavery eventually led to the Fourteenth Amendment, which—as we will soon see—is the cornerstone of modern civil liberties. Without the long American struggle for civil rights, we would have many fewer civil liberties.

Both civil liberties and civil rights became increasingly important to American politics over

● *Legal? Sometimes!*

● *Walter Gobitas with his children, William and Lillian. The Jehovah's Witnesses were expelled from school for refusing to salute the flag.*

the course of the twentieth century. In this section, we look first at why civil liberties matter. We then explain how they grew and spread.

The Purpose of Civil Liberties

Lillian Gobitas was the seventh-grade class president in a Minersville, Pennsylvania, school in 1935. Because she was a Jehovah's Witness, she refused to pledge allegiance to the flag. Lillian was taunted, attacked, and expelled from school. Her father, Walter, sued the school district, and in 1940 the Supreme Court upheld the expulsion (8–1), declaring that "national unity is the basis of national security." The American entry into World War II in December 1941 inflamed the prejudice against the sect. Mobs beat up five Jehovah's Witnesses in Wyoming, burned a Kingdom Hall in Maine, and allegedly castrated a Jehovah's Witness in Nebraska. The Court's ruling seemed to have made matters worse. "They're traitors," declared a sheriff in Maine, "the Supreme Court says so. Ain't you heard?"[4] This is the nightmare for civil liberties advocates: the powerful machinery of government invoked against a minority group.

Three years later, in 1943, the Court reversed itself and ruled that it was unconstitutional to require children to pledge allegiance if it violated their faith. In announcing its new position, the Court made a classic statement of civil liberties: "The very purpose of a Bill of Rights was to withdraw certain subjects from the vicissitudes of political controversy, to place them beyond the reach of majorities and officials."[5]

It has taken a long time for the United States to institute those principles. Civil liberties were barely visible in the nineteenth century. "What I find most dangerous in America," wrote Tocqueville in 1835, "is not the extreme freedom reigning there but the shortage of guarantees against the tyranny of the majority."[6]

The Slow Rise of Rights

The Bill of Rights barely touched American life because it only applied to the national government. The First Amendment begins, "*Congress* shall make no law" prohibiting the exercise of religion or restricting speech. Well, what about the states? Were they also bound by the individual protections in the Bill of Rights?

In 1833, John Barron found out. Barron owned a thriving wharf in Baltimore Harbor until the city diverted the water and left his dock high and dry. Barron sued, arguing that the city had violated the Fifth Amendment by taking his property for public use "without just compensation." The Supreme Court ruled (in *Barron v. Baltimore*) that the Fifth Amendment applied only to the federal government. The Anti-Federalists, reasoned the justices, had demanded the Bill of Rights to protect them from the federal government. Washington could not strip Barron of his property rights—but Maryland or Baltimore could.[7]

The Bill of Rights eventually reached the states thanks to the quest for civil rights. After the Civil War, Congress passed the Fourteenth Amendment (ratified in 1868) to protect the newly freed slaves. Every discussion of civil liberties turns the spotlight on one passage in the Fourteenth Amendment:

> *No state* shall . . . *deprive any person of life, liberty, or property, without due process of law; nor deny any person within its jurisdiction the equal protection of the laws.* [emphasis added]

Look again at the first two words. The amendment directly addresses the states. Pennsylvania, South Carolina, Montana or any other state: none may deprive any person of life, liberty, or property, which are exactly what the Bill of Rights protects. The Fourteenth Amendment *seems* to apply the Bill of Rights to the states. In 1873, the Supreme Court disagreed, ruling that the Fourteenth Amendment applied only to freed slaves and to no one else.[8]

Over time, the Court changed its mind. In 1897, the Court returned to the issue raised in *Barron v. Baltimore* and ruled that state governments could not seize property without compensation. One phrase of the Fifth Amendment now applied to state and local government as well as the federal government. The Supreme Court had "incorporated" the right into the Fourteenth Amendment. The Supreme Court decides, case by case, which rights apply to state governments—a process called **selective incorporation**.

Selective incorporation: The extension of protections from the Bill of Rights to the state governments, one right at a time.

The Court was very slow to force constitutional rights on the states. In 1937, it formally declared its principle for deciding which rights to incorporate: Is the right in question essential to our idea of liberty? If so, the Fourteenth Amendment's due process clause—quoted above—required states to respect that right, and the Court then incorporated, or applied, it to the states.[9] Over time, the Court incorporated almost every phrase of the Bill of Rights beginning with freedom of speech in 1925, continuing with the practice of religion in 1940, and moving to the right to own guns in 2010 (see Table 5.1).[10] In the rest of the chapter, we examine the most important civil liberties and the issues they raise.

THE BOTTOM LINE

» The Supreme Court neatly defined civil liberties in 1943: The Bill of Rights withdraws certain subjects from political controversy and places them beyond the reach of majorities and officials.

» The Bill of Rights did not apply to the states until the Fourteenth Amendment declared that no state could deprive any citizen of life, liberty, or property.

» The Court has applied the Bill of Rights to the states one right at a time between 1897 (no taking of property without compensation) and 2010 (the right to bear arms).

Privacy

We begin with an especially controversial right that, unlike all the others we will examine, is never directly mentioned in the Constitution. Instead, the Supreme Court has ruled that it is implied by the First, Third, Fourth, Fifth, and Ninth Amendments.

Penumbras and Emanations

In the mid-nineteenth century, contraceptives were widely available. Then, in the 1870s, every state, encouraged by the national government, banned them—partly

TABLE 5.1 Incorporation of the Bill of Rights into the Fourteenth Amendment

THE BILL OF RIGHTS	YEAR	KEY CASE
I.* Free exercise of religion	1940	Cantwell v. Connecticut
No establishment of religion	1947	Everson v. Board of Education
Free press	1931	**Near v. Minnesota****
Free speech	1925	**Gitlow v. New York**
Right to peaceful assembly	1937	De Jonge v. Oregon
Right to petition government	1963	NAACP v. Button
II. Right to keep and bear arms	2010	**McDonald v. Chicago**
III. No quartering of soldiers		Not incorporated
IV. No unreasonable search and seizure	1949	Wolf v. Colorado
No search and seizure without a warrant	1961	**Mapp v. Ohio**
V. Right to grand jury indictment		Not incorporated
No double jeopardy	1969	Benton v. Maryland
No forced confession	1964	Escobedo v. Illinois
Right to remain silent	1966	**Miranda v. Illinois**
No seizure of property without compensation	1887	Chicago, Burlington, and Quincy Railroad Co. v. City of Chicago
VI. Right to public trial	1948	In re Oliver
Right to speedy trial	1967	Klopfer v. North Carolina
Right to trial by impartial jury	1966	Parker v. Gladden
Right to confront witnesses	1965	Pointer v. Texas
Right to compel supportive witnesses to appear	1967	Washington v. Texas
Right to counsel in capital punishment cases	1932	**Powell v. Alabama**
Right to counsel in any criminal trial	1963	**Gideon v. Wainwright**
VII. Right to jury trial in civil cases		Not incorporated
VIII. No excessive bail		Not incorporated
No cruel and unusual punishment	1962	Robinson v. California
IX. Rights not limited to rights listed in the first eight amendments		Not relevant to incorporation
X. Powers not delegated to the national government reserved to the states and the people		Not relevant to incorporation

Notice that the First Amendment rights were incorporated early in the process. Most protections for those accused of crimes were applied between 1962 and 1968.
***Boldfaced cases are discussed in this chapter.*

because of fears that immigrants would have more children than native-born Americans. Almost a century later, the director of Planned Parenthood of Connecticut defied that state's ban and dispensed condoms at a birth control clinic in New Haven. The Supreme Court heard the case, *Griswold v. Connecticut*, in 1965, struck down the law, and declared a dramatic new right: the right to privacy.

How could the Court protect privacy if the Constitution does not even mention it? Justice William O. Douglas explained: Rights that are specifically mentioned in the Bill of Rights "have penumbras . . . that give them life and substance." The *penumbras*—literally, the shadows—of the First Amendment create "zones of privacy" in which people have a right to make their own choices free from government interference. So do the "emanations" from other amendments such as the Third Amendment's ban on quartering soldiers in private homes—which, Douglas pointed out, was designed to protect privacy. In addition, the Ninth Amendment declares that other rights exist besides the ones mentioned in the Constitution and that these rights are also "retained by the people." Privacy is one of those rights.

In 1787, when the Constitution was written, no one was thinking about condoms. But if you apply the logic of the Constitution to modern times, the right to privacy—and to contraceptives—emerges. These rights reflect the spirit of the Constitution. After all, concluded Douglas, "would we allow the police to search the sacred precincts of marital bedrooms for telltale signs of the use of contraceptives? The very idea is repulsive." Is it acceptable to interpret the Constitution in this way—reading in rights that are implied but not stated? That question presents one of the great controversies in contemporary legal analysis.

The *Griswold* case itself did not stir much controversy. After all, most people thought married couples had every right to use condoms. In 1973, however, the right to privacy led to one of the most controversial Court decisions ever.

Roe v. Wade

In *Roe v. Wade* (1973), the Supreme Court drew on the right to privacy and struck down a Texas law banning abortion. The Court ruled that the right to privacy is "broad enough to encompass a woman's decision whether or not to terminate her pregnancy"—within the first three months of pregnancy (before the fetus can live outside the womb). During that first trimester, the state governments cannot *regulate* or *infringe on* a woman's right to abortion.

Roe v. Wade changed American politics. It was not immediately controversial. Within a decade, however, two very strong perspectives had emerged. People who supported the decision—known as "pro-choice"—viewed the decision as essential to gender equality, for it enabled women to control when (and whether) they have children. From this perspective, *Roe* opens the door to vocations and careers for women. It protects women's health by doing away with the dangerous "back alley" abortions that desperate women sought out before *Roe* made abortions safe and legal. Democrats, for the most part, are pro-choice.

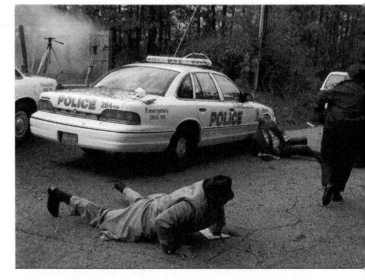

● *The most controversial right. Bystanders take cover after explosions outside an Atlanta family planning clinic in 1997. Decades after the Roe decision, abortion remains the subject of fierce debate, civil disobedience—and occasional criminal acts.*

What Do You Think?

Is There a Right to Privacy?

Are you ready to try your first case? How would you rule in *Griswold v. Connecticut*? Do you agree that there is "a right to privacy" in the Constitution that permitted the Court to strike down the Connecticut ban on contraceptives?

Yes. Although the Constitution does not specifically mention privacy, a modern reading of the document would conclude that privacy is a basic right that the courts ought to protect. In addition, the consequences—a woman's right to control her own pregnancy—is an essential part of gender equality as we understand it today.

No. We have to stick to the simple language of the Constitution itself. We disrespect and even damage the document by reading things into it. Anyone who opposes Connecticut's ban on contraceptives can go to the legislature and lobby them to change it.

What it means. No matter how you voted, you're part of a long intellectual tradition. If you said yes, you agree with a school of thought (which we call *pragmatist*) that says the courts must be guided by the *general ideas* that underpin the Constitution to try and determine the best outcome in a particular case. If you voted no, you're voting with *originalism*, the school of thought that limits judges to considering the document's original intent as explicitly stated in the Constitution's text.

Those who oppose the decision—known as "pro-life"—believe that life begins at conception and that abortion is murder. Many religious activists took *Roe v. Wade* as a call to enter politics. The grassroots campaign to overturn the decision became a powerful force in modern conservatism. Within a decade, the Republican Party had committed itself to overturning *Roe*.

The debate added new intensity to American politics. Activists on each side felt they were fighting for the soul of the nation: on the one side, equality for women; on the other, the rights of the unborn. The intensity has helped politicize Supreme Court appointments. Each new nomination raises the same questions. What is his or her attitude toward abortion? Will it swing the Court?

Planned Parenthood v. Casey

Challenges to *Roe v. Wade* led to a string of Supreme Court decisions. In 1980, the Court accepted a congressional ban on federal funding for abortions. In 1989, it upheld a Missouri prohibition on abortions in public hospitals. In 1992, the Court took up a Pennsylvania law that seemed to directly challenge *Roe* by imposing regulations on women seeking abortions, even in the first trimester. Pennsylvania required a twenty-four-hour waiting period, parental notification for minors, and prior notification of spouses. Many observers on both sides of the issue predicted that the Court would overturn *Roe v. Wade* and permit states to outlaw abortions.

Instead, in *Planned Parenthood v. Casey* (1992), the Court voted (5–4) to take a middle ground. The Court upheld a woman's right to terminate her pregnancy as a "component of liberty." However, it rejected *Roe v. Wade*'s trimester framework, which forbade any state limitations in the first trimester. Now the Court majority allowed states to legislate "measures aimed at ensuring that a woman's choice contemplates the consequences for the fetus." In short, the right to choose an abortion could be balanced—but not overruled—by the state's desire to protect potential life so long as state regulations did not impose "an undue burden" on the woman's choice.

The original *Roe* decision had propounded a **judicial rule**. Rules set clear boundaries between what is lawful and what is not: in this case, the states may not interfere in the first trimester. Now, *Casey* replaced the rule with a **judicial standard**. A standard establishes a more general guiding principle in place of a hard-and-fast rule. What is an "undue burden" on a woman's choice? That's a judgment call.

Judicial rules: Hard-and-fast boundaries between what is lawful and what is not.

Judicial standards: Guiding principles that help governments make judgment calls.

Abortions continue to be fiercely debated—on and off the Court. State lawmakers passed nearly 47 new laws restricting abortion in 2015 alone, an unprecedented number in recent times. And in 2016, North Carolina's legislature passed a law requiring doctors to submit to state regulators ultrasound pictures of fetuses prior to the abortion. A major victory for abortion-rights advocates also came in 2016, as the Supreme Court struck down a Texas law that imposed strict regulations on doctors and abortion facilities.

Sexuality Between Consenting Adults

Does the right to privacy extend to same-sex couples? In 1986, the Supreme Court ruled it did not, upholding Georgia's antisodomy law. However, judicial mores were changing along with wider American culture. In 2003, the Supreme Court reversed itself in *Lawrence v. Texas* and extended the right of privacy to same-sex couples. In striking down a Texas antisodomy law, the majority echoed the original *Griswold* decision: "Liberty protects the person from unwarranted government intrusion into . . . private places." Three members of the Court disagreed and signed on to Justice Scalia's blistering dissent. The decision, they wrote, "calls into question . . . state laws against bigamy, same-sex marriage, adult incest, prostitution, adultery, fornication, bestiality, and obscenity."

Clashing Principles

The privacy cases reflect public opinion. By 1965, most Americans believed that couples should be permitted to use birth control. *Roe v. Wade* appeared to reflect the popular view in the early 1970s, but precipitated an enormous surge defending a right to life. Later decisions balanced the right to an abortion with state restrictions—roughly in line with popular views. It may seem a good idea for the courts to reflect majority opinion. But the Constitution and the Court are designed to stand up to the majority. They are supposed to protect the rights of unpopular minorities, such as Jehovah's Witnesses in the 1940s and gay Americans in the 1980s.

As we will see throughout this chapter, applying the Constitution is never simple. The United States is founded on two ideas that often clash. We believe in government by the people. Yet at the same time, we believe that all individuals are endowed with inalienable rights. The story of civil liberties is the story of managing the collisions between the two great principles—the needs and desires of the community versus the rights of the individual.

● *John Geddes Lawrence (left) and Tyron Garner (right). The police, investigating a gun disturbance complaint, broke into Lawrence's apartment—which had gay posters prominently displayed on the walls. When Lawrence began to argue, the police arrested both him and Garner for "deviant sexual intercourse." In* Lawrence v. Texas *the Supreme Court struck down the Texas antisodomy law for violating the Constitution's privacy protections.*

» The Court discovered a right to privacy implicit in the shadows of the First, Third, Fourth, Fifth, and Ninth Amendments.

» The Court applied the right to privacy to strike down laws banning abortion. In *Roe v. Wade*, the court issued a rule prohibiting states from interfering during the first trimester.

» The Court extended privacy rights to same-sex couples by striking down antisodomy laws in 2003.

Freedom of Religion

The Bill of Rights begins with religion:

> *Congress shall make no law respecting an establishment of religion, or prohibiting the free exercise thereof.*

The First Amendment gives two succinct commands regulating religion. The federal government may not establish an official religion—known as the **establishment clause**. And it may not interfere in religious practice—the **free exercise clause**.

Establishment clause: In the First Amendment, the principle that government may not establish an official religion.

Free exercise clause: In the First Amendment, the principle that government may not interfere in religious practice.

The Establishment Clause

By the time the Constitution was written, Americans were practicing many faiths: Puritans (or Congregationalists) in Massachusetts, Quakers in Philadelphia, Baptists in Rhode Island, Anglicans in Virginia, Catholics in Maryland, and Jews in Newport, Rhode Island. The Constitution posed a threat. What if the federal government imposed a national religion? The First Amendment's establishment clause is designed to prohibit that. But what exactly did it forbid the government from doing? The debate began immediately.

President George Washington (1789–1797) called for a national day of prayer each year. Was that encouraging religion? President Thomas Jefferson (1801–1809) thought so and rejected the practice. The First Amendment, wrote Jefferson, builds "a wall of separation between church and state."[11] When the Supreme Court extended the establishment clause to the state governments in 1947, Justice Hugo Black quoted Jefferson's "wall of separation."[12] Until recently, Jefferson's metaphor guided the Court's efforts.

Jefferson's principle is a difficult guide because there has never been a true wall of separation. The cash in American pockets is inscribed "In God We Trust"; children pledge allegiance to "one nation, under God"; Moses, holding the Ten Commandments, is carved into the Supreme Court building. Congress opens each session with a prayer, and presidents end their speeches with "God bless America"— a sentiment no leader would invoke in England, France, or Japan. Despite these and other interconnections, the courts have tried to separate church and state. The question is how?

The establishment clause is clearly designed to keep government officials from favoring one religion—or religion over nonreligion. In a blockbuster case, *Engel v. Vitale* (1962), the Supreme Court ruled that New York's practice of starting the school day with a nondenominational prayer violated the establishment clause.[13]

● *Debating the establishment clause. The Supreme Court found Kentucky's display of the Ten Commandments unacceptable by a 5–4 vote (left), but a similar display in Austin, Texas, acceptable—also 5–4 (right). What was the difference between the two cases? Justice Breyer, who switched his vote from "no" (Kentucky) to "yes" (Texas) explained: the Texas Commandments had stood for forty years as part of a display about the development of the law, while the Kentucky tablets had been recently erected as a religious statement.*

A long string of controversial decisions followed. Each decision returns to the vexing question of exactly where to construct Jefferson's wall. May public schools introduce a minute of silent prayer or meditation? (No.) May graduation include a prayer? (No.) May students lead prayers at football games? (No.) Can a city or state government display the Ten Commandments? (No definitive ruling has yet taken place.) May a city put up a Christmas display? (Yes, if it includes secular as well as religious symbols—known sarcastically as the "two-reindeer" rule.) And back where this chapter began: May states ensure that business owners citing religious beliefs be free to deny gay people service? (No, a federal judge ruled in 2016.)

In 1971, the Court established a test to guide decisions about separating church and state. In *Lemon v. Kurtzman*, the Court ruled on a Pennsylvania law that paid teachers who taught nonreligious subjects in church-affiliated (mainly Catholic) schools. The Court forbade the practice and promulgated what became known as the *Lemon test* for judging what government actions are permissible. First, the law must have a *secular* purpose. Second, its principal effect must *neither advance nor inhibit religion*. Finally, it must not *excessively entangle* government in religion. Paying the teachers in religious schools was, the Court ruled, an "excessive entanglement," and Pennsylvania could not do it.

As the Court grew more conservative, the Lemon test came under fire. Today, two different perspectives have emerged. **Strict separation** still tries to separate church and state using the Lemon test. An alternative view is known as **accommodation**: Government does not violate the establishment clause so long as it does not confer an advantage on some religions over others. Accommodation is gathering momentum, but until the Court settles on a definitive set of guidelines, establishment clause cases can be unpredictable and even erratic. In a 2014 ruling, for example, the Court (by a narrow 5–4 margin) ruled that the town of Greece, New York, could open city-council sessions with a prayer, reversing lower courts, which held that this practice violated the Establishment Clause.

Free Exercise of Religion

The First Amendment also prohibits government from interfering with the "free exercise" of religion. Once again, the Court's view has evolved over the years.

The first landmark free exercise case was decided in 1963. Adell Sherbert, a Seventh-Day Adventist, refused to work on Saturday because it violated her faith. She was fired. South Carolina rejected her claim for unemployment benefits because she refused other jobs that also required work on Saturday. Claiming that the

Strict separation: The strict principles articulated in the Lemon test for judging whether a law establishes a religion. (See "accommodation.")

Accommodation: The principle that government does not violate the establishment clause as long as it does not confer an advantage to some religions over others. (See "strict separation.")

● Using the neutrality test, the courts struck down a Florida law that forbade the use of animal sacrifices for specifically targeting the Cuban Santeria religion.

state was infringing on her "free exercise" of religion, Sherbert sued the state for her unemployment benefits. In deciding the case, Justice Brennan introduced a two-part test, known as the *Sherbert* or *balancing test*. First, was the government imposing a "significant burden" on an individual's ability to exercise his or her faith? Second, did the government have a "compelling interest" for imposing the burden? In this case, the Court ruled that there was a real burden on Adell Sherbert and no compelling state interest for denying her unemployment benefits.

The Sherbert test lasted until 1990, when the Court took a completely different approach. Two Oregon men participated in a Native American ritual that included taking peyote, a hallucinogen. The men were fired from their jobs at a private drug rehabilitation center and then were denied unemployment benefits for violating Oregon drug laws. The men sued, arguing that they should be exempted from the peyote ban because it was essential to their religious practice. Under the Sherbert test they might have won. However, in *Employment Division v. Smith*, the Supreme Court ruled 6–3 against the two men and, in the process, made it much more difficult to sue the government for interfering with religious expression. In this case, the Court asked simply if the Oregon drug law was a neutral law applied in a neutral way. Yes, the law was neutral. It was not aimed at Native American religious practice because it forbids *everyone* from smoking peyote.

The *Employment Division* case replaced the *Sherbert* balancing test with a *neutrality test*. The new test asks only whether the same law applies to everyone. So long as the law does not target a religious group, the Court will permit it. Obviously, this makes it much more difficult to sue on the basis of "free exercise" of religion.[15]

Religious groups—from the Catholic Church to the *Witches' Voice*—mobilized against the Court's decision. Congress passed the Religious Freedom Restoration

What Do You Think?

May the Christian Youth Club Meet in School?

The Good News is a Christian youth club that wanted to meet in school after class hours. The school district said that this was religious worship and would amount to a public school's endorsement of Christianity. The case went to the Supreme Court. Justices Stevens (who argued against Good News) and Scalia (who supported Good News) each wrote opinions. Which opinion would you sign on to?

Justice Stevens: "Evangelical meetings designed to convert children to a particular faith . . . may introduce divisiveness and tend to separate young children into cliques that undermine the school's educational mission." The school district is right to stop the practice.

Justice Scalia: Religious expression cannot violate the establishment clause when such exercise is (1) purely private and (2) open to all on equal terms. Milford [the school district] was discriminating against a religious group because it allowed other groups to meet.

Testing These Views. As you consider whose side to take, consider how one would decide this case using the Lemon test (with Stevens) or the accommodation view (with Scalia). How did the court actually rule? The answer is in an endnote.[14]

Act of 1993 (RFRA), which required federal and state governments to use the old Sherbert balancing test. In 1997, the Court stepped in again. It ruled that Congress lacked the constitutional authority to order the states to use the balancing test. Congress came back three years later, reaffirming its authority with Religious Land Use and Institutionalized Persons Act (RLUIPA); in addition, some twenty-one states (with four more pending) passed their own RFRA laws—all restoring the Sherbert balancing test. In 2015, however, the Supreme Court reverted to the Sherbert balancing test. A Muslim inmate sued Arkansas, arguing that prison regulations denying inmates the right to grow beards violated his rights to practice his faith. The court ruled unanimously that the state could not burden someone's exercise of religion without showing a compelling state reason.

The decision hardly ended debates in this controversial area—but the general trend has been to restore the traditional balancing test that asks whether the government has a compelling reason to impose a burden (work on Saturday, shave your beard) on religious practices.

THE BOTTOM LINE

» The First Amendment has two religious clauses: The government may not establish a religion, and it may not interfere with the free exercise of religion.

» The courts have ruled on establishment cases by trying to approximate Jefferson's wall separating church and state. The Court requires three things of government action: It must have a secular purpose, neither advance nor inhibit religion, and not excessively entangle government in religion (the three requirements are together known as the Lemon test). A more recent view known as accommodation simply requires that government not promote one religious view over another.

» In protecting the free exercise of religion, the courts traditionally asked if the government had a compelling interest for imposing a burden.

Freedom of Speech

Now, we turn to the most important civil liberty of all, freedom of speech. After its religious clauses, the First Amendment states:

Congress shall make no law . . . abridging the freedom of speech or of the press.

A Preferred Position

Today, the Supreme Court gives the First Amendment a "preferred position" among all the amendments to the Constitution. And among the rights listed in the First Amendment (freedom of speech, religion, press, assembly, and the right to petition government), free speech holds a "preferred position." When freedom of speech conflicts with any other right, the Court generally will "prefer," or protect, speech.[16]

Why do contemporary courts put so much emphasis on the right to express opinions? Because democracy requires vigorous debate. John Stuart Mill, a nineteenth-century English political theorist, put it this way: "However true a doctrine may be, if it is not fully, frequently and fearlessly discussed, it will be held as a dead dogma, not a living truth." Over time, the courts have followed Mill, placing their faith in the free marketplace of ideas.[17]

Hate speech: Hostile statements based on someone's personal characteristics, such as race, ethnicity, religion, or sexual orientation.

When the right to speak out clashes with other rights—as with protecting minors from abusive language—free speech usually wins. The courts will be skeptical of any effort to curb speech, however hurtful. Of course, every right has limits. If you believe in limiting **hate speech**, you will find an argument to support your position later in this section. Much of the debate that surrounds the right to speech is about identifying the boundaries—the limits—of protected speech.

Political Speech

The forceful defense of free speech took a long time to develop. In every generation, political leaders are tempted to stop subversive talk—or harsh criticism. Under the John Adams administration, just ten years after the Constitution was ratified, Congress drafted the Alien and Sedition Acts. Tensions with France were running high, and the acts made it illegal to "print, utter, or publish . . . any false, scandalous, and malicious writing" against the government. The meaning of the acts was brutally simple: criticize the government and face prosecution.

The first modern free speech cases arose during World War I. President Woodrow Wilson had signed the Espionage Act. Charles Schenck, general secretary of the Socialist Party of Philadelphia, was found guilty of violating the act by printing and distributing a document that urged men to resist military recruitment for a war designed, he claimed, to pour profits into greedy Wall Street. Was his freedom of speech abrogated? Under normal circumstances it might be, wrote Justice Oliver Wendell Holmes for a unanimous court in *Schenck v. United States*

COMPARING NATIONS 5.1 — Civil Liberties Around the World

Every democracy protects civil liberties differently. Each makes choices based on its culture, its history, and who wields power. Consider some international differences.

The right to free speech is stronger in the United States. In Germany and France, it is against the law to deny that the Nazis murdered five million Jews between 1941 and 1945. In Turkey, the government will punish you for discussing the Ottoman Turks' genocide of Armenians in 1915. In Thailand, it is a serious crime to criticize the king. In Canada, there are strict limits on pornography because it demeans women. Most Americans despise Nazis, Holocaust deniers, and pornographers. However, the Constitution protects them all—at least in some cases. When it comes to speech, Germany, France, Thailand, Turkey, and Canada all tilt more toward community needs, whereas the United States distinctly emphasizes individual rights.

The United States is unique in protecting gun rights. No other nation explicitly mentions the right to bear arms in its constitution.

The United States puts special emphasis on property rights. For example, the Fifth Amendment forbids the government from taking private property "without just compensation." By contrast, the Canadian constitution does not even mention private property.

Most nations forbid the death penalty. Ninety-eight countries have abolished the death penalty. Almost all industrial democracies have done so (Japan, Taiwan, and Korea are the only exceptions). Abolishing the death penalty is a precondition for joining the European Union (the federation of European nations). In 2015, authorities in the United States executed twenty-eight people in six states (some 3,000 more have been sentenced to executions and are on death row). Only China, Iran, Saudi Arabia, Iraq, and North Korea executed more people—although tyrannical governments are notorious for murdering people outside the criminal justice system and these deaths would not show up in these tallies. Americans debate whether a clause in the Bill of Rights, the prohibition on "cruel and unusual punishment," should push the United States away from the death penalty.[18]

American rights are mostly negative: they tell the government what it may not do. Other constitutions include positive rights—things that the government must do—such as educate all citizens, provide universal healthcare, or ensure that women are well represented in the national legislature.

(1919), but this was wartime. Distributing these documents, Holmes wrote, was like falsely shouting "Fire!" in a crowded theater. Holmes then formulated the most famous test for free speech: speech is not protected if it poses "a **clear and present danger** that it will lead to 'substantive evils.'"

In the early 1920s, many Americans were anxious about foreigners, immigrants, socialists, communists, and anarchists. The Supreme Court hardened the "clear and present danger" test by ruling that judges did not have to "weigh each and every utterance." They could simply determine whether the "natural tendency and probable effect" of the speech was to "bring about something bad or evil"—even if that danger lay in the distant future.[19]

The clear and present danger test stood for decades. Then in *Brandenburg v. Ohio* (1969), the Court complained that "puny" threats, which no one took seriously except "nervous judges," were being declared a "clear and present danger." The issue arose when a Ku Klux Klan leader, Clarence Brandenburg, organized a rally at which Klan members burned crosses, waved guns, and called for "revengeance" against Jews and African Americans. The Supreme Court struck down Brandenburg's conviction and rewrote the clear and present danger test. The state may not interfere with speech, it said, unless the speech "incites imminent lawless action" *and* is likely to actually "produce such action."

The result makes it very difficult to curtail political speech—even when it is highly offensive. Members of the Westboro Baptist Church picket military funerals to protest homosexuality with signs that read "Fag sin = 9/11" and "You're going to hell." Albert Snyder, the father of a Marine killed in Iraq, sued the church. Forty-eight states and numerous veterans groups supported the suit. The Supreme Court acknowledged that the protests were hurtful but protected them as an exercise of free speech. The government may limit the speech only if the bad effects—a lynching, the overthrow of the government, or a terrorist attack—are likely to happen immediately.[20]

The rise of the Islamic State, and its sponsoring terrorist acts around the globe, has caused some to call for a revision of the "clear and present danger" test. Harvard Law professor and former Obama Administration official Cass Sunstein, citing the danger of ISIS attacks, has proposed a new limit on "explicit or direct

Clear and present danger: Court doctrine that permits restrictions of free speech if officials believe that the speech will lead to prohibited action such as violence or terrorism.

Test Yourself: The Simpsons Versus the First Amendment— Which Do You Know Better?

Five rights are listed in the First Amendment, and there are five Simpsons. Thirty-four percent of Americans can name four of the five Simpsons. Only one percent of Americans can name four of the five rights.

How about you? How many First Amendment rights can you name? How many Simpsons? (Answers below.)

(Source: McCormick Tribune Freedom Museum, Chicago.)

Answers: The Simpsons, from left to right: Homer, Bart, Lisa, Marge, and Maggie. First Amendment rights: Freedom of religion, speech, press, and assembly, and the right to petition government.

● *Test yourself: The Simpsons versus the First Amendment—Which do you know better?*

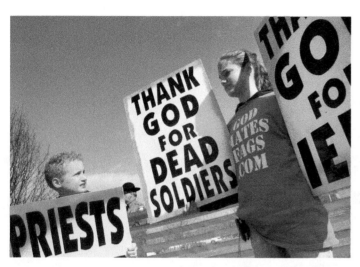

The expansive reach of free-speech protections. Young members of the Westboro Baptist Church join their elders in protests at funerals for U.S. servicemen who died in combat.

Symbolic expression:
An act, rather than actual speech, used to demonstrate a point of view.

incitement to violence, even if no harm is imminent." Others go further: another law professor, Eric Posner of the University of Chicago, has called for making it illegal to share links or even read websites that "glorify" the Islamic State.[21] The Court has not backed off its emphasis on free speech. However the line between supporting ISIS (protected) and assisting it in pursuing terrorism (which is a crime) is increasingly blurry. More on the tradeoffs between civil liberties and protection against terrorism later in this chapter.

Symbolic Speech

When Clarence Brandenburg burned his cross, he engaged in a form of speech known as **symbolic expression**. He was demonstrating a point of view with an act rather than through speech. The First Amendment protects symbolic speech—again, within limits.

In 2003, the Supreme Court identified those limits when it took two cross-burning cases on the same day. The Ku Klux Klan has historically burned crosses to terrorize black neighbors. In Klan lore, the original cross burnings, after the Civil War, signaled the "execution" of a former slave. The Court drew a fine distinction. Individuals may burn crosses to express their views, but not to intimidate others. Sometimes, wrote Justice Sandra Day O'Connor, "the cross burning is a statement of ideology, a symbol of group solidarity. It is a ritual used at Klan gatherings, and it is used to represent the Klan itself." The Constitution protects these symbolic speeches.[22] On the same day, however, the Court upheld the conviction of another cross burner. In this second case, two men had come home after a night of drinking and burned a cross on a black neighbor's lawn. Their act was intimidation. Even if there is no immediate (or clear and present) danger, intimidating people is not protected by the First Amendment.

In 2015, the Supreme Court narrowly upheld (5–4) Texas's refusal to issue a license plate with a Confederate flag. The state of Texas cannot be forced to convey a message; the minority pointed out that Texas had 350 different license plates and by refusing to issue this one the state limited the free speech rights of flag supporters. What do you think?

Burning the American flag is another unpopular symbolic expression. Forty-eight states and the federal government banned flag burning. The Supreme Court narrowly struck down the law by a 5–4 vote. "If there is a bedrock principle underlying the First Amendment," argued Justice Brennan for the majority, "it is that government may not prohibit the expression of an idea simply because society finds the idea offensive or disagreeable."[23] Congress responded by passing legislation defending the flag. The Court overturned that too.

Limits to Free Speech: Fighting Words

Is there any way to rein in cross burning, gay bashing, and other forms of hateful speech? As you can see from Comparing Nations 5.1, other democracies are much tougher on hurtful speech; so are many colleges and universities. The logic is simple: How can you build a good community if some members feel singled out, threatened, or diminished?

● *Is this symbolic speech protected? A closely divided court ruled yes (left) and no (right).*

One legal doctrine offers a limit to hate speech by restricting **fighting words**. The Supreme Court defined these as "personally abusive epithets which, when addressed to the ordinary citizen, are, as a matter of common knowledge, inherently likely to provoke violent reaction."[24] The Court states the principle but has been reluctant to apply it. If the words are political, they must be protected. If hate crime legislation singles out some fighting words (like racial epithets) but not others, the Court will reject it. However, even while the Court keeps striking down the efforts, it reaffirms that there *are* "fighting words" not protected by the Constitution. The key test is that the language does not advance any specific political position. Reformers trying to create codes of decent language generally rely on the logic of "fighting words."

Fighting words: Expressions inherently likely to provoke violent reactions and not necessarily protected by the First Amendment.

What Do You Think?

Free Speech on Campus

Beginning in 2015, a growing swell of on-campus activism aroused intense debates about free speech. Many universities passed or reaffirmed policies listing types of hate speech that were not protected on campus to provide special protection for members of groups that sometimes face intense discrimination—African Americans, Latinos, LGBTQ, and others. These codes in turn encountered fierce opposition. Critics argued that restrictions on speech would create taboo subjects. Anyone condemning or even criticizing homosexuals could be punished or even expelled from college.

Yes. Forbid certain hurtful types of expression. We must protect LGBTQ students, students of color, and other groups who face hatred and violence. Hate speech fractures communities and hurts people. It is frightening and painful to the targeted groups. It poses a threat to teaching and learning.

No. Forbid restrictions on speech regardless of how hurtful. Everyone has the right to an opinion—even if it is a horrible opinion. We can punish criminal behavior, but we should never punish people for simply expressing their views—especially on a college campus, where exploration of ideas is a core value.

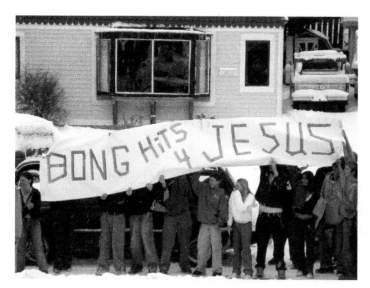

Joseph Frederick was suspended from school for five days for this banner and for five more days because he quoted Jefferson to the principal. The Supreme Court backed the suspension, 6–3.

Limited Protections: Student Speech

Student speech has sparked controversy and litigation. In the 1969 landmark *Tinker* decision, the Court announced that students "do not shed their constitutional right to freedom of speech or expression at the schoolhouse gate." That decision, however, has been qualified in a series of cases that balanced student rights with the schools' educational mission.

In 1965, John (fifteen-years-old) and Mary Beth Tinker (thirteen) violated school rules by wearing black armbands to protest the Vietnam War. They were suspended and told that they could return only when they were ready to abide by the rules. The Supreme Court overturned the suspension and established what became known as the Tinker rule: the students' right to free speech could be curtailed only if it "materially and substantially interferes with the requirements of appropriate discipline in the operation of the school."[25]

In subsequent cases, the Court found that teachers and school officials had an obligation to teach students proper conduct and could regulate speech that was vulgar, indecent, offensive (1986), or inconsistent with the educational mission of the school (1988).[26] A celebrated recent case arose from an incident at Juneau-Douglas High School in Alaska. The school permitted students to leave class and watch the Olympic torch pass through town. One student, Joseph Frederick, unfurled a big banner reading "Bong Hits 4 Jesus," to the merriment of his schoolmates. The principal suspended Frederick for ten days. The Supreme Court upheld the suspension for advocating drugs in violation of the school's antidrug policy.[27]

A new digital frontier has opened in the school-speech debates. Social media and other digital communications allow widespread, lightning fast broadcast of information—as well as malicious gossip, cyberbullying, and cruel rumors. A tenth-grade teacher in North Carolina resigned after students created a fake Twitter profile that portrayed him as a drug addict. Across the country, schools have suspended students for posts deemed inappropriate or illegal.

Ultimately, the First Amendment offers students—in high schools or colleges—less protection than it offers adults. School officials may regulate speech as long as they do not do so arbitrarily.

THE BOTTOM LINE

» Free speech is crucial to democracy, and the Court gives it a privileged position—even against angry public opposition to flag burning, cross burning, or homophobic displays at military funerals.

» Free speech can be curtailed if it poses a "clear and present danger." Today, the Court requires the danger to be both imminent and likely to occur.

» There are limits to free speech, including fighting words and student speech.

Freedom of the Press

Freedom of the press follows most of the same rules as freedom of speech. The written word has always been essential to politics. The form changes—pamphlets during the revolutionary period, newspapers in the mid-twentieth century, and new digital media today. Written words share the "preferred position" enjoyed by speech. Broadcast media are slightly different and subject to federal regulation (as we will explore in Chapter 9).

Prior Restraint

The effort to stop speech before it occurs is known as **prior restraint**. Although the Supreme Court has permitted government officials to punish people for what they have said or printed, it has never allowed federal government agents to gag citizens before they have had their say. In this view, prior restraint is nothing more than a technical term for *censorship*—the practice of dictators who close down newspapers or suppress stories they do not like. Some historians have argued that the real intent of the First Amendment was to forbid censorship.

Prior restraint: Legal effort to stop speech before it occurs—in effect, censorship.

The Supreme Court announced restrictions on prior restraint in 1931 after public officials in Minneapolis shut down a newspaper named the *Saturday Press*, which was published by an avowed racist who claimed that Jewish gangs were running the city. In *Near v. Minnesota* (1931), the Court ruled that the state could not suppress the paper, no matter how obnoxious, but it left the door open to prior restraint for national security reasons. The government would be justified for stopping someone from publishing information about "the number and location of troops in the field," it said, but not for publishing anti-Semitic harangues.

In one famous case of prior restraint, a State Department official leaked a rich archive of classified material, the Pentagon Papers, that exposed the mistakes and deceptions that led the United States into the Vietnam War. The Richard Nixon administration, claiming a threat to national security, went to court to block the *New York Times* from publishing the papers. Within days, the Supreme Court heard the arguments and, by a 6–3 vote, lifted the ban and permitted publication. The majority opinion emphasized the "heavy presumption" against prior restraint.[28]

The shift from print media to the Internet has profoundly changed the logic of prior restraint. In 2008, WikiLeaks, a web-based venue for anonymous whistle-blowers, published internal documents from a Swiss bank that appeared to show tax evasion and money laundering at the bank's Cayman Islands branch. The bank went to court and won a restraining order against publication of the leaked documents. Stopping a newspaper from publishing is straightforward: the court enjoins the publisher. However, because WikiLeaks operates anonymously and globally, it is almost impossible for a court to suppress the information it publishes. In the WikiLeaks case, the court tried to seal the site's American address—but the documents simply appeared on mirror sites.

Former National Security Agency contractor Edward Snowden, wanted in the United States on criminal charges for revealing national secrets online, appears via a Beam robot at a 2016 technology conference. Digital technologies have complicated civil-liberties policies about press freedom.

After two weeks, Judge Jerry White dissolved the injunction and acknowledged that the court's effort had only publicized the documents. There is "a definite disconnect," he commented, "between the evolution of our constitutional jurisprudence and modern technology."[29]

Then in 2013, Edward Snowden, a contractor working for the National Security Agency (NSA), leaked a huge cache of documents detailing the NSA's extensive data collection. The reports, published in the *Washington Post* and the British newspaper *The Guardian*, revealed one controversial secret after another: The United States had listened in on foreign allies such as Chancellor Angela Merkel of Germany; the NSA was collecting metadata on millions of cell phone calls; the PRISM surveillance program was tapping data from IT companies.

Both the WikiLeaks and Snowden stories illustrate how new media renders the government helpless against the spread of embarrassing and potentially harmful electronic information. By flowing anonymously across national borders and court jurisdictions, new media pose dilemmas for every nation as it tries to regulate the written word. The old question was should prior restraint be permitted? The new question is whether it is possible at all.

Obscenity

The First Amendment does not protect obscenity. However, the courts always face the same problem: What is obscene? Justice Potter Stewart put it famously when he said simply, "I know it when I see it." Of course, different people see "it" in different things. The Court's emphasis on free speech leads it to reject aggressive regulation of obscenity.

In *Miller v. California* (1973), the Supreme Court created a three-part test for judging a work to be obscene. The Miller test holds that speech is not protected by the First Amendment if it has all three of these characteristics:

1. "The average person, applying contemporary community standards, would find that the work, taken as a whole, appeals to the prurient interest" (meaning that it is meant to be sexually stimulating).
2. It depicts sexual conduct in a "patently offensive way."
3. The work lacks "serious literary, artistic, political or scientific value."

The Miller test only created new questions. What does it mean to be patently offensive? Offensive to whom? How do we rely on community standards of decency when the Internet and digital media flow across borders?

In recent years, the Court has been hostile to most efforts at banning material. It struck down a congressional effort to ban online material that showed "sexual, excretory activities or organs." In an especially grisly case, it even rejected legislation prohibiting the portrayal of animal cruelty. The ban had tried to forbid "crush videos" in which women wearing high heels crush dogs, cats, and hamsters while engaging in "a kind of dominatrix patter."[30] Congress subsequently rewrote the law to get around this Court ruling and outlaw crush videos.

Feminist scholars have tried to change the framework of this debate. Pornography, they argue, is a form of hate speech. Pornography subordinates women in the same way that hate speech demeans minorities. Nations such as Canada have essentially accepted this perspective. Although U.S. courts have not taken this view, the feminist position continues to be an important part of the debate.[31]

Social media has given rise to a new phenomenon: so-called "revenge porn," in which explicit photos or videos are distributed online without the subject's consent. Revenge porn is now outlawed in a majority of U.S. states, although courts in states like Arizona and Minnesota have struck down these laws. Congress took up a bill in 2016 imposing criminal sanctions on non-consensual pornography. The Supreme Court has yet to weigh in.

The Court, however, flatly forbids child pornography. Abusing minors is criminal. In 2008, the Court upheld a law that forbade efforts to "provide or obtain child pornography." The case involved a man who boasted online, "Dad of toddler has 'good' pics of her and me for swap of your toddler pics, or live cam." He followed up with hard-core images of minors engaged in sexual behavior. Even in this case, two members of the Court disagreed. They argued that the posting violated the laws only if it could be proven that the pictures were really of minors. Simply having the defendant say so was not enough. The First Amendment does not protect child pornography. However, the Court is so sensitive to free speech that even in a case like this one, some justices insisted on being cautious.[32]

Almost anything goes. It is very difficult to win a libel judgment against a publication. Public figures soon learn to deal with outrageous claims; in late 2015, for example, Lindsay Lohan and her mother, Dana, sued Fox news for an on air claim that mother and daughter did cocaine together. The network apologized but, like most defamation suits, this one was thrown out in court.

Libel

There are also limits to the false things one can write or say about someone. Written falsehoods are known as *libel*, spoken falsehoods are known as *slander*. The courts have made it very difficult for public officials or celebrities to win a libel (or slander) judgment. To do so, they must prove not just that a statement was false and that it caused them harm but that it was made with malice or "a reckless disregard for the truth."

Today, the Court allows even outrageous claims, cartoons, spoofs, and criticism directed at public officials and celebrities. By contrast, English law is just the opposite: it puts the burden of proof on the writers to prove the truth of what they have written.

THE BOTTOM LINE

» The rules for freedom of the press reflect those of free speech and strongly protect free expression.

» The courts are especially skeptical of any effort to impose prior restraint. New media make it almost impossible to even try.

» Obscenity is not protected by the First Amendment. The Court has spent a long time wrestling with just what counts as obscenity and now uses the three-part Miller test.

🔘 The Right to Bear Arms

The Second Amendment asserts a uniquely American right. No other national constitution includes the right to bear arms. The text in the Constitution is ambiguous:

> *A well regulated militia, being necessary to the security of a free state, the right of the people to keep and bear arms shall not be infringed.*

On one reading, this amendment simply protects colonial-era militias. On another, it guarantees the right to own weapons. Recently, the Supreme Court has rendered a decisive ruling—by a 5–4 vote—guaranteeing the right to bear arms. Consider each side of the argument.

A Relic of the Revolution?

Skeptics question whether Americans have any right to bear arms at all. The Second Amendment, they say, protected state militias. Early Americans believed that only kings and tyrants kept permanent armies. In a republic, the citizens volunteered for service in local militias that defended their communities and their nation. The Second Amendment, in this reading, is a "relic of the American Revolution"[33] and simply forbids the government from disarming the local militias. It does not involve a constitutional right to tote weapons.

Those who favor this view generally emphasize public safety and gun control. America's high homicide rate, they argue, reflects the easy availability (and the rising caliber) of American weapons. Many cities and some states regulate or limit gun ownership; in 2016, President Obama issued an executive order to expand background check requirements.

The Palladium of All Liberties?

Proponents of gun rights read the same constitutional sentence very differently. As Justice Scalia explained, the Second Amendment has two parts—a preface about militias and a clause that really matters, declaring that "the right . . . to keep and bear arms shall not be infringed." Many see the right to bear arms as the most important right of all—"the palladium of the liberties of the republic," as Justice Story put it. "When all else fails," declared Charlton Heston, actor and longtime honorary president of the National Rifle Association, "it is the one right that prevails. . . . It is the one right that allows rights to exist at all."[34]

The Supreme Court has been moving decisively to defend gun rights. In 2008, the Court struck down a District of Columbia rule that restricted guns in people's homes.[35] In 2010, in *McDonald v. Chicago*, the Court finally *incorporated* the Second Amendment. For the first time, the constitutional right to bear arms applied to state and local governments. The *McDonald* decision seemed to make it more difficult for cities and states to regulate weapons—but in the years since, most state and local restrictions have been upheld. In 2016, a federal appeals court upheld a California law that sharply restricts who may receive a concealed carry permit, strengthening the case for state and local authority.[37]

🔘 *Texas man totes an AK-47 to a demonstration supporting the state's open carry laws*

INFO/DATA: Guns on Campus

The Second Amendment's ambiguous "right to bear arms" guarantee has been a source of much debate virtually since the Bill of Rights was first introduced. College campuses historically have enjoyed low homicide rates.[36] However, after a shooting at Virginia Tech in 2007 left 32 people dead, political science major Chris Brown founded Students for Concealed Carry to lift bans on campuses. The map shows which states allow concealed carry, which ban it, and which leave it up to the campuses to decide.

1. Do you agree that permitting students to carry concealed weapons would make your campus safer? Why or why not?

2. What other actions could be taken to stop gun violence? How do you think the Second Amendment applies to your situation?

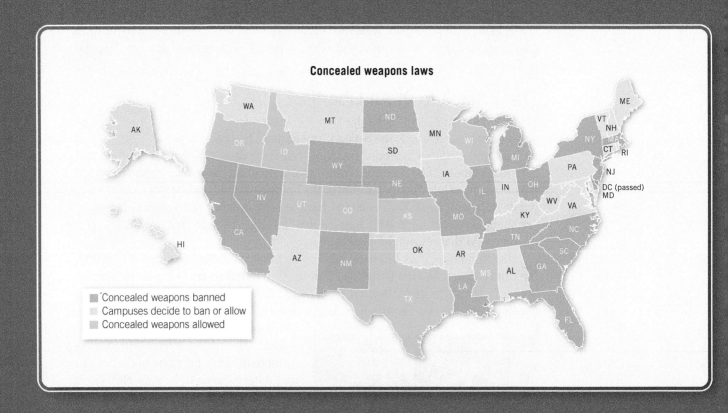

Concealed weapons laws

- Concealed weapons banned
- Campuses decide to ban or allow
- Concealed weapons allowed

Source: National Conference of State Legislatures

Few rights issues have split Americans like the Second Amendment. Conservative and rural Americans generally defend gun rights, which they view as deeply rooted in American culture and essential to personal protection. Liberals fear carnage: domestic disputes turn deadly, children kill their friends, and urban neighborhoods become combat zones. Horrific shootings—such as the 2016 mass shooting at an Orlando, Florida, nightclub—keep this difficult debate on the political agenda.

THE BOTTOM LINE

» Some critics see the Second Amendment as an outmoded defense of citizen militias.

» Others see it as an important individual right—perhaps even the most important right in the entire Constitution.

» In 2010, the Supreme Court incorporated the right to bear arms as an essential individual right, though state and local restrictions have largely been upheld in lower courts.

The Rights of the Accused

The Bill of Rights places special emphasis on protecting people accused of crimes. Four amendments (Four, Five, Six, and Eight) list thirty-one different rights for those who face criminal charges. No other issue gets as much attention. Protecting the accused involves another careful balancing act. On one hand, the courts must restrain law enforcement and defend the constitutional freedoms that define America. Yet too many curbs on law enforcement might lead to more crime. After vastly expanding the rights of the accused in the 1960s, the courts—in step with Congress, presidents of both parties, and most states—now tilt firmly toward law enforcement. However, American incarceration rates are the world's highest and especially affect minority communities—leading to calls for a renewed emphasis on rights.

In this section, we examine the most important (and controversial) protections one at a time. As you read, think about the trade-offs between safe streets and civil liberties. As always, there are solid arguments on both sides of the issue.

The Fourth Amendment: Search and Seizure

The Fourth Amendment protects people from government officials bursting into their houses.

> *The right of the people to be secure in their persons, houses, papers, and effects, against unreasonable searches and seizures, shall not be violated, and no Warrants shall issue, but upon probable cause, supported by Oath or affirmation, and particularly describing the place to be searched, and the persons or things to be seized. . . .*

British officials in the 1770s ransacked people's homes, searching for weapons or smuggled goods. The Fourth Amendment prevents that from happening. Justice Louis Brandeis described it as "the right to be left alone—the . . . right most valued by civilized men."[38] The police may not enter a home unless they go before a judge and explain why they suspect that evidence of a crime can be found in a specific place. The judge determines whether there is "probable cause" to issue the warrant. It sounds simple, but there are large gray areas (see Figure 5.1).

The landmark search and seizure case began in 1957 with a tip that Dollree (Dolly) Mapp was hiding a bombing suspect in her apartment. In addition, the police suspected she had illegal gambling paraphernalia there. The police knocked at her door, but she refused to let them in. They eventually broke the door down, and when she demanded to see a warrant they waved a piece of paper—not a warrant—in the air. The police searched the apartment and the basement. They never found the bombing suspect or the gambling material, but they did discover a suitcase of pornographic material—which was then illegal. Mapp was convicted on obscenity charges. The Supreme Court threw out the conviction and, in *Mapp v. Ohio* (1961, decided 6–3), devised the **exclusionary rule**: Evidence obtained in an illegal search may not be introduced in a trial. Even evidence that clearly proves someone is guilty of a crime may not be used if it was improperly obtained.

Twenty years later, President Ronald Reagan (1981–1989) attacked the exclusionary rule and urged both Congress and the courts to abolish it. John Roberts, the young Justice Department attorney who wrote the memos supporting Reagan's criticism, is now chief justice of the United States. During the Reagan years, the courts began making exceptions to the exclusionary rule. For example, in 1984, police arrested Alberto Leon when they discovered a large quantity of illegal drugs in his possession. Their warrant had expired, but the Supreme Court made a "good faith" exception and permitted the drugs to be introduced as evidence.[39] In 2009, Justice Roberts wrote (in a 5–4 opinion) that there was no need to exclude evidence

Exclusionary rule:
The ruling that evidence obtained in an illegal search may not be introduced in a trial.

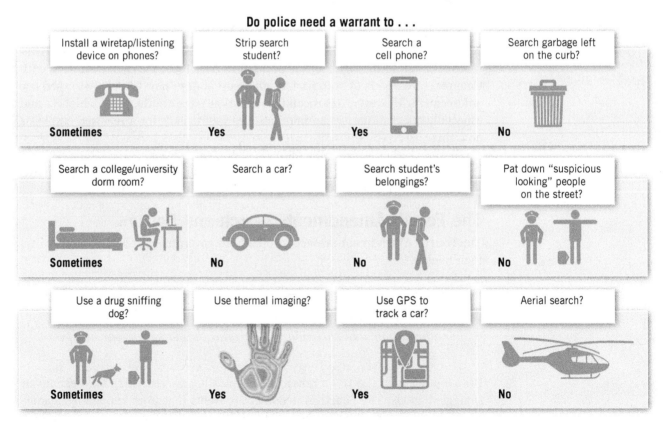

Do police need a warrant to . . .

| Install a wiretap/listening device on phones? | Strip search student? | Search a cell phone? | Search garbage left on the curb? |
| Sometimes | Yes | Yes | No |

| Search a college/university dorm room? | Search a car? | Search student's belongings? | Pat down "suspicious looking" people on the street? |
| Sometimes | No | No | No |

| Use a drug sniffing dog? | Use thermal imaging? | Use GPS to track a car? | Aerial search? |
| Sometimes | Yes | Yes | No |

● **FIGURE 5.1** *When are search warrants required?*

if the police had violated a suspect's Fourth Amendment rights because of "isolated negligence."[40]

In 2011 the Supreme Court crossed an important threshold. It permitted officers to break into a house without a warrant. The officers in the case knocked, identified themselves, and heard movements that sounded like the destruction of evidence of drug use. Only one justice dissented. This ruling would, wrote Justice Ruth Bader Ginsburg, seriously curtail the use of warrants by police. Writing for the majority, Justice Samuel Alito took a hard line. Residents who "attempt to destroy evidence have only themselves to blame."[41]

The Fifth Amendment: Rights at Trials

The Fifth Amendment lists a long series of rights focused largely on criminal trials. Consider them one clause at a time.

> *No person shall be held to answer for a capital, or otherwise infamous crime, unless on a . . . indictment of a Grand Jury.*

Grand jury: A jury that does not decide on guilt or innocence but only on whether there is enough evidence for the case to go to trial.

Before the government can prosecute, it must persuade a jury. A **grand jury** does not decide on guilt or innocence but only on whether there is enough evidence for the case to go to trial. The grand jury meets secretly and hears only from the prosecutor, so, as one New York judge once quipped, a decent prosecutor should be able to get a grand jury to "indict a ham sandwich."[42] As the Supreme Court has never incorporated the grand jury, this provision does not apply to the states. After the grand jury indicts, a petit (or small) jury of six to twelve individuals hears the case, weighs the evidence, and delivers a verdict.

> *. . . nor shall any person be subject for the same offense to be twice put in jeopardy of life or limb.*

Double jeopardy: The principle that an individual cannot be tried twice for the same offense.

An individual cannot face **double jeopardy**, or be tried twice for the same offense. ("Jeopardy of life and limb" refers to the old colonial practice of punishing people by lopping off an ear or damaging other limbs.) Without this provision, the government could simply keep trying people over and over.

Despite this prohibition, individuals sometimes face multiple trials. They can be tried on different charges, tried in federal court after being acquitted in state court, and—if they are acquitted on criminal charges—sued for damages. Darren Wilson, the Ferguson police officer who shot and killed Michael Brown, in November 2014 was acquitted in a Missouri court after a grand jury ruled against bringing criminal charges. The Justice Department then launched a separate federal civil rights investigation into Brown's fatal shooting. This was not considered "double jeopardy" because the civil rights charge was substantially different from the state's criminal manslaughter charge. (In 2015, then Attorney General Eric Holder announced that the Department had not found evidence that Brown was intentionally victimized because of his race, and ended the investigation.) In another famous case, former football star O. J. Simpson was acquitted of murdering his wife and her companion, only to lose a civil judgment for damages to the victims' families.

> *. . . nor shall be compelled in any criminal case to be a witness against himself.*

The Constitution aimed to protect citizens from torture and coerced confessions. The liberal Warren Court tried to put teeth into this right by requiring police officers to inform suspects that they have the right to remain silent, now known as the **Miranda warnings,** after *Miranda v. Arizona* (1966). In this case, the Court ruled that any evidence acquired before the warning would not be admissible in court. The ruling created an enormous outcry. Richard Nixon used *Miranda* in the 1968 presidential campaign as evidence that the United States had grown "soft on crime." Congress tried to pass a law to get around the ruling, which the Court eventually struck down.[43]

Over the past forty years, the courts have limited the *Miranda* rights—permitting confessions made to a police officer posing as another inmate (1990), carving out an exception for public safety (1984), and limiting the rules when defendants take the stand in their own defense (1970).[44]

The controversy subsided long ago, however, and the Miranda warnings have become "part of national culture," as Chief Justice William Rehnquist put it. Every TV cop show ends with the police nabbing the criminal while intoning, "You have the right to remain silent." In fact, some defense lawyers claim, half seriously, the phrase is now so familiar that what defendants actually hear is, "We've caught you, and you're in big trouble now."

Miranda warnings: A set of rights that police officers are required to inform suspects of, including the right to remain silent.

The Sixth Amendment: The Right to Counsel

The Sixth Amendment guarantees a speedy and public trial decided by an impartial jury. It includes another important provision, the right to counsel:

> In all criminal prosecutions, the accused shall . . . have the assistance of counsel for his defense.

The Supreme Court weighed in on this issue in an explosive case known as the trial of the Scottsboro Boys. In 1931 nine young African American men riding a freight train in Alabama were accused of raping two white women. Despite evidence that the charges were false (one woman immediately recanted), angry mobs gathered, and eight of the young men were rushed through trials and condemned to death. In *Powell v. Alabama* (1932), the Court ruled that, at least in a capital case (a case that could end in the death penalty), the defendants are entitled to lawyers and that the lawyers must be given enough time to meet with their clients and prepare their case. The Scottsboro case was a civil rights breakthrough for another reason: None of the African Americans unfairly accused of raping a white woman were executed.

In 1963, the Court expanded the right to counsel to all felony cases. Clarence Gideon, a Florida drifter, was allegedly caught breaking into a poolroom from which he had stolen beer, soft drinks, and the change out of the jukebox. When he came to trial, he demanded a lawyer, but the Florida court denied the request. Gideon was convicted and sentenced to five years, but from his jail cell, working with legal texts, he

● *The Scottsboro Boys, with their attorney Samuel Leibowitz, under guard by the state.*

scrawled an appeal. "Something astonishing . . . happened," wrote Anthony Lewis in a book on the case. "This loser's plea made it all the way to the Supreme Court." In *Gideon v. Wainwright* (1963), the Supreme Court ruled that the Sixth Amendment supported his claim and that the state must provide a lawyer to defend those who cannot afford one. With a competent lawyer, Gideon was acquitted. Attorney General Robert Kennedy commented, "An obscure Florida convict had . . . changed . . . the whole course of American legal history."[45] A network of public defenders soon spread across the country.

In 2012, the Court dramatically increased the scope of the right to competent counsel by holding that defendants have a constitutional right to effective attorneys during plea bargain negotiations (in a 5–4 ruling). Today, almost all federal cases (97 percent) involve a plea bargain, in which the defendant pleads guilty in exchange for a lighter sentence without actually going through a formal trial. The Court ruled that defendants can appeal if the plea-bargain negotiations were not competently handled.[46]

In practice, the right to counsel has grown increasingly difficult to maintain. The public is reluctant to spend tax revenues on lawyers who defend poor men and women accused of crimes. Public defenders face huge caseloads and small salaries—a 2015 Department of Justice study reported legal aid attorneys handle as many as 900 felony cases per year, and in several jurisdictions case load assignments are so high that lawyers average only seven minutes on each case.[47] The attorneys' own clients often disparage them. For all the problems, however, publicly funded criminal defense remains an essential—if endangered—part of civil liberty and American justice.

The Eighth Amendment: The Death Penalty

The Eighth Amendment introduces the question of capital punishment.

> *Cruel and unusual punishment . . . shall not be . . . inflicted.*

Is execution cruel and unusual punishment? Around the world, 101 nations have abolished the death penalty—including all the nations of Western Europe, where it is considered a violation of human rights. In contrast, the United States executed twenty-eight people in 2015 (see Figure 5.2). Although the number of executions has been falling steadily, more than 3,250 men and women have been sentenced to capital punishment and are waiting on death row. Some 60 percent of the American public supports executions, although the number has been slipping over the past fifteen years.

Proponents argue that some crimes are so terrible that justice demands capital punishment. It brings closure to grieving families. It may deter future murders (although there is no definitive evidence one way or the other). Moreover, some criminals are claimed to be so dangerous that they should be executed to protect other prisoners, prison officials, and the general public.

Opponents respond that killing people is immoral and that no government should be given the power to "play God." Because social systems are imperfect some—perhaps many—innocent people will be executed. The system is tilted against African Americans; blacks make up 12 percent of the population but, from year to year, between 25 and 50 percent of those executed.

In 1972, the Supreme Court halted all executions, arguing that state laws were so vague that similar cases produced different outcomes. "The death standards are cruel and unusual," wrote Justice Potter Stewart in *Furman v. Georgia*, "the same way that being struck by lightning is cruel and unusual"—meaning that death

End the Death Penalty?

In a recent case, Justice Stevens called for ending the death penalty. Is capital punishment a form of "cruel and unusual punishment"?

No. Some crimes are so terrible that they require this punishment. Justice demands it. It brings closure to the victims' families. American public opinion supports it. If there is a deterrent effect, executing criminals might save innocent lives. Some criminals are so hardened that they pose a safety threat to other prisoners, to prison officials, and to the public. Finally, multiple safeguards are in place to guarantee that innocent people are not executed.

Yes. It is time for the United States to join the other industrial democracies. Executions are unfair and are meted out almost entirely to poor and black defendants. No government should have this power. Killing is morally wrong, and two wrongs do not make a right. Furthermore, it is impossible to ensure that no innocent people will be killed. The deterrent effect has not been proven. Even the American Medical Association refuses to let physicians participate in administering the death penalty.

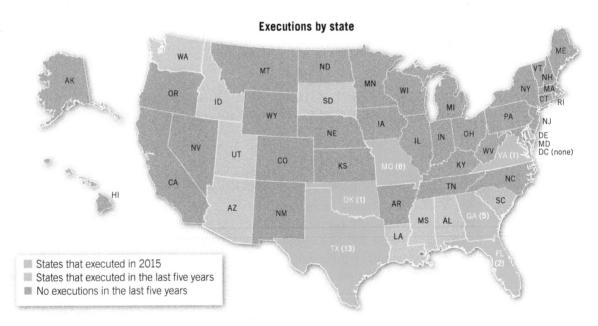

Executions by state

- States that executed in 2015
- States that executed in the last five years
- No executions in the last five years

FIGURE 5.2 *Map of executions in the United States (Death Penalty Information Center).*

sentences seemed to be meted out randomly. Thirty-five states drafted new capital punishment laws using *Furman* as a guide. In 1976, the Court permitted executions to go forward when state statutes included clear criteria to guide judge and jury in weighing death sentences.

Beginning in 1992, a network of law students and their professors began to use DNA evidence to review capital cases. Working together under the name the Innocence Project, they have documented false convictions of over 330 inmates—36 of whom were convicted of capital crimes. All those exonerated have now been released.[48]

The Court has imposed additional death-penalty limits. It has ruled that it is "cruel and unusual" to execute people convicted of crimes other than murder, striking down five state laws that allowed execution for child rape (2008). It has forbidden the execution of mentally ill individuals (2002) and of juvenile offenders (2005). In a much-discussed case, however, the Court ruled that lethal injections did not constitute cruel and unusual punishment despite the claim that they caused "an intolerable risk of pain" (2007).[49]

THE BOTTOM LINE

» The Bill of Rights places special emphasis on the rights of those accused of crimes. Even so, American incarceration rates are the highest in the world.

» The police may not search or seize without a warrant (with minor exceptions); they must inform suspects of their right to remain silent; the accused have a right to legal counsel. The courts have widened the right to counsel, but it is often limited by a lack of funding for public defenders.

» Under current interpretation, capital punishment is not considered "cruel and unusual punishment." However, the number of executions has been falling.

» Between 1962 and 1968, the Supreme Court vastly expanded the rights of the accused. Recent Court decisions have tilted the balance back toward law enforcement.

Fighting Terrorism and Protecting Liberty

USA Patriot Act: Legislation that sought to enhance national security, passed in the aftermath of the September 11, 2001, terrorist attacks.

After the terrorist attacks on September 11, 2001, Congress passed the **USA Patriot Act**. In the fear and emotion of the terrible moment, few criticized the legislation. The act enhanced security by removing restrictions on law enforcement. Removing restrictions, however, means limiting rights. The Patriot Act, the broader campaign against terrorism, and continued terrorism around the world have revived a longstanding national debate: How do we balance civil liberties and public safety?

Terrorist attacks, such as the San Bernardino shootings, raise the question of how to balance national security with privacy rights.

Contacts with Forbidden Groups

In the aftermath of 9/11, the CIA and the FBI came under fire for failing to track and stop the terrorist cells responsible for the deaths of thousands of Americans. The federal government enhanced rules that bar Americans from offering aid to terrorist organizations. ISIS, a terrorist organization, uses Facebook posts, tweets, and grisly beheading videos as recruitment tools. Since ISIS arose in 2014, federal prosecutors have arrested over 80 Americans for traveling or arranging to travel to Syria to meet with ISIS and for planning attacks on American soil.[50] Although the law forbids aiding terrorist organizations, expressing general support for such an organization is protected speech.

As we saw in this chapter's earlier discussion on ISIS and restricted speech, drawing the line between public safety and free speech remains hotly contested. For now, U.S. courts permit the government to prosecute web postings if and when they provide funding or other specialized assistance to terrorist groups. What do you think? Is there an obvious balance between protecting free speech and fighting terrorism?

Surveillance

Domestic surveillance requires a warrant. To prevent terror attacks, however, both the Bush and the Obama administrations permitted the National Security Agency (NSA) to conduct international surveillance without a search warrant. Major controversy erupted in 2013 around the Snowden leaks earlier in this chapter. Snowden revealed that the NSA has been collecting bulk data—over a trillion pieces of information—on phone calls, computer searches, texts, and more. The phone data include the caller, the receiver, the date and time of the call, and the length of the call—but not a transcript of the conversation itself.

Some public officials defended the NSA. Senator Dianne Feinstein (D-CA) put it this way: "New bombs are being devised. New terrorists are emerging. . . . We need to be prepared."[51] The Constitution, argued proponents of the NSA program, permits exceptions to basic rights when "public safety may require it" (Article 1). But even some of the Patriot Act's original sponsors thought that this tilted the balance too far against civil liberties—and trampled on the Constitution. Twenty new bills sprung up in Congress reining in the NSA. In 2015, the USA Freedom Act reauthorized the original Patriot Act—but ended the NSA's collection of telecommunications data.

A new twist came after a husband and wife who had pledged allegiance to ISIS burst into a social service center in San Bernardino, California, and killed or seriously wounded thirty-six people. The terrorists were both killed—but when government officials asked Apple officials to unlock one of their iPhones, the company refused. Apple CEO Tim Cook angrily wrote about the "chilling" violation of privacy the government was asking it to perform. Once again the debate turns on the balance between public safety and privacy rights.[52]

THE BOTTOM LINE

» The response to 9/11 and subsequent terrorist attacks created a debate about the balance between civil liberties and public safety.

» With the Snowdown revelations, controversy rose up about the NSA data collection of phone records and Internet surveillance.

» In 2015, the USA Freedom Act reauthorized the Patriot Act with new limitations—and forbade the use of bulk data collection.

🔵 Conclusion: The Dilemma of Civil Liberties

How should the government balance its duty to keep the public safe, or to uphold public moral standards, with its responsibility to protect civil liberties? This is one of the most important issues facing American democracy today. If we tilt too far toward combating terrorism or outlawing practices considered socially unacceptable, Americans will lose the liberties that have defined the nation since 1776. If we tilt too far the other way, the nation may be vulnerable to attacks or lose its moral core. Getting the balance right is a major challenge facing Americans. The courts take the lead in protecting rights, but elected public officials define the policies that the courts are weighing. Ultimately, the balance between communal needs and individual rights is in the hands of the voters.

Isn't that exactly where it belongs? No. Recall the Supreme Court's judgment in 1943 when it reversed its earlier decision and protected the Jehovah's Witnesses: "The very purpose of a Bill of Rights was to withdraw certain subjects from the vicissitudes of political controversy, to place them beyond the reach of majorities and officials and to establish them as legal principles to be applied by the courts." A core point of civil liberties is to protect the rights of individuals—even if it means overruling the majority of the country.

CHAPTER SUMMARY

🔘 Civil liberties are the limits we put on governing bodies (and the majorities that elect them) so that individuals can exercise their rights and freedom. Disputes are usually resolved by the courts and guided by the Bill of Rights.

🔘 The Bill of Rights did not apply to the states until the Fourteenth Amendment required that *no state* could deprive any citizen of life, liberty, or property.

🔘 The Supreme Court applied the Bill of Rights to the states one right at a time between 1897 (no taking property without compensation) and 2010 (the right to bear arms). This process is known as incorporation.

🔘 The Court discovered a right to privacy implicit (in the shadows) in the First, Third, Fourth, Fifth, and Ninth Amendments. The Court applied the right to privacy to strike down laws banning abortion. In *Roe v. Wade*, the Court issued a rule prohibiting states from interfering during the first trimester. In *Planned Parenthood v. Casey*,

the Court replaced the rule with standard forbidding laws that put "an undue burden" on the right to privacy. The Court extended privacy rights to same-sex couples by striking down antisodomy laws in 2003.

🔘 The Constitution bars government from establishing religion. In one view, this means separating church and state. For many years, the Lemon test guided judicial decisions in cases involving religion. A more recent view requires simply that government not promote one religious view over another. The Constitution also forbids government from interfering with religious practice. The courts traditionally asked if the government had a compelling interest for imposing a burden. Today, they require only that the government action be neutral and apply to everyone. Congress and some state governments have tried to return to the original rule.

🔘 Free speech is crucial to democracy, and the Court gives it a privileged position—even against angry public opposition to flag burning, cross burning, or homophobic displays at military funerals. Free speech can be curtailed if it poses a "clear and present danger." Today, the Court requires the danger to be both imminent and likely to occur. There are limits to free speech involving fighting words, student speech, commercial speech, and obscenity.

● Some critics see the Second Amendment as an outmoded defense of citizen militias. Others see the right to bear arms as an important individual right—perhaps the most important right in the

Constitution. In 2010, the Supreme Court ruled it an essential constitutional right.

● The Bill of Rights places special emphasis on the rights of those accused of crimes. Even so, American incarceration rates are the highest in the world. The police may not search or seize without a warrant, they must inform suspects of their right to remain silent, and the accused have a right to legal counsel. Under current interpretation, capital punishment is not considered "cruel and unusual punishment—but public opinion appears to be slowly changing."

KEY TERMS

Accommodation, p. 135	Fighting words, p. 141	Miranda warnings, p. 151
Civil liberties, p. 126	Free exercise clause, p. 134	Prior restraint, p. 143
Clear and present danger, p. 139	Grand jury, p. 150	Selective incorporation, p. 129
Double jeopardy, p. 150	Hate speech, p. 138	Strict separation, p. 135
Establishment clause, p. 134	Judicial rules, p. 133	Symbolic expression, p. 140
Exclusionary rule, p. 149	Judicial standards, p. 133	USA Patriot Act, p. 154

STUDY QUESTIONS

1. What are civil liberties? How are they different from civil rights?

2. In *Barron v. Baltimore*, the Supreme Court ruled that the Fifth Amendment did not protect a landowner if the state took his property. Why?

3. Describe how the Bill of Rights was applied to the state governments. First, describe the constitutional amendment that directly addressed the states. Then describe the process of incorporation by which the Supreme Court applied the Bill of Rights to the states.

4. Describe how the Supreme Court declared the right to privacy. Discuss the case from a pragmatist's and an originalist's perspective. Would you vote to maintain the right to privacy? Or would you overrule the precedent? Explain your reasoning.

5. Describe the three-part Lemon test for determining whether a state action violates the establishment clause. The late Justice Scalia was highly critical of the Lemon test. What was his view? Do you agree or not? Explain why.

6. Sometimes the Court permits a racist to burn a cross. Sometimes it forbids it. Explain the reasoning in each case. Do you agree with the Court's distinction, or would you rule differently?

7. There are two interpretations of the Second Amendment right to bear arms. Describe each. Which do you support? Why?

8. The Supreme Court gives free speech a "privileged position" among the rights in the Bill of Rights. What does that mean? How does the Court justify that position?

9. Feminist scholars argue that privileging free speech in pornography cases actually undermines free speech. What is their argument? Do you agree or disagree? Explain why.

10. How does the USA Patriot Act raise questions about the balance between public safety and civil liberties? How do you think civil liberties should be balanced with protection against terrorism? If you had to emphasize one goal more than the other, which would you emphasize? Why?

 Go to www.oup.com/us/Morone to find quizzes, flash cards, simulations, tutorials, videos, and other study tools.

The Struggle for Civil Rights

6

ON A HOT SUMMER DAY in Ferguson, Missouri, a police officer confronted a black man accused of stealing some cigarillos from a convenience store. Reports differ about what happened next but there is no doubt how it ended: Officer Darren Wilson fired twelve bullets at Michael Brown. The Ferguson police then left his body bleeding on the street for four hours. The next day vigils turned to protests and then into a movement: "Black Lives Matter."

In the following months, a stunning parade of images flashed before the public: A video of Eric Garner wrestled to the ground on Staten Island, New York, and choked to death as he gasped, "I can't breathe." In Baltimore, Maryland, police arrested Freddie Gray and chained his legs in the back of a police wagon; a week later he was dead of a severed spinal column. In Baton Rouge, Louisiana, Alton Sterling was shot to death by police after being pinned to the ground for illegally selling CDs outside a convenience store. And in a St. Paul, Minnesota, suburb, Philando Castile's last moments of life were recorded by his girlfriend, after a police stop resulted in Castile's being killed. As the death toll of unarmed black people swelled, the Black Lives Matter movement grew. Beneath the protests lay a profound message: A century and a half after slavery was abolished, we still do not feel fully equal and empowered.

We have been here before. Protest movements confronted slavery, fought racial segregation and won civil rights for women, immigrants, religious minorities, and many other groups. They also encountered hostile and sometimes violent opposition—and occasionally turned violent themselves. In 2016, soon after the Sterling and Castile killings, eight police officers were targeted and killed in Dallas and Baton Rouge, ten days apart.

Who are we? We are a profoundly diverse nation, founded on the idea that all people are "created equal" and "endowed" with "unalienable rights" including "life, liberty and the pursuit of happiness." We are also a nation that often does not live up to its noble founding vision.

Civil rights are the freedom to participate in the life of the community—to vote in elections, to enjoy public facilities such as parks, and to take full advantage of economic opportunities like good jobs. People face discrimination when they are denied rights and opportunities because of their race, gender, ethnicity, religion, disabilities, age, or other personal characteristics. Once citizens have won their rights, public attention shifts to protecting them. We covered that topic—known as civil liberties—in Chapter 5. The long

● *Black Lives Matter protesters, pictured here in 2016, invoke the civil rights struggles of the 1960s.*

In this chapter, you will:

● Explore the seven steps to winning civil rights in the United States.

● Review the African American experience that set the pattern for civil rights.

● Assess women's quest for economic and political rights.

● Examine the political experience of Hispanics, Asians, and Native Americans.

● Consider the rights of other groups, including disabled people, same-sex partners, and transgender individuals.

Civil rights: The freedom to participate in the full life of the community—to vote, use public facilities, and exercise equal economic opportunity.

159

battle to win civil rights is perhaps the most powerful story in American history. It reveals the deepest truths about the United States and its values. It tells us who we are—and who we strive to be.

We can view the history of civil rights in two different ways. Some observers see a steady march toward a deeper and richer American equality. Sixty years ago, African Americans were still restricted from voting in many southern states, and many professions were formally closed to them. Today, African Americans are CEOs of *Fortune 100* companies, head elite academic institutions—and one recently served two terms as U.S. president. Forty years ago, only one woman in American history had won a U.S. Senate seat in her own right. Today, the Senate includes 21 women, and the U.S House another 83. The American promise marches relentlessly on.[1]

Other observers, however, believe that there is nothing inevitable about civil rights. Sometimes rights expand, sometimes they contract. Yes, Asians won full rights, but Native Americans did not. African Americans scaled the old barriers, but today they are still more likely to be poor than the rest of the population. They are more likely to face jail time. They have a life expectancy five years shorter than whites—and nearly eight years shorter than Latinos. And, as this chapter's opening underscores, blacks are far more likely than those of other races to be killed by police. There is nothing inevitable about American equality, say proponents of this perspective, and citizens should never take it for granted.[2]

As you read this chapter, ask which view seems most accurate to you: Has the United States advanced consistently toward greater civil rights for all? Or has the progress been unsteady?

Winning Rights: The Political Process

How does a group win political rights? Each civil rights campaign has its own unique history. However, the efforts usually involve the following stages—not necessarily in order.

Seven Steps to Political Equality

1. *A group defines itself.* Discrimination usually stretches back through time and seeps into the way the powerful view others: whites ruled blacks, men took responsibility for "the weaker sex," Indians were "savages," society pitied the disabled, and psychiatrists defined homosexuality as an illness. In the first step toward civil rights, a group embraces its shared identity and redefines itself as a victim of discrimination. Groups usually reject their old, often-demeaning label and find a new name: Negroes, Miss, queers, and cripples became African Americans, Ms., LGBTQ individuals, and persons with disabilities.

2. *The group challenges society.* The next step involves entering the political arena and demanding rights. Civil rights campaigns often go beyond normal politics and include marches, demonstrations, creative protests (like kneel-ins before segregated churches), and even riots.

Civil Rights

Number of black mayors in 1965: **0**
Number of black mayors in 2016: **Over 600**

Percentage of southern students who attended integrated schools eight years after *Brown v. Board of Education* (ruling in 1954): **1**
Percentage of southern students who attended integrated schools eight years after the passage of the Civil Rights Act of 1964: **91**

Percentage of white and black Americans, respectively, who were poor in 1959: **18, 55**
Percentage of white Americans who are poor today: **10.1**
Percentage of Hispanic Americans who are poor today: **24.7**
Percentage of black Americans who are poor today: **25.2**
Percentage of Native Americans who are poor today: **32.2**

Number of Hispanic members of Congress in 1990, 2000, today, respectively: **10, 18, 38**
Number of women elected to full Senate terms between 1920 and 1970: **3**
Number of women serving in the Senate today: **21**
Number of nations with a higher percentage of women serving in their national legislature than the United States (as of 2016): **96**

Year the Supreme Court struck down laws forbidding marriage between blacks and whites: **1968**

Percentages of whites, blacks, Hispanics, and Asians, respectively, married to a member of a different race today: **9, 17, 26, 28**

Percentage of whites, Latinos, and blacks, respectively, who report "a great deal" or "a fair amount" of confidence in the police: **57, 52, 30**

3. *The stories change.* Civil rights always involve a contest over the stories that a society tells about a group. Why does the United States discriminate against people in the first place? Because the majority portrays a group as dangerous, inferior, or helpless. Winning rights requires changing the story. As you read about efforts to secure rights—past and present—be alert to the many different stories we tell about the groups in our society.

4. *Federalism comes into play.* Civil rights politics splashes across local, state, and federal governments. Because many minority groups are concentrated in certain states and regions, discrimination often begins on the local level. Furthermore, state and local officials control many of the policies that affect civil rights: education, law enforcement, and voting rules.

   In other cases, states and localities first introduce reforms: Before the Nineteenth Amendment established women's suffrage nationally, women won voting rights in western states.

5. *The executive branch often breaks the ice.* Presidents can issue executive orders (rules that have the force of law but do not require congressional

Lucretia Mott, who helped organize the Seneca Falls convention for women's rights in 1848, is attacked by a mob of angry men. Women who challenged their own subordination faced violence in the nineteenth century.

approval) that can create opportunities and momentum for a civil rights campaign. President Truman desegregated the U.S. military in 1948, and President Obama extended protections for gender identity in 2014.

6. *Congress legislates a blockbuster.* Typically, it is Congress that passes the great changes that finally secure civil rights and echo through history. The Fourteenth Amendment to the Constitution, ratified in 1868, still dominates every effort to win rights. The Civil Rights Act of 1964 profoundly changed civil rights in the United States.

7. *It all ends up in court.* The courts are the ultimate arbiters of civil rights. Individuals and groups challenge laws they consider unjust. The courts consider what the Constitution requires and weigh the laws, rules, regulations, and private actions for what is permissible and what is not.

Notice how many moving parts there are in the reform process. We have already seen why this is so: American government is unusually fragmented, marked by overlapping actors and institutions all balancing one another. That makes it difficult to change deep social norms such as racial or gender discrimination. Reformers have to win over many different power centers—state legislatures, Congress, governors, the judiciary, the media, and the public.

How the Courts Review Cases

Because civil rights generally end up in court, the judicial framework is important. The courts use three categories for determining whether acts violate "the equal protection of the laws" guaranteed by the Fourteenth Amendment.

Strict scrutiny: The standard by which courts judge any legislation that singles out race or ethnicity.

Suspect Categories. Any legislation involving *race, ethnicity, religion,* or *legal aliens* faces **strict scrutiny**. The Supreme Court is primed to strike down any law that singles out a race or ethnicity or religion unless there is a very strong reason for doing so. The Court will ask: Does the government have a *compelling government interest* in singling out a race or an ethnicity?

Quasi-suspect category: A legal standard that requires governments to have an important state purpose for any legislation that singles out sex or gender. This is not as strong as the *suspect category,* which requires strict scrutiny.

Quasi-Suspect Categories. In 1976, women's advocates won a special category for gender cases: **quasi-suspect categories**. Any legislation—federal, state, or local— that introduces sex-based categories has to rest on an *important state purpose*. This is not as strong a test as a *compelling* interest, but it is still a powerful requirement, one that can touch many aspects of politics, economics, and society. For example, in 1996 the Court ruled that excluding women from the Virginia Military Institute (VMI) did not serve an important state purpose. VMI had to open its doors to women cadets or forgo state funding.

Nonsuspect Categories. Other categories do not face special scrutiny—at least not yet. Legislation based on age, sexual orientation, gender identity, or physical handicaps simply has to have some rational connection between the legislation and a legitimate government purpose. This is the weakest test, but it can still bar discrimination. Using this test, for example, the Court ruled that there was no rational basis for a Colorado constitutional amendment that forbade any protection for gays and lesbians.[3]

This threefold division is the framework for civil rights law. As with almost everything else in American government, politics produced these categories. Groups argued, lobbied, demonstrated, and sued to win stricter scrutiny.

● *A civil rights effort helped lift the ban on women in combat in 2013. As of 2016, women can perform all combat jobs—including Navy SEALs.*

THE BOTTOM LINE

» The battle for civil rights generally involves seven characteristics. The group seeking rights must define itself, challenge society, and change the way it is viewed. The contest for rights spills across all branches of government and involves states, the executive, Congress, and the courts.

» Courts interpret charges of discrimination using three standards: suspect, quasi-suspect, and nonsuspect.

🔵 Race and Civil Rights: Revolt Against Slavery

Few groups in American history have suffered worse treatment than African Americans. By now, the painful images are familiar: Men and women chained in the holds of slave ships, sold at auction, raped at will, separated from their families, and murdered for challenging their oppressors. Even after liberation, black Americans faced another century of repression. In fighting back, African Americans developed the tactics that other groups would use in their own battles for civil rights; black movements forged the laws, amendments, and judicial doctrines that opened the door to civil rights reforms across society. The black quest for freedom included two powerful crusades, one in the nineteenth century and one in the twentieth.

The Clash over Slavery

Slaves were permitted to have churches, and in the early nineteenth century, religion offered leadership, organization, and a powerful message. Black leaders drew on the Christian Bible to compare Africans to the Israelites, bound in slavery but waiting for deliverance to freedom. By the middle of the nineteenth century, the dream of freedom had become a kind of religious faith in the slave quarters.[4] Three additional forces precipitated a national crisis over slavery: a moral crusade for abolition, economic interests, and political calculations.

Abolition:
A nineteenth-century movement demanding an immediate and unconditional end to slavery.

Abolition. An **abolition** movement rose up, branded slavery sinful, and demanded its immediate end. The movement was small and radical, but its newspapers and pamphlets created a furious reaction. Many Americans—in both the South and North—feared the abolitionists would incite the slaves to rebellion. Most people preferred to ignore the issue.

Economics. It was impossible to avoid the slavery question for a fundamental economic reason. As the United States spread west, every new settlement prompted the same question—would it be slave or free? Northerners opposed slavery on the frontier for moral reasons and because it robbed them of the opportunity to claim new lands. Southerners, however, insisted that slavery needed to spread into new states to survive. Because the federal government controlled territories until they became states, the question—slave or free?—constantly haunted Congress.

Politics. Every time a territory applied for statehood it called into question the political balance between slave states and free states in Congress. Because every state has two senators, an equal number of free and slave states permitted the South to defend its "peculiar institution." The slaves (who each counted as three-fifths of a person for the purposes of representation—as we saw in Chapter 3) gave Southern states an additional thirty-six seats in the House of Representatives.

Missouri Compromise:
An agreement to open southern territories west of the Mississippi to slavery while closing northern territories to slavery.

The Senate managed to negotiate the tensions with a series of artful compromises. The **Missouri Compromise** of 1820 drew a line through the Louisiana Territory (see Figure 6.1). All new states and territories north of the line except Missouri

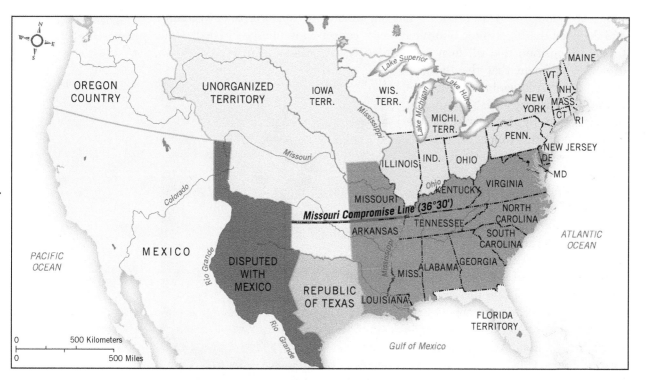

● **FIGURE 6.1** *The Missouri Compromise—all new American territory below the line would permit slavery; all above (except Missouri) would be free.*

would be free; everything south of the line would be open to slavery. In 1845, as Americans moved west, Congress extended the line to include Texas. In 1850, California wanted to enter the Union as a free state. The solution was the **Compromise of 1850**, which permitted California to enter as a free state and turned the decision in Kansas and Nebraska over to the residents—a policy known as popular sovereignty.

Dred Scott v. Sandford

In 1857, the Supreme Court stepped in with a shattering decision that upset all the careful compromises. A slave named Dred Scott sued for his freedom. He argued that he had been taken to live in a free territory before returning to Missouri and that, as a result, he should be free. Chief Justice Roger Taney ruled that Scott was not free, because neither the territories nor the federal government had the power to limit slavery or give a black man rights. What about the Missouri Compromise? Unconstitutional, ruled Taney. Popular sovereignty? Also unconstitutional. The **Dred Scott v. Sandford** decision ruled that no territory could restrict slavery, much less elevate blacks to citizenship.

The *Dred Scott* decision created a political crisis. The Republican Party rose to national prominence by explicitly rejecting it. In 1860, Abraham Lincoln won the presidency on a platform that flatly opposed the extension of slavery into any territories. When Lincoln won, southern states began withdrawing from the United States, and the Civil War erupted. In the four years from 1861 to 1865, more people lost their lives than in all the other American wars combined. However, from the blood and ashes arose a second American founding.

The Second American Founding: A New Birth of Freedom?

In his Gettysburg Address, President Lincoln announced "a new birth of freedom" and declared that the United States had been "conceived in liberty and dedicated to the proposition that all men are created equal." Lincoln expressed a view of self-government that the Declaration had not fully embraced and the Constitution had rejected: "Government of the people, by the people, for the people."[5] With this simple declaration, Lincoln rewrote the American idea of freedom.

Lincoln's bold innovation was institutionalized in four documents. In 1863, Lincoln's **Emancipation Proclamation** freed the slaves—but only in areas that were still rebelling. Ironically, Lincoln freed the slaves in the states where he had no power to enforce his decree. The slaves themselves, however, bolted by the thousands toward the Union Army and transformed it, as one historian wrote, into "a reluctant dragon of emancipation." When the Civil War was finally over,

Compromise of 1850:
A complicated compromise over slavery that permitted territories to vote on whether they would be slave or free. It also included a strict fugitive slave law forcing Northerners to return black men and women into bondage and permitted California to enter the Union as a free state.

Dred Scott v. Sandford:
A landmark Supreme Court decision holding that black men could not be citizens under the Constitution of the United States. It created a national uproar.

Emancipation Proclamation:
An executive order issued by President Abraham Lincoln that declared the slaves in all rebel states to be free.

● *African American troops training at Fort Lincoln (Washington, DC) during the Civil War. The Emancipation Proclamation spurred an estimated 200,000 former slaves to fight for the Union.*

Congress wrote three "Civil War amendments" that gave full legal force to Lincoln's new birth of freedom.[6]

The *Thirteenth Amendment,* ratified in 1865, abolished slavery.

The *Fourteenth Amendment,* ratified in 1868, made anyone born in the United States, crucially including former slaves, a U.S. citizen. The central passage of the Fourteenth Amendment comes in its declaration that *no state shall "deprive any person of life, liberty or property without due process of law; nor deny to any person . . . the equal protection of the laws."* Through this language, as we saw in Chapter 4, the Fourteenth Amendment applied the federal Constitution and the Bill of Rights to the states. The key phrase—the **equal protection of the laws**—would become a core legal weapon in the battle for civil rights. It might be the single most important addition to the Constitution in the last two hundred years. It forbids any law designed to harm a group.

Equal protection of the laws:
The landmark phrase in the Fourteenth Amendment that requires equal treatment for all citizens.

The *Fifteenth Amendment,* ratified in 1870, guarantees the right to vote: "The right of citizens . . . to vote . . . shall not be denied . . . on account of race, color, or previous condition of servitude." Do you notice what is not mentioned? Gender. Women had reasoned that because they were citizens, their right to vote should not be "denied or abridged," but the Supreme Court rejected this interpretation in 1875.

Freedom Fails

What happened to the former slaves? The era after the Civil War began with soaring hopes—and ended bitterly. Black families that had been torn apart during slavery joyously reunited. African Americans formed communities, organized churches, voted, entered politics, and demanded respect from their former owners. Two African Americans were elected to the U.S. Senate and twenty-one to the House of Representatives. However, black empowerment met fierce resistance. Some whites were outraged when the freedmen no longer stepped aside on the sidewalks; many whites faced economic hardship, even ruin, after their land was destroyed and their labor force had disappeared.

Southern state and local governments reacted by passing *black codes.* These regulations tied blacks to the land, restricted their movements, and stripped them of rights like voting, owning guns, and buying property. Legal restrictions were backed up by the violent Ku Klux Klan (KKK), which sought to intimidate former slaves and prevent them from exercising their new rights.

Reconstruction: The failed effort, pursued by Northerners and Southerners, to rebuild the South and establish racial equality after the Civil War.

For a time, Congress supported the former slaves. In an effort known as **Reconstruction**, it tried to rebuild the South around a vision of racial justice. Congress organized a *Freedmen's Bureau* to assist the former slaves. The Civil Rights Act of 1866 guaranteed African Americans the same property rights as white Americans; the Civil Rights Act of 1875 limited private racial discrimination in hotels, restaurants, and theaters.

However, dreams of racial equality began to slip away. The North, weary of the conflict, withdrew the army from the South in 1877. Congress repealed the laws that implemented the Civil War amendments; no national mechanism was left to enforce "the equal protection of the laws." In the *Civil Rights Cases* of 1883, the Supreme Court struck down the Civil Rights Act of 1875, ruling that Congress did not have the authority to stop private discrimination. It took eighty-nine years before the Civil Rights Act of 1964 would find a way around this barrier.[7]

By the 1890s, the state governments had gutted the Fifteenth Amendment right to vote. *Grandfather clauses* forbade people from voting if their grandfathers had not voted; obviously, if a person's grandfather was a slave, he did not vote. Poll taxes required voters to pay a fee that most black people could not afford. **Literacy tests** required voters to read and interpret any passage in the state constitution. These new rules did what violence and intimidation had failed to accomplish—they drove blacks out of politics. African Americans have been the only group in any democracy, notes political scientist Richard Valelly, to enter the electorate and then be cast out all over again.[8]

The white majority built a system of segregation known as **Jim Crow** (named after minstrel shows in which white singers and dancers blackened their faces and pretended to be Africans). Jim Crow laws segregated the races. African Americans could not go to white schools, play in the park, visit the zoo (Thursday eventually became "black day" at many zoos), eat at a white restaurant, stay in a white hotel, drink from a white fountain, go to a white hospital, pray in a white church, or vote.

● Among the brutal techniques used to deny African Americans their civil rights, lynching was the most horrific. Organized white mobs tortured and killed blacks—then left their bodies hanging from a tree or lamppost for days, as a warning to others who might advocate civil rights or racial equality. Here, a 1930s lynching in Indiana.

In 1896, the Supreme Court ruled in ***Plessy v. Ferguson*** that there was nothing inherently discriminatory in requiring separate but equal facilities for the black and white races. "If one race be inferior to the other socially," wrote the majority, "the Constitution of the United States cannot put them upon the same plane." In practice, the facilities were separate but not at all equal.[9]

The entire system of segregation was held in place by the raw brutality of lynching—the ritualized murders of black men (and occasionally women) who had violated the codes. These murders were not crimes of mob passion but organized killings with police directing traffic around the scene and white families posing for pictures around the victim's mutilated body. They served as a horrific way to enforce racial separation. The *Negro Year Book* recorded 1,799 blacks lynched between 1882 and 1920.[10] The white majority directed extraordinary fury at men and women who fell in love across the racial divide—interracial couples threatened the entire structure of segregation.[11]

How could the majority accept such repression? Once again, the white majority repeated a false story about black men's supposed sexual lust for white women. Novels, plays, and films portrayed dangerous black men threatening white women and white culture. The story in its most blatant form provided the plot for one of the seminal works in cinematic history. *The Birth of a Nation* (1915) features lust-filled black men, backed by federal troops, menacing white women until the KKK saves the day. In one of the film's last triumphant scenes, the Klan disarms the skulking black men and stops them from voting. Woodrow Wilson screened the film in the White House, and it became one of the top-grossing films of all time.[12]

By 1915, the dreams of equality had collapsed, and African Americans were, once again, denied almost all of their civil rights. Another generation—black and white together—would have to take up the fight again.

Literacy test: A requirement that voters be literate; in reality, a way to restrict black suffrage.

Jim Crow: The system of racial segregation in the U.S. South that lasted from 1890 to 1965, and that was often violently enforced.

Plessy v. Ferguson: An 1896 Supreme Court case that permitted racial segregation.

see for yourself 6.1

Go online to see clips from *The Birth of a Nation*.

» The clash over slavery eventually led Lincoln to redefine the American idea of self-rule: "Government of the people, by the people, for the people."

» *Institutional changes* marked the rise and fall of civil rights. The president issued the Emancipation Proclamation, Congress passed the Civil Rights Acts, and the states ratified the Thirteenth, Fourteenth, and Fifteenth Amendments.

» The Fourteenth Amendment contains the crucial legal rule for civil rights: "No state shall . . . deprive any person of . . . the equal protection of the laws."

» Later, courts struck down some civil rights laws, Congress repealed laws implementing the Civil War amendments, and the states introduced segregation, which the Supreme Court accepted.

» However, it was *culture*—the terrible stories that white Americans told about their fellow citizens—that fixed the new legal chains in place by inducing the majority to ignore the violations of black rights.

The Fight for Racial Equality

A great population shift marked the next civil rights movement. Beginning in the 1910s, many African Americans left the South and moved to factory jobs in the northern cities—a journey known as the **Great Migration**. By the 1950s, 40 percent of the black population lived in the North, where they faced a different kind of racial discrimination.

Great Migration: The vast movement of African Americans from the rural South to the urban North between 1910 and the 1960s.

Two Types of Discrimination

There are two types of discrimination. Legal discrimination—known as **de jure discrimination**—involves laws that explicitly deny civil rights. By the time the civil rights movement ended, around 1970, Americans had conquered de jure discrimination—an enormous achievement.

De jure discrimination: Discrimination established by laws.

A second type of discrimination—known as "in fact" or **de facto discrimination**—exists without the support of explicit laws and is more subtly embedded in society. De facto discrimination is much harder to address. Today, Americans argue about whether de facto restrictions still exist—and, if so, to what extent.

De facto discrimination: More subtle forms of discrimination that exist without a legal basis.

The Modern Civil Rights Campaign Begins

In 1909, black leaders formed the **National Association for the Advancement of Colored People**, or **NAACP**, and began fighting segregation. During the 1920s and 1930s, they unsuccessfully lobbied the federal government for an anti-lynching bill, protested demeaning images of black men and women in popular culture, and fought for equal inclusion in New Deal programs. In 1941, they finally won the first executive order on race since Reconstruction. President Franklin Roosevelt signed an order barring racial discrimination by defense contractors and created the Fair Employment Practices Committee to ensure compliance. What pushed Roosevelt to act? Black leaders, led by A. Philip Randolph,

National Association for the Advancement of Colored People (NAACP): A civil rights organization formed in 1909 and dedicated to racial equality.

threatened to organize a massive protest march on Washington just as the United States was gearing up to fight the racist Nazi regime in World War II.

Over one hundred thousand black troops fought in the war only to be greeted by racism when they returned home. They added their voices to the call for equality—and helped change the American cultural image of black people. In 1948, Harry Truman desegregated the armed forces, making the military the first racially integrated institution in the United States.

The Courts

The NAACP also went to court and chipped away at Jim Crow laws enforcing segregation. Democratic President Franklin Roosevelt (1933–44) appointed eight Supreme Court Justices during his twelve years in office. The result: a Court sympathetic to blacks' civil-rights claims. In 1944, the Supreme Court struck down the all-white Democratic primary in *Smith v. Allright*, rejecting the idea that a political party was a private organization and could discriminate if it wished to.[13] The Court struck down segregation in many venues—including interstate buses, law schools, and graduate schools—and then took a monumental step.[14]

In May 1954, in ***Brown v. Board of Education***, the Court ruled that segregated schools violated the equal protection clause of the Fourteenth Amendment. In public education, ruled the court, "the doctrine of separate but equal has no place." Separate facilities were inherently unequal.[15]

The media presented *Brown* as a momentous decision. The follow-up to the ruling, however, was far less dramatic: almost nothing changed. The Court did not impose a strong timetable or implementation plan. National officials did little to support *Brown*, and state and local leaders did much to oppose it. A decade after *Brown*, less than 1 percent of the schools in the South had been desegregated.

Where desegregation did occur the results could be explosive. The day before schools opened in 1957, Governor Orval Faubus came out against the desegregation of Central High School in Little Rock, Arkansas. The Arkansas National Guard turned away the nine high school students who tried to enter the school the next day.

The governor backed off in the face of a court order. When the African American students came back two weeks later, the National Guard had been replaced by what the *New York Times* called "a mob of belligerent, shrieking

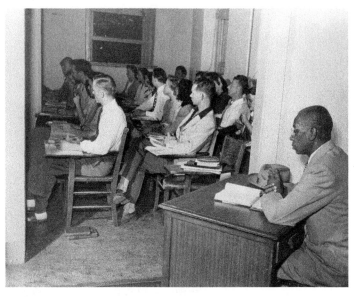

"Separate but equal" for George McLaurin meant a desk in the hallway. McLaurin, who was pursuing his PhD at the University of Oklahoma, sued the university, and the Supreme Court ruled against segregated classes in graduate school.

Brown v. Board of Education: The landmark Supreme Court case that struck down segregated schools as unconstitutional.

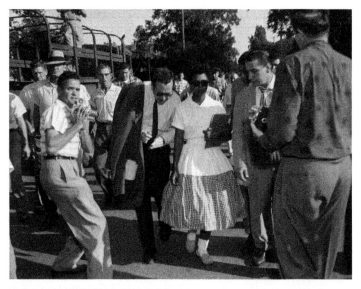

Elizabeth Eckford, one of nine black teens who integrated Little Rock High School in 1957, had to brave a gauntlet of screaming whites.

hysterical demonstrators" shouting racial epithets. President Dwight Eisenhower, a Republican, reluctantly dispatched the 101st Airborne to enforce the court order and desegregate Central High.

Elected officials throughout the South could not help but notice that Governor Faubus had become a local hero among whites and was returned to office for an unprecedented third term. Many white politicians reacted by staunchly supporting segregation. Years later, some white protesters would try and reconcile with the black students they had jeered, and some local politicians would regret what they had said and done. But it was clear at the time that, without political support, even a major court decision like *Brown v. Board of Education* could neither crack segregation nor integrate the schools.

The Civil Rights Movement

What defeated segregation was not the Supreme Court or the paratroopers from the 101st Airborne, but ordinary American people who rose up and seized the moment. There had been scattered demonstrations throughout the country for years, but the organized movement began in Montgomery, Alabama, on a December afternoon in 1955.

Rosa Parks was riding the bus home. The white section filled up, and when a white man got on board, the driver called out that the whites needed another row. Everyone in the first black row was expected to get up. Parks refused to relinquish her seat and was arrested. The local NAACP called a boycott of the Montgomery bus lines and put twenty-six-year-old Martin Luther King, Jr. in charge. That night, King addressed thousands of people from the pulpit of the Holt Street Baptist Church and launched a campaign of Christian nonviolence.[16]

It took more than a year and direct intervention by the Supreme Court to desegregate the buses in Montgomery. But the pattern was set: The Court had opened the legal door. Protesters braved arrest, scorn, and violence to win change on the ground.

In February 1960, four black college students from North Carolina A&T University sat at a white lunch counter and inspired a tactic that spread throughout the South. Within a year, seventy thousand people—black and white—had sat at segregated counters while onlookers jeered, poured ketchup on the sitters, and held cigarette lighters to the women's hair. From lunch counters, the sit-ins spread to movie theaters, parks, pools, art galleries, libraries, and churches.

In 1961, activists came up with a new tactic. Groups of young people rented Greyhound buses and drove as **Freedom Riders** to protest segregated interstate bus lines and terminals. The first bus was pursued by a "citizens' posse" and set ablaze. Angry men tried to hold the doors of the burning bus shut, and the students narrowly escaped—only to get a vicious beating with bats and pipes.

Despite the protests, segregation *still* did not yield. The stalemate was finally broken in Birmingham, Alabama. Young marchers tumbled out of churches and walked, singing and clapping, straight into appalling police violence. Fire hoses sent them sprawling as police dogs

Freedom Riders: Black and white activists who rode buses together to protest segregation on interstate bus lines.

● The civil rights movement took courage. Here, protesters sitting at a whites-only lunch counter have been taunted and doused with ketchup.

snapped and bit. Television blazed the images around the world. The police overreaction horrified the nation.

The Democratic Party at the time was divided between northern liberals and southern segregationists. The Kennedy administration was reluctant to embrace civil rights for it did not want to lose support from Southern Democrats. The images from Birmingham forced the issue, and the administration finally submitted strong civil rights legislation to Congress.

A major obstacle for all civil rights activists is the **free rider problem**. Civil rights protesters faced dog bites, criminal prosecution, and even death; those who stood on the sideline reaped the same political benefits without any risks. Yet, in the early 1960s, hundreds of thousands of Americans (including many whites) ignored cost-benefit calculations and joined protests and marches. Why did they put themselves in harm's way? Was it the idea of freedom? Their moral convictions? Or perhaps it was the communal exuberance of fighting for something larger than themselves.

● Freedom Riders narrowly escaped the burning bus—only to be beaten bloody.

Free rider problem:
A barrier to group or collective action arising because people who do not participate still reap the benefits.

Congress and the Civil Rights Act

Despite the protests, Congress blocked civil rights legislation—as it had done many times in the past. This time, however, activists prevailed. In May and June 1963, a great wave of protests followed Birmingham. Media stories about demonstrations, violence, and arrests fostered a sense of crisis. The **1963 March on Washington** marked the high point of the peaceful protest movement; the entire nation watched Martin Luther King put aside his prepared text and declare, "I have a dream."

In November 1963, President Kennedy was assassinated, and the Civil Rights Act became, as President Lyndon Johnson would put it, a martyr's cause. The **Civil Rights Act of 1964** was powerful legislation. It forbade state and local governments from denying access to public facilities on the basis of race, color, or national origin. The law prohibited employers from discriminating on similar grounds, and barred discrimination in private motels, hotels, theaters, and other public accommodations. There would be no more "black Thursdays" at city zoos or whites-only water fountains. Congress relied on its Constitutional authority over interstate commerce to forbid private businesses from discriminating—no more restaurants or hotels that served only whites.

Opponents sued, claiming that private businesses such as motels should be free to choose their own patrons. The Supreme Court ruled that because motels served people from other states, Congress could use its power over interstate commerce to stop owners from discriminating. Ollie's Barbecue in Birmingham, Alabama, did not have patrons from other states. However, in *Katzenbach v. McClung*, the Court ruled that because it received supplies through interstate commerce, it too fell under congressional jurisdiction. The era when traveling African Americans had to sleep in their cars was finally over.[17]

The Civil Rights Act also empowered the federal government to withhold funds from segregated schools. In less than a decade the number of southern schoolchildren in integrated schools jumped from almost none to over 90 percent (see Figure 6.2). Today, court decisions on civil rights continue to cite this blockbuster legislation.

1963 March on Washington:
A massive rally for civil rights that included Martin Luther King's "I Have a Dream" speech.

Civil Rights Act of 1964:
Landmark legislation that forbade discrimination on the basis of race, sex, religion, or national origin.

see for yourself 6.2

Go online to see Martin Luther King's "I Have a Dream" speech.

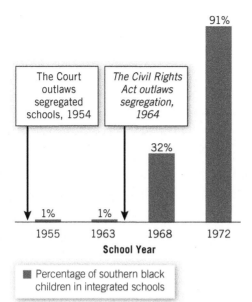

The following year, Congress passed the Voting Rights Act of 1965. This law protected the right to vote, struck down voter suppression tactics like the literacy test, and empowered the attorney general and the U.S. District Court of Washington, DC, to weigh any voting change in suspect areas for its potentially discriminatory effect. The legislation effectively secured the Fifteenth Amendment guaranteeing the right to vote. African Americans surged to the ballot boxes, and in their wake came black elected officials (see Table 6.1). Over time, the number of elected black officials skyrocketed—increasing 129-fold in forty years. However, African Americans, who comprise over 12 percent of the American population, still make up only about 2 percent of all elected officials.

● **FIGURE 6.2** *The Civil Rights Act of 1964—rather than the* Brown v. Board of Education *Supreme Court decision in 1954—led to rapid integration of southern schools.*

Divisions in the Movement

In the summer of 1964 alone, eighty civil rights workers were beaten in Mississippi, four were killed, and more than a thousand were arrested. The unrelenting violence eventually provoked a backlash. After the relentless hostility, harassment, and violence, many activists rejected nonviolent protest and seized instead on **black power**—the idea that African Americans should forget about integration and empower the black community to act on its own. The civil rights movement split over strategy: some continued to follow King and his campaign of nonviolent protest. Groups such as the Black Panthers armed themselves and vowed to answer violence with violence. Still others, like the Nation of Islam, sought separation from whites.

Black power: A slogan that emphasized pride in black heritage and the construction of black institutions to nurture black interests. It often implied racial separation in reaction to white racism.

Eventually, years of frustration burst into urban riots—also known as insurrections—between 1964 and 1969. The deadliest erupted in Los Angeles in August 1965 (34 deaths) and Detroit in July 1967 (43 deaths). Most outbursts had a local cause—often incidents involving all-white police forces. White liberals who had energetically supported civil rights began to turn away from the movement. The era of civil rights gave way to a desire for "law and order"—a slogan that presidential candidate Richard Nixon used to great effect on the campaign trail in 1968.

TABLE 6.1 **Total Number of Black Elected Officials**

	1964	1970	1980	1990	2016
Mayors	0	81	205	314	600 (est.)
Members of Congress	5	9	19	19	48
Total black elected officials in the United States	70	1,469	4,914	7,370	More than 10,500 (est.)
Sources: Congressional Research Service; African American Mayors' Association; Joint Center for Political Studies					

» The NAACP won a series of cases against segregation, culminating in *Brown v. Board of Education*; however, implementation proved difficult.

» In the early 1960s, ordinary men, women, and children—black and white—organized in mass movements to turn the legal promise of the *Brown* decision into a practical reality. As the images from marches became more dramatic, surging public opinion pushed Congress to pass the Civil Rights Act of 1964 and the Voting Rights Act of 1965.

» Taken together, these institutional changes ended de jure segregation in the United States.

» The black movement set the model for future civil rights campaigns by many other groups.

The Post Civil Rights Era

After the successful challenge to *de jure* segregation, civil rights reformers faced the perplexing problems of subtle, *de facto* discrimination. Protesters can kneel in front of a segregated church, but how do they challenge dead-end jobs and shabby neighborhoods?

Affirmative Action in the Workplace

In the 1960s and 1970s, a new approach emerged to assist groups that had faced discrimination. **Affirmative action** involves direct, positive steps to increase the representation (especially in schools and workplaces) of groups that have faced discrimination in the past. The strategy started with race and then grew to redress other forms of discrimination, such as those based on gender and ethnicity. The goal is *equality of opportunity*—giving each person the same chance to achieve success.

Affirmative action: Direct steps to recruit members of previously underrepresented groups into schools and jobs.

Litigation and legislation pushed affirmative action forward. Because it was difficult to prove discrimination in any one hiring decision, the Supreme Court propounded a doctrine called **disproportionate impact** in 1971. Companies could not use hiring or promotion mechanisms that created, as the Court put it, "'built-in headwinds' for minority groups [that] are unrelated to measuring job capability." A company with no minority managers would be suspected of those "built-in headwinds."[18]

Disproportionate impact: The effect some policies have of discriminating, even if discrimination is not consciously intended.

Affirmative action raises difficult issues. It appears to guarantee *equality of outcome*: reserving jobs or opportunities for individuals based on their race or gender. Is this necessary to right past wrongs? If so, for how long? And are these remedies—extended to minorities and women—unfair to white men?

Affirmative action soon sparked a backlash and the Supreme Court began to narrow its use. In 1986, the Court warned that such programs could be used only in cases of "severe discrimination" and should not "trammel the interests of white employees."[19] By 1995, a more conservative Court rejected the entire idea of explicitly setting aside places for members of racial groups.[20]

In cities like Boston, the school busing program led to protests, riots, and even killings. In 1976, these protesters attacked Ted Landsmark, an African American attorney.

In 2009, the New Haven, Connecticut, fire department began requiring a written exam for promotions. The top scorers on the test were all white. If the city accepted the test results, black and Hispanic firefighters could sue under disproportionate impact, arguing that the test created "headwinds" unrelated to fighting fires. When New Haven threw out the results, white firefighters who had scored well on the test sued. The Court agreed, 5–4, that New Haven should not have dismissed the results. The case is difficult because both sides have a good argument: The New Haven fire department needs diverse leadership, but ignoring the test results seems unfair to the individuals who did well.

Affirmative Action in Education

Civil rights advocates believed that if children from different races and ethnicities went to school together, they would shed the prejudices that marked their parents and grandparents. The problem, however, was that because many children lived in single-race neighborhoods, local schools were inevitably segregated. One solution, known as **school busing**, aimed to achieve racial integration by driving students to other neighborhoods. Busing declined after the 1980s, but observers still disagree about whether the effort was a noble and often-successful experiment in getting young children over the racial divisions of the past or a disastrous mistake that whipped up racial animosity by using children to right old social wrongs.

School busing: An effort to integrate public schools by mixing students from different neighborhoods.

What Do You Think?

Higher Education and Affirmative Action

One of the most difficult problems in politics is how to make up for past injustice. What do we, as a society, owe to groups who have faced violence and discrimination for many generations? Consider higher education—the path to success in contemporary society. Which of the following positions would you support?

I favor affirmative action *for as long as it takes.* People who have faced many years of discrimination deserve affirmative action in education for as long as it takes for members of the group to catch up to the rest of society.

I favor affirmative action *with an end in sight*. People who have faced discrimination should get affirmative action in higher education for a fixed period. But how long should that period run? In *Grutter v. Bollinger* (2003), the Supreme Court implied that the correct period should last roughly three generations, or sixty years (1965–2025). Do you agree? If not, how much time would you allow?

I favor affirmative action only *if it doesn't set back others*. People who have faced discrimination should get special educational opportunities if and only if it does not harm other people's chances. Can you think of some ways to do this?

I am against affirmative action once discrimination has ended. Even if a group has faced past discrimination, its members should not get any special treatment. Once the discrimination ends, they must compete like everyone else. But how do you measure the end of discrimination? By the passage of a law or by practice in society?

Another controversy arose over affirmative action programs that reserved places in universities for members of minority groups. Many schools sought to make up for past discrimination and at the same time enhance the diversity of their student body. These quotas, too, created a backlash.

One landmark education case focused on the medical school at the University of California at Davis, which held sixteen places in its entering class of one hundred for members of minority or economically disadvantaged groups. Allan Bakke, a white man who had been rejected by the medical school, sued, arguing that his academic scores were higher than the scores of minority applicants who had been accepted. In a 5–4 decision in *University of California v. Bakke* (1978), the Supreme Court ruled in favor

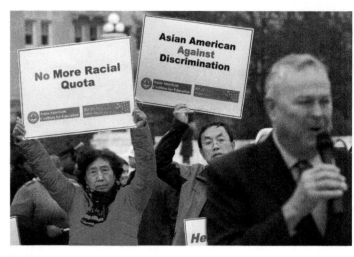

● *Protesters outside the Supreme Court challenge the University of Texas plan to expand diversity. In* Fisher v. The University of Texas *(2016), the Court upheld the Texas affirmative action program.*

of Bakke; setting a quota, as the university had done, violated the equal protection guarantee of the Fourteenth Amendment. Although the Court barred racial quotas, it accepted the use of race as a "plus" factor in the admissions process. After years of litigation, in 2016 the Court narrowly upheld the use of affirmative action in college/university admissions decisions.[21]

The Court has painfully picked its way through the minefield of equal opportunity. Crucial questions abound: How does a nation make up for past discrimination? How much is owed to people who have been terribly mistreated for generations? How long should preferential programs last? And what about people who feel they are losing out today because of efforts to address past injustice?

THE BOTTOM LINE

» To make up for past discrimination, legislatures and courts turned to affirmative action in the 1960s and 1970s. Employers and schools that had previously excluded Hispanics, Native Americans, or African Americans now set aside places for them.

» The courts initially sponsored affirmative action programs but are increasingly skeptical of any race-based categories, including those designed to ameliorate past injustice.

Women's Rights

In the early nineteenth century, an American woman had no political rights. She could not vote, serve on a jury, or enter into a contract after marriage. Her husband controlled her property, her wages, and even her body. Husband and wife are one, mused Justice Hugo Black, and "that one is the husband."

Suffrage

The struggle for women's rights in the United States has been interconnected with the fight for racial equality. When women joined the abolition movement, they quickly grew frustrated by the barriers that confronted them. They could lecture to women but not men (for that would be "promiscuous"); they could join abolitionist societies but not be elected officers.[22] The first American gathering for women's suffrage, the 1848 **Seneca Falls Convention**, grew directly from the gender barriers in the abolition movement.

Seneca Falls Convention: The first convention dedicated to women's rights, held in July 1848 in Seneca Falls, NY.

In the 1870s, the women's movement gained momentum. The Women's Christian Temperance Union attacked alcohol as a cause of male violence against women. It championed voluntary motherhood (no more marital rape), suffrage for women, and decent wages. Two other groups focused on winning the vote. Led by Carrie Chapman Catt, the American Woman Suffrage Association emphasized winning voting rights state by state. The National American Woman Suffrage Association (NAWSA), galvanized by Alice Paul, fought for a constitutional amendment that would give every American woman the right to vote.

Success came first in the West, beginning with the Wyoming and Utah Territories, which granted women the vote in 1869 and 1870, respectively. By 1916, women voted in every state of the West and Midwest except New Mexico. The issue remained contentious, however. Four northern states voted to reject suffrage during the 1916 presidential election, and the South remained strongly opposed for fear that women would oppose segregation (see Figure 6.3).

During World War I, women took on new roles throughout the economy. Led by Alice Paul and NAWSA, they increased the pressure for suffrage. Paul was jailed for her activism. Eventually, President Woodrow Wilson grudgingly supported suffrage as a "wartime measure." The Nineteenth Amendment—giving women the right to vote—cleared Congress over stiff opposition in the Senate and was ratified by the states in 1920.

● **FIGURE 6.3** *Before the Nineteenth Amendment, women had full voting rights in the West, limited rights in the Midwest, and almost none in the South and East. For women, winning the vote took a difficult political campaign that lasted more than eighty years.*

Although they had secured suffrage, women were slow to win political office. In the first fifty years after the amendment, only three women were elected to the U.S. Senate for full terms. During the 1970s–80s, beginning at the local level and reaching Congress in the 1990s, the number of women officeholders soared (see Figure 6.4).

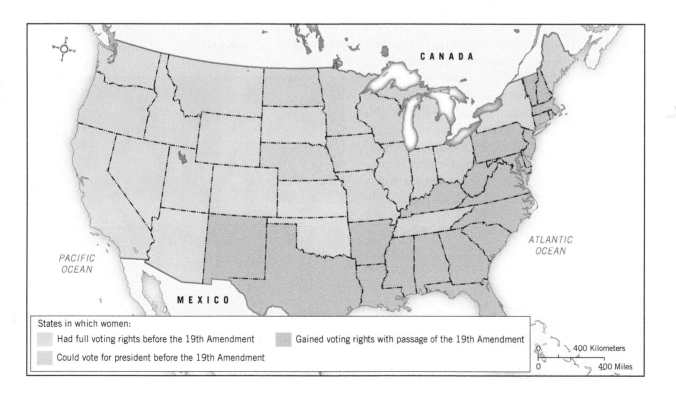

States in which women:
Had full voting rights before the 19th Amendment
Gained voting rights with passage of the 19th Amendment
Could vote for president before the 19th Amendment

Women in state legislatures, 1971–present

Despite these gains, the United States in 2016 ranked 94th worldwide in the percentage of women in its legislature (see Comparing Nations 6.1). In the United States, people decide for themselves whether to run for office—regardless of what party leaders think. Women are less likely than men to leap into the contest. When they decide to run, they are more likely to face opponents from their own party in the primaries. The good news is that women who do run win just as often as men do.[23]

The Civil Rights Act of 1964

The breakthrough in the struggle for gender rights slipped into the Civil Rights Act of 1964. This landmark law, as we have seen, was designed to bar racial discrimination. Congressman Howard Smith, a segregationist from Virginia, proposed adding a single word—"sex"—to the legislation with the hopes of making a mockery of the entire bill and killing it. The tactic did not work, and the Civil Rights Act passed, barring discrimination based on "race, color, religion, *sex* and national origin."

At the time, no one predicted that the gender provision in the Civil Rights Act would have the same far-reaching consequences for gender rights as *Brown v. Board of Education* had for African Americans—but it did. As with the Supreme Court decisions on race, the Civil Rights Act merely opened the door to gender change. The women's movement had to seize the opportunity.

At first, officials ignored the gender provision. The **Equal Employment Opportunity Commission** (**EEOC**), which monitored compliance with the Civil Rights Act, considered it a "mischievous joke perpetrated on the floor of the House of Representatives." In response, a network of women organized the **National Organization for Women** (**NOW**), drawing directly on the tactics of the civil rights campaign—demonstrations, rallies, lobbying, and litigation.

Congress and the EEOC began to pay attention. For example, in 1972, Congress passed federal education amendments that denied federal

● **FIGURE 6.4** *Number of women in state legislatures. Note the steep rise in the 1970s–1980s and the leveling out after 1992.*

Equal Employment Opportunity Commission (EEOC): Federal law enforcement agency charged with monitoring compliance with the Civil Rights Act.

National Organization for Women (NOW): An organization formed in 1966 to take action for women's equality.

● *The cheering players and fans do not realize how the Civil Rights Act changed their world.*

COMPARING NATIONS 6.1	Percentage of Women in National Legislatures: Selected Countries	
WORLD NATION % WOMEN IN RANK		**LOWER (POPULAR) HOUSE**
1	Rwanda	63.80
2	Bolivia	53.10
3	Cuba	48.90
11	Iceland	41.30
26	Germany	36.50
48	United Kingdom	29.60
53	Afghanistan	27.70
62	Iraq	26.50
64	Canada	26.00
73	China	23.60
85	Pakistan	20.60
97	Kyrgyzstan	19.20
98	United States	19.10
117	North Korea	16.30
129	Venezuela	14.40
136	Russia	13.60
143	India	12.00
157	Japan	9.50
175	Iran	5.90
187	Yemen, Qatar	0.00

Many countries outdistance the United States in the percentage of women in national legislatures: note Saudi Arabia, where women are not allowed to drive, a few places ahead of the United States. (Source: Inter-Parliamentary Union; authors' compilation.)

funds for programs that discriminated against women (Title VI) and that required equal athletic opportunities for men and women (Title IX). Underfunded women's sports programs began getting the same treatment as the men's varsity programs.

Notice how a single piece of legislation can have far-reaching consequences. The next time you watch a women's basketball game on national television, thank Congressman Smith for dropping the word "*sex*" into the Civil Rights Act of 1964.

Equal Rights Amendment

The politics of Civil Rights spilled into other areas of gender politics. Feminists had introduced an **Equal Rights Amendment** (**ERA**) in Congress every year between 1924 and 1972. The amendment was simple: "Equality of rights under the law shall not be denied . . . on account of sex." By 1972, it had become uncontroversial, and Congress passed it by lopsided margins. Five years later, the ERA was just three states short of ratification. Then Phyllis Schlafly, a Republican activist from Florida, organized the STOP ERA movement. Schlafly argued that the ERA threatened traditional family life. "What the libbers don't understand," said Schlafly, is "that most women want to be a wife, mother, and homemaker."[24] By **reframing the issue**, Schlafly stopped the Equal Rights Amendment in its tracks. The ERA legislation is still reintroduced every year in Congress—but it has not even come to a vote in over thirty years. Eleven states have passed their own Equal Rights Amendments.

The Courts

The women's movement also echoed the black civil rights movement in targeting the courts. Led by Ruth Bader Ginsburg (now a Supreme Court justice), advocates challenged discriminatory state laws, case by case. Because gender was a *nonsuspect category*, the courts upheld any state law as long as it had some "rational connection to a legitimate state purpose." In a series of cases, culminating in *Craig v. Boren* in 1976, the Court lifted gender into a new category of *heightened scrutiny*—not as rigorous a test as the scrutiny the courts give racial classifications, but a more rigorous test than that applied to other social groups. Ironically, the case—a major victory for women's rights—involved men challenging an Oklahoma statute that set the drinking age for beer as eighteen for women and twenty-one for men.

The courts also applied the prohibition on gender discrimination in the Civil Rights Act to sexual harassment. In 1998, the Supreme Court expanded the protection by ruling that an employee did not have to prove a specific instance of sexual harassment if there was a hostile workplace environment, which might include sexual advances, lewd comments, or general attitudes. The Court ruled that even if employers were not aware of specific instances of harassment, they remained liable for the general culture of the workplace.

Women's advocates raised the issue of differential pay more than a century ago. Today, women working full time earn, on average, four-fifths as much as men—although the exact amount of the disparity is hotly disputed and varies from 75 percent to 95 percent, depending on the methodology.[25] In a famous case, Lilly Ledbetter sued after a nineteen-year career as a supervisor with Goodyear Tire Company because she had been paid less than men in the same position. A jury found Goodyear guilty of pay discrimination, but the Supreme Court reversed the judgment by a 5–4 vote. The majority ruled that Ledbetter should have sued within 180 days after Goodyear set her pay—long before she knew about the salary differential. In 2009, President Obama signed equal-pay legislation—known as the Lilly Ledbetter Act—that permits an employee to sue 180 days from her last paycheck (resetting the clock each time she gets a lower paycheck).[26]

Recent Supreme Court decisions, however, have made it more difficult to sue businesses for discrimination. In a major case decided in 2011, the court turned down a **class action** suit brought against Wal-Mart. The suit alleged that the

Equal Rights Amendment: An amendment, originally drafted by Alice Paul in 1923, passed by Congress in 1972, and ratified by thirty-five states, that declared: "Equality of rights . . . shall not be denied or abridged . . . on account of sex."

Reframe the issue: To redefine the popular perception of an issue; to show it in a new light with a new set of costs or benefits.

Class action: A lawsuit filed on behalf of an entire category of individuals, such as all people in public housing in a state or all the female managers of a large company.

TABLE 6.2 Women CEOs of *Fortune 500* Companies

Year	2000	2005	2010	2016
Women CEOs	3	9	15	22

company systematically discriminated against women by offering them less pay and fewer promotions. The Supreme Court ruled—once again by a 5–4 margin—that simply showing that women received less pay was not enough to prove discrimination. Rather, the plaintiffs (the women suing) needed to demonstrate a specific company-wide policy that set lower wages for all the women involved in the class action.[27]

Progress for Women—But How Much?

There had never been a woman Supreme Court justice until Ronald Reagan named Sandra Day O'Connor to the bench in 1981; today, three of the nine justices are women. In 1964, 9% of American women got bachelor's degrees (compared to 16% of men); today 37% of women do (and just 30% of men). There had never been a woman CEO of a Fortune 500 company until 1972. In 2000, the number had inched to three. By 2016, 22 women were heading Fortune 500 companies—a still not very inspiring 4.4% (see Table 6.2).

Gender politics raise provocative questions about social roles and power. When women demanded the right to vote in the mid-nineteenth century, they met anger and violence. Today, issues such as abortion, equality, and women's rights in the workplace continue to generate conflict.

Once again, American society has witnessed extraordinary progress. The American dream seems alive and well. At the same time, we still have a long way to go to reach gender equality—in many ways the American dream remains an aspiration more than a reality.

What Do You Think?

Reproductive Politics

When birth control pills went on the market in 1960, they seemed revolutionary. For many women, reported *Time* magazine, "the pill spells freedom from fear."[28] Four years later, the Supreme Court struck down bans on condoms. Controlling pregnancy made professional careers easier to manage. Reproductive rights became far more controversial when the Supreme Court ruled, in *Roe v. Wade* (1973), that laws banning abortion violated a woman's right to privacy. The decision sparked intense political reaction on both sides. Some women organized to defend *Roe v. Wade*; others entered politics to fight it.

A basic right! Legal abortions are an essential part of gender equality and should be protected. It is not right that women in some states enjoy genuine choice while those in other states face many barriers and few providers.

A Balancing Act! States should decide how to balance protection of the unborn with a woman's right to choose. It makes sense that more conservative states introduce more restrictions.

No Right At All. I do not believe women have a right to privacy in this case. I would advocate overruling *Roe v. Wade* and permitting states to outlaw abortion if the majority wishes to do so.

THE
BOTTOM
LINE

» In nineteenth-century law, women's political rights operated through their husbands. When women organized to win rights, they met with ridicule and violence.

» Women first won voting rights in the states—especially in the West and Midwest—before finally securing the Nineteenth Amendment, which guaranteed the right to vote regardless of gender.

» The Civil Rights Act of 1964 bars gender discrimination. As with the civil rights movement of the 1950s and 1960s, the women's movement organized to take advantage of legal changes. The law transformed American gender roles in political and professional life.

» Following *Roe v. Wade* in 1973 and the unsuccessful fight for the Equal Rights Amendment in the mid-1970s, gender politics became especially controversial, spilling into many other issues.

Hispanics

Hispanics, or Latinos (we use the words interchangeably), play a powerful and growing role in American politics and culture. Today, Hispanics are the largest minority group, making up 17.4 percent of the American population—up from just 6.4 percent in 1980.

Latinos have long faced discrimination in the United States. Latinos were already living in the Southwest—in Arizona, California, New Mexico, and parts of Colorado, Nevada, Utah, and Texas—before the United States took those lands from Mexico in 1848. As white settlers poured into the new territories, they often displaced Latino residents from their homes and farms. As the nation urbanized, Latinos were pushed into segregated schools, excluded from jobs, and barred from housing in white neighborhoods. They also faced hostility and violence. During World War II, after sensational newspaper headlines reported that Mexicans had beaten up a sailor, thousands of soldiers and sailors raged through Los Angeles attacking Mexican men. The police did not intervene.

Today, despite enormous success in achieving the American dream, Hispanics still face challenges. They are incarcerated at a much higher rate than white non-Hispanic Americans. They are more likely to be poor, less likely to have health insurance, and underrepresented in almost every political venue.

Challenging Discrimination

Latinos adapted many of the tactics of the black civil rights movement. They organized the League of United Latin American Citizens (LULAC) in 1929. Like the NAACP, the organization fought segregation through lawsuits. In *Mendez v. Westminster*, decided in 1947, the court struck down Latino school segregation in

● *During the early twentieth century, Latinos began to organize for civil rights. This replica of a 1929 Texas restaurant sign helps illustrate why.*

● *Cesar Chavez organized the farm workers.*

Chicanismo: A defiant movement expressing pride in Latino origins and culture in the face of discrimination.

United Farm Workers (UFW): An influential union representing migrant farm workers in the west.

Orange County, California; the case was an important precursor to *Brown v. Board of Education* and involved some of the same lawyers.

During the 1960s, young Latinos launched more active protests. In 1968, high school and college students called a massive student strike that reverberated throughout the Southwest. The students pushed LULAC and other mainstream Latino organizations to fight more aggressively against discrimination and challenged immigration policies that restricted movement across the Mexican border. Many young people took a slur against Mexicans, *Chicano*, and turned it into a movement they labeled **Chicanismo**—a defiant pride in their heritage and culture.

At the same time, the **United Farm Workers** (**UFW**) organized the most vulnerable population—migrant workers who picked crops up and down the West Coast. The UFW became a symbol of Latino mobilization. Throughout the 1960s and 1970s, traditional organizations such as LULAC, activist students, and farm workers challenged discrimination. Their efforts prepared the way for the entry of Latino elected officials into every level of government.

Today, the central questions for Latino politics turn on immigration, language, and—perhaps most important—just how the very diverse Hispanic population might mobilize together for political action.

The Politics of Immigration

Despite Hispanics' long heritage in the land, Hispanic politics is wrapped up with immigration. Although the United States is an immigrant nation, the door to foreigners has historically swung from wide open to shut tight. Restrictions in the 1920s strictly limited immigration—President John Kennedy sadly noted forty years later that America no longer offered a beacon for immigrants. After his assassination, Congress lifted the restrictions, in 1965, and a new era of immigration began. Today, one in eight American residents was born abroad.

Ancient Fears.　Immigrants always trigger the same fears: They will undermine American values and culture; they will take away jobs; they will cling to their own languages, and remain loyal to their countries of origin and their supposedly un-American ideas. Today, this concern has focused especially on Hispanic Americans, by far the largest immigrant group. Republican presidential candidate Donald Trump's attacks on Mexican immigrants set a nasty tone for the 2016 election.

Three Categories.　Immigrant groups fall into three different categories with very different legal claims on civil rights.

1. Those who were born in the United States or have become American citizens (roughly 65 percent of the Latino population) claim the same rights as any citizen. They are in the same protected legal category as African Americans. Any law that singles them out is "suspect" and subject to strict scrutiny by the courts.

2. Foreigners who have not become citizens fall into a second category known as resident aliens. They may work in the United States and they pay taxes, but they cannot enjoy the benefits of citizenship: Aliens may not vote in most elections and many government safety-net programs, such as Medicaid, explicitly exclude them.

3. Some immigrants are unregistered—that is, they are not legal residents of the United States. Many arrived on a temporary visa, got a job, settled down, and simply remained after their legal time in the country expired. Others crossed the borders illegally (more than 330,000 people were caught doing so in 2015, compared to 1.64 million in 1999).[29] Undocumented aliens have no constitutional rights and, when caught, are subject to immediate deportation. The nonpartisan Pew Hispanic Center estimates that the number of undocumented aliens in the United States is 11.3 million (3.5% of the American population) and that three in four are Latino.

Undocumented Immigrants.   The debate over the rights of illegal aliens is intense and often angry. Some argue that undocumented immigrants are part of the American economy and society. They live in fear of jail and deportation. As a result, many are wary of going to a hospital, visiting their children's school, or reporting crimes against them. American policy, proponents of this viewpoint argue, should bring these Americans out of the shadows. We should permit them driver's licenses (12 states, including California, Illinois, and Maryland, plus the District of Columbia currently do so); we ought to encourage them to go to universities (see Figure 6.5). Ultimately, the United States ought to give its undocumented a path to legal status. A movement urges the undocumented to "come out" and announce their immigration status, to show fellow Americans "that we're not taking away from this country but contributing to it."[30]

Opponents respond that the undocumented are breaking the law and should not be rewarded for unlawful behavior. Many argue that immigrants take jobs. Some people feel anxiety about America becoming a majority–minority nation,

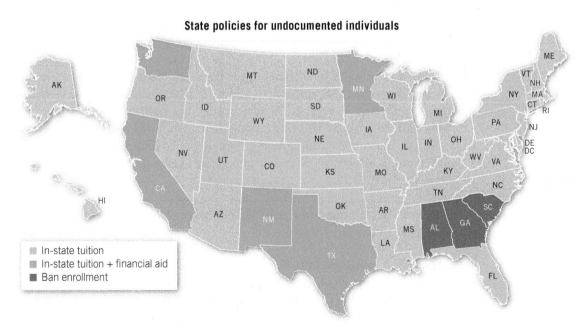

State policies for undocumented individuals

■ In-state tuition
■ In-state tuition + financial aid
■ Ban enrollment

● **FIGURE 6.5** *State higher education policies for undocumented individuals.*

although careful studies show that immigrants tend to work hard and commit fewer crimes than permanent residents.

Even Hispanic citizens whose families have lived on American soil for many generations consider immigration a defining political issue. It has thrust their community into controversy. It leads police to single out Latinos, a practice known as **racial profiling**. Hispanic immigration is a major contributor to the fundamental American question: *Who are we?*

In 2012, President Obama signed an executive order—bypassing a deadlocked Congress—that gave young undocumented aliens temporary work permits and removed the threat of deportation against them. Well over one million undocumented immigrants have benefited from the program; a Supreme Court ruling in 2016 threw into jeopardy the Obama Administration's plan to expand the program. The immigration debate, more than two centuries old, rages on today.

Racial profiling: A law enforcement practice of singling out people on the basis of physical features such as race or ethnicity.

Language Controversy: Speak English!

As long ago as 1752, Benjamin Franklin worried that there were so many Germans in Philadelphia that "instead of them learning our language, we must learn theirs or live as in a foreign country." In recent decades, Spanish language use has become a major issue. In 1974, the Supreme Court ruled in *Lau v. Nichols* that equal protection required schools to assist students whose primary language was not English. Many school districts established bilingual education programs. Opponents argue that bilingual education divides the community, undermines traditional American culture, and disadvantages students who fail to learn English.

Political Mobilization

Hispanic Americans face other challenges. More than one in five live below the poverty line—two and a half times the rate for non-Hispanic whites. They have less health insurance coverage and face tensions with law enforcement.[31]

When they turn to politics to address these issues, Latinos face both barriers and advantages. The biggest barrier lies in the nature of the Hispanic community itself. In fact, *Hispanic* is a misnomer. Hispanic people come from many different places, each with its own interests and concerns (see Figure 6.6).

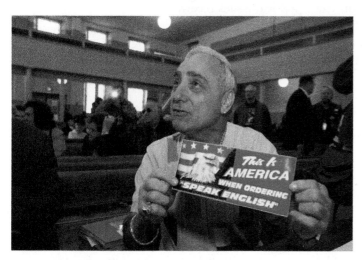

● More than 250 years after Benjamin Franklin expressed his concern, the owner of Geno's Steaks in Philadelphia announces that people should speak English. This is a hot issue—and always has been.

For Mexican Americans, who are concentrated in the Southwest, the politics of immigration looms very large. In contrast, Puerto Ricans, the second-largest Hispanic population in the United States, are American citizens by birth; immigration is less relevant to them. Salvadorans, now the third-largest Latino group, face the problems of more recent immigrants— poverty, social integration, and community building. Cuban Americans offer still another contrast. They have high average incomes and generally do not share the same political concerns as most other Hispanic groups. In fact, Cuban Americans traditionally stand apart by strongly voting Republican—though the youngest generation now breaks evenly between the parties. Dominicans focus on economic and education achievement.

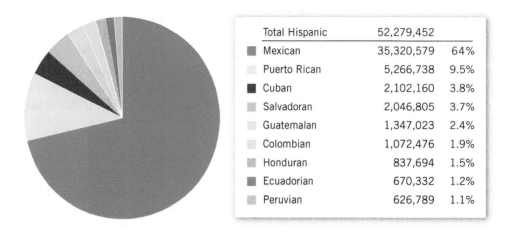

Total Hispanic	52,279,452	
Mexican	35,320,579	64%
Puerto Rican	5,266,738	9.5%
Cuban	2,102,160	3.8%
Salvadoran	2,046,805	3.7%
Guatemalan	1,347,023	2.4%
Colombian	1,072,476	1.9%
Honduran	837,694	1.5%
Ecuadorian	670,332	1.2%
Peruvian	626,789	1.1%

● **FIGURE 6.6** *Countries of origin—Latinos in America. Most Latinos who live in the United States were born here. This figure shows their national heritage. (U.S. Census)*

Is there a common political denominator across this diverse population? Today, a pan-Latino movement seeks to find common ground and mobilize voters around issues that transcend any one country or group. Shared political influence, if Latinos seek to exercise it, figures to be formidable: The Hispanic population has grown three times faster than the general population in the last two decades. Latino leaders note that Mexican American voters moved California decisively into the Democratic column in the last fifteen years.

In 2006, when the Republican-led Congress proposed tough new restrictions on undocumented aliens, massive demonstrations sprang up around the United States. In the past, Latino protesters had waved Mexican flags and symbols. This time, they marched under a sea of American flags. Researchers who were undertaking a major survey of Hispanic Americans at the time discovered that the protests made Hispanics feel significantly more American.[32] After Donald Trump's anti-immigration comments in the 2016 presidential campaign, more than 200,000 Latinos joined an online protest.

The surge in demonstrations reflects the convergence of three important trends: the rapid growth of the Latino population, a sense of shared identity within that population, and an increasing identification with the American homeland. This combination may prove to be one of the most important political developments in future elections, determining not only who gets elected but which political issues receive attention. In the 2016 election, Latinos accounted for roughly 11 percent of the vote and went two to one for Hillary Clinton. Still turnout remained relatively low among Latino voters—posing a major challenge to activists and community leaders.

THE BOTTOM LINE

» Latinos, the largest immigrant group, have been the fastest growing population in the United States; the rate of increase has slowed in recent years.

» Latinos are a diverse people with different national identities, histories, cultures, and concerns. As with African Americans and women, Hispanic Americans have won civil rights advances in recent decades—and suffered setbacks.

» A key political question is whether Latinos will mobilize around shared interests and concerns. If they do, they will become an even more formidable political force.

Asian Americans

Asian Americans are the third-largest minority in the United States after blacks and Hispanics and, according to the U.S. Census Bureau, have for three years been the fastest growing (see Figure 6.7).[33] Unlike Latinos, they do not share a common language; unlike African Americans, they do not share a common historical experience. As you can see from Figure 6.7, Asian Americans range from Indians to Vietnamese, from Koreans to Laotians.

As a group, Asian Americans have the highest education level and the highest median personal income of all American population groups. However, the statistics mask as much as they reveal, for Asian Americans range from Indian Americans with high income and education levels to Hmong from the mountains of Laos with income levels about one-third the U.S. average.

Anti-Asian Discrimination

Asians have a long history of negotiating the complicated American lines between "us" and "them." Among the first Asians to arrive in the United States were Chinese railway workers in the nineteenth century. When the economy deteriorated in the 1880s, American-born workers turned against these immigrants. Congress passed the Chinese Exclusion Act in 1882 barring Chinese immigrants and declaring Chinese people ineligible for citizenship. By 1917, Congress had extended the ban to "all natives of Asia including the whole of India." The California Alien Land Law of 1913 forbade "aliens ineligible for citizenship"—that is, Asian immigrants—from owning land. Each restriction came amid painful stereotypes. The Chinese were excluded because, as one California congressman put it, "His ancestors have bequeathed to him the most hideous immoralities. They . . . are so shocking and horrible that their character cannot even be hinted."[34]

After the Japanese attack on Pearl Harbor in 1941, President Roosevelt ordered the army to round up Japanese Americans and place them in cold, flimsy, miserable internment camps. They lost their liberty, jobs, property, and bank accounts. The Supreme Court upheld the internments.

The wartime camps marked only the most extreme case. San Francisco's Chinatown was the first segregated neighborhood; eventually Chinese Americans, Japanese Americans, and Filipino Americans along with black Americans would all be restricted to limited areas. Schools, too, were segregated. In San Francisco,

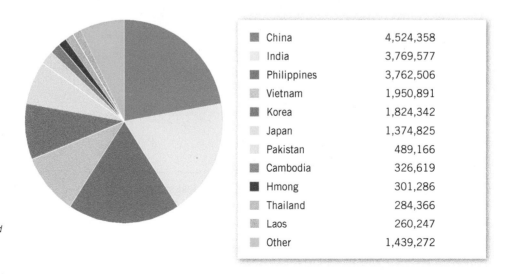

China	4,524,358
India	3,769,577
Philippines	3,762,506
Vietnam	1,950,891
Korea	1,824,342
Japan	1,374,825
Pakistan	489,166
Cambodia	326,619
Hmong	301,286
Thailand	284,366
Laos	260,247
Other	1,439,272

● **FIGURE 6.7** *Countries of origin. The national identities of the 14.9 million residents of the United States who come from an Asian heritage in the last U.S. Census.*

separate schools for Chinese Americans were established in the 1880s and maintained until the *Brown* decision. Across the United States, Asian Americans found themselves straddling the racial binary of black and white, particularly in the Jim Crow South.[35]

Perhaps the oddest cultural twist of all is the stereotype that emerged in the 1960s. Many Asian groups—once despised and singled out for exclusion—began to be perceived as the "model minority": a hardworking group that makes its own way without any demands for rights or privileges. It may seem that this is a "good" stereotype, but there is no such thing. By reducing each person to nothing more than a member of a group, stereotypes demean individuals and stoke social tensions.

● *Japanese Americans were interned in work camps during World War II; the Supreme Court upheld this treatment.*

Political Mobilization

Unlike Latinos or African Americans, Asian Americans do not form a majority in any federal electoral district except Hawaii—although some districts in California come close. Thus, Asian Americans must reach out to other groups and build broad coalitions to win elections.

Is there anything to tie together the vast populations and interests—from Indian to Laotian—that are combined under the "Asian American" (or "Asian/Pacific Islander") label? Perhaps. Heightened security in the face of terror threats has resulted in more scrutiny of minority and immigrant groups. And attacks on immigrants, stirred up during the 2016 election, may very well unite recent immigrant groups around the cause of civil rights and dignity.[36]

THE BOTTOM LINE

» Asian Americans, the third-largest minority group in the United States, are the fastest growing.

» Asian Americans have faced discrimination—including today, the image of "a model minority" that, as with any stereotype, is simplistic and hurtful.

» Asian Americans are a tremendously diverse group made up of people who, on the surface, appear to have little in common with one another. The key to their political effectiveness as a group lies in finding (and acting on) common interests as well as forging ties to other groups.

🧍 Native Americans

The original natives of the United States own the saddest story about rights denied. Before the Europeans arrived, an estimated ten million American Indians lived on the land that would become the United States. As the colonists spread, they introduced deadly diseases, denied indigenous peoples' sovereignty, fought bitter wars, and slowly pushed the tribes from their ancestral lands.

The Lost Way of Life

The dark side of American expansion was "Indian removal." As European settlers moved west, Indian tribes were forced from their homelands. Alexis de Tocqueville watched along the banks of the Mississippi as an immense tribe of Choctaws—tired, cold, and hungry—were forced westward. He described their journey, in the middle of winter, in the most moving passages of *Democracy in America*: "It is impossible to imagine the terrible afflictions of those forced migrations. . . . There is famine behind them, war ahead, and misery everywhere." He described the Indians' dogs, who suddenly realized they were being left behind and, with a mournful howl, plunged into the icy river and struggled to swim after their masters.[37] By the time the United States stretched from coast to coast, less than a million of the estimated ten million natives remained.

Recent historians have warned us against simply seeing Native Americans as the passive victims of American westward expansion. The Indians built their own empires and, at times, forced the white settlers to retreat. During King Philip's War (1675–1678), natives destroyed or damaged one in five Massachusetts villages. (The war was named after the Native American leader Metacomet, known to the English as "King Philip.") Between 1750 and 1850, the Comanches dominated economic and military life in the Southwest and pulled white settlers, Spanish colonies, and other tribes into what amounted to an imperial system. Some Iroquois tribes, hoping to preserve their lands, cultures, and independence, sided with the British during the American Revolution. Tecumseh (a Shawnee warrior) forged an alliance of Native American peoples across the Midwest to resist American expansion. With much blood and conflict, the federal government had forced most of the Native Americans into reservations by the late 1800s.

On the reservations, the tribes were pushed to adapt European lifestyles. The Dawes Act of 1887 divided reservation lands into individual parcels to destroy traditional ownership customs and encourage farming. Boarding schools educated and assimilated native children. By halting the transmission of cultural legacies, it was hoped that whites could "kill the Indian" and "save the man." Even Sitting Bull, famed Lakota seer and fierce opponent of white settlement, sent his son to be educated to ensure him a place in an uncertain future.[38]

Indians and the Federal Government

Native Americans have an ambiguous legal status. In 1831, the Supreme Court ruled that Indian tribes were "**domestic dependent nations**"—essentially, a separate people but without the rights of an independent nation. Native Americans were not considered citizens and were not protected by the Constitution until Congress passed the Indian Citizenship Act in 1924. Even today, their legal status remains ambiguous. Of a total Native American population of some two million in the Continental United States, about half live on tribal reservations, which are independent jurisdictions subject to federal but not state governments. These Indians are both American citizens and members of self-governing independent lands. Another three million Alaskan natives became U.S. citizens when Alaska joined the union in 1959.

Domestic dependent nation: Special status that grants local sovereignty to tribal nations but does not grant them full sovereignty equivalent to that enjoyed by independent nations.

● Assimilation of Native Americans, often forced, was official U.S. government policy well into the twentieth century. Pupils at Carlisle (PA) Indian Industrial School, c. 1900.

The primary connection of Native Americans on reservations to American government is bureaucratic rather than electoral. The Bureau of Indian Affairs (BIA) is responsible for Native American issues. The early placement of the bureau offers a telling symbol: It was part of the Department of War. Later, Congress moved it to the Department of the Interior, whose chief purpose is to promote and protect natural resources and public lands. Native Americans joke that BIA stands for Bossing Indians Around.

Social Problems and Politics

Native Americans face difficult social problems. Their poverty rates are approximately three times higher than the national rates and stand at 32.2 percent—well above any other American group. Life on the reservations is especially difficult. Most are located in rural areas with few jobs or resources. Native Americans tend to suffer from low education levels, high infant mortality rates, and lower life expectancies.

Native Americans civil rights politics divides roughly into two camps. The *ethnic minority* perspective argues that Indians should engage American democracy and mobilize for rights and equality. The alternative is the separatist *tribal movement*, which advocates withdrawing from American politics and society and revitalizing Native American culture and traditions.

The 1960s civil rights protest movements spread to Native American activists. Led, in some cases, by the American Indian Movement (or AIM), tribes occupied the Bureau of Indian Affairs in Washington, DC, for six days in November 1972. They "captured" Alcatraz Island in San Francisco Bay and occupied the site of the infamous prison for nineteen months between 1969 and 1971. They seized control of the village of Wounded Knee on the Pine Ridge Indian Reservation, the site of a massacre of Indians in 1890, for seventy-one days, declared the reservation a sovereign nation and exchanged occasional gunfire with federal marshals. During this Wounded Knee Incident, AIM brought its grievances before the United Nations General Assembly.

Native Americans and the Courts

As with their contemporaries in other civil rights struggles, Native Americans fought for legislation and sought judicial redress. In *United States* v. *Sioux Nation of Indians*, the Court ruled in 1980 that the federal government wrongly allowed lands reserved to the Sioux to be settled without purchasing them for fair market value. The settlement awarded, including a century's worth of interest, was approximately $105 million. Now totaling over $1 billion, the settlement remains unclaimed, as doing so would relinquish the Sioux Nation's claim to the disputed lands. In another closely-watched case, the Supreme Court ruled in 2016 that Native American courts retained the authority to rule on suits brought by tribal members against non-tribal businesses.[39]

In recent years, some tribes have used their exemption from state laws to create highly profitable gambling businesses and resorts. The Supreme

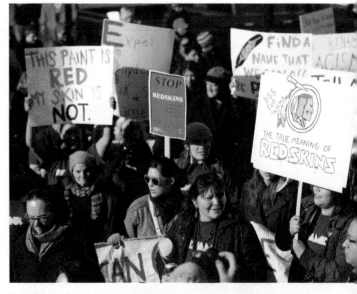

● The cultural clash spills into sports. In 2015, a federal court ruled that the Washington National Football League team's "Redskins" name was no longer protected under U.S. trademark law. Across the country teams debated names and mascots that, in the eyes of many, disparage Native Americans.

Court ruled in 1987 that because tribes are considered sovereign entities, they are free from state prohibitions on gaming.[40] According to the gaming industry, 233 of the nation's 565 tribes run casinos. Whether this is a positive development—for the tribes, for the communities around them, and for the United States—is a matter of much dispute.

THE BOTTOM LINE

» Native Americans lost their way of life in the face of colonial settlers' disease, armies, and forced removal.

» The Supreme Court gave American Indians a special status: a separate people without rights. Although they retain the special status, Native Americans became U.S. citizens in 1924.

» Native Americans support two different civil rights strategies: The ethnic minority approach argues for winning political rights and benefits. The tribal movement approach prefers to withdraw and to emphasize a separate Indian society and culture.

Groups Without Special Protection

The idea of demanding rights has spread to other groups that were not mentioned in the Civil Rights Act and have never received special scrutiny from the courts.

People with Disabilities

Section 504: An obscure provision in an obscure rehabilitation act that required all institutions that received federal funds to accommodate people with disabilities.

Before 1970, children in wheelchairs did not go to school, and most blind children never learned how to read. People with disabilities lived outside mainstream society. A political breakthrough came in an unnoticed provision that liberal congressional staff slipped into an obscure bill. **Section 504** of the 1973 Rehabilitation Act borrowed language directly from the Civil Rights Act of 1964 and applied it to the disabled: "No . . . handicapped individual . . . shall, solely by reason of his handicap, be excluded from participation in, or be denied the benefits of . . . any program or activity conducted by an executive agency." Suddenly, any university receiving federal funds—and all government agencies—had to accommodate the handicapped.

Section 504 gave activists a political focus. When the government was slow to issue regulations, for example, sit-ins at regional offices pushed the matter forward. Notice the dynamic: Congressional staffers dreamed up a change, giving advocates a focus for action. People with handicaps and their advocates soon mobilized for widespread change on every level of government. Local health boards, planning agencies, and school officials all began hearing from the advocates. The political pattern resembles that followed by African Americans after *Brown v. Board of Education* and feminists after the Civil Rights Act: Government action provided new legal rights; the group then organized and demanded further change.

Advocates went from requesting welfare benefits to demanding civil rights. The process culminated in 1990, when Congress passed the Americans with Disabilities Act (ADA). The ADA forbade companies of twenty-five or more employees from discriminating against handicapped people. It also required companies to make "reasonable accommodations" for a wide range of disabilities (see Figure 6.8).

Unlike racial discrimination, however, a business can avoid making accommodations if it would be expensive or inconvenient to do so. Courts constantly weigh the costs and benefits of making accommodations in specific places. What is reasonable to ask a firm or a store or a university to do to accommodate special needs? Even with this delicate balancing of costs and access, the ADA created what amounts to a massive affirmative action program for people with disabilities. Public transportation, schools, shops, and businesses all must help facilitate a normal, mainstream life for people with special needs.

Sexual Orientation

The movement for same-sex rights began with a riot. In June 1969, police raided a New York City gay bar named the Stonewall Inn. Traditionally, gay people had responded to such raids with shame. This time, however, the gay community broke the unwritten rules. The Stonewall riot marks the moment that the LGBTQ community stopped apologizing and proudly affirmed its identity. Four years later, in 1973, the American Psychiatric Association removed homosexuality from its list of mental disorders.

When activists turned to politics, their first targets were state antisodomy laws. These criminalized gay sex (and, as we saw in Chapter 5, were finally struck down by the Supreme Court in *Lawrence v. Texas*).[41]

In the early 1980s, gay communities were devastated by a mysterious plague—AIDS. At the time, no one knew what the illness was or how it was transmitted—only that it was invariably deadly. In every city, gays organized to confront AIDS: They established links to the medical community, local governments, and social service networks. The terrible disease pushed gay groups into local politics and forced them to develop political skills.

Few recent changes in American politics and culture are as dramatic as the transformation of same-sex civil rights. In 1993, the newly elected Bill Clinton ran into a firestorm in Congress when he promised to open the military to gay men and women. The compromise policy, known as "don't ask, don't tell," permitted gay individuals to serve as long as they kept their sexual orientation hidden. Eighteen years later, the Obama administration ended the policy. The relatively quiet reaction in Congress is a mark of changing cultural norms.

Meanwhile, Vermont created shock waves in 2000 by permitting same-sex civil unions—giving gay couples the same benefits and responsibilities as married couples. Three years later, Massachusetts became the first state to permit same-sex marriage. Other states followed—and the 2015 Supreme Court *Obergefell v. Hodges* decision enshrined gay marriage as a civil right nationwide. Few civil rights areas—in politics, law, or public opinion—have evolved as quickly as this one.

Gender Identity

Transgender Americans have moved out of the cultural shadows and opened another front—gender identity—in the long American struggle for civil rights. Prominent transgender public figures such as Laverne Cox, Janet Mock, and Caitlyn Jenner have won popular acclaim. Transgender citizens, however, still face harassment,

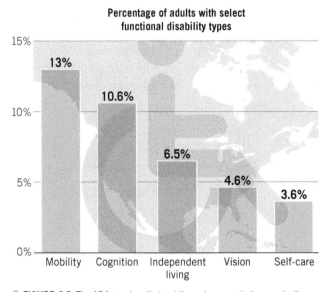

Percentage of adults with select functional disability types

● **FIGURE 6.8** *The ADA requires that public and many private organizations accommodate the wide range of disabilities in the United States.*

discrimination, violence, and sexual assault. Forty-one percent of one national sample reported attempting suicide.[42]

Transgender activism focuses on educating fellow citizens and ensuring basic civil rights. In 2015 Governor Jerry Brown of California signed the School Success and Opportunity Act, ensuring that transgender students can fully participate in all school activities, sports teams, programs, and facilities that match their gender identity.[43]

THE BOTTOM LINE

» People with disabilities used an obscure bureaucratic rule to mobilize, and eventually won sweeping civil rights with the Americans with Disabilities Act. The goal is to mainstream disabled people as much as possible.

» The gay (and lesbian) movements were born in a burst of pride and anger in 1969. Gays were the first to confront AIDS—a harrowing plague (in its early years) that pushed them into politics and community building.

» Gay, lesbian, bisexual, and transgender communities have moved from taboo toward the mainstream. Barriers to military service, civil unions, and marriage have eroded. The conflict over marriage and childrearing remains a flash point of contemporary culture wars, as does transgender status.

The Fight for Civil Rights Goes On

How close has the United States come to achieving racial equality and civil rights? A few key indicators measure how the past half-century of movements has changed America—and how far we still have to go.

African Americans once faced violence, segregation, poverty, and exclusion at every turn. Fifty years ago, there were no black mayors in the United States. There were only five black members of Congress. Most professions were closed to blacks. It was an enormous cultural milestone when the Brooklyn Dodgers signed Jackie Robinson to play major league baseball (to the taunts and curses of both fans and players). These barriers to equal opportunity vanished long ago.

The original civil rights movement also inspired a host of other groups—and provided them with new legal structures like the Civil Rights Act of 1964 and the Voting Rights Act of 1965.

Yet, the data—on poverty, employment, health, education, incarceration rates and more—suggest that despite great progress, the struggle for many groups continues. Let us look at two main arenas—political equality, in the form of voting rights; and social and economic equality, focusing on health, income, and incarceration.

Voting Rights Today

During the 2016 election, sixteen states introduced restrictions on voting: they required voter ID, eliminated same-day voter registration, limited early voting, reduced the number of polling stations, and imposed other restrictions. Proponents argued that these measures were necessary to reduce voting fraud. Critics claimed that they disproportionately affect black, Latino, and young voters—and were put in place to depress the vote of groups that tend to vote Democratic.

The Supreme Court made restricting the vote easier in 2013 when it struck down the central requirement in the Voting Rights Act of 1965: Now, southern states that had once denied African Americans the vote were no longer required to clear voting rights changes with the federal Justice Department. "Our country has changed," Chief Justice Roberts declared for the majority.[44] Congress now must specify exactly where there is a pattern of discrimination before the federal government can intervene. The solid Republican majorities in both House and Senate are not likely to do so.

Economic and Social Rights Today

Equality has many dimensions. Are Americans more equal when it comes to health, wealth, and social justice? Again, we find a mixed story: much progress and a very long way left to go.

Health. Health is the most basic indicator of social equality. In 1935, enormous differences separated black and white life expectancy: Whites lived 9.8 years, or 15 percent, longer than African Americans. By 2014, that racial difference had fallen by more than half: A white baby would live on average 78.9 years; that is more than four years longer than a black baby and two years longer than a Native American. As Table 6.3 shows, however, an Asian or Hispanic child has a longer average life expectancy than whites do.

Income. In 1959, just before the sit-ins began, 55 percent of African Americans lived in poverty. By 1979, the poverty rate among blacks was 31 percent, and today it is 26 percent. Few groups at any time in history have experienced such a rapid rise out of poverty as African Americans did between 1959 and 1980. Yet for the entire half-century, the black poverty rate has remained roughly three times the white poverty rate. The percentage of Hispanic and Native Americans who live in poverty is closer to the black rate than the non-Spanish-speaking white (see Table 6.4). The racial difference closely tracks the enormous rise in inequality between 1970 and today.

For a different perspective, turn to the CEOs in the top 500 corporations. As we saw earlier, there are 22 women in that corner office. There are also nine Hispanics, nine Asian Americans, five blacks, and no Native Americans. The number in 1995 for every one of these groups: zero. Although there remains a long way to go, Americans of every description keep pushing the boundaries of civil rights.

TABLE 6.3 Average Life Expectancy by Ethnic and Racial Group

Asian American	86.5
Hispanic	82.8
White	78.9
Native American	76.9
African American	74.6
Source: Kaiser Family Foundation	

TABLE 6.4 Percentage of People in Poverty, by Race (U.S. Census)

White	10%
Hispanic	24%
African American	27%
Native American	28.3%
Source: Kaiser Family Foundation	

INFO/DATA: Political Equality: Voter Turnout Rates by Race and Ethnicity

One bedrock of political equality is voter turnout, the percentage of voters who turn out to cast their votes. Elected officials are more likely to attend to the interests of individuals who are likely to go to the polls and support them. As a result, efforts to advance political equality have rested in part on increasing the voter turnout among ethnic and racial minorities.

1. How has the turnout of ethnic and racial minorities changed over time?

2. Are there still gaps today? What groups have the highest turnout today? How is this likely to influence the policy decisions made by elected representatives?

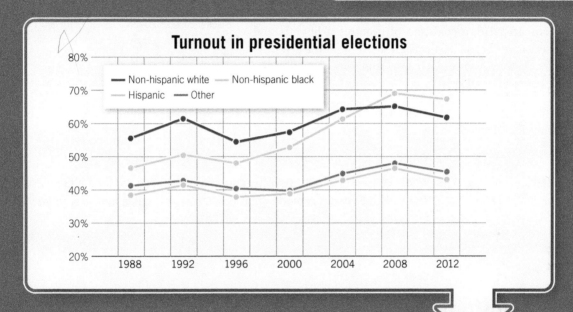

Turnout in presidential elections

Legend: Non-hispanic white, Non-hispanic black, Hispanic, Other

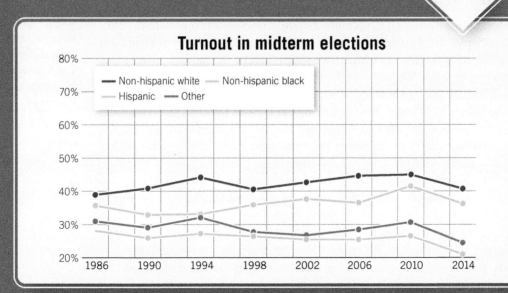

Turnout in midterm elections

Legend: Non-hispanic white, Non-hispanic black, Hispanic, Other

Source: United States Election Project

194

Incarceration. One final twist to the American civil rights story introduces a new source of alarm. As Figure 6.9 shows, African American men are seven times as likely to be in jail as whites. Latinos are three times as likely. Is this "**The New Jim Crow**," as civil rights advocates have argued?

Some suggest that people of all races benefit from tough law enforcement. But most observers believe that the United States has gone too far in sending people to jail—especially for minor offenses. Studies repeatedly suggest a racial bias throughout the criminal justice system, starting in the way Americans perceive criminals. For example, when subjects were asked to "imagine a drug user," 95% pictured a black person. In reality, 72% of users are white.[45] There are subtle forms of racial and ethnic discrimination at every stage of the criminal justice system. In 2016, a coalition of prominent liberals and conservatives began a campaign to overhaul the criminal justice system. A formidable new front has opened in the long battle for civil rights.

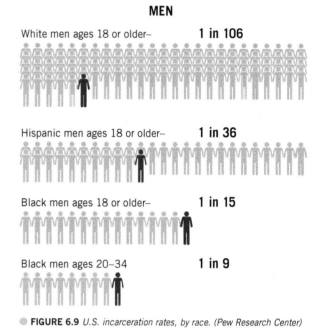

MEN

White men ages 18 or older– **1 in 106**

Hispanic men ages 18 or older– **1 in 36**

Black men ages 18 or older– **1 in 15**

Black men ages 20–34 **1 in 9**

● **FIGURE 6.9** *U.S. incarceration rates, by race. (Pew Research Center)*

THE BOTTOM LINE

» Voting rights remains a source of fierce political debate today.

» When we turn to health, poverty, and criminal justice, we find a familiar story: The United States has made great progress—and has a long way to go to achieve full civil rights.

Conclusion: Civil Rights . . . By the People

The New Jim Crow: the idea that mass incarceration of African Americans has the sweeping effects of Jim Crow discrimination laws. The term was the title of a book by Michelle Alexander.

Race. Gender. Latinos. Asians. Immigrants. Native Americans. People with disabilities. Sexual orientation. Transgender individuals. The struggle for civil rights—in many ways, the struggle to secure American ideals—spans the nation's history and engages every generation. We have seen how each group described here reached for civil rights. We also have seen how true civil rights still remain something to fight for.

No American idea is more powerful than the idea of inalienable rights, and none generates more arguments. Government actions are crucial in settling the arguments about rights. One important lesson to draw from this chapter is that laws and court cases have far-reaching consequences. The 1964 Civil Rights Act, for example, ended *de jure* segregation, focused the women's movement, changed gender relations in schools and workplaces, and inspired the disabilities rights movement—and its influence continues even today.

The Supreme Court has been crucial across the last half century of debates. Prior to Justice Scalia's death in February 2016, our divided Court—four conservative justices, four liberals, and one swing vote leaning to the conservative side—reflected a deeply divided society. Liberals argue that American society must ensure that past discrimination does not hobble future generations. Conservatives, in contrast, are skeptical of any program that benefits some individuals simply because of race, gender or any other factor.

America's civil rights movements mark an extraordinary attempt to overcome centuries of injustice, targeting minority and marginalized groups of all types. But did the nation do enough to give every member of society a genuine opportunity to succeed? Has America, as Justice Roberts declared, truly "changed?"

Ultimately, the power to make a change lies not with the Court or the Congress or the government but with the people. The *Brown* decision became an enormous force for change only after the civil rights movement sprang into action. Throughout this chapter, we have seen people rise up to transform the politics of rights— marching into violence in Birmingham, prodding a reluctant government to implement the gender provisions in the Civil Rights Act of 1964, waving American flags over immigrant rights in Chicago, holding sit-ins to hurry implementation of disability rules in Washington, and fighting back when the police raided a gay bar in New York City. It was the people who helped shape the meaning of the legislation and the court decisions. Through their passion and their activism, the people are constantly pushing the United States to live up to its founding ideals.

Each generation faces the same challenge of civil rights. That challenge is what drew the two of us to political science. It is our own hope that the mostly young adults reading our book will, like so many Americans in the past, lead the United States toward greater civil rights.

CHAPTER SUMMARY

● The battle for civil rights generally includes seven stages. A group seeking rights must define itself, challenge society, and change the cultural story. The contest for rights spills across the different levels of federalism and the different branches of government: The executive branch can break the ice, Congress is the key to deep social change, and the courts are the final arbiters of civil rights.

● The Fourteenth Amendment contains the crucial legal rule for civil rights: "No state shall . . . deprive any person of . . . the equal protection of the laws."

● A great mass movement rose up in which ordinary men, women, and children turned the legal promise of the *Brown v. Board of Education* decision into a practical reality. Protests eventually led to the Civil Rights Act of 1964 and the Voting Rights Act of 1965. The black civil rights movement set the model for future civil rights campaigns by many other groups.

● To make up for past discrimination, legislatures and courts turned to affirmative action in the 1960s and 1970s. The courts, and the public, have become increasingly skeptical of these programs.

● Women first won voting rights in the states— beginning in the West—before finally securing the Nineteenth Amendment, which guarantees the right to vote regardless of gender.

● The Civil Rights Act of 1964 bars gender discrimination. The women's movement organized to take advantage of these legal changes. The results transformed American gender roles in political and professional life. Following *Roe v. Wade* (in 1973) and the Equal Rights Amendment (in the mid-1970s), gender politics became especially controversial.

● Latinos, the United States' largest immigrant group, are a diverse people with many different national identities, histories, cultures, and concerns. A key political question is whether they will mobilize around shared interests and concerns. If they do, they will become a formidable force, poised to advance civil rights claims.

● Asian Americans are the third-largest minority group in the United States and now comprise 5 percent of the population. They are also a tremendously diverse group.

● Native Americans lost their way of life in the face of disease, armies, and settlers. The Supreme Court gave them a special status: a separate people without rights. Though they retain the special status, they became U.S. citizens in 1924.

● People with disabilities leveraged an obscure bureaucratic rule, used it to mobilize, and eventually won the sweeping rights of the Americans with Disabilities Act.

● The gay (and lesbian) movements were born in a burst of pride and anger in 1969. Gays were the first to confront AIDS—a harrowing plague (in its early years) that pushed them into politics, health provision work, and community building. Gay, lesbian, bisexual, and transgender communities have moved from taboo to mainstream. Nevertheless, the conflict over marriage and childrearing remains a flash point of contemporary culture wars.

KEY TERMS

1963 March on Washington, p. 171
Abolition, p. 164
Affirmative action, p. 173
Black power, p. 172
Brown v. Board of Education, p. 169
Chicanismo, p. 182
Civil rights, p. 159
Civil Rights Act of 1964, p. 171
Class action, p. 179
Compromise of 1850, p. 165
De facto discrimination, p. 168
De jure discrimination, p. 168
Disproportionate impact, p. 173
Domestic dependent nation, p. 188

Dred Scott v. Sandford, p. 165
Emancipation Proclamation, p. 165
Equal Employment Opportunity Commission (EEOC), p. 177
Equal protection of the laws, p. 166
Equal Rights Amendment (ERA), p. 179
Free rider problem, p. 171
Freedom Riders, p. 170
Great Migration, p. 168
Jim Crow, p. 167
Literacy test, p. 167
Missouri Compromise, p. 164

National Association for the Advancement of Colored People (NAACP), p. 168
National Organization for Women (NOW), p. 177
The New Jim Crow, p. 195
Plessy v. Ferguson, p. 167
Quasi-suspect category, p. 162
Racial profiling, p. 184
Reconstruction, p. 166
Reframe the issue, p. 179
School busing, p. 174
Section 504, p. 190
Seneca Falls Convention, p. 176
Strict scrutiny, p. 162
United Farm Workers (UFW), p. 182

STUDY QUESTIONS

1. Name the seven steps involved in civil rights campaigns. Give examples of three, drawing on historical material in this chapter or your own reading/studies.
2. Describe the Civil War amendments. Why was the Fourteenth Amendment so important?
3. What was Jim Crow legislation? What happened to Jim Crow practices?
4. Describe the sit-ins and Freedom Rides of the civil rights movement. What was their point?
5. Describe three effects of the Civil Rights Act of 1964.
6. What is affirmative action?

   For further reflection: Write your own Supreme Court decision. Would you accept affirmative action in your college or university? Why or why not?

7. What are undocumented aliens?

   For further reflection: What should the United States do about undocumented aliens?

8. What is the Lilly Ledbetter Law?

   For further reflection: Why do you think President Obama chose this to be the first law to sign as president?

9. Although same-sex marriage has won national acceptance in courts and public-opinion polls alike, LGBT people continue to face discrimination. Discuss recent examples of limits on gay or transgender citizens' civil rights, and how these might be redressed.

 Go to www.oup.com/us/Morone to find quizzes, flash cards, simulations, tutorials, videos, and other study tools.

Public Opinion

IN 2000 VERMONT became the first state to recognize same-sex civil unions. Although the legislation did not permit marriage, it did give same-sex couples the same rights and duties as married couples. The state immediately erupted in protests. Signs sprang up across the state urging local people to "Take Back Vermont." The biggest issue in the next election, held later that year, was whether to repeal the law. Opponents won a majority in the Vermont House (which promptly voted to repeal), but the Vermont Senate preserved the reform. At the time, only one in three Americans approved of same-sex marriage. No state permitted it.

While Vermonters were battling it out, a friend called us and asked whether the law was going to survive. Would the law still be there, she asked, in a year? Neither of us, back in 2000, could have even dreamed of what was to happen during the next decade.

What happened was a revolution in public opinion. The change began with the millennials (as noted in Chapter 1, born roughly between 1983 and 2001). When pollsters began to ask their opinion, their answers surprised most observers: 51 percent approved of same-sex marriage in 2003. Overall public approval of same-sex marriage increased from 31 percent in 2001 to 55 percent in 2016—an enormous shift (see Figure 7.1). What accounts for the change? Well, a new generation had different opinions. Today, millennials' approval is 73 percent, while only 38 percent of people over 65 approve of same-sex marriage (see Figure 7.2).[1]

With public approval rapidly rising, state legislatures began passing same-sex marriage laws and courts struck down bans on same-sex marriage. In one courtroom after another, justices ruled that the bans violated the Fourteenth Amendment's guarantee of "equal protection under the laws." Finally, the Supreme Court struck down all state bans on same-sex marriage.

What happened? Legislatures and courts responded to shifting popular views. Although we expect legislatures to weigh public opinion, courts are supposed to protect rights regardless of how people feel about them (that's why federal justices are appointed for life). But in this case, public opinion also seemed to drive the courts forward. A change in public opinion helped inspire a major shift in policy.

Or take another case of changing public opinion. Twenty years ago, only one in four Americans supported legalizing marijuana. Then the number

A revolution in public opinion: same-sex marriage.

In this chapter, you will:

- Explore the sources of our opinions about public issues.

- Reflect on the role of public opinion in a democracy.

- Understand the uses of public opinion in politics and government.

- Explore how public opinion is measured.

07-Morone-Chap07.indd   199
19/11/16   12:51 PM

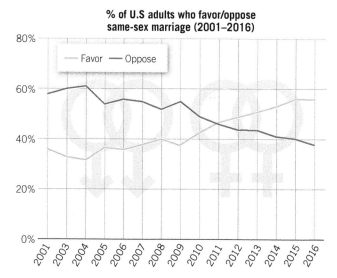

% of U.S adults who favor/oppose same-sex marriage (2001–2016)

Favor — Oppose

● **FIGURE 7.1** *Support for same-sex marriage has risen dramatically. . . .* (Pew Research Center; Gallup.)

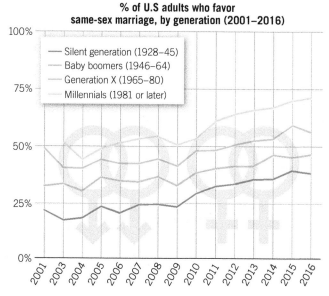

% of U.S adults who favor same-sex marriage, by generation (2001–2016)

— Silent generation (1928–45)
— Baby boomers (1946–64)
— Generation X (1965–80)
— Millennials (1981 or later)

● **FIGURE 7.2** *. . . with millennials setting the pace (Pew Research Center).*

began to rise. Why? Once again, pollsters started asking a new generation with a very different outlook (see Figure 7.3). People born after 1981 strongly support legalization (71% in 2015); even Republican millennials agree (63% approve of legalization). That is a far cry from the oldest cohort where only 35 percent approve of legalization.

In both cases, a new generation led a change in public opinion. And that change, in turn, led to new government policies. By 2016, thirty states and the District of Columbia had legalized marijuana in some form—up from zero twenty years ago.

Who are we? The world's oldest democracy. Public opinion takes us to the very heart of self-rule: The people's views matter in government. Isn't this exactly the way it should be?

Not necessarily. Remember that the Constitution limits direct popular rule through the Electoral College, lifetime appointment for federal judges, the system of checks and balances, and many other institutions. American government is designed to balance public opinion and the judgment of public officials.

No democracy can ignore its people for long. But public opinion raises a lot of tough questions: Can we trust the people to have informed opinions? Or are members of the public simply parroting their friends, or professional talking heads, or some vague idea? What happens when the public is divided? How to tell when public opinion is correctly measured? And even if we know precisely what the public thinks, perhaps politicians should do what they believe is the right thing, regardless of the polls.

These are the questions we discuss in this chapter. They all revolve around the most basic issue in any democracy: How responsive should the government be to the people's views?

🔍 Sources of Public Opinion

Public opinion is simply the sum of individual beliefs and opinions. Your views about the right to carry firearms, whether to raise the minimum wage, global

BY THE NUMBERS
Public Opinion

Year that "public opinion" was first mentioned by a public official (in France): **1788**
Year the French Revolution began: **1789**

Percentage of the American public unable to name their House member in 1960
and 2013, respectively: **47, 35**
Percentage of millennials and the "Silent Generation" (aged sixty-five and over),
respectively, who approve of marijuana legalization: **70 , 32**

Percentage of these generations, respectively, who believe abortions should be legal
in all or most cases: **58, 46**

Percent of these generations, respectively, who would rather have a smaller govern-
ment providing fewer services: **38, 64**
Percentage of baby boomers, Gen X, and millennials, respectively, who expect that
Social Security will provide no benefits by the time they retire: **28, 50, 51**

The authors' predicted probability that there will be no Social Security by the time
the millennial generation retires: **0.001**
Highest average approval rating recorded by Gallup for any president across their
entire term (John F. Kennedy): **70.1**
Lowest average approval rating of a president (Harry Truman): **45.4**
U.S. Congress (Republican-controlled) approval rating, July 2016 (Gallup): **13%**
Gallup daily index for Americans "with a lot of happiness/enjoyment," 2015: **61%**

Proportion of Americans expecting another terrorist attack in the next five years,
October 2011, 2016 (CNN, Quinnipiac): **32, 79**

warming, and whether *Game of Thrones* is too violent for television—along with the views of everyone else in the country—make up public opinion. The central question for this chapter is what role your preferences ought to play when public officials make policy. But before ponder-ing that, we turn to a more basic question: Where do your opinions come from? Let us take a look at some classic sources.

Political Socialization

Why do white Americans trust the police more than black or Latino Americans? Why do some of your friends—but not others—support a strong military? Why is one classmate a com-mitted libertarian and another completely un-interested in politics? We call the many forces that shape our political attitudes and values **political socialization**.

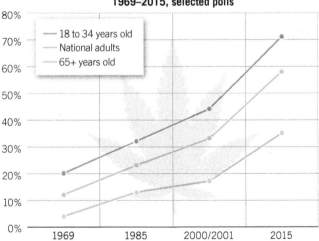

% support for legalizing the use of marijuana, by age group, 1969–2015, selected polls

- 18 to 34 years old
- National adults
- 65+ years old

● **FIGURE 7.3** *Millennials set the pace again: growing support for legal marijuana—now spreading across the nation thanks to changing public opinion.*

Political socialization: The process by which individuals acquire their political values and outlooks.

President Lyndon Johnson (LBJ) once remarked, "Tell me where a man comes from, how long he went to school, and where he worships on Sundays, and I'll tell you his political opinions."[2] LBJ, a big-talking Texan, may have exaggerated a bit. But basic life details—such as race, age, gender, ethnicity, and level of education—are all strong agents of socialization. And, yes, as Johnson claimed, they help predict where people stand. Let us look at some of the major sources of political socialization.

Parents and Friends. Many people absorb the political attitudes of their parents and caregivers. Mark Losey, running for a U.S. House seat, told his audiences a typical story about how he chose his party: As a child he used to go walking on his grandfather's farm. On one of those walks, recalls Losey, I asked, "'Grandpa, are we Democrats or Republicans?' My grandpa, who grew up on a farm during the height of the Great Depression, paused. 'Before Roosevelt became president, our family almost starved to death,' he replied. 'Grandpa Wren is still a Democrat. So am I.'"[3] Of course, some people—a minority—react against the attitudes they grew up hearing as children. Senator Orrin Hatch, a Utah Republican, was raised a staunch Democrat. In college, recalls Hatch, "I learned that personal responsibility . . . was supremely better for businesses and individuals than an intrusive federal government that led to personal dependency."[4] That belief turned him into a Republican. Social networks—friends and colleagues—exert a major influence in shaping public opinion. We tend to adopt views expressed by the people around us.

Education. Education is a major agent of socialization. Many of us were influenced by our teachers, going right back to kindergarten when students begin to say the Pledge of Allegiance. Those who stay in school past college are more likely to be Democrats—those with advanced degrees identify as Democratic, 57 percent to 35 percent Republican. Indeed, college professors in the United States are roughly five times more likely to identify as liberals than conservatives.[5]

Gender. Gender also has a major effect on political views. Women are more likely to oppose nuclear power plants, fracking to extract natural gas, genetically modified foods, and testing products on animals. As you might guess from these examples, women lean Democratic by an average of five percentage points. That may not sound like much, but if only women were allowed to vote in American presidential elections, the only Republican candidate who would have won in the last forty-five years is Ronald Reagan in 1984.

Race. As we have already seen, race plays an enormous role in American politics and history. African Americans are more churched, more economically liberal, and more Democratic. Hispanics tend to be socially conservative on issues such as abortion (see Figure 7.4) but liberal on government services (see Figure 7.5). They also have trended strongly toward the Democratic Party.

Friends, past times, and public rituals all influence political socialization.

Religion. Religion shapes public opinion on major value questions—from support for food stamps to views about abortion. White evangelicals vote strongly Republican (between 70 and 80%). Catholic voters tend to be split. Black Protestants, Latino Catholics, Jews, and Muslims all trend decidedly Democratic.

Life Events. As we grow up, major events shape our outlooks. The plunge into a great depression (in the early 1930s), the attack on Pearl Harbor (in 1941), the assassination of Martin Luther King (1963), the 9/11 terrorist attack (2001), the severe economic downturn beginning in fall 2008—all have the potential to socialize the young people who are just forming their political opinions. The result, of course, is that each generation grows up with its own background, technologies, and expectation.

In sum, there is much truth in Lyndon Johnson's crack about understanding how a person votes. He just did not have enough variables to give a full account of political socialization. Family, friends, education, gender, race, what you have experienced—tell us all those things and we can make a pretty good guess about where you stand politically.

Party

Party preference has become an even stronger predictor of individual opinions than factors such as race and religion. Most politically active Americans register as either Democrats or Republicans and generally stay committed to their party. In recent years the differences between the parties has grown on almost every issue. "From immigration reform to food stamps to student loans," commented one respected pollster, "Republicans and Democrats inhabit different worlds."[6] Your party tells us more about your opinions than even strong demographic factors like race and religion.

For a time, political scientists believed that elected officials were far more partisan than the public at large. Political scientist Morris Fiorina and his colleagues argued that, at least on cultural issues such as abortion, most Americans are moderates. More recent polling suggests a major surge in partisan divide within the public.

Views on abortion, by religion and nativity
% of Hispanics in each group who say abortion should be illegal in all or most cases OR legal in all or most cases

	All–mostly Illegal	All–mostly Legal
All Hispanics	53%	40%
Catholic	54%	38%
Evang. Prot.	70%	24%
Mainline Prot.	46%	45%
Unaffiliated	35%	58%
Attend worship services		
Weekly+	69%	25%
Monthly/yearly	46%	44%
Seldom/never	35%	58%
Foreign born	58%	33%
U.S. born	43%	49%
General public	40%	54%

FIGURE 7.4 *Hispanics tend to be socially conservative on issues such as abortion and religious observance . . .*

Role of government
% of Hispanics in each group who prefer smaller government with fewer services or a bigger government with more services

	Smaller, fewer services	Bigger, more services
All Hispanics	53%	40%
Mexican	54%	38%
Puerto Rican	70%	24%
Cuban	46%	45%
Salvadoran	35%	58%
Dominican	35%	58%
Catholic	54%	38%
Evang. Prot.	70%	24%
Mainloine Prot.	46%	45%
Unaffiliated	35%	58%
Men	54%	38%
Women	70%	24%
Foreign born	54%	38%
U.S. born	70%	24%
General public	40%	54%

FIGURE 7.5 *. . . but liberal on the role of government.*

TABLE 7.1 **Party Affiliations by Income Level**

FAMILY INCOME	REPUBLICAN	DEMOCRAT	INDEPENDENT
$150,000+	29	29	38
$100,000 to $149,999	30	30	37
$75,000 to $99,999	30	29	38
$50,000 to $74,999	27	30	38
$40,000 to $49,999	24	33	40
$30,000 to $39,999	19	33	43
<$30,000	17	35	42
Source: Pew Research			

Self-Interest: Voting Our Pocketbooks

Some experts believe that economic self-interest matters most. Whether you are rich or poor, you will try to increase your wealth. According to this perspective, people with more money will vote for lower taxes, while people with less will vote to expand social programs.

In practice, economic interests are important—but they are only one factor among many. In a book entitled *What's the Matter with Kansas?*, economist Thomas Frank points out that Kansas has some of the lowest average incomes in the country but votes for a congressional delegation made up exclusively of Republicans who support cutting taxes and social programs. If these voters focused on their economic interest, argued Frank, they would be more likely to vote for Democrats. As he discovered, public opinion does not simply spring out of people's wallets. Although poorer Americans are more likely to affiliate with the Democratic Party, wealthier Americans are equally divided between the parties (see Table 7.1). But there are enough exceptions that we have to look further if we want to fully understand the roots of public opinion.

Political elites: Individuals who control significant wealth, status, power, or visibility and consequently have significant influence over public debates.

● *In 2015, Kanye West disclosed his presidential ambitions, but deferred his entrance into the race and instead backed 2016 presidential candidate Hillary Clinton.*

Elite Influence

Stop for a moment and think about whom you listen to when you make up your mind about an issue. Many people turn to friends and family. A series of studies, most notably by the political scientist John Zaller, suggests that people also look to **political elites**. Americans routinely receive signals from political leaders and embrace those that are consistent with their prior beliefs.[7]

The greatest influence is wielded by figures who have the most credibility. Some people look up to "experts" such as academics or media personalities such as Megyn Kelly or Anderson Cooper. Others follow very visible public figures such as Oprah Winfrey or Kanye West.

When elites compete to shape members of the public's views on issues, they are trying to *frame* the issue—to give the issue a particular slant. For example, when obesity became a source of widespread popular concern, many leaders joined the food industry in framing the issue as one of personal responsibility: Obesity is, they said, a problem of self-control. The simple solution: eat less, exercise more.

Others framed the problem as a "toxic food environment"—too much high-fat, low-nutrition food is available cheaply, from fast-food drive-throughs to convenience stores to school cafeterias. As the public health consequences of obesity became clearer, the toxic food environment perspective gained traction. The framing battle reached a fever pitch when New York Mayor Michael Bloomberg proposed banning sugary drinks larger than sixteen ounces—prompting cheers from public health advocates and conservative critics sounding off against the nanny state.

Wars and Other Focusing Events

Americans pull together during crises. Tragedy, terrorist attacks, and the start of wars generally produce consensus—and a spike in the government's approval ratings. Franklin D. Roosevelt faced plenty of opposition when he tried to arm Britain against Germany after World War II broke out—until December 7, 1941. On that day, the Japanese bombed Pearl Harbor, galvanizing public support for the war effort. Six decades later, nearly 90 percent of Americans backed the decision to invade Afghanistan a few weeks after the September 11, 2001, terrorist attacks on the World Trade Center and the Pentagon.

Wars inspire a strong sense of "we're all in this together," a nationalist sentiment that has characterized public response to wars in almost every country. But that sentiment typically fades over time. Consider the U.S. conflict in Iraq. After President Bush launched the war in March 2003, almost 80 percent of the public approved. Four years later, approval for American involvement in Iraq had fallen to barely 30 percent.[8]

Most dramatic events have a similar, if smaller, effect on public opinion. After a gunman brandishing semi-automatic weapons murdered twenty first graders and teachers in Newton, Connecticut, backing for gun control spiked—58 percent of the public supported action. Within a year, the support had faded away and action on gun control once again divided the nation (see Figure 7.6). Similar effects were evident after the tragic series of shootings in June and July 2016, including at an Orlando gay dance club and sniper killings of five police officers in Dallas. Savvy political scientists discount the spikes in public opinion, knowing that the poll numbers generally come back down again.

see for yourself 7.1

Go online to see John Oliver criticizing "Big Sugar" companies. (flash required)

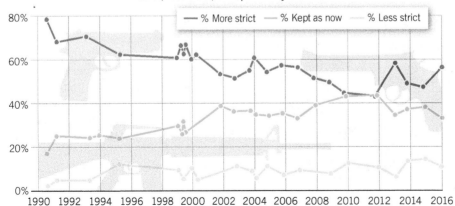

In general, do you think the laws covering the sale of firearms should be made strict, less strict, or kept as they are now?

— % More strict — % Kept as now — % Less strict

● **FIGURE 7.6** *Percentage who approve of enhanced gun controls (Gallup).*

THE BOTTOM LINE

» Political socialization refers to the factors that shape our political opinions. These include family, friends, education, gender, race, religion, and major life events.

» Party identification has become the most reliable predictor of public opinion in recent years.

» Self-interest and political elites also influence political attitudes.

» How issues are framed can shift individual and collective views.

» Dramatic events, especially wars, also have a powerful role in shaping our opinions.

Measuring Public Opinion

How do we know what the people are thinking? Professional polling firms such as Gallup, major media organizations, partisan outfits, and academic research centers all jostle to provide the most up-to-date polls. Candidates for office commission private polls to tell them how they are performing; presidents and governors retain pollsters to gauge public opinion on various policy items. Let us take a look at why good polling techniques are important, how reliable polls are designed, where not-so-good polls cut corners, and—most important—how to recognize each kind.

Early Polling Bloopers

Well-designed scientific polling techniques might have averted polling's first major embarrassment. Back in 1920, a magazine named the *Literary Digest* helped introduce the idea that polls could predict presidential elections. The magazine relied on postcards sent in by subscribers. Until 1936, it could brag that it had never failed to predict the winner. Then, in October of that year, the *Digest* forecast a lopsided defeat for incumbent President Franklin D. Roosevelt—who went on to win the biggest landslide in a century (he took every state but two). Why was the *Literary Digest* so far off base? Because its readers tended to be wealthy people who did not like President Roosevelt or his policies. The biggest polling blooper ever? The 2016 election. Scores of polls gave Hillary Clinton a solid lead. Reading the polls, some experts declared her election up to 99 percent probable. One of the great questions about the election: How could all the polls be so wrong?

Polling 101

Imagine that you are hired to conduct a public survey about preferences in the next mayoral election. Where do you start? You could ask a few friends in your American government class whom they plan to vote for, but that would not offer you a reliable way to predict the winner. Here is how you could improve your poll.

The Random Sample. One foolproof way to predict the election would be to interview every voter. That would take too much time and cost too much. Instead, pollsters select a random selection of individuals who reflect the entire population. All people should have an equal chance of being interviewed. Otherwise, your results will be as misleading as the *Literary Digest* poll (skewed to the wealthy)—or as

see for yourself 7.2

Go online and listen to excerpts from Roosevelt's fiery 1936 campaign speech, helping him overcome opposition among wealthier voters.

Random sample: A sample in which everyone in the population (sampling frame) has an equal probability of being selected.

INFO/DATA: Surveys Face Growing Difficulty Reaching and Persuading Potential Respondents

Political campaigns and major issues surfacing for debate now attract dozens of polls from a dizzying host of sources, with news stories of all types routinely citing polling results. Yet even as professional pollsters expand in number and influence, Americans' willingness to participate in polls has plummeted.

1. Is it problematic that all three rates (contact, cooperation, and response) displayed in the infographic have fallen sharply over the last fifteen to twenty years? Can we trust poll results based on shrinking percentages of the population?

2. Could you imagine ways to reverse this decline in cooperation with pollsters? What would incentivize *you* to spend twenty to thirty minutes on the phone with a polling organization?

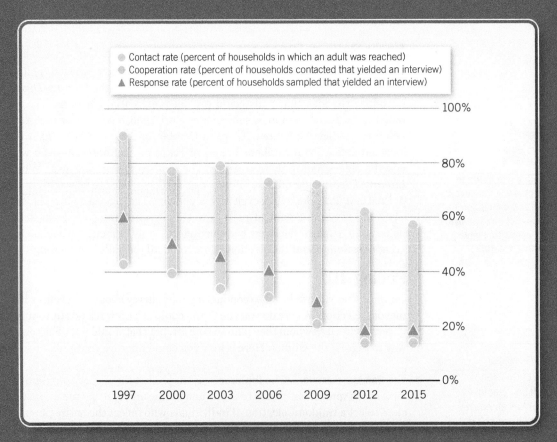

- Contact rate (percent of households in which an adult was reached)
- Cooperation rate (percent of households contacted that yielded an interview)
- Response rate (percent of households sampled that yielded an interview)

Source: Pew Research

website polls that invite anyone to cast a vote (skewed to the kinds of people who surf to that site).

Sampling frame:
A designated group of people from whom a set of poll respondents is randomly selected.

Demographic group: People sharing specific characteristics such as age, ethnicity/race, religion, or country of origin.

Likely voters: Persons identified as probable voters in an upcoming election. Often preferred by polling organizations, but difficult to specify with great accuracy.

Sampling Frame. Professional pollsters are careful to construct an accurate **sampling frame**—the types of people they plan to survey. If your poll is to accurately reflect public views, your survey respondents must reflect the population. That means they must vary in *age, education, income, race* or *ethnic group, gender,* and many other factors so they reflect the population that will vote in the mayoral election. Asking only your classmates would bias the poll toward college-educated and younger people. A good representative survey includes **demographic groups** in rough proportion to their presence in the population.

Refining the Sample. You also will have to make a related sampling decision. Do you want your poll to represent *all* city residents, or only those who will probably turn out and vote? Choosing **likely voters** will more accurately predict the outcome of most elections—but determining exactly who will come out makes the pollster's job more difficult. Perhaps this is where they went wrong during the 2016 election.

Timing. Before you start knocking on doors or dialing numbers consider the *timing* of your survey. When do you conduct the poll? If you do it during the day, people with jobs will be away from home or unable to talk; if you conduct a telephone poll on a Friday evening, you are unlikely to find many younger residents at home—skewing your results to older people's opinions.

Framing effects: The influence, on the respondent, of how a polling question is asked; changes in wording can significantly alter many people's answers.

Wording. Once you have chosen your sampling frame and decided when to ask questions, you face an even more important question: What exactly will you ask? If this were a chat with your classmates, you might ask simply, "Who do you support in the 2017 mayoral election?" But surveys must take into account **framing effects**: The *way* pollsters ask a question often influences the response.

For example, researchers from the Pew Research Center asked people to choose between a tax cut and "funding new government programs." The public overwhelmingly picked the tax cut, 60 percent to 25 percent. Then the pollsters adjusted the question and asked people to choose between a tax cut and funding for "programs on education, the environment, health care, crime fighting and military defense." Now, 69 percent opted for the government programs and only 22 percent for the tax cut. The wording made all the difference. Slight rephrasing can dramatically change the results. Does government provide too much assistance to the poor? Only 6 percent say yes. Does government provide too much *welfare* (which is the same question with a new word)? Now, 40 percent say yes. In another Pew poll, 51 percent of respondents favored "making it legal for doctors to assist terminally ill patients to end their lives," but only 44 percent favored "making it legal for doctors to assist terminally ill patients to commit suicide."

In other cases, these wording biases can be subtle. In obscure political races (other than

Mocking bias in the polls.

COMPARING NATIONS 7.1 **Top Global Threats: Polling Around the World**

When people in different nations are asked about the greatest global threat, Americans and Western Europeans point to Islamic terrorism; South Americans worry about global climate change; Eastern Europeans fear Russia; and Russians are concerned about economic instability. (Pew Research Center)

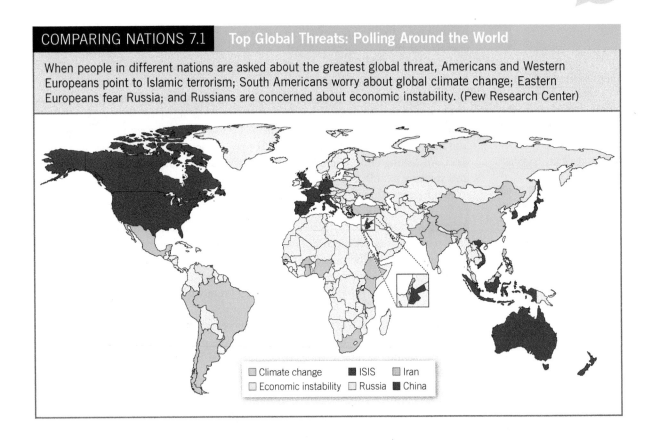

| Climate change | ■ ISIS | Iran |
| Economic instability | Russia | ■ China |

president, governor, or big-city mayor), many survey respondents prefer the candidate who is named *first*, no matter what party or other identifying details are included in the question. A really good poll will pretest the questions to sniff out the subtle biases that creep in with different wordings and will reverse the order of the questions to negate biases associated with question ordering. International polling also has grown more sophisticated (see Comparing Nations 7.1).

Lies, Damn Lies, and Polls. Campaigns or advocacy groups often *want* to skew their survey results and use framing effects to their advantage. Some polls actually try to influence respondents' views. These surveys—which do not even pretend to be legitimate efforts to measure opinions—are termed **push polls**. Such "polls" have more impact on unsuspecting respondents because they are campaign advertisements masquerading as scientific surveys.

For example, people who answered the phone in South Carolina during the 2016 Republican primary heard an automated voice ask standard questions: What's your age? Which candidate do you support? Then, for those who indicated support for Senator Marco Rubio, they were asked: Did you know Rubio is "for letting 11 million illegal immigrants stay in the U.S." and "for letting Syrians cross the border freely"? That is not a serious question; it's an attack—or a push poll.[9]

Technology and Error. Younger Americans are especially hard to reach and survey. Can you guess why? Many young people—and 47 percent of all phone users—rely on mobile phones rather than landlines.[10] To save time and money, most professional pollsters use *automated* dialing for landline calls. Machines dial dozens of

Push poll: A form of negative campaigning that masquerades as a regular opinion survey. Usually conducted by a campaign or allied group; features strongly critical or unflattering information about an opponent.

FIGURE 7.7 *Sampling errors decline with larger sample sizes. (MEER Research)*

numbers at once; when a caller answers, the "robo-dialer" transfers the call to a human surveyor to ask the preapproved polling questions.

Sampling Error and Response Bias.   Finally, you have collected the raw data from all of your surveying. Time to tell the world about the details of your poll? Not so fast. You still need to determine your poll's **margin of sampling error**, a statistical measure of how accurate your results are. By carefully designing their poll, national surveys are able to achieve small errors with as few as one thousand respondents (see Figure 7.7).

Pollsters also must consider **response bias** in publicizing their findings. Studies show that some respondents purposely mislead pollsters. Response bias can reflect animosity toward pollsters or the all-too-human tendency to align with "acceptable" views. Survey questions that might elicit unpopular attitudes, such as racism or sexism, can lead respondents (consciously or unconsciously) to shift their answers in a more socially acceptable direction.

A classic example of response bias arose when Tom Bradley, the first African American mayor of Los Angeles, ran against a white candidate, George Deukmejian, for governor of California in 1982. Bradley had a comfortable double-digit lead in opinion surveys as Election Day approached—but lost the race. Today pollsters must be alert to what is now known as the Bradley effect: The possible inclination of some survey respondents to avoid appearing racist or racially motivated.

Sample size, framing effects, and margin of error: account for all these, and you are well on your way to conducting a truly scientific public opinion survey. One important reason to understand the design of polls is so that you can distinguish the good from the bad. Table 7.2 summarizes some of the tips in this section.

How Did They Do?   The pollsters failed to accurately predict the results of the 2016 presidential election. In the days before the election, national polls showed a close race—with most giving the Democratic candidate Hillary Clinton a two to seven point lead and fewer handing Republican candidate Donald Trump a smaller lead. The real debacle, however, was at the state level, where polls failed to show Trump's strength in key swing states (see Table 7.3). What went wrong? Some argued that polls overestimated Democratic turnout; others suggested that the Bradley effect may have come into play; while many pollsters began to reassess their methodology in search of a systemic error.

Margin of sampling error: The degree of inaccuracy in any poll, arising from the fact that surveys involve a *sample* of respondents from a population, rather than every member.

Response bias: The tendency of poll respondents to misstate their views, frequently to avoid "shameful" opinions such as sexism or racism.

Bandwagon effect: When people join a cause because it seems popular or support a candidate who is leading in the polls.

Boomerang effect: The discrepancy between candidates' high poll ratings and election performance, caused by supporters' assumption that an easy win means they need not turn out.

TABLE 7.2	**Tips on Reading Polls**

1. *Check out the margin of error.* Then reread the poll that figures it in. A 3 percent margin of error means plus or minus 3 percent—turning a 50 percent approval rating into one of 47 to 53 percent.

2. *What is the timing?* The further away from Election Day, the less meaningful the results.

3. *The random sample is the gold standard.* If the respondents chose themselves (by deciding to take the survey), then it may be fun to read . . . but it is probably not an accurate picture of the public.

4. *What is the sample size?* Be wary of polls that interview a small number of people. For a national poll, 1,000 to 1,500 respondents are typical. If the margin of error is too large (say over 5%), then approach the poll with caution.

5. *Compare across polls.* Because every poll has biases, read a range of polls, toss out the extreme findings, and take an average of the rest.

TABLE 7.3	**Polling Error in Swing States, 2016**

STATE	TRUMP'S AVG POLLING MARGIN	MARGIN OF TRUMP'S VICTORY	AVG ERROR IN POLLS
Ohio	+2.0	+8.6	+6.6
Wisconsin	−5.4	+1.0	+6.4
Pennsylvania	−3.7	+1.2	+4.9
North Carolina	−0.7	+3.8	+4.5
Michigan	−4.0	+0.3	+4.3
Florida	−0.6	+1.3	+1.9
Source: FiveThirtyEight.com			

Do Opinion Surveys Influence Us?

Might the profusion of polls also affect the decisions we citizens make—including how to vote? Evidence suggests that they do. Candidates who are leading in the polls tend to pick up support from voters who were undecided or who weakly supported the opponent. The **bandwagon effect** in polling varies considerably from place to place and election to election. It can be exaggerated by media coverage: In 2016, one article after another attributed Donald Trump's unexpected nomination to the bandwagon effect.[11]

The idea that positive poll results inspire people to support a leading candidate has been around for a long time. Pollsters staunchly resist suggestions that their "objective science" of measuring opinion influences outcomes. But the fact has stubbornly remained resistant to efforts to dislodge it.

A close cousin of polling's bandwagon effect is the **boomerang effect**. Here, a candidate who has been consistently ahead in opinion surveys performs more

Talking POLITICS

TYPES OF POLLS

Benchmark polls. Conducted by a campaign as the race begins, these surveys provide a basis for comparison, or a "benchmark," for later polls. With a benchmark number, candidates can tell if their likelihood of winning is rising or falling.

Straw polls. Informal polls carried out by local party organizations or news outlets; they often involve actual (nonbinding) votes cast by party members. Media organizations (and the straw poll winners) report straw poll results, especially during presidential primaries.

Brushfire polls. Internal surveys conducted by a campaign once election season begins. They provide details about how a candidate is performing; if things are going poorly, the campaign can work to put out the "brushfire" of opposition (which burns swiftly and potentially spreads fast).

Exit polls. Performed on Election Day, both by campaigns and news organizations, these surveys intercept voters as they exit the voting location. Media reporters often rely on exit polls to call results for one or the other candidate, even if ballots haven't been officially counted.

Calling the Election Early?

Imagine that you are the news director of a local network TV station. It's election night, one of the biggest days of the year for political news. Reliable exit polling suggests that a local race—for mayor, or state senate, or maybe the U.S. House—is breaking overwhelmingly for one candidate. Your reporters are pushing you to let them announce that result on the air, beating other local stations to the punch. They have the information and accuse you of censoring them. What do you do?

Let the polls close first. If we announce the result before the polls close, some unknown number of voters will not vote, affecting the election outcome. The national TV networks and cable news stations have agreed to hold off announcing results from a specific state until the polls close.

Go for the scoop. It's important to win the television ratings race. Some media organizations report exit polling results while voters are still waiting to cast their ballots. And doing so reflects a basic American value: Freedom of the Press.

poorly than expected on Election Day. The logic is that supporters see a big lead for their candidate, figure that he or she will win without any difficulty, and so do not bother to vote.

Scrambling the issue further, some voters also appear to follow the *opposite* of the bandwagon effect. America loves rooting for the underdog—the one we do not expect to win—and this tendency also appears in public opinion polling. The **underdog effect** is invoked when a candidate losing in the polls performs better than expected. There is less empirical evidence for this phenomenon than for the bandwagon effect, but enough examples exist that the term has stuck.

Underdog effect: Sympathy for a candidate behind in the polls, contributing to a higher-than-predicted vote total—and sometimes a surprise election victory.

THE BOTTOM LINE

» Scientific surveys have come a long way since their origins in 1936. Professionals now design well-specified polls that capture popular views with a high degree of accuracy.

» Indeed, poll results can affect public opinion, in ways ranging from the bandwagon effect to the underdog effect.

» Sampling errors, response bias, and other potential flaws inevitably confer a measure of uncertainty on any survey.

Public Opinion in a Democracy

If the public is to have a meaningful role in governing, political leaders must listen to their views. But here is the uncomfortable question: Do the people know enough to shape government decisions? We have seen that the founders were wary of the public when they framed the Constitution. The question continues to provoke disagreement. Is the public rational and capable of self-government? Or are we ignorant masses? Let us look at two different views.

Ignorant Masses

"The masses are asses!" insisted Walter Lippmann in his pathbreaking book *Public Opinion* (published in 1922). Lippmann, a well-known political journalist and cultural critic, dismissed the young "science" of public opinion as undeserving of the name. In his view, the typical American was distracted by celebrity shenanigans and minor scandals, rarely followed policy issues closely enough to understand the details, and yet readily offered up personal views on any topic. Paying attention to the uninformed masses was no way to run a country. Lippmann, along with many others, believed that governing involved technical decisions that were best left to well-trained experts.[12]

Some modern thinkers embrace a similar view. Most Americans cannot answer basic questions about our political system—like how many justices are on the Supreme Court (nine) or the name of their representative in Congress. As a result, critics describe America as an "ignorant democracy." Popular whims and cleverly packaged slogans, they say, win out over serious political deliberation.[13] Public opinion, in this view, is a tool for manipulation by savvy message consultants and political marketers.

In 1960, four University of Michigan professors published a book that hit America like a thunderclap. Not only were most citizens uninformed, but even more damning, *The American Voter* described the scientific poll—the instrument widely used to capture public opinion by the 1950s—as all but useless. One of the authors, Philip Converse, later coined the term **nonattitudes** to describe the response of many Americans to polls. When people were asked the same questions at different times, they tended to change their answers—sometimes radically. Moreover, changes in their responses were random: People did not switch their positions in response to new information or in changing contexts, but rather offered up different and even diametrically opposed views for no apparent reason.[14]

> **Nonattitudes:** The lack of a stable perspective in response to opinion surveys; answers to questions may be self-contradictory or may display no ideological consistency.

The American Voter shook the confidence in the value of both public opinion and the scientific methods used to measure it. If Americans spewed random thoughts in response to survey questions, what use were opinion polls? This perspective extends right down to the present. A more recent political-science study, *The American Voter Revisited*, drew very similar conclusions: Americans remain politically ignorant. Popular historian Rick Shenkman summed up this gloomy perspective in the title of his bestseller: *Just How Stupid Are We? Facing the Truth About the American Voter.*[15]

Recent research in political psychology echoes this pessimistic view. Milton Lodge and Charles Taber argued that citizens evaluate political leaders and issues by relying on "unconscious political thinking." People are very sensitive to subtle cues—hearing the word "President" before Clinton/Trump, patriotic music in campaign ads, or the inflection of the broadcaster's voice as she reports a story. In effect, subconscious attitudes drive public opinion. People rationalize preconceived biases rather than making rational choices. They may not even be aware of why they are making the choices they make. In short, political psychologists add more reasons to be skeptical about the people's wisdom in governing the nation.[16]

The Rational Public

Many other commentators defend the American public, arguing that ordinary Americans, not elite technocrats, are the best judges of what government should do. This alternative view arose in the 1980s, most prominently captured in a book-length response to *The American Voter* called *The Rational Public.*[17] The authors,

Can We Trust the Public?

Which side makes more sense to you: *The American Voter*, which concludes that the public is clueless? Or *The Rational Public*, which insists, on the contrary, that the people are the wisest political actors? The answer to this question is crucial for the practice of democracy.	**I believe the public is thoughtful and informed.** Are you and your friends contributors to a thoughtful American viewpoint based on your interest in politics or your daily experience?	**I believe the public is clueless.** Or are you more likely to offer clueless "doorstep opinions" that change in unpredictable ways depending on your mood at the time?	**Both.** Like Condorcet, do you believe that both positions contain valuable insight and that when we add up all our friends and neighbors, what emerges is the "wisdom of crowds"?

Benjamin Page and Robert Shapiro, recognized that—yes—most voters are generally inattentive to policy issues and uninformed about political details. However, measured across large groups of people, public opinion moves in coherent, stable ways that signal shared views about policy issues. Although a single voter or poll respondent may hold inconsistent or even self-contradictory notions, these are submerged in the collective outlook of tens of millions of voters. Taken as a whole, the public can differentiate among alternative policies, in ways that accurately reflect its shared values and beliefs.

Information shortcuts:
Cues about candidates and policies drawn from everyday life.

Page and Shapiro argued that most of us use **information shortcuts** to arrive at reasonable judgments about politics and government. These shortcuts often derive from our direct personal experience. Homeowners grasp the importance of interest-rate changes, and shoppers feel inflation's effect on rising prices. Both homeowners and shoppers develop an intuitive sense of the performance of the economy. Likewise, citizens notice the impact of other policy outcomes on their daily lives, as when trains or buses run on time or mail arrives late. Through a steady and often unwitting process of making everyday evaluations, voters and poll respondents can arrive at reasonably well-established positions on candidates or policy issues.

Is there any way to reconcile the two views—ignorant individuals on the one hand, a rational public on the other? The journalist James Surowiecki offered one solution, summarized by the title of his book: *The Wisdom of Crowds*. Even if any one individual does not have clear views, argued Surowiecki, a large crowd, taken together, adds up to a rational public. In fact, a random collection of people is actually wiser than a group of experts when it comes to devising the best solution to a policy dilemma.

Surowiecki builds on work by the French thinker Nicolas de Condorcet, who in the eighteenth century demonstrated that although each member of a jury may have only a slightly better chance of accurately judging guilt or innocence than would a random coin flip, taken as a majority, the jurors are likely to reach a correct decision. Similarly, a collection of people may exhibit a wide diversity of political opinions, including many that are poorly informed or even eccentric. Overall, however, if the group is of sufficient size—at least a few dozen—and members feel free to speak their minds, they will zero in on a good collective decision. Often these are innovative, outside-the-box solutions. Experts, on the other hand, are typically trained in similar ways and are subject to **groupthink**: They tend to reinforce one another's existing prejudices.

Surowiecki illustrates his point by going back to an old country fair in England. A prize was offered to whoever could guess the correct weight of a giant ox on display. Cattle experts weighed in with their own well-founded opinions, but all were considerably off the mark. More than eight hundred locals offered up guesses as well. Although no one hit the correct weight (1,198 pounds), an average of the crowd's collective estimate came out at 1,197—just one pound below the correct total, and much closer than that offered by any agricultural or farming expert.[18]

Groupthink: The tendency among a small group of decision makers to converge on a shared set of views; can limit creative thinking or solutions to policy problems.

● *How much does this ox weigh? Ordinary fairgoers' collective guess outperformed that of agricultural experts in a famous nineteenth-century contest—a testament to the power of aggregated public opinion.*

THE BOTTOM LINE

» Since the founding era, some Americans have viewed public opinion as an unreliable, even dangerous, guide to government policymaking based in part on voter ignorance.

» Others argue that, in practice, a "rational public" is the best source of democratic decision making.

» One way to combine these clashing views is to focus not on what individuals know about politics but on how many different popular views add up to the "wisdom of crowds."

🔒 Public Opinion and Governing

The optimistic view about the crowd's wisdom restores traditional hopes about self-rule. However, if public opinion is to guide government, three conditions must be met.

1. The people know what they want and guide government decisions.
2. The public can clearly communicate its desires to political leaders.
3. Political leaders pay attention to public views—and respond.

That three-step process reflects the argument for public opinion's vital role in democratic governance. Each step, however, is full of difficulties. Let us consider each in turn.

Do the People Know What They Want?

Although opinion polls suggest that the public have distinct preferences, public views often fail to provide a guide for policymakers. For example, after the economic collapse between 2008 and 2010, polls showed that a majority of Americans were angry at Wall Street banks. By large margins, the public favored tough legislation: slash financial industry CEOs' pay, throttle back on trading in exotic financial instruments that few people understand, and make banks pay for the economic mess they helped create.

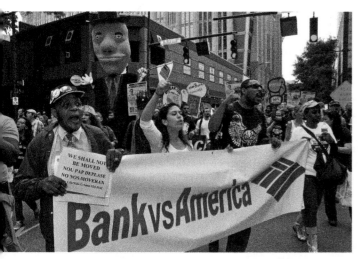

● Public opinion alerted politicians to the anger at big banks—but did not provide an answer for what to do about it.

But when Congress and the Obama administration tried to translate this public discontent into concrete legislative solutions, popular consensus evaporated. Should we regulate derivatives as we do stocks and bonds so that their trading is transparent? Half the public said yes, half said no. Limit CEOs' pay or the multimillion-dollar bonuses the financial wizards receive each year? Maybe, or maybe not, Americans told surveyors. Deep in the details, the crowd did not seem to have much wisdom after all. In the end, the "Dodd-Frank" bill regulating the financial industry that passed Congress in summer 2010 satisfied few. Today, the American public gives low marks to both that Dodd-Frank regulatory effort *and* to the large Wall Street banks that the law is designed to monitor.[19]

Does the public know what it wants? In a general way, it arguably does. But political leaders have to supply the policy specifics.

How Do the People Communicate Their Desires?

It is difficult for the people—even a clear majority—to convey their views to policymakers. None of our instruments for adding up and transmitting millions of people's views are particularly effective.

Survey research:
Systematic study of a defined population, analyzing a representative sample's views to draw inferences about the larger public's views. Also termed *opinion poll.*

Mandate: Political authority claimed by an election winner as reflecting the approval of the people.

As we have seen, **survey research** can offer snapshots of public opinion on policy issues. However, polls have margins of error; they can be spun to advance partisan interests; and they offer general impressions, not a guide to crafting policies and making decisions—as we just saw in the case of widespread public anger at Wall Street.

Of course, democracies also rely on elections. Candidates who win often claim they have a **mandate**: The people have spoken. But it is difficult to translate an election into support for any single policy. Congressional Republicans, victorious in the 2014 midterm election, claimed a mandate to eliminate the 'Obamacare' law and lower tax rates significantly. They had little success while Democratic President Obama was in office. Normally, it is difficult to translate electoral victory into policy. Watch carefully to see if Republicans can achieve these goals with a Republican president in the White House.

Interest groups and political parties also work to collect and transmit popular views. However, their messages about what the people want generally come with a partisan spin.

Do Leaders Respond to Public Opinion?

On the surface, the answer seems to be unambiguous: yes! Opinion surveys are everywhere, and politicians seem hooked on them. American politicians spend more on pollsters, by far, than leaders of other nations.

Approval rating: A measure of public support for a political figure or institution.

Our national campaigns collectively spend upward of one billion dollars annually on polling. All members of every institution you will read about in this book— senators, presidents, lobbyists, even judges—avidly consume polls about their performance, as well as about the hot issues of the day. **Approval ratings**, which are routinely reported for top U.S. political figures and national institutions, can boost a leader's power when ratings rise and weaken his or her standing when they fall.

During the Clinton administration, presidential pollsters such as Mark Penn were described as having "close to veto power" on some policy decisions.[20] The president reportedly heard from his polling staff even on such matters as where he and his family should go on vacation.

However, attention to public views does not necessarily mean that politicians slavishly follow the poll results. Rather, polls guide political leaders in their efforts to persuade the public to embrace their own views—and criticize the opposition and their ideas.[21]

Polls clearly matter in setting the **policy agenda**. Public opinion helps shape which topics governing officials pay attention to in the first place. If the public thinks something is important, political leaders will usually respond.

Policy agenda: The issues that the media covers, the public considers important, and politicians address. Setting the agenda is the first step in political action.

Big changes in public opinion have an especially significant effect on Congress. Members are often reluctant to legislate in the face of strong popular opposition. Americans may ignore many topics, but when large numbers of us pay attention to something, politicians generally respond. That is exactly what we saw at the start of this chapter with same-sex marriage and legal marijuana.

Public opinion also enables presidential actions that might otherwise be blocked. Theodore Roosevelt (1901–1909) was a popular president, but he had to abandon his ambitious plans for a national system of protected forest in the eastern United States because of public indifference. His less popular successor, William Howard Taft (1909–1913), signed the Forest Reserve Act into law. How did Taft succeed? After a massive forest fire known as the "Big Burn" raged across three western states and killed more than one hundred young firefighters, public opinion swung decisively in support of environmental protection. If you have hiked on the Appalachian Trail, vacationed in the Smoky Mountains, or gone leaf-peeping in New England, you have benefited from a program made possible by shifting public opinion.

● *You can enjoy this trail today thanks to a shift in public opinion back in 1910.*

THE BOTTOM LINE

» If public opinion is to guide politics, three conditions must be met: The public must know what it wants, its views must be effectively communicated, and leaders must pay attention.

» Even strong public opinion may not be specific enough to offer policy guidance.

» U.S. government officials devote more resources to polling operations than do top officials in other nations.

» All government officials constantly have to weigh doing what they think is best against doing what the public desires. Popular views can help set governing agendas. Polls often guide officials not in selecting a policy, but in determining how best to win over the public to their policies.

🔘 Conclusion: Government by the People

The Declaration of Independence states a powerful ideal that has inspired each generation of Americans: the consent of the governed. Lincoln memorably reaffirmed this national commitment in his Gettysburg Address: "government by the people." Self-rule appears to demand that public opinion guides—or at least influences—national officials.

Public opinion surveys are widely used to understand the popular mind. Scientific techniques have made polls more accurate. However, rising costs, low response rates, the difficulty of predicting turnout, and hostility can all make polls miss.

A great debate swirls around public opinion itself. Many have considered it whimsical or uninformed—even the framers of the Constitution were skeptical of public opinion. Other scholars respond that collective decisions—the wisdom of crowds—are better decisions than those made by well-trained experts.

Of course, the public can always be better informed. Our information age provides ever more polling data. But more information is not always better. Research by Barry Schwartz, a psychologist, shows that an overabundance of choices and details tends to paralyze individual citizens, rather than empower them.[22] The current torrent of polls, many of them carefully slanted by advocates or politicians trying to influence us, spews out overwhelming reams of data. Rising political scientists (like you) and activists alike need to hone their skills at reading polls—drowning out the noise, picking the more accurate reflections of public sentiment.

For all the din of politics and polls, remember the examples that began this chapter. Massive shifts in public opinion—as with same-sex marriage and marijuana reform—profoundly affect public officials. A rising generation's attitudes quietly influence our public policies.

Still, no amount of public opinion can replace the central act of governance: elected leaders, with an eye to public sentiment (and all the surveys measuring their approval ratings) who make the choices. Public officials have a major effect in setting the agenda, framing issues, and signaling popular views. They can take the lead in encouraging us to be better stewards of democracy.

CHAPTER SUMMARY

🔘 Scientific surveys have come a long way since the *Literary Digest* in 1936. Professionals now design well-specified polls that capture popular views with a high degree of accuracy. However, be cautious when reading polls, such as those without a well-defined sample (for example, online surveys). Always pay attention to the margin of error when interpreting results.

🔘 Political socialization is the study of the forces that shape public opinion. The most important are family and friends, race, gender, religion, economic interests, demographics, party affiliation, the view of political elites, and defining events like war.

🔘 In a democracy, public opinion should guide the government. But are the people capable of self-rule? From the Constitutional Convention to contemporary social scientists, many experts consider public opinion to be uninformed and unreliable—and therefore a dangerous guide to decision making.

● Others respond that the public, taken as a whole, is a rational, reliable source of government decisions. Even if individuals do not know much, there is wisdom in crowds.

● The United States devotes more resources to polling operations than other nations. Polls have become the everyday mechanism for gauging public opinion.

● Public officials generally balance public opinion with their own beliefs about the best decisions. If they are seen as overly faithful to poll results, the paradoxical result may be that their approval rating falls. Polls often guide administrations, not in selecting a policy, but in determining how best to win over the public to its policies.

● Popular views can be especially important in setting the agenda: If something seems important to the public (and the media), politicians respond. Congress, in particular, pays attention to spikes in public opinion. Presidents find it easier to get their policies passed when public opinion is strongly in favor of that policy.

KEY TERMS

Approval rating, p. 216
Bandwagon effect, p. 211
Boomerang effect, p. 211
Demographic group, p. 208
Framing effects, p. 208
Groupthink, p. 215
Information shortcuts, p. 214

Likely voters, p. 208
Mandate, p. 216
Margin of sampling error, p. 210
Nonattitudes, p. 213
Policy agenda, p. 217
Political elites, p. 204

Political socialization, p. 202
Push poll, p. 209
Random sample, p. 206
Response bias, p. 210
Sampling frame, p. 208
Survey research, p. 216
Underdog effect, p. 212

STUDY QUESTIONS

1. "The masses are asses," wrote one observer of American politics. He was summarizing a perspective that public opinion is not a reliable guide to government. Why, exactly, is public opinion unreliable? Be sure to include the effect of *The American Voter*.

2. Some scholars believe that public opinion is a legitimate guide to government decision making. Summarize this alternative view, noting the argument made in *The Rational Public*.

3. For further contemplation: Which of these perspectives on public opinion seems more powerful to you? Do you believe the public is basically ignorant? Or collectively wise? (Yes, it is okay to opt for a bit of both.) Defend your answer.

4. *"Public officials must always balance public opinion with their own beliefs."*

a) Explain why.
b) What problems face political leaders who *always* follow the polls in deciding what to do?
c) What problems face political leaders who *never* follow the polls in deciding what to do?
d) How can polls help leaders who already know what they want to do?

5. Define the following terms: *push poll*; *sampling frame*; *margin of error*; *Bradley effect*.

6. What does it mean to "frame an issue"? Illustrate using the issue of obesity.

7. For further contemplation: Describe another example of "issue framing." You can pick another example from this book, a hot-button issue from news headlines, or an issue that has arisen on your campus or in your community. In each case, describe the alternate frames.

 Go to www.oup.com/us/Morone to find quizzes, flash cards, simulations, tutorials, videos, and other study tools.

Political Participation

8

KELI CARENDER had a pierced nose, performed in a Seattle improv group, and passionately hated government spending. She tried calling her congressman to complain about an Obama administration proposal—but his mailbox was full. So Keli did what Americans have been doing for 200 years—she organized a protest. In February 2009, a smattering of people showed up—not enough to eat all the pulled pork she had brought along as a symbol of, well, government pork (or excessive spending).

A week after the little rally, former bond trader Rick Santelli launched into a rant on a CNBC business show, the Squawk Box: "What we're doing in this country now is making [the founding fathers] roll over in their graves. . . . We need . . . a Tea Party!" And, bang, Keli Carender's Seattle protests—and groups like hers across the United States—had a name. Before long, people were standing outside the White House waving symbolic teabags.

By the summer, the Tea Party protests were roiling American politics. When Seattle Congressman Norman Dicks held a town hall meeting to discuss health reform, Keli Carender was in the packed room. "If you're so keen to forcibly take . . . my money and give it to someone else based on their supposed need then you come and take this $20 bill from me." As she waved the bill, the room erupted.

The Tea Party attracted conservative activists opposed to the Obama administration—and government spending in general. These heartfelt conservatives soon began to draw funding from conservative donors; Democrats dismissed the conservative group as "Astroturf" (manufactured support) rather than true grassroots engagement. But there was no denying their intensity—or the influence they won in the Republican Party. The Tea Party activists resisted compromise and attacked politicians who bargained away conservative principles—even bringing down the top two Republicans in the House, Speaker of the House John Boehner (in 2015) and Majority Leader Eric Cantor (2014). These activists forcefully championed individualism (recall the contest between individualism and solidarity we discussed in Chapter 2).

Other groups arose on the other side of the issue. Occupy Wall Street challenged inequality and injustice. Moral Monday protests denounced limits on voting rights and spending cuts in North Carolina—then spread to other states. Democratic presidential candidate Bernie Sanders stunned the political establishment in 2016 by drawing tens of thousands to rallies calling for

● *The Tea Party rallies*

In this chapter you will:

● Explore the longstanding paradox of America exhibiting strong *and* weak political participation.

● Learn the three types of participation: traditional politics, direct action, and civic engagement.

● Examine why people participate.

● Identify the benefits and drawbacks of an emerging "clickocracy," as political engagement moves online.

● Consider whether there can be too much popular participation in a democracy.

221

● *Tea Party meetings, like this one in Sharon, Kansas, spread across the nation.*

more government and *higher* taxes on the wealthy to diminish inequality. But, so far, none have proved as successful as the Tea Party in setting the agenda and electing candidates to office.

Who are we? Heirs of the revolutionary Americans who took to the streets and town centers to throw off the British yoke? A nation where every generation finds new ways to participate? A country where thousands show up to political rallies to cheer long-shot candidates? A democratic nation where most people do not even bother to vote? We are all of these.

Participation in public life is always changing. The millennial generation, like many before them, have found new ways to participate that revolve around social media—we call it **"clicktivism"** or hashtag politics, and it takes many forms. Perhaps your friends dumped ice water on their heads and challenged people in their network to do likewise or pay up for a good cause? That too is a form of public participation.

Clicktivism: Democratic engagement in an online age: point your mouse or scan a QR code, click, and you have donated funds, "liked" a candidate, or (in some states) even cast your vote.

see for yourself 8.1

Go online to see Keli Carender confront her congressman.

Traditional participation: Engaging in political activities through the formal channels of government and society.

How We Participate

We start with a paradox: In some ways, Americans are highly engaged in politics, while in other ways Americans are downright apathetic. In this chapter, we will explore the many pathways to participation in the political system. Some stretch back over two hundred years. Others are just emerging on the political scene today. Altogether, they break into three broad categories: traditional participation, civic volunteerism, direct action.

Traditional Participation

The 2016 election campaign fired up millions of people. Hillary Clinton aimed to be the first woman president, Marco Rubio the first Latino, and Donald Trump the first with no prior government experience. Many of these candidates' supporters engaged in traditional politics. **Traditional participation** means getting involved in politics through formal government channels—organized by federal and state constitutions and developed over time. Voting, working for a candidate, signing petitions, or writing letters to the newspaper are all ways of becoming active (see Table 8.1).

Voting. Voting is the foundational political participatory act in any democracy. Yet over 90 million eligible Americans did not in 2016. If you have voted, you know the basic drill. First, register to vote. Some states make it much easier than others: Eleven states and the District of Columbia permit registration and voting on the same day. Oregon became the first state to automatically register voters.

Second, cast your vote. Only a few years ago, this meant arriving on Election Day at your assigned polling place. But today, thirty-two states now permit early voting—and more than a third of the ballots are cast before Election Day. Washington and Oregon conduct elections by mail. If you do vote on Election Day, bear in mind

BY THE NUMBERS

Political Participation

Percentage of Americans under thirty expressing trust in U.S. government, 2015: **25**
Percentage of Americans under thirty expressing trust in U.S. government, 1961: **81**

Percentage of U.S. college students who volunteer for public service, including informal volunteering like helping neighbors, 2015: **82**

Percentage of baby boomers (aged fifty to sixty-eight, roughly) who volunteered when they were of college age, 2015: **44**

Percentage turnout of voting-age population, U.S. presidential election, 1840: **80**
Percentage turnout of voting-age population, U.S. presidential election, 1940: **63**
Percentage turnout of voting-age population, U.S. presidential election, 2016: **56.8**

Percentage donated to U.S. election campaigns by the top 0.5 percent (one half of one percent), 2015–2016: **70.3**
Percentage of campaign contributions that came from small donors for Bernie Sanders, Donald Trump, and Hillary Clinton: **77, 70, 17**

Estimated number of political-themed blogs, 2001: **500**
Estimated number of political-themed blogs, 2016: **more than 100,000**

TABLE 8.1 **Rates of Traditional Political Participation**

22% of Americans have attended a political meeting on local, town, or school affairs.
13% have been an active member of a group that tries to influence the public or government.
10% have attended a political rally or speech.
7% have worked or volunteered for a political party or candidate.
7% called into a live radio or TV show to express an opinion about a political or social issue.
1.7% have donated to political campaigns.
0.03% have donated $200 to political campaigns.
Source: Pew Research Center

that some states limit voting facilities—creating long lines, which will discourage some voters. In November 2016, voters waited over three hours in Phoenix, Arizona, and up to five in Fishers, Indiana. (Recall from Chapter 3 that the Constitution leaves most election details up to the states.)

Once you get to the head of the line, you may encounter polling workers. They are usually unpaid volunteers—another form of political participation. They will

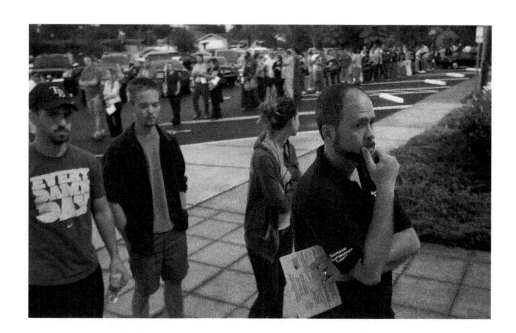

Why is voting turnout low in the United States? Perhaps it is because some governments make it difficult. Here, the long voting lines in Florida.

direct you to a voting booth, often adorned with distinctive blue curtains. Inside, you find one of many different voting mechanisms. Some jurisdictions use touch screens; some states use voting machines with levers; and in others you mark paper ballots much as the first U.S. voters did in 1789 (although there were no curtains back then—everyone voted in public). In 2016, an allegedly Russian-sponsored hacking of Democratic Party servers led to concerns about electronic voting machines being tampered with, and even calls for a return to paper balloting.[1]

If many different offices are listed on the ballot, perhaps along with an issue referendum or two (which we discuss later in this book), it might take you several minutes to work your way down the ballot and make all your choices. In local elections featuring just a handful of races, you may finish voting in thirty seconds or so.

Electoral Activities.   Voting is an important but limited form of political participation. Beyond voting, Americans engage in other **electoral activities.** They volunteer to get out the vote for favorite candidates. They go to meetings and rallies. They post signs on their lawns and bumper stickers on their cars. They donate money.

Electoral activities: Public engagement in the form of voting, running for office, volunteering in a campaign, or otherwise participating in elections.

Political Voice.   Engaging politically continues after the election is over. According to Pew Research, one in five Americans contacts a government official in the course of a typical year. They get in touch about potholes, immigration policy, trade deals with Asia, or the school lunch menu. Obviously, the key is finding the right official: Do not call the White House about potholes or the mayor's office about an international trade deal. To the surprise of many people, legislators—and especially members of Congress—devote considerable time to constituent inquiries.

If Americans are low in voting turnout, they are quick to express political opinions, exercising their First Amendment rights. On average, Americans exercise their **political voice** more often and more openly than citizens of many other advanced democracies. Chinese Americans protest the *Jimmy Kimmel Show* (for an alleged anti-Chinese skit), students demonstrate against products made in sweatshops, and small business owners contribute campaign funds to politicians challenging Obamacare. In addition, Americans, particularly millennials, sometimes

Political voice: Exercising one's public rights, often through speaking out in protest or in favor of some policy change.

try to express their voice through the market—buying local or not buying at all from companies who exploit workers or spoil the environment.

Civic Voluntarism

Not all participation runs through politics. Many Americans—young, middle-aged, and seniors alike—volunteer for causes or donate money for local charities. These are forms of **civic voluntarism**, working together to address problems through society.

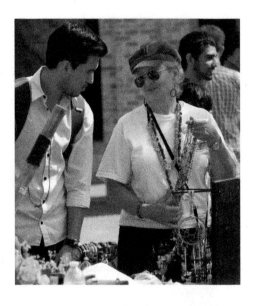

Civic voluntarism has a long pedigree. When the French visitor Alexis de Tocqueville, who we met earlier in this book, traveled through the United

Getting involved in civic action comes in many forms. Here vendors like Ruth Wagner were part of the Earth Day celebration at the University of Texas at Brownsville.

States in 1831–1832, he was struck by Americans' propensity to get involved. In *Democracy in America*, Tocqueville repeatedly remarked on the way Americans join together to build roads, schools, and hospitals; in France, he noted, such projects would require elaborate layers of government approval—and in England, would need the patronage of a lord.[2]

Civic voluntarism: Citizen participation in public life without government incentives or coercion (speaking at a town meeting vs. paying taxes, for example).

Americans still volunteer for causes at higher rates than citizens of other democratic countries. And the millennial generation—again, adults between late teens and early thirties—is the most active in modern U.S. history when it comes to volunteering their time for worthy causes. Over the past decade, the proportion of teenagers who volunteer has more than doubled. Résumé padding for career advancement? Recent studies say no, or at least not exclusively. Figure 8.1 shows the major reasons millennials get involved.

Voluntary engagement comes in many forms. People serve in a food bank, teach English as a second language, join a volunteer fire department, or help raise money for high school basketball uniforms. Many Americans respond to crowd funding requests on sites like Kickstarter, GoFundMe, and others.

Volunteers may not see their work as political, and indeed, getting involved is often related to a hobby or enthusiasm rather than public spirit. Whatever the motivation, voluntary activity tends to draw people into the common sphere. And once there, the payoff is clear. If you volunteer, you are more likely to vote, pay attention to political affairs, and otherwise engage in public life. As we saw in Chapter 1, successful democracies require a vibrant civic spirit.

Direct Action

When people feel that the traditional forms of participation are not working, they sometimes seek change outside of normal channels and take direct action. This is the world of demonstrations, marches, armed standoffs, and riots.

Protest politics can invoke the highest American aspirations. Or they can reflect nativism, prejudice, and unbridled anger. The

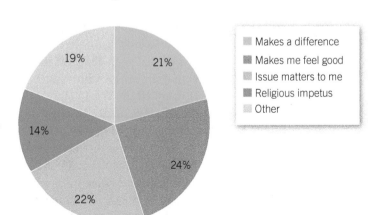

- Makes a difference
- Makes me feel good
- Issue matters to me
- Religious impetus
- Other

21% 24% 22% 14% 19%

FIGURE 8.1 *Americans aged 15 to 25: Reasons for volunteering. (Brookings Institution)*

Would You Have Protested?

Go back to the Civil Rights protests pictured on pages 170–171— young people at a sit-in are humiliated, those on a Freedom Bus beaten and almost burned alive. College students carried out the sit-ins and Freedom Rides. A question for you—one we often ask ourselves: **If you were in college between 1960 and 1962, would you have joined in?** It would have taken conviction, courage, and (for most students) a willingness to ignore parents horrified by the risks.

What would you have done? Explain why. Now consider the protests taking place on campuses today. How are they similar? How are they different? Have you considered taking part yourself? Explain why.

Direct action: Participating outside of normal political and social channels through civil disobedience, demonstrations, and even riots.

goal is generally to call attention to a cause and to foster a movement around it. Of course, direct action can blur into electoral politics. Protests can foster political movements that then penetrate national institutions, as we saw with the Tea Party at the start of the chapter.

Occasionally, direct action goes further and violates the law—sometimes through proud acts of **civil disobedience**. Protesting slavery in 1849, Henry David Thoreau urged his countrymen: "if [the law] requires you to be the agent of injustice to another, then, I say break the law. Let your life be a counter friction to stop the machine." Martin Luther King picked up this theme in his eloquent letter from a Birmingham jail, where he explained to white liberals why black Americans would break unjust laws rather than waiting quietly for reform.

Civil Disobedience. Protesting laws one considers unjust by refusing to obey them—and accepting the punishment.

The line between traditional participation and direct action can blur. Recall that the First Amendment guarantees the right to assemble—although local authorities normally require a permit before people can march in the street. We label all marches and demonstrations direct action—whether the protesters have a permit (making their assembly legal) or not (making it civil disobedience).

Direct action is not always part of the proud democratic legacy. Violent protests in Seattle cost an estimated $20 million—and put antiglobalization on the political agenda. Opponents of the Affordable Care Act threw rocks through a Colorado member's office window when he voted aye. Were they taking political action? Recklessly destroying property? Or both?

Finally, direct action also includes a dark legacy of violence and injustice. Recall how the entire system of Jim Crow was kept in place by a tradition of lynching—a form of American terrorism.

More common, great American rallies mark high points in our political history. Environmental activism offers a classic example. After millions of Americans gathered to promote cleaner air and water at the first Earth Day in April 1970, Congress passed major clean air legislation within a month, and a Clean Water Act soon after that. That kind of political voice is the lifeblood of American democracy.

Voter turnout: A measure of what proportion of eligible voters actually cast a legitimate ballot in a given election.

An Underlying Question

Recall one finding from the last chapter: Public opinion surveys repeatedly show that most Americans do not know much about politics. In a sense, this chapter extends that finding by showing how **voter turnout** rates are comparatively low in the United States: under 60 percent in presidential elections and under 40 percent—often well under that mark—in congressional midterm elections. Low voting rates mark a vital puzzle, especially when they are coupled with relatively high levels of direct action. Perhaps the level of citizen participation reflects the rules that govern the system; perhaps low turnout is less a result of individual motivation and more the result of electoral institutions (there's that second "I" from Chapter 1 again). After all, rules can make it easier or more difficult for citizens to participate.

In the past some states actively restricted the vote, often to keep African Americans away from power. For example, Mississippi had very high barriers to voting; in 1938, the two million citizens of the state (49% of them black) cast a total of only 35,439 votes for all five seats in Congress.[3] Limits at work in that era, like poll taxes and literacy tests (more on those below), no longer exist. But critics still ask: Do government officials *want* the public involved in their work? High participation rates make a democracy more robust—but they also slow things down and raise more controversy. Of course, raising the barriers to traditional participation always invites the larger disruption of direct action.

Throughout the chapter we will return to this question: Is the American system a miracle of mass participation? Or one designed to limit citizen access? Or, in the spirit of American federalism, is it a state-by-state patchwork of both these things?

THE BOTTOM LINE

» Traditional participation involves engaging politics through formal government channels. Voting is the most familiar form of traditional political participation.

» Americans participate in politics year round. One in five contacts a public official in the course of a year.

» Civic voluntarism is a form of engagement with public life that operates outside of government—but enhances democracy.

» Direct action seeks change by going outside the formal channels of government. It has a long legacy in the United States that goes back to the founding and includes some of the nation's great reform movements.

Why People Get Involved

Political scientists pay particular attention to who gets involved, how much, and why. Americans participate with extraordinary vigor in many aspects of public life. Approximately 28 percent—more than one in four Americans—contacts a political official. This is more than twice the percentage of citizens of the United Kingdom who reach out to their officials. Although only seven to eight percent of Americans volunteer on political campaigns, this compares favorably to the percentage of Canadians—between two and three percent.[4] Yet whether we are voting, volunteering, or expressing our political voice, some Americans feel more inspired to participate than others. What explains this higher likelihood of engagement in political activity?

Five main factors spur individuals to participate: Their personal background—especially age, wealth, and education; the influence of *family members* or close friends; the civic engagement and mutual trust that surrounds them—what social

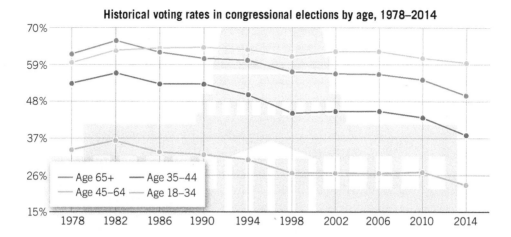

Historical voting rates in congressional elections by age, 1978–2014

● **FIGURE 8.2** *Voter turnout in Congressional elections, by age. (U.S. Census Bureau, Current Population Survey)*

Social capital: Relations between people that build closer ties of trust and civic engagement, yielding productive benefits for the larger society.

scientists term **social capital**; *mobilization efforts* by advocacy groups and political parties; and—perhaps most surprising—*receiving benefits* from government. Let us look at each in turn.

Background: Age, Wealth, and Education

Age.   Age is a strong predictor of political engagement: older people vote more often. Figure 8.2 displays voting rates for different American generations. Notice that *young* adults vote less, in election after election. At the same time, some evidence suggests younger voters are more likely to try and influence politics through direct action, are far more likely to engage in clicktivism, and practice greater political expression than did young Americans in recent decades (see Figure 8.2).

Wealth.   Income is another strong predictor of political participation. Top earners tend to be much more involved in public life than those farther down the income ladder—and the higher the income, the more likely individuals are to get involved in politics. The wealthiest one percent of the top one percent (0.01%) contributed over a billion dollars (around 29% of all donations) in 2014 to political campaigns.[5]

Americans' behavior has run in cycles: Sometimes, the political system permits (and even facilitates) vast differences in wealth—what Mark Twain called a gilded age. National resources flow to those at the top. At other times, a backlash develops against growing inequality. In these egalitarian eras, national and state policies limit the accumulation of outsize wealth. However, in every era, wealthy people have more access to political leaders and more influence over politics.

Education.   Education also predicts political involvement—and education closely tracks income. As Figure 8.3 shows, the more education, the higher the voting levels. Less than 30 percent of people who did not finish high school normally vote in presidential elections, whereas citizens with a college degree are more than twice as likely to vote. Voters with less education, however, played a critical role in 2016 due to their strong support of Donald Trump.

People with a college degree are typically more politically involved in other ways than those who did not finish high school. Because many civic acts require advanced social, managerial, and bureaucratic abilities, they tend to correlate with higher levels of education.

Race.   If we were writing this book fifteen years ago, we would have had to add another major category: race. Traditionally, African Americans voted in lower

INFO/DATA: Higher Engagement and Ideology

Americans are drawn to participate in politics for many different reasons, as this section shows. In recent years, some Americans have become polarized ideologically, moving to the conservative and liberal extremes. How will this influence politics? The extremes—the most liberal or the most conservative people—are especially active in politics.

1. Those at both ends of the spectrum in this infographic ("consistently liberal" and "consistently conservative") are responsible for a larger proportion of political participation than the proportion of the population they comprise. In which activities are they slightly more active? In which are they far more active? Why do you think that is?

2. Building on Question 1, do you think it is *desirable* to have disproportionately high participation among the very conservative and the very liberal? What effects might their greater engagement have on American politics? On elections? On legislation? On the courts? What happens if only the most intense partisans turn out for one (or both) party's primaries?

	Consistently liberal		Mixed	Consistently conservative		NET% consistently left or right
Total public	12%	22%	39%	18%	9%	21%
Among those who always . . .						
Vote in general	14%	19%	31%	21%	14%	28%
Vote in primaries	16%	16%	28%	21%	18%	34%
Among those who in the past two years have . . .						
Contacted official(s)	19%	18%	27%	21%	15%	35%
Donated money	26%	18%	22%	19%	15%	41%
Attended event(s)	20%	20%	29%	18%	13%	33%
Volunteered	24%	21%	28%	14%	13%	37%

Source: Pew Research Center

229

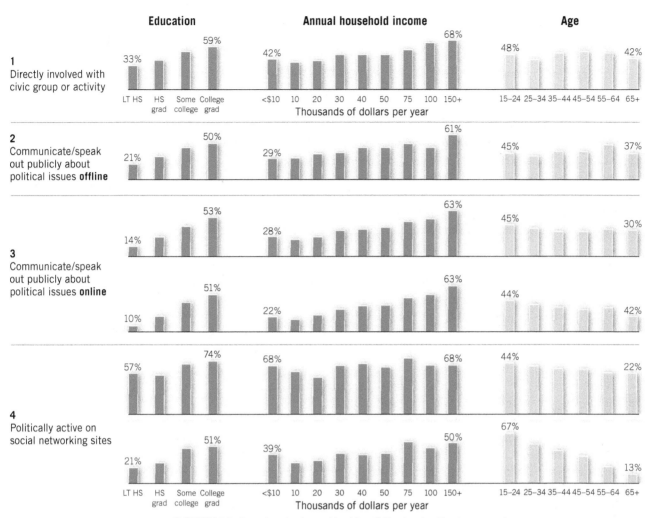

FIGURE 8.3 *Percentage involvement in civic activities by education, income, and age.*
(Pew Research Center)

Note: "LT HS" indicates the population with less than a high school education.

Social capital on the big screen. Characters from It's a Wonderful Life, *a 1946 film that portrays the power of social networks and civic engagement.*

numbers than white Americans. Gradually, however, the gap began to close, and in 2012, for the first time in American history, black Americans voted at a slightly higher rate than white Americans. Latinos and Asian Americans, however, still vote at a lower rate than whites. Just under 50 percent of eligible voters in these communities cast ballots, for reasons researchers still debate.[6] However, as their numbers grow, they are becoming an increasingly important political force.

Friends, Family, and Social Capital

Another way to predict whether someone will vote or volunteer is to find out whether their parents and closest friends do. On average, someone whose family or peers vote regularly is likely to do so as well. An even more powerful inspiration is being *asked* to vote, volunteer, or otherwise exercise political voice by people close to you. Political science studies find that face-to-face encouragement is the most reliable route to political activity. Being asked to vote, even by a stranger, as long as it is in person, tends to get results.[7] This finding appears to hold for many forms of participation—and in many nations. Protesters are often part of personal networks.

The type of community you live in also seems to make a difference. In areas in which neighbors are more trusting and civic participation is strong, people are more likely to get involved—both in local activities, such as block watches or school fundraisers, and in voting for national office. Such communities, organized around a commitment to building social capital, tend to house happier, healthier residents. Through active communication and a strong foundation of trust among citizens, Americans can realize the benefits of engagement on a wide scale.

People who live in areas high in social capital are more deeply involved in activities such as book clubs, community gardens, and bowling leagues and spend more time connecting informally with one another than in places where people live more anonymously and watch a lot of television. It may sound simple: A key to political participation is to live in a highly participatory community. But transforming a neighborhood into one with strong social capital—or sustaining civic connections once they exist—is no easy task. How might you help to cultivate a spirit of engagement in your surrounding community?

In one neighborhood in the city of San José, Costa Rica, residents developed their own technique for boosting social capital. The neighborhood had experienced a sharp rise in crime. Residents got together and agreed to leave for work a few minutes earlier each morning, taking that extra time to greet and talk at least briefly with their neighbors. The practice became informally known as *El Ley del Saludo* (Law of the Greeting), and it helped reduce crime markedly—as well as

● *Social capital in Detroit where residents in low-income neighborhoods joined together to paint vacant homes.*

Talking POLITICS

HOW MOBILIZERS SEE US

Political strategists and mobilizers have a language of their own. Below are some of the terms you'll hear if you work in advocacy or campaign politics long enough.

• **Grassroots:** A movement for political reform that is sparked at the local level, "from the ground up"— figuratively speaking, from the grassroots.

• **Astroturf:** A movement for reform that *appears* to be grassroots but is actually mobilized by political professionals.

• **Dog whistling:** Using insider, "coded" language to rouse constituents or interest-group members who care strongly about an issue. (The rather rude analogy is from training dogs, which hear high-frequency whistles that other animals—including humans—cannot.)

• **Actorvist:** A professional actor involved in political issue campaigns, an increasingly valuable way to win attention for one's cause. Leonardo DiCaprio, who speaks out on environmental issues, and Jessica Biel, on the rights of women and girls around the globe, are just two of the many "actorvists" engaged in American policy mobilization efforts today. Also sometimes heard is "raptivist," a term describing rappers who get involved in political causes.

boost voting rates and other markers of political participation. Likewise, a low-income area of Detroit banded together and used social media to call out people dumping trash in their neighborhood. Once they began taking action, they found new ways to get involved: They painted vacant homes and started community gardens in the empty lots.[8]

Connections between family and participation may run deeper than our tendency to imitate the behavior of those closest to us. Recent studies suggest that we may *inherit* a tendency toward political participation. In other words, your desire to vote or volunteer is determined by your genes—but only partly.[9] Political involvement is shaped by several influences simultaneously, so genetic inheritance, as with the level of social capital in a community, is only one factor among many.

Political Mobilization

Political mobilization: Efforts to encourage people to engage in the public sphere: to vote for a particular candidate (or donate money, work on the campaign, etc.) or to get involved in specific issues.

Party organizations have traditionally done the work of **political mobilization.** Both major parties remain powerful sources of encouraging millions of people to get involved—especially at election time. (We'll talk about political parties, and the work they do in our political system, in Chapter 11.) On **issue advocacy** campaigns, however, when professional and amateur organizations seek to attract public involvement in a specific cause, interest groups have become our mobilizers in chief. At times, issue advocacy campaigns and social movements take over a party—exactly what happened with the Tea Party Movement and the Republican Party.[10]

Issue advocacy: Organized effort to advance (or block) a proposed public policy change.

In the eyes of professional political mobilizers—advocacy groups, campaign strategists, and other members of the enormous Washington, DC–based "political industry," each of us is a potential resource. Activists constantly test ways to inspire people to sign a petition, write our congressional representatives, get out and vote, or otherwise engage politically.

Government Beneficiaries

A fourth factor encouraging participation in public life may strike you as odd at first glance: receiving some type of government benefits. If, for example, your grandparents get a monthly Social Security check, your older brother or sister was covered by your parents' health insurance·past age twenty-one, or you receive a federally guaranteed student loan (which keeps interest rates low), you are a beneficiary. Receiving such support can boost active participation later in life. Researchers have shown that when the government rewards service—as when returning soldiers receive free or discounted college tuition through the GI Bill—recipients are considerably more likely to get involved as volunteers and to exercise their public voice.

However, not all government programs are alike. As political scientist Joe Soss has shown, programs that treat beneficiaries with respect generate social capital. But programs aimed at poor people—called "means tested" because government officials check on your income (or means) before approving the benefits—appear to depress political participation.[11]

These spurs to participation all focus on individual factors. Being asked, imitating your parents and friends, responding to incentives, or receiving government benefits influence your inclination to engage in the public sphere. There is a larger backdrop to participation as well.

Context

Major shifts in the economy and in politics affect both the intensity and favored types of participation. In the rural South during the 1950s, for example, an infestation of boll weevils (tiny insects that feed on cotton plants) devastated the cotton crop. Many African American subsistence farm workers, their livelihood gone, moved to southern cities where they became recruits for the Civil Rights movement. In part because of the boll weevil, they became deeply involved in politics.

Context deeply influences opportunities for political engagement.[12] During some historical periods, Americans have been more likely to engage in public life than at other times. For example, workers (in the 1930s) and students (1960s) flocked into direct action politics in massive numbers. Today—with Americans organizing across the political spectrum, including on many college campuses—we appear to be in another high participation moment.

THE BOTTOM LINE

» Participation in politics and government is influenced by personal factors: background characteristics such as income and education; family, and friends and social capital; political mobilization; and receiving government benefits from programs that treat beneficiaries with respect (like Social Security).

» Americans participate in political life at very different rates. A few engage passionately, a larger number are moderately engaged, and the majority of us are only sporadically involved. This contributes to the appearance of high *and* low participation in the United States.

» Political mobilization also is influenced by the larger social and historical context.

What Discourages Political Participation?

Let us go back to the American paradox: Although Americans are more actively engaged in politics then citizens of other nations, voter turnout in the United States is low (see Comparing Nations 8.1). Why? Political scientists list many reasons:

- Elections are held on Tuesdays—when many people work. Many other nations vote on weekends.
- The U.S. holds more frequent elections—national, state, and local.
- The U.S. also holds primary elections, which are staggered throughout the year in different states.
- Finally, registering to vote can be burdensome and complicated.

Economist Anthony Downs famously asked why anyone should vote. His theory, the **paradox of voting**, suggests that it makes little sense for an individual to expend the time and resources necessary to vote. One person is not going to change an election. The paradox: apparently rational people show up by the millions to vote

The paradox of voting: For most individuals, the cost of voting (acquiring necessary information, traveling to polling site, and waiting in line) outweighs the apparent benefits. Economic theory would predict very low voter turnout, given this analysis.

● *Americans vote almost anywhere: in schools, churches, mosques—and pool rooms.*

COMPARING NATIONS 8.1 — Voter Turnout in Selected Countries

The United States has one of the lowest voter turnout rates in the developed world. Most stable democracies register voter turnout rates in the 65 to 80 percent range, far higher than America's. In one of the top five countries, Australia, voting is *compulsory*—required by law. In the U.S., while a high percentage of registered voters turn out to vote, a much lower percentage of the voting age population are actually registered to vote.

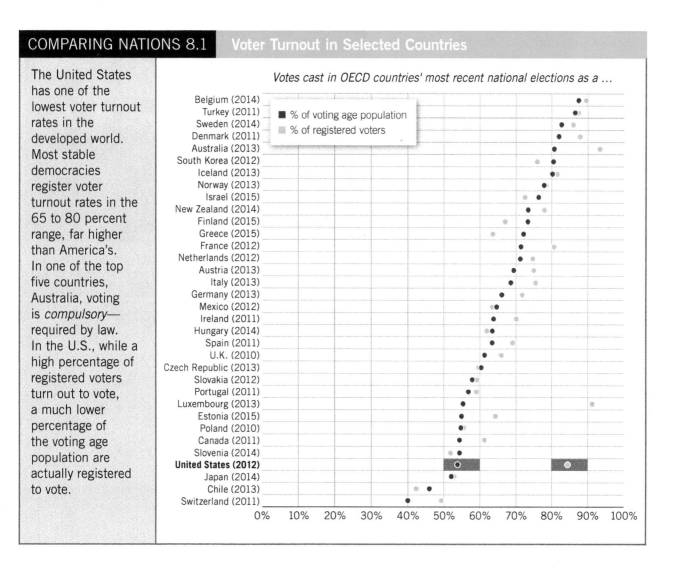

Votes cast in OECD countries' most recent national elections as a ...

■ % of voting age population
▨ % of registered voters

Belgium (2014)
Turkey (2011)
Sweden (2014)
Denmark (2011)
Australia (2013)
South Korea (2012)
Iceland (2013)
Norway (2013)
Israel (2015)
New Zealand (2014)
Finland (2015)
Greece (2015)
France (2012)
Netherlands (2012)
Austria (2013)
Italy (2013)
Germany (2013)
Mexico (2012)
Ireland (2011)
Hungary (2014)
Spain (2011)
U.K. (2010)
Czech Republic (2013)
Slovakia (2012)
Portugal (2011)
Luxembourg (2013)
Estonia (2015)
Poland (2010)
Canada (2011)
Slovenia (2014)
United States (2012)
Japan (2014)
Chile (2013)
Switzerland (2011)

0% 10% 20% 30% 40% 50% 60% 70% 80% 90% 100%

each year. Downs could have said the same thing about joining a protest march or posting online. Here again, Americans regularly take to the streets or post petitions on Facebook. Why?

However, as we saw in the previous section, people get many benefits from participating: a sense of involvement, of duty performed, of belonging to a community. So some political scientists flip the question: Instead of asking why people vote, they ask the opposite: Why don't **more** people vote? There are four broad reasons to explain why people of all ages, income levels, and educational backgrounds do not participate in political life: alienation, barriers to participation, complacency, and shifting mobilization patterns.[13]

Alienation

Alienation from public life may be described as a feeling of powerlessness, or an inability to control one's own political fate. Most alienated people ignore politics. When they get involved, it is usually not through traditional channels but through direct action—intense and even violent protest. Historically excluded groups, such as African Americans, are most likely to report a sense of alienation.[14] Younger people and recent immigrants also feel higher levels of alienation. Recently, alienation levels have soared among white men who failed to finish high school.

These findings raise a basic question: Do some groups feel alienated because they lack a history of participation? Remember, one predictor of whether a person will get involved in politics is whether his or her parents or peer group are actively engaged. Or perhaps immigrants, minorities, and young people *want* to participate in politics and feel alienated because they are shut out? In a moment we will look further at institutional barriers that discourage participation.

A sense of alienation from politics and government also can come in less extreme forms. The sheer number of elected offices and the

Congressman Joe Wilson (R-SC) became an instant celebrity when he shouted, "You lie!" during President Obama's speech to Congress in September 2009. Such angry displays may play a role in turning people off conventional politics.

high frequency of U.S. elections can result in public weariness and eventually disengagement, especially when campaigns feature seemingly endless negative advertisements.

Sharp partisan differences also play a role. In *Why Americans Hate Politics*, political analyst E. J. Dionne noted a widening gulf between liberals and conservatives in U.S. political debates. The angry debates accompanying this polarization have led many Americans to "hate politics and politicians." The millennial generation appears to be particularly uncomfortable with the high levels of conflict between the parties.[15]

Finally, alienated citizens charge the political establishment with focusing on matters that do not solve real problems facing the people. Government officials, they contend, seem more interested in winning arguments, election victories, and appeasing the rich and powerful. They do not address the deeper problems that many people care about—growing inequality, lost opportunity, a sense of being left behind, or the erosion of the nation's moral fabric. The 2016 presidential election featured two candidates, Donald Trump and Bernie Sanders, who embodied this alienation—and stunned political observers (including your authors) with their unexpected success. Trump's victory was one of the great election upsets in American history.

In countries with totalitarian or oligarchic political systems, alienation can become pervasive. Large majorities of the population are turned off completely from government and politics. Compared to such places, Americans exhibit much lower levels of alienation (see Comparing Nations 8.2). But the phenomenon is present in the United States. Looming changes in American society raise important questions about alienation. As the United States becomes a "majority–minority" country, will white voters tend to feel more alienated? Will minority groups feel less alienated?

Institutional Barriers

When Will Walker, a young black farmer, arrived to cast his vote in Tuscaloosa, Alabama, in 1964, he was first required by state law to pass a literacy test, one supposedly designed to prove that he was capable of exercising political judgment. None of the white voters streaming past Will to the voting booths had to take such a test. Will shrugged and turned to the paper before him, brandished by an unfriendly poll worker. He had brushed up on his basic U.S. government facts, and he

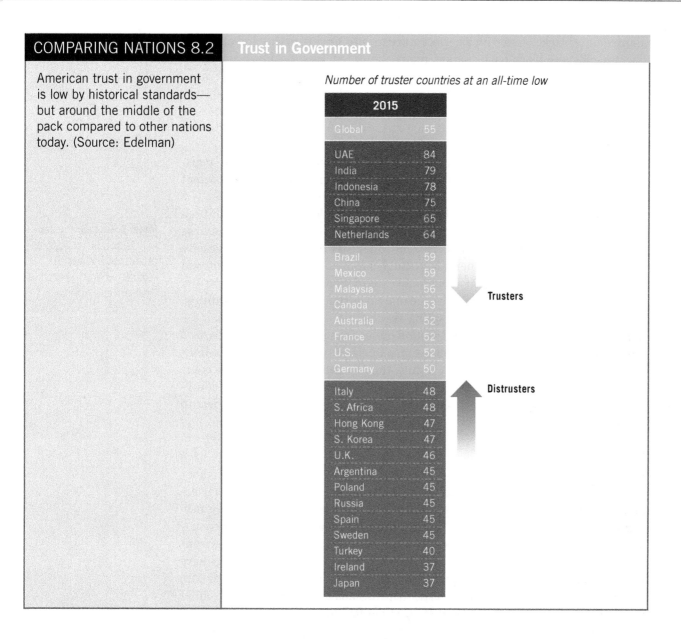

COMPARING NATIONS 8.2 | Trust in Government

American trust in government is low by historical standards—but around the middle of the pack compared to other nations today. (Source: Edelman)

Number of truster countries at an all-time low

2015	
Global	55
UAE	84
India	79
Indonesia	78
China	75
Singapore	65
Netherlands	64
Brazil	59
Mexico	59
Malaysia	56
Canada	53
Australia	52
France	52
U.S.	52
Germany	50
Italy	48
S. Africa	48
Hong Kong	47
S. Korea	47
U.K.	46
Argentina	45
Poland	45
Russia	45
Spain	45
Sweden	45
Turkey	40
Ireland	37
Japan	37

Trusters

Distrusters

knew plenty about the various candidates running for election. Yet no amount of studying could have prepared Will for questions like these:

- The electoral vote for president is counted in the presence of two governmental bodies. Name them: _____ and _____.

- The president is forbidden to exercise his or her authority of pardon in cases of _____.

- If the president does not wish to sign a bill, how many days is he or she allowed in which to return it to Congress for reconsideration? _____ days.

- At what time of day on January 2 each four years does the term of the president of the United States end? _____

Will filled out as many of the twenty questions as he could; he did better than most political science majors might today. But he was turned away from the polls. Alabama allowed only black voters with a perfect score to vote. Owing to this and other deliberate efforts to block participation, many counties across the Jim Crow South featured voter registration rates among African Americans that approached zero.

Most of these overtly racist obstacles to participation were eliminated during the 1960s. Nevertheless, some critics continue to point out structural barriers to participation in American public life, such as the disenfranchisement of individuals convicted of a crime, even after they have served their sentence.

The incentives and barriers to voting can be subtle: How difficult is it to register? How long does voting take place? How long are the lines in the different precincts?

Democrats have generally tried to simplify voting rules. They have sponsored reforms such as the National Voter Registration Act of 1993, usually referred to as the **motor voter law**, which permits citizens to register to vote when they receive their driver's license. On the other side, Republicans in many states have tightened restrictions on voting. They argue that more careful monitoring reduces fraud and that voting should be treated as a privilege that takes time and energy. Accordingly, many states have introduced new voting regulations: tougher identification requirements, limits on same-day registration, reductions in the voting periods, and so on. Opponents call this voter suppression and charge that it is an effort to limit young people, minorities, and others from voting. In 2016, a federal appeals court ruled unconstitutional North Carolina's voting restrictions, passed by a newly-Republican legislature the year before. The debate about institutional barriers to voting goes on.

> **Motor voter law:** Passed in 1993, this act enables prospective voters to register when they receive their driver's license.

Complacency

Some people do not participate because they are satisfied with their lives. Without problems they want solved, why bother to get involved? Research shows, for example, that large membership-based interest groups tend to attract more new members and receive a boost in financial contributions when the group's core issues are threatened. After a big oil spill or new warning about global warming, environmental groups attract more public interest. (In recent years, mass shootings have resulted in expanded membership applications to the National Rifle Association, as gun supporters fear government restrictions.) When those concerns drop out of the news, the groups find it hard to mobilize their followers.

● Why don't more American's vote? Perhaps its the barriers we put in their way. These cartoons mock new registration requirements (left) and the Supreme Court's decision to end safeguards that protected voting in Shelby v Holder (right).

A different view of political apathy comes from the economist John Kenneth Galbraith, who coined the phrase "culture of contentment" to describe America. His view was that the upper-middle class and those at the top of the wealth distribution will fight hard to sustain their "contented" way of life. Those who are less well-off will be increasingly discouraged from participating in political life.[16]

Is there still a culture of contentment in pockets of American life? What do you think? Do you see evidence of contentment complacency around you?

Shifting Mobilization Patterns

Before the 1960s, when political parties were Americans' main source of political mobilization, wealthy and poor people were organized to participate in roughly similar proportions. The main focus was on getting people out to vote, so intensive door-to-door canvassing at election time was the norm. A surge in advocacy-group organizing since the 1960s has boosted the public's collective voice in politics. Movements on behalf of consumer rights, the environment, and many other causes represent major gains in public leverage.

These gains, however, have primarily benefited the relatively well-off, who can devote resources of time and money to public involvement. Political sociologist Theda Skocpol noted that "Americans who are not wealthy or higher-educated now have fewer associations representing their values and interests, and enjoy dwindling opportunities for active participation."[17]

This shift from parties to advocacy groups as the main agents of political mobilization adds up to a **circle of nonparticipation**. If people are so disengaged that they do not affiliate with either political party, party organizers are unlikely to reach out to them at election time—because they might vote for the wrong side.

Circle of nonparticipation: Resistance by political parties to mobilizing disengaged Americans to vote—because their lack of involvement makes their allegiance to one or the other party suspect.

THE BOTTOM LINE

» Participation in civic life tends to vary by age, income level, and education.

» Several other factors have fueled a decline in Americans' political participation in recent years. These include alienation, barriers to participation, complacency, and shifting mobilization patterns.

» The tendency to disengage is most pronounced among millennials, which includes most college students today.

New Avenues for Participation: The Internet, Social Media, and the Millennial Generation

The millennial generation is the most wired group in history. New technologies have engendered new forms of participation—liking a candidate's Facebook page, commenting on an online opinion piece, or following tweets by political commentators during presidential debates. Today, political participation has expanded to include online activities and social media. As we saw earlier, advocates have a new word for this style of participation: clicktivism—democracy enhanced through mouse clicks and social media. Like many new styles of politics, clicktivism has triggered a hot debate.

Is clicktivism a powerful new form of participation that can change the way we do politics for the better? Or is it a threat to popular government? Or, less dramatically, does "participating" from behind a laptop or on a smartphone screen negatively affect the experience of civic involvement? Once again, there are multiple sides to the story. Some observers predict a vibrant new era of citizen participation. Others take a much less sunny view and warn about fragmented communities, central government control of emerging outlets, and viral malice.[18]

Scenario 1: Rebooting Democracy

First, optimists begin by pointing out how *active* Internet users are. People seek out news, follow links, and access a world of information (see Figure 8.4).

Second, people can easily respond. The Internet offers multiple opportunities for talking back: tick the "Like" icon, comment angrily or wittily on a political blog, or communicate with a network of like-minded people. Democracies, when they are working well, *hear* their people. New technologies give individuals many opportunities to exercise their political voice.

Third and related, the Internet vastly expands the range of commentary. Traditionally political pundits were limited to a small circle of well-known personalities and authors. Today, if you have something to say, you can launch a blog, send a tweet to dozens or hundreds (or millions) of followers, or post news stories or opinions for your Facebook friends. Some have had terrific success. The *Daily Kos*, launched by Markos (Kos) Moulitsas Zúniga, boasts millions of visitors per month. Other familiar sites include the *Drudge Report* (conservative), *The Huffington Post* (liberal), and *The Blaze* (conservative). Of course you do not need a blog—Vine and YouTube videos go viral all the time. People post petitions on change.org. Upworthy's clickbait headlines have drawn seven million eyeballs to the realities of inequality in the United States.

Fourth, as we will see in Chapter 9, the new media democratizes news production. Rather than wait for a news van and reporters, bystanders capture important events and upload them. Suddenly, everyone sees a shooting or an angry candidate blurt out a racial slur.

Fifth, the Internet offers new ways for politicians and parties to reach out. Barack Obama refined this technique and turned his 2008 and 2012 campaigns into a kind of movement, galvanizing millions of carefully targeted followers. Others learned the lesson and adapted the technologies. Donald Trump treated his Twitter followers—eventually growing to more than 10 million—to a daily stream of pungent observations and stinging insults.

In sum, optimists argue that social media and other Internet-based sources promote active users; link people to one another; permit citizens to bypass the talking heads and make their own comments; and offer politicians a powerful tool to mobilize, connect, and collect. None of these factors ensures that clicktivism will help refresh American democracy. But they suggest a great deal of promise.

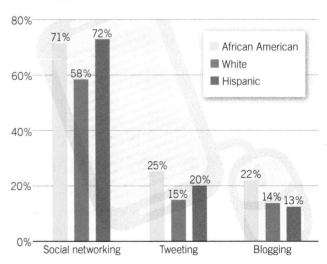

● **FIGURE 8.4** *Who is socially active online? A view by race and ethnicity. (Pew Research Center)*

Scenario 2: More Hype and Danger Than Democratic Renaissance

All this potential, however, might be squandered. Technological change may not enhance democracy and, according to some skeptics, is already harming it. Critics level three main charges against the Internet and social media as keys to political participation.[19]

First is the sustained power of *central control*, by governments or corporations, over the Internet and its users. "Facebook has more power in determining who can speak and who can be heard around the globe than any Supreme Court justice, any king or any president," noted law professor Jeffrey Rosen. Social media companies determine what speech violates their community standards, when to cooperate with security agencies, and how to monetize information about your shopping habits.[20] Competing with public officials and tech companies for control are cyber-criminals, as hackers constantly seek to steal sensitive political information (the Pentagon, for example, is attacked by hackers an estimated 100,000 times *per day*).[21]

Second, with more than one billion websites on the Internet, the sheer volume and variety of available information are mind-boggling. The resulting chaos can overwhelm participation as well as enhance it. Researching or following a specific topic often involves wading through a forest of posts by authors with difficult-to-verify credentials, contradictory accounts, and deliberate misinformation. One term for this is **din**.

Try to do an Internet search for this chapter's topic, "political participation" and related terms, for example. As of 2016, we found some 27.9 million relevant Internet sources. Which ones provide valuable or even usable details about participation in the public sphere? Merely to scan each site for one minute would take fifteen and a half years.

Third, the Internet incubates lies, malice, and falsehood. Rumors start and spread. Racism, anti-Semitism, misogyny, and character assassination all flourish in the hyper-connected, often-anonymous new media. No, 2016 presidential candidate Chris Christie did not say that women's Viagra "will only increase lesbianism"; no, Syrian forces did not secretly "invade" New Orleans in 2015–16; no, Kid Rock did not sneak into a 2016 Hillary Clinton campaign rally and shout "Vote Donald Trump!" All are falsehoods that metastasized on the Internet. The democratic promise of the Internet comes with a dark side.[22]

In sum, critics worry that the Internet and social media will have a corrosive effect on American democratic participation. They point out that the government monitors Internet behavior in many countries, including the United States; meanwhile, corporations gather information from every click of the mouse. Yes, people can post and blog, but not many develop an audience. Finally, the speed and connectivity of the Internet can lead to misinformation and malice as easily as communication and community—and users may grow overwhelmed by the sheer volume of information.

Does Social Media Increase Political Participation?

Although it is important to respect the downsides of every form of participation, the new social media have become a fact of political life. They open more and more opportunities for broad participation and policy innovation. For example, Mobile, Alabama, engages Instagram to fight urban blight. Fairfax County, Virginia, uses social media to boost pet adoption rates. Government "hackathons" invite people to

Din: Shorthand for the sheer volume of information and noise generated by online sources; can be a disincentive to participate politically.

TABLE 8.2 Social Network Site (SNS) Users Participation Rates

	% OF SNS USERS WHO HAVE DONE THIS	% OF ALL ADULTS WHO HAVE DONE THIS
"Like" or promote material related to political/social issues that others have posted	38	23
Encourage other people to vote	35	21
Post your own thoughts/comments on political or social issues	34	20
Encourage others to take action on political/social issues that are important to you	31	19
Belong to a group that is involved in political/social issues, or working to advance a cause	21	12
Follow elected officials, candidates for office or other elected officials	20	12
Source: Pew Research Center		

pitch their civic-improvement ideas. And everywhere citizens use smart phones to publicize what their public officials are doing. Social media users are also more likely to participate in politics than the general public (see Table 8.2).

What explains this correlation between social media and participation? Perhaps individuals who are inclined to become involved in politics are more likely to be social media users. Or do people get engaged by what they see and hear online—and then act on it? Or is there a bandwagon effect—watching others comment on posts or joining groups stimulates individuals to jump in and do likewise?

● *How will millennials change political participation in American democracy?*

The bandwagon effect has been successfully employed in the past to encourage voter turnout and other kinds of political participation. In Barack Obama's 2008 presidential campaign, an advisory group recommended that the campaign's messages encouraging supporters to vote on Election Day be revised to read "A Record Turnout Is Expected." This proved more effective than other types of appeals.[23]

Skeptics point out that although the bandwagon effect within social media may galvanize participants in the short-term; it is unclear whether it will sustain traditional political engagement. Although the critics offer valuable caveats, participation via new social media is here to stay. It will continue to morph and change—and with it the ways we participate in government.

How the Millennial Generation Participates

Millennials vote less than other age groups both in the United States and in many other nations. They are less likely to get involved in political campaigns. They do not identify strongly with either political party—half of millennials call themselves independents. That is far more than any other generation—no other age cohort goes over 40 percent independent (see Figure 8.5). Millennials are also more likely to identify as liberals than does any other generation.[24]

Millennials participate in their own distinctive way. They volunteer their time and energy to serve the public. From working in hospitals to helping out in programs for at-risk kids—young adults today volunteer at unusually high rates. And they are willing to endorse government more than any other generation. Should we

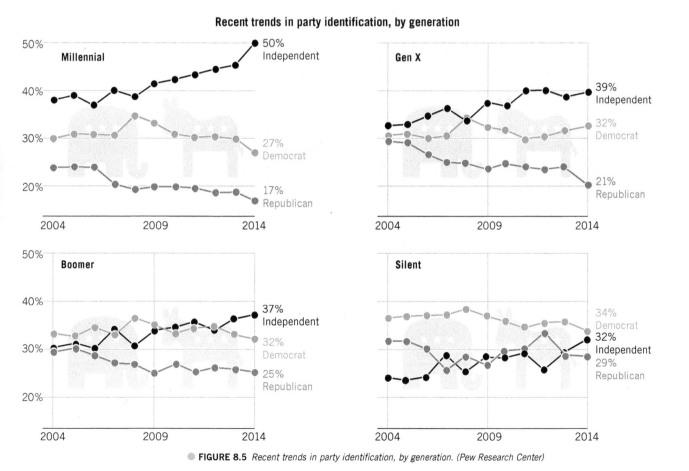

Recent trends in party identification, by generation

FIGURE 8.5 *Recent trends in party identification, by generation. (Pew Research Center)*

have a bigger government doing more things such as guaranteeing healthcare for all? Only the millennials says yes. In contrast, 64 percent of the silent generation, enjoying the two largest government programs—Social Security and Medicare—say no (see Table 8.3). Why?

Younger generations display a higher level of trust in public officials, but relatively low levels of trust in their fellow citizens (see Figure 8.6). When asked whether "Most people look out for themselves," 70 percent of millennials agreed—in contrast only 40 percent of "matures" (Americans over sixty-five) agreed. A similar gap was present for the statement "Most people would take advantage of you" (56% of millennials, compared to 29% of matures). Millennials also called themselves less patriotic—49 percent said yes compared to 75 percent of boomers (patriotic) and 81 percent of the oldest generation.[25]

How does a generation that is skeptical of their fellow citizens but not of government participate? You probably know the answer to that: through social media and the Internet. This is a generation of "digital natives" who comment on politics, capture (and upload) the world around them, and network online. For millennials and the generations that follow, the future of political participation lies in the question we posed above: How will clicktivism affect our democracy?

As we saw in the last chapter, this is the generation that has already rewritten national attitudes on issues ranging from same-sex marriage (68% approval) to legalizing marijuana (69% approval). A strong majority (55%) believe undocumented immigrants ought to have a chance to become citizens. Millennial political voice has already changed public policy—and it will continue to do so.

Political scientists have one concern about this generation. Alternative forms of political participation—both direct action and online—are powerful forces for disruption and change. However, they cannot produce stable, long-term democratic governance. A generation skeptical of the political system participates at low levels, and participation trends tend to persist over time. Young America is diverse, eager to build social capital by volunteering, and feels strongly about many political issues. But it has not been moved to translate that energy into traditional modes of political action.

The great question is why? Perhaps the new generation finds subtle political barriers to participation built into the political process—complicated election rules, long lines, reduced voting periods, and so on. Or perhaps the fault lies with the parties that they are so disinclined to join: Negative advertising drives down turnout and the issues themselves may not address a new generation's major concerns, including debt, education, employment, and inequality. Research suggests another

TABLE 8.3 Support for Bigger Government Highest Among Younger Generations

WOULD YOU RATHER HAVE . . .			
	SMALLER GOVERNMENT, FEWER SERVICES	BIGGER GOVERMENT, MORE SERVICES	DEPENDS
Gen X	51	40	9
Millennials	38	53	9
Boomer	59	32	8
Silent	64	22	14
Source: Pew Research Center			

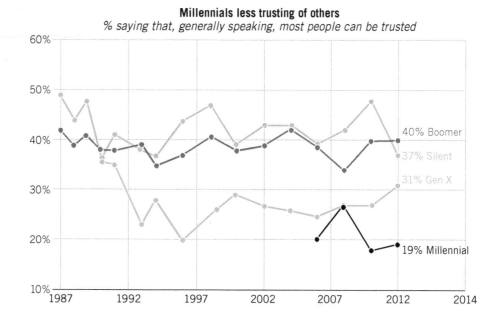

Millennials less trusting of others
% saying that, generally speaking, most people can be trusted

40% Boomer
37% Silent
31% Gen X
19% Millennial

FIGURE 8.6 *Millennials less trusting of others. (Pew Research Center)*

possibility that those high-volunteering millennials also are much more apt than previous generations of young Americans to switch their interests swiftly among different policy areas: fighting homelessness today and advocating for cleaner water tomorrow. Such dizzying shifts makes it difficult to develop a sustained interest in any particular topic—and, ultimately, any sustained interest in civic action more generally.[26] Finally, it may simply be that the online generation is less interested in collective solutions and traditional politics. What do you think?

THE BOTTOM LINE

» The Internet, and especially social media, has launched a revolution that is changing the way Americans participate politically.

» An emerging age of activism and connection may refresh American democracy—or troubling developments may diminish it.

» New methods of participation are emerging online.

» Millennials participate in these new methods, but are less likely to vote, belong to a party, or get involved in traditional politics.

Conclusion

Participation is always in flux. Today, young Americans are less likely to participate in traditional politics—voting at lower rates than other generations did, for example. At the same time, millennials volunteer, build social capital, and engage politically through social media.

A rising generation that spurns traditional politics bodes trouble for popular government. It reminds us of Ben Franklin describing the newly formed government: "A republic, if you can keep it" (Chapter 1). Keeping the republic means revitalizing the traditional channels of political participation.

Should Voting Be Required by Law?

Americans vote at relatively low rates. One proposal is to require voting (you'd risk a fine by not voting). Countries where voting is required have much higher participation rates.

Yes! A vibrant republic requires active participation by the people. If everyone voted, elected officials would genuinely represent all the people. It would make our politics more inclusive. And it would avoid a grave danger: Apathetic people soon lose their rights and liberties.

No! Voting is a privilege as well as a right. People ought to inform themselves and take the extra effort to cast a vote. We shouldn't make voting too easy—it's probably a good thing if uninformed people stay home. It makes politics and governing more efficient.

Not sure? Today, political observers make arguments on both sides. Democrats are usually eager to expand voting—and are usually in the yes column. Republicans have increasingly been voting no on this issue. You'll probably have a stronger opinion by the time you've finished this book.

When our behaviors threaten ourselves or those around us, should public officials step in to help encourage the "right" kind of participation? Governments have intervened in other areas such as using resources such as electricity and water more responsibly, for example, or boosting our inclination to save money for retirement. Traditionally, governments have adopted coercive, top-down answers, relying on official regulations: Everyone *must* conserve water by taking shorter showers, or everyone *must* wear a seat belt or use a motorcycle helmet. Some governments, in fact, require their citizens to vote. Should we? (See What Do You Think?)

Americans resist such restrictions on individual behavior. When we participate in politics, it tends to be on our own terms, not because laws or political leaders require us to.

Another possibility is to provide gentler nudges toward participation. Faced with a wide array of choices, most of us tend to go with the simplest option. Take the example of organ donations. In most countries around the globe, consenting adults can choose to have their vital organs preserved in case of unexpected death and donated to needy recipients. Spain had a relatively low proportion of organ donations in the early 1990s, but within a decade, its rate of donations had soared. The shift saved many lives. How did Spain manage it? By changing the default option. Previously, Spanish citizens—like Americans today—had to "opt in" to organ donor programs, a process involving several steps. Spain's government shifted to an "opt out" default, so that Spaniards were presumed organ donors unless they went through the process of indicating otherwise. Should state governments find a way so that citizens who turn eighteen have to opt out of voting? What about other forms of participation?

Whatever you think of these nudges, Americans today face the task of revitalizing the formal channels on participation. There is enormous political energy across the political spectrum—from the effervescence of the Tea Party and Trump supporters on the right to the call for social justice on the left. The key to the future lies in finding a way to channel that energy into everyday politics. Finding a way to make traditional politics vital and relevant is the key to "keeping the republic."

CHAPTER SUMMARY

● Participation in civic and political life is a longstanding American tradition—helping, in the view of nineteenth-century visitors like Tocqueville, to distinguish the United States as a rising nation. Today, although Americans still exhibit higher levels of voluntarism than citizens of other countries, our rates of participation in politics and government have fallen to disturbing levels.

● People participate in public life in three broad ways:
First, by participating through traditional political mechanisms: Voting, going to rallies, contributing to campaigns, contacting public officials.
A second mode of participation involves contributing to civil society through volunteering and getting involved in the community.
Third, Americans have been quick to get involved in direct action when traditional mechanisms seem unresponsive. This is the politics of demonstrations, protest movements, and even armed confrontations.

● Whether someone engages in civic life depends on both personal factors—those with politically active family members and close friends, or with higher education levels, are more inclined to participate—and political context. During periodic outbursts of direct participation, many people who might ordinarily stay on the sidelines are drawn to participate.

● Another key to this push–pull of participation: Americans simultaneously get involved in civic affairs, especially in their local communities, and express high dissatisfaction with U.S. government institutions. That dissatisfaction helps to drive down participation in direct political activity like voting.

● Millennials exemplify this tension: They engage in voluntary public service activities at record rates but tend to mistrust politics and government. They also increasingly connect with others through social media, a force that is transforming political participation in fast-evolving (and, for the most part, poorly understood) ways.

● Mass engagement in politics and other civic activities is the lifeblood of American democracy, helping to explain why analysts are so anxious to expand participation.

KEY TERMS

Circle of nonparticipation, p. 238
Civic voluntarism, p. 225
Clicktivism, p. 222
Din, p. 240

Direct action, p. 226
Electoral activities, p. 224
Issue advocacy, p. 232
Motor voter law, p. 237
Paradox of voting, p. 233

Political mobilization, p. 232
Political voice, p. 224
Social capital, p. 228
Traditional participation, p. 222
Voter turnout, p. 226

STUDY QUESTIONS

1. This chapter describes three forms of political participation: traditional political participation, civic volunteerism, and direct action. Describe each. Which do you think is most important? Why?
2. What are some of the benefits of participating in civic and political life? Why do so many Americans—especially younger people in their teens and twenties—choose not to participate through formal mechanisms?
3. Why do many Americans have a difficult time articulating a sense of the "public," compared to private life or affinity groups?
4. Describe the factors that encourage and discourage political participation.

5. Forms of direct participation appear to be rising even while voting rates remain low. What explains this paradox?

6. What features distinguish the millennial generation when it comes to participation in civic and political activities?

7. Do you consider social networking sites a source of *enhancing* or *discouraging* participation in public life? What evidence might you consider in support of your claim?

8. What explains the strong turn in recent years to "nudges" in U.S. policymaking? Does this trend strike you as a benefit or a drawback for American democracy?

 Go to www.oup.com/us/Morone to find quizzes, flash cards, simulations, tutorials, videos, and other study tools.

Media, Technology, and Government

9

IN 1961, THE AMERICAN MEDICAL ASSOCIATION

enlisted Ronald Reagan, then an actor, to help fight President John F. Kennedy's healthcare plan. Reagan cut a record (on vinyl) that the medical association sent (by snail mail) to every physician's home. "If this program passes," warned Reagan, "one day we will awake to find that we have socialism. . . . We will spend our sunset years telling our children and our children's children what it was like in America when men were free." The record asked doctors' wives to invite their friends, serve coffee, play Reagan's message, and then write letters to Congress opposing government health insurance. Congress voted down the program, although another version passed four years later and is now known as Medicare.

In 1993, the Health Insurance Association of America aired television ads opposing President Bill Clinton's health plan. The ads featured "Harry and Louise," a pleasant middle-aged couple who were concerned that national health insurance would create a bureaucratic monster and wreck their healthcare. "They [the Washington bureaucrats] choose," intones a voice at the end of the ad. "You lose." Congress soon buried the Clinton health proposal. It took nearly two decades until a later president, Barack Obama, succeeded in getting a comprehensive healthcare plan passed.

In 2016, Republican presidential nominee Donald Trump took to the social media platform Twitter to publicize his vow to end that health law, known as "Obamacare." In 140-character bursts, Trump channeled outrage at this Big Government intrusion—and issued other promises, such as one to build a 45-foot wall along the U.S.–Mexican border. As Trump's Twitter following swelled to over twelve million, his health-policy plans and attacks on opponents also were retweeted and commented on positively by thousands of followers.

Each snapshot captures the media technology of a different era—and the politics they have channeled. In 1961, a recording reached an elite audience, which responded by mailing letters to Congress. In 1993, a TV ad ran in select markets and then spread further on television via pundits—and helped bring down a signature presidential policy initiative. In 2016, a posting instantly reached millions of Twitter followers, generating reaction in new media

● *Reporters swarm Senator Bob Corker (R-Tenn.) seeking his comments on the results of key presidential primaries.*

249

Donald J. Trump
@realDonaldTrump

 Following

I will bring our jobs back to America, fix our military and take care of our vets, end Common Core and ObamaCare, protect 2nd A, build WALL

● *From LP record albums to tweets: evolving media technologies have changed American politics—and journalism.*

see for yourself 9.1

Go online to hear Reagan's "Operation Coffee Cup" recording.

see for yourself 9.2

Go online to see the Harry and Louise ad.

New media: On-demand access to information and entertainment through digital devices that also features interactive participation with content.

formats (Instagram, blogs, Facebook) and traditional ones (newspapers, radio, TV). Three major changes mark the evolution of issue campaigns across more than fifty years:

- First, *the media keeps delivering information faster and faster.*

- Second, *today's media includes many more voices and formats.* This dramatic expansion in outlets also has contributed to a more polarized public, as people choose sources that align with their interests or ideological outlook.

- Third, *the new media permits the public to be much more active.* You can comment on an Instagram or Facebook posting more easily (and in more ways) than you could respond to a record in 1961 or a TV commercial in 1993. Ordinary Americans also are far better able to act as media watchdogs and information providers, by recording and posting events on their cell phones—supplying coverage formerly controlled by large media outlets.

What is the media?[1] It is all the ways people obtain information about politics and the wider world: Instagram, television, Facebook, radio, newspapers, Google searches, blogs, Twitter, and more. Media outlets are the major information bridge between citizens and government.

Every change in the media affects politics. The rise of radio, television, and the Internet each had a profound impact on American political culture. Fifty years ago, everyone heard the same newscast and took part in the same debate. Today, each position on the political spectrum tunes in to its own news source and links to its own network. A key question looms above the **new media**: Does the vast expansion in outlets enhance democracy? Diminish it? Or perhaps some of both?

Who are we? From the very start of this book, we have seen that the United States is an immense, ongoing argument over political ideas. The media brings the people into political debates; it is the great link between leaders and citizens. The national media reflects America itself: raucous, fast-changing, multilingual, multicultural, forceful, loud, and lucrative. It communicates in many languages at home. It broadcasts America to the world.

BY THE NUMBERS
The Media

Number of daily newspapers in print in the United States in 1850: **254**
Number in 1900: **2,226**
Approximate number in 2017: **1,200**
Expected number in 2020, according to the Congressional Research Service: **700**
Estimated number of African American–owned newspapers: **200**
Number of African American–owned newspapers that print daily editions: **0**

Percentage of Republicans and Democrats (respectively) who expressed trust in the media, 1998: **52, 59**
Percentage of Republicans and Democrats (respectively) expressing trust in media, 2016: **14, 51**

Number of television channels in most homes outside of major cities in 1960: **3**
Number of television channels received by the average home today: **189**
Rank of CNN, Fox News, ESPN and HGTV (respectively) among the most-watched cable channels, 2016: **1, 2, 3, and 6**

Percentages of African Americans, Hispanics, and whites, respectively, who use social network sites, according to a Pew study: **65, 65, 56**
Number of journalists for broad-interest websites (such as Slate.com) accredited to cover the U.S. Senate, 2009: **2**
Number accredited in 2016: **more than 90**
Online searches for political news carried out on mobile devices, 2009: **0 percent**
Online searches for political news carried out on mobile devices, 2016: **Over 50 percent**

Media and American Democracy

Media outlets perform three essential functions in a democratic system: providing information, acting as a public watchdog, and helping shape the political agenda. Let us take a closer look at all three.

Providing Information

First, media coverage *informs the public*. Without media bridging the gap, the public would be ignorant of most political events: most of us cannot attend important sessions of Congress, the Supreme Court, or even our local city or town council—much less keep track of the literally thousands of policy issues and public problems that government addresses each year. When the media does its job well, we are more informed voters, more avid politics watchers, and more engaged citizens.

Are there limits to this information providing role? Imagine that you are a Republican with lots of Democratic friends. You come across a detailed news story that crushes one of their cherished beliefs. You send it to them with a snide comment—and what happens? Rather than changing their minds, the story simply reaffirms what they already believe. Researchers have shown that new information rarely influences people who already have strongly held opinions. Instead, new information reinforces existing opinions, regardless of the content of the story.

However, news items can have an impact on people who have not yet made up their minds. About a third of the public does not have strong political views and is less likely to follow the news. This group *is* open to influence by the media. Here is a paradox: The news media is most likely to influence the people who pay the least attention to it. Because this group does not follow politics and government very closely, only news stories with a **loud signal** are likely to reach them and influence their views. A loud signal means that a news story gets *broad media coverage* and delivers an *unambiguous message.*

Loud signal: Media stories with very broad coverage and an unambiguous message.

Watching Political Leaders

Public watchdog: Media coverage that alerts the public when a problem arises in politics or society.

Second, the media serves a **public watchdog** function, scrutinizing government for corrupt or illegal acts, misleading statements by leaders, failed consumer protections, and other flawed decisions or government processes. During the 2016 election, candidates' public statements (whether issued on social media, during debates, or in campaign appearances) were scoured by media outlets for accuracy and consistency. Was a candidate misleading the American public? Reporters kept careful score.

Politicians often complain about media coverage, but Donald Trump fought back directly, denouncing journalists who criticized his views or even those who asked debate questions he considered unfair. Megyn Kelly, for example, a reporter for Fox News, was a target of Trump's ire after posing a debate question about his record of demeaning public references to women. For the next several months, Trump referred to Kelly as "crazy@megynkelly" on Twitter. Serving as a watchdog for democracy has never been easy. As technology changes, media efforts to inform the public have had to adapt as well.

Shaping the Political Agenda

Editors and reporters have enormous influence on what Americans think *about*. Media executives listen to the political din and pluck out one or two stories to headline and a dozen others for the second tier. Those become the topics that politicians address, Congress investigates, talk shows debate, and you discuss and tweet and blog. When an issue commands such attention, we say it is on the political agenda, also known as the **policy agenda**. If something you care about—homelessness, immorality, or animal cruelty—is not being discussed, it is unlikely that political leaders will pay attention to it. The first step toward political action is to get your issue onto the policy agenda.

Policy agenda: The issues that the media covers, the public considers important, and politicians address. Setting the agenda is the first step in political action.

Setting the agenda is one of the most important influences the news media has on American politics. Politicians, think tanks, interest groups, citizens, and experts all try to influence the agenda. Sometimes they succeed; far more often they fail. In 2013 following Edward Snowden's leak of classified government documents, demonstrations against government spying caught the media's attention. As the news reverberated, the demonstrations multiplied and grew. The coverage kept the

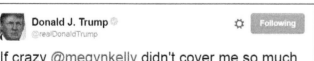

Donald J. Trump
@realDonaldTrump
Following

If crazy @megynkelly didn't cover me so much on her terrible show, her ratings would totally tank. She is so average in so many ways!

● Reporters serving as "watchdogs"—reporting on political leaders' foibles and misdeeds—can become targets of sharp coverage themselves.

issue of government data collection firmly on the national agenda. As we will see in Chapter 17, getting onto the agenda is only the first step in the long political process.

Does the public attend to an issue because the media covers it? Or does the media cover an issue because the public is focused on it? In a classic study, two political scientists asked subjects what issues they thought were most important. Then the researchers broke the subjects into groups and, over four days, gave each group a different version of the nightly news emphasizing different issues—pollution, defense, inflation, and so forth. For the most part, the issues that the subjects saw on the news became more important in their own minds.[2] When the media focuses on an issue, its importance—or salience—generally rises in the public perception.

Those issues that rise onto the agenda and dominate the news affect public perceptions of candidates and officials. This influence is known as **priming**. For example, because the Republican Party is identified with smaller government, stories about government incompetence *prime* the public to see the world through Republican eyes. Stories about the plight of the elderly or the hard-working poor prime voters to think along Democratic Party lines.

There are many ways to cover an issue, and each offers a slightly different perspective. When the media chooses a particular slant, we say it is **framing** the issue. House Speaker Paul Ryan, a conservative Republican, addressed poverty in a series of 2016 speeches and policy papers. Conservative media outlets applauded Ryan's approach, framing the issue as one of communities determining their own destiny in fighting poverty, rather than the ineffective federal government. Outlets on the left decried Ryan's "heartless" effort to slash existing anti-poverty programs and trash the government-supported "safety net" on which many poor Americans depend. Both sides felt they would benefit politically if they could frame the issue their way.

Priming: Affecting voters' or poll respondents' perception of candidates or public officials by raising issues that are perceived to enhance or diminish the candidates.

Framing: The way an issue is defined; every issue has many possible frames, each with a slightly different tilt in describing the problem and highlighting solutions.

● *Media framing battles are carried out on every front: social media such as Twitter and Instagram, paid advertising in print and on the air, and humorous cartoons. Here, cartoonist Joe Heller weighs in on the gun control debate.*

Often, media framing is invisible to the public because it reflects the dominant social values of the time. The issue of equality was once framed as a problem concerning white men: Could they achieve the American dream in an industrial system devoted to profits? Later, mass social movements reframed the issue as one that spoke directly to race, ethnicity, and gender.

In short, framing defines the nature of the problem, organizes potential solutions, and wipes out alternative policies. A lesson all political (and business, non-profit, etc.) leaders learn quickly: if you are not actively shaping the terms of debate, your opponents will do so. A recent academic article's title puts it perfectly: "Frame or Get Framed."[3] Media coverage plays a crucial role—often, *the* crucial role—in issue framing.

THE BOTTOM LINE

» A vast change is underway in media formats, driven by rapid technological advancement.

» Media outlets continue to perform essential democratic functions, providing information, acting as "watchdogs" to protect the public trust, shaping what news is reported (agenda setting), and describing how it is reported (framing).

» Who performs those functions—once mainstream media outlets, now potentially anyone armed with a smartphone and Facebook page or Twitter account—is increasingly up for grabs.

U.S. Media Today: Traditional Formats Are Declining

Media technology changes quickly, and each change remakes the connections between citizens and their leaders. The media affects the news we get, the arguments we hear, and the deliberations we engage in.

Where People Go for News

Our lead story is simple. Fifty years ago, three national networks and the daily paper all delivered essentially the same news to an audience with few options for challenging (or even responding to) reporters' coverage. Most households subscribed to one newspaper. Your grandparents' choices were simple: tune in or not. Today, new technologies give Americans a host of options that are shaking up both media and government.

As Figure 9.1 shows, Facebook has replaced television as the top source of news for Americans under the age of 50. Back in 2002, TV was the chief source of news for 82 percent of the public; that figure has fallen to below 50 percent for all but Americans over 55. Newspapers and magazines continue a long slide from their one-time dominance. In contrast, radio hangs on—almost everyone listens to it, in the car or on podcasts.

What are the implications of this shifting media world? Social media sites such as Facebook or Instagram do not perform their own reporting: They rely on a combination of links to traditional news sources and public comments. New media

Among millennials, Facebook far exceeds any other source for political news

% who got news about politics and government in the previous week from . . .

Millennial		Generation X		Baby Boomer	
Facebook	61%	Facebook	51%	Local TV	60%
CNN	44	Local TV	46	NBC News	47
Local TV	37	CNN	45	Fox News	47
Google News	33	Fox News	36	ABC News	44
ABC News	32	NBC News	35	CNN	43
Fox News	30	ABC News	32	CBS News	39
NBC News	27	MSNBC	27	Facebook	39
Yahoo News	27	CBS News	27	MSNBC	33
MSNBC	22	Yahoo News	25	PBS	26
CBS News	19	NPR	21	NPR	22

● **FIGURE 9.1** *Sources of political news. (Pew Research Center)*

formats include podcasts (which audiences can access on their own schedule, not when media producers decide to air reports); "stories" as brief as six seconds, on outlets such as Vine; and crowd-funded reporting. More than 200 stories are now funded each year through Kickstarter and similar sources; this removes traditional gatekeepers such as producers and editors from the work of agenda setting, or deciding which issues receive priority coverage.

What does this fast-changing landscape mean for the media, for politics, and for democracy? We can learn more by focusing on developments in each of the major media.

Newspapers and Magazines: Rise and Decline

Newspapers have always been midwives to American democracy. The *Federalist Papers* (still the most important commentaries on our Constitution) first appeared as newspaper articles in the *New York Independent Journal*. George Washington subscribed to ten newspapers. His most famous communication, the Farewell Address, was actually a letter addressed to his "fellow citizens" and printed in the papers.

The First Mass Media. In the 1830s, newspapers became the first **mass media**— just when the vote expanded to include all white men. Papers cost one penny and reflected the raucous and often-corrupt politics of the era. The *New York Herald* broke with the stodgy past, hired reporters to go out and dig up facts, and gave the readers just what they wanted—murder, fire, suicide, and crime. That profit-driven journalism disgusted the old elites but made the *Herald* the most widely read newspaper in the world. One New York rival, the *Tribune*, listed Karl Marx as a foreign correspondent. Another, the *Aurora*, hired as a local reporter Walt Whitman, already the foremost poet in New York.

Newspaper influence grew throughout the nineteenth century. The Spanish-American War, in 1898, is known as the first media-driven war because banner

Mass media: Information and entertainment for broad popular audiences including newspapers, magazines, radio, and television.

● *The power of the media, 1898. No one was sure why the American battleship* Maine *exploded. But the newspapers left no doubt that it was "Spanish treachery." Notice the prominent mention of Assistant Secretary of the Navy Theodore Roosevelt. He would become a hero during the war—and the nation's next president.*

headlines blamed Spain for sinking an American battleship in Havana Harbor (there was no evidence for the charge) and helped bully the McKinley administration into the conflict. The papers developed comic strips to stretch their markets to the many immigrants who did not speak English well. By the turn of the century, there were more than 2,200 newspapers in the United States.[4]

Even after the rise of radio and television, newspapers remained the major source for gathering and disseminating news, especially local news. A typical metropolitan newspaper ran seventy stories in a day, including national, local, and business news—add sports and society news and the total ran to more than a hundred. By contrast, the half-hour television news had time for only ten or twelve stories. Now, after more than two centuries at the center of the news media, the newspaper is waning, with magazine circulation falling as well. The advertisers who once guaranteed profits have migrated to the Internet, and so have readers.

The result is a dramatic decline in big-city newspapers. Between 2000 and 2015, American newspapers slashed 40 percent of their staff, especially foreign correspondents and those covering local beats.[5] Some major papers stopped printing and have moved entirely to the Internet. Occasionally an "angel investor" comes along—Jeff Bezos, the Amazon founder and chief executive officer, spent $250 million in 2013 to buy the *Washington Post* and its affiliated papers—but such investments are rare.

Should We Worry?   There is much to celebrate about reading the news online. It is up-to-the-minute and invites active readers who can click a Facebook link, read content from, say, the *Wall Street Journal*, post a comment back on Facebook, debate classmates in an online chat room, and then surf over to YouTube for a clip from a TV network—or one posted by an eyewitness. The reader, not the editor, chooses the material. The Internet permits readers to respond, to share, to network, and to learn more.

Media analysts see two problems with this scenario. First, newspapers still do the vast majority of basic reporting. Web-based outlets add background, links, and multiple perspectives, but it all begins with stories developed by reporters. If newspapers cannot generate revenue, they will not survive. Where will we get the basic facts and stories? Will the reporting function migrate to another media institution? This is already happening in some cases, with online reporters for sites such as Vox or Slate.

Second, important stories may get lost. Newspapers always covered the "hot" topics (war, murder, and high school sports) along with less exciting civic issues (such as school board meetings and wetland controversies). Because everything was bundled together into one package, the popular stories paid for the civics lessons. As newspapers downsize staff and try to sell their stories by the piece on the Net, there may be no way to subsidize coverage on limited-interest (but very important) issues such as education.

Third, newspapers and other traditional media tend to include a variety of viewpoints: conservative and liberal columnists. Facebook and other web-based sources write algorithms that automatically filter stories based on viewer preferences, emphasizing newsfeed items that fit into a user's worldview.

Radio Holds Steady

● Roosevelt used the new medium—radio—to speak directly to citizens in their homes. The result: the rise of the personal presidency. The change in the media helped introduce a change in our politics.

The first commercial radio stations began airing in the 1920s. President Franklin Roosevelt seized the new technology during the Great Depression of the 1930s and delivered weekly radio addresses known as "fireside chats." The talks were informal, as if the president were talking to his listeners right by their own firesides. Hearing Roosevelt's voice changed the relationship between Americans and their president. The people grew to expect a personal connection. Indeed, political scientists link this development to the rise of the **personal presidency**.

Personal presidency: The idea that the president has a personal link to the public. Made initially possible by twentieth-century media.

The radio also gave new immediacy to wartime reports during World War II—and to baseball games. It accelerated the velocity of news and information. The medium made the nation, and the world, a smaller place.

The radio era lasted just thirty years. By the mid-1950s, television had displaced it. However, radio still has a role in national politics. Conservative talk radio arose in the late 1980s after the Reagan administration cleared the way (we discuss the government connection later in this chapter). After Rush Limbaugh—a talented, loquacious, pugnacious host—syndicated his daily talk show, a stream of other conservatives followed him onto the airwaves. Limbaugh pioneered the argument that became an article of conservative faith: The rest of the media is biased, so dial in here. Liberals tried to counter with their own talk shows, but their efforts foundered, perhaps because liberals are less likely to complain that the media is biased.

The main demographic for talk radio is middle-aged, white, male, and conservative.[6] One exception to radio's rightward tilt is National Public Radio (NPR). Its audience, over twenty-six million listeners a week, is loyal and remains steady in numbers. Roughly 15 percent of NPR's funds come from the federal government, prompting ferocious criticism from conservatives, who argue that taxpayers should not be supporting "liberal" radio shows. Supporters respond that rural areas often have no other source of radio news. (And a Duke University study showed that NPR programs tend to hew close to the political center.)[7]

Today, podcasts also have sustained radio as a news provider, as Americans of all ages now listen to podcasts at twice the rate they did just a few years ago.

Television: From News to Infotainment

Television burst onto the American scene in the 1950s and revolutionized both entertainment and politics. President John F. Kennedy sensed TV's power and gave the first live press conference in February 1961. An incredible sixty-five million people—one in three Americans—tuned in. The young, charismatic president was a natural TV performer, and, once again, a new media technology intensified the

○ *Kennedy pioneered the televised news conference—and his approval rating soared to 70 percent. Presidents now had to be telegenic in live performance. Once again, the media had shifted the expectations and role of the presidency.*

link between the people and their president. Vice President Lyndon Johnson offered an ironic symbol of the new, visual era when he tried to hide his 250 pounds with a girdle.

The Rise of Cable. Two networks, CBS and NBC, monopolized the television news business during the 1960s and 1970s. Interested Americans all watched the same version of the day's events, solemnly read during the evening news shows by celebrated anchors.

Technology broke the monopoly. Cable stations came online in the 1980s and began to reach for small slices of the network audience. They lingered on the fringe of the media until 1991, when an upstart network, CNN, showed a live video of American rockets exploding into Baghdad, the capital of Iraq, at the start of the Gulf War. CNN introduced a new model: It reported news all day long. No more waiting until 6 p.m. for the national network news. A new format was born: the twenty-four-hour news cycle. Thirty years ago, White House staff, and the reporters who covered them, all relaxed when the news cycle ended around 5 p.m. Today, the cycle never ends.

In 1996, Rupert Murdoch launched Fox News, a network with a conservative slant. As Republican viewers headed for Fox, other cable networks—most notably MSNBC—moved to the left and developed shows with a liberal spin. Eventually, cable channels filled every niche along the political spectrum—Fox offerings such as *Hannity* on the right, shows like *Hardball with Chris Matthews* in the center, and *Last Week With John Oliver* and the *Rachel Maddow Show* on the left (see Figure 9.2).

see for yourself 9.3

President Obama and Zach Galifianakis discuss Obamacare, flanked by potted palm trees.

Infotainment. As cable channels proliferated, the line between news and entertainment began to evaporate. Late night talk shows got into the political act. Hosts gleefully lacerated the political losers of the day. Politicians responded by lining up as on-air guests. A major threshold of the new era was crossed when Senator John McCain, the Republican nominee for president in 2008, announced his candidacy on the *Late Show with David Letterman*—with bandleader Paul Shaffer in pink shades blasting out "Hail to the Chief." In 2014, President Obama appeared with comedian Zach Galifianakis to encourage Americans to sign up for health insurance exchanges.

Amid this colorful scene, network and cable news are gaining viewers, after several years of declines. This partly reflects the irresistible spectacle of Campaign 2016: CNN, for example, during the height of the 2016 Republican and Democratic primary battles, attracted six times its viewers during the same week a year earlier (nearly 3 million, vs. 480,000).

Overall, the TV picture reflects the state of the entire American media. A broadly shared view of the world, as interpreted by the nightly network news, has shattered. TV now runs the gamut from left to right and from formal news to frothy entertainment. The line between news and entertainment continues to blur—leading to the hybrid now known as **infotainment**.

Infotainment: The blurred line between news and entertainment.

Most trusted television news sources

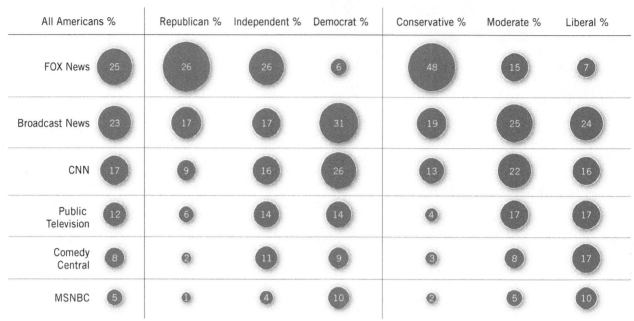

	All Americans %		Republican %	Independent %	Democrat %		Conservative %	Moderate %	Liberal %
FOX News	25		26	26	6		48	15	7
Broadcast News	23		17	17	31		19	25	24
CNN	17		9	16	26		13	22	16
Public Television	12		6	14	14		4	17	17
Comedy Central	8		2	11	9		3	8	17
MSNBC	5		1	4	10		2	5	10

● **FIGURE 9.2** *Political polarization fuels Americans' belief that the media (especially that favored by the other side) is biased. Here, trust levels vary by political outlook. (PRRI/Brookings)*

🔒 The Rise of the New Media

When Marco Rubio, who for a time was polling highest among Republicans in the 2016 presidential primary, announced his candidacy, he first sent a Snapchat to supporters. Hillary Clinton posed for thousands of selfies, each uploaded to Facebook and Instagram. And nobody tweeted like Donald Trump. What lasting effects on the media sector will these latest technologies produce? Some observers predict a new era of citizen participation.

The Internet and social media sites turn us all into potential news providers. Traditional news always awaited the arrival of a camera team. Now anyone can record an event on his or her phone, post it to Facebook or Instagram or Twitter (or all three), and watch it go viral.

Likewise, new technologies enable us to trace events that were much harder to track when people communicated via (untapped) telephones. Today, public officials' texts or email trails can connect them to scandalous revelations. The revelation in 2016, via more than eleven million leaked emails, of secret offshore accounts and other illegal deals enabled by a Panama bank cost the Icelandic prime minister his job and embarrassed hundreds of political and industry figures worldwide, including dozens in the United States. The "Panama Papers" scandal was only possible because modern technology enabled the massive release, on the secrets-sharing site WikiLeaks, of information—immediately picked up on social media and then by mainstream news reporters.

Still, the new outlets primarily rely on old media sources, which they are choking off. Yes, the new media generates important stories, including those on widely read platforms such as Politico and Buzzfeed. But these topics—like almost every other story—became important when traditional media focused attention on them. The list of the top fifteen websites includes mostly traditional players such as CNN, *The New York Times*, NBC, and *The Washington Post* (see Table 9.1).

TABLE 9.1	Top-Visited News Sites, April 2016	
RANK	DOMAIN	UNIQUE VISITORS
1	Yahoo! News websites	175,000,000
2	Google News	150,000,000
3	*Huffington Post*	110,000,000
4	CNN	95,000,000
5	*NYTimes.com*	70,000,000
6	Fox News Digital Network	65,000,000
7	NBC News	63,000,000
8	*Mail Online*	53,000,000
9	*Washingtonpost.com*	47,000,000
10	*The Guardian*	42,000,000
Source: Alexa News Aggregation		

Search engines and Internet portals link mainly to stories posted by traditional news sources—most of those populating Table 9.1. Both mainstream media and citizens worry that the portals and search engines grab the revenue. News aggregators such as *Huffington Post* or *Daily Beast* rely on the same old news sources but avoid paying them, while also generating their own content. The people who gather the news—for old and new media alike—find it difficult to eke out a livable salary. As these sources cut their own costs, news coverage gets thinner and less reliable. Ultimately, the old media's downward spiral affects most of the stories that people read on their laptops and cell phones.

THE BOTTOM LINE

» Thirty years ago, a few outlets—three networks, a weekly news magazine, and the local newspaper—delivered roughly the same news. Today, media outlets cater to every perspective—left, right, and center. Americans no longer share a single source of news.

» Previous waves of rising "new" media—newspapers, radio, and television—changed the nature of news reporting and altered political institutions such as the presidency.

» Today all these now-traditional institutions are in serious decline. Newspapers and magazines, network and local television, and radio are all losing ground as the place Americans go for news. Internet sources, especially social media platforms, are taking their place—especially among young people.

» The new media raises a major question: Do the benefits—the ability of everyone to contribute to "the news" and increased transparency—outweigh the dangers of losing traditional reporting sources? And can new media invent revenue sources that enable funding of investigative and longform journalism?

Is the Media Biased?

"What you have to do in order to earn the approval of the people in the media," declared Rush Limbaugh, is "to adopt their causes," such as global warming. "And it really helps if you take a position opposite me." Conservative media draws strength from a furious charge: The mainstream media is too liberal.[8] Forty-four percent of Americans believe this view (see Figure 9.3).

On the other side, liberals also charge the media with bias. In his book *What Liberal Media?*, Eric Alterman complained that the news corps rarely challenged the rich, the powerful, or the status quo. Mainstream media outlets breathlessly track the stock market but underplay stories about the rise of inequality. They ignore labor issues, child poverty, and homelessness. All the right's charges about media bias are, from this liberal perspective, intended to force the mainstream media to lean over backward to prove they are not biased.[9] Today, just two in ten Americans think the media is too conservative.

Which is it, in your view? A powerful left-wing media out to destroy conservatives? Or timid reporters, editors, and producers who are collectively bullied by the right?

Reporters Are Democrats

Conservatives are correct about the press corps' personal attitudes. Reporters in the mainstream media are more liberal than the country as a whole. Roughly 85 percent of journalists align with Democrats or Independents, compared to about 60 percent of the population. Although most reporters call themselves independent (especially those in the local media, where the number runs well above 60 percent), very few—just 7.1 percent, as of a 2014 study summarized in Figure 9.4—are self-described Republicans. Moreover, the press corps tends to vote for Democratic presidential candidates.

However, dozens of studies about election campaigns fail to show a systematic bias among mainstream media reporters in favor of Democratic candidates. Scholars have searched for bias in coverage, in statements, and in the types of stories that are aired. A few studies in some elections have found favoritism, but most do not. There have been fewer studies of media bias outside of elections. Perhaps reporters'

Americans' perceptions of media bias

In general, do you think the news media are too liberal, just about right, or too conservative?

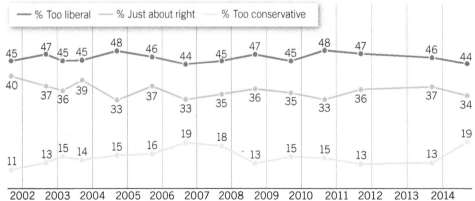

● **FIGURE 9.3** *Only a third of Americans believe the media is unbiased. (Gallup)*

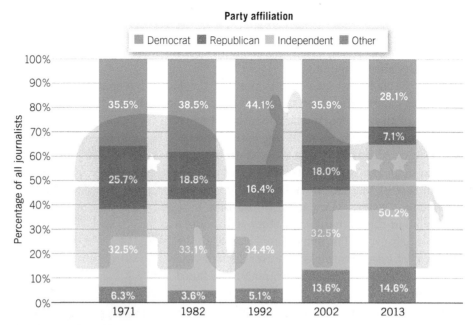

FIGURE 9.4 *Party affiliation of journalists. (Indiana University)*

views creep into their coverage of policy fights or presidential speeches—for example, in their framing which issues matter? Researchers find no reliable evidence to suggest that. However, there is hard evidence of a much deeper bias that runs through the news media—the need to attract a larger audience. We suggest that the media is indeed biased, but not in the way either side imagines. The principal bias arises in the media's real purpose: attracting coverage and making money. Media outlets print or say or film with an eye to drawing an audience.

Profits Drive the News Industry

What does the media actually sell? The answer is not news about government actors or election campaigns. Media sells its audience to advertisers. As a result, the prime directive is to expand the audience. When ratings rise, the business prospers; when they fall, networks replace anchors and newspapers cut staff. These financial realities give the news media a strong incentive to pitch its own politics near the views of its audience. For the large networks, that means the political center, where most Americans are comfortable. And, that is why both the Left and the Right complain about bias; the center *is* to the left of conservatives and to the right of liberals.

At the same time, each publication and network seeks its own audience. More conservative communities usually tune in to more conservative sources, and the current media is, as we have seen, divided into strong partisan niches.

In short, the market forces each news source toward the politics of its audience. That pressure is just the start of the market's influence on the media. Other market biases include the search for drama, conflict, and scandal.

Drama Delivers Audiences

Journalists find it more difficult to generate audience excitement about a school board meeting or a healthcare proposal. Miners trapped below the earth, on the other hand, pull people to their televisions and radios. A good drama must have a narrative arc with a beginning, middle, and end. It should have a protagonist (the miners), pathos (anxious spouses), a villain (the coal company or the government regulators), drama (will they be rescued before they run out of air?), an ending (tired but jubilant miners hugging their families), and a take-home message (we need to worry about mine safety).

Do not be fooled by the political moral at the end of the episode. Real mine safety raises complicated—and potentially boring—policy issues that will not attract much of an audience. You can be sure that when the state legislature debates mine safety, the cameras and reporters will be off chasing the next drama.

Local news gets much of its drama from crime. A classic rule of thumb guides the local TV news: "If it bleeds, it leads." Many good things may have happened that day, but the lead story will feature the most grisly event. The images are familiar to the point of cliché—a breathless reporter live on the scene, yellow tape blocking the area, grim-faced cops or firefighters in the background, weeping relatives in a daze, and perhaps a blank-faced perpetrator blinking into the camera.

The need for drama transforms election coverage as well. Election reporting rarely focuses on the issues—an audience turnoff. Instead, it is all about the drama of the protagonists, their families, their strategies, their dirty tricks, and their blunders. Elections have a built-in narrative arc with all the familiar features: a *beginning* (the candidates throw their hats into the ring), a *middle* (who is ahead? who had the best week?), a *conclusion* (someone wins), and a *take-home message* (the loser had a fatal flaw that other candidates should avoid). In 2016, media outlets debated whether Americans' thirst for drama-filled coverage led reporters and editors to provide Donald Trump with more free publicity than any other candidate.[10]

Political debates—whether about the environment, gun rights, education, or taxes—generally reflect the same pressure to build a narrative. Regardless of the issue, media coverage focuses on drama and conflict, heroes and villains, winners and losers. This tendency exacerbates media bias. For example, as political scientist Justin Wolfers demonstrated, despite a dramatic drop in U.S. crime rates over the past twenty years, most Americans believe that crime is actually rising.[11] The constant coverage, especially on local news, of crime misleads viewers to imagine that criminals are running rampant everywhere.

Check out your favorite news website. Can you see the dramatic narrative that frames the lead story? Pundits criticize the news for lacking substance. However, as a student of political science, you have learned to examine the *institution* and its incentives.

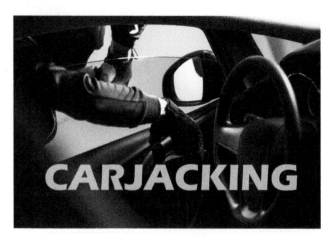

● *Media outlets, driven by a bottom-line concern for expanding audiences, tend to emphasize sensational stories—especially about violent crimes such as carjacking. This image led the news in West Palm Beach, Florida, although car thefts had fallen by 66 percent over the previous two decades.*

North Carolina Congressman: Bruce Springsteen Is a "Bully" for Canceling Concert

4:41 PM PDT 4/8/2016 by Paul Bond

● *Conflict sells. After a controversial North Carolina law curtailing LGBTQ rights passed in 2016, more coverage was devoted to critics of the new law (the National Basketball Association moved its All-Star game from Charlotte; companies such as Google and American Airlines issued denunciations; artists cancelled concerts) than to the complicated details of the law itself.*

The media, seeking a large audience to serve up to advertisers, covers whatever attracts the most attention. Simply calling for serious coverage will not change the incentives built into the media market.

Sex and Scandal

Nothing attracts an audience like a scandal—and the bigger the name involved, the bigger the media bonanza. President Bill Clinton's sexual involvement with a White House intern received enormous coverage. A scan of sixty-five newspapers of the time revealed that this scandal averaged more than a story a day for the entire year. During the coverage, CNN quadrupled its average rating. By the end of the year, 97 percent of the public could identify the president's alleged lover, while only 12 percent knew who was chief justice of the United States.[12]

Long lists of politicians have become entangled in sex scandals. In recent years alone, a New York congressman resigned in disgrace after tweeting a photo of his private parts to female fans (and then had a subsequent mayoral campaign derailed for repeat episodes); Alabama's governor, who won office as a virtuous "family values" candidate, was impeached in 2016 after recordings were released of his sexually suggestive phone conversations with his top political adviser, who was also married. Each time a scandal breaks, the press goes into overdrive. Jon Stewart offered the perfect description: Watching the media is like watching little kids play soccer. They all go running in a pack after the ball. Unless the politician is very nimble, the herd destroys their target and then moves on in search of the next scandal.

Investigative "Bias"

Other media biases have to do less with market and more with the profession of journalism. Two are especially powerful: skepticism and objectivity. Back in the early 1960s, Washington reporters were a small, white, male club with a code that winked at extramarital affairs in the White House or falling-down drunks in Congress. Then a series of events transformed the media's stance toward powerful men and women: The moral intensity of the civil rights movement, administration efforts to manipulate the press during the Vietnam War, and the **Watergate scandal** all made the old accommodations seem irresponsible. How could reporters go easy on segregationists or liars?

Watergate was especially significant in fostering skepticism. Reporters investigated a burglary of Democratic Party headquarters that led directly to the White House. President Nixon had secretly taped conversations in the Oval Office, and while pursuing the case of the botched burglary, the Supreme Court forced the release of the tapes. Their content stunned Americans. Now the public could hear their president order aides to "stonewall" the Watergate investigations. Even more shocking, the presidential tapes bristled with ethnic slurs, anti-Semitism, and foul language. (The newspaper transcripts were full of the notation "expletive deleted.")

In response, reporters redefined their roles. Rather than acting as chummy insiders, they became skeptics, aiming to pierce through official propaganda and find the hidden truth. Relations between the press and politicians turned adversarial. Each time the members of the press felt misled by an administration, their skepticism grew. For example, George W. Bush insisted that Iraq owned dangerous weapons that threatened the United States. (It did not.) Barack Obama promised Americans, "If you like your health plan, you can keep it." (Not all could.) The reporter's mission became uncovering lies and bad behavior.

see for yourself 9.4

Go online to see President Bill Clinton claim that he did not have sex with a White House intern.

Watergate scandal:
A failed effort in 1972 by Republican operatives to break into Democratic Party headquarters in the Watergate office complex in Washington, DC. President Nixon tried to cover up the event—eventually causing him to resign from the presidency.

The Fairness Bias

The effort to be fair introduces an unexpected bias. Reporters energetically try to present both sides of each issue. However, when issues do not have two equal sides, the effort creates the impression of a debate that does not exist. Companies that market tobacco, unhealthy foods, or toxic products, for example, have learned that they do not need to win the debate. They simply sponsor research and then announce that there are two sides to the issue. The fairness bias then leads the media to report the two sides as equivalent—even if one of the sides was manufactured by an interested party.

see for yourself 9.5

Watch John Oliver on the "false equivalency" among scientists in the climate change debate.

THE BOTTOM LINE

» Both conservatives and liberals complain of media bias. However, the media generally reflects the politics of its audience—which is to the left of conservatives and to the right of liberals.

» The media's deepest bias comes from its need to win ratings and appeal to advertisers. That puts an emphasis on drama, scandal, and conflict—exacerbating partisan political divisions.

» Media efforts to be balanced can introduce their own biases, such as "fairness."

How Governments Shape the Media

We have seen how technology constantly changes the media. The media, in turn, changes politics. In this section, we examine how political rules shape the development of the media.

Democratic nations organize their media in three different ways: First, the *government can fund* media outlets. This **public ownership** model is familiar in many nations—but not the United States. Second, the government can *regulate* the media to ensure that it operates in the public interest. Third, the government can stand aside and let the *market* guide the media; the assumption of the market model is that private companies will give the people (and the advertisers) what they want.

Public ownership: A situation in which media outlets are run by the government and paid for by tax dollars.

The First Amendment Protects Print Media from Regulation

You have already encountered the primary political rule governing print media—the First Amendment: "Congress shall make no law . . . abridging the freedom of speech or of the press." As we saw in Chapter 5, the Supreme Court has been strict about forbidding government interference with the press. It is very difficult to censor news (a practice known as prior restraint), to convict someone of slander or libel (spoken or written lies), to restrict pornography, or to forbid hate speech. Reporters are also fierce in protecting their sources. A *New York Times* reporter, Judith Miller, went to jail for three months rather than reveal her source for a story about a CIA agent named Valerie Plame.

Market forces and audience feedback impose the limits that do exist. American newspapers, paid for by local advertisers, generally reflect local mores. They are tame compared with, for example, the English tabloids. Web-based news outlets likewise reflect the outlook of their parent companies and of their audience. New-media consumers can respond swiftly to coverage they see as biased or inappropriate, through "comments" sections and organized Twitter and Facebook campaigns. When the gossipy site Gawker printed an article outing a gay Condé Nast executive, readers tweeted a torrent of objections, calling the story an unwarranted example of "gay shaming." Gawker soon removed the article and issued a promise to uphold higher standards in the future. (Soon after, in 2016, Gawker was driven bankrupt by another business leader, Peter Thiel, who had been outed on the site; Thiel secretly financed lawsuits against Gawker.)

Regulating Broadcasters

Radio and television fall into a separate category. They have been subject to government regulations from the start. As radio stations spread in the 1930s, their signals began to interfere with one another. In 1934, the Franklin Roosevelt administration created the Federal Communications Commission (FCC) to referee the industry. The agency was founded on a basic political philosophy: the airwaves belong to the public. The FCC would license stations on a given frequency—preventing signals from overlapping—but in exchange, stations were required to be "socially responsible." When a station secured or renewed its license, it had to show that it operated in the public's interest. When television emerged, the FCC expanded its jurisdiction to include it.

Fairness doctrine:
Regulation that required media outlets to devote equal time to opposite perspectives.

In 1949, the FCC issued an important regulation, the **fairness doctrine**. The fairness doctrine required radio and TV stations to give equal time to each side of a public issue. The rule reflected the era's expectations: sober, nonpartisan coverage of news and politics. Even though it was not strictly enforced, the fairness doctrine led stations to shy away from political controversies altogether; that way, they avoided the bother of achieving a balance.

In the 1980s, the Reagan administration challenged the entire idea of public responsibility enforced by regulatory agencies. It promoted a different political philosophy, viewing media as a private commodity rather than as a public good: end government regulations and let the consumers use the market to enforce what they value. The FCC repealed the fairness doctrine in 1983. The consequences were huge. Under the fairness doctrine, each talk show with a point of view had to be balanced by another talk show from the opposite perspective. A station that broadcast conservatives such as Rush Limbaugh would be required to air an equal amount of liberal programming. Repealing the rule opened the door to the media landscape we have today: a rich and raucous menu of news and politics that reaches across the political spectrum.

As with Internet news outlets, government regulation of new media operating in cyberspace is evolving as technology changes. In 2015, following a vigorous debate pitting new-media

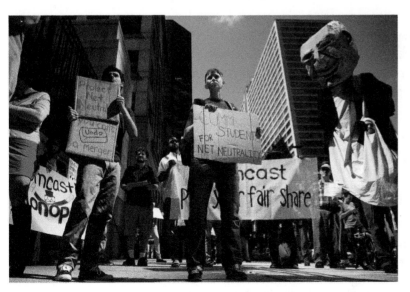

● Debate continues over whether higher paying customers should receive preferred broadband service, or whether the Internet should remain "neutral"—same access and streaming rates for all.

companies such as Netflix and large Internet service providers such as Comcast against consumer rights advocates, the FCC established "net neutrality" rules. High speed Internet service was reclassified as a telecommunications service, tightening FCC supervision—and mandating that providers cannot guarantee faster service to higher paying customers.

Protecting Competition

The market model is based on competition. If one corporation captures too much of the market, might it diminish consumer choice? This question arose when corporations moved to control companies across different media markets—print, radio, and television. Some observers warned that a few companies may come to dominate and stifle the marketplace of ideas. The top two radio companies, Clear Channel and CBS, control so many stations that they broadcast to a larger audience (263 million strong) than all twenty-four of the remaining radio networks combined. **Consolidation**, from this perspective, threatens free speech and fair debate.

Those who favor deregulation respond that today's media takes so many different forms, from radio stations to online news, blogs, and tweets, that stiff competition for consumer attention is inevitable. The **Telecommunications Act of 1996** reflected this second view and permitted many forms of cross-ownership. However, the debate about media consolidation continues.

> **Consolidation:** The process whereby a media company grows, acquires other companies, and threatens to dominate the market.

> **Telecommunications Act of 1996:** A major overhaul of communications law that opened the door to far more competition by permitting companies to own outlets in multiple media markets such as radio, television, and magazines.

THE BOTTOM LINE

» Democratic nations organize their media in three ways: government ownership, regulation, and markets. The United States has historically relied on the latter two models, regulation and markets.

» The First Amendment protects print media from most government regulation.

» Broadcast media in the United States was originally regulated by agencies such as the FCC, which imposed the fairness doctrine—a reflection of a less partisan era. The FCC is still active, as the "net neutrality" debate demonstrates, but its control has fragmented.

» Deregulation, new technologies, and the rise of multiple media have created the spectrum of perspectives and views that mark American media today. At the same time, a handful of giant media companies now control much of the content we see and hear. This contributes to our partisan and conflicted politics.

Media Around the World

The American media is different from that of other nations. (Have you noticed how many times we have said that about American politics?) Most nations began with government-operated broadcast media—the one option the United States has little pursued. However, the differences may be eroding. The American media has gone global, and in some countries, leaders even complain about the "Americanization" of their media.

INFO/DATA: Media Consolidation

Thirty years ago, dozens of companies provided national, state, and local media coverage. Today, just six companies control the vast majority of media content.

1. Is this problematic in your view? Why or why not?

2. Does the rise of new media make this consolidation more or less problematic? Why or why not?

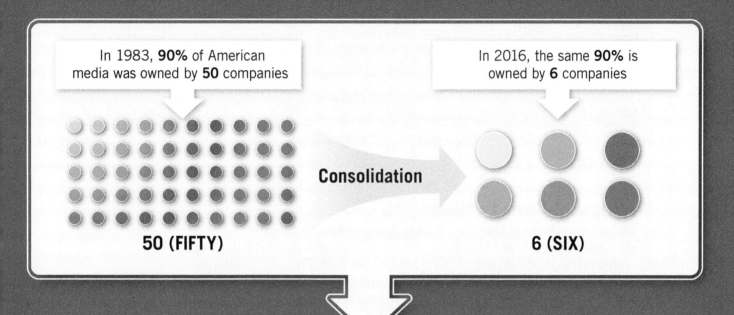

In 1983, **90%** of American media was owned by **50** companies

In 2016, the same **90%** is owned by **6** companies

Consolidation

50 (FIFTY)

6 (SIX)

These **6 (SIX)** media giants control **90%** of what we **READ & WATCH & LISTEN** to

COMCAST	NEWSCORP	DISNEY	VIACOM	TIME WARNER	CBS
Notable Properties	Notable Properties	Notable Properties	Notable Properties	Notable Properties	Notable Properties
NBC	FOX	ABC	MTV	CNN	CBS
Universal Pictures	Wall Street Journal	ESPN	Nickelodeon	HBO	Showtime
Focus Features	New York Post	PIXAR	Paramount Pictures	TIME	Smithsonian Channel

Source: Frugal Dad

268

TABLE 9.2 **Public Television—Abroad and at Home**

COUNTRY	% OF NATION'S DAILY AUDIENCE	TAXES PAID FOR PUBLIC TV PER PERSON
Denmark	69%	$130
UK (BBC, Channel 4)	50%	$90 (BBC only)
Germany	40%	$130
France	30%	$51
Australia	19%	$34
Netherlands	35%	$50
Norway	32%	$133
Canada	9% (English speaking) 17% (French speaking)	$30
Japan	17%	$54
United States	1.2%	$3.75

. . . and even that $3.75 is extremely controversial in the United States.
Source: Benson and Powers[13]

Government-Owned Stations

When radio developed in the 1920s, leaders in many democratic nations worried about the new medium's potential power. What if demagogues seized the airwaves? Elites felt that radio should inform and uplift citizens. Rather than leave radio programming to private entrepreneurs, most democratic countries introduced public stations that were owned by the government and funded through taxes. When television arrived, public media operated those stations too. To this day, the publicly owned BBC is the largest network in Britain, drawing 33 percent of the TV market; in contrast, the largest commercial network draws just 22 percent.[14] Most other democracies also have popular public stations funded by tax dollars and much smaller private sectors—with fewer stations—than the United States. This robust public media contrasts with the United States, in which public television draws less than 2 percent of the TV audience. Table 9.2 shows just how different the American media is on this issue of public ownership.

The Rise of Commercial Media

In the past thirty years, commercial media has developed around the globe. In many places, privately owned stations are drawing audiences away from public broadcasting.

Some European leaders criticize the rise of commercial media. Although it is popular with audiences, they call it crass and exploitative. Some believe it signals a much-feared "Americanization" of European culture. This last charge may seem unfair, as it is Europeans who developed reality TV, and the sexploitation on Italian game shows makes the American version look positively mild. Complaints about Americanization do, however, underline a key point. Although public broadcasting is still powerful in many nations (i.e., Britain, Germany, and Scandinavian countries), the American media model—private ownership—now poses a real challenge to the old public broadcasting model.[15]

An incident in China illustrates how the new media can shake up information control in small ways. In 2011, a young girl typed a message on the Chinese microblog *Sina Weibo* that read, "What's happening to the high-speed train? It's crawling slower than a snail." Five days later, another high-speed train was rammed from behind, killing thirty-nine people and injuring 192. Messages from inside the wrecked train, also posted to the microblog, described bloodshed, chaos, and slow response; they were reposted up to one hundred thousand times. The official state-run media tried the usual narrative—bad weather, a heroic response, many saved. An incredible twenty-six million posts from ordinary Chinese citizens overwhelmed that story. Both government and news agencies apologized, changed their approach, and launched an investigation into the crash. As one state-run newspaper put it, the government responded to its "netizens."[16]

The apology in China suggests that new media can shake up authoritarian governments and censorship. At the same time, the Chinese government continues to crack down on "outside media" sources. Facebook, Google, YouTube, and Twitter are all blocked in China, and new rules in 2016 required all images and words from even partly foreign-owned companies to be approved by government agencies before being viewed or read in China.[17]

Censorship

An entirely different media model dominates authoritarian nations: The government directly controls the media and censors every story. This has historically been common practice around the world. Government censorship limits open inquiry, information, and political debate and has always been the tool of tyrants. Democracies can only operate with the free flow of ideas and information.[18]

New media challenges the ability of authoritarian regimes to control information (see Comparing Nations 9.1). When the Internet is shut off or blocked, innovative networks can spring up to spread the news while new technologies permit people to receive content outside official channels. A key question for the future is whether (and how) citizens in authoritarian countries will successfully seize the democratic potential of new media forms. Whatever the answer, the crucial link between media and popular government extends far beyond the United States to every nation in the world.

American Media in the World

American media industries have enormous reach and power. In one typical week in May 2016, *Captain America: Civil War* was the highest grossing film in twelve of twenty-seven countries tracking box-office receipts, from China to Brazil to Australia; *The Angry Birds Movie* was on top in another dozen countries, such as Russia and South Africa; and *Zootopia* led in Japan. American television has a similarly wide influence. And the U.S. media model itself, with its emphasis on markets and consumer choice, has had a major impact in both democracies and authoritarian nations. The fear of "Americanization," expressed by opinion leaders in many nations, demonstrates the dominance of American media.

Concerns about "Americanization" intersected with censorship fears when, apparently in response to a Sony Pictures film that poked fun at the North Korean dictator Kim Jong-Un, North Korea launched a cyberattack on Sony's internal computer network so devastating that the company canceled the film's mainstream release. Curious viewers, however, turned to the Internet to watch the film, and the film became Sony's most successful digital release ever.

To be sure, every nation has its distinct media. Governments remain a major media player in most industrial nations. Looking abroad illustrates the strength of the American media—as well as just how unique the American media model remains. Few other nations have organized a system of private entrepreneurs operating within a framework of very light (and heavily criticized) regulatory oversight.

THE BOTTOM LINE

» Rapidly changing media outlets link citizens to their politics around the world. An open media is a vital key to making democracy work.

» The American model of media as private enterprise is spreading. However, most other democracies retain more government regulation than the United States.

» Authoritarian nations censor their news reporters. Increasingly, new media forms are challenging government control of the news, for better and for worse.

Understanding the Media in Context: War, Terrorism, and U.S. Elections

Every aspect of the media's influence on politics is on full display during two dominant American events: military conflicts, including responses to terrorism; and election campaigns. Framing issues, emphasizing drama and "infotainment," the fragmenting of story lines in our new-media age: all these come to the fore.

Covering Wars and Terrorism

When America engages in military conflicts, reporters are right there, embedded with the troops. Mathew Brady's portraits of Civil War carnage and destruction helped establish photography's mass appeal. Wars and terrorist attacks feature no shortage of drama, of course, playing naturally to media's inclination to cover

● *Vietnam War coverage. Images such as these—a South Vietnamese general shooting a handcuffed Vietcong prisoner in the head, and Vietnamese children fleeing a U.S. napalm attack on their village—were debated both as too violent for American viewers in the 1960s and as arousing antiwar protests.*

Media coverage of terrorist attacks: the aftermath of terrible Orlando shooting in 2016. Might 24/7 reporting exacerbate the chances of further attacks?

striking conflicts. Questions arise in every war about whether media is "sensationalizing" the conflict by providing particularly gruesome images.

Such worries are joined by concerns that wartime media coverage not give "aid and comfort to America's enemies," as a U.S. general warned darkly during the Vietnam conflict. Debates were sparked during the Iraq War by media reports of alleged American military misdeeds, such as "waterboarding" torture or mistreatment of prisoners at the notorious Abu Ghraib detention facility. Did the coverage portray U.S. soldiers unfairly, and diminish support for the war back home? What responsibility do journalists have for balanced reporting, including atrocities by our wartime enemies?

Media coverage of terrorist attacks also arouses an array of questions about journalistic ethics. Should the media faithfully report on any government claim about foiled terrorist attacks, for example? Some experts worry that extensive media coverage of terrorist attacks may actually heighten the chance of a subsequent attack, as misguided actors seek journalistic fame through terrible crimes. Should the Islamic State, for example, be given the media's "oxygen of publicity" for beheadings and other horrific acts?

Political science research suggests that reporting inadvertently *does* lead to further terrorist acts. In a 2016 study, Professor Michael Jetter concluded that a *New York Times* article about a terrorist attack in any specific country increased the number of ensuing attacks in that same country by as much as 15%. Jetter calculated that each additional *Times* article—or other mainstream global coverage—resulted in between one and two casualties from another terrorist attack within the next week.[19]

The Campaign as Drama

Along with wars and terrorism, media influences politics when it focuses on U.S. election campaigns: As noted earlier, media covers electoral campaigns like horse races—with constant predictions of who will cross the finish line first. As a result, coverage of presidential campaigns now devotes much less time to the candidate's actual views. In 1968, the average clip of a candidate speaking on the news, called a **sound bite**, ran uninterrupted for over forty seconds. Today, the average clip has fallen to under eight seconds. After those eight seconds, you might see the candidates gesture and move their lips, but those are just the backdrop for the anchor or pundit's analysis, which is often centered on (you guessed it!) why the candidate is winning or losing.

Sound bite: A short clip of speech taken from a longer piece of audio. Often refers to a brief excerpt from a speech by a candidate or politician.

Throughout the campaign, reporters' antennae are always up for gaffes and hints of scandal. When one appears, the entire media throngs to it. Every speech and every debate is carefully combed over for blunders; sites such as "FactChecker" review all candidates' claims during stump speeches and debates. Does this media whirlwind really matter to election outcomes? The short answer: rarely. Effective campaigns develop rapid-response teams that can deal with whatever crisis gusts through the media on that day.

Donald Trump's insults and misstatements during the 2016 campaign kept him in the media spotlight. Trump claimed erroneously to have seen "thousands of Muslims cheering in New Jersey" as the Twin Towers fell on 9/11, and characterized Mexican immigrants as "in many cases, criminals, drug dealers, [and] rapists." His X-rated bragging on an Access Hollywood recording caused him to drop in the polls. Yet for many, his statements shaped his image as someone who tells it like it is. Sometimes the missteps stick, though. Hillary Clinton came under fire for her use of a private email account during her time as Secretary of State. Though an FBI investigation brought no charges, polls suggested her credibility suffered badly. And Democrats angrily charged that the FBI's decision to reopen the investigation ten days before the election may have thrown the election to Trump. Gaffes and scandals are part of life on the campaign trail, and effective politicians learn how to blunt them—or even turn them to their advantage.

see for yourself 9.6

Go online to see Donald Trump deflect criticism about remarks he made in 2005.

Candidate Profiles

Campaign coverage often features a powerful narrative. The media sketches a profile of each candidate—simplistic, exaggerated, and very hard to escape. That image then shapes future coverage. Once the portrait develops, it reverberates through the world of infotainment. Behavior that "fits" immediately gets airtime, reinforcing the narrative.

The media first pictured Bernie Sanders as a fiery, nothing-to-lose insurgent, whose critiques of U.S. financial institutions attracted progressive Americans, especially college students and other young voters. Hillary Clinton became an Establishment figure, with reporters noting her long history in Washington institutions such as the State Department, the U.S. Senate, and the White House as First Lady. As the primary season shaped up as an anti-Establishment year in both parties, Sanders's surprising staying power was in part thanks to the framing of his candidacy by reporters.

Campaigns respond to shrinking sound bites by creating visual images that will speak louder than the inevitable punditry. Waving flags, cheering crowds, or bales of hay down on the farm all convey images—regardless of media voiceovers.

Campaigns spend extraordinary sums on advertising. Some ads have become classics, usually because of their wicked stings. In 1988, Republicans skewered presidential Democratic nominee Michael Dukakis with an ad featuring Willie Horton, a convicted murderer who was released from a prison on a weekend-furlough program approved by then-Governor Dukakis. While on release, Horton committed a rape; the story was used to paint Dukakis as a hapless, "soft-on-crime" liberal. Political advertisements become especially effective if they seep into the news coverage and become part of the campaign narrative. That can amplify the signal enough to reach the voters in the middle who are not paying much attention.

New media raises the prospect of great changes in campaigning. Social media outlets such as Facebook and Twitter give candidates a targeted way to circumvent the mass media and speak directly to supporters. Online messaging creates a sense of movement, of belonging. It offers a way to mobilize supporters behind a cause without relying on traditional media coverage. Ironically, the mainstream media eagerly reports on successful new media campaigns—amplifying that success by publicizing it.

» Reporting on war and terrorism has long attracted more viewers than almost any other political story. Ethical questions about the nature of media coverage continue to reshape editors' approach to these dramatic stories.

» Media coverage of campaigns reflects the general patterns of the contemporary media. It emphasizes drama, conflict, and the horse race narrative.

» Campaigns attempt either to influence the media or to bypass it and speak directly to supporters. These efforts in turn become part of the media coverage.

Conclusion: At the Crossroads of the Media World

The media reflects the United States—and broadcasts it to the world. American media has many critics. Conservatives blast the mainstream media's "liberal bias"; progressives lament Fox News and Rush Limbaugh; still others criticize the violence or the vulgarity on prime time, or worry that terrorist attacks will be encouraged by relentless media coverage. We should remember what makes the American broadcast media unusual: It has always been a commercial enterprise. For better or for worse, whatever draws an audience survives and flourishes.

America's media reflects the nation and its people. The fifth-largest network in the United States is the Spanish-language Univision. In fact, the dozen Spanish-speaking networks on American television today boast a total of more than 260 affiliates. Together, they reach more local stations than any one of the major networks. And the foreign-language media does not stop at Spanish. In San Francisco, Comcast offers thirty-five foreign-language channels, and the Dish satellite menu includes a hundred foreign-language stations. Sixty million Americans (including one of your authors) have at least one parent born abroad, and the media reflects that reality.

What else does the media tell us about who we are? Here is another important indicator: The ten largest religious networks have more than 350 affiliates. The largest, INSP (formerly the Inspiration Network), reaches an estimated 81 million households. By way of comparison, ESPN reaches 94 million.

As we have seen, television in every demographic is being squeezed by the Internet and the new media. Netflix, for example, now reaches some 43 million American households, and by some estimates will be the largest U.S. "TV network" within the next few years. And, in this booming new category, it is America's young people who are driving the change—pioneering new technologies and picking winners and losers among sites and applications. What once appeared to be a great digital divide is now shrinking, as African American and Latino youth catch up to white youth. In forums such as Twitter, they have even nudged their way to the top of their demographic.

All of these features add up to a nation at the crossroads of the media world. The United States consumes programs and programming in hundreds of languages. All that content offers one answer to our question, *Who are we*?: a multinational and multicultural society, bustling with changes and beaming its images to

Does the Media Enhance Democracy?

	Agree.	**Disagree.**	**Unsure.**
Return to the question that opened this chapter. When you think about the American media, what do you see for the future of democracy and politics? Are you with the optimists or the pessimists?	A booming media enhances American democracy. Media offers new ways to process news, build networks, and interact with leaders. All of this works as a robust new form of political action.	Media harms democracy. The babel of voices hastens national decline by chasing sensation and fomenting conflict. New media in particular erodes our news-producing capacity, increases inequalities, and offers dark corners that incubate malice.	Of course, the answer may lie somewhere in the middle, but keep the range of possibilities in mind as you monitor the media in the years ahead.

the world—through television, cinema, blogs, Instagram posts, streaming Netflix shows, and tweets.

Pessimists lament the collapse of our national community. Every political side now has its own news shows. Americans do not just disagree about their values—they do not even hear or see the same reality. Mainstream newspapers and networks are losing money, and as a result, their capacity to collect the news is declining. As the details about national and international events get sketchier, the void is filled by loud, ill-informed opinions. The entire news apparatus dashes after drama, conflict, and scandal. Important issues such as education, the environment, and impartial analysis of the healthcare system are downplayed in this chase for an audience, with victory going to the loudest or the most outrageous.

To pessimists, the new media only hastens the demise of the old reflective politics that permitted leaders to work together, forge compromises, and address our national problems. Today's media—fragmented, declining, sensationalist—exacerbates the conflicts in American politics.

In contrast, optimists see a thriving democracy in which people are active and engaged. Debates in Washington may be long and loud, but that only reflects an energetic nation undergoing enormous change. As media outlets expand, people's choices grow richer. Today, the United States has a broad lineup of news, information, and analysis. Members of the traditional media try to present objective reports as best they can. Cable channels and radio stations get partisans excited about their ideas and their parties. And new media—Internet-based outlets such as Twitter and Facebook—permit people, especially young people, to engage in political dialogue as never before. The media stirs up the best features of American politics: broad participation and strong opinions that leaders cannot help but hear.

CHAPTER SUMMARY

● The media—and the stories editors and users choose to emphasize—helps set the political *agenda*, *prime* the electorate, and *frame* issues.

● Media stories affect public opinion—primarily among people who do not have strong opinions. Because these people tend to pay less attention to the news, stories with clear signals (heavy coverage, a strong perspective) will change their views.

● Media platforms have expanded from the traditional television, radio, and newspapers to include online news sites, podcasts, Facebook, Twitter, and more.

● Media technology changes very rapidly, and each change reshapes the connection between citizens and their leaders—a crucial criterion for democracy. A big question runs through this chapter: Does today's media strengthen American democracy or weaken it?

● News sources are changing. Newspapers, magazines, television, and radio are all facing very different business models, and rushing to fill the void with new formats such as on-demand streaming and podcasts. Online news is rising fast. Today, it is the number one source of news for people under thirty. The enormous number of news sources spans the political spectrum and blurs the line between entertainment and news.

● Yes, the media is biased. Reporters in the mainstream press are less conservative than the general population, but they do not seem to tilt election coverage. The deepest bias—across the entire news media spectrum—comes from the media's purpose: It is a business that needs an audience to generate revenue. Therefore the news emphasizes drama, conflict, and scandal.

● In most other democracies, the government ran the first radio and TV stations and still plays a large role in the media world, although commercial media is rising. In authoritarian countries, the new social media poses a threat to the old model of information control and press censorship.

● The new social media is changing the nature of news and information. On the upside, users are more active. They can choose, respond, report, comment, critique, create, and share. Candidates and parties have new ways to connect. On the downside, the ready availability of news on the Internet has challenged the pay models of traditional print outlets, leading to a new media environment that facilitates the spread of rumors and even lies. All this means that we as a society do not share the same news.

● This influence gives it considerable power over American politics. Whether that power is used for the public benefit is a much-debated question—perhaps most sharply when it comes to covering urgent topics such as war, terrorism, and election campaigns.

● In many ways, the media reflects America. What we watch and hear tells us who we are.

KEY TERMS

Consolidation, p. 267

Fairness doctrine, p. 266

Framing, p. 253

Infotainment, p. 258

Loud signal, p. 252

Mass media, p. 255

New media, p. 250

Personal presidency, p. 257

Policy agenda, p. 252

Priming, p. 253

Public ownership, p. 265

Public watchdog, p. 252

Sound bite, p. 272

Telecommunications Act of 1996, p. 267

Watergate scandal, p. 264

STUDY QUESTIONS

1. Where do most Americans get their news—local television, network television, newspapers, or the Internet?

2. Which sources do millennial Americans rely on most for their news?

3. Name two problems most analysts see in the decline of the newspaper. Do you agree that these are problems? Why or why not?

4. How is the American media biased? Describe three of its biases.

5. Name three ways in which the American media is different from that of other nations. Be sure to consider the questions of ownership, objectivity, and investigation.

6. Choose a news source and look at today's headlines. Can you find a "media narrative" in these stories? Do you see a narrative arc, drama, conflict, good guys, and bad guys? Can you come up with a more objective way to present the story?

7. Research a potential Senate or House candidate for the 2018 midterm election. What does she or he stand for? Now design a campaign commercial for that candidate. Put him or her in the best possible light using visuals and voiceovers. Post your creation on YouTube.

8. Pick a story. Read its coverage in the *New York Times*. Now compare this coverage with that of two other sources: the BBC and Al Jazeera. Identify at least one difference in the way the other two outlets covered the story.

 Go to www.oup.com/us/Morone to find quizzes, flash cards, simulations, tutorials, videos, and other study tools.

Campaigns and Elections

THE FUNDRAISING FIGURES were startling. Jeb Bush, the former governor of Florida, had raised a whopping $116 million in his run for the presidency. The primaries were still a year away, but before the voting even began, Republican party insiders were setting up the winner by providing money, endorsements, and little changes in the rules (e.g., the timing of the debates). Everything seemed to point to Bush's nomination. Then, the conventional wisdom collapsed.

Donald Trump, a brash, abrasive reality TV and real estate personality, broke all the rules of campaigning: He did not raise money, he did not build a serious campaign organization, and he barely ran any commercials. He was crude and insulting—to Latinos, African Americans, U.S. prisoners of war, women, immigrants, Republican elder statesmen, newscasters, and donors. He challenged his party on fundamental issues and simply shrugged away what he did not know about politics and policy. Yet he won primary after primary. White voters from economically distressed communities, particularly men, flocked to his side. Despite the cold shoulder from almost every past Republican presidential candidate ("trickle-down racism," charged one), Trump won the nomination, and then shocked everyone all over again by winning the White House.[1]

In the Democratic Party, the results of primaries also appeared to be set in stone. Hillary Clinton raised almost as much money as Jeb Bush. Washington Democrats were enthusiastic about her campaign: She would finally break the greatest of all gender barriers, and she knew the workings of government inside out. Then Senator Bernie Sanders of Vermont, a rumpled, little-known, seventy-four-year-old with a Brooklyn accent also defied all expectations. Sanders championed democratic socialism, lashed the rich, and blasted the Democratic Party for ignoring everyday people. He won twenty-one states and came close to upsetting Mrs. Clinton's sure-fire victory. Both parties experienced something similar: Angry voters, who felt left behind in the American political economy, rose up and challenged the status quo. They voted for long-shot candidates who had tossed out the usual campaign playbook.[2]

● Republican Donald Trump looms behind Hillary Clinton at their second debate, held 'town hall' style. The question for political scientists and citizens alike: How much did the debates—or the campaign—really matter?

279

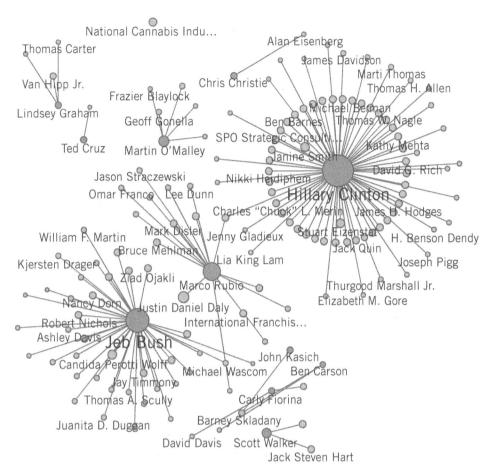

● *A year before the convention Hillary Clinton and Jeb Bush had lined up strong financial backing from major lobbies. Neither Bernie Sanders nor Donald Trump had lined up any big donor support. (Open Secrets)*

Sometimes, political scientists suggest, campaigns barely matter. More fundamental factors—such as the economy, war and peace, media coverage, and the sitting president's approval rating—determine who wins the election. Not the hyped-up, media-saturated, roller-coaster campaign. Yet in this case, the campaign and the manner in which it was run certainly seemed to shape the outcome: Do campaigns matter, and if so, how much?[3]

Yes, campaigns can decide elections. This chapter will show you how and why. Of course the underlying fundamentals have a big impact: They tell you who has a good chance and who faces an uphill battle. But within that framework, the voters—and the fundraisers and the media—take a large number of candidates and winnow them down until the United States has its president.

Meanwhile, thousands of other races take place for positions from U.S. senators to judges to municipal drain inspectors. Elections make American government. *Who are we?* A nation of elections. Americans vote more often and for more officers—on every level of government—than the people of almost any other nation. Through elections, Americans choose leaders, guiding philosophies, programs and policies, and the nation's attitude toward the rest of the world.

The wild election of 2016 directly raised a question we have been asking throughout this book: How democratic is the process? Both Donald Trump and Bernie Sanders charged that the electoral process was "rigged"—biased in favor of the status quo and designed to rein in real (and disruptive) grassroots initiatives. Their challenges pose an overarching question for campaigns and elections in the United States: Is the electoral system, the rules that govern our voting, designed to reflect the people? Should it better reflect public views? Or perhaps, as some of the founders thought, American electoral machinery should be *less* sensitive to the whims of public opinion.

BY THE NUMBERS
Campaigns and Elections

Year of first election with universal white male suffrage in most states: **1828**
Year in which Senators were first chosen by the people in all states: **1914**
Years in which American women first voted (in New Jersey): **1797–1807**
Year in which women in all states could vote: **1920**

Number of people filing to run for president in 2016: **1,812**
Number filing as Republican candidates: **305**
Number filing who were "serious" Republican candidates: **17**
Number filing as One Earth, Prohibition, Communist, and Libertarian candidates, respectively: **4, 5, 33, 56**
Number of candidates named Prince of Darkness, Satan Lord of the Underworld H. Majesty: **1**

Sequential rank of Iowa and New Hampshire in presidential primary season: **1, 2**

Percentage of U.S. population that is non-Hispanic white, 2016: **61.4**
Percentage of Iowa's and New Hampshire's population, respectively, that is white: **91, 93**

Typical cost of 30-second CNN commercial during prime time, 2016: **$5,000**
Cost of 30-second prime-time commercial during 2016 Republican primary debates: **$200,000,**
Cost of one thousand yard signs, North Dakota at-large House district: **$3,500**

Percentage of Americans who think money has too much influence in political campaigns (2016): **84**
Percentage of voting-age population who turned out, 1912: **58.8**
Percentage of voting-age population who turned out, 2016: **54.8**
Number (and percentage) of House or Senate incumbents who lost in 2016: **4 House, 2 Senate (1.2%)**
Percentage of incumbent losers who typically join Washington lobbying firms: **33**

Time, place, and manner clause: The constitutional clause that delegates control of elections to the state governments.

How Democratic Are American Elections?

The Constitution ignored a crucial matter: Who votes and how. It left the election details—the **"time, place, and manner"**—up to the states. That means a slightly different election system in each state. For example, women won the vote in Wyoming in 1890; but in New York, they had to wait another thirty years.

Government by the people can be measured along multiple dimensions: How often do people vote? How many positions do they vote for? What role does money play in the process? The American electoral process is distinctive along each of these dimensions.

Frequent and Fixed Elections

One way to hold public officials accountable is to require them to face the public frequently. The United States schedules elections for national office more often than most other democratic countries. House members are chosen every two years, presidents every four, and Senators every six. Add state and local elections (for governor, mayor, state legislature, city council, and so on), and there is never a year in the United States without major elections.

This tally only covers our general elections. Count all the primary contests, and, in some years, the election calendar stretches through the year. In 2016, for example, Iowa held its caucuses on February 1, and the process continued until the people elected President Donald Trump more than nine months later.

Many parliamentary democracies have a five-year ceiling on the term for national officials. The chief executive, usually a prime minister, decides when elections will be held: He or she must "call" an election within five years of the last election. The built-in uncertainty allows officials to shape the calendar to their preferred schedule. In contrast, American national elections are on a fixed date (chosen back in 1845), except when an officeholder resigns or dies. On the first Tuesday after the first Monday in November of every even-numbered year, we elect all House members and a third of the Senate; every fourth year, we elect a president.

COMPARING NATIONS 10.1	Election Timetables for National Government	
How does the United States compare to other selected advanced democratic countries in election frequency?	**FREQUENCY**	**GOVERNMENT BODY**
	2 years	**U.S. House of Representatives**
	3 years	House of Representatives in Australia, New Zealand, El Salvador
	4 years	Parliaments in Argentina, Costa Rica, Germany, Japan, South Korea, Switzerland; **U.S. president**; president and lower chamber of legislature in Brazil
	5 years	Parliament in Ireland; president in South Korea; congress in Peru; *maximum term* for prime minister (and parliaments) in Canada, Denmark, France, Italy, United Kingdom, many others
	6 years	Argentinian, Australian, and **U.S. senators**
	8 years	Senators in Brazil and Chile

Nothing—war, economic depression, terrorist attacks, or other major emergencies—has changed that schedule. The states, however, still fix the date of the primaries for every office from president to the collector of county deeds. The frequency of elections tilts the U.S. electoral system in a more democratic direction.

Do you see any drawbacks to frequent elections? All that campaigning consumes a great deal of public officials' time, as well as scarce resources (we'll get to the cost of elections in a minute). Critics also worry that it is more difficult to focus on policymaking when House members are constantly running for reelection. As a Canadian prime minister once remarked: "In your system, you guys campaign for 24 hours a day, every day for two years. You know, politics is one thing, but we have to run a government."[4]

Over 520,000 Elected Officials

Not only are American elections unusually frequent compared to most countries, but an enormous *number* of positions are elected. From presidents to municipal drain inspectors, Americans elect their public officials. And the roster of elected positions continues to expand. The United States was the first nation to choose its chief executive by popular election—even if the founders hedged by adding the Electoral College to the process. American judges also were the first to face the voters, more than a century ago. Today, thirty-nine states elect judges (87 percent of all state judges). No other country elects judges, as they are supposed to be above politics. Critics charge that fundraising and campaign promises compromise the impartiality of state judges. But elections remain the American way.

To better grasp the number of elective offices in the United States today, see Table 10.1, which lists elected officials representing the residents of Iowa City, Iowa.

TABLE 10.1 **Who Do You Vote for in Iowa City?**

NATIONAL OFFICIALS	
1 U.S. president	
2 U.S. senators from Iowa	
1 U.S. representative from Iowa's Second District	
STATE OFFICIALS	
1 Iowa governor	
1 Iowa lieutenant governor	1 Iowa secretary of state
1 Iowa attorney general	1 Iowa state treasurer
1 Iowa agriculture secretary	1 Iowa state auditor
1 Iowa state senator	1 Iowa state representative
COUNTY OFFICIALS	
1 county supervisor	1 county sheriff
1 county treasurer	1 county attorney
1 county auditor	1 county recorder

(continued)

TABLE 10.1 *(Continued)*

TOWNSHIP/CITY OFFICIALS (IOWA CITY IS BOTH A CITY AND A "TOWNSHIP")
1 township clerk
3 township trustees
7 school board members
4 education agency directors
7 city council members (who in turn elect one member as Iowa City mayor)
9 agriculture extension members
1 soil and water conservation commissioner
7 Iowa Supreme Court justices (appointed for one year by governor, then must win a public "retention election" every eight years)

Count them up: there are fifty-eight elected officials for Iowa City alone. That number is one measure of democracy in action. Some argue, however, that this is *too much* democracy. From Anchorage, Alaska, to Zapata, Texas, there are more than 520,000 elective offices at the local, state, and national level. That is roughly one official for every 420 Americans eligible to vote. Too many? What do you think?

Financing Campaigns: The New Inequality?

In a democracy, all voters should have an equal say in selecting the winner. Legally, each registered American voter can show up at the polls only once per election. But there is growing concern about the ever larger sums of money flowing through U.S. elections. Do big contributors have more influence over elections?

Too Much Money? Each election breaks the spending records spent in the last one. Candidates for national office in 2012 (Congress and the Presidency) spent $6 billion, and figures for 2016 ran even higher. Each midterm congressional election also spends more than the last (see Figure 10.1).

Do we spend too much? Many critics say yes. Public officials on every level devote enormous amounts of time and energy to raising money. As a result, some people fear that wealthy people may be able to bury candidates and (more important) political issues that they do not like. Nonprofit organizations, such as the Sunlight Foundation, argue that a few wealthy donors have more influence than millions of voters. And the public agrees. Polls consistently show overwhelming majorities want to reduce the role of money in U.S. elections.

On the other side, both the Institute for Justice and the American Civil Liberties Union argue that

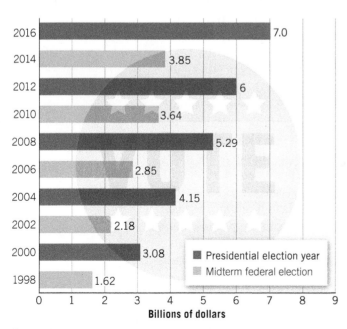

● **FIGURE 10.1** *The cost of national elections (inflation-adjusted dollars). Every federal election breaks the record for money spent. (Open Secrets)*

Too Many Elected Positions?

Yes, there are too many elective positions. The public is asked to vote too often. Few voters can learn about so many races. The United States should appoint more experts to handle the technical aspects of government.

No, we need to encourage people to vote more often. With U.S. voting rates so low, reducing the number of elected officials would be unhealthy for our democracy. Voting permits the people to hold their public officials directly accountable.

donating to campaigns is a form of free speech. Americans have a right to financially support campaigns as means of expression. Moreover, think about those campaign numbers in context: The approximately $7 billion spent on national races in 2016 (president, 435 House and 33 Senate) was less than two-thirds of what Americans spent at Taco Bell that year, and less than a third of the estimated amount spent on pornography during the same year. When the Supreme Court's 2014 *McCutcheon v. FEC* ruling allowed even more funds to pour into campaigns, there was little public outcry. Americans oppose the rising tide of campaign cash, but for most, the issue is not a high priority. What do you think: Is contributing to campaigns a citizen's right? Or is it turning our democracy over to the wealthy?

Democracy for the Rich?   Do the wealthy dominate elections—perhaps even squeezing out the people's influence? Concerns about this dominance can be divided into two parts: First, the fear that one political party will unfairly stack the deck in its favor; and second, the fear that influence (exercised by individuals or corporations) is unevenly distributed in ways that add up to dangerous inequities.

Some groups do contribute mainly to one party. For example, labor unions financially back Democrats (by a ten-to-one margin, in recent elections), and some industries—such as oil and gas companies—largely support Republican candidates. But most business sectors traditionally split their donations about evenly between the two major parties. The largest-spending group of corporate donors, finance/insurance/real estate (FIRE) companies gave a bit more to Democrats in 2008 and tilted slightly Republican (50 percent to 46 percent) in the 2010 midterms. Then, in opposition to new regulations introduced by the Democrats (known as Dodd Frank), they turned Republican. By 2014, the industry was sending 63 percent of its donations to Republican candidates. The traditional pattern was clear: Most corporate sectors wanted a seat at the table in both parties. Are the Republicans now pulling ahead? If so, it has only begun to show in total spending.[5]

The two major parties spent at roughly equal levels in recent elections—with a slight (but growing) edge to Republicans at most levels—though not in the race for president. Democrats raised more money than Republicans in the presidential contest ($734 million to $562 million). However, Republicans outspent Democrats in races for Senate ($363 million to $3i9 million) and House (527 million to $432). In statewide races across the country, Republicans outspent Democrats by about 10 percent (in 2014).[6]

Beyond partisan balance lies the concern that some people, companies, or points of view gain unfair advantage because office holders are reliant on campaign funds. In any campaign, a small number of people (fewer than one in two thousand)

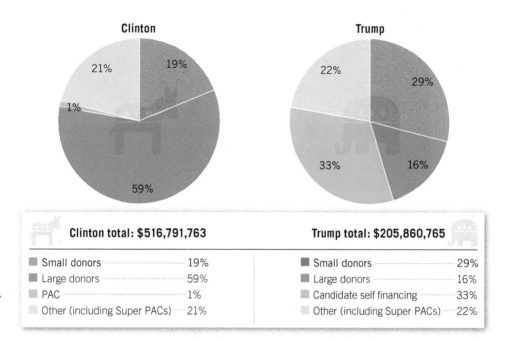

FIGURE 10.2 *Sources of funds, by type of contributor, October 2016 presidential campaign. (Open Secrets)*

donate more than $200 to a candidate. Critics worry that the need to raise funds—always more and more money—is always on the elected official's mind. Won't office holders be especially sensitive to those people's concerns? Many activists insist that it must, but research has not yet found a definitive link between contributions and political influence. Figure 10.2 summarizes the sources of the 2016 presidential campaign donations for Clinton and Trump during the primary elections.

Major Donors: Easier to Give.   Shaun McCutcheon, a conservative Alabama businessman was frustrated by the campaign finance laws that limited his donations to $1,776 per candidate and $48,600 overall. He wanted to give more. McCutcheon sued claiming that his constitutional right to support candidates and causes had been violated. In 2014, the Supreme Court agreed, effectively ending limits on an individual's total donations—the top contributor in 2016 gave $67 million (to Democrats).

What is left after the Court's ruling is a patchwork of regulations. No one may contribute more than $2,700 to any individual candidate. One way around that limit is through **bundling**: convincing colleagues and friends to donate at or near the maximum amount, then delivering all the checks together. Presidential campaigns sign up hundreds of bundlers.

There are also organizations designed to donate. Many corporations and advocacy groups form **political action committees** (**PACs**) to make legal donations to candidates. PACs, which by law must comprise fifty or more contributors, may legally contribute $5,000 per election cycle to any one candidate (the primary and the general election are considered different cycles effectively raising the limit to $10,000).

Want to contribute still more? In a landmark 2010 case, *Citizens United v. FEC*, the Supreme Court struck down laws limiting "independent" political spending by corporations and unions: The **super PAC**, formally known as "independent expenditure-only committees," was born. Super PACs may raise unlimited sums from virtually any source—business firms, unions, or individuals—and spend as much as they like to openly support or oppose political candidates. Unlike traditional

Bundling: A form of fundraising in which an individual persuades others to donate large amounts that are then delivered together to a candidate or campaign.

Political action committee (PAC): An organization of at least fifty people, affiliated with an interest group that is permitted to make contributions to candidates for federal office.

Super PACs: Organizations that are permitted to raise and spend unlimited amounts of money to promote a candidate or publicize a cause. However, they may not directly contribute to a candidate or coordinate with a campaign.

INFO/DATA: Money in Elections: The New Rules

Since 2010, the Supreme Court rulings in *Citizens United v. FEC, McCutcheon v. FEC,* and others have weakened the limits on campaign contributions and enabled Super PACs to emerge. Although per candidate and per PAC limits still exist, the caps on the number of candidates or PACs a donor can contribute to have been lifted.

1. How has the lifting of contribution caps changed the total amount of money that may stream into an election cycle? How does the lifting of caps affect wealthy donors who hedge their bets by contributing to multiple candidates?

2. How will this impact elections and democratic representation overall?

		2010	**2016**
Candidates	Limit for each candidate	House and Senate candidates $5,200 each	House and Senate candidates $5,400 each
	Limit for all candidates in an election cycle?	**YES** Total possible contribution: $48,600	**NO** Total possible contribution: $2,527,200
Party committees	Limits	$74,600	$1,197,400
PACs	Limit for each PAC	$5,000 each	$5,000 each
	Limit for all PACs	**YES** Total possible contribution: $74,600	**NO** Total possible contribution: $Millions
Number of super PACs		0	Over 2,300

Sources: Washington Post Information Graphics; Open Secrets

527 groups: Organizations governed by Section 527 of the federal tax code; they are allowed to raise and spend unlimited amounts for "issue advocacy" but are forbidden to coordinate their efforts with any candidate or campaign.

PACs, they may not contribute directly to (or coordinate their efforts with) individual political candidates.

Another source of campaign-related funds are **527 groups**, named for the section of the U.S. tax code that regulates them. 527 groups are forbidden from advocating directly on behalf of any candidate's election but can accept and spend unlimited amounts for "issue advocacy." They may not explicitly support or oppose a candidate, but the ads they run can be indirectly supportive—or scathing. "Senator Jones is a tree killer who hates the environment" is an acceptable message a 527 group may broadcast; "Vote against Senator Jones" is not.

PACs, super PACS, bundlers, 527s: In the 2016 presidential contest, these outside groups spent an estimated $1.04 billion—beyond the roughly $1.5 billion raised by the presidential campaigns. Each innovation raises a fresh round of questions about democracy and campaign spending. As the limits on campaign spending are eliminated, a handful of very wealthy individuals can keep a candidate's primary campaign going.

Does this help or hurt democracy? Does contributing funds to a legislator "buy" anything valuable for donors? Should the system be changed to reduce the influence of monetary contributions? Or is spending money on campaigns a vital form of free speech? We will come back to these questions at the end of this chapter.

THE BOTTOM LINE

» Are American elections truly democratic? Americans vote more often than the citizens of most other democracies.

» Americans vote for more offices—from state judges to school board members—than people in other democracies. Some critics argue that we vote on too many offices.

» The most familiar question about American democracy today focuses on the role of money in election campaigns. PACs, super PACs, and 527s have become fixtures in national elections. Recent court decisions have significantly expanded the ability of wealthy donors and outside groups to spend large sums in support of their preferred candidates, party, and causes.

Presidential Campaigns and Elections

The presidency is the greatest electoral prize. Presidential candidates receive a crush of media and public attention. Front runners attract large audiences wherever they go, and candidates become an instant campaign case study if they win their party's nomination. Small wonder that every four years, so many political leaders catch "presidential fever" and declare their candidacy.

Who Runs for President?

Onetime candidate Morris "Mo" Udall, who ran in 1976, said afterward, "You have to be a little crazy to run for president." Along with the positive aspects of a campaign (if you like attention, that is), seeking the presidency is expensive, privacy-shredding, and exhausting. Yet in every presidential race, dozens take up the challenge. Some are third-party hopefuls, representing various ideologies or causes.

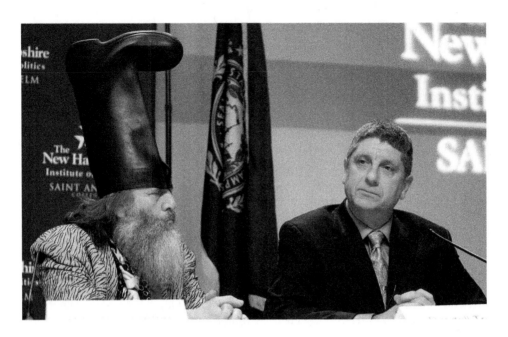

Vermin Supreme placed fourth in the 2016 New Hampshire Democratic primary before running as an independent candidate in the general election, promising funds for time travel research, zombie alert preparation, and a pony for every American.

Libertarian Party candidate Gary Johnson, Green Party candidate Jill Stein, and other more colorful independents ran in the 2016 race.

Serious presidential candidates generally have experience as elected officials—and in the last half-century, both parties have always nominated candidates with one of three offices on their résumé—vice president, governor, or senator—at least until Donald and 2016. Four points about successful candidates in the past (see Table 10.2):

Senators usually lose. Barack Obama was the first senator in forty-eight years to win a presidential race. Five senators were nominated for president and lost between 1964 and 2004. Another five senators sought the Republican nomination in 2016: All failed to win that prize.

Vice presidents have the best record. Seven sought the White House in the last fifty years; all won their party's nomination, and three went on to win the presidency.

Governors are the new winners. Before Jimmy Carter won in 1976, no governor had won the presidency since Franklin Roosevelt in 1932. In fact, only two governors had been elected in the entire twentieth century. Since 1976, however, four out of our seven presidents have come from governors' mansions. What changed? As we have seen again and again, after the upheaval of Vietnam, civil rights, and Watergate, Americans lost their confidence in Washington, DC, and its insiders. Governors from both parties win by claiming they were successful state executives untainted by the mess in Washington.

Traditionally, no one else gets nominated or elected. Every election season, people from other positions toss their hats into the ring. There is almost always a member of the House and often a businessperson. They never win modern presidential elections. The last president to come directly out of the House of Representatives? Andrew Jackson back in 1828. Businesspeople with no experience in elected office? None had ever won the presidency until Donald Trump won in 2016. It takes enormous political talent to run the contemporary gauntlet from primaries through the general election and into the White House. In all American history, Donald Trump is the first newcomer to navigate the political process. How did he do it? Read on.

TABLE 10.2 The President's Résumé

YEAR	WINNER	PREVIOUS POSITION	LOSER	PREVIOUS POSITION
1960	John Kennedy	Senator	Richard Nixon	Vice president (1953–1961)
1964	Lyndon Johnson	Vice president (1961–1963)	Barry Goldwater	Senator
1968	Richard Nixon	Vice president (1953–1961)	Hubert Humphrey	Vice president (1965–1969)
1972	Richard Nixon	Incumbent	George McGovern	Senator
1976	Jimmy Carter	Governor	Gerald Ford	Vice president/incumbent
1980	Ronald Reagan	Governor	Jimmy Carter	Incumbent
1984	Ronald Reagan	Incumbent	Walter Mondale	Vice president (1977–1981)
1988	George H. W. Bush	Vice president (1981–1989)	Michael Dukakis	Governor
1992	Bill Clinton	Governor	George H. W. Bush	Incumbent
1996	Bill Clinton	Incumbent	Bob Dole	Senator
2000	George W. Bush	Governor	Al Gore	Vice president (1993–2001)
2004	George W. Bush	Incumbent	John Kerry	Senator
2008	Barack Obama	Senator	John McCain	Senator
2012	Barack Obama	Incumbent	Mitt Romney	Governor
2016	Donald Trump	Real Estate Developer, Reality TV star	Hillary Clinton	Secretary of State, Senator, First Lady

The Three Phases of Presidential Elections

Presidential campaigns involve distinct stages. First, the *nominating process*, in which each party chooses its contender, is often drawn out over years of campaigning followed by some six months of state-by-state primary elections. Second, the two major *party conventions* take place during the summer of an election year. Finally, the *general election* features the final battle for the White House and kicks off in earnest after the conventions. Each stage requires very different political strategies, played out amid the white-hot lights of national—and global—media coverage.

Winning the Nomination

The presidential nominating process is grueling. Candidates must master the nominating process's elaborate rules and primary election calendar to have any hope of success. Remember that each state determines its own primary election date through careful negotiation with the national parties. Every four years, states jockey to schedule their balloting near the front of the line. Holding a primary early in the process, before the nomination is decided, attracts attention—and gives the

What Do You Think?

Why Iowa and New Hampshire?

Starting around two years before each presidential election, the nation's most powerful politicians and skilled campaign advisors travel to two small states. By tradition, Iowa's caucuses and New Hampshire's primary are the first two presidential contests held every four years—giving them an outsized influence in the process. If you win or perform better than expected in one or both, you're launched toward the nomination. If you do badly in both, your campaign is in trouble. Should they continue to have such an important say in choosing the president?

Yes. Small states like these test the candidates' abilities through one-on-one meetings with small groups—a very different type of test than they face in the media campaigns reliant on heavy fundraising that follow in the large states. In these states, we can get to know the men and women behind the slick media presentations.

No. Iowa ranks thirtieth in population and is 93 percent white; New Hampshire forty-second in population and 95 percent white. Two highly unrepresentative states eliminate many candidates before any large state has even had a chance to vote.

---

voters an important say in selecting the nominee. Back in 1992, national party leaders scheduled multiple elections on a single date, known as **Super Tuesday**, hoping to keep the contest from dragging out too long; in 2016, that "Super" day was March 1, when twelve states held primaries or caucuses. By then, six states had already voted.

Both parties require that a winning candidate amass a certain number of convention delegates, assigned proportionately based on state population—and loyalty to the party in the last election. In the 2016 Republican race, for example, Texas had 155 delegates, Alabama had 50, and Vermont 16. In the past, Republicans used a **winner-take-all** system, under which the winning candidate receives all the delegates for that state. Democrats, in contrast, have generally employed a system of **proportional representation**, allocating delegates based on the proportion of the vote a candidate wins. In 2016, the GOP primaries required proportional representation until mid-March when states could chose to allocate all their delegates to the outright winner (seven states did so) or to anyone who scored over 50 percent of the state and congressional districts. Why all this rigmarole? Republican Party activists wanted a process that did not get decided too soon—before their candidate had been fully tested (as happened with John McCain in 2008)—but they did not want the contest to drag out so long as to damage the winner (Mitt Romney in 2012).

In the 2016 Iowa Caucus, for example, Ted Cruz won 27.6 percent of the vote, followed by Donald Trump (24 percent), Marco Rubio (21 percent), Ben Carson (9.3 percent). They reaped 8, 7, 7, and 3 delegates, respectively. Seven weeks later, in Florida's winner-take-all primary, Trump took 45.7 percent of the vote and won all 99 delegates.

The traditional rules are clear: Primary season candidates must make strong first impressions, compete well in state after state, avoid errors or outrageous statements in a dozen or more debates, and manage a campaign team that, as the contests continue, can swell to thousands of people. They also may have to carefully calibrate their issue positions.

In 2016, Donald Trump broke the rules. He made outrageous statements. He did not build a campaign team. He casually announced and discarded policy

Super Tuesday: The date on the presidential primary calendar when multiple states hold primaries and caucuses.

Winner-take-all: The candidate receiving a simple majority (or, among multiple candidates, a plurality) receives all electoral votes or primary delegates. Sometimes called "first-past-the-post."

Proportional representation: The allocation of votes or delegates on the basis of the percentage of the vote received; contrasts with the winner-take-all system.

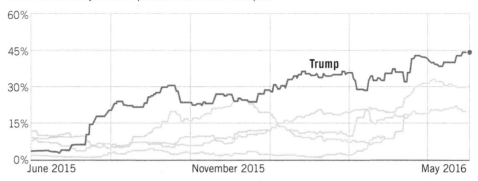

Trump's support in the polls grew steadily over time
Other candidates jostled for position but couldn't compete

Trump

June 2015 November 2015 May 2016

● **FIGURE 10.3** *American support for Trump during primary. Light blue lines indicate support for other candidates in the Republican primary. (NBC News)*

positions. So, why did he win the primary? Political scientists and media pundits alike are still pondering this question, but three good points have been raised.

First, Trump emphasized American economic decline even as the Obama administration touted a solid growth rate. Trump understood that many individuals felt left out of the economic recovery—and he targeted his pitch directly to them. These individuals formed a vital component of his early base of supporters.[7]

Second, the American public already knew Trump well as a businessman and celebrity. From his first cameo appearance on the popular sitcom *The Jeffersons* to his own reality television show, *The Apprentice*, Trump had been entertaining Americans for three decades—and until the 2016 campaign brought on intense media scrutiny, Trump had been a symbol of economic success to many.[8] As a result, he dominated the media news cycle throughout the election—and as we saw in Chapter 9, Trump's misstatements continued to place him in the limelight.

Finally, an unprecedented number of candidates ran in the 2016 Republican primary—and the strongest candidates were deeply divided. Traditional Republican candidates such as Jeb Bush and John Kasich squared off against new Tea Party candidates Ted Cruz and Ben Carson. Trump capitalized on this lack of consensus, gaining support as they remained divided and winning primaries often with a low plurality of the vote (see Figure 10.3).

Democratic candidate Bernie Sanders's unexpected success can be attributed—in part—to the nature of voter turnout in primary elections. Far fewer Americans turn out for primary elections than for general elections, and those who do vote tend to be more ideologically driven than the more centrist fall electorate. Conventional political wisdom holds that candidates must therefore run more to the extreme—farther left for Democrats, farther right for Republicans—to capture the nomination and then move back to the middle for the general election. Sanders ran to the left of Clinton, appealing to social democrats.

The end of primary season generally enables both nominees to reintroduce themselves, while their opponents try to define them in a negative way. Both jobs (positive reintroduction and negative definition) are much easier with relatively unknown candidates than with well-known figures such as Donald Trump or Hilary Clinton.

Organizing the Convention

Political party conventions showcase the party's presidential nominee on a national stage; they also gather party insiders from across the United States for several days

see for yourself 10.1

Go online to see the 1960 Nixon–Kennedy debate.

of meetings and celebration. Advocacy groups and corporate interests flock to the conventions as well. Everyone jockeys to be noticed by a potential future president and his or her closest advisers.

When it works well, the convention can provide the nominee an **electoral bounce**, a boost in the polls that lasts from a few days to several weeks. The 2016 conventions gave Donald Trump, whose Republican Party met in Cleveland a month before Democrats convened, a short-lived electoral bounce of a percentage point or two. His own campaign missteps and a political star-studded Democratic convention gave Hillary Clinton a bounce of her own, vaulting her into a lead she never relinquished in the polls—until Donald Trump defied expectations and swept into office on election night.

Electoral bounce: The spike in the polls that follows an event such as a party's national convention.

The General Election

In the past, presidential nominees typically took a break for vacation after the conventions, held in July or early August, and resumed campaigning after Labor Day weekend (in early September). Since 2000, however, the campaigns have continued with virtually no pause. With just three months between the convention and Election Day, every hour matters. Campaigns lose no opportunity to stage a media event, approve a Facebook post, criticize the opposing candidate, or meet with donors to gather more cash.

General elections usually feature three debates between the nominees, as well as a vice presidential debate. These contests are among the most widely watched political events on the political calendar. Pundits scrutinize the performances and count up the gaffes. The truth, however, is that most viewers have already made up their minds and debates normally have only a slight impact on the race—unless the race is close.

The first televised presidential debate, held in 1960, featured Republican Richard Nixon (the sitting vice president) and Senator John F. Kennedy, the Democratic nominee. More than seventy million Americans tuned in—some two-thirds of the adult population at the time. Though listeners who heard the debate on the radio told pollsters that Nixon had won narrowly, on TV, the charismatic Kennedy seemed the winner.

At each stage of the election, style can matter as much as substance. Some critics blame the media for focusing on outrageous statements and insults or emphasizing which candidate is rising or falling in the polls.

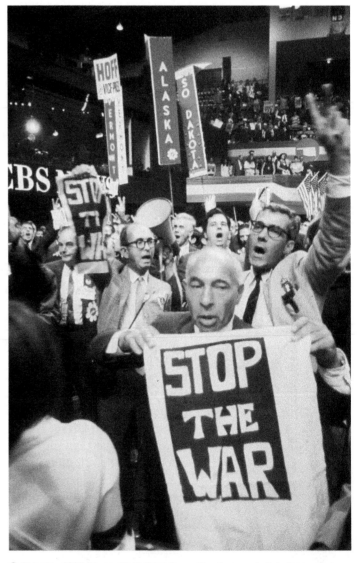

● *Chicago—1968 Democratic National Convention. Angry protests both in and outside the hall created an image of disarray and crisis. Democrats had won nine of the previous eleven presidential elections, but this convention symbolized the collapse of the old Democratic coalition. Republicans would take the White House in five of the next six elections.*

Over 70 million Americans tuned into the Kennedy and Nixon debate in 1960—launching the age of televised campaigning. The more charismatic Kennedy won the White House by the slimmest of margins—.001 percent.

Winning Presidential Elections

Along with the candidates themselves—their speeches, gaffes, debate performances, and responses to the many unexpected events that occur on and off the campaign trail—a variety of factors help determine the winner. Some are under candidates' control, such as raising sufficient funds to mount a worthy campaign; others are a matter of luck and circumstance.

Economic Outlook. Economic factors such as the unemployment rate, economic growth (or decline), and stock market trends have a powerful place in many voters' minds. Bill Clinton's headquarters in 1992 featured a whiteboard displaying a reminder to campaign staffers: "It's the Economy, Stupid." If the economy is performing poorly, the party holding the presidency is likely to suffer.

Even under fairly good economic conditions, the growing difference between the haves and the have-nots proved to be a major issue—with many people in both parties identifying against the "haves." In 2016, Bernie Sanders appealed to Democratic frustrations with America's growing inequality.

Demographics. Once upon a time, each party worked to build a winning coalition by relying on its base of likely supporters and reaching out to undecided groups. That remains the conventional idea. After the 2012 election, the Republican Party did an "autopsy" to explain why they had lost the presidential race and lost ground (two seats) in the Senate. One major conclusion: The party had to appeal to more young people and minorities, especially Hispanics. In 2016, Republican primary voters spurned that advice and turned to a candidate who shouted out the perils of immigration and disparaged immigrants. A party that had been older, whiter, and more male doubled down on that base: White males. White voters had not given a Democratic nominee more than 43 percent of the vote in thirty-five years—only 39 percent had voted for President Obama in 2012. Now Republicans aimed to get even more of the white vote. The criticism of immigrants fed the narrative of economic insecurity, propelling Trump to victory in the primaries. Rather than pivot for the general election, Trump doubled down on anti-immigrant rhetoric and policies such as a border wall with Mexico.

Hillary Clinton responded by emphasizing inclusion. Tim Kaine, her vice presidential pick, introduced himself to the Democratic convention in both English and Spanish.

Clinton won the primaries on her strength among black and minority voters. But in the general election, her base failed to turn out—as they had for President Obama. Clinton overwhelmingly won the black vote (with an estimated 88%), Latino (65%), Asian (65%) and people under thirty (55%). But she only managed 37% of all whites voting—and lost the Electoral College as white voters in the rust belt states—Pennsylvania, Wisconsin, Michigan, and Ohio—abandoned the Democratic Party.

War and Foreign Policy.   Most Americans pay far more attention to domestic issues—especially those that touch their pocketbooks—than foreign ones. Occasionally, however, foreign-policy issues become pivotal, especially when the nation is at war. Hillary Clinton came under heavy fire for a terrorist attack in Benghazi, Libya, that killed four American embassy officials during the time she served as secretary of state. Republicans capitalized on this episode: Their 2016 convention featured speakers who had survived the attack and a mother of one of the victims. All blamed Clinton.

On the other side, Democrats—and most Washington insiders—were aghast at Trump's foreign-policy statements. He appeared to question U.S. support for NATO allies, the backbone of America's post–World War II security policies. Diplomats feared that Trump's apparent admiration for Russian leader Vladimir Putin would serve as a green light to Russia, already knee-deep in Ukraine, to swallow other bordering nations such as Latvia and Lithuania.[9] Such off-the-cuff remarks raised concerns about Trump's ability to lead the United States in the international arena. Voters who rated foreign policy a top priority voted two to one for Clinton.

Projecting toughness can backfire if it is not convincing. When Michael Dukakis opposed George H. W. Bush in 1988, he climbed into an M1 Abrams tank for a photo opportunity; clad in a helmet several sizes too large, peering uncertainly from the tank, Dukakis created a comical image that gave some voters pause about his ability to fit the commander-in-chief role, especially after the Bush campaign ran mocking advertisements.

see for yourself 10.2

Go online to see the Dukakis/tank campaign advertisement.

Domestic Issues.   Every presidential candidate has a list of favorite programs and strategies. Bill Clinton discussed education, energy, Medicare, and Medicaid so often that his staff started calling his campaign E2M2. Hillary Clinton emphasized immigration reform, campaign-finance reform, and improving U.S. infrastructure like bridges and highways. Trump's plans were generally vaguer but promised job creation and a hard line on immigration. The candidates' issue preferences are important, not because they will decide the election (which is highly unlikely), but because they set the agenda for the presidency.

Sometimes, incendiary issues die in flames. One staple of past presidential campaigns, opposition to same-sex marriage, faded in 2012 and largely vanished by 2016. Why? As we saw in Chapter 8, public opinion had turned on the issue.

The Campaign Organization.   One truism that every would-be president knows is that it is essential to assemble a team of talented, loyal advisors capable of charting a plan for victory. Yet this obvious task can be immensely difficult in practice. Building a large, multistate organization—often from scratch—is an enormous job that tests every candidate's executive skill.[10]

● *Clinton campaign headquarters in 2016. Volunteers still play a vital role in campaigns, particularly in get out the vote initiatives, but professional advisors are critical to success.*

see for yourself 10.3

Go online to see the controversial "Daisy" political advertisement from the 1964 Johnson campaign. (requires Flash)

Political scientist Samuel Popkin has shown that a strong campaign chief of staff can be a decisive factor in whether campaigns thrive or founder.[11] Among other advisors who can make a key difference in any modern presidential race are skilled communications professionals. Back in 1964, during the *Mad Men* era, Madison Avenue advertising executive Tony Schwartz created the "Daisy" ad for President Lyndon B. Johnson. Deployed against the lesser-known Republican Senator Barry Goldwater, the controversial ad implied that Goldwater was too extreme to be trusted with nuclear weapons. Again, Donald Trump was unusual in that he relied largely on his own instincts and the advice of his family—despite Republican pleas that he defer to seasoned political managers and repeated shake-ups of his senior advising team.

There is no sure recipe for winning a presidential election. They occur so rarely—the 2016 contest is only the eighteenth since World War II—and involve such an immense array of influences that journalists, academics, and political professionals spend the several years following each election trying to make sense of the outcome. Explaining why one candidate or another won a race is exceeded in difficulty only by predicting that outcome in advance.

Who Won and Why.   Once the votes were all counted, Hillary Clinton was over a million votes ahead of Donald Trump. But, once again, the Electoral College, which we discussed in Chapter 3, produced a different outcome.

White working-class people (especially men) turned away from the Democratic Party that they had long supported. White people without a college education favored Trump by more than two to one. Suburban and rural America went Republican, too, balancing out the heavy Democratic vote in the cities. For the first time in 28 years, Republicans won Pennsylvania, Michigan, and Wisconsin—destroying what had been Democratic strongholds. Rust Belt states—states in the northeast and Midwest that used to be the industrial heartland of the United States but have declined economically—turned Republican. Trump's emphasis on jobs and opposition to free-trade agreements—which many blame for the economic decline—appealed to voters in these states. Political scientists will study the election for a long time: Did racism, nativism, and misogyny play a role (as Donald Trump's language might suggest)? Why has the gap between urban and non-urban populations grown so large? Why do whites continue to abandon the Democratic Party? Will millennials (and minorities) continue to vote left—and if so, what will that mean for the future? Bottom line: For now, Republicans have taken control in the White House, in Congress, and in most state governments.

Predicting Presidential Elections

Do you want an easy way to start a conversation with strangers? Ask which candidate will win the next presidential election. Predicting presidential outcomes is a national pastime, attracting pollsters, political scientists, pundits, and all the rest of us.

Social scientists have developed sophisticated models predicting presidential elections. Some even go so far as to say that most of the campaign excitement is irrelevant: Their models predict which party will control the White House in all but the closest elections.

What goes into a model? Each has a slightly different recipe but most political science models focus on *national conditions* emphasizing "bread"—how fast the economy grew, especially in the three quarters before the election; "peace"— how many Americans died in combat overseas; and "fatigue"—or how long the incumbent party has held the White House (Donald Trump's in the past sixty years only one candidate was elected after his party controlled the presidency for two terms). Some models add presidential approval rankings and other factors (like opinion polls).

Another approach parses the voting *demographics.* In 2016, the white vote, which typically breaks Republican, fell from 72 to 70 percent of eligible voters. Meanwhile, voters who lean Democratic grew: Hispanics rose from 10 to 11 percent of all voters, Asians from 5 to 6 percent, and black voters held stable at 13 percent. Those changes helped boost the Democratic Party's presidential chances.

How did the political science models do? In 2012, twelve out of seventeen top models got the results right though only four anticipated the size of Obama's victory (51 percent to 46 percent). In 2016, the top five models were less reliable. Clinton won the popular vote count by 0.004 percent. Two of the leading models forecast a Trump victory of 4.8 percent and 2.8 percent; three others picked Clinton by 4 percent, .8 percent, and 1.2 percent. In sum, only two models got within 2.5 percent of the final outcome—though, thanks to the Electoral College, they pointed to the wrong winner.

The models apply only to the general election, when the field is already down to two candidates. Primaries—with multiple candidates competing across many states—are still too complicated for predictive models.

In short predictive models are useful for fueling the great national conversation and for offering a picture of the underlying fundamentals—who has the advantage, who has an uphill climb. But as the 2016 election dramatically showed, models cannot predict unusual campaigns or unexpected strategies. At least sometimes, campaigns make all the difference.[12]

THE BOTTOM LINE

» Presidential elections, despite their grueling intensity and duration, attract many aspirants every four years.

» Nearly all serious candidates for the presidency are experienced politicians. Senators tend to run most frequently, but vice presidents and governors have been the most successful party nominees in recent decades. No candidate without any experience in the public sector has ever won the presidency—until Donald Trump.

» The three phases of the campaign—the nominating process, party conventions, and the general election—require different political strategies.

» Election outcomes are influenced by many factors: economic performance, war and peace, advisors and organization, the coalition of supporters, and the candidate's own personality and performance. Add to this the role of accident and luck, and election outcomes are often difficult to predict.

Congressional Elections

In contrast to the focus on two presidential candidates, congressional elections feature a colorful kaleidoscope of races across the country. Every two years, all 435 House districts hold an election, with an additional thirty-three or thirty-four Senate seats in play as well. The result is a political junkie's dream.

TABLE 10.3	**Requirements for Running for Congress**
Age	Successful House candidates must be at least twenty-five years old to take office; senators must be at least thirty.
Citizenship	House candidates must have been a U.S. citizen for at least seven years; Senate candidates for at least nine.
Residence	Candidates must live in the state, though not necessarily the House district, where they are seeking election.

Candidates: Who Runs for Congress?

Almost anyone can seek a seat in Congress. Convicted felons, rodeo clowns, and little known college professors have all won unexpected victories. As Table 10.3 shows, there are few limits on candidacy.

Contending seriously for a seat in Congress is a different story. Winning an average House race costs over $1.7 million; to make it to the Senate, you will need on average $10.5 million. (These figures differ depending on district and state, of course.) Most successful candidates spend long hours on the phone raising money. The time commitment requires freedom from the long working hours that most jobs demand. The personality traits that inspire candidates to run for Congress— self-confidence, leadership ability, and interest in politics—increase as people move up the ladder of educational and economic success.

Even so, Congress is not a rich person's club. Most members are not from blue-collar backgrounds; however, in contrast to many other democracies, congressional races attract relatively few top American business leaders, wealth holders, or celebrities—there are not many Mark Zuckerbergs, Warren Buffetts, or Oprahs in Congress. The sociologist C. Wright Mills noted long ago that House and Senate races represent the "middle levels of power" in America. And when the famous or wealthy mount a run, they do not always win. Maryland businessman David Trone spent more than $12 million of his own money seeking the Democratic nomination for an open House seat in 2016; he finished second. World Wrestling Entertainment CEO Linda McMahon spent $100 million on her two failed Senate races in 2010 and 2012. On the other hand, former *American Idol* star Clay Aiken won his 2014 race for Congress in North Carolina following the sudden death of his Democratic primary challenger Keith Crisco.

Each time one party targets a Senate candidate, the other party matches it. The price tag for the 2016 Senate races ran up to $120 million in Pennsylvania and over $100 million in little New Hampshire—breaking the old record, $114 million in North Carolina's 2014 election. The results reflected what political scientists have long found: Money alone rarely swings congressional elections.[13]

If neither money nor celebrity guarantees a seat, here is a more promising shortcut to Congress: be related to a member. One in eight

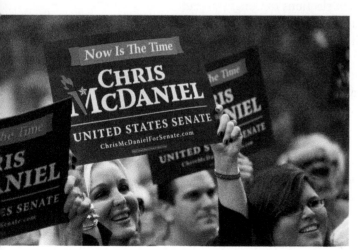

Little-known Tea Party conservative Chris McDaniel forced six-term senator Thad Cochran of Mississippi into a Republican primary runoff in 2014 by attacking Cochran's longtime strength: bringing federal dollars to his state. In the end, Cochran prevailed.

Left: Frederick Frelinghuysen, New Jersey delegate to the Continental Congress (1779) and later U.S. senator (1793–1796). Right: Frederick's great-great-great nephew Rodney Frelinghuysen has served in the U.S. House since 1995. He is the sixth Frelinghuysen to represent New Jersey in Congress.

members of Congress have relatives who already served (including twenty members who hold their parent's seat). House Republican Rodney Frelinghuysen is the sixth family member to represent New Jersey, going all the way back to the 1780s when his great-great-great-great-grandfather served in the Senate. Between 1947 and 2011, there was always a Kennedy in elective office in Washington. Other families—Bush, Adams, Roosevelt, Clinton—have built dynasties over the years.[14]

Still, political amateurs dominate each crop of new candidates challenging sitting members of the House for their seat. Typically, about one in six of these challengers is an elected official, usually from the state legislature; another 10 percent or so serve in nonelected government positions—often as former congressional staff. The remaining candidates—generally around three-quarters of the total—are new to government service. Senate candidates, because they run statewide, tend to be more experienced. Most are political veterans.

Women on average are just as likely as men to win elections to Congress—but fewer run. Why? The parties are slower to recruit them as candidates, and women are less likely to seek election. One study shows that when a woman announces her intention to run, she is more likely to draw primary challengers than a man.[15] Members of large minority groups (African Americans, Latinos, and Asian Americans) tend to run much less often than Caucasians, proportionate to their share of the population, but their ranks are growing, especially in the House Democratic Caucus.

Talent and experience are vital in congressional races. Party leaders know that recruiting skilled candidates with a stronger political background and better education gives them a leg up in the contest between Democrats and Republicans for power in Congress. A candidate's background also has an impact on the quality of representation in Washington. How well Congress carries out its work depends on the political ability of its members.

The Power of Incumbency

If you talk to sitting members of Congress about reelection, you will see the worry wash over their faces. House and Senate officeholders face a more volatile

see for yourself 10.4

Go online to hear Senator George Allen's "macaca moment."

Incumbency advantage: The tendency for members of Congress to win reelection in overwhelming numbers.

American electorate than they did a quarter-century ago: Voters are less predict-able and harder to reach through traditional advertising. Now that virtually every utterance is digitally preserved, candidates have to be more careful about what they say. The popular Senator George Allen of Virginia, cruising with a twenty-point lead in 2006 against little-known Democratic challenger James Webb, was caught on videotape at a campaign rally calling an Indian American Webb staffer "macaca," a slang racial insult. The clip ran everywhere from CNN to the *Colbert Report*. Allen tried to deny it, to laugh it off, and eventually apologized, but he could not shake the media storm and wound up narrowly losing—dooming his presiden-tial aspirations as well. Allen never recovered. Since then, many candidates have been caught saying embarrassing things that come back to haunt them.

Despite this more treacherous electoral environment, most incumbent House and Senate members fare very well in their quest for reelection. Even in 2010, when Republicans won back the House in the largest Republican landslide since 1890, more than nine of every ten incumbents won another term. At first glance, this **incumbency advantage** is a mystery. As we explore in Chapter 13, Americans overwhelmingly give Congress a thumbs down. The 113th Congress (which took over in 2013) recorded the lowest approval ratings in modern history, sinking as low as 9 percent in one poll. Yet in the subsequent 2014 election, incumbents run-ning for reelection won 96 percent of the races in the House and 89 percent in the Senate (see Figure 10.4). Congress was scarcely more popular in 2016, yet again incumbents won more than 90 percent of the time in both chambers.

What explains these consistently high incumbent success rates? For one thing, members have become very skilled at running *against* Congress. They position themselves as reasonable individuals fighting against a dysfunctional institution. And the way Congress operates—stalemate on the big issues, lots of little favors to constituents—makes the stance an easier sell. "I'm for expanding aid to needy chil-dren," say liberal members, "but I can't get it past the Republicans on Capitol Hill. Oh, and how about that new aquarium I funded?" GOP members tell a similar

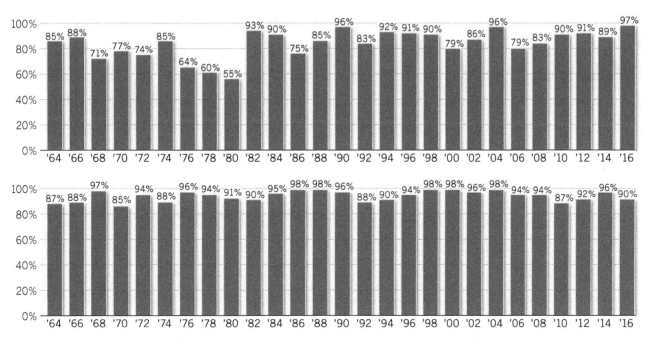

● **FIGURE 10.4** *Senate (top) and House (bottom) reelection rates, 1964–2016.*

story. Here, moreover, is one place where funding makes a great deal of difference. Most races feature very well-funded incumbents running against underfunded challengers. In short, members are attentive to constituents, raise a great deal of money, and already have staff and name recognition. Most win reelection. Here is the paradox: People despise Congress but defend their own representatives.[16]

Congressional Election Results

Along with incumbents' tendency to win reelection, congressional elections feature additional intriguing patterns. One of these concerns **midterm elections**, or those elections held in a nonpresidential year. In most elections, the president's party loses congressional seats—termed **midterm loss**. In the last forty midterm elections (going back to 1938), the president's party picked up seats in either chamber of Congress only five times—and only a few seats each time. In contrast, the president's party lost double-digit House seats eight of twelve times—including huge swings in 2010, 1994, and 1974 (see Table 10.4).

Another intriguing pattern involves elections when America is at war. Although we might expect voters to "rally around the flag" and support the president's party during wartime, in fact, the opposition usually wins seats in the congressional elections following a war's outbreak. This was true of both world wars, as Presidents Wilson and Franklin Roosevelt, respectively, saw their parties suffer big House and Senate losses in the first election after war was declared. In 1950, five months after America's entry into the Korean War, President Truman's Democrats lost twenty-eight House and five Senate seats—and the subsequent presidential election—in 1952. Less than a year after President George H. W. Bush swiftly won the first Gulf War in 1991, he was tossed out of office in favor of Bill Clinton and the Democrats, who picked up seats in both the House and the Senate.

Midterm elections: National elections held between presidential elections, involving all seats in the House of Representatives, one-third of those in the Senate, thirty-six governorships, and other positions.

Midterm loss: When the party of the president loses seats in Congress during the midterm elections. This has occurred in almost all midterm elections.

TABLE 10.4 Midterm Congressional Election Results, 1970–2014

ELECTION YEAR	PRESIDENT	SEAT GAIN	
		HOUSE	SENATE
2014	Obama (D)	R+13	R+9
2010	Obama (D)	R+63	R+6
2006	G. W. Bush (R)	D+30	D+6
2002	G. W. Bush (R)	**R+8**	**R+2**
1998	Clinton (D)	**D+5**	(No change)
1994	Clinton (D)	R+54	R+8
1990	G. H. W. Bush (R)	D+8	D+1
1986	Reagan (R)	D+5	D+8
1982	Reagan (R)	D+26	(No change)
1978	Carter (D)	R+15	R+3
1974	Ford (R)	D+48	D+3
1970	Nixon (R)	D+12	**R+1**

The president's party has won seats in a midterm election only four times in the past forty-two years.

President Wilson declares U.S. entry into World War I. A year and a half later, his Democratic Party would be punished in congressional midterm elections.

What are the reasons for this wartime effect—the opposite of what we might expect? It appears that a war's patriotic "rally effect" fades away swiftly. Wartime brings anxiety, tension, sacrifice, and even panic. Such emotions attach to the administration that led us into conflict, fairly or unfairly. The opposition party capitalizes at congressional elections time.

Redrawing the Lines: The Art of the Gerrymander

Fifty-one Democrats in the Texas House fled the state and holed up in Oklahoma in May 2003. Legislative leaders called the Texas Rangers, the Federal Aviation Administration, and the Department of Homeland Security to "round 'em up and bring 'em home." What was going on?

Republicans had won control of the Texas legislature, and they immediately whipped out their red pens to redraw the congressional districts. Democrats claimed that Tom DeLay (R-TX), the Republican majority leader in the U.S. House, had masterminded a plan to stack new districts to assure Republican winners. Because the Democrats in Texas knew they were going to lose a vote that they considered unfair, they took off to deny the majority a quorum (the number of members a legislature needs to have present to do official business).

Indeed, when the Democratic state legislators finally limped home, they lost the vote over redistricting. As a direct result, five Democrats lost their seats in the U.S. House in the 2004 elections.

Membership of the House of Representatives has been fixed at 435 for over a century. The American population keeps shifting, and after every ten-year census, U.S. House representatives also have to deal with **reapportionment**. First, the census determines which states have gained or lost population, and then House seats are reapportioned accordingly. In 2010, Texas gained four new seats, Florida gained two, and New York and Ohio each lost two. Each state has the job of redrawing the boundaries of the election districts in a process called redistricting. Sometimes two U.S. House representatives will find themselves running against one another when their districts are combined.

In a **gerrymander**, the party in control of the state legislature draws the lines to help itself. See Figure 10.5 for a hypothetical example of how this works.

Imagine a state called PoliSciLand that has two districts that are 100 percent Republican (A and B) and one district that is 100 percent Democratic (C): PoliSciLand thus sends two Republicans and one Democrat to Congress. Then an enterprising Republican on the redistricting committee says, "Hey, we're the majority in this PoliSciLand legislature. Let's redraw the congressional districts our way."

Check out the result: By drawing the district lines horizontally instead of vertically, Republicans take the Democratic district and split its voters into three different congressional districts. Instead of one district with 100 percent Democratic voters and two that are 100 percent Republican, PoliSciLand now has three

Reapportionment: Reorganization of the boundaries of House districts, a process that follows the results of the U.S. census, taken every ten years. District lines are redrawn to ensure rough equality in the number of constituents represented by each House member.

Gerrymander: Redrawing an election district in a way that gives the advantage to one party.

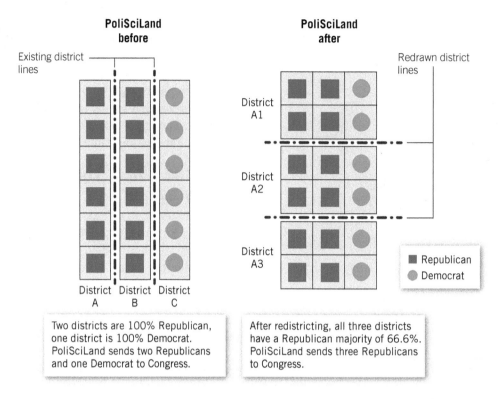

PoliSciLand before

Existing district lines

District A   District B   District C

Two districts are 100% Republican, one district is 100% Democrat. PoliSciLand sends two Republicans and one Democrat to Congress.

PoliSciLand after

Redrawn district lines

District A1

District A2

District A3

■ Republican
● Democrat

After redistricting, all three districts have a Republican majority of 66.6%. PoliSciLand sends three Republicans to Congress.

● **FIGURE 10.5** *How gerrymandering works—a hypothetical case of highly political redistricting.*

districts, each 33 percent Democratic and 66 percent Republican. Without a change of mind by a single voter, our imaginary PoliSciLand state now has three House Republicans . . . and no Democrats.

The term *gerrymandering* goes back to 1812, when Massachusetts governor Elbridge Gerry signed a bill that redrew the districts to help his party. One of Gerry's new districts looked like a salamander, which at that time was seen as a sort of mythical dragon. "Gerry" + "salamander" = "gerrymander," and a great American contribution to the art of politics was born.

Today, with sophisticated information technology, state legislatures can carefully craft political boundaries. Two main techniques are "packing," or placing all the like-minded voters into one district, and "cracking," or spreading them out so that they form a minority in many districts. Our imaginary PoliSciLand cracked the Democratic district.

Savvy political observers carefully watch who wins the state legislatures in the round years ('10, '20, '30, . . .), because those results determine the majority that gets the job of redrawing the lines after the census numbers are announced. This is especially difficult if your state is losing population.

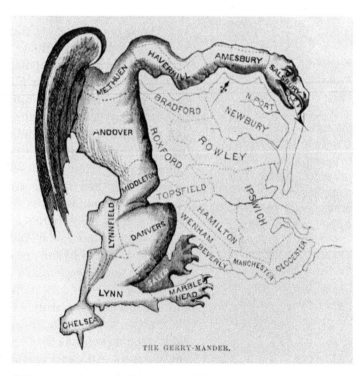

THE GERRY-MANDER.

● *The original gerrymander: Massachusetts, 1812.*

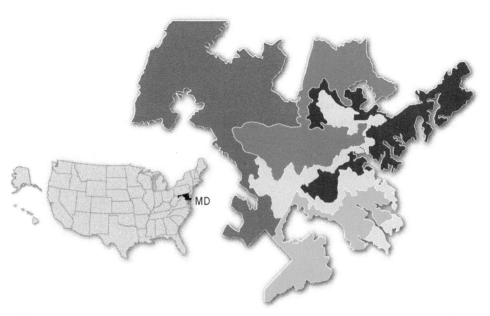

● **FIGURE 10.6** *Maryland's congressional districts, 2014.*

Redistricting processes in most states are messy and politically charged. Many results look at least as bizarre as the original gerrymander. See, for example, Maryland's arrangement after the latest round of redistricting, shown in Figure 10.6. Together, the political parties have perfected the practice—although lately Republicans have come to dominate on the state level and in the process became masters of the form: During the 2012 election for the House of Representatives, the Democrats beat the Republicans by 1.7 million votes, but lost the chamber by 33 seats. And in 2014, a Republican landslide year, the party won 52 percent of the votes but reaped 57 percent of the seats.

As you can see, the election contest usually begins in earnest—long before anyone starts running—when the state legislature sits down to draw the district. That has led some observers to quip that Americans elect their leaders but members of Congress select their voters.

Nonpartisan Districting and Minority Representation

Some reformers would like to put the whole process of drawing electoral districts into the hands of a nonpartisan commission that would divide states into natural communities and not tilt to any political side. California passed a law to do just that after the 2010 census. State legislative districts were redrawn by a "Citizens' Redistricting Commission" rather than by elected politicians, who naturally seek to protect their personal and partisan interests. The result was compact, contiguous districts faithful to existing geographic communities—and a lot of angry legislators at the state and U.S. House levels, who had to scramble to figure out their new district lines.

After the 1990 census, some states used the process to enhance the number of black representatives. They created majority–minority districts packed with African American voters, and these districts proved highly likely to send African American representatives to Congress. White Republicans strongly supported the effort because packing black Democratic voters into some districts left the surrounding areas more Republican. The overall effect was an increase in Republican representatives, alongside the expected increase in black legislators.

Was that a good deal for African American Democrats? For black Democrats, it was an anguishing call because it split two sides of their political identity. It gave them more black representatives, but fewer Democrats. Given the long, painful heritage of racial exclusion, many African Americans saw a good argument for pursuing majority–minority districts. In 1995, the Supreme Court ruled that race could not be the predominant factor in creating congressional districts, and this packing was halted.[17] Despite dire predictions, the black congressional caucus continued to grow, jumping from twenty-nine House members in 1995 to forty-eight after the 2016 election.

THE BOTTOM LINE

» Every two years, all 435 House seats and a third of the Senate seats are up for election.

» Very few restrictions govern who may run—and some candidates are true characters.

» House and Senate incumbents have powerful built-in advantages when running for reelection.

» The president's party generally loses House and Senate seats during the midterm elections following the president's victory. Presidents who declare war also tend to see their party lose seats in the subsequent elections.

» Decennial redistricting of House seats can result in some strangely shaped—and politically motivated—districts, known as gerrymanders. Redistricting tends to further increase the advantage of incumbency.

» Both parties gerrymander. In 2010, Republican control over state legislatures led to election districts that gave the Republicans an advantage in the House of Representatives.

Congressional Campaigns

Congressional candidates continue to navigate a changing political landscape, with the rise of new media, the influx of ever-greater sums of money into elections, and other developments. Over the past four decades, we can trace a shift to **candidate-centered elections**, in which Americans view their choice as less between parties and more between individual candidates, based on personality, ideology, and appeal. In this section, we examine how these trends are shaping the way candidates run for Congress.

The Rise of Candidate-Centered Elections

In most advanced democracies, political parties remain the primary engines of campaigns and elections, mobilizing voters and choosing slates of candidates to run under the party banner. If you ask a friend or classmate from another country who runs the government back home, they will usually respond with a party name: Tories, or Socialists, or Liberal Democrats. For a time, the combination of expanding presidential primaries, beginning in 1972, and the ability of candidates to use

Candidate-centered elections: A political system in which individual candidates decide to run, raise their own money, and design their own strategy—as opposed to party systems, in which political parties play these roles.

television to bring their images and words directly to the public greatly reduced the influence of parties in campaigns for the presidency and Congress.

Why is the United States so different from other major democracies? In part because we have so many contenders for so many positions—national, state, and local. As the number of elected positions grows, it is harder for the two major parties to organize such a large set of nominating processes. Moreover, candidates for most offices first face a primary election, which is essentially an individual effort to capture their party's nomination. Candidates also must raise large sums of money to finance their campaigns, as you saw earlier in this chapter, and this step diminishes their dependence on party organizations. Finally, the expansion of the Internet, smartphones, and social media give candidates a presence that appears to liberate them from party databases, outreach, and fundraising.[18]

However, for the past three decades, another trend has limited the candidates' independence. Although individual candidates still control their own destiny—deciding to run, raising their own money, choosing their issues, organizing their team—the American population has grown increasingly partisan. And the party bases, which vote in the low-turnout primaries, are increasingly intolerant of party members who stray from party positions. Republicans who will vote for a tax increase or Democrats willing to compromise on environmental standards have become endangered political species.

How to Run for Congress

Having mastered the broad outlines of U.S. national campaigns and elections, perhaps you are pondering your own race for a local position or even for Congress. How can you make that first run a successful one? Here we highlight four keys to winning a congressional election—*money, organization, strategy,* and *message.* Even if you are not planning to be a candidate, remember these as you watch House and Senate races shape up in the coming months.

Key 1: Money. First and foremost, you will need funds to mount a legitimate challenge—up to two million dollars in many House districts and five or six times that if you are running for Senate. Where does all the money go? TV advertising, along with radio and direct mailing take a big chunk, followed by database and demographic data, consultants, offices, phone banks, computers, and lawn signs. Unless you are wealthy (or married to a rich person), you are going to have to "dial for dollars." Your staff will prepare **call lists** and you will spend your days desperately packing your war chest.

Call list: A long list of potential donors who candidates must phone.

To boost your chances of winning and reduce the cost of campaigning, you may want to wait and run for an **open seat**—one with no incumbent running because of a sitting member's retirement or death. Taking on an incumbent costs more each election cycle.

Open seat: A seat in Congress without an incumbent running for reelection.

Key 2: Organization. You also will need a well-constructed team to run for Congress. Somebody has to recruit and train all those speechwriters, fundraisers, supportive community leaders, get-out-the-vote experts, and volunteer envelope stuffers. Until the advent of candidate-centered politics in the 1980s, parties took care of most of that work. The local Republican or Democratic organization provided the knowledge and manpower to mount a campaign. Today, challengers like you usually have to create an organization from scratch. Yes, the parties get involved in a handful of high-profile races, pumping in funds where possible and

Name recognition: An advantage possessed by a well-known political figure, a political celebrity.

providing occasional strategic advice. But most often the candidate and core supporters build an organization.

There is a side benefit to the expense of assembling a talented campaign organization. Political insiders see hiring established pollsters, media experts, and so forth as the sign of a competitive campaign. Funders, recognizing a possible winner, will start directing more money your way. Although most new congressional candidates publicly decry the "professionalization" of campaign politics, they usually hire established members of the Beltway insiders' club.

Key 3: Strategy. A fat bankroll and seasoned organization cannot compensate for a common rookie mistake—the lack of a well-conceived campaign strategy. Uncertainty is a central fact in every election, given fast-shifting political winds, opponents' moves, and the power of unexpected events. Incumbent members tend to stick to the strategy that got them there last time. Challengers must invent a strategy that plays well to their political and personal strengths.

Two elements of successful congressional campaign strategies are vital: building a coalition of supporters and connecting with voters. Every state or district includes "influentials," such as local business leaders, political activists, religious leaders, and spokespeople for identity groups. Strategically attracting some of them—and, presumably, their voting followers—is essential to victory. A coalition-building strategy also targets broader groups likely to vote for a party's candidate. During the 1980s and 1990s, House Republican candidates in district after district forged coalitions of conservative, middle-aged, white, Protestant, relatively affluent voters. By 2006, this reliable lineup had fragmented in many places, and Democrats won forty-seven of forty-eight contested House seats to retake control of the chamber. By 2010, the Republican coalition was back, now fueled by Tea Party activists and featuring a larger proportion of lower-income, disaffected white voters. Notice how fast the winds shift in contemporary electoral politics. In the 2014 midterm, that same coalition again boosted Republicans and helped them capture both chambers of Congress. In 2016, the Republican coalition appeared to fracture. Many wealthier, pro-business GOP donors refused to back Donald Trump. Paul Ryan, the top House Republican, refused to campaign with him. However, white voters—especially rural and less educated white voters—flocked to Trump's side. Will Donald Trump forge a new Republican coalition? Will the Democrat coalition regroup? Stay tuned!

Candidates primarily contact voters through the media. Candidate strategies need to include plenty of high-profile events, such as speeches before substantial crowds and press conferences engaging new ideas for helping the district or state. All of these occasions can attract reporters without cost to the candidate. If you cannot build crowds because of your low **name recognition**, you may resort to more creative approaches. If you are a Democrat, try calling party supporters Katy Perry, George Clooney, or Alicia Keys; if you are Republican, try Patriots quarterback Tom Brady, actor Jon Voight or Willie Robertson from Duck Dynasty.

Paid advertising is also a cornerstone of any successful strategy, but marketing a House or Senate candidate involves more than big-budget TV ads. Your campaign will need a smart social media strategy, as outlets such as Google banner ads are inexpensive ways to reach large numbers of potential voters.

Be careful not to fall into the "technology trap," though: Campaign professionals insist that old-fashioned politicking is still essential to victory. As a House challenger in 1974, Bill Clinton announced his intention to "shake every hand in the

Talking POLITICS

CAMPAIGN LINGO

If you're running for Congress, you will want to know what your advisers are talking about. Here are a few insider terms from the campaign trail.

• **Robocall:** Automated phone call used to contact thousands of voters simultaneously; may feature a recorded message by the candidate or a popular party leader—or an attack on the opponent.

• **Advance team:** Campaign staffers who arrive at the site of major events (e.g., a speech) a day or more ahead of time to organize the site and build crowds.

• **Field/GOTV:** The staff and volunteers who engage one on one with the public on behalf of the candidate.

• **Retail campaigning:** Attracting supporters or votes one by one, through door-to-door visits or small meetings. More efficient strategies are *wholesale* campaigning, whereby candidates can reach hundreds or thousands at once through a speech, targeted advertisement, or robocalls.

• **Oppo:** Conducting research on the opposition to identify weakness.

• **Text-to-donate:** Use of text messages to donate funds to a campaign. Tightly regulated by the Federal Election Commission: for example, donations to any one candidate are limited to $50 per phone billing period.

district." Clinton lost that race but employed the strategy in his next race for Arkansas governor, which he won. Said one voter, "I'd go to the store—there was young Bill Clinton. Go to the movies—there he was at the entrance, hand out. Eventually I told him I'd vote for him if I just didn't have to shake his hand anymore!" Studies generally show that knocking on someone's door is still the best way to earn their vote.[19]

Another traditional approach will receive attention from your trusted oppo researchers and strategists: **negative campaigning**. This usually involves strewing seeds of doubt in voters' minds about your opponent's policy positions, ethics, and character. Much as you may find this strategy repugnant, "going negative" works. Expect that the other side's opposition researchers will strive to portray you in the least flattering light possible. It is a lot easier to play offense than to defend against attacks, no matter how unfair.

In 2016, Donald Trump spent less on ads than any other serious contender (see Figure 10.7). Why? His shocking remarks and jibes at other candidates made headlines and provided him with free media coverage. The final result: lower turnout in 2016.

Key 4: Message.   Meeting the voters is important—but they also need a reason to vote for you. Candidates with a clear, powerful rationale for why they are running can sometimes topple better-financed and more elaborately organized opponents. In 2014, an unknown economics professor with a shoestring budget ($200,000) named David Brat upset House Majority Leader Eric Cantor who had raised 5.4 million in the Republican primary of a conservative Virginia district. Brat's message? His opponent had become a Washington insider and compromised on conservative principles.

In the relatively rare case that a first-time challenge like yours is victorious, what can you expect as a freshman member of Congress? (Yes, *freshman*: the term is the same as in high school or college, and the learning curve is just as steep!) What comes next?

Negative campaigning:
Running for office by attacking the opponent. An unpopular tactic that is nevertheless very effective.

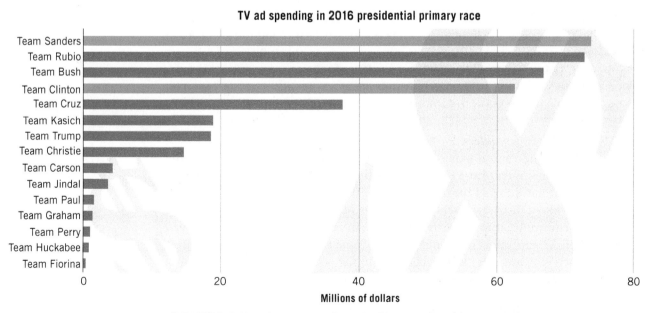

TV ad spending in 2016 presidential primary race

● **FIGURE 10.7** *Money isn't everything: Trump and Clinton were both outspent on the way to their nomination victory.* (NBC News)

A *new campaign*, starting immediately. For House members, election looms just two years away. Senators have a more relaxing six years—but must run state-wide, which in high-population or sprawling states is very time consuming. Winning an election to become a congressional "sophomore" can be especially difficult. The legendary House speaker Sam Rayburn told each incoming House freshman class that "a member of Congress can be elected by accident, but seldom reelected by accident." Voters back home will watch a first-term member especially close, as will his or her colleagues on Capitol Hill.

As a sitting representative or senator, you may join your colleagues in denouncing Washington as corrupt and in need of reform. Such a message has short-term electoral appeal, but it has corroded Americans' support for their national legislature in recent decades. And this decline in support raises an important concluding question: Is the American electoral system in need of reform? And if so, how?

THE BOTTOM LINE

» To run successfully for Congress, follow a few vital steps: raise sufficient funds (and then raise more), organize a talented and loyal team, develop a strategy that plays to your strengths, and hone your message.

» If you and your team do a splendid job and luck is on your side, you may be a first-time congressional victor; well done! Next up: start all over again, with a new campaign.

❽ Conclusion: Reforming American Elections

Does the U.S. electoral system work? In this chapter we highlighted a variety of concerns—from gerrymanders to incumbency rates to the influence of money in politics. Is it a problem that we keep sending the same representatives back to Congress, up to 98 percent of the time? Is it a problem that big spenders often win elections? Many reforms have been proposed to address problems such as these.

Start with *gerrymanders*. We could try and end partisan battles over House districts by asking neutral panels to draw the lines—as California did after the 2010 census. Reformers praise the idea of moving away from bluntly partisan gerrymanders designed to pad the majority party. Why not create rational, compact, community-based districts? Such proposals are often defeated by a simple problem: Who can we trust to draw the districts? In many states, voters have been skeptical of nonpartisan experts and prefer to leave the issue to state legislatures or governors, who are, after all, accountable to the public. The debate continues, however, heating up each time one party draws up another outrageous election district.

Next comes *money*. Do we really want our legislators spending hours each day, every day, raising funds? Do we want them piling up so much cash that no one can afford to run against them? Although the current system is highly unpopular, there is little agreement about how to change it. Once simple reform, proposed by Democrats in 2016: forbid anonymous donations (known as "dark money") and let the public know exactly who is funding that oppo (negative research) shop. More ambitious reformers call for publicly financed elections, in which (as in most other advanced democracies) the government provides equal funding to each candidate and allows relatively small donations from the public, typically under two hundred dollars. This would create a much more even playing field between incumbents and challengers. Several states—including Arizona, Connecticut, and Maine—have passed laws to enable public funding for congressional and other statewide elections, although court challenges have brought the constitutionality of these laws into question. The court was closely divided in these cases and a shift of just one seat would have a major impact on campaign finance laws.

We also saw concerns in this chapter that money buys donors unfair influence. What about co-chairing a fundraiser? Surely that earns a House or Senate member's heartfelt gratitude. Or perhaps you sign on as a bundler, pulling in tens of thousands of dollars for a presidential or congressional candidate. Surely that candidate will owe you once he or she reaches office. The connection seems obvious to many critics.

Nevertheless, political scientists, examining the data from every angle, have had a very hard time proving anything like direct "pay-to-play" schemes— contributing to a campaign in expectation of a policy payoff after the election. The best that analysts have been able to show is that big donors enjoy personal access to a House member or senator. Tracing actual votes, or other legislative favors, to contribution patterns has so far come up empty. However, subtle forms of influence, especially over small issues (e.g., items in the tax code) are difficult to measure and prove. Money makes it difficult to upset incumbents— and fundraising distracts elected officials by soaking up enormous time and energy. Large donors can help protect incumbents who support their perspective. And even if researchers have not been able to uncover a direct connection between money and influence, many argue that the politician's insatiable need to raise funds keeps many issues on the political backburner—politicians are wary of hurting their donors.[20]

Complaints about corporate influence in Congress go far back in American history. In this satirical cartoon from 1889, cartoonist Joseph Keppler suggested that large corporate trusts were the real "bosses of the Senate." It took decades, but the Senate of that era was reformed. Does ours need reform too?

Campaign finance reform polls well, but it also has strong critics. They argue that contributing to campaigns is a form of free speech. If a candidate excites you, why shouldn't you send money to him or her? This is the logic upheld by the Supreme Court in the *Citizens United v. FEC* and the *McCutcheon* cases—both discussed earlier in this chapter.

The greatest disagreement rests on who can spend: Should we give large organizations—such as corporations and labor unions—the same right to free speech as citizens? The Supreme Court in *Citizens United* reaffirmed the argument that corporate or labor union contributions to campaigns are protected as a form of free speech. Another concern is that a single very wealthy individual can simply bankroll a candidate, or target a candidate, especially on the state level where relatively small amounts of money and negative research can sink a legislator or a judge. Congress has been reluctant to move boldly toward finance reform, with many Republicans being especially skeptical. And the Supreme Court (by a 5–4 majority) has been equally skeptical and, in the name of protecting speech, has overruled the bipartisan legislation that Congress had once crafted. The debate remains intense, but the institutional barriers to finance reform, in both Congress and the courts, have gotten steeper.

Along with redistricting and campaign finance reform, some analysts have proposed *term limits*. The president is limited to two terms, as are many governors. Why not limit members of Congress to, say, twelve years of service? The problem with this reform is that good legislating takes skill. Term limits clear out legislators just when they have learned how to become effective. Starting in the 1990s, many states added term limits for their state legislators and some of these states are now considering repeal. While the reform has been credited with leading to a steady infusion of fresh blood, this turnover also makes for an inexperienced legislature, transferring power to lobbyists—who do not have term limits and can build up memory and help "guide" the steady flow of rookie legislators. Proponents of term limits reply that we must find some way to restore Congress to the people. Incumbents become most savvy at staying in office—term limits would open up Congress to fresh ideas and talent.

These are three of the most popular reform ideas. Individual states have tried versions of each, but nationally we still have gerrymandering in most states, few (and declining) limits on campaign spending, and no term limits for Congress. Candidates for national office must raise millions of dollars to be seen as serious contenders, and as a result, almost everyone wins reelection to a partisan Congress that often bogs down in stalemate—and receives worse grades than almost any other institution in American life.

Is the system broken? Or is it doing what it has always done: muddling through just fine? We will look at this issue from different angles when we study Congress in Chapter 13 and the presidency in Chapter 14.

Whether the system needs reform or not, campaigns and elections provide avenues to participation for the many groups in American society. Every system, and every change, creates a new configuration of winners and losers. Despite all the barriers, occasional waves sweep new people and new ideas into office. Each generation of Americans decides whether to shake up the system of campaigns and elections or to leave things in place. Every election brings new excitement, new voters, and new ideas into American politics. We hope that you get engaged with our electoral system—it is the one and only way to ensure government by the people.

CHAPTER SUMMARY

• Elections—free, fair, competitive elections—define democracies. They give the people a say over who governs them.

• A key question in this chapter is: Are American elections democratic enough?

American electoral systems are unique because:

- The number of positions that we vote for is huge—over 520,000.

- We vote often compared to other nations.

- Federal elections for the House of Representatives take place every even-numbered year.

- In some places, there are elections every single year.

• The Constitution puts the states in charge of running elections, instructing them to manage "the time, place, and manner."

• In the last sixty years, all presidents have had one of just three jobs on their résumés: vice president, governor, or senator. Donald Trump became the first president in American history with no public sector experience.

• The road to the White House passes through three stages: primaries, the party convention, and the general election.

• The most familiar question about American democracy today involves the role of money in election campaigns. PACs, super PACs, and 527s have become fixtures in national elections.

• Econometric models have become better predictors of which party will control the White House. They explain the underlying fundamentals—who is favored, who has an uphill climb. They cannot predict primaries or unusual turns.

• The only constitutional limits to running for Congress are age, citizenship, and residency in the state.

• Winning a race for Congress takes money, organization, constituent service, name recognition, and a good knowledge of the district.

• Every ten years, the state legislatures redraw the congressional districts to keep up with changes in the population. The *gerrymander* is a district that is redrawn to help one party. Across time, some striking patterns have emerged in congressional elections: The president's party loses seats in the midterm elections, results have grown more volatile (with the party in power shifting often), and war spells trouble for the president's majority.

KEY TERMS

527 groups, p. 288
Bundling, p. 286
Call list, p. 306
Candidate-centered elections, p. 305
Electoral bounce, p. 293
Gerrymander, p. 302
Incumbency advantage, p. 300

Midterm elections, p. 301
Midterm loss, p. 301
Name recognition, p. 307
Negative campaigning, p. 308
Open seat, p. 306
Political action committee (PAC), p. 286

Proportional representation, p. 291
Reapportionment, p. 302
Super PACs, p. 286
Super Tuesday, p. 291
Time, place, and manner clause, p. 281
Winner-take-all, p. 291

STUDY QUESTIONS

1. Describe the limits that the Constitution places on popular participation in elections. What one federal office could the people originally vote for directly? Which people were generally not permitted to vote?

2. For further study: Is the American system of elections democratic enough for the twenty-first century? Defend your position by pointing to features that make it more (or less) democratic.

3. Who decides about who can vote?

First describe what the Constitution says about the matter in the "time, place, and manner" clause.

Next, consider the role of constitutional amendments in the voting process. How many are about expanding the vote? Does this add up to a history of great reforms? Or is it a slow expansion of the vote to different groups?

4. Describe the American system of campaign finance. What are PACs? How about super PACs?

What influence did the 2014 *McCutcheon v. FEC* Supreme Court decision have on the system?

5. For further study: What is campaign finance reform? Make an argument for or against campaign finance reform. If possible, explain how recent research supports your argument.

6. Describe the three stages of a U.S. presidential campaign. What were some highlights of each stage during the rollicking 2016 contest?

7. You have decided to run for Congress. What four things will your campaign need to be successful?

8. What is negative campaigning? Why do candidates rely on it so heavily?

9. For further study: If you were running for Congress, would you use negative campaign ads against your opponent? Why or why not?

10. Describe three reforms that have been suggested for campaigns and elections in the United States. Now, pick one and argue for or against it. Be sure to defend your position.

 Go to www.oup.com/us/Morone to find quizzes, flash cards, simulations, tutorials, videos, and other study tools.

Political Parties

CONGRESSMAN RON MACHTLEY, a moderate Republican from Rhode Island, enjoyed playing basketball with his congressional colleagues. Because his family and friends were all back home, Washington was a lonely place; the ball games were a great way to relax. One day, in the early 1990s, a couple of serious-looking men delivered a blunt message from the new Republican House leader, Newt Gingrich (R-GA): "No more basketball. You're playing with the enemy—Democrats." Gingrich believed that Republicans had grown comfortable in the minority, where they had languished for most of the last sixty years. The path back to power, he believed, required fire and resolve.

Ron was stunned. He had heard about a time when Democrats and Republicans used to battle it out during the day and then adjourn to a Capitol Hill bar for bourbon and tall tales. Members of the two parties worked together to craft legislation—including landmark laws. The Senate passed the Civil Rights Act (1965) thanks to Northern Republicans; five years later, Congress passed the Clean Air Act, a blockbuster environmental bill, almost unanimously (there was only one negative vote) and it was signed into law by Republican President Richard Nixon. In 1997, the Republican majority worked with Democratic President Bill Clinton to extend health insurance to seven million children.

Cross-party majorities were not unusual because there was as much difference *within* each party as there was between the parties. The Democratic Party appealed to very conservative southerners and very liberal northerners; Republicans also stretched across the political spectrum. In the early 1990s, almost as many Republicans (86 percent) as Democrats (93 percent) agreed that the "nation needed stricter environmental laws and regulations."[1]

Those days are over. Liberals sorted themselves overwhelmingly into the Democratic Party, conservatives went to the Republicans, and now **partisanship** touches every aspect of politics. The difference between parties is greater than any of the other divisions we normally measure in American politics—among people of different race, income, education, religion, or gender. Today 93 percent of Democrats continue to call for stronger environmental regulations. But the number of Republicans who still do so has plummeted a whopping forty-seven points and party leaders infuriate Democrats by mocking

● *Senator Rand Paul bats for the Republican Congressional baseball team, which ended a 7-year losing streak to the Democrats in 2016. Gone are the days of bipartisan basketball teams.*

In this chapter you will:

● Learn about the role of parties in governing America.

● Explore the two-party system and compare it to political parties in other nations.

● Review the rise and evolution of parties.

● Investigate why people identify with one party (or why they don't).

● Analyze the great paradox: Why Americans embrace parties and reject partisanship.

● Reflect on whether or not the United States has grown too partisan.

Partisanship: Taking the side of a party or espousing a viewpoint that reflects a political party's principles or position on an issue. Often decried by those who wish the parties would work together.

climate change as "a hoax" and "the triumph of extremism over common sense." In a 2016 Pew study, 70 percent of politically engaged Democrats said that the Republican Party made them feel "afraid"; the corresponding GOP figure was 62 percent.[2]

Although the parties have changed, their basic purpose remains the same. *A political party is an organization with a public following, established to win elections, generally by promoting a set of principles.* Political parties organize American government around competing ideas. However, many Americans dislike the name-calling and disagreement—the partisanship—that accompanies politics.

Americans have always had a love–hate relationship with parties. They were not mentioned in the Constitution because the founders feared them. President George Washington warned against their "destructive," "frightful," and "fatal" consequences. Thomas Jefferson, who helped organize the first party (against big government), insisted, "If I could not get to heaven but with a party, I would not go there at all."[3]

The deep corruption of the nineteenth-century political parties seemed to justify the early fears (cynical politicians used to half-jokingly urge supporters, "Vote early, vote often"). Today, Americans remain disdainful of parties and partisans: One survey found that nearly 90 percent of respondents identified "too much partisan infighting" as a chief obstacle to effective U.S. government.

Despite corruption and disdain, parties are essential to American government. As voting rights spread in early America, political parties stepped in to organize the new voters around the major questions of the day: Big government or small? Slavery or abolition? When should immigrants get to vote? Parties gave the people a choice. By the mid-1800s, political parties—the rival engines of democracy—were the largest and most influential political organizations in the nation. Today, national elections, congressional votes, policy decisions, judicial rulings, state government, and our own political opinions are all stamped by party influence.

Who are we? A deeply partisan people who helped invent the modern political party. Parties provide a vital link between Americans and public officials, and many form lifelong party attachments. Yet Americans also are quick to denounce partisanship, never more so than today, when partisanship has reached extremely high—perhaps unprecedented—levels (see Figure 11.1).

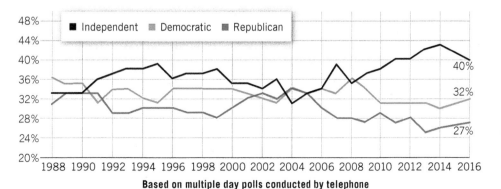

Based on multiple day polls conducted by telephone

● **FIGURE 11.1** *Trends in party identification. (Gallup)*

Has partisanship gone too far? Does it impair effective self-rule? Or, despite conventional wisdom, does it enhance democracy? These are the central questions about parties and American politics today.

Political Parties and U.S. Government

In February 2016, Justice Antonin Scalia, a powerful conservative voice on the Supreme Court, died. President Obama nominated Merrick Garland to replace him, but the Republican majority in the Senate announced it would not consider any nominee submitted by President Obama. They would wait until after the presidential election in November. Their resistance was rewarded when Republicans won the 2016 election—and, with it, the right to replace Scalia. Stories such as this one might tempt you to echo President George Washington: Do we really need parties? The answer is yes. Let us see why.

What the Parties Do

Love them or hate them, political parties are an essential part of American government. They are responsible for five major jobs: championing ideas, selecting candidates, mobilizing voters, organizing post-election government, and integrating new voters into the political process.

Parties Champion Ideas.   U.S. politics reverberates with ideas, as we saw in Chapter 2, and every candidate takes a position on scores of issues. How do voters keep all these positions straight? In effect, parties create a brand that gives people an easy way to find candidates who roughly share their views. If you strongly support environmental activism, a path to citizenship for undocumented immigrants, robust social programs, a woman's right to choose, public radio, and high-speed rail, you are probably a Democrat. If, on the other hand, you care more about lowering taxes, reducing the size of government, getting tough on undocumented aliens, supporting morality and traditional families, and outlawing abortion, you are probably a Republican. You prefer to mix and match from the lists? You're likely an independent who belongs to neither party—but be warned, political scientists believe most independents actually regularly vote for one party. Each party has its language and symbols. Do people in a group raise their voices when they say "under God" in the Pledge of Allegiance? They are likely to be Republicans, participating in a conservative ritual. However parties—and what they believe—are always evolving. Every election introduces new ideas and goals—such as free universal college education or a hard crackdown on illegal immigration.

Parties Select Candidates.   Parties choose the candidates who will run for election. Republicans began with seventeen contenders running for president in 2016 and voted, state by state, until they had selected Donald Trump as their candidate. The two major parties select candidates to run for office at every level of government—except local government, which often relies on **nonpartisan elections**.

Parties Mobilize the Voters.   Party leaders work to get the people to vote for their candidates. The parties raise money, hire consultants, craft advertisements, take polls, and organize phone banks. They also have become adept at suppressing the other side's votes through negative advertising.

Nonpartisan election:
An election in which candidates run as individuals, without any party affiliation. Many towns and cities feature nonpartisan elections.

BY THE NUMBERS

Political Parties

Percentage of Americans who identified as Democrats, Republicans, and independents, respectively, September 2016 Gallup poll: **32, 27, 40**

Percentage of Americans who identified as Democrats, Republicans, and independents, respectively, November 2005 Gallup poll: **34, 33, 30**

Percentage of Republican vote that came from white voters in 2000 and 2012, respectively: **88, 87**

Percentage of Democratic vote that came from white voters in 2000 and 2012, respectively: **64, 55**

Percentage of white, black, and Latino voters, respectively, who supported Donald Trump in 2016 (according to exit polls): **58, 8, 29**

Percentage favorable/unfavorable rating of Republican Party, August 2016: **36/58**

Percentage favorable/unfavorable rating of Republican Party, July 2005: **46/45**

Percentage favorable/unfavorable rating of Democratic Party, August 2016: **44/46**

Percentage favorable/unfavorable rating of Democratic Party, July 2005: **52/38**

Smallest proportion of Senate seats held by a major party (Federalists, 1821–1823): **4** (out of 48)

Largest number of House seats held by any party (Democrats, 1937–1939): **334**

Largest midterm pickup of seats in the House of Representatives in the past seventy-five years (Republican Party, 2010): **63**

Total number of national parties fielding a presidential nominee, 2016: **9**

Total number of parties (other than Republican or Democratic) getting at least one electoral vote in the last forty-five years: **0**

Parties Organize Governing Activity After the Election. Once the election is over, each party works to enact its signature programs. Leaders set agendas, line up votes, and organize their teams in Congress (as we will see in Chapter 13), in presidential administrations (as we will see in Chapter 14), and in the state governments (as we saw in Chapter 4).

Parties Help Integrate New Groups into the Political Process. Parties are important agents of **political socialization**, transmitting basic lessons about politics and government (the details may differ depending on the party). Party messages have attracted immigrants, young voters, evangelical Christians, high-tech entrepreneurs, and many more into the American polity. Parties provide crucial communication links between 325 million Americans, spread across a continent, and their elected leaders. Savvy party leaders are always looking for overlooked groups they can rally to their cause. Barack Obama galvanized black Americans who, in 2012, turned out at higher rates than whites for the first time in American history. Four years later, Republican nominee Donald Trump galvanized white males without a college degree—who felt abandoned by both Democrats and Republicans.

Political parties provide an efficient, effective solution to these five issues.[4] Is there anything especially distinctive about the American **party system**? Yes: the United States is unusual because it relies on just two major parties.

Political socialization: Education about how the government works and which policies one should support; provided by parents, peers, schools, parties, and other national institutions.

Party system: The broad organization of U.S. politics comprising the two main parties, the coalition of supporters backing each, the positions they take on major issues, and each party's electoral achievements.

● Parties socialize new groups into politics. When evangelical Christians started getting involved in politics in the 1970s and 1980s, Republican leaders were there to show them the ropes. Here, President Ronald Reagan speaks to evangelical leaders.

● Barack Obama supporters celebrate his presidential reelection in 2012. For the first time in history, African Americans voted at a higher rate than white voters.

Two-Party America

In January 2017, all 435 members of the House of Representatives, ninety-eight out of one hundred senators, and all fifty governors were either Democrats or Republicans. Why is the United States so resolutely devoted to the number "two" when it comes to party politics?

One reason for this two-party tradition rests on American ideas. As we saw in Chapter 2, Americans long ago embraced a set of national ideals. Each side of these great debates is typically associated with one of the two major parties. For example, most Republicans see liberty as freedom from government, while most Democrats fight for programs that will help free needy people from want. The two parties each rally around one of the two classic definitions of liberty—what we described as negative and positive liberty, respectively.

As you know by now, institutions invariably reinforce ideas. In this case, the winner-take-all electoral rules, described in the previous chapter, keep third parties out. The Libertarian or the Green Party may amass a great many votes; but even a party that wins 20 percent of the national vote but does not win an outright majority in any state or congressional district is shut out of both Congress and the Electoral College. In contrast, most other democracies operate multiparty systems. Proportional representation systems (see Chapter 10) give small parties an incentive to compete.

The result is simple and dramatic: The rules push every group to join one of the two major parties. When candidates decide to break out of the two-party system, they are accused of being "spoilers"—attracting voters from the party that is more sympathetic to their cause and, as a result, throwing the election to the party that does not share their philosophy at all. This is precisely what happened in the 2000 presidential election. In Florida, Republican George W. Bush won 48.847 percent of the vote, Democrat Al Gore won 48.846 percent of the vote, and Green Party candidate Ralph Nader won 1.635 percent of the vote. Even though Bush won by only 0.001 percent, because our system is "winner-take-all," he commanded all twenty-five Electoral College votes and won the presidency. What did disappointed Democrats realize? Ralph Nader and the Green Party had drawn just enough liberals away from the Democrats to throw the election to the Republicans—who were far less sympathetic to Nader's causes. The Florida experience only reinforced a key institutional lesson: work within the two parties.

COMPARING NATIONS 11.1 — Organizing Electoral/Governing Systems

The international community features a colorful array of party arrangements, with at least subtle differences between every nation. But a few main organizational styles tend to predominate, and each produces a different style of party politics.

Nonpartisan systems: Today, some Persian Gulf states—the United Arab Emirates, Oman, and Kuwait—outlaw political parties and officially run on a "nonpartisan" basis, though a traditional tribal family rules in each of the three nations. A few Pacific island nations also are nonpartisan, partly because their populations are so small that elected officials can personally represent their constituents.

Single-party systems: Only seven formal single-party states, in which only one party is allowed to contest national elections, exist today, ranging from China to Eritrea. Another forty-plus countries feature "single-party dominance" systems, in which minor parties are allowed but one powerful party wins national elections.

Two-party systems: The United States is the largest and longest-lived two-party state; other examples are Jamaica and Malta. Elsewhere, as in the United Kingdom and Spain, two parties have long runs of dominance, but parliamentary rules open the door to third parties.

Multiparty systems: The vast majority of the world's countries are governed along multiparty lines, from India to Italy and Japan to Tokelau, a tiny group of Pacific islands with about 1,400 inhabitants and three political parties. Government in multiparty systems usually involves a coalition of two or more parties, with frequently shifting alliances and complex power-sharing arrangements.

Other institutional forces help keep the two main parties at the center of American politics. State laws determine who gets on the ballot, and they often make it very difficult for a minor party candidate to be listed. In Florida, for example, after reforms in 2011 that *eased* restrictions, a third party still needs to collect more than 112,000 notarized signatures simply to list its candidate on a presidential primary ballot—a high bar for a small party.

The advantage of America's two-party system: It is predictable and stable. In nations with many parties, each election is followed by negotiations among the parties trying to form a majority. Today in Germany, the majority coalition has two parties; in Israel, it has six; and in India, the "National Democratic Alliance" governing coalition elected in May 2014 includes twenty-nine parties. Sometimes a single group pulls out of the governing coalition and forces a new election.

There also are disadvantages to two-party dominance in the United States.[5] For starters, it is less representative. In 2014, almost 25 percent of the voters in Massachusetts voted for Republican

● The Die Partei is a satirical party in Germany. Their campaign poster mocks the political discussion ("Bla, Bla, . . .") and then promises: "If you vote for us, we will execute the 100 richest Germans." In the 2014 elections, the party won a seat to the European Parliament—the first satirical party to win representation.

congressional candidates. Is it fair to end up with nine Massachusetts Democrats—and no Republicans—in Congress? Voters in Germany or Japan or other proportional representation systems generally have more choices for national or local office; people passionate about a cause—immigration, the environment, religion, free markets—can often find a party devoted to their cause (see Comparing Nations 11.1). Perhaps you're wondering if we have ever made room for additional parties? The short answer: No.

Third Parties in American Politics

Theodore "Teddy" Roosevelt is one of the most colorful figures in U.S. political history: A military hero who suffered from asthma and a big-game hunter who adopted an orphaned bear cub (giving rise to the familiar "teddy bear"). When Roosevelt came out of retirement to run as a Progressive Party candidate, he became the only third-party presidential candidate to come in second—but he still got clobbered by Woodrow Wilson, who won 435 electoral votes to Roosevelt's 88.

Table 11.1 lists all third-party presidential contestants who gained more than 5 percent of the popular vote or more than ten electoral votes since 1840. It is a short list, without a single candidate who came close to winning. Even in 2016, after much publicity, the Libertarian Party candidate managed just 3%. And most third parties lasted just one term (or four years) at the national level. Roosevelt's Progressive Party, for example, elected some fifteen members to Congress and spearheaded important reforms but dissolved within four years. The Tea Party, which has attracted considerable attention, is not in fact an organized national party, but a label that candidates adopt to signal their conservative views.

On the state level, Minnesota marks one of the few third-party gubernatorial successes in modern American politics. Jesse Ventura, a former professional wrestler (known as "The Body"), rode his blend of outsized personality and blunt common sense to the governor's mansion as a Reform Party candidate in 1998. In the last

TABLE 11.1 The Road to Nowhere: The Most Successful Third-Party Presidential Contenders, 1840–2016

ELECTION	THIRD-PARTY CANDIDATE(S), PARTY	PERCENTAGE OF POPULAR VOTE (NO. OF ELECTORAL VOTES)
1856	Millard Fillmore, American (Know-Nothing) Party	22% (8)
1860	John Bell, Constitutional Union Party	12.6% (39)
1892	James Weaver, People's Party	8.5% (22)
1912	Theodore Roosevelt, Progressive Party Eugene Debs, Socialist Party	27.4% (88) 6% (0)
1924	Robert La Follette, Progressive Party	16.6% (13)
1948	Strom Thurmond, States' Rights (Dixiecrat) Party	2.4% (39)
1968	George Wallace, American Independent Party	13.5% (45)
1980	John Anderson, National Unity Party	6.6% (0)
1992	Ross Perot, United We Stand Party	18.9% (0)
2016	Gary Johnson, Libertarian Party	3% (0)

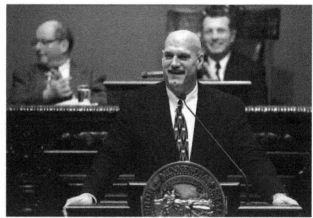

● *Wrestler-turned-governor Jesse Ventura, a member of the Reform Party.*

quarter-century, four other states have elected governors outside the major parties: Alaska (1990, 2014), Connecticut (1990), Rhode Island (2010), and Maine (1994, 1998). All four winners were independents rather than representatives of third parties.

Despite their history of electoral failure, minor parties are valuable contributors to American government. They provide a vehicle for people to express alternative views. This helps dissidents get a hearing, expands civic engagement, and perhaps minimizes the potential of anger and violence that arise when a cause is ignored. Third-party movements have often injected strong and controversial views into the major parties. They have fought for the abolition of slavery, the direct election of senators, votes for women, laws eliminating child labor, the prohibition of drinking, the income tax, limits on immigration, and smaller government.[6] When a third party cause becomes popular, one of the major parties tends to adopt it—as they did with every issue in the previous sentence.

THE BOTTOM LINE

» America's two-party style has endured for over two hundred years, with Democrats and Republicans as the main standard-bearers since 1856.

» The election rules explain the dominance of the two parties.

» Third parties arise periodically to challenge two-party dominance, but none has ever managed to break through.

🔒 America's Party Systems: Origins and Change

Political parties are always evolving. Every few decades the entire U.S. party system changes—the winners, the losers, the ways the parties organize, and the issues they debate. In short, the party system gets a makeover. We can identify at least six distinctive "party systems" stretching across American history.

Beginnings: First Party System (1789–1828)

Early Americans tried to avoid political parties. But they disagreed on a crucial issue: How strong should the central government be? In the first administration, President George Washington, Secretary of the Treasury Alexander Hamilton, and Vice President John Adams all pressed for a strong national government. Representative James Madison and Secretary of State Thomas Jefferson resisted central power. Each side rallied supporters—and political parties were born.

Candidates soon identified as either Federalists (for strong national government) or Democratic-Republicans (for states' rights and limited national power). The Federalists controlled the first three administrations. The immensely popular Washington ran unopposed in the first two presidential campaigns (even his opponents never criticized him directly, choosing to attack those around him instead); John Adams, Washington's vice president, won the third election.

In 1800, Democratic-Republican candidate Thomas Jefferson won a bitter, razor-thin victory over President John Adams. This was the first time the White House changed party hands. For the rest of the first party period, the Democratic-Republicans dominated national politics, winning the next six presidential elections and dominating Congress for twenty-four years (see Table 11.2). The Federalists bitterly noted that Jefferson had won by carrying the slave states whose Electoral College count was inflated by adding three-fifths of a vote for each slave (discussed in Chapter 3). Small wonder that slaveholders held the presidency for most of the next forty years.

TABLE 11.2 | Overview of the Six Party Systems

Notice that the sixth party system—our own—is very unusual in one way: no party dominates. This is especially true in recent times. Democrats have an edge in the Presidency while Republicans have an edge in the House and Senate.

	YEARS IN CONTROL					
	PRESIDENT		HOUSE		SENATE	
	FEDERALIST	DEMOCRATIC-REPUBLICAN	F	DR	F	DR
1. 1789–1828	12	28	8	26	12	22
	DEMOCRAT	NATIONAL REPUBLICAN/ WHIG	DEM	NR/WHIG	DEM	NR/WHIG
2. 1829–1860	24	8	24	8	28	4
	DEMOCRAT	REPUBLICAN	DEM.	REPUB.	DEM.	REPUB.
3. 1861–1896	8	28	6	30	14	22
4. 1897–1932	8	28	10	26	6	30
5. 1932–1968	28	8	32	4	32	4
6. 1969–present						
a) 1969–1992	4	20	24	0	18	6
b) 1993–present	16	12	6	20	11	15

The first party system began with a distrust of party politics. George Washington struggled, through the first two administrations, to project a nonpartisan image. The idea did not last long. Party newspapers were soon showering opponents with insults that would make modern politicians blush. Politics occasionally turned deadly. Aaron Burr, a Democratic-Republican who served as Jefferson's first vice president, despised Hamilton and his Federalist followers, especially after Hamilton campaigned vigorously (using a pseudonym) against Burr's run for New York governor in 1804. Hamilton criticized Burr's character at a private dinner party, word got around, and the two fought a duel on a hot July day in 1804. Hamilton was fatally wounded, further hobbling a Federalist Party already in decline. The party limped along until 1816, but after 1800 it never won a presidential election.

The first party system set a durable pattern: Two main parties contesting elections and building coalitions. One party (in this case, the Democratic-Republicans) dominated until evolving rules swept in a new constellation of parties, ideas, and supporters—in short, a new party system.

Rise: Second Party System (1828–1860)

When Andrew Jackson won the presidency in 1828, some twenty thousand Democrats (many of them angling for government jobs) swarmed into Washington for his inauguration. Supreme Court Justice Joseph Story, watching the spectacle, spoke for many of the old-style gentry: "The reign of King Mob seemed triumphant."[7] What he was really seeing was the birth of modern party politics.

In just three decades, political parties had evolved into a form that we would recognize today. Party competition grew fierce, voting rights expanded to most white males, and enthusiastic party members threw themselves into politics. These hallmarks of America's second party system remain the backbone of our party practices today.

"The rise of the common man" came with significant downsides: It meant fewer rights for the small population of free blacks (90 percent of African Americans were still slaves). And, as we discuss in Chapter 15, political connections—known as the spoils system—dictated the distribution of jobs at every level.

Party names changed along with the institutional shifts. The Federalists had vanished. Jefferson's old Democratic-Republicans split into two factions in the 1820s. Supporters of Andrew Jackson adopted the "Democratic" half, while a separate faction aligned with a brilliant young Kentucky politician, Henry Clay, called themselves "Whigs"—after a British term associated with opposition to tyranny—in this case, "King Andrew."

The new era saw renewed debates over the ideas that had arisen during the founding era. The Democrats favored small farmers, the rising urban workers, local control. Whigs had an expansive view of capitalism and supported a national plan (known as the American System) to knit the country together through canals, railroads, and other internal improvements. Democrats promoted aid for the needy, especially to widows of soldiers who had fought in the War of 1812 and later the Mexican War.

g. Ernte und Verpackung von Baumwolle in Louisiana.

● From 1800 to 1860, the slave population grew from 893,000 to four million—giving the slaveholding states additional representatives and Electoral College votes and helping to boost the Democratic Republicans over the Federalists during the first party period.

Whigs favored allowing the strongest to emerge from life's struggles without government aid. Democrats favored a genocidal policy of Indian removal; Whigs opposed it. Democrats embraced immigrants; nativists drifted to the Whigs and then formed a short-lived but powerful third party, the American, or Know-Nothing, Party.

There was no federal safety net during this pre-Civil War period. Hence, Democratic Party officials, especially in urban areas, often provided basic services in exchange for votes (the basis for the urban party machines that would grow extremely powerful by the late 1800s).

Both parties foundered on the question of slavery. Neither, however, could duck the issue. As the United States spread west, every new territory and state raised the same terrible question: Should slavery also be permitted to spread? Factions formed within each party over this question. In the early 1850s, the Whigs, who had attracted the strongest opponents of slavery, collapsed. Out of the Whigs' demise a new party system arose—and clarified the future of slavery in the United States.[8]

War and Reconstruction: Third Party System (1860–1896)

Abraham Lincoln helped form a new party—the antislavery Republican Party. The Republicans strongly supported free labor (which today we call capitalism) and insisted that new western settlements should be free of slavery (free soil), because slavery's expansion would undermine the people's right to work for themselves (free labor). After Lincoln won the presidential election of 1860, the southern states feared the end of slavery, and the nation soon entered the Civil War.

During the war, Lincoln skillfully deployed the Republican Party on behalf of the Union forces. He drew on party members to recruit soldiers, name officers (party connections helped), negotiate for war supplies, and sell war bonds to finance the war effort. With no similar party apparatus in the South, Confederates faced a much more difficult task.[9]

After the war, Republicans again drew on the party to help rebuild the nation. "Radical Republicans" promoted black rights, helping to boost many former slaves into Congress and statehouses under the Republican banner. Democrats, fighting back in the South, denounced Reconstruction's "excesses" and often resorted to violence and racist tactics that tried to limit the freedom of the former slaves to travel, to vote, or to seek employment.

After winning the war, Republicans dominated elections between 1864 and 1880. By the end of Radical Republican rule in 1877, each party had developed a strong regional identity. Democrats controlled the former Confederate states, which became known as "the Solid South" because they reliably voted Democratic, while the Republicans grew strongest in the Northeast and the Midwest. During the 1870s and 1880s, large numbers of European and Asian immigrants streamed into the cities, where municipal

THE FREEDMAN'S BUREAU!

AN AGENCY TO KEEP THE **NEGRO** IN IDLENESS AT THE **EXPENSE** OF THE WHITE MAN. TWICE VETOED BY THE **PRESIDENT**, AND MADE A LAW BY **CONGRESS**.

SUPPORT CONGRESS & YOU SUPPORT THE NEGRO. SUSTAIN THE PRESIDENT & YOU PROTECT THE WHITE MAN

● *Reconstruction featured a hotly fought battle between the parties. Although Republicans promoted images of racial harmony and national economic health, Democrats warned of impending doom. This caricature was part of the racist campaign designed to show that the former slaves were not prepared for freedom—a false charge backed by violence that eventually helped defeat efforts at racial reconstruction.*

Party machine:
A hierarchical arrangement of party workers, often organized in an urban area to help integrate immigrants and minority groups into the political system. Most active in the late nineteenth and early twentieth centuries.

Party boss: The senior figure in a party machine.

governments featured well-developed **party machines**—powerful political organizations. Managed by **party bosses**, party machines provided immigrants with such basic services as food, shelter, jobs, contacts, and a sense of belonging. In exchange, the party could count on a block of all-important votes once immigrants became naturalized citizens. The machines grew notorious for bribery and corruption. In some places they paid men to vote, stuffed ballot boxes, permitted repeat voters, and engaged in terrible brawls on Election Day.

Reformers eventually cleaned up city politics (although the hardiest machines lasted well into the twentieth century) through a series of institutional reforms that included banishing the parties themselves from urban elections. Today, parties remain crucial on the national and state level, but many cities have nonpartisan elections. In fact, you can measure how strong the urban reformers have been in any city by checking whether the parties still operate in local elections.

Business and Reform: Fourth Party System (1896–1932)

At the end of the third party period, national elections had become very close. Then, in 1896, a renewed Republican Party, sometimes tagged the "millionaires' party," swept back into control. However, after President William McKinley was assassinated in 1901, his vice president, Theodore Roosevelt, stepped into the White House and challenged the "millionaires' club."

The great debates of the fourth party system featured support for the status quo and business on the one side and pressures for political and economic equality (championed by the Progressive movement) on the other. Should women be given the vote? Should the government regulate emerging corporate giants such as Standard Oil or the Central Pacific Railroad? Should judges be elected? On the state level, should the government regulate child labor? Should it limit the workday for men and women? To the Progressive reformers, led by Theodore Roosevelt, the answer was yes, yes, yes.

THE "BRAINS"
THAT ACHIEVED THE TAMMANY VICTORY AT THE ROCHESTER DEMOCRATIC CONVENTION.

● *A caricature of William M. "Boss" Tweed of New York City. Tweed epitomized the corrupt and powerful party bosses of the nineteenth and early twentieth centuries. Bosses organized urban populations, especially immigrants, and dominated city government.*

This period also focused on the question of whether liquor should be prohibited. More than one in six Americans had been born abroad; drinking became associated with immigrants, big cities, political corruption, and spousal abuse. Republicans supported both Prohibition and women's suffrage. In every state where women won the vote, statewide prohibition followed within a year. Southern Democrats became fervent Prohibitionists after race riots and lynching were blamed (unfairly) on black men drinking. A constitutional amendment whipped through Congress and the nation, and America banned the sale of alcohol beginning in 1920. A wave of crimes associated with bootlegging—illegally transporting liquor to sell on the black market—rocked the cities, while rural districts went dry with little complaint (or violence). Democrats soon became advocates of repealing Prohibition. So did Republican businessmen who were afraid that Prohibition meant the birth of big government in America.[10]

● *One policy both parties agreed on for most of the fourth party system: prohibiting the sale of alcohol. The 1920s became a boom time, marked by rising new industries such as advertising, automobiles, and electricity. Then the economy collapsed in 1929–1930, taking down Prohibition and the entire "fourth party system" as well. (Source: history.com)*

Depression and the New Deal: Fifth Party System (1933–1968)

Another President Roosevelt, Teddy's distant cousin Franklin, helped define the fifth party system. The Great Depression (1929–1941) unhinged party politics, crippling a Republican Party associated with business interests and economic incompetence.

After three years of economic misery, Roosevelt frankly blamed the "unscrupulous money changers" and "self-seekers"—the old "millionaires' club"—for the nation's "dark days." Roosevelt's **New Deal** focused on jobs, infrastructure, government aid to the elderly (Social Security), temporary assistance for the needy (unemployment insurance and welfare), and new federal government agencies to manage it all. Roosevelt's Democratic Party reaped the electoral rewards, reshaping party coalitions.

New Deal: Broad series of economic programs and reforms introduced between 1933 and 1936 and associated with the Franklin Roosevelt administration.

The Democratic Party coalition included an unusual mix of interests: the Solid South; the big-city machines with their ethnic supporters; labor unions (the Democrats sponsored legislation that permitted the movement to grow); farmers, who saw agricultural prices rise during these years; and—perhaps most surprising—African Americans.

African Americans had been loyal to the Republican "**Grand Old Party**" (**GOP**) since Lincoln signed the Emancipation Proclamation. From the party's free-soil origins in 1856 up through the 1920s, the GOP was seen as the party of civil rights; it had championed widespread change in the South after the Civil War. Republican governments in the western states gave women the vote long before the Nineteenth Amendment extended it to women in Democratic strongholds. Now, Roosevelt's employment programs, along with early efforts to reduce racial segregation, won many black voters to the Democratic Party. However, there was a tension within the base of the Democratic Party: liberals, labor unions, and African Americans

Grand Old Party (GOP): Longstanding nickname for the Republican Party; ironically, bestowed early in the party's history, in the 1870s.

What Do You Think?

Does the 2016 Election Suggest a New Party System?

What do the results of the 2016 presidential election tell us about the immediate future of the party system? Is one party or another poised to establish dominance and break away for a long period of time?

Yes. Donald Trump's election means that the Republicans have won the White House in three of the last five elections, they have held the House for 8 years, the Senate for four years, and dominate the state governments. The electorate is Republican now.

Probably not. Remember that the Democrats won the popular vote in the presidential election. Control of the political system has swung back and forth with neither side breaking through.

No. Republicans may have won—but it was a very close call. Elections are still won and lost by a hair. And millennials may have been on the losing side—but their influence will only grow. Demographic changes herald a very different future.

pressured the party to expand social programs and civil rights, while southern Democrats struggled to rein in social programs and supported segregation. Democrats kept the coalition together—and hung on to their southern majority—for another thirty years, but as they became known as the party of civil rights, white southern voters shifted to the GOP. As the Democratic coalition began to crumble, a new generation of Republicans rose up with fresh ideas for America.

The Sixth Party System: The Parties at Equal Strength (1969–Present)

President Richard Nixon (1969–1973) and, later, Ronald Reagan (1981–1989) developed a "southern strategy" to win middle-class white votes. They emphasized small business, limited government, and a more market-oriented vision. The Republican Party had always had a conservative wing, but now this wing rose to dominance. By 1981, Republican president Ronald Reagan had launched a direct assault on the fifth party system through a powerful new conservative mantra: Government is not the solution to our problems. Instead, said the rising Republican coalition, government is the source of the problem. By the 1980s, the parties had lined up in their contemporary ways: on economic and social issues alike, Democrats leaned left, Republicans right.

Republicans had controlled the fourth party period and Democrats the fifth. The current party era introduces something new: Neither party is in control. Instead, very close elections swing party control back and forth. The new era, the sixth party system, is the era of very close elections. And with very close elections comes growing partisanship.

The most influential president of this period was Ronald Reagan and his new pro-market, antigovernment philosophy. Eventually, even Democrats began to abandon their old philosophy and echo Reagan. Democratic president Bill Clinton announced that "the era of big government is over," and upon entering office, President Obama promised to end government programs that "don't work."[11]

"Want to learn about the Wonders of Democracy? Here's a crash course."

 The sixth party system. The seesaw fight for control diminishes cooperation between the parties.

Perhaps the United States will experience close elections for a long time to come. However, this sixth party period is already one of the longest. Political historians are watching carefully to see if one party or the other is poised to break away, establish dominance, and start a new party era. Perhaps Donald Trump's victory and the strong run by Bernie Sanders in 2016—both party outsiders—suggest that the coalitions of the sixth party system are unraveling. What do you think?

Why the Party Period Matters

Why should we care what party system we are in? Because a new party system means new politics—and new national rules. The coalitions of voters, ideas, and political leaders determine how America is governed. Will we adopt universal health insurance or encourage more private-sector healthcare? Will tax cuts allow business to apply the savings to hiring new workers? Will we round up and deport undocumented people or give them a path to citizenship? These and many other decisions depend on the party—and the ideas—in power.

THE BOTTOM LINE

» Two main parties have always dominated U.S. party politics—and since 1856, they have been the same two, Republicans and Democrats.

» The two parties—and the contest between them—regularly reboot the party system. Each change in party system means a change in the voters who make up each party and the ideas that inspire them.

» We count at least six party systems since the founding of the United States. The latest, which began in 1969, is the period of very close elections.

» Political historians are watching closely for the rise of the next party system.

Party Identification . . . and Ideas

Party identification: Strong attachment to one political party, often established at an early age.

Many Americans feel strongly attached to their party. That attachment is called **party identification**, and it deeply affects how individuals see politics. Where do party identities and differences come from? And exactly who is attached to each party?

Building Party Identification

As we saw in Chapter 7, political socialization and party loyalty often start with family. Party identification also is shaped by who you are. In Chapter 10, we saw that the Republican Party today is mostly white while the Democratic Party, in contrast, is increasingly diverse (see Figure 11.2). Gender also distinguishes the parties. Republicans draw an equal number of men and women. Democratic voters and officeholders, on the other hand, tend to be women—by a three to two margin. White males are a minority among Democratic House members.[12]

Other traits also make a difference, such as where you live (urbanites lean Democratic, suburbanites Republican). Even personality seems to matter. Recent studies suggest that people who exhibit more "openness" (eagerness to explore new experiences) and "agreeableness" (a very social outlook) are more likely to be strong Democrats. Those who measure high in "conscientiousness" (strong sense of duty, discipline, impulse control) and "emotional stability" (even-temperedness) tend to

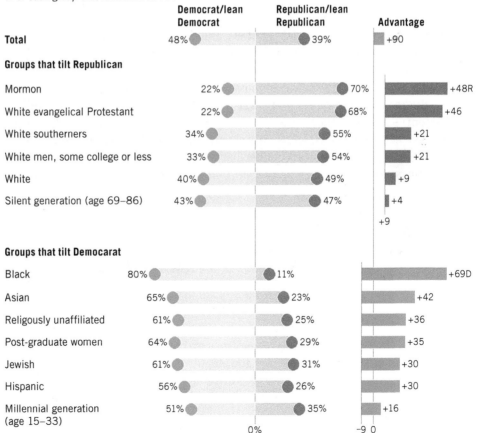

Strong groups for Democratic and Republican parties
% of each group that identifies as . . .

	Democrat/lean Democrat	Republican/lean Republican	Advantage
Total	48%	39%	+90
Groups that tilt Republican			
Mormon	22%	70%	+48R
White evangelical Protestant	22%	68%	+46
White southerners	34%	55%	+21
White men, some college or less	33%	54%	+21
White	40%	49%	+9
Silent generation (age 69–86)	43%	47%	+4
			+9
Groups that tilt Democarat			
Black	80%	11%	+69D
Asian	65%	23%	+42
Religously unaffiliated	61%	25%	+36
Post-graduate women	64%	29%	+35
Jewish	61%	31%	+30
Hispanic	56%	26%	+30
Millennial generation (age 15–33)	51%	35%	+16
	0%	–9 0	

FIGURE 11.2 *Party demographics. White, male, evangelical Protestant or Mormon voters are more likely to vote Republican while Asian, female, and young voters are more likely to vote Democrat. (Pew Research Center)*

be stronger supporters of the Republican Party.[13] Think about your own personality: Does it fit with this recent political science wisdom?

Another influence on party affinity is political context—put simply, what is happening in national politics when a voter forms attachments. Certain political moments seem to carry magic for a political party—John Kennedy's 1960 election drew millions into strong identification as Democrats, as Ronald Reagan's election in 1980 did among Republicans.

Although political historians are always alert to a sea change, no mass shift in party identification has shown up for the last twenty-five years. Currently, poll numbers show that around 30 percent of the electorate identifies as Democratic and between 23 percent and 28 percent as Republican, depending on the poll. Recently, we see a surge in independents who are weary of both parties. Recent polls show that over 40 percent of registered voters identify as independents. Why? One reason may be the intense conviction among the party faithful.

Still one factor may shift the balance in favor of the Democratic Party: When Ronald Reagan whipped Jimmy Carter in the 1980 presidential election, the electorate was almost 90 percent white; by 2016, the white electorate was down to 73 percent—and falling.[14]

The Power of Party Attachment

Party identification shapes three key aspects of public involvement: voting/political participation, "filtering," and ideology.

Voting/Participation. Your Democratic or Republican party identity tends to be a very strong predictor of your voting habits. In 2016, for example, 89 percent of Democrats voted for Clinton while 90 percent of Republicans voted for Trump. Analysts measuring the strength of party attachment find that strong partisans tend to be very loyal **straight-ticket voters**, sticking with their party's candidates right down the ballot. Their opposite? **Split-ticket voters**, who make their choices candidate by candidate.

Voting rates are higher among those with strong party identification than among the rest of the public. Of the 221 million eligible voters, only 60 million (27 percent)—typically, those who are most committed—voted in the 2016 primaries. The key to every election is turning out the party's **base voters**—those who are highly unlikely to vote for the other party—while winning over the independents. Conventional wisdom used to hold that independents were in the middle.

Straight-ticket voter: Votes for the same party for all offices on a ballot.

Split-ticket voter: Votes for at least one candidate from each party, dividing his or her ballot between the two (or more) parties.

Base voters: Party members who tend to vote loyally for their party's candidates in most elections.

What Do You Think? **Personality and Party**

Consider your own personality and party preference. Does recent political science research help predict your views—and the views of the people around you?

Yes. I believe that Democrats are more likely to seek new experiences and Republicans are more likely to emphasize duty and discipline.

No. I think there are different traits that explain party identification. (Please specify which traits you think matter most.)

Interests, not personality. I don't believe personality predicts politics. We are rational creatures pursuing our own self-interest regardless of personality.

Not anymore. Today, most lean strongly toward either the Democratic or the Republican Party.

Filtering. Party identification also plays a *filtering* role. Filters choose what signals in the media environment people are liable to accept or reject. As one political scientist wrote, "people tend to *project* favorable characteristics and acceptable issue positions onto the candidates of the party they favor."[15] In a set of experiments, social scientists asked respondents to rate a generic series of political candidates ("Candidate A," "Candidate B," etc.), based on photos and fairly detailed personal and political biographies. Each of the candidates was sometimes described as a Democrat, sometimes as a Republican, and sometimes as an independent. The study found that self-identified Democrats (especially strong partisans) liked the candidates described as Democrats the best, and the same result occurred for Republicans: The candidate's policy positions, appearance, family background, and so forth were all far less important than the party label.

Ideology. The parties take divergent views on issue after issue. This creates the polarization we described at the start of the chapter. Should we provide government support to people who cannot take care of themselves? Democrats say yes (75 percent); Republicans say no (only 40 percent agree). Should we make every effort to improve the position of minorities, even if it means preferential treatment? A majority of Democrats say yes (52 percent), while just 12 percent of Republicans agree. Do you doubt the existence of God? Republicans are more likely to say "no" (92 percent) than Democrats (77 percent). On all these indicators, differences between the parties have more than doubled in the past fifteen years.[16]

Of course, even with the growing intensity of party ideology, no party is a monolith. Each includes multiple factions with different—sometimes very different—ideas. Let us take a look at the issue factions within the parties today.

Republican Factions

Republicans are often lumped together as conservatives, but significant differences exist. Consider five prominent Republican factions.

Religious Traditionalists. Some conservatives support a return to what they consider America's Christian origins. Traditionalists oppose abortion, affirmative action, and same-sex marriage; they support school prayer, gun rights, and restrictions on immigration. Most members of the "religious Right" are traditionalists; many view the Bible as a guide to social and political life that is every bit as important as the Constitution.

Libertarians. Libertarians are strong defenders of individual liberty who promote minimal government intrusion into personal rights. Most libertarians follow a laissez-faire economic theory and are passionate advocates of free markets. They call for abolition of the Internal Revenue Service and the Federal Reserve Bank (which regulates interest rates and the money supply). Libertarians reject federal involvement in education, environmental regulations, transportation, healthcare, old age pensions—you get the idea. That may sound conservative, but because libertarians oppose all government they are liberal on social issues. For example, libertarians believe the federal government has no business deciding whether you can have an abortion, smoke pot, or marry someone of the same sex. Although there is an independent Libertarian Party in many states, most libertarians vote Republican.

Conservative Populists. These men and women feel left behind by economic and cultural changes. They are skeptical of elites in both parties, believing Republican elites to have turned their back on true conservative values. They view unfettered entrepreneurship as a source of job growth, strongly oppose immigration, and fear international trade deals. The populists are strong nationalists, and respond to calls to shake up the system. Donald Trump effectively appealed to this sector in the 2016 election.[17]

Neoconservatives. Neoconservatives support strong U.S. intervention to spread democracy and free markets around the world. The "neocons" believe that the United States—as the world's only superpower—should exercise its muscle to help improve the world. This view slipped from favor in many quarters after its proponents, led by Vice President Dick Cheney, strongly advocated the U.S. invasion of Iraq in 2003. But it has deep intellectual roots and remains a mainstay of Republican foreign policy.

Fiscal Conservatives. This faction supports tax cuts, opposes government spending, and identifies the large U.S. budget deficit as a central political concern. Some fiscal conservatives have threatened to shut down the government rather than increase the U.S. debt limit. Many aim to reduce the size of the federal government. Many of the Tea Party Patriots that have recently energized the Republican Party fit into this category.

Moderates. Moderates, a once-proud Republican faction, appear to be heading toward extinction. Moderates tend to be fiscally conservative but will consider tax increases along with spending cuts. They are relatively liberal on social and international issues. A sliver of the Republican Party (4 percent) calls itself "liberal." Many Republican Party members dismiss moderates as RINOs: Republicans in Name Only.

Democratic Factions

Democrats also encompass very different groups. One in five labels him or herself "conservative."

Progressives. Progressives occupy the left wing of the Democratic spectrum. Progressives are often skeptical of military action and wary of corporate power. They are strong environmentalists, embrace universal healthcare, support immigrant rights, advocate a woman's right to reproductive freedom, often champion gun control, and are especially concerned about economic inequality. They rally around Senator Elizabeth Warren and voted for Senator Bernie Sanders in the primaries.

The Civil Rights Caucus. Many Democratic Party members trace their political commitment to the spirit and the memory of the civil rights movement. They advocate for groups that have historically faced discrimination, especially racial minorities, recent immigrant communities, and women. They

see for yourself 11.1

Watch Donald Trump's populist supporters jeer immigration, free trade, and other targets during the campaign (*warning: includes some profane/ violent images*).

● *Every party has fringe groups. Strong language about immigration during the 2016 primaries brought white nationalists back into the national spotlight when some endorsed Donald Trump.*

build "rainbow" coalitions, fight against discrimination, social injustice, and racial inequality. Both Barack Obama and Hillary Clinton won their primaries with muscular support from this group.

Organized Labor. Unions are shrinking, but they have been a core Democratic constituency since the 1930s. They strongly support jobs programs, infrastructure projects, and workers' rights. Labor tends to oppose globalization and free trade, and they often break with progressives on environmental issues and immigration questions. As a result, Republicans have made major inroads, especially among white working men.

"Third Way" Proponents. In the 1990s, some centrist Democrats embraced a *Third Way* between the farther-left progressives in the party and Republican conservatives. For example, they sought to reduce the number of abortions while legally protecting women's right to choose. They sought to balance environmental protection with "smart growth." The "third way" theme was important during the Bill Clinton years and slid into obscurity afterward. With Hillary Clinton's defeat to an economic populist, the third way might well be over.

Deficit Hawks. Another declining faction, the deficit hawks support efforts to reduce the U.S. federal deficit. This wing of the Democratic Party usually proposes a combination of tax increases and spending cuts to achieve its aim. As with their GOP fiscal-conservative counterparts, they are not especially attentive to social issues. The deficit hawks were active in Obama's first term. Today, concern with inequality (championed by the progressive and civil rights groups) has almost completely eclipsed Democrats' focus on national deficits.

We have just described eleven major factions across the two parties. If we add variations across states and regions, we multiply the perspectives. The groups remind us that the parties are often boisterous combinations of views. Perhaps you find none of these perspectives appealing? Then you might be an independent, along with over 40 percent of American voters.

Organizing the Parties

With so many factions, running a party is a complicated job. The work falls on three different groups: the party organization, the party in government, and the party in the electorate. Like most American institutions we have studied in this book, each of these groups has a national, a state, and a local dimension. By now you will recognize the classic feature of American political institutions: a very complicated organizational chart.

Party platform: The written statement of a party's core convictions and issue priorities. Generally revised every four years, in time for the national party convention.

The Party Bureaucracy. The central organization for both parties is a national committee—the Republican National Committee (RNC) and the Democratic National Committee (DNC). These committees raise funds for the party, coordinate election strategies, decide which local races to fund, organize a national convention every four years, and prepare the **party platform**—the party's statement of purpose and its position on issues. If you are a candidate for a prominent office—from senator to mayor—your success may rest in large part on your ability to persuade the **party organization** to contribute funds to your campaign.

Party organization: The portion of a political party that includes activists, state/local leaders, and affiliated professionals such as fundraisers and public relations experts.

The committees also issue and enforce the party's rules for primary elections, from the presidential level downward. Important members of the DNC and RNC include the state party chairs and vice chairs, who are the most faithful activists in each party.

Traditionally, the party's organizational leaders are anonymous insiders that oversee the primary process. Then, during the 2016 primaries, Bernie Sanders charged that the Democratic National Committee (DNC) was openly siding against him. A blockbuster email trove, published by Wikileaks (apparently the result of a Russian intelligence hack) proved him right as high-level staffers wrote things such as "he's never going to be president." With their behind-the-scenes activity exposed, DNC Chair Debbie Wasserman Schultz and other staffers resigned in disgrace.

Party in Government. The **party in government** gets the recognition. These are the government officials in each party—elected leaders, appointed officers, individuals running for political office, and their staffs. The party in government struggles to enact the policies they support—and to stop their rivals from enacting theirs.

There is a constant struggle for influence within each party in government. Presidents usually command their own party, though members of the party may challenge them if the administration's policies grow unpopular. There is constant jockeying to become the face of the party that does not control the White House. Congressional leaders, governors, and presidential candidates all vie to put their own stamp on the party. Throughout the 2016 campaign, Republican Speaker of the House Paul Ryan and presidential candidate Donald Trump jockeyed to be the voice of the party. Each was slow to endorse the other.

> **Party in government:** The portion of a political party's organization that comprises elected officials and candidates for office.

> **Party in the electorate:** The largest (and least organized) component of a political party, drawn from the public at large: registered members and regular supporters.

Party in the Electorate. What is left after the party organization and officeholders? We are! Each party's followers make up the **party in the electorate**.

The Big Tent. The media generally focuses on the famous party names. Political parties thrive, however, when all their elements—the organization, the officeholders, and the public supporters—work together. That means sharing the same message, getting enthused about shared principles, and even embracing the party symbols—right down to the bumper stickers.

American federalism makes unanimity difficult. Local officials run the party in each state. Democrats in a conservative state like Alabama often have more in common with many Republicans in their own state than they do with liberal Democrats in San Francisco or New York. The same is true for the more liberal Republicans in New York or Massachusetts.

The party organizations always make tactical calculations: Do they put their resources in a few swing states that they have a good chance of winning in the next election cycle? Or should they spread their resources across many states—even long shots—with the hope of slowly building up their party in places where it does not often win?

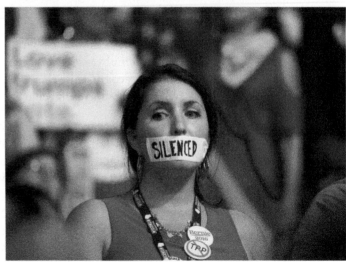

● Party in the electorate: (top) delegates at the Republican convention boo Ted Cruz for failing to endorse Mr. Trump; (bottom) Sanders supporters at the Democratic convention protested the bias of the DNC. The role of the conventions is to bring the different factions together.

Federalism pushes each of the two major parties to adopt a "big tent" approach: spread themselves wide, embrace followers of divergent views, and hope any resultant ideological muddle does not turn off too many party members. However, many party members reject the big tent approach and insist on sticking to their political principles—which can make for tumultuous politics within each party.

THE BOTTOM LINE

» A substantial majority of voting-age Americans identify strongly with one of the two major parties. Others declare themselves independents—their numbers have been rising.

» Our powerful sense of party identification is a result of many factors, including parental influence, political context, and even personality type.

» Party identification in turn helps shape our voting patterns, the ways we filter political information, and our bedrock ideas about politics and government.

» Each party features several ideological factions, with most politically aware Americans aligning with one or two of these.

» Each party includes three groups: the party organization, the party in government, and the party in electorate.

Talking POLITICS

PARTY ICONS AND SYMBOLS

Democratic donkey: Roosters and donkeys were the first Democratic icons, dating back to Jacksonian times, in the 1830s. The brilliant American cartoonist Thomas Nast began drawing the Democratic Party as a donkey in the 1870s, which popularized the association.

Republican elephant: This originated directly from the pen of the inventive Nast in November 1874. Republicans until then had used an eagle as their party symbol; the eagle still designates GOP candidates on ballots in Indiana, New York, and West Virginia.

Party Competition . . . and Partisanship

Parties began to lose their influence over politics and government in the mid-1960s. Interest groups muscled in on party territory, mobilized voters, and shaped issue positions. Americans began to identify with movements and organizations—civil rights, environmentalism, the right to life, and libertarianism. The parties floundered. By the 1970s and 1980s, political observers were publishing books such as *The Party's Over* and *The Decline of American Political Parties.*[18] The central role of parties in organizing elections also slipped, with the rise of the "candidate-centered election" that we saw in the preceding chapter. Political scientists warned that there was not enough partisanship in the American system—if the parties became too much alike, they could not offer the voters a meaningful choice.

Parties Rise Again

Just as political science analysts declared the death of parties, however, their revival began. During the 1980s, changing congressional rules shifted power from committee chairs back to party leadership, strengthening the parties in Congress. A huge influx of money into politics further revitalized party organizations, buoyed by the widespread adoption of PACs in the 1980s, 527 committees in the 2000s, and super PACs in the 2010s (see Chapter 10). The DNC and RNC, along with the congressional campaign organizations, became the chief recipients of campaign funds—and directed them in turn to candidates, who became more dependent on the parties as a result.

The parties also became ideologically purer. Each party was now organized around a clear set of ideas and principles. Each side could concentrate on defeating its foes rather than on negotiating the differences within its own ranks.

Competition and Partisanship Intensifies

Today the two parties are thriving, contesting very close national elections. The three presidential elections between 1996 and 2004 featured the closest trio of successive races since the 1880s. Since 2000, the presidency has changed hands three times, the Senate four times, and the House twice—again, something that has not happened since the nineteenth century. The close contests have made parties more important and partisanship more intense (see Table 11.3).

In the past, partisan differences on Capitol Hill were blurred by factions within each party. Democrats were so bitterly divided over civil rights that they could barely hold a **party caucus** during the 1950s and 1960s. Today, those differences within the parties have almost disappeared. Party factions remain, as we saw earlier, but party members are far less diverse in their views. The strongest divisions are now between the two parties. By 2010, every single Republican in the U.S. Senate was to the right (in terms of voting record) of even the most conservative Senate Democrat. For the first time, ideological conflict in both the House and the Senate breaks down perfectly along party lines. This partisan divide makes the political contest—over ideas, programs, and even the meaning of America—louder and angrier than it has been in more than a century. No matter where you look, partisanship within government is rising. It is also increasing among the public.[19]

It is not clear who influences whom. Are partisan officials fanning the flames of party differences among Americans? Or do activists within each party push their leaders to take stronger positions against the opposition? Or perhaps media outlets such as Fox News and MSNBC, catering respectively to conservatives and liberals, have driven us into our party corners? The answer to all three questions is probably yes.

| **TABLE 11.3** | **Party Control of U.S. National Institutions** |

Eight changes of control in eight elections is an unusual level of turnover.			
		PARTY IN CONGRESSIONAL MAJORITY (SIZE OF MAJORITY)	
ELECTION YEAR	CONTROL OF PRESIDENCY	SENATE	HOUSE
2000	**R (Bush)**	**50–50 (later +1 D)***	R (9 seats)
2002	R (Bush)	**R (2 seats)****	R (24 seats)
2004	R (Bush)	R (10 seats)	R (29 seats)
2006	R (Bush)	**D (2 seats)**	**D (37 seats)**
2008	**D (Obama)**	D (19/20 seats)	D (79 seats)
2010	D (Obama)	D (6 seats)	**R (49 seats)**
2012	D (Obama)	D (10 seats)	R (34 seats)
2014	D (Obama)	**R (8 seats)**	**R (60 seats)**
2016	R (Trump)	R (4 seats)	R (47 seats)

*After May 2001, when Senator Jim Jeffords switched parties, Democrats controlled the Senate.
**Party control switched after that year's election.

Party caucus: A meeting of all House or Senate members of one or the other main party, usually to discuss political and policy strategies.

Talking POLITICS

PARTY ICONS AND SYMBOLS (Continued)

Red/Blue: Widely used by the media and the public—and party insiders—to designate states that tend to vote Republican (red) or Democratic (blue), the red/blue "tradition" dates back only to 2000, when the major broadcast networks used these colors to indicate whether GOP candidate George W. Bush or Democratic nominee Al Gore won a state.

Abraham Lincoln: As an early Republican adherent in the 1850s, Lincoln appears as a party icon more often than other figures associated with the GOP. Ronald Reagan has been catching up fast—especially as the South has gone Republican.

Thomas Jefferson/Andrew Jackson: These were especially iconic figures on the Democratic side. Most state Democratic parties held an annual Jefferson–Jackson Day celebration. One problem: They were slaveholders. As the progressive and civil rights groups rise in the Democratic Party, so does skepticism toward Jefferson and Jackson.

INFO/DATA: Party Control by State

Only one of the fifty states—Utah—has been exclusively red (controlled by Republicans) or blue (controlled by Democrats) over the past twenty-five years. As this infographic displays, most states have at least some periods of split party control, and a few have bounced back and forth between GOP, Democratic, or split control.

1. What is the history of party control of the state you are from (or where you currently attend college)? Based on your knowledge of state politics, what forces help explain changes and/or consistency in this control over time?

2. While all three branches of the national government are in Republican hands, many states are still controlled by Democrats. Is this division a good thing? Would we be better off if the United States were more like other nations and the same policies were implemented across the nation? Why or why not?

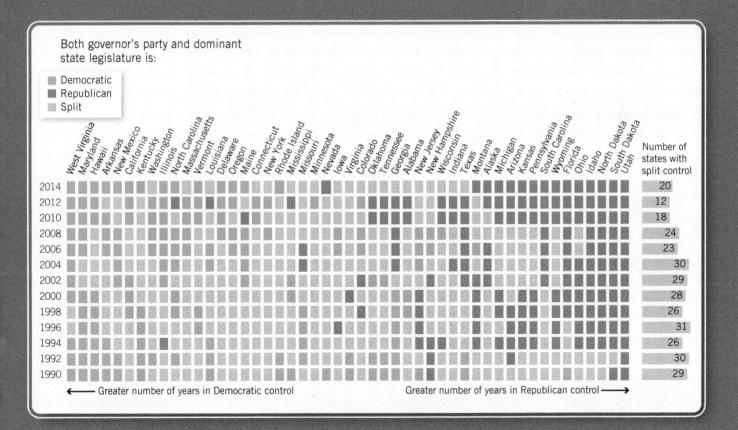

Source: The Washington Post

Should we worry about the rise in partisan differences? Does it make governance worse? Public opinion surveys repeatedly report Americans' dismay at partisan disagreement, even while we fan the flames of party polarization. What is it that Americans are so worried about?

First, party divisions lead to gridlock—a slowdown in government's ability to get things done. Second, bitter partisanship, as one commentary put it, "breeds bad public policy."[20] Third, a toxic partisan climate is said to drive more public officials away from government service, because less partisan members of Congress retire early in the face of incivility and relentless conflict. And fourth, it leads to disenchantment among the public.

Is partisanship really generating these types of bad government outcomes? Some political scientists break with popular wisdom and argue that the fears of partisan breakdown are exaggerated: American government—with its checks, balances, and federalism—was designed to move incrementally. Delay is part of the normal process. **Divided government** (when at least one house of Congress is controlled by a party different from that occupying the White House) has always been loud, divisive—and unexpectedly productive.[21]

> **Divided government:**
> Periods during which at least one house of Congress is controlled by a party different from the one occupying the White House.

Moreover, partisanship has not made congressional service less attractive. Retirements in the 2000s actually lagged behind the pace of the 1980s and 1990s, and the average length of House or Senate service rose slightly in the 2000s. Is partisan rancor driving the "best and brightest" out of politics? This argument is not supported by counting up years of service.

Today, most political scientists contest this optimistic view. The parties clash over almost everything and increasingly, on every level of government. Divided government increasingly yields political paralysis. The political standoff led to a government shutdown in October 2013, and an unprecedented drop in the nation's bond rating in 2011. It meant the Supreme Court had to muddle through with eight members for over a year in 2016–17. Even if divided government worked in the past, the partisan differences have grown too intense to be good government. Moreover, the partisan intensity drives away everyone but the shrinking party bases—as the millennial generation's experience grimly testifies.

Which side is right? For now, be aware that there are two sides to the argument about whether rising partisanship is harming American government. However, as the debates go on, social scientists—like the general public—tilt increasingly toward the pessimistic perspective.[22]

What Do You Think? Partisanship

| Should we be trying to diminish partisanship? | **Yes, partisanship is harmful.** Partisanship leads to paralysis. Worse, it is turning people off from politics, and that will create problems for us in the long run. | **No, partisanship is healthy.** The problems of partisanship originate from strong ideas and close elections. These arguments are useful and part of the democratic process. We should encourage intense views and strong arguments—that's what introduces bold new ideas. | **Maybe.** Some partisanship is useful, but today the parties are taking disagreement too far. |

THE BOTTOM LINE

» After declining thirty to forty years ago, the main political parties are now both thriving—and are highly competitive. Recent national elections have featured narrow margins of victory in presidential races and frequent shifts in party control.

» This competition has helped fuel a rise in partisan differences, evident among both national policymakers and the U.S. public.

» Most Americans—and many social scientists—believe that partisanship is affecting the quality of American government. The intensity of the conflict, they believe, will weaken our institutions.

Conclusion: A Party System Ripe for Reform?

Calls for reforming the U.S. party system are as old as the system itself. George Washington and other founders called for an end to partisan spirit before parties even arose. Yet parties swiftly became vital to American government and have remained vital (with some ups and downs) through the years. Their success, however, has not stemmed the tide of reform proposals. Here are three of the most commonly voiced proposals. As always, we invite your own ideas. Can you think of other ways to reduce the partisan conflict?

1. Proportional Representation.   As we saw earlier, America's winner-take-all system elects the highest vote recipient in each of 435 single-member House districts—and that reduces to almost zero the number of House or Senate members who are not from one of the two major parties. A proportional representation system provides minor parties with representation equivalent to their electoral support. You would soon have representatives of the environmental party, the pro-immigration party, the anti-immigration party, and the libertarians. Would this change be a good thing?

Supporters claim that moving to proportional representation would give voters more choices, possibly increasing voter turnout. It would enhance policymaking by ensuring that a wider spectrum of options is considered, better reflecting the nation's ideological and civic diversity. Many advocates predict that more women and minority-group representatives could be elected.[23]

2. Reduce the Barriers to Third-Party Competition in Elections.   If not a wholesale switch to a proportional representation system, why not make it easier for minor parties to be listed on the ballot? Why not let them join major-party candidates onstage in debates? Multiple parties might reduce the level of conflict and force groups to compromise and reach out across party lines. They might bring change and fresh ideas into American politics.

On the other hand, perhaps the two parties have effectively managed the head-spinning diversity of America. Opening the floodgates to numerous minor parties might make it even more difficult to achieve consensus.

3. Reduce Partisanship in Government. Reformers promoting this approach sometimes call for a "postpartisan" American politics. Ideas include limiting negative campaigning (unfortunately, this is hard to do, because negative campaigning works), reducing the role of outside advocacy groups in campaigns (attempts to do so have been struck down by the Supreme Court), and adopting public financing (implemented in a few places, but without notable reduction in partisan polarization), and a growing list of organizations who support candidates in the middle.

So far, the attempts at unity have been swamped by disagreements. If partisan differences are to decline in intensity, the change is likely to originate with our public officials—or with voters who punish partisan-style governance at the next election. Neither governors nor governed have shown much inclination to change their practice: condemn partisanship while fiercely embracing one party and its ideas.

Here is a slightly different way to think about parties and partisanship. Consider the rich history of party politics in America that we have traced across six party systems. Those 225 years have often seen a spirit that the Greeks called *agonistic*— a willingness to disagree with your adversaries while acknowledging their views as legitimate. This spirit means engaging wholeheartedly in a process of debate. In a democracy, successful political ideas must not just be rationally sound. We must also contest them, and we do this through party competition. Perhaps *stronger* parties, providing clear alternatives and articulating "core commitments" in a forthright way, is an antidote to our current gridlock and hyperpolarization.[24]

After all, the United States has always been a nation based on ideas—and intense disagreements about what they mean. The great debate that now occupies the parties has been going on for more than two hundred years. The important goal is that as many citizens as possible all join in. The greatest dangers come not from strongly held views but from apathy among the citizens. That, in the long run, might be the greatest risk of our charged partisan times.

CHAPTER SUMMARY

● America's two-party style has endured for over two hundred years, with Democrats and Republicans its main standard-bearers since 1856.

● The foundational American ideas and the organization of our elections help explain the dominance of the two parties.

● Third parties arise periodically to challenge two-party dominance, but none has ever managed to break through.

● The system of two parties—and the contest between them—is regularly rebooted through the birth of new party systems. Each change in the party system means a change in the voters making up each party and the ideas that inspire them.

🔵 Historians count at least six party systems since the U.S. founding: the Federalist era, the Jacksonian era, Civil War and Reconstruction, the era of rising business and Progressive reform, the New Deal, and (beginning around 1972) a contemporary period of roughly equal balance between the two major parties.

🔵 A substantial majority of voting-age Americans identifies strongly with one of the two major parties. Others declare themselves independents.

🔵 A powerful sense of party identification is a result of many factors, including parental influence, political context, and even personality type.

🔵 Party identification in turn helps shape our voting patterns, the way we filter political information, and our bedrock ideas about politics and government.

🔵 Each party features roughly five ideological factions, with most politically aware Americans aligning with one or two of these.

🔵 Republicans include traditionalists, conservative populists, libertarians, neoconservatives, fiscal conservatives, and moderates. Democratic factions include progressives, the civil rights caucus, organized labor, deficit hawks, and third-way proponents.

🔵 Each major party must work to unite under one "big tent" their key figures and followers. These include the *party in government* (elected politicians, their staffs, and affiliated political professionals), the *party organization* (party chairs, the national committees, and the state party leaders), and the *party in the electorate* (the millions of people who identify with the party).

🔵 American parties are highly decentralized: state and local party leaders largely run their own organizations, independent of national headquarters.

🔵 Most Americans—and many social scientists—believe that partisanship is affecting the quality of American government. The intensity of the conflict, they believe, will weaken our institutions.

🔵 Perhaps a long period of deep conflict will have this type of dangerous effect. However, strong debates are healthy in a democracy. Remember, the United States is a nation based on ideas—and intense disagreements about what they mean. The great debate that now occupies the parties has been going on for more than two hundred years. The important thing is that as many citizens as possible join the debate.

KEY TERMS

Base voters, p. 331
Divided government, p. 339
Grand Old Party (GOP), p. 327
New Deal, p. 327
Nonpartisan election, p. 317
Partisanship, p. 315

Party boss, p. 326
Party caucus, p. 337
Party identification, p. 330
Party in government, p. 335
Party in the electorate, p. 335
Party machine, p. 326

Party organization, p. 334
Party platform, p. 334
Party system, p. 318
Political socialization, p. 318
Split-ticket voter, p. 331
Straight-ticket voter, p. 331

STUDY QUESTIONS

1. What are the two main reasons American politics is usually limited to two political parties?
2. Which reason do you consider a more important explanation for the two-party system? Explain why.
3. What is proportional representation?
4. For further contemplation:

a) Would you support introducing proportional representation in Congress?
b) What would be the effects of this switch?
c) Explain why these effects would help or harm American democracy.

5. Describe four functions that parties serve in the American electoral process.

6. What are the three separate parts of the party organization? Explain what each part is responsible for.

7. Choose any one party system in American history.
   a) Describe the era.
   b) Which party, if any, dominated the era?
   c) What replaced the party system you have chosen? (If you chose the present era, do you see any signs that this system is ending?)

8. What is party identification? Name three factors that influence party identification.

9. Describe three factions in each political party today.

10. For further contemplation:
   a) What does partisanship mean?
   b) Explain why many Americans worry about partisanship.
   c) The authors suggest the fears of partisanship may be exaggerated. Do you agree with this suggestion or not? Explain why.

 Go to www.oup.com/us/Morone to find quizzes, flash cards, simulations, tutorials, videos, and other study tools.

Interest Groups

YOU HAVE BEEN HIRED as a new congressional staffer—and today is your first day at work on Capitol Hill. (Congratulations!) You arrive during a wildly busy legislative season. The office is bustling, and nobody has time to get you oriented. In fact, you barely know where you are assigned to sit . . . and now the legislative director has asked you to prepare a detailed analysis of "air," or at least that's what you heard her say. A sympathetic colleague explains that she meant "AIRR," which Google tells you is the Aviation Innovation, Reform, and Reauthorization Act. Your diligent Internet search doesn't turn up anything more than that; the bill hasn't yet been introduced. And your analysis is due by tomorrow morning.

Where to begin?

Quick, call the Congressional Research Service, the research arm of Congress. They're glad to help you out, they say—but it will take a few weeks. *Weeks*? You have hours, at best.

You feel like slinking out of the office before anyone notices and disappearing into a completely different career. Then salvation arrives on your desk, in the form of an elegantly bound, meticulously researched report on the AIRR. All the details you need on aviation reform—which House and Senate members are pushing which views, the politics involved, even the technical details—are laid out clearly. As you debate whether to cry or laugh with relief, you wonder: Who *wrote* this? You look around to thank your angel of an officemate. Not here, your colleagues smile: over on **K Street**. An aviation interest-group lobbyist sent it directly to you. As this chapter shows, that elegant, informative, and timely report is at the heart of what interest groups do in Washington.

Interest groups have become so central to American government that it is difficult to imagine our system without them. At the same time, lobbyists and the interest groups they represent consistently receive among the lowest approval ratings of any professionals, in or out of politics.

Who are we? We are a nation of too many lobbyists and special interests. Or are interest groups positive contributors to American democracy? Pause and consider: How many interest groups work on *your* behalf? None, you say? Or perhaps one or two advocate for causes you care about—such as the environment or tax relief or the Catholic Church? In fact, like most Americans, you are represented by dozens of groups—advocates who push for clean air, safe

- Learn what interest groups do in American government—and how they do it.

- Reflect on whether interest groups wield too much power.

- Trace the historical roots of interest-group activity, and see how lobbyists have changed (preview: they are no longer exclusively older white men).

- Examine the multiple roles that lobbyists play.

- Consider whether interest groups are good for America.

K Street: A major street in downtown Washington, DC, that is home to the headquarters for many lobbying firms and advocacy groups—and thus synonymous with interest-group lobbying.

● *Interest groups in action. Max Montrose of MedicinalMarijuana.TV lobbies a Colorado state senator; as more states legalize marijuana use, interest-group activity in this area has grown rapidly.*

345

food, affordable federal student loans, and most everything else you care about. Your college or university probably has representatives who lobby to promote the school's concerns—at the state capitol and in Congress. Your student fees or tuition may help pay for their work. Even your favorite subject, political science, has a national association based in Washington, DC, with several advocates on staff. Whether you know it or not, you are a participant in what one expert terms our "interest-group society."[1]

More than two centuries ago, James Madison warned against interest groups—he called them "factions"—in *Federalist* no. 10, calling them the "mortal disease" that have always killed off popular government. His solution? *Increase* the number of interest groups. That way, none would become too powerful and they would have to work together to accomplish anything. Increase the number of groups? That is one piece of advice the United States has certainly taken.

Special interest:
A pejorative term, often used to designate an interest group whose aims or issue preferences one does not share.

Concern about **special interests** has surged periodically since Madison published his famous warning. Jacksonian Democrats, Progressives, New Dealers, 1960s radicals, Bernie Sanders supporters in 2016: many reform groups across U.S. history expressed a fear that a few select groups (usually big business) were getting fat off the rest of us. All of the outcry obscures a basic truth: Interest groups are not just "them"—they are us.

The United States is an interest-group society, with interest groups woven into the fabric of our government. The central puzzle in this chapter is whether interest groups' influence saps American government of its vigor and fairness—as most people believe—or whether interest groups perhaps enhance American democracy.

BY THE NUMBERS

Interest Groups

Estimated number of interest groups engaged in U.S. politics: **More than 200,000**
Number of members claimed by National Rifle Association: **4.5 million**
Number of member companies, American Petroleum Institute: **650**
Number of national interest groups active on defense issues: **795**
Number of national groups active on welfare issues: **47**

Number of lawyers practicing in Washington, DC, 2016: **89,427**
Number of lobbyists who registered with Congress, 2015: **11,165**
Estimated percentage of former members of Congress who now work as Washington lobbyists: **43**

Percentage of registered lobbyists who serve only public interest clients: **33**
Total spending reported by healthcare interest groups, 2015: **$503,649,480**
Total spending on lobbyists reported by the city of Dallas, Texas, 2015: **$280,000**

Total amount spent on lobbying by the Chamber of Commerce, 1998–2016:
$1.3 billion
Median pay, top 100 best-paid Washington nonprofit lobbyists, 2015: **$545,867**

Interest-Group Roles in American Politics

What does it take to become an interest group? Dozens of lobbyists pursuing members' goals on Capitol Hill? Inside political connections galore? A million motivated supporters? It is much simpler, actually: We define an **interest group** as *an organization whose goal is to influence government.*

Notice two important elements in that definition. The first is *organization*: a collection of wheat farmers begins to resemble an interest group only when they meet regularly to jointly discuss and manage their concerns. The second is *influence government*: Plenty of organized groups have no contact with public officials. When those wheat growers join the American Farm Bureau Federation and press Congress for subsidies to keep crop prices stable, then they are an interest group.

At least two hundred thousand interest groups are active in American politics today. About three-quarters of those are public advocacy or citizen groups; the remainder represents private (usually corporate) interests. The American Association of Retired People (now officially, AARP), which represents nearly forty million Americans, is an example of an interest group. It provides financial services, insurance products, discounts at hotels, and information to people aged fifty and over. It also hires lobbyists to influence the government.

Given that interest groups seek to influence government, how do they carry out that work? Along three main paths: informing, communicating, and mobilizing.

Interest group: An organization whose goal is to influence government.

Informing Members

Interest groups like the AARP and American Farm Bureau Federation perform three main functions for their members. First, groups *inform members about political developments.* The American government is sprawling—House members each represent more than 710,000 people, on average. Interest groups have become a primary link between the public and its government. Groups provide access through which members can stay informed. Most of us do not have the time to keep up with complicated government policies—even those directly affecting our career or personal interests.

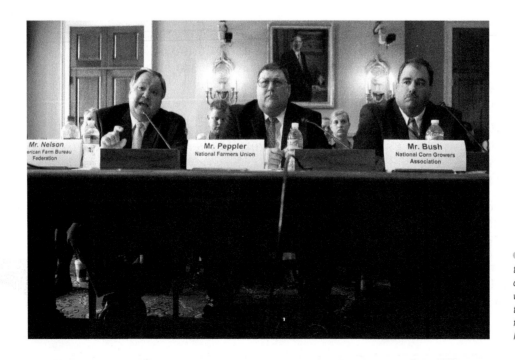

Mr. Nelson
erican Farm Bureau
Federation

Mr. Peppler
National Farmers Union

Mr. Bush
National Corn Growers
Association

● *Lobbyists representing farmers testify before an Agriculture committee on Capitol Hill. The were participating in a hearing over the safety net for American farmers—part of the 2012 Farm Bill.*

Communicating Members' Views

A second main role interest groups play is to *communicate members' views to gov-ernment officials*. Interest groups may communicate directly with these officials, but often they gain access by hiring **lobbyists**. Put simply, a lobbyist is a person who contacts government officials on behalf of a particular cause or issue. Plenty of people try to influence government—such as college students, who fan out across their state capital for a "Lobby Day" each year, asking legislators to oppose higher student fees or appropriate more funding for science labs. Professional lobbyists, who are paid by clients to influence lawmakers, generally enjoy greater access to the halls of power than does the average American.

Lobbyist: A person who contacts government officials on behalf of a particular cause or issue.

The AARP hires lobbyists to communicate members' views to government on a wide range of issues affecting seniors, from Social Security benefits to disability insurance.[2] In 2006, when President Bush tried to add a new prescription drug benefit to Medicare, Democrats thought they had the votes to block the legislation on Capitol Hill. Then the AARP threw its weight behind the bill—and it passed.

Mobilizing the Public

Third, interest groups *mobilize the public*—that is, they encourage groups of people to act politically. They develop TV ads, urgent direct-mail alerts, Facebook post-ings, and tweets, all meant to provoke action.

Many Americans care deeply about abortion policy, for example. Most are not satisfied merely by voting every two or four years for candidates who share their position. Pro-life and pro-choice groups offer members frequent opportunities to *do something* on this issue of personal concern. Interest-group mobilization activ-ity happens on many issues, from gun rights to climate change. Contributing funds, writing letters, organizing rallies and protests, exchanging ideas with others of similar views, and winning audiences with policymakers: Interest groups facilitate all these means of political participation.

When groups mobilize their members, they are often pushing their own spe-cific angle, of course. A few years ago, the Food and Drug Administration proposed regulations to reduce teen smoking. Tobacco company lobbyists mounted a big

Two perspectives on tobacco policy. This cartoon caricatures government antismoking policy as an assault on freedom while real crimes go unnoticed. Tobacco companies have been active in supporting the proliferation of such images.

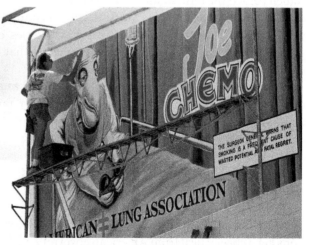

Antismoking groups create stark images of their own. One recast Joe Camel, the cartoon figure used to promote Camel cigarettes, as "Joe Chemo."

"education" campaign aimed at both the public and lawmakers about the dangers of a giant, out-of-control federal bureaucracy meddling with people's freedom to smoke. Public health groups pushed back with graphic advertisements showing the ravages of smoking—amputations, voice boxes, and death.

How well represented by interest groups are your specific political concerns? If you care about something that is already on the government agenda, groups are very likely promoting your view in Washington. More obscure topics—and less powerful interests—may be less likely to get a hearing. However, if you have strong opinions about a policy that seems to be overlooked, do not despair. American political history is full of "crackpots" who believed in outlandish things—ending segregation, cleaning up polluted rivers, putting airbags in every car, slashing personal income-tax rates—that eventually won out.

Indeed, through their work informing members, communicating views to political officials, and mobilizing the public, interest groups play an important (if controversial) role in democratic societies.

What Do Interest Groups Do for Democracy?

Whether our interest-group system represents all (or most) people is a heated debate, both among political scientists and across the public. Some, in a view called **pluralism**, hold that as long as the American political process is open to a wide range of different groups, then government policies should roughly correspond to public desires. No single set of interests dominates our system, pluralists insist, and all the different groups pushing and tugging allows the collective good to shine through. You might see this view as a latter-day update of James Madison's argument in *Federalist* no. 10: The answer to the problem of interest groups is—more interest groups.

Pluralism: An open, participatory style of government in which many different interests are represented.

Two pessimistic theories respond to the pluralists. First, *hyperpluralists* fear that there are so many interests and groups that the entire system is bogging down in stalemate. Any time a group proposes a new project—education reform, a new highway, privatizing Social Security, or fighting climate change—there is always another group ready to oppose it because they do not want to pay the taxes or fear harm to the environment. Hyperpluralists see gridlock. The journalist Jonathan Rauch coined the term **demosclerosis** to describe the sheer number of lobbyists at work in Washington. *Demo* is the Greek root meaning "of the people" (think *democracy*). *Sclerosis*—well, we should keep our arteries clear of dangerous sclerotic plaque. Rauch, echoing hyperpluralists, suggests that the American body politic is endangered by the immense buildup of lobbyists.[3]

Demosclerosis: The collective effect of the vast number of Washington lobbyists in slowing the process of American democratic policymaking.

Others worry that the playing field is tipped too far toward the richest and most powerful people. This **power elite theory** portrays a group of wealthy, influential Americans—mostly from the corporate sector—who mingle with one another regularly and thus promote their shared ("class") interests in government. Most of the power elites live and work in cities other than Washington, DC, so business lobbyists do the day-to-day work of influencing government on the elite's behalf.

Power elite theory: The view that a small handful of wealthy, influential Americans exercises extensive control over government decisions.

Power elite analysts look at events like the $125 billion U.S. government bailout of big banks in 2008–2009—using public tax dollars—and conclude that corporations get a special deal from American government. As 2016 presidential candidate Bernie Sanders repeated in speech after speech, nobody bailed out the more than one million property owners who lost their homes, many of them because of the same subprime-mortgage crisis that devastated the banks.

Sierra Club volunteer Alex Burke organizes signs to hand out near the local Environmental Protection Agency offices, on the first of two days of public hearings held by the EPA on President Barack Obama's plan to cut carbon dioxide emissions by 30 percent by 2030.

Power elite theorists, in contrast, see interest groups as part of a cozy, interlocking network that perpetuates themselves in power.

One political-science analysis of Washington interest-group spending came up with numbers that gave new life to the elitist perspective. Lobbying, these researchers wrote, is dominated by business: 53 percent of the lobbying organizations and 72 percent of the expenditures represent business interests. In contrast, public interest lobbying weighs in at about 5 percent of lobbying efforts. And groups supporting less privileged people employ just 2 percent of the lobbyists in Washington. The results, this study suggests, reflect the conclusion of a famous political scientist back in 1960: this chorus "sings with a decidedly upper class accent."[4]

Which view—pluralist, hyperpluralist, or power elite—is correct? Political scientists cannot say for sure. It is difficult to tell whether big business or other powerful groups successfully turn policies in their direction on a regular basis. For every bank-bailout example that affirms the power of elites in the American system, another story seems to suggest the opposite—that small business or retired people or environmental advocates prevail. Perhaps each of these theories captures part of the truth.

We return later in this chapter to the question of how well Americans are represented in general. By now you have a taste of the central issue: the extent of interest groups' influence in American politics and policymaking.

THE BOTTOM LINE

» Interest groups, or organizations that seek to influence government, employ lobbyists to pursue benefits for their clients or membership.

» Groups serve their members by communicating political information to them, analyzing and relating members' views to policymakers, and mobilizing people to act politically.

» A long debate continues among pluralist, hyperpluralist, and power elite theorists about whether the collective public is well represented by interest groups.

🎱 Types of Interest Groups

Interest groups can do a good job promoting their members' personal interests. How well are larger groups of Americans—truck drivers, for example, or Latinos or CEOs or homeless people—represented in the interest-group system? What about the U.S. public as a whole? To answer such questions, let us look at the various types of interest groups, and who they represent.

Political scientists divide the teeming world of interest groups into three main categories: *economic* groups, which exist primarily to serve members' financial interests; *citizen* groups, which are organized to advance the public interest (as they define it) or a particular cause or political viewpoint; and *intergovernmental* groups, featuring one level or branch of government seeking to influence another.

Economic Groups

Economic groups seek financial and other resource benefits for their members; we can further classify them into three subcategories (see Table 12.1). *Business* groups promote the interests of corporations. Most large companies have their own in-house lobbyists—Google, for example, employs ten registered lobbyists in its Washington office alone—and also hire lobbying firms with expertise in their industry to work on specific projects. Google pays more than twenty other groups to lobby on issues such as protecting high-tech patents, cybercrime, net neutrality, and immigration (Google hires engineers and other experts from all over the world).

Labor groups represent workers from nearly all large industries in the United States. The largest is the National Education Association (NEA), with more than 2.7 million members, most of them public school teachers. Next largest, at 1.5 million members, is the Service Employees International Union (SEIU), representing many service industries such as healthcare, hospitality (e.g., hotels and restaurants), and public employees. Both the NEA and SEIU, like other labor groups, engage in various programs to benefit members. But their greatest focus is on higher pay and better benefits for their members. This effort mainly targets employers, but they also lobby government—primarily to pass regulations affecting working conditions, like a higher minimum wage or safety improvements.

A third class of interest groups primarily concerned with economic interests is **trade associations** and professional groups, introduced earlier in this chapter.

Trade association: An organized group representing individuals and businesses that belong to the same industry.

TABLE 12.1 Types of Interest Groups

CATEGORY	PRIMARY PURPOSE	EXAMPLE
Business groups	Economic benefits for a company or firm	Google (10 in-house lobbyists; hire 20+ additional lobby firms)
Labor groups	Economic benefits for labor union members	National Education Association (2.7 million members)
Trade or private associations	Economic benefits for businesses or professionals in a given sector	American Petroleum Institute (oil and gas company members)
Citizen groups; also called public interest groups	Organize and mobilize like-minded individuals around a shared passion, political viewpoint, or cause	Sierra Club, Christian Coalition
Intergovernmental groups	Advocate for one level or branch of government to another	National Governors Association

These organizations represent several—or even hundreds—of companies or professionals in a specific sector. The American Petroleum Institute (API) is a Washington-based trade association representing oil and gas companies: the API lobbies for tax benefits, favorable trade deals, and reducing costly regulations on their members. To join the American Architects Association, one must be—you guessed it—an architect; similarly, lawyers join the American Bar Association and doctors the American Medical Association. Although these groups are well-known, many associations are obscure: take a guess, for example, at what PATH International represents.[5] Others may use a name that masks their purpose: a few years ago, an association called Citizens for Better Medicare spent millions of dollars lobbying for changes to Medicare, the national health insurance law. Eventually media accounts noted that the "citizen" members were actually drug companies, health insurers, and large hospitals.

Citizen or Public Interest Groups

What about interest groups not organized primarily to serve members' economic interests? Hundreds of thousands of *citizen groups*, also called *public interest groups*, exist in American politics. They cover the political spectrum, and represent practically every conceivable issue and group of people, even those at society's margins: the National Alliance to End Homelessness, for example, is a well-respected Washington interest group. Single-issue organizations, such as People for the Ethical Treatment of Animals (PETA), fit into this category, as do those established to promote a political viewpoint, such as the American Conservative Union.

Citizen groups do not have a built-in constituency (most lawyers join the American Bar Association), and so must work hard to recruit and retain members. Public interest organizations, as the economist Mancur Olson recognized a half-century ago, must address the problem of *free riders*. There is no evident reason that a rational person should join a citizen group, pay dues, and spend time in meetings, when others are willing to bear the costs of organizing the group, mobilizing members, and lobbying on behalf of a cause like clean air or consumer safety.

Log on to the website of a public interest group you find appealing—Greenpeace or the National Rifle Association (NRA) or Habitat for Humanity, which builds homes for needy people around the globe. Alongside the rhetoric about global warming or the right to bear arms, you will see major swag available. Tote bags, curated trips to Yosemite, gun-safety videos, teddy bears, travel mugs—all free or discounted for joining. (Ironically, the NRA also offers its members accidental-death insurance.)

In political science terms, these **material benefits** are a key part of what citizen groups provide. Such benefits help attract new members, whose dues provide part of the funds needed to keep the lights on and lobbyists on board. Others join because of **expressive benefits**: The group expresses values that its members share, such as social justice or individual freedom. Still other people may join an interest group for **solidarity benefits**. Think of your own experience as a Girl Scout or fraternity member: It can feel very powerful to be part of the group. Interest-based organizations tap into that feeling and engage members based on shared social fellowship.

Trade associations are subsidized by their sponsoring firms. Members of the American Petroleum Institute, for example, pay annual dues based on the size of their organization, starting at $1,525 and rising to tens of thousands of dollars. Citizen groups are partly supported by members, but their dues are much less, averaging around fifteen dollars. Larger donations might come from foundations, government grants, or wealthy individuals, who are called "angels" in the interest-group world.

The best-known angels are big-spending donors who usually align with one or the other political party and who financially support interest groups. Charles

Material benefits: Items distributed by public interest groups as incentives to sign up or remain a member.

Expressive benefits: Values or deeply held beliefs that inspire individuals to join a public interest group.

Solidarity benefits: The feeling of shared commitment and purpose experienced by individuals who join a public interest group.

and David Koch are prominent conservative funders. They sponsor Republican candidates for all levels of office, and run ad campaigns designed to inoculate their energy companies from political backlash. An "angel" on the other political side, George Soros, secretly funneled millions of dollars into anti-Soviet resistance movements during the 1970s and 1980s. Not so secretly, Soros later became a major funder of liberal advocacy groups, from America Coming Together to MoveOn.org. In our highly polarized politics, angels such as Soros and the Koch brothers face bitter criticism from partisans on the other side.

Intergovernmental and Reverse Lobbying

Public officials also act like interest groups and promote their own views. Some engage in **intergovernmental lobbying**, pushing their counterparts in other branches to support their policy aims. The White House maintains a legislative-affairs office to promote its views on Capitol Hill, staffed with former top House and Senate staffers. Even the president needs lobbyists!

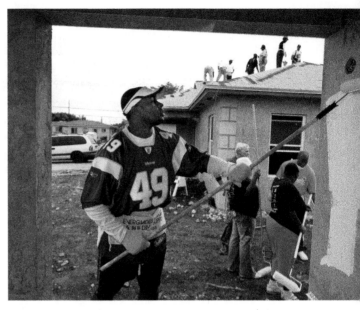

● *Minnesota Vikings Tony Richardson paints a Habitat for Humanity home in the Liberty City area of Miami, Florida. NFL players from the league volunteered to assist workers as part of the Super Bowl XLI Community Impact Program.*

Presidents and Congress are also frequent targets of intergovernmental lobbying from state and local officials. The National Governors' Association (NGA) includes all fifty states' governors—conservative and liberal alike. Because states share a strong interest in federal funding for social programs (Medicare, Social Security, Medicaid), infrastructure programs (e.g., highways, bridges, and schools), and many other concerns, the NGA is in constant contact with the White House and Congress.

Government officials also lobby interest groups, an activity termed **reverse lobbying**. Executive and legislative leaders alike regularly convene closed-door meetings of key interest groups before moving forward on a policy proposal. Hearing from all sides can generate useful information and ideas, and also may establish a compromise that wins support to push legislation through Congress.

Reverse lobbying can be controversial. Barack Obama used this approach to health reform in 2009–2010, when he directed advisors to meet secretly with groups representing the insurance industry, pharmaceutical companies, hospitals, physicians, and other primary stakeholders. Republicans charged that Obama and Democratic allies had "bought off" these groups—reverse lobbying run amok.[6]

Intergovernmental lobbying: Attempts by officials in one part of the government to influence their counterparts in another branch, or at a different (state or local) level.

Reverse lobbying: Attempts by government officials to influence interest groups on behalf of their preferred policies.

THE BOTTOM LINE

» Interest groups come in several types: Those pursuing primarily *economic* concerns include business and labor groups, along with trade and professional associations.

» *Citizen* groups include those promoting broad causes (consumer rights, civil liberties) and single-issue advocates such as the National Rifle Association, as well as ideological groups.

» Governments also lobby each other, as well as engaging in "reverse lobbying"—working with interest groups to advance desired aims.

🔒 Interest Groups Past and Present

America's interest-group society has deep roots in our history. The First Amendment is among the most familiar American political creeds. Freedom of religion, speech, assembly, and the press are ingrained in our national mind. Most schoolbooks do not mention the final clause of that amendment, however: the right to "petition the government for a redress of grievances." The first amendment in the Bill of Rights guarantees the right to lobby.

After the Constitution was ratified in 1789, the first Congress gathered—and so did petitioners seeking benefits. As journalist Jeffrey Birnbaum described, "After each legislative day, hogsheads of wine and port poured freely at sumptuous meals of mutton, pork, duck, and turkey. Dinner linens are snowy white; the cutlery is burnished & English, and the check was paid by the wealthy merchants of the day."[7] These merchants were among the original economic interest groups in American politics.

As early as the 1750s, journalists lining the halls outside Britain's House of Commons were called "lobbyists." In the early 1830s New York, the "Empire State," had the largest population and most business activity. Albany, the capital, was a constant target of privilege seekers, who became known as "lobby-agents." President Andrew Jackson, or someone on his White House staff, shortened this to "lobbyist" and hurled it pejoratively at national bankers. The name stuck, and spread to anyone seeking to influence government.

1960s Advocacy Explosion

Although economic interest groups have a long history in the United States, the number of professional lobbyists remained at a few dozen for a century, then gradually rose to perhaps two thousand by the 1950s. Public interest groups also arose during this period, but because they were organized around a specific objective—banning liquor sales or winning benefits for Civil War veterans—the enthusiastic membership melted away once the legislative battles were done.

Then the old ways changed. Demonstrations for civil rights and against the Vietnam War roused massive numbers of Americans in the 1960s and 1970s. This spirit of public engagement spread to other areas: the environment, consumer rights, access to healthcare, protecting life.

These movements required organizers to channel all that public passion to attain results. Enter professional public interest lobbyists. Advocacy groups such as the Sierra Club and the NAACP had existed for decades, but they expanded both their membership and political activities. As Washington churned out regulations, political and economic life became more complex—requiring a guide to explain all the intricate new rules to small businesses, farmers, local officials, and others. Enter the expert insider lobbyists. Big corporations, the target of many of these new rules (Make safer products! Stop polluting the environment! Increase gas mileage! Protect worker safety!), realized they needed louder voices in Washington as well. Enter the corporate lobbyists. Their demands also issued forth: Lower our taxes! Protect us from competition! Help us create jobs!

Advocacy explosion: A vast and relatively swift increase in interest groups active in Washington, DC, beginning in the mid-1960s.

The result of all this expanded public, government, and lobbying activity: an **advocacy explosion**. After the mid-1960s, the number of professional, full-time lobbyists swelled to tens of thousands (see Comparing Nations 12.1). Critics who already feared interest-group power were doubly alarmed by the growth of an elaborate "politics industry" in Washington, DC.

COMPARING NATIONS 12.1 The Spread of American-Style Lobbying

Though other countries also ramped-up legislative volume and complexity during the 1960s, none has anything like America's interest-group society. Parliamentary democracies in Europe and Asia organize public and private interests into a few "peak groups," whose representatives sit with national officials to slice up the pie—deciding formally how much business and labor should get. These groups are often financed by the government and work more like collaborative partners than multiple opposing sides in a legislative scrum.

This political style leaves far fewer openings for interest groups. As a result, only the United States features lobbying *firms*, filled with hundreds of lawyer lobbyists and their support staffs. Lobbying practices overseas are beginning to more closely resemble American styles, largely because U.S. lobbying outfits increasingly locate their offices in other national capitals. Ironically, the United States is exporting what may be the least popular feature of American government.

Young and Plugged In

For many Americans, the mental portrait of a lobbyist involves a potbellied, middle-aged fellow swapping yarns with his old pal the congressman. That stereotype may fit an earlier era. In recent years, lobbying has become a lot more female and a lot more youthful. Women now make up nearly half of Washington lobbyists and increasingly dominate social issue areas like healthcare and consumer rights.[8]

By the late 1990s, the *Wall Street Journal* noted, in a piece called "Young Guns," that the world of lobbying was shifting to "20-somethings and 30-somethings" who had advanced degrees in policy studies and technical expertise—a far cry from the backslappers of an earlier era. After Republicans won control of Congress in the 1994 election, the *Washington Post* profiled the new lobbying power in town, characterizing these interest-group representatives as "young, conservative, and very plugged in."[9]

THE BOTTOM LINE

» Interest-group activity in the United States stretches back to the beginning of the republic; our modern system of thousands of highly active groups dates to the "advocacy explosion" of the 1960s–1970s.

» Various reform efforts have done little to curb the activity and power of lobbyists.

» In recent years, younger Americans and women have increasingly populated Washington's interest-group ranks.

Interest-Group Lobbyists in Action

Another Monday morning in Washington, DC, and all over the capital, lobbyists are starting their workweek. Some head straight to Capitol Hill to catch up with any staffer (or, ideally, Senate or House member) they might bump into. Others gather in boardrooms for breakfast with lobbyists sharing similar interests—protecting the environment or promoting family values—to review the week's

● *Lobbyists work at all levels of government. Here, they pack a hearing in Lansing, Michigan, on the state's electricity laws.*

urgent legislation. Some pore over blogs and online news sources, sifting through the latest opinions and posting a few of their own. And several dig into an ongoing research project, gulping coffee to help break through the morning fog.

The Multiple Roles of Lobbyists

Lobbyists wear many different professional hats. Some interest groups are large enough to hire specialists—staff members dedicated to researching policy issues or developing media advocacy campaigns. Lobbying firms also hire outside scientists, consultants, and other experts to assist them. But most Washington representatives juggle several roles: it's all part of the job.

Researchers. The typical interest-group representative spends significant time every day studying political trends, monitoring government programs, and analyzing policy information. As the huge farm bill moves through Congress in anticipation of action in 2017–2018, various agricultural trade associations prepare detailed briefing books for each House and Senate office.

Such research work can be very expensive. Between 2001 and 2014, the American Petroleum Institute, a trade group for the oil and natural gas industry, spent some $36 million on a single study refuting the link between benzene (a vapor produced by burning gasoline) and cancer.

Witnesses. Most congressional committee hearings feature testimony—on both sides—from interest groups most concerned about the issue. Executive agencies convene similar gatherings on how to implement a law, again featuring lobbyist experts. Far more lobbyists *attend* congressional hearings, following every utterance and move. Experienced Washington eyes can watch this crowd—a questioning look to a senator's aide here, a note passed to a witness there—and predict whether the committee will be favorable or unfavorable to the legislation under discussion.

Lobbying coalition: A collection of lobbyists working on related topics or a specific legislative proposal.

Issue campaign: A concerted effort by interest groups to arouse popular support or opposition for a policy issue.

Astroturf lobbying: An attempt by interest groups to simulate widespread public engagement on an issue.

Position Takers. Washington representatives for various groups routinely issue statements outlining their organization's position on important legislation. In January of each year, for example, the powerful U.S. Chamber of Commerce—which represents more than two million U.S. businesses—holds a press conference to announce the group's main goals for the coming legislative season.

Coalition Builders. Affiliated groups often band together in **lobbying coalitions**, allowing them to share information and split the labor of contacting lawmakers. More than twenty-five groups joined a coalition in 2016–2017 to advocate for government-subsidized Internet connections for low-income Americans. Observers dubbed it the "strange bedfellows coalition," because it included both large telecommunications companies such as AT&T and Verizon and public interest groups that usually fight against big business, such as Common Cause and the Center for Media Justice.

Social Butterflies. There is a social side to the lobbying job as well. One interest-group representative we know starts his weekday mornings in Longworth Cafeteria, on the House side of Capitol Hill. Strategically located at a central table, he greets the stream of Members and staffers as they pick up a morning coffee or bagel, exchanging the latest political gossip.

Grassroots Campaign Builders.   Join an interest group, and you will receive a steady stream of appeals to write your representative or senator: to protect gun ownership, to stop teen smoking, to recognize Palestine as a country, and so on. Interest groups mount these **issue campaigns** as part of their attempts to attract public support from across the country—from the "grassroots," as the term goes. Sometimes these appeals can backfire. Back in the 1980s, Texas senator Lloyd Bentsen labelled one transparent Washington-based effort to mobilize Texans as "**astroturf lobbying**"—a caustic dismissal of artificial attempts to mimic grassroots-style public concerns.

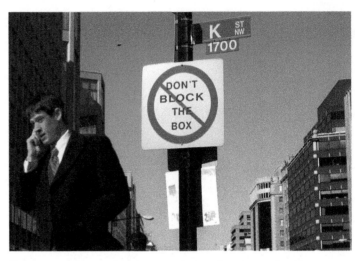

● *Lobbyists' offices on K Street. Although "K Street" remains shorthand for Washington lobbying, in reality, most interest groups in the capital locate their offices elsewhere.*

Three Types of Group Representatives

A big divide exists in Washington between lobbyists who represent *economic interest groups* and those who represent citizen groups or intergovernmental lobbying offices. So far, we have treated each type as similar. But their professional styles, and the demands on their time, are often different.

If you ran into Heidi Wagner on campus, you might well mistake her for a student. Wagner is quick-witted and loves indie and hip-hop music. Unlike any of your classmates, though, she is listed as one of "Big Pharma's 625 Washington Lobbyists" in a report published by the advocacy organization Public Citizen. Wagner is a highly talented healthcare lobbyist who represents a global pharmaceutical firm. Wagner exemplifies one type of private interest-group actor, the *single-firm lobbyist*. Though she collaborates with many other healthcare lobbyists, Wagner ultimately works for—and is paid by—one employer.

Now meet Tom Dobbins, lobbyist for the American Composites Manufacturing Association. He represents dozens of firms that make composites: everything from high-tech fiberglass boat hulls to carbon-reinforced materials that support our skyscrapers. Dobbins is a *trade association lobbyist*, working for a collection of firms in the same type of business. Because tobacco farmers or automakers or composites manufacturers share common interests in Washington, it makes sense to have one or a few lobbyists represent their concerns.

After working for a single firm or trade association for a few years, many lobbyists go into business for themselves, representing a range of clients (usually in one issue area, though some high-profile lobbyists work across fields). These *independent lobbyists* are known in Washington-speak as "hired guns," though most of them hate that term.

Independent lobbyists, unless their firm goes out of business or their client stream dries up, have a guaranteed income stream—sometimes a very large one. For example, Tom Donohue, the chief lobbyist for the U.S. Chamber of Commerce, earns more than $6 million a year.[10]

WASHINGTON LOBBYING

Drop: Set of brochures and position papers left behind by a lobbyist after visiting a legislator's office.

Fly-in: A series of Washington meetings, usually on Capitol Hill, organized by lobbyists for their out-of-town clients.

Bird-dogging: Posing tough questions to an elected official, often at a public event. Advocacy groups often engage in this tactic to advance their cause and win attention.

Gucci Gulch: Areas outside the House Ways and Means and Senate Finance committees, which deal with lucrative tax and revenue issues; the hallways are lined with high-priced lobbyists wearing Gucci clothing and expensive shoes.

Rainmakers: Lobbyists adept at raising funds for politicians

Talking POLITICS

(*continued*)

or causes; when they collect large sums, they are said to be "making it rain."

Third House: In Washington, as well as many state capitals, lobbyists are viewed (not necessarily positively) as a co-equal "third branch" of government, given their expertise and access.

Nonprofits Don't Lobby?

For many citizen groups, the very word "lobbying" has a dirty connotation. Few public interest leaders describe themselves as active lobbyists. Moreover, one study found, "most nonprofits don't know how to lobby and, worse, think that it entails cutting shady deals with sleazy characters."

Yet to successfully advocate for a group's interests, it is all but essential in to-day's American political system to make one's case to lawmakers in state capitals or in Washington. As the same study concluded, "to make the changes they want to see in the world, nonprofits must learn to lobby . . . and they may even learn to love it."[11] Failing to engage in organized political pressure can doom an otherwise-promising advocacy strategy. Whether cleaning up a local river, providing social services to immigrants, seeking English-only laws, or planning a march on the state capitol or White House, to succeed, citizen-group advocates must include lobbying as part of their plan.

THE BOTTOM LINE

» Lobbyists perform a wide range of roles, from researchers to social butterflies.

» Private sector lobbyists can represent a single firm or a trade association, or set up in business for themselves as independent lobbyists.

» Citizen groups are often loath to engage in "lobbying," but they must to succeed.

🛇 Interest Groups and the Federal Branches of Government

Iron triangle: The cozy relationship in one issue area between interest-group lobbyists, congressional staffers, and executive branch agencies.

The traditional model of Washington power brokers depicted a closed process dominated by **iron triangles**—tight, durable links among powerful interest groups, congressional committee chairs and their staff, and administrative officials.

Consider one example: *farm subsidies*. For decades, many American farmers—growing crops from corn to tobacco—have received "price supports," or subsidies worth millions of dollars, from the U.S. government. Critics charge that this practice is a huge giveaway of taxpayer dollars. (Agricultural experts explain that weather and other uncertainties endemic to farming make a system of crop insurance and production management necessary.) During the 2014 farm bill reauthorization, many expected that farm subsidies would be cut sharply. After all, conservative Republicans and deficit hawk Democrats were strongly focused on reducing government spending. But when the smoke cleared, the price supports remained in place, if in somewhat altered form.

In some accounts, a classic iron triangle explains the staying power of farm subsidies. Congressional staffers on the agriculture committees in the House and Senate (Point A in Figure 12.1) have close relationships with lobbyists for various farm groups (Point B), who encourage them to appropriate funds managed by Agriculture Department bureaucrats (Point C). Farm lobbyists establish friendly connections with Department of Agriculture officials as well. If the executive branch (C) balked at implementing subsidies, it might find its congressional appropriation cut the following year—so it keeps the programs humming along. The combination of executive branch, legislative branch, and lobbyists—the iron triangle—is unstoppable.

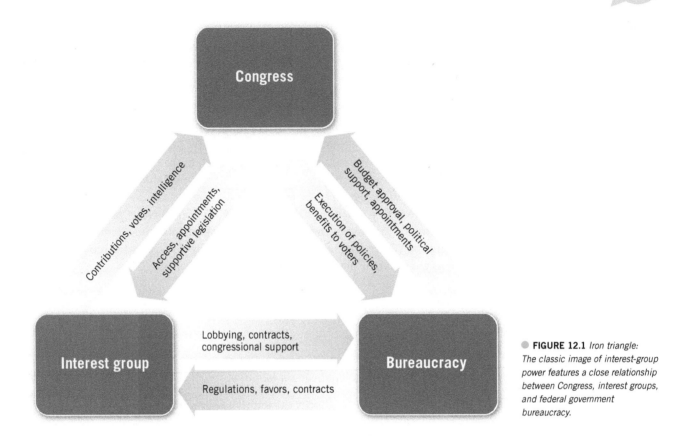

● **FIGURE 12.1** *Iron triangle: The classic image of interest-group power features a close relationship between Congress, interest groups, and federal government bureaucracy.*

Washington actors often serve sequentially (and sometimes even simultaneously) as policymakers, lobbyists, and formal party officials—a phenomenon termed the **revolving door** that helped facilitate the rise of iron triangles.

Farm policy, given its long-established players, may be the last vestige of an old system. Iron triangles proliferated around Washington into the 1960s, given the relatively closed environment of national policymaking. The subsequent "advocacy explosion" initially brought more lobbyists into closer contact with Capitol Hill staffers, which ensured the triangles' survival for a while.

Revolving door: The tendency of Washington's most seasoned lobbyists to move from government work (e.g., as a presidential advisor) to lobbying and back again.

Rise of the Issue Network

Over the past thirty years, iron triangles have largely given way to a very different image of looser, more open **issue networks**. A flood of new lobbyists representing more and more positions, in addition to growing numbers of congressional staffers, have broken apart the cozy triangles. Political scientist Mark Peterson charts a "radical change" beginning in the 1980s, as triangles dissolved into a "far more diverse and open system" that featured "looser, less stable, less predictable, and more diverse patterns of interaction and decision."[12]

Issue network: Shifting alliances of public and private interest groups, lawmakers, and other stakeholders all focused on the same policy area.

Figure 12.2 illustrates an example of an issue network focused on telecommunications policy. Notice how much more complicated than a simple triangle this network is. Welcome to the life of a Washington lobbyist today! To negotiate these networks—to faithfully represent members and attract new clients—modern interest-group representatives cannot count on a few reliable contacts with the chair of a congressional committee and a bureaucrat or two. Instead, they must cultivate connections across Capitol Hill and in multiple executive departments and agencies. They also may have to master the byzantine ways of the judicial branch.

Education
Teachers union, national PTA, schools, Department of Education, Catholic education groups

Social Welfare
Liberal groups, community-based organizations, Benton Foundation, ALA, rural health clinics, RAC, AHA

Telecommunications
Local telephone companies, long distance companies, USTA, COMPTEL, NCTA, FCC, USAC, NTIA, White House, commerce committees in Congress, CBO, CRS, court, Department of Justice, FTC, cellphone companies, VoIP providers, lawyers, lobbying firms

Conservative groups
Heritage Foundation, PFF, CES, Cato Institute, National Taxpayers Union

High-tech industry
Wireless Infrastructure Association (PCIA), Apple, IBM, Software Information Industry Association (SIIA), Gates Foundation

● **FIGURE 12.2** *Today, scholars generally see a more extensive network of actors influencing policy than that pictured by the classic iron triangle. Here, the issue network that influences telecommunications policy. (Based on Berry and Wilcox)*

Interest Groups and the Courts

Iron triangles and issue networks portray interest groups engaging with the two elective branches, Congress and the presidency. What about the courts, which—as you will see in Chapter 16—have a major role in federal and state policymaking? By law and custom, interest groups have almost no access to Supreme Court justices and very little connection to other federal (or senior state) judges. But interest groups still manage to weigh in on judicial decision making, even without seeing judges in person to make their case. They do so in three main ways.

Lobbying on Judicial Confirmations.   One way to shape court decisions is to influence the central players—to help determine who gets *appointed* as Supreme Court or federal judges. Each federal judge is approved by the Senate. That process used to be routine—the longest-serving current justice, like many of his predecessors, was approved unanimously. Today, however, every Supreme Court nomination immediately prompts a multimillion-dollar confirmation fight. Interest groups spend heavily on public campaigns to influence the presidents who choose judges and the senators who confirm—or block—a president's choice.

Filing Amicus Curiae ("Friend of Court") Briefs. Groups interested in a pending case are permitted to—and sometimes invited by a court to—write up legal memos, or "briefs," arguing their position on the case. Major cases attract dozens of such documents: in 2015–2016, when the Supreme Court reviewed affirmative action in the *Fisher* case involving the University of Texas, hundreds of groups and individuals filed more than seventy-five different amicus curiae briefs.

● *Choosing a justice. Supreme Court nominee Merrick Garland arrives for his Senate hearings, held in a room filled with lobbyists for interest groups—many of which spent millions of dollars seeking to influence the confirmation battle.*

Sponsoring Litigation. It can be very expensive to take a case to court. Researching the relevant issues, paying the lawyers, and pursuing litigation through multiple appeals can cost millions of dollars. Interest groups often take up a legal cause, contributing both money and expertise. When the Supreme Court agreed to review establishment clause rules about what counts as state sponsorship of religion—for example, whether government funds can go to Catholic schools or whether a state courthouse can post the Ten Commandments—interest groups such as the American Civil Liberties Union (liberal) and the Federalist Society (conservative) provided substantial expertise and financing.

THE BOTTOM LINE

» Lobbyists working in specific areas sometimes still form "iron triangles" with congressional staff and executive branch officials.

» More fluid "issue networks" featuring lobbyists as central players increasingly characterize today's complex policymaking environment.

» Successful federal lobbyists master political information gathering and analysis, engage in political campaigns, and form close ties with one of the two major parties.

» Interest groups also lobby the judicial branch by funding confirmation battles, filing amicus curiae briefs, and financing litigation.

Interest Groups and Power

Should Americans worry that interest groups are intimately involved in the details of policymaking, writing bills, and shaping legislative outcomes? Senator Henry F. Ashurst, an Arizona Democrat, once admitted bluntly: "When I have to choose between voting for the people or the special interests, I always stick to the special interests. They remember. The people forget."[13] If members of Congress are voting with or otherwise directly influenced by lobbyists, this unelected set of central actors deserves our close scrutiny—and perhaps alarm.

Lacking hard evidence about interest groups' power—Did this bill pass because lobbyists said it should, or did it pass regardless of all their politicking?—we fall back on typical measures of what matters in national politics: *numbers* and *money*. Washington insiders gauge the status of a White House agency or a special congressional committee based partly on how many staff it has. If interest groups are spending a lot to influence lawmakers, their financial input may be a clue to the return their clients are getting on their investment.

How many lobbyists work in Washington? Around 11,500 professionals registered as congressional lobbyists in 2016, but that number represents a fraction of the total. Lobbyists can avoid registering if they spend less than 20 percent of their time on "lobbying activities," a loosely defined term. Although legal penalties apply to those failing to disclose lobbying work, not one criminal case has been filed under this law. One interest group's expert offers a figure closer to 100,000, based on all the grassroots advocates, political consultants, trade association representatives, and others who can claim to be under the 20 percent threshold.[14]

Tens of thousands of lobbyists, all chasing members of Congress and their staffs, as well as White House and executive branch officials—many commentators see these numbers as decisive evidence of interest-group influence. Interest groups are increasingly active in state and local government as well. Companies that used to focus on Washington are diversifying: Google had lobbyists in just two states in 2006; today they have expanded to 30 states.[15]

Ultimately, if you measure the influence of interest groups by simple numbers, then this sector is certainly powerful. Do the numbers suggest an ability to win policy goals? Not necessarily. Recent research suggests that, as lobbying networks become denser, interest groups are better able to block undesirable legislation, but not to advance new aims.[16] That "veto power" underscores how central interest-group lobbyists have become to national, state, and local government. But the widespread notion that lobbyists are writing most bills and arranging laws' passage: No research substantiates that claim.

Interest Group Spending

Interest groups big and small, from Wall Street financial interests to California almond growers, spend an estimated eight billion dollars each year attempting to influence Washington policymaking. This does not include spending on political campaigns, an issue discussed later in this chapter.

This $8 billion figure is inexact. Official Senate and House records indicate that *registered* lobbyists reported spending nearly $3.25 billion on lobbying activities in 2015 (see Figure 12.3). Because many of those seeking to influence Congress never bother to register, analysts estimate that total spending is about 2.5 times the reported amount.[17]

Clients of private groups and members of public groups together provide those billions of dollars, which are spent on lobbyists' salaries, research costs (remember that neatly bound report!), the expense of running a Washington office, travel, and so forth. Table 12.2 lists the top-spending interest-group clients for 2015. Of the various sectors represented (healthcare, oil/gas, etc.), most of these big spenders are corporate interests. Does that fuel the "power elite" view? Or is it merely a waste of money, since business appears to lose plenty of policy battles?

When an issue of great importance to a group or industry arises in Washington, affected groups tend to boost their spending. In 2009–2010, Congress debated a climate change bill aimed to reduce Americans' use of coal and oil. Sharp spending increases on lobbying were reported by oil companies, coal-mining industries, and

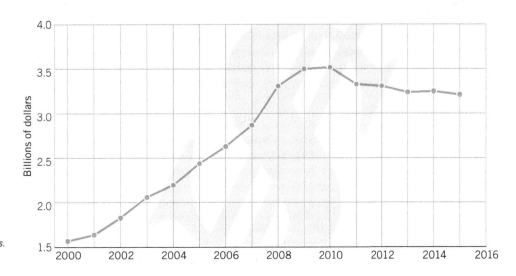

● **FIGURE 12.3** *Trends in spending by registered lobbyists, 2000–2015, in billions of dollars. (Center for Responsive Politics)*

| TABLE 12.2 | **Biggest-Spending Lobbying Clients, 2015** |

LOBBYING CLIENT	TOTAL AMOUNT SPENT
U.S. Chamber of Commerce	$84,730,000
National Assn. of Realtors	$37,788,407
Blue Cross/Blue Shield	$23,292,049
American Medical Assn.	$21,930,000
Boeing Co.	$21,921,000
General Electric	$20,920,000
American Hospital Assn.	$20,687,935
Business Roundtable	$19,250,000
Pharmaceutical Rsrch. & Mfrs. of America	$18,920,000
National Assn. of Broadcasters	$17,360,000
National Assn. of Manufacturers	$16,950,000
Alphabet Inc. (Google parent company)	$16,660,000
AT&T Inc.	$16,370,000
Comcast Corp.	$15,680,000
CVS Health	$15,230,000
Source: Center for Responsive Politics	

electric utilities. At the largest lobbying firm for utilities, Edison Electric Institute, spending jumped by 50 percent in one year, from $7 million to $10.5 million.

Some analysts look at these hikes in spending and conclude that they prove interest groups' extensive political influence. But the truth is more complicated. We might ask, for example, what the energy industry got for all its spending. Although no climate change law passed in 2010 (and still has not, more than seven years later), was this lack of success due to lobbying opposition?[18]

Our conclusion about all that money: It probably did not influence many votes. On a high-profile issue such as climate change, most members of Congress have very strong views: liberals fiercely support the legislation (unless they think it does not go far enough), while conservatives are equally strongly against it. You can predict most of the votes. What are the lobbyists spending funds on, then? They are supporting the members who agree with them, or trying to "soften up" the few members who might be persuadable on this topic. If members need facts for their speeches, lobbyists are there to provide background. That is why, in our story at the beginning of the chapter, that invaluable report landed on your desk.[19]

A clearer sign of lobbying heft may be an adjustment in a policy or specific bill. Energy companies, for example, successfully pushed to include an "offset program" in climate change legislation that allowed them to invest in projects to remove carbon dioxide from the atmosphere if they were unable to meet reduced emissions targets. This technical policy change underlines an important truth: The more

INFO/DATA: Interest Group Campaign Spending: Sector Totals, 2015–2016

Lobbyists' hundreds of millions of dollars in campaign spending is displayed in this infographic by sector. Note the dominance of financial interests (category 1) and business (4); also worth noting is that contributions to the top seven sectors can be divided roughly equally between Democrats and Republicans.

1. Does money translate into influence? Many critics allege that interest groups, especially in ■ the top-ranked sectors, are "buying" preferred policy outcomes. How would we know if this were true?

2. Think back to Chapter 10's discussion of campaign spending. Should we limit interest-group spending ■ in elections? Eliminate it altogether? What would the main obstacles be to achieving such a goal?

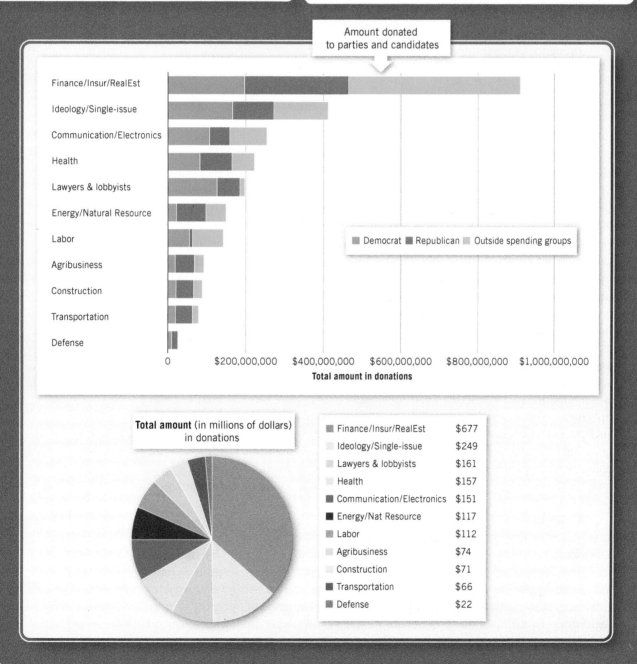

Amount donated to parties and candidates

■ Democrat   ■ Republican   ■ Outside spending groups

Total amount in donations

Total amount (in millions of dollars) in donations

Sector	Amount
Finance/Insur/RealEst	$677
Ideology/Single-issue	$249
Lawyers & lobbyists	$161
Health	$157
Communication/Electronics	$151
Energy/Nat Resource	$117
Labor	$112
Agribusiness	$74
Construction	$71
Transportation	$66
Defense	$22

Source: Center for Responsive Politics

obscure the provision, the better the chances of winning it. The less the public is aware of a topic, the more room Congress has to deliver favors.

Regulating Interest Groups

All this talk of influence leads naturally to questions about how interest groups are regulated. What are lobbyists forbidden to do in pursuit of their policy goals? For a long time, the answer was "not much." Until 1946, there were no real limits on lobbying action, though out-and-out bribery—clearly exchanging votes for money or other favors—was prohibited. That year, Congress passed the **Federal Regulation of Lobbying Act**, which required lobbyists seeking influence in the House or Senate to:

Federal Regulation of Lobbying Act: The initial U.S. statute spelling out requirements on lobbyists active in Congress, which was passed in 1946.

- *Register with Congress.* An office was opened in the Capitol—although today registration is online—for lobbyists to fill out forms (first annually, and eventually every three months) listing all clients on whose behalf they sought to influence Congress.

- *Report the amount and sources of income derived from lobbying Congress.* This line-by-line list is supposed to include all of a lobbyist's clients and how much each paid, but some lobbyists exploit the rules to keep some of their clients out of sight.

Notice the absence of any restrictions on lobbying activity. In theory, a lobbyist could accept a large sum from one client and pass those funds on to a member of Congress as a "gift." The 1946 law merely required interest-group representatives to identify both themselves and the source/amounts of their payments for lobbying.

Tighter restrictions on gift giving were imposed in 1995, following public clamor about presents, meals, and travel "junkets" for members of Congress paid for by interest groups. The House banned virtually all gifts. On the Senate side, inexpensive items such as T-shirts and other trinkets were still allowed—up to a value of fifty dollars per year for any senator from a given lobbyist. This **gift ban** law was designed to make it more difficult to "buy" favors from a member of Congress. Members and lobbyists insisted that gifts were simply tokens of friendship and esteem; critics thought otherwise.

Gift ban: A regulation that eliminates (or sharply reduces the permitted dollar amount of) gifts from interest groups to lawmakers.

Loopholes in the 1995 law swiftly appeared. The House prohibition on lobbyists buying meals for congressional members or their staff was clarified to cover only meals consumed while sitting down, presumably at a restaurant. "Finger food," such as hors d'oeuvres eaten standing up at parties, was a legitimate expense—enabling lobbyists to continue attending or even sponsoring fundraising events for congressional members. Lobbyists also could pay for a meal with lawmakers as long as the member or staffer was a "personal friend." Imagine how many new friendships were born after that ruling!

Stories like the "finger food exception" inspired a fresh round of popular outrage, sparking Congress to revisit interest-group lobbying reform. In 2007, a new Democratic majority closed many of the loopholes in the gift ban and barred senators from lobbying their former colleagues for two years after leaving the Senate. Yet today, despite continued public criticism, "junkets" and other excesses remain: interest groups continue to sponsor plentiful trips for members of Congress or state legislators. In 2016, House and Senate members took more than two thousand lobbyist-funded trips, at a cost of more than $6 million.

THE BOTTOM LINE

» Because of the difficulty of directly measuring interest-group influence in government, researchers turn to metrics like number of lobbyists and the amounts of funds they spend on lobbying.

» Beginning in the mid-1960s, an advocacy explosion saw lobbyist numbers climb dramatically. Resources devoted to lobbying also rose sharply.

» Despite their extensive presence and billions of dollars in spending, lobbyists are not likely to change congressional minds on high-profile votes; their role is more akin to supporting the members who are already on the same side. Special favors are easier to win on obscure or highly technical topics.

» Regulations on interest-group activity are relatively limited in the United States. They have been tightened lately, but loopholes remain.

Are Interest Groups Bad or Good for America?

Americans remain deeply cynical about the work of interest groups in our national polity, even as we write checks to groups involved in the causes we care about. What is wrong with interest-group activity in American government? Throughout this chapter we have explored the question of influence—whether lobbyists have too much say in national politics. Here we summarize four primary concerns, raised at various points in this chapter.

Four Concerns About Interest Groups

1. Corruption. The close connections between lobbyists and federal lawmakers arouse concerns about the unfair advantage enjoyed by lobbyist-insiders over ordinary citizens. As we saw earlier, interest groups devote more than $8 billion annually to influence policymaking and help direct hundreds of millions more to campaigns for Congress and the presidency. Does this add up to corruption at the core of American government?

Jack Abramoff would fit right into a nineteenth-century lobbyist's portrait: well connected, high-living . . . and thoroughly corrupt. Over more than a decade of lobbying, "Casino Jack" flouted the rules by spending millions of dollars to offer lawmakers lavish international trips, expensive meals and parties, and other illegal perks. When the scandal broke, more than one hundred members of Congress and several state officials hastily returned or donated to charity campaign contributions from Abramoff. The powerful House majority leader Tom DeLay (R-TX) resigned his leadership position because of close ties to the disgraced lobbyist.

Abramoff's case seems to demonstrate the widespread corruption of interest-group lobbying. But, ironically, it may reflect just the opposite. In Washington, with an alert news media always ready to leap on a scandal, no other lobbyist in recent years has been charged with anything similar.[20]

2. Division and Demosclerosis. Critics also worry about interest groups' divisive influence. Former Harvard president Derek Bok wrote that "America no longer seems diverse; it seems divided into innumerable special interests . . . gray power, gay power, red power, black power; the sun belt and the frost belt; environmentalists and hard hats; industrial groups, professional groups, educational groups: all more conscious of their rights, all more aware of their claims on the rest of society. This process seems less and less satisfactory, either to participants or to the whole public."[21]

Bok's view taps into an old debate about whether individual preferences add up to the "public good." Does any collective interest transcend the selfish demands of specific interest groups? Alexis de Tocqueville praised Americans' tendency to form voluntary associations to achieve political ends. Modern public interest groups, however, seem like pale shadows of the lively civic bodies Tocqueville applauded.

A related concern, introduced earlier in this chapter, is "demosclerosis": the fear that the crush of lobbyists hinders decisive political action. Interest groups, say their critics, clog the arteries of our political system, creating the political equivalent of a stalled heart: gridlock. On the 2016 presidential campaign trail, former Florida governor and presidential son and brother Jeb Bush blasted the "swarms of lobbyists" holding sway in Washington—until reporters noted that he had once registered as a lobbyist himself.[22]

3. Accountability. America's leaders are accountable to the people, thanks to our frequent national elections. Furthermore, the recall power allows the public to vote leaders out of office before they have finished the term they were elected to. Interest-group lobbyists face no such public accountability, despite their significant roles in influencing debates and policymakers. No lobbyist is elected by the people, and few legal controls regulate their activities.

4. Restricted Access. Interest groups are an increasingly important way of bringing public concerns before our national officials. Yet not all segments of the population are equally represented: Some political science research suggests that barriers to representation have become higher as interest-group mobilization has expanded in recent years.[23] Unequal access is the result. Political sociologists Theda Skocpol and Vanessa Williamson summarized the concern: "Over the past few decades, attentive and well-resourced business lobbying organizations [have] gained enormous influence over what issues came up for debate, and they were able to block or insert critical provisions in legislation making its way through Congress and in rules taking shape within administrative agencies."[24]

Though blatantly corrupt acts like Abramoff's may be rare, on this view the real scandal is not in lavish trips or fancy meals. Instead, the U.S. political system may face a more fundamental problem: the proliferation of interest groups and lobbyist bias tilts democracy toward the wealthy and the powerful.

These four arguments constitute a sobering set of critiques, fueling the pressure for reform that has occupied Congress in recent years.

Four Defenses of Interest Groups

There is another side of the story—one not often told in a contemporary political discourse that portrays interest groups as agents of corruption and inequality—that may help to moderate this negative view. Early in this chapter we looked at how interest groups may be useful to you and other group members; let us turn now to the possible benefits that interest groups provide for all of us.

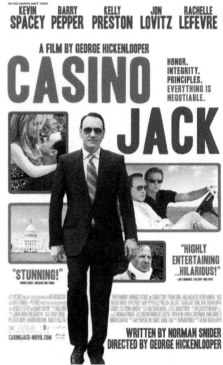

Interest-group corruption, Hollywood style: Kevin Spacey as disgraced lobbyist Jack Abramoff.

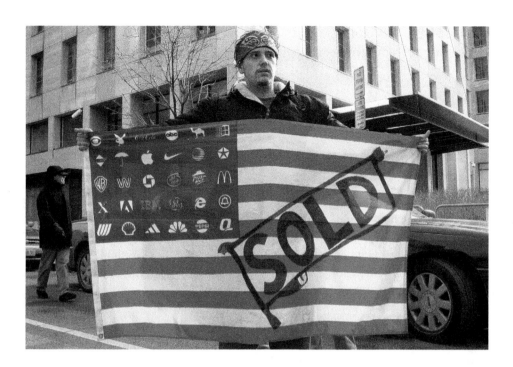

Do interest groups representing large corporations have greater access—and therefore power—than other groups? This protester certainly thinks so.

1. More Democratic Representation. In this view, the proliferation of interest groups, and their tight links with party officials, furthers the democratization of American politics. The growing number of groups over the past three decades translates into better representation of a wide range of interests. Not *all* interests, however: People seeking assistance from government typically must possess some combination of resources, organization, and a favorable political context.[25] Even so, advocates' ability to negotiate the system—and link directly to lawmakers and party leaders—means that many Americans and their interests are well represented today.

2. Communication and Information. Conveying citizen views to officials and providing the population with information about government activities are essential features of any democratic polity. Such two-way communication is facilitated by constant exchanges between interest groups and the members or private clients they represent. Thanks to technological advances in communication, as well as innovative tactics developed in part by interest groups, any interested citizen has vast quantities of information available with only a few mouse clicks.

Likewise, Capitol Hill and the executive branch are inundated with information about public (and corporate) concerns—ideally permitting lawmakers to analyze more information and hear more points of view before reaching a decision. Additional information and new perspectives can inform both public and official preferences, thus enhancing the democratic deliberative process.

3. Mobilizing and Organizing the Public. America's mass political parties originally came into existence to mobilize the vast number of voters entering the system after the expansion of suffrage beyond property holders. Parties still play an important mobilizing role, but their work is supplemented in essential ways by interest groups. Issue advocacy, along with other group activity to mobilize public concern, appears to spur at least modest increases in turnout among voters.[26] It also may encourage more participation in other respects, as citizens are inspired to write their members of Congress and otherwise get involved.

What Do You Think?

How Much Influence Should Interest Groups Have in American Government?

	Less influence.	**About the same amount.**	**More influence.**
Think about the four concerns and the four defenses described in this section and about our discussion of influence a few pages back. Then ask yourself: How much influence *should* interest groups have in American government?	Interest groups and lobbyists are a serious problem for democracy and good government, and their influence must be limited—or the power elite will continue to control politics and policy in America.	Madison's observation long ago still holds: limiting groups' ability to form and seek influence is worse than the excesses of lobbying influence. We should, however, vigorously enforce existing regulations on lobbying.	Despite their poor reputation, interest groups enhance democracy and good government. As pluralists rightly note, when the public wants something from government, interest groups help us obtain it.

4. Stability. The flip side of demosclerosis—in which the crush of lobbyists slows down our separated-powers system of policymaking—is *stability*. One virtue of the U.S. system, in some people's eyes, is its remarkable longevity. Approaching 230 years after the Constitution was ratified, we see relatively few changes in our basic way of carrying out national government.

James Madison's fundamental concern about factional influence led him to recommend the proliferation of interests and sects, preventing any handful of powers from gaining enduring control over public policy. The legacy of that view exists today: Interest-group activity is so extensive, featuring strong positions on every side of most issues, that the policymaking system inches along very slowly. It is difficult to mount innovative new policy programs, or even pass new legislation, given the army of lobbyists and formal party leaders seeking to rewrite, add amendments to, or kill outright most bills.

In summary, the interest-group story is a paradoxical one. One principal result of all the heaving and pushing, effort and striving, by thousands of lobbyists in Washington may be greater stability in policy formation and governance. Whether the four benefits described here outweigh the dangers we described above is the ultimate puzzle of interest groups and democracy.

THE BOTTOM LINE

» Critics of interest groups in American governance variously claim that they are corrupt, too numerous, lack accountability through elections or other means, and/or enjoy access to lawmakers that ordinary citizens usually can't achieve.

» Supporters of interest groups might respond that they enhance democratic representation, help communicate popular views to public officials (and in turn report on government actions to their members), mobilize people for action, or that their sheer numbers enhance the stability and predictability of American government.

🔴 Conclusion: Interest-Group Influence Revisited

To help spur your thinking on the essential matter of group influence, we end with a final question: How might we better tap the potential benefits of interest-group activity while minimizing the dangers? If national policymakers work to keep the political process open and transparent, their efforts can enable more groups to gain access—and to help ensure something like a level playing field for all of us.

Public officials can also strive to ensure that the least well-off sectors of our society—typically those poorly represented by interest groups—receive enhanced representation. As you have seen throughout this book, some Americans are uneasy about a government that stitches together a safety net of welfare benefits, healthcare, and other essential services for people down on their luck. The powerful and the wealthy have plenty of voices looking after their concerns in Washington. A fair system can ensure that the thousands of groups that support the least powerful will get the sanction and resources needed to make our interest-group society one that embraces every member.

CHAPTER SUMMARY

🔵 Interest-group lobbying has long been a vital feature of U.S. government and politics. Lobbyists are deeply engaged in all parts of our policymaking system, and groups have sprung up to represent virtually every imaginable professional, personal, and identity-based interest, providing their members with information about federal policies and conveying those members' concerns to Washington. Yet Americans hold lobbyists in very low regard.

🔵 Public anxiety centers on interest groups' reputed power to affect policymaking. Groups spend billions of dollars each year to advance their views, and lobbyists swarm over Washington (and, increasingly, state capitals) in vast numbers. It is not clear, however, what all this activity adds up to.

🔵 Although critics insist that lobbyist influence in shaping government outcomes is extensive, political science research has not turned up definitive evidence in support. And the proliferation of groups on all sides of most issues tends to mean that even if one sector (e.g., business) gains

the upper hand in Washington, the pendulum eventually swings to the other side, and other sectors (e.g., public interest groups) win a string of policy victories.

🔵 A long history of interest group involvement in American national and state politics was punctuated by an "advocacy explosion" that began in the 1960s. In recent years, interest-group representatives have been getting younger— and many more women have entered the lobbying profession. Today, lobbyists perform a wide range of roles, from testifying on policy issues before Congress to acting as full-service "concierges" on behalf of their private or public interest clients. Advocacy or membership groups have a harder time retaining members and must appeal to a mix of benefits: material, solidarity, and expressive.

🔵 Interest groups are active in all three branches of government; in each, they both seek and provide information—the currency of politics. They also work on (and help finance) political campaigns and are closely intertwined with the leadership of both the Republican and the Democratic parties.

The central presence of interest groups in the halls of government has led—across U.S. history—to calls for reform, including banning lobbyists altogether. At least partly balancing the dangers that interest groups pose are a set of benefits they provide, including boosting democratic representation and contributing to the long-lived stability of American politics and governance.

KEY TERMS

STUDY QUESTIONS

1. What is an interest group, and what are their main roles in the American political system? What are the different types of interest groups? How did the groups (and the lobbyists they employ) proliferate so widely in American national politics?

2. Name the three main theories about the effects of interest groups (pluralism, for example, is one). Describe each.

3. After reading the chapter, which of the theories in Question 2 seems to you most accurate? Justify your answer.

4. Describe the traditional iron triangle. Explain the issue network that has now replaced it in large part.

5. What is the free rider problem? Name three types of benefits that interest groups provide to overcome the free rider problem.

6. Describe three ways that interest groups try to affect Supreme Court decisions.

7. One of the most important elements to lobbying success is gathering information. Explain how and why.

8. Describe four primary concerns about interest groups (summarized at the end of the chapter).

9. Describe four defenses of interest groups. Are there any you would add, based on your reading?

10. Researchers have not made much headway in specifying interest-group influence. Can you imagine any better ways to accurately measure lobbyists' influence on American policymaking?

11. Think of the interest group that represents you the best. Is it a group that works on a specific issue, such as gun control or lower taxes? Or is it one representing a specific "identity" group, as in women or Latinos or LGBTQ people? Or is it a geographically based organization, concerned with the interests of Texans or New Englanders or mountain states residents? Or, perhaps, is the group organized around a partisan or ideological perspective? Why is that group your preferred representative?

12. What do you think the effects might be of the trend toward younger and more female lobbyists? Can you imagine any changes in how lobbyists do their work or the effect of interest groups on the policy system?

 Go to www.oup.com/us/Morone to find quizzes, flash cards, simulations, tutorials, videos, and other study tools.

Congress

SENATOR TED CRUZ (R-TX) stood before the Senate and spoke for 21 hours. He blasted the Obama Administration, pledged to "speak until I am no longer able to stand," traded insults with Democrats, and even read Dr. Seuss's *Green Eggs and Ham*. Senator Cruz was leading a brash plan to defund the Affordable Care Act (ACA; also known as Obamacare). The battle offers a snapshot of partisan conflict that entangles Congress today.

The ACA story had begun in the House of Representatives in March 2009. Over four months, three different House committees produced two different bills. The Speaker of the House at the time, Nancy Pelosi (D-CA)—the first female Speaker in American history—worked to combine elements of both bills into a single Act. Pelosi and her top lieutenants met with different groups in the House: conservative Blue Dogs, the liberal Progressive Caucus, the Congressional Black Caucus, the Hispanic Caucus, abortion opponents, and others. Each wanted to add to or subtract from the bill. After bargaining for seven feverish months, Pelosi brought the legislation to the House floor; after a fierce all-day debate (with sparks flying about whether abortion would be covered), the legislation squeaked through by a vote of 220 to 215 as the clock moved toward midnight.

In the Senate (with its one hundred members), two more committees produced two *more* bills—making five different versions, each one topping a thousand pages. The Senate majority leader, Harry Reid (D-NV), then hammered out a compromise Senate-style: Reid met not with separate groups but one by one with individual senators, searching for the magic sixty votes. After eight months of negotiating, and compromise, an exhausted Senate voted yes at 7:15 a.m. on December 24. Now, the House and Senate had to negotiate the differences between their bills: add three more months of horse trading and negotiation. Throughout the process, only one Republican voted for the legislation. When the ACA finally passed, the very next day Republicans introduced legislation to repeal the new law. This is, to put it mildly, an excruciating way to manage a legislative branch. The new law energized the Republican Party, which won control of the House in 2010, the Senate in 2014, and the presidency in 2016.[1]

When Ted Cruz launched into his day-long filibuster, he and his conservative allies tried a new tack: They threatened to cut funding to the federal

- Learn what Congress does.

- Reflect on how well Congress represents the people.

- Examine the internal workings of Congress.

- Consider the importance of skilled congressional leadership.

- Think about the problems that face Congress—and some possible solutions.

● *U.S. Senate Majority Leader Mitch McConnell (R-KY) promises an active legislative agenda as a new congressional session gets underway. Bitter party polarization in recent years, resulting in legislative inaction, has led scholars to term the modern Congress a "broken branch" of government.*

373

government. Indeed, on October 1, the start of the new fiscal year, the government shut down. From Yellowstone Park to the National Institutes of Health (which funds biomedical research), all nonessential government services came to a halt. As public criticism grew, the Republican House leadership backed down.[2]

The government reopened, but the partisan tensions did not go away—nor have they since. Observers note something dramatic: the 112th (2011–2012) and the 113th (2013–2014) Congresses each were close to breaking the record for passing the fewest laws in history. The list of stalled major legislative initiatives continues: In 2016, for example, Congress took no action on several issues receiving majority support in public-opinion polls, including restricting assault weapons, allocating significant funding to fight the mosquito-borne Zika virus, or even passing a federal budget. To top off this dismal record, the Senate, for the first time in modern history, refused to even consider a president's nominee to the Supreme Court.

Many analysts now dub Congress the "broken branch" of American government. They criticize the Senate for its archaic filibuster and the House for its angry partisanship. As one respected former Congressman put it, "People are fretting about everything from control of our borders to stagnant wages and the spread of ISIS. On Capitol Hill, no one seems particularly concerned."[3] Only after the 2016 election, with Republicans controlling both chambers of the 115th Congress and the presidency, did it appear possible that the gridlock might ease.

Who are we? A vibrant people who are suspicious of government. Congress builds that suspicion right into its governing process: It is very difficult to introduce important changes. This raises the key question about Congress today: Is it indeed "the broken branch of government"? Or does it reflect the spirit of the American nation by slowing the government down and ensuring that deliberation and stability are the rule? Keep these two different views in mind as we explore Congress.

🗩 Introducing Congress

The Constitution places Congress at the center of American government. The document's first and longest article provides a detailed accounting of legislative organization and authority (Table 13.1).

This is a formidable set of powers. For most of American history, Congress ruled. After the Civil War, President Andrew Johnson brooded in the White House while Congress passed bill after bill redefining the nation, including the postwar Constitutional amendments ending slavery and guaranteeing voting rights to black Americans—which President Johnson ineffectually opposed. A half-century later, when Senator Warren Harding won the presidential election of 1920, one of his old Senate buddies told him to "sign whatever bills the Senate sends you . . . and don't send bills for the Senate to pass."[4]

By the middle of the twentieth century, however, Congress had become increasingly deferential to the White House, especially in foreign affairs. Today, the nation looks first to the president to manage the economy, deploy troops, address

BY THE NUMBERS

Congress

Percentage of Americans who approved of Congress, fall 2016 polls: **13**
Percentage of House members re-elected in 2012: **90**
Percentage of House members re-elected in 2014: **95**
Percentage of House members re-elected in 2016: **97**
Percentage of Senators re-elected in 2006: **79**
Percentage of Senators re-elected in 2016: **90**

Number of African Americans in the Senate, 1950: **0**
Number of African Americans in the Senate, 2017: **3**
Number of African Americans who have ever served a full term in the Senate: **3**

Number of women in the House of Representatives, 1949: **7**
Percentage of those women who were Republicans, 1949: **57**
Number of women in the House of Representatives, 2017: **83**
Percentage of those women who were Republicans, 2017: **25**
Percentage of women in European legislatures (average): **35**
U.S. rank out of 189 countries, for number of women in national legislatures: **97**

Annual salary for Member of Congress: **$174,000**
House Speaker Paul Ryan's annual salary: **$223,500**
Former Majority Leader Eric Cantor's 2015 compensation (after losing his 2014 GOP
   primary and leaving Congress): **$3.4 million**

TABLE 13.1 Constitutional Powers of Congress

From Article 1, Section 8 (unless otherwise noted).*
Financial. Power to raise revenue through taxes and borrowing, pay national debts, "provide for the common defense and general welfare," and regulate trade and commerce among the American states and with other countries.
Legal. Power to establish U.S. citizenship laws, regulate bankruptcy laws, issue U.S. money, punish counterfeiters, establish a patent system ("to promote the progress of science and useful arts"), fix national weights/measures standards, and enact laws subject to presidential approval. Impeach presidents and federal judges.
Institutional. Power to organize the judicial and executive branches, establish a postal system (Article 2, Sec. 2), set up and control the national capital (since 1797, in Washington, DC), admit new states, and exercise control over U.S. territories (Article 3, Sec. 3). Alter or amend the time, place, and manner of states' election laws related to congressional elections (Article I, Sec. 4).
National defense. Power to declare war, regulate rules for prisoners of war, and raise and fund the U.S. Army, Navy, and other defense forces.
Additional congressional powers are provided by constitutional amendment. For example, the Thirteenth (1865), Fourteenth (1868), and Fifteenth (1870) Amendments authorize Congress to enforce African Americans' civil rights, as you read in Chapter 6.

crises, and pursue policy objectives, although Congress retains its powers to introduce, debate, and pass all legislation. We call health reform "Obamacare" even though Congress worked out most of the details.

Still, Congress remains near the center of American government. Presidents may command more public attention, but they need cooperation from the House and Senate to advance their policies. We judge presidents in part on whether their programs win approval from Congress, as you will see in Chapter 14. Moreover, Congress's importance extends far beyond the vital responsibility of lawmaking. As much as any other actor or institution in U.S. government, it is Congress that answers the question, *Who are we?*

Two Houses, Different Styles

Congress reflects two faces of the American people in its basic makeup. Like most other national legislatures, Congress is bicameral comprising "two houses." The *House of Representatives* is the larger chamber and includes 435 members, divided among the states based on population size, along with six nonvoting delegates from Washington, DC, Puerto Rico, American Samoa, Guam, and other U.S. territories. All 441 House members serve two-year terms, and each represents a district of around seven hundred thousand people.

115th Congress: The Congress elected in November 2016, meeting in 2017–2018. The first Congress met in 1789–1790. Each Congress is elected for a two-year session and numbered consecutively.

The House is organized around a relatively clear set of rules and procedures. The majority party wields centralized control through a powerful leadership team. In the **115th Congress** (which holds office during 2017–2018), Republicans are in the majority; this makes the GOP leader the Speaker of the House (currently Paul Ryan) and permits him to control which issues reach the **floor**, and frequently to get them passed.

Floor: The full chamber, either in the House of Representatives or the Senate. A bill "goes to the floor" for the final debate and vote.

The Senate is made up of just one hundred members, two from each U.S. state, each elected for a six-year term. The Democrats lost the Senate in 2014, Republicans retained a slim majority after 2016.. Back in the nineteenth century, an old truism (sometimes attributed to Mark Twain) declared "every senator a little king."[5] To this day, each Senator possesses a remarkable degree of autonomy, especially compared to the average House member. Any senator—even the most junior—is able to halt the entire body's consideration of a bill merely by placing a **legislative hold** on it.

Legislative hold: An informal way for a senator to object to a bill or other measure reaching the Senate floor. The action effectively halts Senate proceedings on that issue, sometimes for weeks or longer.

For example, the Senate must vote approval for every U.S. ambassador nominated by the president. Normally, this is a routine formality. Cassandra Butts, an experienced government worker, was proposed in 2014 as new ambassador to the Bahamas. She excitedly awaited confirmation. Months, then years came and went: first Senator Cruz put a hold on all nominations of State Department officials because he was upset about a U.S. treaty with Iran. Then Senator Tom Cotton (R-Arkansas) put holds on Butts as well as nominees for ambassadors to Sweden and Norway. What troubled Senator Cotton? A complaint about a Secret Service leak of private information, unrelated to Butts or the Bahamas. Cotton wanted the administration's attention, so he did what any senator may: bring the body to a halt with a one-man veto.[6]

Filibuster: Rule unique to the U.S. Senate that allows any senator to hold the floor indefinitely and thereby delay a vote on a bill to which he or she objects. Ended only when sixty senators vote for cloture.

Popular American culture, in films such as *Mr. Smith Goes to Washington* featuring a noble **filibuster**—"democracy's finest show"—celebrates the lone senator standing up bravely for justice. But much of the time these stands involve narrowly focused issues, such as Senator Cotton's.

The two congressional chambers present a familiar contrast in the United States. Americans, as we saw in Chapter 2, embrace direct democracy—and the centralized House can move swiftly on national legislative priorities. Americans also fear government power and seek stability: enter the independent senators, slowing legislation down with filibusters and holds. Legend has it that Thomas Jefferson, who had been in Paris during the Constitutional Convention, asked George Washington why the Constitution established two chambers in Congress. "Why," responded Washington, "do you pour your tea into the saucer?" "To cool it," replied Jefferson. "Just so," returned Washington, "we pour House legislation into the senatorial saucer to cool it." Whether the exchange actually took place, it neatly captures the traditional contrast between House and Senate.[7]

● *Swearing in a new Congress.*

An essential question for Americans today is whether the Senate is too good at the task of cooling legislation. Cooperation between the two parties, essential for getting around the filibuster, has diminished—the tone in the once courtly Senate now increasingly resembles the partisan House. Across the United States, schoolteachers, police officers, state health officials, and everyone else dependent on federal funding had to wait for agonizing months in 2016 while the Senate and House bickered over a federal budget while missing deadline after deadline. Imagine trying to plan for a new school year or organize a Mars launch with no idea what your budget will be. Do we need a more nimble and responsive government in the twenty-first century? Or is the senatorial function of slowing things down more important than ever?[8]

see for yourself 13.1

Go online to see Senator Smith's noble filibuster in *Mr. Smith Goes to Washington*.

The House and Senate Each Have Unique Roles

The Constitution also grants each branch a measure of unique authority. All budget measures must originate in the House (because until 1913 it was the only chamber elected directly by the public; now both are). The House holds the power to impeach public officials—including the president—for "high crimes and misdemeanors." After the House impeaches (or indicts) an officeholder, the Senate holds a trial and decides whether to remove him or her. The Senate has exclusive authority over two important matters. The president negotiates treaties with other countries, but the Senate must approve them by two-thirds majority. Sixty-seven votes is a very high bar in today's politics, and, as we will see in Chapter 14, presidents have found some creative ways around it.

What Do You Think?

Senate Filibusters

Should senators be allowed to hold up legislative initiatives indefinitely, or at least until their opposition can round up sixty votes to stop their stalling action? What do you think?	**Yes.** Filibusters ensure independence and protect minority rights. They are also a time-honored tradition. Slowing government down remains a good idea.	**No.** The sixty-vote rule makes a mockery of simple majority rule and causes gridlock, slowing policy-making to a crawl. It is time to rewrite Senate rules and end the filibuster.	**Not sure.** You may want to ponder this question as you read the rest of the chapter.

The Senate also has sole power to review presidential appointments—the Constitution calls it "advice and consent." Each nominee for the Supreme Court, for example must win confirmation by the Senate. Here is another place where some political scientists see a broken branch: In 2016 there were seventy-three court vacancies, including one on the Supreme Court. The Republican Senate blocked the Democratic White House's appointees. Again the question: A broken branch? Or a healthy limit on an administration that had already appointed 325 federal judges to lifetime posts (including two to the Supreme Court)?

THE BOTTOM LINE

» Congressional powers, as granted under the Constitution, are extensive and very clearly defined.

» America's Congress is bicameral: The House has 435 members (plus six nonvoting members) who are elected every two years. The one hundred senators serve six-year terms.

» The two houses of Congress reflect different national priorities. Populists appreciate the responsive House; advocates of stability embrace the more deliberate Senate, where rules like the filibuster make it more difficult to pass legislation.

» Less legislation and more partisanship has Congress watchers debating: Is this a broken branch of government?

Congressional Representation

Members of Congress represent their constituents in multiple ways. They must live in the same state or district—which is known as *geographic* representation. They share views about political issues—or *substantive* representation. Another angle is *descriptive* representation, which measures the extent to which they resemble the people they represent in terms of race, ethnicity, gender, age, national origin, and so on. Citizens sometimes have to choose between descriptive representation (she is the same gender, race, ethnicity, and/or religion as I am) and substantive representation (she does not look like me but believes what I believe).[9]

Does Congress Reflect America?

A half-century ago, every senator was white. Only two African American members sat in the House of Representatives. Today, Congress more closely resembles the country it represents—in some respects.

As Figure 13.1 shows, the Congressional Black Caucus (one of several **congressional caucus** groups) has now grown to include forty-eight members (including two nonvoting representatives from Washington, DC, and the Virgin Islands). Among House Democrats, nearly one in four representatives is black. Latinos have had a slower time breaking into Congress, but their recent rise in numbers is also striking. Thirty-eight members are Hispanic. Thirteen members are Asian and two are Native American.

Despite the growth, Congress has a long way to go before it reflects America. Overall, only 21 percent of the House and just 9 percent of the Senate are members of racial minorities—compared to 36.7 percent of the population.

see for yourself 13.2

Go online to access an interactive map of African Americans in the House and Senate throughout U.S. history.

Congressional caucus:
A group of House or Senate members who convene regularly to discuss common interests; they may share political outlook, race, gender, or geography.

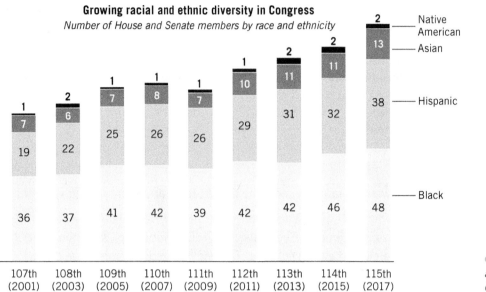

Growing racial and ethnic diversity in Congress
Number of House and Senate members by race and ethnicity

FIGURE 13.1 *Growing racial and ethnic diversity in Congress. (Pew Research Center)*

What Do You Think?

Who Really Represents You?

Which do you consider more important—descriptive or substantive representation?	**Descriptive representation.** Race, ethnicity, gender, sexual orientation, and/or class are crucial to representation. Someone cannot really speak for me if he or she has not experienced the world as I have.	**Substantive representation.** It doesn't matter if someone looks like me as long as he or she effectively represents my views. Someone who does not share my political outlook is not going to represent me well.	**Not sure.** There may be no right answer to this question—political theorists have long argued about which to emphasize. Think about how you might combine these two positions.

Jeannette Rankin (R-MT) was the first woman elected to the House, in 1916. She fought for women's suffrage, Prohibition, and workers' rights during her first term. Many years later, in 1941, Rankin returned to the House for a second term (by then, there were six other female members). As a confirmed pacifist, she was one of fifty members to vote against U.S. entry into World War I, and the only member to vote against declaring war on Japan after the attack on Pearl Harbor in 1941.

Among historically underrepresented groups, the number of women in Congress has risen most rapidly. The House had twenty female members in 1966, thirty by the late 1980s, and eighty-three in 2017. Still, just 20 percent of the House, compared to 52 percent of the nation, is female. In the Senate in 2017, there were a record twenty-one women—also 21 percent of the chamber. The United States ranks ninety-seventh among legislatures around the globe on the percentage of women in the larger national chamber (our House). Some nations *require* a certain percentage of women. That is easier to do in a parliamentary system, where the parties choose the candidates, than in the United States, where candidates declare themselves and run in primary elections for the nominations.

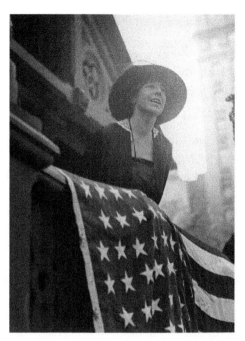

Representative Jeannette Rankin (R-MT), the first woman in Congress. She was first elected in 1916—before the Nineteenth Amendment legally enfranchised women in all states.

These numbers are a far cry from parity. On the other hand, we might marvel at how things are changing. When your parents were in school, female, black, or Latino members of Congress were a rarity—and their political science textbooks did not even mention the fact. Today, the numbers are at an all-time high.

The religious makeup of Congress has changed dramatically over the last half-century. Until recently, it was overwhelmingly Protestant: In one telling remark, a House member asked in 1958 why the Israelis and Arabs could not settle their differences "like good Christians."[10] Today, Catholics make up 31 percent of Congress (reflecting their proportion of the population); Jews represent 5 percent of the House and 9 percent of the Senate (more than two times the percentage in the population); there are sixteen Mormons, two Muslims, two Buddhists, one Hindu, and one atheist in Congress today. The most religiously diverse Congress in U.S. history reflects the growing diversity of America itself.

The descriptive question—Does Congress look like the American people?—reflects just one mode of representation. Some critics question the value of this idea (consider this matter yourself in What Do You Think? Who Really Represents You?). If you are a conservative, evangelical woman who deeply believes in the right to life, you may not be thrilled to hear that Nancy Pelosi (a liberal who strongly supports abortion rights) is the most powerful woman in the House of Representatives. She represents you descriptively (you are both women) but not substantively (you share few of the same ideas or policy preferences). You might say that former Speaker Pelosi does not represent your interests at all.

Trustees and Delegates

Each member of Congress—in fact, every representative in any organization—faces the same conundrum: Do what you think is right? Or do what your constituents want?

Do the Right Thing. One view holds that representatives owe us their best judgment. They sit in the House or Senate, with considerably more information than their constituents. Just like your doctor or your lawyer, your House and Senate members' job is to pursue what is best for you. And if you disagree with the result, you can always vote for their opponent in the next election. This perspective is known as the *trustee* view of representation.

On a lot of issues, members of Congress must rely on their best judgment, or that of their staff. Constituents often have no strongly held views. Most people do not care whether their senators voted to approve the president's choice for deputy undersecretary of commerce, or whether the technical corrections bill updating an obscure public law passes.

Do What the People Want. Another view holds that true representation involves House or Senate members faithfully following popular preferences. A lot of choices before Congress have to do with basic values. You do not need more information to know how you feel about the right to own guns, or whether healthcare is a universal human right. A legislator, according to this view, should take voting instructions directly from his or her constituents. This is the *delegate* view of representation.

Political scientists recognize that the rules help tilt individuals one way or another (here is the institutional perspective again). When the Constitutional framers required members of the House to run every two years, they favored the delegate view: Pay close attention to the people, or you will be out of a job. Each senator has six years between elections; the rules practically instruct them to be trustees, to act as they think best.

What ultimately makes for good representation? The theoretical answer is simple: *Representatives effectively pursue their constituents' substantive interests.* The trick comes in figuring out what those interests are and promoting them through the complicated legislative process. Eventually, at election time, the people will judge whether their members of Congress effectively pursued their interests. To political scientists, this is how a well-operating representative system works.

This theorizing barely registers with most members of the House and Senate. They come to Congress with a clear perspective that informs nearly all of their important votes. They rarely stay up late at night pondering what stance to take on gun rights or on national health insurance. The answers are part of their basic philosophy, forged years before they arrived in Congress. Most politicians do not pander—at least not on large, visible issues. They know what they believe, and despite popular wisdom, they rarely say merely what they think their audience wants to hear.[11] However, a great outcry from the constituency over an issue will often moderate a member's strongly held views. It is often safer to do nothing and blame the other members for the outcome.

What Do You Think?

Two Views of Representation

The trustee and the delegate views are both legitimate ways to represent people. Do what you think best—or do what the people tell you to do. On every issue, each representative must decide how to weigh these two key factors. Ask yourself how you would act as a member of the Senate or House.

Delegate. I take my voting instructions directly from my constituents. I don't think I would be properly representing them if I didn't follow their wishes.

Trustee. I am more inclined to be a trustee and do what I believe to be the right thing on behalf of my constituents. If they disagree, I will have to persuade them in the next election campaign.

Not sure. Perhaps the answer depends on the issue. If you take this middle ground, think about the types of issues that would make you a delegate or a trustee.

» Members of the House and Senate represent Americans in multiple ways. These include the following:

1. *Geographic representation*: Constitutional election rules say members must live in the state or district they represent.
2. *Descriptive representation*: Does the assembly look like the people?
3. *Substantive representation*: Do members of Congress effectively pursue constituent interests?

» Along with these different styles of representation, members can act as delegates or trustees. Representatives can faithfully follow what the people want or do as their political experience, instincts, and core principles dictate.

Getting to Congress—And Staying There

How do members of Congress spend their days? From occasional glimpses of C-SPAN, you might imagine Congress as a sustained feast of debates, but members of the House and the Senate spend relatively little time on the floor. Table 13.2 displays the typical workweek of a member of the House, taken from a survey. Not a lot of time left for quietly contemplating the major issues of the day, is there?

The Permanent Campaign

Congressional members spend a great deal of time on the campaign trail. House members face the voters every two years—more frequently than most other national legislatures. Even senators, with a more comfortable six years between races, must keep their campaign operation, especially fundraising, humming along. Notice, in Table 13.2, that the members spend as much time raising money as they

TABLE 13.2 **Average Division of Time of a U.S. House Member**

Meeting with staff (mostly in Washington)	19%
Meeting with constituents (mostly in district)	19%
Ceremonial events (in district; some in Washington)	15%
Fundraising calls/meetings	9%
Committee meetings (hearings, member meetings)	8%
Floor action (votes, debates, morning business)	7%
Office work (email, reading, legislative drafting)	6%
Informal talks (with colleagues, lobbyists, media)	6%
Caucus meetings (all-party or subgroup gatherings)	5%
Other (miscellaneous)	5%
Source: Congressional Management Foundation	

do on committee meetings or floor action. Does this constant pressure to attract donations and remind voters of their virtues discourage members of Congress, or potential candidates, from running? As we saw in Chapter 10, most representatives stay in office a long time. And when a seat in either chamber opens because of retirement or death, a long list of office seekers from both parties is usually ready to run.

A major dispute at the Constitutional Convention involved whether the people could be trusted to vote directly for members of Congress. Recall the original compromise: House members would be elected directly, while senators were to be insulated from the whims of public opinion and chosen by state legislatures.

As western states joined the Union, their legislatures turned Senate elections over to the people (westerners were also first to grant women the vote); the entire nation began voting for senators in 1913 when the Seventeenth Amendment was ratified. Did the state legislatures pick more elevated senators than the people did (as the constitutional framers expected)? Not necessarily. In the very first congressional elections, for example, Virginia's legislature passed over James Madison for the Senate; the people of his district had better sense and elected him to the House, where he immediately pushed through the Bill of Rights.

Another important influence on U.S. House elections is **reapportionment**. As we discussed in Chapter 10, every ten years the U.S. census determines which states have gained or lost population, and because each district is the same size, House seats are reapportioned accordingly. In 2010, for example, Texas gained four new seats, Florida gained two, and New York and Ohio each lost two. The new districts are drawn by the state legislature, and, as we saw in Chapter 10, fierce political battles surround the way lines are drawn.

Reapportionment: Reorganization of the boundaries of House districts, a process that follows the results of the U.S. census taken every ten years. District lines are redrawn to ensure rough equality in the number of constituents represented by each House member.

Home Style: Back in the District

New members of Congress—and most long-serving representatives and senators, for that matter—spend a lot of time back in their district or state. Often they are literally returning home to families who have decided to stay in San Francisco or St. Louis or Scranton, rather than making the move to Washington. Today, over 100 conservative House members proudly refuse to settle into a Washington residence and sleep on a cot in their office. Most members leave Washington on Thursday evenings and only return on Monday evening or even Tuesday morning, unless House or Senate votes are scheduled on a Friday or Monday.

Back home in their constituency, members are kept hopping. District staff line up events for them to attend every morning, afternoon, and evening. Members spend this time meeting with constituents, giving talks about Washington issues (and hearing plenty of advice about how to do things better), cutting ribbons on new ballparks or office buildings or schools, visiting with local party leaders and elected officials, and—as always—raising funds for their next election.

A Government of Strangers

In the past—before jets, advanced technology, and modern campaigns—members of Congress lived in Washington. Senators or representatives worked together during the day and socialized at night and over the weekends. In fact, a bar for members, called the Hole in the Wall, was located between the House and Senate chambers.

Today, most legislators are not in Washington long enough to get to know one another. They dash in, spend three days packed with congressional business, and dash home. This schedule makes it very difficult for Congress to get things done, because it is now a collection of strangers. The tortured legislative process—described at the start of this chapter—is further complicated by the lack of personal relations.

Why do the members insist on rushing home each week? Because it helps them win re-election—an ever-present concern for most members. In fact, when political scientists build models to explain and predict congressional behavior, they often assume that re-election is a member's primary goal. We consider this an exaggeration. Many members are genuinely pursuing their political ideals. But there is no denying that the pressure for re-election significantly shapes congressional behavior.

THE BOTTOM LINE

» Members of Congress are always running for office. Fundraising takes up a particularly large amount of time and attention.

» Members pay special attention to their home style: Most go back to their constituency every week—compressing normal congressional business into the period from Tuesday through Thursday.

» Congress has become an institution of strangers who do not know one another. Most members focus intensely much of the time on re-election.

Congress at Work

When members of the House and Senate do gather in Washington, they have a staggering to-do list: managing the nation's legislative business, investigating executive branch activities, staging public hearings about everything from auto safety to U.S. aid to Zimbabwe. And, of course, raising money for re-election. How—and where—do they accomplish all that work?

The City on the Hill

The huge Capitol building is perched on an actual hill; its majestic marble dome dominates the Washington skyline. Traditionally, no building in the District of Columbia except the Washington Monument may be taller. The Capitol building is also the heart of a small city within a city. Six grand office buildings house the members and their staff; the newer buildings feature offices the size of basketball courts. Three ornate structures house the Library of Congress, which has mushroomed from Thomas Jefferson's personal book collection into the largest library in the world.

This City on the Hill also includes a dozen restaurants, two gyms, a chapel, a bank, a post office, and a warren of "hideaways": small unmarked offices for the personal use of senior members. Add another half-dozen staff "annex" buildings, several elegant townhouses rented most nights for fundraising events, a small high school for congressional pages—young men and women who scurry around the House and Senate floor running errands for members—and even a subway, to shuttle the members back and forth between their office buildings and the congressional chambers.

Inhabitants of this "city" include the 541 members of Congress, along with more than 22,000 staff members, who range from well-paid senior policy experts to summer interns; the Capitol police force, 250 members strong; and the U.S. poet laureate, a Congress-appointed position whose occupant receives a beautiful office in the Library of Congress. And do not forget the thousands of lobbyists. It all adds up to a very busy place.

How much are members paid? As of 2017, the rate is $174,000 for House and Senate members, a figure frozen since 2009.[12] That is more than four times what the average American makes (see Table 13.3). Leaders earn a slightly higher salary; House Speaker Ryan is the highest paid at $223,500. Constituents frequently complain that congressional salaries are too high. Note, however, that comparable leaders in other areas—from business managers to academic deans—make much higher salaries. If your primary professional aim is to make money, running for Congress is not your best bet.

Congressional staff members are a major presence in this company town. Until 1893, most members of the House had no staff support; beginning in 1891, senators were allotted one part-time staffer, paid six dollars per day. As Congress became more professional, it saw a steady increase in assistants, researchers, committee experts, legal counsel, and the like. By the 1990s, House and Senate staff leveled off and then started to decline from a high of around 27,000 total staff members to about 22,000 today.

Each House and Senate member has a chief of staff, a legislative director, a press secretary, a scheduler, and a host of other office staffers, including legislative correspondents (LCs) who handle the huge volume of constituent requests that pour into each member's office. Many college graduates take entry-level positions

TABLE 13.3 **Annual Average Salaries by Profession**

CEO, top 500 company	$12.9 million
NBA player	$4.9 million
NFL player	$2.11 million
U.S. president	$400,000
Four-year university president/chancellor	$385,909
Physicians	$182,700
Senior U.S. executive branch official	$199,700
Member of Congress	**$174,000**
Pharmacist	$118,470
Personal financial advisor	$108,090
Registered nurse	$69,790
Plumber	$53,240
Social worker	$49,150

Note: All figures as of 2016.
Source: Data from Bureau of Labor Statistics and U.S. Office of Personnel Management

Congressional staff at work. Staff members (standing) brief their House bosses before the start of a Budget Committee hearing.

(like the LC), because there are many opportunities to move up quickly. We have both spent time working with congressional staff—it is an exciting job for the men and women, many of them right out of college, who dominate staff positions.

In addition, each summer, thousands of college students descend on Capitol Hill to work, usually without pay. It is not glamorous activity, but congressional offices hum with excitement and offer a ringside seat on one of the most fascinating institutions in the world.

New staffers arriving on the Hill soon hear the most common question: not *"What do you do?"* but *"Who are you with?"* Working for a congressional leader, a committee chair, or a nationally known figure can catapult even new staffers up the Washington pecking order. Many staff members feel a rush when an important bill they helped craft passes or when they prepare their boss to succeed on a major news show or when they simply hear that their member met with the president.

Capitol Hill life runs on a unique rhythm. Congress usually remains in session from the beginning of January through early August; members return after Labor Day and rush to finish for the year in early October during election (even-numbered) years, because they are anxious to focus on their campaigns. In nonelection years, the session lasts longer—Obamacare passed the Senate on December 24 in 2009—a nonelection year. When in session, the Hill buzzes with action, especially when members are in residence Tuesday through Thursday. Staffers work late into the night, while lobbyists and media swarm around the Capitol.

Members of Congress know that they stand in the vortex of history. Every move—such as the deep bow made by clerks carrying House bills to the Senate and vice versa—reflects a legacy that may stretch as far back as the Virginia House of Burgesses, which first convened in 1619. In fact, new members of Congress make a candlelight visit to that historical site as part of their orientation.

Minnows and Whales: Congressional Leadership

When Lyndon Johnson (D-TX) served as Senate majority leader in the 1950s, he divided colleagues into two camps: "whales," who could influence landmark legislation, and "minnows," who dutifully followed others. Most "whales" are chairs of important committees or part of the formal leadership structure.

The House and Senate feature very different leadership styles. The smaller, more collegial Senate—where any member can request a hold and bring the entire body to a halt—usually requires patient, consensus-minded leadership. Majority leaders do not so much lead as manage Senate procedures, cajoling and pleading proud senators to move legislation along. Recently, the traditionally consensual Senate has begun to sound more like the partisan House, making it still harder to forge agreements. The larger House, run on majoritarian principles, permits much tighter central control from the Speaker and other top leaders; perhaps because the whole body is up for election every two years, the House has traditionally been the more partisan branch.

House Leadership

Democrats and Republicans each choose a party leader from their ranks. When a new Congress opens after an election (in January of odd-numbered years), the majority party votes its leader to the top post in Congress, the **Speaker of the House**. In 2010, the Republicans captured the House, and John Boehner (R-OH) replaced Nancy Pelosi as Speaker. In 2015 Boehner stepped down amid division in the Republican-led House and Paul Ryan was voted in as the Speaker. Ryan was again elected speaker at the start of the 115th Congress. The Speaker serves as the public face of the House. He or she is simultaneously an administrative officer, a political spokesman, and a party leader.

As chief administrative officer of the House, the Speaker presides over the chamber on special occasions (e.g., when a president delivers the State of the Union address to Congress). The Speaker rules on procedural issues, chooses members for committees, assigns legislation to committees, and "maintains order and civility"—although civility is increasingly difficult to maintain.

The Speaker sets the House's agenda and determines which bills are considered and when. Speakers negotiate with the Senate and executive branch. And they help manage the Rules Committee, which sets the terms of the debate for every piece of legislation that reaches the House floor. Speakers sometimes work with Rules to hold the majority together or derail opposition on important votes.

As leaders of the majority party, Speakers spin issues in their party's favor and serve as the party's public face. That leads the opposition to try and diminish them—to portray them as partisan or ruthless. It takes a nimble politician to juggle the different roles the Speaker must play. Newt Gingrich brilliantly designed the 1994 Republican victory in Congress after forty straight years in the minority. However, he proved to be more effective as a rebel than as Speaker. His combative persona and fondness for the limelight quickly made him a controversial figure—and hurt the new Republican majority's image. In contrast, John Boehner tried to build consensus in his party, but was undone by ultra-conservative young Republicans impatient for change.[13]

The House majority leader is the second in command. He or she acts as the majority party's floor manager, negotiator, and spokesperson. The majority leader also serves as the Speaker's eyes and ears, tracking party members' actions and preferences. Kevin McCarthy (R-CA) currently holds this position.

The number-three position is the majority whip. Whips are responsible for party discipline—ensuring that Republicans vote the way the leadership wants them to. The term *whip* comes from the British Parliament, which long ago borrowed the term from fox hunting, where the "whipper-in" was responsible for keeping the pack of hounds together—and yes, those fox hunters did the job by cracking whips. The majority whip leads a team of nine deputy whips, each responsible for members from a different region. Frank Underwood, the ruthless politician on the Netflix show *House of Cards*, started the series as majority whip.

> **Speaker of the House:**
> The chief administrative officer in the House of Representatives.

● *Outgoing Speaker Nancy Pelosi D-CA) passes the gavel to incoming Speaker John Boehner (R-OH) who is momentarily overcome with emotion. Boehner himself was pushed aside less than five years later.*

The minority generally has the same leadership structure, with one big difference: no Speaker. The top Democrat in the 115th Congress, minority leader (and former Speaker) Nancy Pelosi is joined by the minority whip in trying to thwart the Republican majority.

House whips have a challenging time persuading their proud, talented colleagues to vote the way they want. They do a lot of arm-twisting and deal-cutting—and they have to be creative. Back in the 1970s, minority whip Leslie Arends (R-IL) needed one more GOP vote to win an important agriculture bill. One Ohio Republican, knowing the bill was unpopular with his constituents, simply flew home. When Arends discovered his crucial vote was missing, he called an Ohio radio station and persuaded the DJ to announce, every fifteen minutes: "If anybody spies Representative Jones, who should be representing us in Washington but isn't, tell him he's supposed to be in Washington tomorrow for an important vote." Jones flew back the next morning and sheepishly voted with his fellow Republicans.

Senate Leadership

When you think about the Senate, take all the difficulties involved in managing the House—and quadruple them. Senate rules, such as the filibuster and the hold, give each individual senator a great deal of autonomy. The Senate leadership must turn to personal skills, especially an ability to negotiate with colleagues, to advance their party's goals.

The senators elect a majority leader—currently Mitch McConnell (R-KY). However, the Senate leader does not even formally preside over the chamber. The Constitution gives that job to the vice president (VP). In practice, vice presidents rarely show up in the Senate, appearing mainly for very important votes (because the VP can break a tie) and on ceremonial occasions. Likewise, the **president pro tempore** (currently Orrin Hatch, R-UT) has presiding authority at certain formal occasions. Otherwise, every senator presides in turn over the body, serving rotating half-hour stints. A staff member stands by the presiding member's side, helping him or her to negotiate the complex rules.

President pro tempore:
Majority party senator with the longest Senate service.

After Hillary Rodham Clinton, elected to the Senate from New York in 2000, served her first half-hour in the Senate's presiding chair, she told colleagues it was "the most difficult thing I'd ever done in politics."[14] Perhaps she would change her mind now, after a grueling presidential campaign preceded by service as Secretary of State. But then-Senator Clinton's line emphasizes how tortuous the Senate rules can be. ·

Senate whips from both the majority and minority parties serve the same functions as in the House—though they command much less power to demand party discipline, again owing to the Senate's individualistic ways. This difficulty extends right up to the majority leader. It is hard to set the Senate's agenda or command floor action in a context of unlimited debate and amendments, with the constant threat that any one senator will place a hold on legislation or mount a filibuster. The best that majority leaders and their team can muster is to influence which policies will be considered on the Senate floor, and in what order, though that is usually done in consultation with the minority leader. If the minority leader indicates that an item will be subject to a filibuster or a hold, the majority leader normally passes over it and moves to the next item on the agenda.

Committees: Workhorses of Congress

The regular duties of congressional lawmaking play out mainly in committees. Committees draft legislation, sponsor hearings, oversee the executive branch, and draft the federal budget. Every year, the administration sends its priorities to Congress. Leadership duly assigns issues to committees, where many die a quiet death. Even after Obama won a big re-election victory in 2012, congressional committees buried such presidential priorities as gun control, environmental regulation, and (in the House) immigration reform.

The Enduring Power of Committees

Table 13.4 lists the types of congressional committees, which have not changed in more than a century. In fact, legislative committees were invented in the very early days of the United States; the British Parliament still has nothing resembling the extent and power of congressional committees. Committees have been remarkably resilient—despite decades of pressure for reform. How have they managed to duck calls for change?

Two reasons: First, inertia—it is hard to remake Congress, given the layers of tradition and complex rules. Second, in their own way, committees work. Individual members devote extensive time to fundraising, paying attention to constituents, and shuttling in and out of Washington. The committee system permits busy members to specialize and become expert on a narrow range of topics (especially in the House, where members typically serve on one committee). In short, committees enable Congress to devise fairly sophisticated legislative solutions to the many issues competing for attention.

The committee system is yet another way American government separates powers. It means that Congress winds up with multiple centers of authority, making the legislative process slower and harder for the public (and the media) to follow. But the division of labor allows an institution—with distracted, busy members— to accomplish more. By dividing the labor of its members, the 114th Congress was able to dispatch more than 11,644 items, although that number is down from 24,285 forty years ago.

The standing committees (see Table 13.5) provide a main avenue to send favored services, or "pork," home to a representative's district. Members of the Appropriations Committee—which decides how U.S. funds are spent—are known as "cardinals," like the ruling cadre in the Vatican. Other members approach them, hat in hand, to request **earmarks** in the form of items in appropriations bills: a dam in this district, funds for highway construction in that one. Appropriations

Earmark: A legislative item, usually included in spending ("appropriations") bills, that directs Congress to fund a particular item in one House member's district or a senator's state.

TABLE 13.4	**Congressional Committee Types**

Standing committees: Permanent bodies, with fixed jurisdiction (Table 13.5 lists them all). House and Senate standing committees vary widely in prestige: The oldest are traditionally the most influential, though some newer ones (such as Intelligence, created after 9/11 in both chambers) deal with significant topics. Standing committees are further divided into multiple *subcommittees*, organized around areas of expertise.
Select committees: Created to investigate a particular issue; these exist for a defined period of time. Also called *special committees*. A select committee to investigate the terrorist attack on the U.S. Embassy in Benghazi, Libya, was convened from 2014–2016, for example.
Joint committees: Made up of both House and Senate members to address topics of continuing importance. These committees can remain in place for decades; the Joint Committee on Taxation has existed since 1971, for example. *Conference committees*, introduced later in this chapter, are temporary joint committees.

TABLE 13.5 House and Senate Permanent Committees, 115th Congress

U.S. HOUSE COMMITTEES	U.S. SENATE COMMITTEES
Agriculture	Aging (Special)
Appropriations	Agriculture, Nutrition, and Forestry
Armed Services	Appropriations
Budget	Armed Services
Education and the Workforce	Banking, Housing, and Urban Affairs
Energy and Commerce	Budget
Ethics	Commerce, Science, and Transportation
Financial Services	Energy and Natural Resources
Foreign Affairs	Environment and Public Works
Homeland Security	Ethics (Select)
House Administration	Finance
Intelligence (Permanent Select)	Foreign Relations
Judiciary	Health, Education, Labor, and Pensions
Natural Resources	Homeland Security and Governmental Affairs
Oversight and Government Reform	Indian Affairs
Rules	Intelligence (Permanent Select)
Science and Technology	Judiciary
Small Business	Rules and Administration
Transportation and Infrastructure	Small Business and Entrepreneurship
Veterans Affairs	Veterans Affairs
Ways and Means	

members saw their power diminished in 2012, after the 112th Congress's decision to outlaw earmarks took effect; within a year, however, Congress began to find creative ways to fund the practice.

The committee system makes Congress far more efficient. But there is also a harsher reality. The committee system fragments Congress into small fiefdoms, hides action from public view, and makes it relatively easy to do little favors for well-placed constituents (a tax break or a phone call to get a pesky regulator to back off). The fragmentation also makes it still more difficult to pass major legislation or to address large national problems. Only about 6 percent of the bills and proposals that make it into committee ever make it to the floor.

The organization of Congress raises, once again, the dilemmas of American democracy: Is the system biased toward the powerful? Does the bias against action frustrate the popular will or simply reflect the American wariness of government (or both)? What do you think?

Leadership and Assignments

After the 2016 Congressional election, many House members found excuses to check in with the Speaker: Along with fond holiday wishes, they were jockeying for preferred committee assignments. The Speaker assigns members (and chairs) to each committee—a vital decision, given all the power committees wield. Over in the Senate, the decision involves more give-and-take but ultimately rests in the majority leader's hands. Minority party assignments are recommended by minority leaders in both chambers.

Members compete fiercely to join the most influential committees. Once they are on a committee, representatives and senators often stay for many years—gaining power and influence, and aspiring to become chair. Traditionally (but not always), the chair is the longest serving committee member. Members generally seek to join committees that reflect the concerns of their district. When political scientist David Price (D-NC) won a seat in Congress, his colleagues at Duke University wondered just how his committee assignment would reflect his expertise. Price, already a savvy politician, requested a seat on the House Banking (now Financial Services) Committee because his district has a strong banking and financial service sector. [15]

Skilled committee chairs are able to broaden the jurisdiction of their committee by claiming pieces of bills that are referred to many different committees. As we saw in the chapter opening, five different committees won jurisdiction over Obamacare. Each committee has its own process. Each has its own political slant. Committees can bury a bill, completely rewrite it, report out an unrealistic version, or boost the chances of success with a strong bill.

Jurisdictional squabbles can erupt into battles for influence between committees when their responsibilities overlap. The House and the Senate each have different committees for Homeland Security, Intelligence, and Foreign Affairs. Sometimes they all hold hearings on the same issue, and because legislation is assigned to every committee that has jurisdiction over the topic, overlapping authority means multiple committees wrestling to shape the same legislation. See Comparing Nations 13.1 to find out how this legislative process differs from that in other countries.

COMPARING NATIONS 13.1 A Unique U.S. System

The American style of multiple committees claiming jurisdiction is very unusual. If the British Parliament wants to consider major environmental or tax legislation, it forms a special committee to craft the law—and the majority party in the House of Commons follows the lead of the prime minister, who it elected to his or her post.

In Japan, the bureaucracy writes laws and the Diet (Japan's national legislature) passes them—no subset of Diet committee members examines and rewrites legislation. Only in the United States do we have this scrum of committees, clashing with one another throughout the process.

» Congress is a little like a small city. Its citizens include the 541 members of Congress, 22,000 staff members, and an army of lobbyists. The city includes its own amenities, traditions, and slang.

» Congressional leadership in the House includes a Speaker, majority and minority leaders, and ten whips. Successful leaders in the House impose discipline on their party members. The Senate allows far more individual action. Party leaders and whips have fewer institutional tools with which to impose discipline.

» Congressional committees are the workhorses of Congress. They have proved efficient and adaptable over the years. However, the committee system also fragments Congress, hides action from public view, accommodates well-placed constituents looking for individual favors, and makes it difficult to pass major legislation.

Legislative Policymaking

As the Affordable Care Act's convoluted passage testifies, congressional lawmaking can be boiled down to five words: *Complex process. Difficult to win.* The last ten years (or, as you now know to say, the last five sessions of Congress) saw thousands of bills submitted each year (see Figure 13.2). How many made it all the way through the process? Less than 3 percent.

Why even bother pursuing legislative wins? There are other ways to make policy. As we will see in the following chapters, presidents can issue executive orders (Chapter 14), bureaucrats can write regulations (Chapter 15), and activists can go to the courts (Chapter 16). But nothing else has the status—symbolic as well as legal—of an act of Congress. That is why the bills keep coming despite the long odds. What happens once a bill is proposed?

Americans complain about the nation's failure to face up to global warming. Or our broken public education system. Or our inability to ban abortion, regulate assault rifles, or reduce the federal budget deficit. Pundits explain these failures by invoking "American attitudes" or "American culture" or "powerful lobbyists." Here is a more accurate explanation: Congressional rules make it very hard to do any of these things—even when a majority of legislators (and the nation) are in support.

Drafting a Bill

Anyone can petition Congress to consider a bill, but only members of the House and Senate have the right to introduce one. Every piece of legislation needs at least one primary sponsor, whose name is publicly inscribed on the first page. Major bills are often referred to by the sponsors' names, with some creative exceptions (see Table 13.6).

Bills can feature any number of co-sponsors, or members who agree to have their names listed as

● **FIGURE 13.2** *Bills introduced in Congress (114th as of November 1, 2016). (Source: GovTrack)*

TABLE 13.6 **Examples of Creative Legislative Titles**

PROMESA (2016): Using the Spanish word for "promise," sets up a U.S. control board for financially troubled Puerto Rico, rather than providing budget relief.
"EGO (Eliminating Government-funded Oil-painting) Act" (2013): Ban federal funding of official portraits of government officials.
"Pass a Budget Now Act" (2012): Cut congressional pay for each day that a budget resolution (an overview of spending/revenue targets for the coming year) fails to pass.
"Personal Responsibility in Consumption Act" (2006): Immunize fast-food companies against lawsuits by obese consumers.
"What Really Happened Act" (2002): Require instant TV replay in all major sports.
Note: Only the first of these bills passed.

supporters. The main sponsors usually try to sign on many members, especially powerful ones like committee chairs, as co-sponsors. A loose rule of thumb: The more co-sponsors a bill has, the higher the likelihood of passage.

Anything can be introduced as legislation—no matter how far outside the box. Congressman Ron Paul (R-TX) once introduced a bill mandating that the Treasury buy a one-inch-wide strip of land stretching down the middle of the United States from Canada to Mexico. All goods or people crossing that line would be charged a toll, declared Representative Paul, eliminating the need for any other taxes or government fees. The bill did not make it out of committee.

Bills' sponsors rarely write the legislation themselves. Some bills include language taken from state legislation, or even other countries' parliaments. Congressional members "borrow" legislative language from each other, adapting colleagues' bills for their own use. Most serious bills go to the experts at the Congressional Research Service (CRS) for drafting help. Bill drafters also consult with outside experts, including executive branch officials, lobbyists, and academics. And members especially enjoy copying themselves; as each new session begins many congressional offices participate in a time-honored ritual: dust off and reintroduce bills that failed last time.

There is a great art to bill drafting. Writing legislation necessitates major political choices. How much money should we ask for in spending bills? How far can we change current laws? Do we dare test existing constitutional limits? Many bills include bargaining chips—provisions the sponsors are willing to negotiate away to win over the skeptics. Legislation to reduce average elementary school class sizes might also feature a sentence promising healthier lunches in all public schools. When the serious bargaining starts on Capitol Hill, that line may be dropped to satisfy budget hawks who always focus on the costs. Drafters are also aware that if the law passes, it may very well end up involved in litigation, which puts a premium on clarity and precision.

Once the bill is drafted and the co-sponsors have signed on, it is ready for the next step: submission.

see for yourself 13.3

Go online to view an example of a congressional bill, its description, supporters, and status.

Submitting the Bill

The more traditional Senate typically introduces bills as the legislative day opens, around noon on Tuesdays, Wednesdays, and Thursdays. Let's take a peek inside the chamber.

The presiding officer taps his or her gavel, bringing the stir of conversation to a halt. Members pause as the Senate chaplain recites a prayer. A swirling bustle breaks out as the chaplain concludes. Routine administrative motions (such as approving records of the previous day's proceedings) are followed by morning hour statements—short speeches that celebrate home state achievements. A constituent is turning 100 years old, or a softball team has won the state title.

Watch carefully: A senator snaps her fingers. A page (usually a high school student trained for this role) dashes down the aisle, takes the senator's document, and places it in a flat wooden tray beside the bill clerk. The clerk writes a number on the first page (bills are numbered serially, starting each session with S.1), notes the senator's suggestion for committee referral, and places it in a tray. That night it is printed. A bill has been born!

The House is less ritualized, in keeping with its democratic spirit, but bill introduction continues to be an old-fashioned practice. Representatives carry proposed bills themselves down to the rostrum. They hand their legislation to the clerk or drop it in a mahogany box, called the "hopper." From there, bills are delivered to the Speaker's office, where they are assigned a number—starting each session with H.R. 1—and referred to committee.

Committee Action

As we have seen, committees are the congressional workhorses. The House leadership normally assigns each bill to committees with authority (or jurisdiction) over the area affected by the proposed legislation—recall that the "Obamacare" bill went to five different committees. Once they are assigned a bill, the committees perform four major tasks.

Committee hearing: A way for committees to gather information as legislative policymaking gets underway. Hearings usually feature witnesses who submit testimony, make an oral presentation, and answer questions from members of Congress.

1. Committees Hold Hearings on Policy Topics.   Witnesses submit written testimony for staff members and reporters to read; unless they are important individuals, they are limited to a five-minute presentation at the **committee hearing**. When they begin, a little green light goes on; at the four-minute mark, a yellow light goes on. At five minutes, a red light blinks. Nervous rookies stop mid-sentence; veterans ignore the lights and talk serenely on—until the chair bangs the gavel.

The staff carefully puts together a list of who is testifying at each hearing. Witnesses generally include White House officials and cabinet heads—whose testimony has to be cleared with the Office of Management and Budget (OMB; introduced in Chapter 14 as "the agency that says no"). At many hearings, officials try to stick to their authorized script while critical Senate or House members pummel them knowing full well that the government witness cannot express any views that were not cleared by the OMB.

Celebrities are popular witnesses, attracting media attention to what might otherwise be a low-profile event. Angelina Jolie has appeared before Congress five times on international aid issues; Alexis Ohanian, co-founder of the social

Celebrity congressional witnesses include . . . Elmo! Elmo "testifies," with the help of Representative Duncan Hunter (R-CA), before the House Education Appropriations subcommittee in support of funding for school music programs.

networking site Reddit, testified against a bill to curb online piracy; Michael Crichton, author of *Jurassic Park*, *Westworld* and other thrillers, explained a few years ago that global warming was pure fiction. More often, witnesses include interest-group lobbyists, think tank experts, academics, and pollsters reporting public opinion on the issues.

Hearings also can get tough. When the CEOs of three big U.S. automakers went to Congress for a bailout, their trouble began when Representative Brad Sherman (D-CA) needled them about flying to Washington on corporate jets while claiming that their companies faced bankruptcy.

Rep. SHERMAN:	I'm going to ask the three executives here to raise their hand if they flew here commercial.
Mr. MULALLY [Ford CEO], Mr. WAGONER [GM], Mr. NARDELLI [Chrysler]:	(No response.)
Rep. SHERMAN:	Second, I'm going ask you to raise your hand if you're planning to sell your [private] jet . . . and fly back commercial.
Messrs. MULALLY, WAGONER, NARDELLI:	(No response.)
Rep. SHERMAN:	Let the record show no hands went up.
Rep. ACKERMAN:	It's almost like seeing a guy show up at the soup kitchen in high-hat and tuxedo. . . . I mean, couldn't you all have downgraded to first class or jet-pooled or something to get here?

Other members asked the CEOs if they would give up their hefty compensation packages and work for one dollar a year. Nardelli, the Chrysler chairman, declined with a muttered, "I'm good." The CEOs learned their lesson: When they next testified before Congress, they rode to Washington in cars manufactured by their company.

2. Committees Prepare Legislation for Floor Consideration. Committees are the primary source of policy development in Congress. Members and committee staff, drawing on their collective knowledge, assess and revise each bill that comes before them.

Major rewrites of bills occur in **committee markup sessions**, when the committee gathers to work through the legislation's language, line by line. The result, called a "chairman's mark," is hot property among lobbyists, public advocates, and other interested parties; it contains many of the details that will become law if the legislation wins approval.

Committee markup session: A gathering of a full committee to draft the final version of a bill before the committee votes on it.

Following markup, the committee holds a vote on whether to report a bill to the full House or Senate. When the Senate Judiciary Committee considered immigration reform in 2013, it considered 301 amendments—and incorporated ninety-two into the bill before passing the bill by a vote of 13 to 5. All that work in just one Senate committee—and remember that at least one other committee (and usually more) is negotiating another version of the same legislation.

Committee votes are pivotal moments in a bill's career, as important as roll-call votes on the floor. If a bill is voted down in committee—not reported, in Congress speak—it is usually dead. Those voted up by a narrow margin probably face tough sledding on the floor, and the Speaker may decide never to bring the closely divided measure up for a vote. Then the bill dies even though it won a majority vote in committee.

3. Committees Also Kill Legislation. Of the more than four thousand bills referred to the forty House and Senate standing committees each year, about one in eight sees any action at all. Items judged less important or not particularly urgent—or not politically viable—may be quietly deleted. Well into modern times, bills often died in committee without any public acknowledgment of how members voted. A key reform of the 1970s required all committees to keep full records of important votes.

4. Committees Exercise Oversight. Congress's work is not done when legislation passes. House and Senate standing committees monitor the executive branch, making sure cabinet departments and agencies perform their roles properly. This supervision can be a high-stakes activity: Oversight hearings investigate scandals; review major issues such as cybersecurity and protection against terrorism; and evaluate presidential appointees. Committees also continue to monitor the programs that they have passed.

Note that, as with lawmaking, the committees of Congress are the front lines in this vital interplay between the legislative and executive branches.

Floor Action

Unanimous consent:
A Senate requirement, applied to most of that body's business that all senators agree before an action can proceed.

After a successful bill makes it through committee markup (where it is amended but remains recognizable) and is approved by one or more committees, its next stop is the House or Senate floor. Once it gets there, its chance of becoming law has increased dramatically. Of bills that make it to the floor, more than half are enacted. But legislation may take a long time to achieve floor consideration—leaders rarely call up a bill until they think they have the votes to win.

FBI Director James Comey (right) and Homeland Security Secretary Jeh Johnson testify before the U.S. House of Representatives committee on homeland security regarding terrorist threats to the United States. Comey became a central figure in the 2016 election campaign with his investigation of Hillary Clinton's potential misuse of classified emails.

Getting to the Floor. Floor procedures in the House and Senate are very different. After a Senate committee approves a bill, it is placed on the "business calendar," from which it will be called up for consideration on a timing schedule worked out by the majority and minority leaders. Only bills that receive **unanimous consent**—agreement by all senators—can be brought to the floor. One "nay" and the bill is put on hold.

In the House, the majority party leaders exert more control over which issues make it to the floor. They may start by rewriting the legislation—sometimes because multiple committees have passed different chairman's marks and cannot come to agreement among themselves. Other times, the Speaker, majority leader, and fellow leaders rewrite a bill to get the measure through.

Once it confirms a bill's language, the House Rules Committee issues a directive governing the process for the bill: For example, which type of amendments may be proposed from the floor. The membership of the Rules Committee is tilted to favor the majority party, and the committee chair works closely with the Speaker to ensure that floor action will follow the leadership's wishes. The Senate, in contrast, allows virtually unlimited consideration on the floor; amendments of all kinds just keep on coming.

In both chambers, once bills make it to the calendar, they can get stuck there—for an entire session, in some cases. A logjam of legislation may be the reason. Or it might be the result of coordination issues between House and Senate, given the requirement that legislation has to move through both chambers. Bills also may be bottled up in the Senate because of the "unanimous consent" requirement. Achieving 100 percent agreement to allow a bill to come up for a vote often involves elaborate negotiations.

On the Floor. Eventually the calendar clears, and a bill's moment for floor consideration arrives. Supporters hope their measure will be taken up in the House and Senate around the same time, knowing that plenty of legislation makes it only to one or the other chamber during a session—another form of death sentence. For example, the Senate passed an ambitious bill in 2016 to address an "epidemic" of opioid (strong painkiller) addiction and abuse. However, the House was more skeptical. Conservatives opted for an approach that favored stronger law enforcement, rather than preventative health policies. House committees then voted out eighteen different "small bore" opioid reforms that might have served as the basis of negotiation with the Senate. In the end, the House never even voted on the Senate's measure. On the other side, bills to prohibit taxpayer funding for abortion, to cap government spending, and to repeal the Affordable Care Act all sailed through the House—and vanished when the Senate failed to act on them.

In both chambers, floor action on legislation follows the same broad procedures. First, a bill is assigned a floor manager—usually the main sponsor, but on big issues, the chair of the committee or subcommittee that reported the bill takes up this role. The manager handles amendments as they come up and controls the time for debate. Majority and minority party members each have a specific number of hours and minutes to discuss the legislation, determined in the Senate by agreement between party leaders and in the House by the Rules Committee.

Then the political maneuvers really start. In both House and Senate, floor action involves amendments, procedural moves, and eventually a final vote—all accompanied by a lot of talk along the way. Members rarely change any votes with their eloquence. But floor speeches are not empty oratory. Congress watchers know that who chooses to speak, and what they say, matters. "I rise to support H.R. 835" is very different from "I rise to thank my good friend for introducing this excellent bill, H.R. 835; I have just a few questions about it." Each statement offers valuable clues about the likely outcome. Whips listen especially closely and adapt their floor strategies to secure a majority in support of party approved amendments and the final vote for passage.

The real audience for much of the speechmaking is the constituency back home eager to see their representatives fight for (or against) an issue. At times, however, the members snap at one another. Members of the minority often express frustration at the hardball tactics of the leadership. In 2016, the Senate considered six gun-control measures in the wake of a horrific mass murder at an Orlando dance club. House Republican leaders, however, refused even to hold committee hearings

House Democrats demanding floor action on gun control.

Cloture vote: The Senate's only approved method for halting a filibuster or lifting a legislative hold. If sixty senators—three-fifths of the body, changed in 1975 from the original two-thirds—vote for cloture, the measure can proceed to a vote.

on the issue—leading furious Democratic members to stage a rare sit-in on the House floor.

The rules in the House permit leaders to introduce creative strategies to get their legislation through. They can extend the time allocated for debate (while a few more arms are twisted). They sometimes permit members to vote "yes" on multiple contradictory motions knowing only one (the last vote or the one with the most votes) will really count; this procedural antic permits members to tell angry constituents, "don't blame me, I voted for that bill" (yes, they did—but they also voted against it when it really counted).

Senate leaders, far from inventing new rules, are more likely to breathe a sigh of relief after steering a bill past the potential member holds and simply getting it to the floor. There, a related danger lurks: the filibuster. A senator may halt all activity in the chamber by refusing to yield the floor; the only way to stop him or her is through a **cloture vote**, which requires the approval of three-fifths of the Senate—sixty votes.

Filibusters used to be rare events. Between 1927 and 1960, there were only eighteen efforts to break a filibuster (or cloture filings). Not a single one succeeded in *invoking cloture*, or stopping the filibuster and permitting a vote on the issue. As you can see in Figure 13.3, the effort to invoke cloture was more common in the 1970s (which averaged thirty-two filibusters every two-year session); it became a common tactic in the 1990s and 2000s when both Democratic and Republican majorities averaged seventy-two cloture filings (seeking to break a filibuster) a session. The new Republican minority (2007–2015) broke all records and averaged 161 cloture filings a session. Sixty votes has effectively become the new Senate threshold for passing legislation.

The Vote

Once amendments are voted down or adopted, the time for speeches has expired, and the leadership reckons it has a winning majority, it's time for a final floor vote. On uncontroversial matters, a **voice vote** of all members is sufficient. But several dozen votes each session are judged important enough to require a **roll-call vote**. In the Senate, a clerk still calls the roll, alphabetically scrolling through senators by last

— Cloture filings [sixteen senators request vote to end filibuster]

— Cloture invoked [filibuster stopped]

Session of Congress

FIGURE 13.3 *Cloture votes are votes to end a filibuster. When they are successful, cloture is invoked and the filibuster ends. Notice how they used to be rare events. The 113th Congress (2013–2014) broke the all-time record for cloture votes (which is one way to measure the number of filibusters) by almost doubling the previous record. (Source: U.S. Senate)* name, with each responding "yea" or "nay" (or "present," if they wish to abstain). Because the much larger House would take hours to vote if it proceeded in this way, roll calls are now done electronically. Representatives use a card about the size of a credit or ATM card that they plug into kiosks located around the House chamber.

Roll-call votes on major bills are among the most important public acts a member of Congress performs. These votes attract a great deal of attention from constituents, lobbyists, potential opponents, and media alike. Political scientists also find them compelling, in part because they provide a handy data source (hundreds of votes each session, each with a clear yes/no alternative). Despite years of roll-call analyses and some elaborate theories, we are not very good at predicting vote outcomes. Whips and other nose-counters in Congress perform better than most academic models.

Voice vote: A congressional vote in which the presiding officer asks those for and against to say "yea" or "nay," respectively, and announces the result. No record is kept of House or Senate members voting on each side.

Roll-call vote: A congressional vote in which all members' votes are recorded, either by roll call (Senate) or electronically (House).

Conference Committee

Legislation must pass the Senate and House in identical form to be ready for presidential signature. If different versions of a bill pass—and technically a single comma in a five-hundred-page bill counts as a "difference"—a conference committee must reconcile them. These special sessions, made up of lawmakers from both chambers, provide a golden opportunity for disgruntled members or attentive lobbyists to revisit a bill. Interested parties who failed to get a favorite item included during committee or floor action now have another chance. "An apple and an orange could go into conference committee," lamented President Ronald Reagan, "and come out a pear." No joke: The conference can write an entirely new bill.

House–Senate conferences, if successful, yield a single version of a bill. Each chamber then has an "up-or-down" floor vote—no further amendments permitted. Opponents in the Senate may launch another filibuster, hoping to win over new members who object to the compromises made with the House. If the majority beats the filibuster in the Senate and a majority of both houses votes in favor, the bill has passed Congress.

● Conference committee in action. With staffers at the ready and the media recording every utterance (and lobbyists crowded in the halls outside), a Senate–House conference committee works to resolve differences on a bill.

Presidential Action: Separated Powers Revisited

Even after all that, legislation still faces another hurdle. No bill becomes law until the president signs it. On important issues, the signing ceremony often takes place in the White House Rose Garden. Presidents sign multiple copies of the bill, handing out pens to the original sponsors and other high-ranking congressional members in attendance.

Presidents can also **veto** legislation. Here is yet another place a bill can falter. If the president says no, Congress has one more shot at passing the legislation. It is a high bar, though. To deny or override a veto, both chambers need a two-thirds majority: at least sixty-seven senators and 291 members of the House have to say no to the president. Only in this way can a bill become law without a presidential signature. Figure 13.4 summarizes the process of how a bill becomes a law.

Veto: The constitutional procedure by which a president can prevent enactment of legislation passed by Congress.

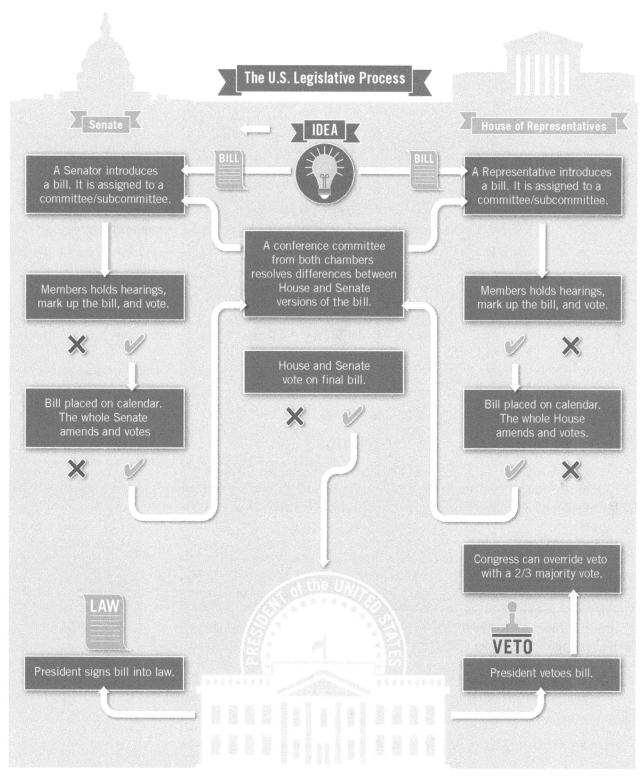

● **FIGURE 13.4** *How a bill becomes a law.*

We will cover more details about veto practices in Chapter 14 on the presidency. Fortunately for most legislative advocates, presidential opposition is rare: George W. Bush vetoed just twelve bills during his eight years as president; President Obama had exactly the same record, twelve vetoes, as he entered the last month of his eight years in office.

» Transforming a policy idea into a federal law is extremely difficult. Why bother? Because legislation remains the central act of American domestic government. Important laws have far-reaching consequences.

» The power of an officially sanctioned law inspires the introduction of thousands of bills in Congress each year. Most proposed legislation (97%) never gets through the process and becomes law.

» Congressional committees are the central actors in legislative policymaking, holding hearings and marking up (or deleting) bills to prepare them for floor action.

» Floor procedures are another intricate part of the process. Once passed by both House and Senate, legislation may still face a conference committee, a presidential veto, or both.

Why Is Congress So Unpopular?

Congress, the "people's branch," might be expected to win the most public support among our national political institutions. Not even close—it is by far the least popular branch. For a half-century, polls have reported the popularity of Congress, the sitting president, and the Supreme Court, along with other institutions. Since the 1970s, Congress has come in last in virtually every survey, often by a great margin. Today, Congress is less popular than at any other time in modern history and less popular than, well, almost anything—including the Internal Revenue Service, witches, zombies, and hipsters (see Figure 13.5).[16] And yet, as we saw in Chapter 9, Americans re-elect over 90 percent of their representatives, year after year. Why?

Constituents tend to like their own representatives and senators, who receive far higher approval numbers than Congress as a whole. And individual members have become adept at raising money (to drive off talented challengers) and running against the Congress they serve in. But what makes the institution itself so unpopular? The public dislikes both partisan fighting and gridlock. Let us look more carefully at each complaint.

Partisan Polarization in Congress

Congress has exhibited partisan differences since its origins. Strong party disputes, fueled by regional and racial divisions led nineteenth century members to carry swords, pistols, or Bowie knives into chambers. Following a rousing antislavery speech by Senator Charles Sumner of Massachusetts in 1856, a southern House member, Preston Brooks, slipped onto the Senate floor and beat Sumner unconscious with a cane. Sumner was unable to resume his Senate duties for nearly three years.

INFO/DATA: Historic Partisan Polarization

For more than one hundred years, the Senate and House tended to shift together ideologically: When one became more conservative (moving to the right on the infographic), so did the other and vice versa. In recent years, the two chambers have displayed unprecedented levels of ideological difference.

1. Most commentary decries partisan polarization across the chambers of Congress. Are there any advantages to such a wide ideological divide?

2. Think about yourself and your politically engaged friends and relatives. Do you prefer highly partisan candidates? What impact might your choices have on the work of Congress?

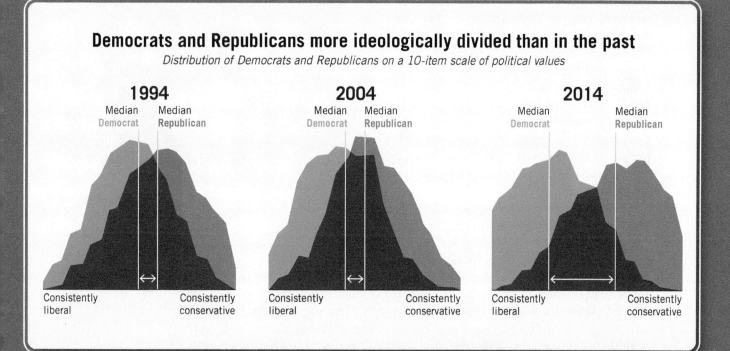

Democrats and Republicans more ideologically divided than in the past

Distribution of Democrats and Republicans on a 10-item scale of political values

1994 — Median Democrat / Median Republican — Consistently liberal / Consistently conservative

2004 — Median Democrat / Median Republican — Consistently liberal / Consistently conservative

2014 — Median Democrat / Median Republican — Consistently liberal / Consistently conservative

Source: Pew Research Center

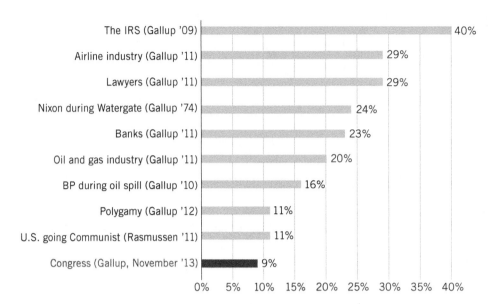

The IRS (Gallup '09) — 40%
Airline industry (Gallup '11) — 29%
Lawyers (Gallup '11) — 29%
Nixon during Watergate (Gallup '74) — 24%
Banks (Gallup '11) — 23%
Oil and gas industry (Gallup '11) — 20%
BP during oil spill (Gallup '10) — 16%
Polygamy (Gallup '12) — 11%
U.S. going Communist (Rasmussen '11) — 11%
Congress (Gallup, November '13) — 9%

0% 5% 10% 15% 20% 25% 30% 35% 40%

● **FIGURE 13.5** *Public approval of Congress, compared to other institutions, ideas, and individuals. By late 2016, Congress's approval rating had climbed to 20 percent; it fell as low as 7 percent in 2014. (Gallup)*

Subsequent combat in the House or Senate was mostly, but not entirely, limited to words. During the 1950s and 1960s, large Democratic majorities in both chambers masked differences—mostly between southern conservatives and liberals from other regions of the country—within the Democratic caucus. Cross party conflict rose during the 1980s, as Republicans became more competitive within Congress. When the GOP won control of the Senate in the 1980s, it marked the first time the party had held a majority for more than two years since 1930.

The fault lines cracked open further after 1990, when Republicans challenged the Democrats for control of the House for the first time in almost forty years.[17] Political scientist Barbara Sinclair demonstrated that the proportion of House votes in which a majority of Democrats voted against a majority of Republicans increased by more than 50 percent during the 1990s and early 2000s.[18] In a similar telling measure, party cohesion—the proportion of each party's House or Senate members who vote with the party majority—remained at or above 90 percent each year after 1990, after historically varying from the mid-60s to the low 80s. In other words, the parties in Congress were digging in against each other, with fewer and fewer members willing to look for middle ground or vote with the other side.

SOUTHERN CHIVALRY — ARGUMENT versus CLUB'S.

● *Congressional partisanship, Civil War era–style. A northern cartoonist vividly renders the 1856 caning of Senator Sumner.*

Titles and subtitles of recent books about Congress underscore the point: *Fight Club Politics: How Partisanship Is Poisoning the House of Representatives*; *The Broken Branch: How Congress Is Failing America and How to Get It Back on Track*; *Republic, Lost: How Money Corrupts Congress*; *Too Weak to Govern*; and *It's Even Worse Than It Looks.*[19]

There are two perspectives on polarization. Most political scientists believe the parties are now, for the first time, sorted by ideology. Republicans are conservative, and Democrats are liberals; this encourages both parties to be more partisan.

What Do You Think?

Is a Partisan Congress a Good Thing?

Should Congress seek more cross party agreement? The answer may not be so obvious—especially if you view politics in terms of principles, not merely the pursuit of self-interest. Today's "partisan" Congress features a significant ideological divide between conservative Republicans and progressive Democrats. Partisanship helps guide how members pursue the goals they believe in and try to persuade the public. What do you think?

Yes, a partisan Congress is a good thing. It permits the public to choose between very different political philosophies. The two parties represent different visions of America. That's better than two parties that basically say the same things.

No, Congress has gotten too partisan. The parties may disagree with one another, but they do not reflect the views of most Americans. Most people are moderates who do not feel well represented by the strong party views that fail to listen to the other side. American government should be a government of compromise.

It depends. The context matters. For example, in times of economic suffering, people should put aside their political philosophy (whether pro- or antigovernment) and legislate relief. But on other matters (such as abortion or gun control) members should stick to their principles.

Others see "asymmetrical polarization": The Republicans, inspired by a fiery conservative movement, are the ones who have pressed the partisan fight in the name of their ideals.[20]

Divided Government

How to explain the rise in partisan "gridlock" in our era? Divided government, say some. Divided government occurs when each party holds at least one of the three nationally elected branches: the presidency, the House, or the Senate. Include state governments and the courts, and party division and gridlock get even worse. One or both houses of Congress led by a party opposed to the president, the argument goes, will result in a legislative standoff—as well as more aggressive congressional investigations of the White House. The argument makes intuitive sense, but some scholars have traditionally gone counter to the conventional wisdom.

Political scientists David Mayhew and Keith Krehbiel have separately shown that divided government is actually no less productive in terms of legislative achievements than is unified government—when the presidency and both houses of Congress are in the same party hands.[21] Neither scholar denies the existence of gridlock or policy stalemate, but they do not attribute it to divided government. When the chips are down, they each argue, the political process works. Disruptions and breakdowns occur, but usually in the short term. The crises, in Mayhew's words, are "short-term, limited, tolerable and correctable."

Many other political scientists think otherwise. Sarah Binder, a scholar at the Brookings Institution, questions these results. Divided government, in Binder's view, leads directly to stalemate. Others have argued that perhaps divided government worked more smoothly in the past. However, the recent polarization has brought "the virtual disappearance of regular order in Congress."[22]

The conclusion is simply that careful scholars disagree. However, the endless battle over health reform—still raging years after the legislation passed—as well as inaction on a host of other important issues (from the environment to immigration, from wage stagnation to tax reform) has even the optimists thinking twice about Congress's ability to solve its conflicts today.

As you observe Congress in the future, keep both perspectives in mind. Watch to see if, after all the dramatics and the finger pointing, the two sides quietly agree on legislation—especially toward the end of the sessions. If so, it reflects a more optimistic view: divided we govern. If not, you will know that the pessimists made the right prediction and that Congress has proven to be "the broken branch."

THE BOTTOM LINE

» Congress has grown more partisan. Today, the parties themselves are more ideologically consistent. This makes for sharper conflict, but it also gives people clearer choices.

» Does divided government lead to more gridlock? Political scientists disagree. Some have argued that it does not; "Divided we govern," they insist. Others have argued that recent developments—such as the growing ideological purity of the parties and the regular use of the filibuster—signal that divided government now means an inability to solve America's problems.

Some Popular Reforms—And Their Limits

Should we care that Americans do not like Congress? Many observers—and thoughtful members—worry that continued public disapproval will erode the effectiveness of Congress as an institution. Our national legislature will not disappear as a result of unpopularity, but the laws Congress enacts will have less sanctity, compel less attention and obedience, if the institution passing them is increasingly viewed as corrupt. Others worry that potential political talent, especially our best and brightest young people, are discouraged by continued deep public disapproval from considering a congressional career (as either staffers or members). Still another danger: that a deadlocked Congress will permit power to leak into the executive branch which will increasingly make policy on its own. We will explore how in Chapter 14.

Each year, reformers propose various fixes to improve Congress. We have already discussed two such reforms: increasing third parties and imposing term limits (see Chapter 10). Here we discuss two other popular reforms: limits on lobbyists and public education about what Congress really does.

Limit Lobbyists

Americans have called for years for reductions in lobbyists' influence in Congress. Both the 104th (1995–1996) and 109th (2007–2008) Congresses passed extensive lobbying reforms, including bans on gifts and meals that lobbyists once provided to members. Both reform packages were greeted with yawns from the public: Congressional approval ratings actually dropped after each was implemented.

Public disapproval of Congress.

James Madison, no fan of large bureaucracies, considered the possibility of minimizing interest group factions in *Federalist* no. 10 (see Chapter 3 and Appendix III). Madison came to a surprising conclusion: Because it is inevitable that groups will pursue their own interests, liberty is best protected if there are many groups pursuing their interests right out in the open. That way, the different interests will check one another and people will have a choice among a great many different perspectives. The solution to special interests: more special interests.

True, he could not possibly have imagined the vast array of interests swarming over Capitol Hill today. But, as we discussed in the previous chapter, one person's special interest is another's cherished protector of a vital program. Lobbyists represent virtually everyone. And in the real world, they link together our vast public and the complicated structures of national governance.

Even so, congressional organization—with its arcane ways, complicated processes, and multiple committees and subcommittees—creates a great many opportunities for special interests to quietly win favors and block things they do not like. The problem is not their power over the big issues, on which members have strong views and votes are in the limelight, but in the minute details or obscure items to which few pay attention, even though millions of dollars (or other favors) can be gained or lost with a few strokes of a legislator's pen.

What is the solution to such deals and favors? Perhaps James Madison had the best answer. When energy companies seek special favors, environmental groups blow the whistle (and vice versa); when hospitals seek higher pay, taxpayer groups challenge their arguments. Perhaps the solution to the problem of interests really is more interests. That would mean reforming the way Congress does business—to make sure that a wider array of interests are heard on every issue—rather than focusing on eradicating lobbyists' engagement.

Educate the Public

Some reform proposals include an earnest plea for better education about Congress. Many Americans do not know their House member's name, cannot begin to explain how bills become law, and do not even know how many senators come from each state. Perhaps with a little more knowledge, the public would be more sympathetic.

Political scientists John Hibbing and Elizabeth Theiss-Morse argued, on the other side, that Americans' real problem with Congress is not lack of knowledge. The underlying problem is deeper: Americans dislike logrolling and bargaining; we dislike committees and bureaucracy; we dislike political partisanship (and parties); we despise interest groups. Americans disdain the slow pace of congressional lawmaking: we disapprove of multiple stages, veto points, and extended House and Senate debates—which inevitably involve hashing things out, bickering, and back-scratching. Or, to put it differently, concluded Hibbing and Theiss-Morse, Americans disapprove of democracy in practice. Although Americans love democracy in the abstract and demand transparency in politics, we do not enjoy watching the congressional process playing out with all its messy give-and-take.[23]

The Real World of Democracy

This chapter has tried to make clear how difficult, complex, and often muddled congressional policymaking is. Our ultimate goal: to increase your appreciation for the messiness of democracy, as carried out in the people's branch. Another way to view all the bargaining, partial solutions, noisy debates, horse trading, and compromising is as faithfully representing a diverse, divided American public. Congress is, on balance, the most open, most public institution in our system of government. It is also full of flaws and limits.

Why, in the end, are people's opinions of Congress so dismal? Perhaps the public laments how hard it is to get legislative results from Congress despite glowing promises on the campaign trail. Or perhaps it is discomfort with the essential realities of democracy in the real world: noisy debates, stops and starts, compromise and logrolling. Part of the fault also lies with the individual members who have learned to glide to re-election, year after year, by running against the institution they serve in.

THE BOTTOM LINE

» Some popular reforms propose limiting the influence of lobbying groups in Congress.

» Others emphasize the importance of educating the public, so that Americans can exercise greater oversight and develop a deeper understanding of the workings of Congress. We would recommend education about the "messy" nature of legislating in a diverse democratic nation.

Conclusion: Congress and the Challenge of Governing

Here is how we sum up the story of this chapter: Congress, as an institution, does some important things very well—representatives and senators are remarkably adept at looking after individuals who request help. Direct constituent service, at home in the district and state, is often superb. That is one reason why re-election rates are so high.

But as our individual needs have become better supported, Congress has grown less capable of solving the big societal problems—such as immigration, healthcare, government spending, inequality, wage stagnation, global warming, or the byzantine tax code. By any measure, Americans' collective aspirations are at least as important as our personal concerns. The overarching question we have asked throughout this chapter is whether the U.S. Congress has lost its ability to achieve big collective aims, or whether it still muddles through precisely as the Constitutional framers intended.

In the past, Congress has certainly proven capable of broad achievements. Medicare and Social Security, to take two of the largest congressional programs, have cut the rate of poverty among elderly Americans by more than half and provided seniors with extremely generous health benefits.

Genuine democratic, popular government can be chaotic, muddled, and sometimes repugnant. But it is essential. Our representatives in Congress must find a way to continue to fulfill their democratic duties. The representatives in the people's branch will have to find a way to govern together—and to win back popular approval—if American democracy is to flourish in the future.

CHAPTER SUMMARY

⬤ Congress operates under extremely complicated rules that make action difficult. The overarching question for this chapter is whether Congress still works the way it is supposed to—blunting too much government action. Or whether it has become "the broken branch."

⬤ America's Congress is bicameral: the House of Representatives contains 441 members (435 voting; six others represent territories like Guam and Puerto Rico) elected every two years; in the Senate, one hundred senators serve six-year terms.

⬤ The two chambers of Congress reflect different national priorities. Populists appreciate the responsive House; advocates of stability embrace the more deliberate Senate.

⬤ Members of the House and Senate represent Americans in multiple ways. These include:

- *Geographic representation*: Constitutional election rules say members must live in the state or district they represent.

- *Descriptive representation*: Does the assembly look like the people?

- *Substantive representation*: Do members of Congress effectively pursue constituent interests?

⬤ Members of Congress are always running for office. Fundraising takes up a particularly large amount of time and attention. Members pay special attention to their home styles: Most go back to their constituency every week—compressing normal congressional business into the period from Tuesday through Thursday.

⬤ Congress is increasingly an institution of strangers who do not know one another well.

⬤ Congressional leadership in the House includes a Speaker, majority and minority leaders, and ten whips. Successful leaders in the House impose discipline on their party members. In the Senate, party leaders and whips have fewer institutional tools with which to impose discipline.

⬤ Congressional committees are the workhorses of Congress. They have proved efficient and adaptable over the years. However, the committee system also fragments Congress, hides action from public view, advantages well-placed constituents looking for individual favors, and makes it difficult to pass major legislation.

⬤ Floor procedures are another intricate part of the legislative process. Once passed by both House and Senate, legislation may still face a conference committee, a presidential veto, or both.

⬤ Congress has grown more partisan. Today, the parties themselves are more ideologically consistent. This makes for sharper conflict, but it also gives people clearer choices.

⬤ The difficult path to legislation raises the key question about Congress: Should we cheer the difficult process as a way to limit government? Or should we worry that the institution is not up to addressing America's vital problems?

KEY TERMS

115th Congress, p. 376

Cloture vote, p. 398

Committee hearing, p. 394

Committee markup
    session, p. 395

Conference committee, p. 394

Congressional caucus, p. 378

Earmark, p. 389

Filibuster, p. 376

Floor, p. 376

Legislative hold, p. 376

President pro tempore, p. 388

Reapportionment, p. 383

Roll-call vote, p. 399

Speaker of the House, p. 387

Unanimous consent, p. 396

Veto, p. 399

Voice vote, p. 399

STUDY QUESTIONS

1. Discuss the following reforms:
   a) There should be public financing for all congressional elections, even if that means raising taxes.
   b) The Senate filibuster should be abolished.
   c) There should be more limits on lobbyists' access and/or influence.

2. How did Congress lose so much power to the president? Are there ways to get some of that power back? Should power be more balanced between the two branches?

3. Why is Congress today so partisan? Can you think of ways to reduce partisanship? Are there any advantages to drawing strong partisan lines between Republicans and Democrats?

4. Should it be easier to pass laws through Congress? What, if any, benefits do all the checks and balances provide?

5. Why is Congress so unpopular with the American people? In your view, does Congress deserve its low approval ratings?

 Go to www.oup.com/us/Morone to find quizzes, flash cards, simulations, tutorials, videos, and other study tools.

The Presidency

GEORGE WASHINGTON, the first president of the United States, faced a problem. He had to find a way to persuade thirteen independent-minded states to think of themselves as one unified nation. Washington decided to foster unity by touring the new country—a grueling journey in the 1790s. He set out with assistants, slaves, horses, and dogs. As the party approached each town, the president mounted a great white steed and cantered handsomely into the cheering throngs, his favorite greyhound trotting at his side. Washington named the dog Cornwallis, after the British general who surrendered to end the Revolutionary War. Poor Cornwallis the greyhound died while touring the southern states, but his name reminded the people that they were part of a proud and independent nation. Everywhere Washington went the people greeted their president with ringing bells, cheers, songs, speeches, parades, and flags. The crowds felt, at least for a day, like Americans.[1]

Who are we? Each president offers a different answer. Washington may be our greatest president, not because of his domestic programs or foreign policies—critics were scathing about both. Instead, Washington embodied the new nation. He championed American ideals, spoke to national aspirations, introduced new ideas, and personified the nation's sense of identity—both to Americans and to the world. All presidents do the same, some more successfully than others. Each offers a different answer to the question: *Who are we?*

The president's role is difficult partly because Americans rarely agree about who we are. The United States are often the *Un*-United States. Washington took slaves on his unity tour. Didn't slavery violate the new nation's ideals? Many Americans knew that it did.

More than 225 years after Washington's tour, a new president embodied a new America. For the first time, a man with no experience in public or military service took the oath of office. Donald Trump immediately faced a decision: drone strikes. Drones are sophisticated unmanned aircraft. "Pilots" sit in dark, air-conditioned rooms around the world and remotely fly the aircraft as they streak across faraway skies in places like Afghanistan, Pakistan, or Yemen. The drones upload vivid images and can launch Hellfire missiles or laser-guided bombs at targets halfway around the globe. Between 2009 and 2016, American operators used drones to kill nearly 3,000 people.

● *President Trump speaks about his policy positions.*

In this chapter, you will:

● See how the Constitution defines the presidency.

● Focus on presidential power.

● Learn what presidents do.

● Reflect on presidential popularity—and greatness.

● Consider the personal side of the office.

● Tour the Executive Office of the President, and meet the team around a president.

Is the program effective in fighting terrorism? On his first day in office, President Trump had to decide. Drone attacks have decimated terrorist organizations, killing more than sixty leaders and almost two thousand foot soldiers. On the other hand, drones have killed hundreds of civilians, sparking fury at the United States. Stories of American missiles massacring schoolchildren, hospitals, or a wedding party inflamed anti-American sentiment. Some Americans—both conservatives and liberals—argue that the drone attacks actually recruit more terrorists than they kill.

The drone program demonstrates the extensive power of the modern presidency. Today, the American executive can approve the death of an enemy on the other side of the world.[2] The power of the office raises the same question the delegates debated at the Constitutional Convention: How much authority should the president have?

Washington's tour, the election of President Trump, and the drone program all illustrate three essential features of the American presidency:

The president personifies America. More than any other individual, presidents tell us who we are—and what we are becoming.

The president injects new ideas and themes into American politics. Our discussion of Congress emphasized the institutional rules of the game; the presidency puts more focus on individuals and ideas.

The president has enormous powers—at least on paper. That authority, and how presidents use it, raises a fundamental question: Is the presidency too powerful for a democratic republic? Or is the office too weak to do what Americans demand of it? Perhaps the same president can be both too strong and too weak at different points. Keep this question of authority in mind as you read the chapter.

Defining the Presidency

Time travelers from the nineteenth century would easily recognize today's Senate or the Supreme Court. However, the modern White House would stun them. The presidency is the branch of the federal government that has changed the most over the decades.

One hundred fifty years ago, Americans could walk right in the front door of the White House and greet the president. In 1829, during President Andrew Jackson's inauguration, supporters mobbed the mansion and forced the president to climb out a window for his own safety; aides placed tubs with whiskey and orange juice on the lawn to lure the crowds outside. When William Henry Harrison won the presidency in 1840, so many men milled about the White House hoping to get a government job that the president-elect could not find an empty room to meet with his cabinet.

Today, there are no more mobs in the White House. Presidents have redefined their roles and renegotiated their powers. The presidency is a different institution. To this day, each president has the opportunity to reshape the office. One reason the presidency is so fluid lies in the job description. By now, you know where to look for that: the Constitution.

The Presidency

Number of presidents in the last 80 years: **14**
Split between Republican/Democratic presidents in the last 80 years: **7 from each party**

Length, in months, of the shortest presidency (William Henry Harrison): **1**
Length, in months, of the longest presidency (Franklin D. Roosevelt): **145**

Number of years by which Franklin D. Roosevelt's lifespan was shorter than that of the average person at the time: **12.4**
Number of presidents younger than Barack Obama when they were elected: **2**

Election year of last president without a college education (Harry S. Truman): **1945**
Election year of last president with no formal schooling (Andrew Johnson): **1865**

Birth year of first president to be born in a hospital (Jimmy Carter): **1924**

Year in which first woman (Victoria Woodhull) ran for president: **1872**
Year in which women could first vote for president nationwide: **1920**

Number of presidents who lost the popular vote but still won the election: **5** (John Quincy Adams, Rutherford B. Hayes, Benjamin Harrison, George W. Bush, Donald Trump)

Number of presidents who were sons or nephews of prior presidents: **4** (John Quincy Adams, Benjamin Harrison, Franklin D. Roosevelt, George W. Bush)
Average winning proportion of the popular vote in the last ten presidential elections: **50.5%**
Average winning proportion of the Electoral College vote in the last ten presidential elections: **69.7%**

Highest presidential approval ratings (percent) ever recorded by Gallup (for Harry Truman, George H. W. Bush, and George W. Bush, respectively): **91, 89, 89**
Lowest approval ratings recorded by Gallup at end of a full term (for Harry Truman, Jimmy Carter, and George W. Bush, respectively): **31, 34, 34**
Highest approval ratings at end of a full term (for Bill Clinton, Ronald Reagan, and Dwight Eisenhower, respectively): **66, 63, 59**

Estimated proportion of presidents who have had extramarital affairs: **1 in 3**

Number of presidents to hold a patent: **1** (Abraham Lincoln, for an invention to free boats trapped on a sandbar)

Defined by Controversy

The Constitutional Convention's delegates faced three tough questions when they defined the presidency (for more detail, see Chapter 3). First, *should the United States even have a president?* Traditional republics feared executive power—the ark of monarchs. The founders feared the English king was too powerful, but also worried that the state governments were too weak. Their job was to find a happy medium. In the end, they selected a single president and established simple

A different era. After Andrew Jackson's inauguration, Americans crushed into the executive mansion to shake hands with the president—who was forced to escape through a window. Today, elegantly dressed supporters attend inaugural balls.

qualifications for the post: a natural-born citizen at least thirty-five years old who had lived in the United States for at least fourteen years.

Second, *how long should the president serve?* The delegates at the Constitutional Convention considered terms of four, six, seven, eight, eleven, and fifteen years. Alexander Hamilton passionately argued that presidents should be elected for life. They settled on four years, with no limit on the number of terms. Washington would set a precedent when he stepped down after his second term, dazzling his contemporaries by walking away from power. For a century and a half, American presidents followed Washington's example and served no more than two terms—until Franklin D. Roosevelt broke the pattern and won four elections between 1932 and 1944. The Twenty-Second Amendment, ratified six years after Roosevelt's death in 1945, bars presidents from serving a third term.

Third, *how should the United States choose its president?* Delegates to the convention feared that the public did not know enough, that the state legislatures were too self-interested, and that Congress would become too powerful if given the task of appointing the executive. They finally settled on a roundabout method, the Electoral College, which you encountered in Chapter 10: The states each get electoral votes equal to the members in their congressional delegation. Political scientists still debate the Electoral College because it distorts the popular vote. Even very close popular votes look lopsided in the Electoral College. Bill Clinton managed only 43 percent in 1992 (in a three-way race), and Ronald Reagan got 50.7 percent (again, in a three-way race) in 1980. Yet the Electoral College made these contests look like routs, with Clinton receiving 69 percent and Reagan a whopping 91 percent of the Electoral College vote. Moreover, this voting procedure has put the loser of the popular vote in the White House five times, most recently in 2016.

The President's Powers

Article 2 of the Constitution, which defines the presidency, seems puzzling at first glance. Article 1 meticulously defines everything Congress is empowered to do: The instructions run for fifty-two paragraphs. In contrast, Article 2 says very little about who the president is or what the president does. Thirteen short paragraphs define the office. This vague constitutional mandate is one reason why the office keeps evolving.

The Constitution is especially concise when it gets to the heart of the presidency: the powers and duties of the chief executive. It grants the president a limited

TABLE 14.1 The President's Powers Are Balanced by Congress

The president is commander in chief of the army, navy, and state militias. But Congress has the power to declare war, set the military budget, and make the rules governing the military.
The president can grant pardons and reprieves for offenses against the United States.
The president can make treaties (with the approval of two-thirds of the Senate), appoint ambassadors (with the advice and consent of the Senate), and select Supreme Court justices and other officers (again, with Senate approval).
The Constitution also authorizes presidents to solicit the opinions of their officers (the cabinet members) and requires presidents to report on the state of the Union.

number of **expressed powers**, or explicit grants of authority. Most are carefully balanced by corresponding congressional powers. Table 14.1 summarizes this balance.

Expressed powers: Powers the Constitution explicitly grants to the president.

The president draws real authority from a simple phrase at the end of the section: "Take care that the laws be faithfully executed." Congress votes on legislation and then sends it to the executive branch to put into effect. In other words, Congress grants **delegated powers** to the president. For example, Congress passes legislation that aims to improve hospital care. It delegates power to the executive branch, which issues a detailed rule saying that hospitals will receive lower federal payments if patients develop infections after surgery.

Delegated powers: Powers that Congress passes on to the president.

Modern presidents claim a third source of authority: **inherent powers**. These are not specified in the Constitution or delegated by legislation, but are implicit in the vague Article 2 phrase, "The executive power shall be vested in a president." During crises, presidents have often seized new "inherent" authority. During the Civil War, for example, President Lincoln took a series of unprecedented military actions with no clear legal basis. He imposed censorship, ordered a naval blockade, and issued orders while Congress was not in session. After the 9/11 attacks, President Bush exercised inherent powers to engage in foreign surveillance, to detain enemy combatants without hearings, and to authorize coercive interrogation (which critics called torture). After presidents claim inherent powers, the Supreme Court generally weighs whether they have overstepped the constitutional boundaries of their authority.

Inherent powers of the presidency: Powers assumed by presidents, often during a crisis, on the basis of the constitutional phrase "The executive power shall be vested in the president."

Executive agreements: An international agreement made by the president that does not require the approval of the Senate.

Modern presidents have expanded presidential power in informal ways. As we shall see later in this chapter, presidents regularly issue executive orders, negotiate **executive agreements** with other nations, claim **executive privilege**, and issue signing statements—all ways of bypassing Congress. Throughout this chapter we will encounter subtle ways the presidents have used their office to expand their power.

Executive privilege: Power claimed by the president to resist requests for authority by Congress, the courts, or the public. Not mentioned in the Constitution but based on the separation of powers.

The result is a very fluid definition of presidential power. Presidents regularly renegotiate the limits of the office through

● President Franklin Roosevelt vastly increased the power of the presidency—here a cartoon mocks his request for more authority in his second term.

COMPARING NATIONS 14.1 — Chief Executives' Power

Although presents have expanded their authority over time, chief executives in parliamentary systems, those used in most other democracies, typically are granted these powers. U.S. presidents long to exercise any of these.	*Emergency decree powers*: Executives' authority is greatly expanded in national emergencies (and they typically get to decide what counts as an "emergency").
	Partial (line-item) *veto*: Prime ministers and other foreign leaders are able to strip out individual legislative provisions that they find objectionable.
	Exclusive right *to introduce certain kinds of legislation*, especially budgets.
	The ability to *dismiss the legislature and call new elections*.

their actions at home and abroad. Crises generally expand the presidential role. More than any other institution, the presidency is a constant work in progress. The arc of presidential history begins with a modest constitutional grant of power that has grown through the years.

This discussion brings us back to the question we posed at the start of the chapter: Has the president become too powerful? We turn to that question in the next section.

THE BOTTOM LINE

» Presidents serve a four-year term and can run for re-election once.

» They are elected indirectly, via the Electoral College.

» The president has three types of powers: *expressed* in the Constitution, *delegated* by Congress, and *inherent* in the role of chief executive.

» In theory, Congress passes laws and the president executes them. In reality, presidents constantly negotiate the limits of their power—which often expands during crises.

Is the Presidency Too Powerful?

The constitutional framers wrestled with the same issue we debate today: *power*. How much authority do presidents need to protect the nation and get things done? When does the office's reach violate the idea of limited government?

An Imperial Presidency?

During George Washington's national tour, a few Americans fretted about his nine stallions, gold-trimmed saddles, personal attendants, and all that adulation. Washington, they whispered, was acting more like a king than the president of a homespun republic. They were articulating a constant American theme: The president has grown too mighty. Flash forward two centuries. When President Obama visited Africa, hundreds of Secret Service agents arrived in advance, an aircraft carrier with a fully staffed medical trauma center sailed offshore, and military cargo planes hauled in fifty-six support vehicles including fourteen limousines. The presidential party included lawyers, secretaries, speechwriters, and chefs. U.S. fighter jets flew in shifts, providing continual air cover. American presidents travel almost like emperors.[3]

Presidents have constantly redefined the authority of their office—setting off critics who charge that they have gone too far. Washington's successor, President John Adams, did not have to worry about cheering crowds. Critics mocked the chubby second president as "His Rotundity." Adams attracted so little attention that he regularly swam naked in the Potomac River (until a

The president arrives in Los Angeles aboard Marine One—surrounded by support aircraft.

female reporter allegedly spied him, sat on his clothes, and demanded an interview). Even Adams, however, aroused widespread fears about executive power when he signed the Alien and Sedition Acts, which gave the executive broad powers to deport "dangerous aliens" and punish "false, scandalous, and malicious" speech. The president seemed to be trampling the First Amendment by silencing criticism.

Many presidents have stretched the limits of the office. One approach, the **unitary executive theory,** defends the expansion of power. This view holds that the Constitution puts the president in charge of executing the laws, and therefore no one—not Congress, not the judiciary, not even the people—may limit presidential power when it comes to executive matters. Many executive decisions demand swift, decisive, and sometimes secretive action. Only an empowered president, the argument goes, can make those instantaneous calls.

The unitary executive theory is controversial. Arthur Schlesinger, Jr., a celebrated historian, warned of an **imperial presidency**. Very powerful presidents, he feared, become like emperors: They run roughshod over Congress, issue secret decisions, unilaterally deploy force around the world, and burst past the checks and balances limiting presidential power. Critics worry that imperial features have become part of the presidency itself. Republicans bitterly argued that the Obama Administration's overreach had created an imperial presidency. Now Democrats say the same about the Trump era. Despite the opposition, as Congress and the Supreme Court deadlock, more power appears to be flowing to the president.[4]

At issue are two vital principles: We need a president who is strong enough to lead the country and face our problems. But if presidents become too strong, we lose our republican form of government. This is a deep paradox of American politics: *We need powerful leaders; we fear powerful leaders.*

Unitary executive theory: The idea that the Constitution puts the president in charge of executing the laws and that therefore no other branch may limit presidential discretion over executive matters.

Imperial presidency: A characterization of the American presidency that suggests it is demonstrating imperial traits, and that the republic is morphing into an empire.

A Weak Office?

At the same time, the presidency also can seem very weak. Every modern president has complained about his inability to get basic goals accomplished. Congress, the courts, the opposing political party, the media, interest groups, and bad luck can all humble a president. Since 1960, only four (of ten) presidents have completed two full terms. What kind of "imperial" presidency is that?

Presidents often appear weakest when they wrestle with domestic issues. Even under the best of circumstances, as we saw in the previous chapter, it is difficult to get major legislation through Congress. Presidents' vetoes can be overridden, and Congress retains the power of impeachment. The president nominally runs the executive branch, but the bureaucracy is immense and often difficult to control—and cabinets are staffed by officials the Senate must approve. Introducing changes through the American political process is extremely difficult, even for the savviest presidents.

For a case study in the weak presidency, take Jimmy Carter. Congressional relations turned frosty early in his term after Carter unexpectedly vetoed a spending bill. Carter's major legislative proposals stalled on Capitol Hill. Then the economy soured; interest rates spiraled toward 20 percent, and unemployment topped 10 percent. Gas prices soared, forcing customers in some regions to wait in long lines at gas stations.

Carter did not seem to have an answer to all the woes besetting the nation. A mischievous editor at the *Boston Globe* captured one reaction to Carter's speech when he designed a mock headline, "Mush from the Wimp." By mistake, the headline ran in the *Globe*'s first edition.[5] A few months later, militant Iranian students took fifty-three Americans hostage at the U.S. embassy in Tehran and held them for 444 days. A weak president seemed to be completely overwhelmed by events all around him.

Back and forth goes the debate. Is the president getting too powerful and breaking free from popular control? Or is the president not up to the job of governing a superpower? To answer these questions, let us take a closer look at just what presidents do.

» Americans want a powerful president; simultaneously, Americans fear a powerful president.

» The executive branch has grown far stronger over time, especially when it comes to foreign policy.

» In significant ways, presidential power also is limited, especially when it comes to solving domestic problems.

What Presidents Do

Over time, presidents have taken on many jobs. Some are described in the Constitution. Others arise organically during national crises. Presidents seize still other powers as they jockey for political advantage. By now, the president has accumulated an extraordinary number of hats (and helmets).

Commander in Chief

The Constitution lays it out simply: "The president shall be the Commander-in-Chief of the Army and Navy of the United States and the militia of the several states, when called into the actual service of the United States." Congress declares war and presidents manage it.

For many years, the United States had a small standing army and called men and women to service in wartime. The size of the army jumped thirty-eight-fold during the Civil War and thirty-six-fold during World War I. After each war, the army quickly demobilized. This approach reflected classical theory. In great republics like Athens and Rome, citizens took up arms when enemies loomed and then returned home when the crisis had passed—just as George Washington had done during the American Revolution. Peacetime armies were, according to the traditional perspective, a recipe for empire or monarchy.

This tradition changed after World War II, when the United States faced off against the Soviet Union in the Cold War. An army of around 250,000 (after World War I) grew into a force of over two million and spread across the globe. Back in 1835, Tocqueville mused that the Constitution gave the president "almost royal prerogatives which he has no occasion to use." Now the occasion had arrived, and the president's power grew.

Today, America's active-duty force numbers over 1.3 million, with another 850,000 in reserve (Figure 14.1). Military spending fell sharply between 2011 and 2015—partially because of troop reductions in Iraq and Afghanistan—but began to rise again in 2016.

Even with these cuts, the defense budget ran over $625 billion in 2016—not including the Department of Veterans Affairs, the Department of Homeland Security, intelligence agencies, and other related efforts. The military operates about 750 installations that span the globe. In short, the commander in chief oversees the world's largest fighting force. That role, by itself, makes the president one of the most powerful individuals in the world.

Meanwhile, checks on the commander in chief have faded. The Constitution authorizes Congress to declare wars, but since the nuclear age dawned in 1945, presidents have rarely waited for Congress to act. Facing the doomsday threat of nuclear missiles, military response time is measured in minutes—too fast for congressional deliberation.

FIGURE 14.1 *The military and how it grew, 1800–2015: Traditionally, the United States called soldiers to war and then demobilized after the war. The United States began to play a global role after the Spanish-American War. (Historical Statistics/Statistical Abstracts)*

In an effort to regain some of its authority, Congress passed the War Powers Act in 1973, requiring congressional approval after troops had been deployed for sixty days. That is a far weaker check than the constitutional power to declare war. It concedes the president's authority to unilaterally deploy troops; Congress does not get its say until American men and women are already in combat—when it is very difficult to vote no. Moreover, presidents have been contemptuous of the War Powers Act.

In Libya, American forces helped demolish Muammar Gaddafi's air defense system. That turned the tide in favor of the rebels. But after doing the job, the United States turned control of the skies over to its allies. Congress demanded that the administration seek congressional approval under the War Powers Act. The Obama administration refused, arguing that the United States had no ground forces in combat. Ten members of Congress sued President Obama in federal court for violating the Constitution and the War Powers Act. The Court dismissed the case, arguing that Congress possessed sufficient constitutional powers to resolve the issue.

Presidential powers have always waxed during wartime. Franklin D. Roosevelt's attorney general once commented, "The Constitution has not greatly bothered any wartime president."[6] Two developments since then have further increased the president's military authority: America's powerful military machine, always poised for deployment, and the perception of perpetual threat—first from the Soviet Union, now from terrorists. However, when wars drag on and become unpopular, the president's powers seem to fade. Congress holds hearings and cuts military budgets; public approval ratings decline; protests spring up.

Presidents are deeply engaged by their military role. They start each day with a security briefing that reviews all the dangers stirring around the world, they have a large national security staff, and—the great symbol of our nuclear age—they are never more than a few feet away from "the football."

If you see the president in person, or a wide-angle shot on television, you can glimpse a military officer standing about twenty feet away and clutching a medium-size black briefcase, known as "the football." What is in the bag? The answer is classified, but over the years the public has learned that it is a mobile communications center locked into the American nuclear arsenal. Every minute of every day, the American president is steps away from a kit that would enable him or her to launch an attack that could obliterate any nation from the face of the Earth.

Top Diplomat

The Constitution gives presidents the lead role in foreign affairs. Presidents and their

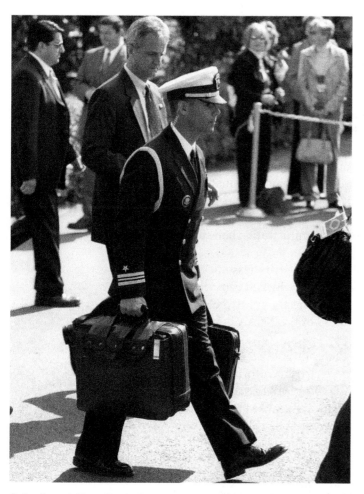

A uniformed officer with "the football"—a briefcase that contains launch codes for the nuclear arsenal. The football is never more than a few feet away from the president.

international advisors set an overall framework for the U.S. role in the world. Some administrations emphasize international alliances; they work closely with foreign powers and build multinational institutions. Others prefer to go it alone—they ignore the United Nations and are reluctant to sign treaties for fear that they will bind the United States to foreign governments.

Foreign policy issues bombard each president. Should the United States take the lead on global warming or reject international agreements in favor of bulking up domestic manufacturing? Should we press foreign governments on social justice issues (e.g., the right to unionize without facing violence) when negotiating trade agreements? Should we try to broker peace in the Middle East? Respond to aggression such as Russia's intervention in Syria? What should be done about rogue states with nuclear weapons or terrorist organizations like the Islamic jihadist group ISIS? Presidents and their team constantly meet, discuss, threaten, and negotiate with nations near and far.

Should the United States intervene to try and stop the bloodshed in Syria? Another tough decision for the president. (Source: Daily Mail)

Foreign diplomacy is not just about trouble spots. The State Department manages 305 embassies, consulates, and diplomatic missions around the world. Presidents must hash out American relations with nearly two hundred nations that range from "special friends" to distant allies to avowed enemies. Intricate questions arise about how to approach each country: Should the president shake hands with our nation's enemies? Every smile or snub sends a diplomatic message. A president sets the tone and the policy for all these relationships.

Global statecraft is full of unexpected snares. When the newly elected President Obama met then–British Prime Minister Gordon Brown for the first time, the English press howled about "humiliation." Brown had given Obama a valuable pen carved from the timbers of a nineteenth-century British warship; Obama's gift was a pile of DVDs. Did the then popular president really mean to humiliate the relatively unpopular prime minister? Certainly not; the new administration had simply slipped up.

Two years later, the Obama administration had learned its lesson. When new Prime Minister David Cameron came calling, Obama whisked him via Air Force One ("the first foreign leader to ride on the presidential aircraft," cheered the English press[7]) to a courtside seat at the first round of the NCAA basketball championship.

Foreign policy crises differ vastly from everyday domestic politics. Passing laws is a long, complicated process full of compromise and constraint. During international crises—hostage situations, terrorist attacks, the outbreak of war—all eyes turn toward the president and his team. Often presidents must make fast decisions with immediate consequences. John F. Kennedy captured the intensity, a few weeks after taking office, in a late-night phone call to former vice president Richard Nixon during his first international crisis. "It really is true that foreign affairs is the only important issue for a president to handle, isn't it?" queried Kennedy. "I mean who gives a shit if the minimum wage is $1.15 or $1.25 compared to something like this?"[8]

The First Legislator

The Constitution includes presidents in the legislative process. It authorizes them to *recommend measures* for Congress's "consideration," report to Congress *information on the state of the Union*, and *veto legislation* they oppose.

Recommending Measures. Until modern times, presidents generally avoided legislative affairs. In 1840, William Henry Harrison devoted his inaugural address—the longest in history—to denouncing the insatiable love of power creeping into the presidency. He pledged to honor congressional authority by avoiding legislative involvement. Dwight Eisenhower (1953–1961) was the last president to try to leave legislation to Congress. His cabinet officers complained, and before long Eisenhower was recommending measures—and blasting Congress when it failed to approve them.

Today, presidential candidates define the legislative agenda long before they arrive in office. President Donald Trump talked during his campaign about prominent policy priorities, including immigration restrictions, reversing health reform, and altering trade agreements. Each president begins their term with a few legislative priorities. However, many others inevitably arise. Congressional leaders have their own lists. Top White House advisors lobby for favorite programs. And unexpected issues constantly spring up and require presidential attention.

State of the Union. The Constitution invites the chief executive to report on the state of the Union "from time to time." Today, the "SOTU address," as insiders term it, is an annual event, delivered with great fanfare before Congress, Supreme Court justices, and a national television audience. The speech announces the president's legislative program for the year.

Following the SOTU address, each program undergoes a second round of debates within the administration: Does it really fit our budget? Can we make it work smoothly? Did Congress cheer or yawn when the boss rolled it out? What was the public reaction? Most policies have friends and enemies in the administration—and if you get your favorite idea funded, I may not get mine. The process is a polite version of a knife fight. Proposals that survive go up to Capitol Hill, where they face the long, complicated congressional process we described in the last chapter.

Presidential "Batting Average." Only members of Congress can formally propose a law, so presidents rely on supporters in each chamber to submit their bills. The White House has a congressional liaison team to negotiate and cut deals. Generally hidden from public view, the liaison is a key role in the modern presidency. No matter how talented a liaison might be, frustration inevitably sets in. To the executive branch, legislators seem overly parochial as they focus on their states and districts. Still, most presidents quickly learn the same lesson: work closely with Congress. Managing relations with House and Senate members is one of the most important presidential skills.

● *Across the ideological divide: President Ronald Reagan (a Republican) and Speaker of the House Tip O'Neill (D-MA) negotiate the budget. The liberal and the conservative loved to swap Irish stories—often long into the night.*

426

We can measure each president's legislative success—generally referred to as the batting average (Table 14.2). There are many different ways to keep score: successful passage as a proportion of all the bills the president endorses, of the most important bills, or of bills that the other party opposes. You can see that when the same party controls the White House and Congress, known as unified government, the batting average is much higher, usually around .800. When the opposition party controls Congress (divided government), the average usually falls below .500. Some political scientists have argued that divided government makes for a more effective legislative process. But notice how divided governments (the light blue lines) have been yielding less agreement in recent years. President Obama enjoyed the highest batting average in the past seventy-five years when both houses of Congress were Democratic, and the second lowest average when he faced a divided Congress. Recall that the two parties are much more uniformly opposed to one another today than in the past, when each party had both conservative and liberal wings.

TABLE 14.2 **Presidential Batting Average: Measuring the Proportion of Congressional Bills on Which the President Took a Position That Passed**

PRESIDENT	PARTY	YEARS IN OFFICE	CONGRESSIONAL CONTROL	PERCENTAGE OF CONGRESSIONAL VOTES SUPPORTING PRESIDENT'S POSITION
Ronald Reagan	R	1981–1986	Mixed control (R Senate, D House)	67.4%
Ronald Reagan	R	1987–1989	Democrats control Congress	45.4%
George H. W. Bush	R	1989–1993	Democrats control Congress	51.8%
Bill Clinton	D	1993–1994	Democrats control Congress	86.3%
Bill Clinton	D	1995–2000	Republicans control Congress	48.1%
George W. Bush	R	2001–2006	Republicans control Congress	80.9%
George W. Bush	R	2007–2008	Democrats control Congress	43.0%
Barack Obama	D	2009–2010	Democrats control Congress	92.0%
Barack Obama	D	2011–2013	Mixed control (D Senate, R House)	52.8%
Barack Obama	D	2015–2016	Republicans control Congress	35.7%

▓ *President's party controls Congress*
▒ *Opposition party controls Congress*
░ *Congress split*

Veto power: The presidential power to block an act of Congress by refusing to sign it.

Override: The process by which Congress can overcome a presidential veto with a two-thirds vote in both chambers.

Veto. When Congress passes a law, presidents have the authority to sign or **veto** it (*veto* means "I forbid" in Latin). As we saw in the last chapter, a veto blocks the legislation unless two-thirds of both chambers vote to **override** it, a very high bar. Presidents have ten days to return the legislation to Congress with a message explaining why they have rejected it. If the president does nothing, the bill becomes law in ten days.

The veto is a formidable weapon. In the last eighty years, presidents have rejected more than 1,400 bills. Congress managed to override just sixty times: a congressional "batting average" of 4 percent. Recently the veto has become a more partisan weapon, as conflict between the parties has escalated. Franklin D. Roosevelt, Harry Truman, and Jimmy Carter all flourished the veto pen against a Congress controlled by their own party; in their first two years, the three presidents struck down seventy-three, seventy-four, and nineteen bills, respectively. In contrast, the most recent presidents—Clinton, Bush, and Obama—*combined* vetoed a total of two bills against their own party majorities in their first two years (see Figure 14.2). Barack Obama vetoed only two bills in his first six years in office. You would have to go back to 1822 (James Monroe) to find fewer vetoes. During his final two years in office (2015–2016), after Republicans gained control of the Senate, he vetoed ten more bills.

A president's veto rarely comes as a surprise. As Congress works on a law, the president's congressional liaisons are ever present. Administration officials may threaten a veto to shape the legislation in favorable ways. When negotiations get especially intense, the president can also go public and threaten Congress. Congressional leaders in turn can threaten to bury a bill the president wants, or openly defy a president to veto popular bills. After all the back-and-forth, presidents have developed yet another strategy: They can voice their displeasure while signing bills into law.

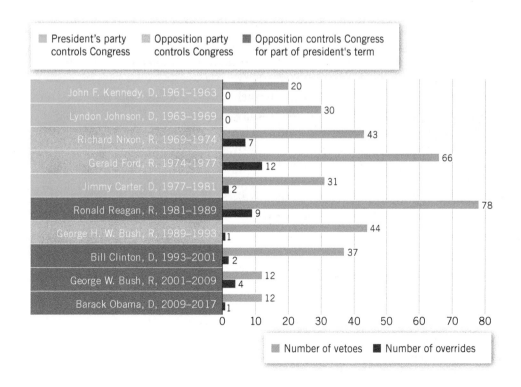

● **FIGURE 14.2** *Presidential vetoes and overrides. Note that vetoes were far more common fifty years ago, even when the same party controlled Congress and the White House. Congress rarely manages to override a presidential veto. (U.S. Senate)*

Signing Statements. Bill signing has become a great Washington ritual, especially for popular legislation. Congressional sponsors flank the president, who has a big pile of pens to hand out to the program's key supporters while cameras capture the smiling moment.

In recent decades, presidents have increasingly issued **signing statements** as they sign a bill into law. These statements may offer their administration's interpretation of the law—one sometimes at odds with Congress's expressed ideas. Senator Obama, like most Democrats, criticized the signing statements. Once he was elected president, however, he continued the practice, though he only issued a total of thirty-three statements as president. Unless the Supreme Court rules on the matter, this may become another example of the pattern: Presidents redefine their own office and expand its powers.

Chief Bureaucrat

As chief bureaucrat, the president has the powers to make appointments and issue executive orders.

Appointments. The Constitution gives the president the power to appoint the men and women of the executive branch of government, subject to confirmation by the Senate. President Washington took the top officers of the major departments and organized them into a cabinet to advise him. The original cabinet included four officers: the secretaries of war, treasury, and state, and the attorney general. By 1800, the executive branch comprised two hundred officeholders.[9]

Today, the executive branch includes fifteen departments and 2.7 million employees—a number that has remained the same for fifty years; add the military and the executive branch tops four million. Presidents appoint some four thousand **political appointees** who direct the executive agencies; the rest are **civil servants** who stay on from one administration to the next. We will explore these officials and their agencies in Chapter 15.

Executive Orders. As chief executive, presidents wield powers that do not need to go through Congress. They can sign **executive orders**, with the force of law, setting guidelines for federal agencies. Contemporary administrations issue thirty to forty executive orders a year. Some are simply instructions for operating the executive branch: setting up a new council or office, for example. Others involve controversial decisions. They can be issued with fanfare or executed secretly. Recent executive orders have required government action dealing with the impact of climate change, lifted blocks preventing companies from trading with Cuba, and stopped the deportation of young, undocumented immigrants (blocked by the courts).

Use of executive orders has expanded considerably in recent years. Some presidential scholars, as well as critics of expanded presidential power, suggest that executive orders are unconstitutional—the Constitution never mentions them. However, courts generally permit

Signing statements: Written presidential declarations commenting on the bill that is being signed into law—often including criticism of one or more provisions.

Political appointees: Top officials in the executive agencies, appointed by the president.

Civil servants: Members of the permanent executive branch bureaucracy who are employed on the basis of competitive exams and keep their positions regardless of the presidential administration.

Executive order: A presidential declaration, with the force of law, that issues instructions to the executive branch without any requirement for congressional action or approval.

● *Appointments Power. President-elect Trump and his team were considering some four thousand appointments to top executive branch positions before taking office.*

INFO/DATA: Executive Orders Issued by Each President, Per Day in Office

Presidential power is exercised in many forms. Although the Constitution separates power among the branches, presidents dating back to Abraham Lincoln have issued executive orders that have the force of law but do not require congressional approval. Notice the increased usage of these orders during the Theodore Roosevelt administration, as well as a decline in recent years.

1. Should presidents hold this autonomous power to act through executive orders, or does it violate the spirit (and perhaps the letter) of the Constitution? Does a gridlocked Congress make the practice necessary? Or will it lead to an overly active government?

2. Choose a political topic you care about (environmental sustainability, gun rights, etc.). Research whether recent presidents have issued executive orders related to your topic. What are the advantages and drawbacks to presidents exercising their will in this way?

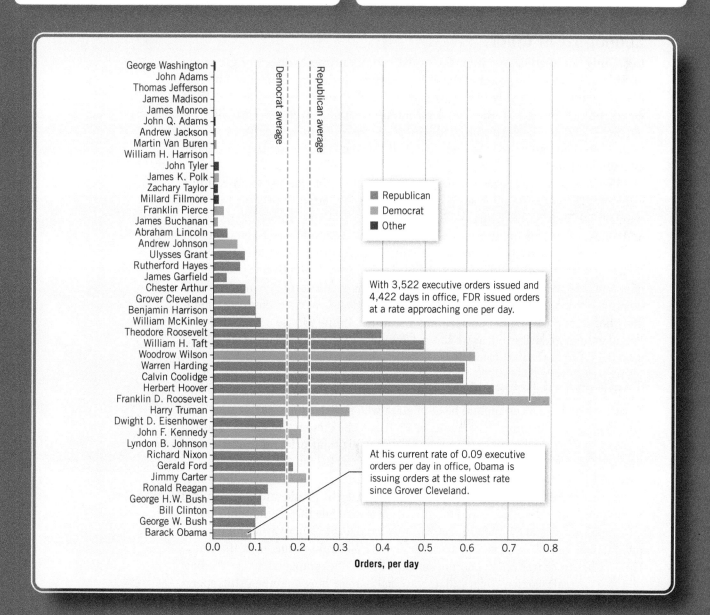

With 3,522 executive orders issued and 4,422 days in office, FDR issued orders at a rate approaching one per day.

At his current rate of 0.09 executive orders per day in office, Obama is issuing orders at the slowest rate since Grover Cleveland.

Legend:
- Republican
- Democrat
- Other

X-axis: Orders, per day (0.0 to 0.8)

Presidents listed (top to bottom): George Washington, John Adams, Thomas Jefferson, James Madison, James Monroe, John Q. Adams, Andrew Jackson, Martin Van Buren, William H. Harrison, John Tyler, James K. Polk, Zachary Taylor, Millard Fillmore, Franklin Pierce, James Buchanan, Abraham Lincoln, Andrew Johnson, Ulysses Grant, Rutherford Hayes, James Garfield, Chester Arthur, Grover Cleveland, Benjamin Harrison, William McKinley, Theodore Roosevelt, William H. Taft, Woodrow Wilson, Warren Harding, Calvin Coolidge, Herbert Hoover, Franklin D. Roosevelt, Harry Truman, Dwight D. Eisenhower, John F. Kennedy, Lyndon B. Johnson, Richard Nixon, Gerald Ford, Jimmy Carter, Ronald Reagan, George H.W. Bush, Bill Clinton, George W. Bush, Barack Obama

Vertical reference lines: Democrat average, Republican average

Source: The American Presidency Project and authors' compilation.

the orders as part of the "inherent powers" of the presidency. The Supreme Court has only struck down eight executive orders—two of Bill Clinton's and, five of Franklin Roosevelt's, and one of Barack Obama's—out of more than 13,700 going back to the Washington Administration.

Barack Obama used orders for more technical purposes until Republicans took control of the House in 2011. Then the White House began to make policy through executive orders, signing 126 by the end of 2016. For example, when Congress voted down the DREAM Act, which offered a path to citizenship for some undocumented aliens, President Obama issued an executive order designed to stop deportation (and allow work permits) for young, undocumented men and women who had been brought to the United States as children. After the president later expanded the program to include adults, the Supreme Court deadlocked on that expansion's constitutionality in 2016; that stopped the expansion, though legal debates continue.

Some observers worry that, once again, Congress is slowly losing authority while presidents—from both parties—use a traditional form of executive power to expand the scope and authority of their office.

Economist in Chief

Economic authority is one item the Constitution definitely does *not* grant the president. It places the power of the purse—taxing, spending, borrowing, and regulating commerce—firmly in congressional hands. However, during the Great Depression of the 1930s, the Roosevelt administration seized responsibility for putting the nation back to work, launching one recovery program after another. "Take a method and try it," insisted Roosevelt. "If that fails, try another. . . . Above all try something."[10]

The idea soon took root: The president was responsible for a smooth-running economy. The year after Roosevelt died, Congress legislated the Council of Economic Advisers (CEA) to help presidents oversee the economy. Today, the president and a host of staffers monitor economic conditions. White House economists vet every plan and proposal for its impact on American prosperity; they help formulate policy on almost every issue—taxing, spending, trade deals, and the projected costs of a new federal holiday. Every new administration crowds more economists into its ranks. When Donald Trump won the election in 2016, media accounts immediately began speculating about who might lead the White House economic team. Presidential popularity and, as we saw in Chapter 10, the party's chances of holding onto the office in the next election are heavily influenced by economic conditions.

The Head of State

Most nations have a ceremonial head of state who stands above partisan politics and represents the nation. The queen of England, the emperor of Japan, and the president of Israel all play this nonpolitical role while their prime ministers make the policies that govern their countries. Citizens of the British Isles do not need to check their political affiliation when they sing "God Save the Queen"—she represents them across the political spectrum. In contrast, the presidents of the United States play both roles. They stand for the nation even while they fight for one party.

Presidents spend a lot of time in their ceremonial role. They throw out the first pitch during the World Series, spare a turkey every Thanksgiving, light the White House Christmas tree and menorah, smash a bottle of champagne across the bow of a new aircraft carrier, congratulate national heroes, host championship sports teams, and embody America every time the Marine Corps Band plays "Hail to the

The president as head of state. President Bill Clinton and First Lady Hillary Clinton wear traditional kente cloth. They are waving to thousands of cheering Ghanaians. With them is then–president of Ghana, Jerry Rawlings.

Chief." When presidents travel abroad, they represent all Americans, not just their party or their supporters.

Party Leader

George Washington repeatedly warned the country against political parties and the strife they bring. However, by his second term, rival parties were not-so-quietly emerging. As suffrage spread beyond landowning gentlemen, parties grew into the largest political organizations in America. They created yet another role for the president: party leader.

This role sharpens the tension we described in the last section. There is a very fine line between leading the nation (and standing for everyone) and leading the Democrats (which means defeating Republicans).

Presidents must perform complicated balancing acts to avoid charges of blatant partisanship (levelled by the other party) and failing to adequately support their party colleagues. During George W. Bush's presidency, Democrats complained that the president was using the war on terror to defeat Democrats and build a permanent Republican majority. Republicans, in turn, accused Barack Obama of leaking classified information about the death of Osama bin Laden for political gain. Each side accuses the other of taking politics to unprecedented extremes.

Can anything tamp down the partisan conflict? Yes: the secret ingredient is fear. When a president grows very popular, opponents will often go along out of fear that the voters might punish them if they do not. Presidents who get more votes in a district than a House member, or more votes in the state than a senator, can be very persuasive—as long as their poll numbers remain high.

The Bully Pulpit: Introducing Ideas

President Theodore Roosevelt was bursting with ideas, opinions, exhortations, and warnings. He called the presidency itself a "bully pulpit" (today we might say "awesome brand multiplier"). Roosevelt knew that an active president has the country's ear, an opening to introduce and promote new ideas.

Most presidencies are marked by a few big ideas. In his inaugural address, John F. Kennedy called the nation to public service. "Ask not what your country can do for you," said Kennedy. "Ask what you can do for your country." As the second-youngest president in history (after Theodore Roosevelt), Kennedy projected youthful energy and vigor. The president's ideas seemed part and parcel of the man himself. Ronald Reagan championed a very different idea when he called government the source of our national problems; individuals pursuing the American dream and trying to get rich were, he declared, the real source of national vitality. Successful presidents arrive in office with powerful ideas—and persuade the public to embrace new visions of our political life.

A sign of a fading party is a cupboard bare of ideas. When Jimmy Carter won the White House in 1976, a member of his transition team wrote a strange memo. The new administration, he said, must educate its appointees about President-elect Carter's "goals and philosophy." The Democrats of that era were so vague about their ideas that the president's staff thought it necessary to instruct its troops about what their new leader stood for.[11]

More than any other political office in America, the presidency rises and falls on ideas. "The power of the presidency," as one scholar famously put it, "is the power to persuade."[12] Persuasion involves the ability to put something new before the public, the power to take an unfamiliar notion, and get the whole nation to talk about it. Throughout this book, we have focused on the power and importance of ideas in American politics. The presidency is the institution best geared to inject new ideas into our great national conversation.

● *Theodore Roosevelt called the presidency a "bully pulpit." No other office is more effective for introducing new ideas. Here, TR takes full advantage of his pulpit.*

The Impossible Job

How can anyone juggle so many different presidential roles? The honest answer is that no one can. Even great presidents cannot handle all their jobs well all of the time. Still, this is what we demand of our chief executive.

Each presidential role requires different strengths and skills. No person will have them all. The bully pulpit can help: bold ideas bring together the many threads of this huge task. They make a presidency coherent. Without that, presidents may seem overwhelmed by the job, skittering from one task to another without a broader sense of purpose or vision.

Finally, note one theme that runs through every role: Presidential authority has grown in every aspect of the office. The president's many roles are one more way to measure the swelling power and importance of the office. That brings us back again to the central paradox of the executive: The presidency grows ever more powerful, yet the role has grown so large that no one person can perform every aspect of it well.

THE BOTTOM LINE

» The president wears many hats and helmets. Some are specified in the Constitution. Others have developed over time.

» Presidential roles include commander in chief, top diplomat, first legislator, head bureaucrat, economist in chief, head of state, and party leader. Presidents also are uniquely situated to introduce new ideas—tying together these many different roles.

» The president's authority has grown in every one of these roles. At the same time, it is difficult to do so many different things effectively.

Presidential Leadership: Success and Failure in the Oval Office

Presidents try to manage perceptions of their performance. They address the public, use (and bypass) the media, schedule eye-catching events, and rely on polls to hone their message. How do we know if they have succeeded? We will examine three different measures of presidential achievement: polls, historical rankings, and the great cycles of political time.

Managing the Public

Going public: Directly addressing the public to win support for oneself or one's ideas.

As the only nationally elected official (excepting the vice president, who is elected as a package with the president), presidents develop a relationship with the people, which they cultivate by **going public** by directly addressing citizens to win support. Each new form of media—radio, television, Twitter, Pinterest—shifts the way presidents go public.

John F. Kennedy demonstrated the full power of the media when he held the first live, televised press conference in February 1961. It was a smash hit, with sixty-five million viewers; Kennedy's approval ratings climbed to 75 percent and stayed high for sixteen months. Kennedy had shifted how presidents connect to the public: people saw him, heard him, and related to him directly. Few people gave Donald Trump much chance in the 2016 Republican primary, much less the general election. What did they overlook? His savvy in going public.

Today, presidents continue to look for ways to connect with Americans. They call town hall meetings, travel across the country, and give speeches before large crowds. They speak directly to the camera from the Oval Office. Their office tweets supporters. You can follow them on Instagram or Facebook. Each of these actions is an effort to win the public over—sometimes for a specific policy, sometimes for a broad presidential agenda.

see for yourself 14.1

Go online to see President Ford's unfortunate stumble. (Flash required)

Presidents "go public" primarily through the media. Each effort is designed to control the spin that filters out through newscasts, talk shows, and Twitter feeds. Especially talented communicators, such as Ronald Reagan or Barack Obama, are able to further expand the informal powers of the presidency through their presence on mainstream and social media outlets.

Images are often more important than words. Presidents hug disaster victims, play basketball with the troops, or wave to cheering throngs holding American flags in a foreign nation. The image can turn negative in an instant. President Johnson playfully lifted his beagle by the ears in front of the press (cruel!). President Ford slipped and fell in public (clumsy!). President George H. W. Bush threw up at a state dinner in Japan (you can imagine!). In a complicated world, a single picture can distill popular perception. Images have an impact—positive or negative—when they seem to

Lyndon Johnson lifting his beagle by the ears. The president was trying for a lighthearted moment but quickly felt the backlash from outraged pet lovers.

reveal the president's true strengths or weakness. The key point is simple: *Presidents constantly try to manage their image in the public eye.*[13]

Our 24/7 media era, described in Chapter 9, complicates the effort to touch the public. On the one hand, it is easier than ever to communicate. However, the velocity of the news cycle means that most efforts only linger a few hours before they are displaced by the next story. A generation ago, an important presidential address might dominate the news for several days. Today the sheer volume of information flowing through the media means that only the most important events will command attention for long. The president's message now requires constant repetition, amplification, and—to grip viewers—a touch of novelty and drama. Going public is a rapidly changing art form.

The White House runs a sophisticated polling operation that guides its outreach efforts. The president's daily schedule frequently includes briefings from the administration's pollster. The president's team scrutinizes the findings, not to develop new policies but to recalibrate the ways it presents its message. Despite polls to the contrary, President Obama doubled down on healthcare reform and same-sex marriage. An administration's goals do not change, but the language and the pitch of its messages are heavily poll tested in the constant search for the most effective way to communicate to the public.[14]

Approval Ratings

Every week, another wave of polls reports how Americans view the president's performance. These are used widely, inside and beyond Washington, as a rough barometer of the administration's success. Any one poll can be misleading (as we saw in Chapter 8), but if you eliminate the outliers—the occasional polls that are much higher and lower than the others—and scan the rest, you will have a snapshot of the administration's ratings that are reverberating through the media and around Washington.

What Do You Think? | **Ranking the President**

You've seen a variety of presidential rankings by historians, political scientists, and statistical experts. Time for you to weigh in, on the most recently departed president. Where, in your opinion, does President Obama rate alongside the previous forty-three presidents to hold the office?

Among the greats. Obama entered the presidency during a time of grave economic difficulty, and his success steering the nation to safer financial shores, pushing through a landmark health reform act (which eluded other presidents, Democrats and Republicans alike, for nearly 100 years), taking executive action on clean air, ending U.S. war in Iraq, and signing a pact to deny Iran nuclear weapons qualifies him as among the very best presidents in U.S. history.

In the middle. Obama's important achievements, noted at left, are balanced by his frequent inability to advance his agenda. Yes, he faced a staunch opposition party—but the most successful presidents are able to overcome opponents and move their ideas and policy priorities forward.

Near the bottom. The Obama administration has produced one failure after another: an expensive and intrusive health reform law, an economy that has stayed stuck in neutral for too many years, and an incoherent and weak foreign policy that has led to the rise of antidemocratic forces. History will judge him poorly.

A president riding high in the polls finds governing easier. The press corps and Washington insiders are slightly more deferential. Members of Congress watch the president's popularity in their own states and districts and think twice about opposing them. As the president's approval sinks, criticism rises. Congressional allies back away. Press coverage turns sour. The late night talk shows serve up mockery.

All administrations run through polling cycles; no president stays above 50 percent approval for an entire term. Average out differences across administrations and roughly the same pattern generally emerges: High approval scores at the start, usually above 60 percent; a slow decline that bottoms out midway through the second year; a gradual ascent and peak toward the end of the fourth year (see Figure 14.3). With luck, it rises above 50 percent in time for re-election. A dip after re-election and a rise at the end. Each individual administration offers its own unique variations—with general economic performance especially affecting the general approval level. The Obama administration precisely fits the general profile—rising back above 50 percent during the last year.[15]

Dramatic events create spikes in approval (or disapproval). The two highest ratings on record reflected boosts for George H. W. Bush after a quick, dramatic victory in the First Gulf War, and for his son George W. Bush after he responded to terrorist attacks on the World Trade Center in September 2001 by standing defiantly on the rubble with a bullhorn, surrounded by cheering firefighters and cleanup crews. Each Bush peaked at an 89 percent approval rating in Gallup polls. Such spikes in popularity are usually temporary. A year after his military triumph, George H. W. Bush's approval rating had fallen below 40 percent, and he lost his re-election campaign. The younger Bush narrowly won re-election but ended his time in office tied for the lowest ratings of all modern presidents after a full term.

Polls offer immediate public feedback, but they do not reflect an administration's historical importance or long-term success. For that we can turn to a different type of poll.

see for yourself 14.2

Go online to see President George W. Bush's dramatic bullhorn speech at Ground Zero.

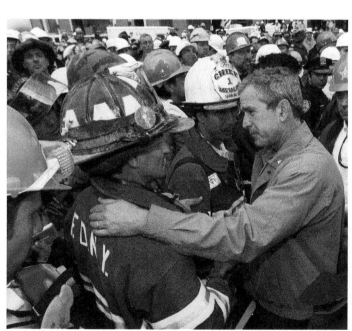

● *George W. Bush visits the scene of the 9/11 terrorist attack. The dramatic days following the attack drove President Bush's approval ratings to one of the highest levels ever recorded by Gallup.*

Presidential Greatness

Back in 1948, historian Arthur Schlesinger, Sr., asked a panel of historians to rank the presidents. Their choice for the top three: Abraham Lincoln, George Washington, and Franklin D. Roosevelt.

Poll after poll followed—we list four different versions in Table 14.3. In each, a different panel of historians and political scientists ranks the presidents in order from great to failed.

Liberals and conservatives rarely disagree about how the presidents rank. Ronald Reagan is an exception, though his ratings from left-leaning scholars have climbed in recent polls. Such agreement returns us to the question: What makes a great president?

There are plenty of answers. President Harry Truman said that all the great presidents were especially decisive. Political scientists Marc Landy and Sidney Milkis suggested that

436

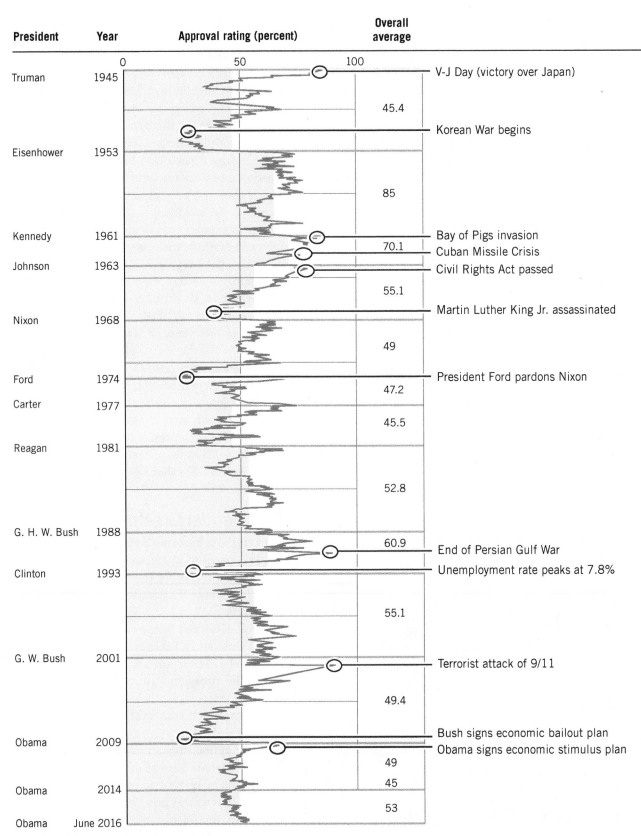

President	Year	Approval rating (percent)	Overall average	
Truman	1945			V-J Day (victory over Japan)
			45.4	
Eisenhower	1953			Korean War begins
			85	
Kennedy	1961		70.1	Bay of Pigs invasion
				Cuban Missile Crisis
Johnson	1963			Civil Rights Act passed
			55.1	
Nixon	1968			Martin Luther King Jr. assassinated
			49	
Ford	1974			President Ford pardons Nixon
			47.2	
Carter	1977		45.5	
Reagan	1981			
			52.8	
G. H. W. Bush	1988		60.9	End of Persian Gulf War
Clinton	1993			Unemployment rate peaks at 7.8%
			55.1	
G. W. Bush	2001			Terrorist attack of 9/11
			49.4	
Obama	2009			Bush signs economic bailout plan
			49	Obama signs economic stimulus plan
Obama	2014		45	
Obama	June 2016		53	

● **FIGURE 14.3** *Presidential job approval. Every administration goes through polling cycles—rising and falling in public esteem. Note how approval ratings are affected by important events and political decisions. (Gallup)*

TABLE 14.3 **Rating the Presidents**

Here are the results of four independent polls by historians and political scientists (you can find dozens of them). Historian Arthur Schlesinger polled historians in 1948; his son, Arthur Schlesinger, Jr., repeated the exercise with historians and political scientists in 1996; the United Kingdom Center for the United States Presidency provided rankings from a foreign scholarly perspective; and the American Political Science Association conducted a survey in 2015.

	POLITICAL PARTY	SCHLESINGER (1948)	SCHLESINGER, JR. (1996)	USPC 2011	APSA 2015
George Washington	None	2	2	3	2
John Adams	Federalist	9	11	12	15
Thomas Jefferson	Dem-Repub.	5	4	4	5
James Madison	Dem-Repub.	14	17	14	13
James Monroe	Dem-Repub.	12	15	13	16
John Q. Adams	Dem-Repub.	11	18	20	22
Andrew Jackson	Democratic	6	5	9	9
Martin Van Buren	Democratic	15	21	27	25
William H. Harrison	Whig	—	—	—	39
John Tyler	Whig	22	32	37	36
James K. Polk	Democratic	10	9	16	19
Zachary Taylor	Whig	25	29	33	33
Millard Fillmore	Whig	24	31	35	37
Franklin Pierce	Democratic	27	33	39	40
James Buchanan	Democratic	26	38	40	43
Abraham Lincoln	Republican	1	1	2	1
Andrew Johnson	Democratic	19	37	36	41
Ulysses Grant	Republican	28	24	29	28
Rutherford Hayes	Republican	13	23	30	30
James Garfield	Republican	—	—	—	31
Chester Arthur	Republican	17	26	32	32
Grover Cleveland	Democratic	8	13	21	23
Benjamin Harrison	Republican	21	19	34	29
William McKinley	Republican	18	16	17	21
Theodore Roosevelt	Republican	7	6	5	4
William H. Taft	Republican	16	22	25	20
Woodrow Wilson	Democratic	4	7	6	10
Warren Harding	Republican	29	39	38	42
Calvin Coolidge	Republican	23	30	28	27

TABLE 14.3 *(continued)*

	POLITICAL PARTY	SCHLESINGER (1948)	SCHLESINGER, JR. (1996)	USPC 2011	APSA 2015
Herbert Hoover	Republican	20	35	26	38
Franklin D. Roosevelt	Democratic	3	3	1	3
Harry Truman	Democratic	—	8	7	6
Dwight D. Eisenhower	Republican	—	10	10	7
John F. Kennedy	Democratic	—	12	15	14
Lyndon B. Johnson	Democratic	—	14	11	12
Richard Nixon	Republican	—	36	23	34
Gerald Ford	Republican	—	28	24	24
Jimmy Carter	Democratic	—	27	18	26
Ronald Reagan	Republican	—	25	8	11
George H. W. Bush	Republican	—	24	22	17
Bill Clinton	Democratic	—	20	19	8
George W. Bush	Republican	—	—	31	35
Barack Obama	Democratic	—	—	—	18

great presidents redefine the presidency. Our view is that great presidents redefine America; they reshape the way the nation sees itself.[16] Or, to put it slightly differently, *great presidents tell us who we are*. Their definitions of America resonate with the public and endure over time.

Greatness in Context: The Rise and Fall of Political Orders

Presidents are by no means masters of their destiny. The times make the presidents as much as they make the times. Individual presidents fit into national cycles of politics and power. Presidential scholar Stephen Skowronek has described each presidency as part of a great historical pageant: the rise and fall of **political orders**. A political order is a set of ideas, institutions, and coalitions that dominate an era.[17] In Skowronek's telling, orders rise and fall in three steps. Every president fits somewhere in the cycle.

Political order: The set of institutions, interests, and ideas that shape a political era. Great presidents reconstruct the framework, launching a new order.

Step 1: A New Order Rises. Outstanding leaders take over the presidency and shake up the political system. An Abraham Lincoln, Franklin D. Roosevelt, or Ronald Reagan introduces a fresh philosophy of government. He leads a political party with new allies and new ideas into power. The public responds enthusiastically to this bold break with old political ways.

Step 2: The Order Refreshed. Every governing coalition eventually grows tired. The great president who boldly articulated its themes is gone. Many of the original goals are won. New problems arise that have nothing to do with the philosophy that fired up the party in the first place. The ideas begin to look out of date; the great coalition begins to unravel. In fortunate times, a new leader will come along and infuse the party with a fresh variation of the old philosophy, renewing the aging order.

Step 3: The Old Order Crumbles. No order lasts forever. Over time, the party finds its ideas increasingly irrelevant. The old order feels outdated, a political dinosaur.

Every president comes to Washington with fresh hope and promise. Political historians look back and see that each operates within a cycle. Some (Lincoln, Roosevelt, Reagan) take office as the head of a new coalition with fresh ideas. Others come to Washington at the end of an era (Herbert Hoover, Jimmy Carter). They face a far more difficult governing challenge. To some extent, the rankings we see in Table 14.3 reflect each president's place in political time.

THE BOTTOM LINE

» Presidents try to manage public perceptions of the job they are doing. They get immediate feedback from polls. A president's place in history, however, usually does not emerge right away.

» Great presidents change the way Americans see themselves. They change what government does. They forge a new answer to the question, *Who are we?*

» Individual presidents don't completely control their own destiny. They operate in the historical cycle of political orders.

The Personal Presidency

In at least one respect, the presidency is very simple: It is always about one individual. At the heart of the enterprise stands a person with strengths and weaknesses, quirks and foibles. The personalities of our presidents have imprinted their administrations in many ways, big and small.

Presidential Style

James Madison was just a bit over five feet tall and weighed less than one hundred pounds. He wore tall hats to add height, dressed entirely in black, and never owned more than one suit at a time. He was both diminutive and timid. Early historians blasted him for his cautious leadership during the War of 1812. But scholars have warmed to Madison. Historians now believe that the war helped define America as a united nation. Madison was guided by a fierce attachment to the Constitution that he had drafted. He believed that the office was greater than the man. Who better than a small, shy, modest, black-clad figure to avoid too much "personality" in the presidency?

Or take some darker personal qualities. . . .

Secluded in his hideaway office across the street from the White House, the fireplace crackling as the air conditioner hummed, Richard Nixon scribbled on yellow legal pads into the night. He was brilliant—and often paranoid. Nixon usually dealt directly with four or five aides; their job was to keep others at bay. Sitting alone, writing away on his yellow pads, he dreamed up stunning ideas.

At the time, the United States was locked in a cold war with two great communist powers, Russia and China. Nixon calculated that our two enemies were bitterly opposed to one another as well. He negotiated secretly with China. When the Russians discovered the thaw between China and the United States, they feared being left out in the cold. They too pursued closer relations with the United States. Nixon had invented a way to ratchet down the bitter cold war by playing off our enemies against one another.

Nixon also cooked up a national health insurance plan that serves as a model (for Democrats) to the present day. But, sitting alone and often drinking heavily into the night, he also stoked the personal fears that ultimately cost him the White House.

Or consider a very different political genius. . . .

● *Ronald Reagan: This sunny, folksy, patriotic, old-fashioned storyteller introduced a new conservative era.*

Ronald Reagan loved to tell stories. He told them to make a point, to deflect people from saying things he did not want to hear, to reorient a conversation that was going the wrong way, or—well, just because he loved telling them. "He could drive you crazy [telling] . . . the same stories over and over again," reported Congressman Dan Rostenkowski (D-IL). "He really made no show whatsoever of listening to arguments. . . . He saw reality, not as a thing to bow to but a thing that could be changed and shaped."[18]

Was it really true that, during World War II, army bureaucrats granted Reagan's unit permission to destroy a warehouse full of useless files, "provided copies are made of each paper destroyed?" Who knows? The parable was irresistible: Government bureaucracies choke the life out of any enterprise.[19]

Such tall tales went to the heart of Reagan's successes and failures as president. He focused on parables rather than policies. His airy indifference to the analytic world of evidence and arguments freed him to repeat his handful of moral lessons, impressing them on American discourse. Such tales helped him reframe American politics in terms of a more rugged individualism that scorned handouts and collective action. He made it work because he wrapped that individualism in a nostalgic vision of America.

Madison's republican simplicity, Nixon's brilliance and paranoia, Reagan's pointed storytelling and gauzy vision of American free enterprise all shaped the way they governed and the mark they left. This kind of territory used to be the province of historians and anthropologists, not political scientists. But we know that it is vital to acknowledge—and study—the personal dimension of the presidency.[20]

What Do You Think?

The President in Action

Watch the current president in action, delivering speeches and interacting with staff and family.

How would you describe the president's personal style? What are its elements? Think about the ways they seem effective, and what their shortcomings appear to be.

Young man, older man: Barack Obama as president-elect and late in his presidency.

The Burden of the Office

For another truth about the presidency, compare photographs of almost any president at the start and then at the end of their time in office: It is an exhausting job that takes a visible toll on the incumbents. Fourteen presidents and former presidents died during the twentieth century; eleven passed away prematurely. Eight of them fell more than seven years short of expected life spans for men of their age. Presidents before they take office usually appear young, handsome, and smiling; by the time they step down, they often look careworn and gray.[21]

These morbid health statistics remind us that the Oval Office houses a vulnerable human being. Presidents get sick, take dubious drugs, drink to excess, have affairs, contemplate suicide, fret about ailing parents, burn with insecurities, and bury people they love. None can escape the human condition. All wrestle with an extremely difficult job.

Personal frailties have an impact on presidential successes and failures, on wise choices and mistakes. Presidents are usually very talented—or they would not have gotten to the White House. As with all people, however, they have strengths and weaknesses, great skills and blind spots.[22] Confronting their very real personal limits returns us to a central question of this chapter: Has the president developed too much power for one person to handle?

THE BOTTOM LINE

» Although presidential scholars generally focus on ideas and institutions, the presidency also has a critically important personal dimension.

» All presidents exhibit a distinctive personal style.

» Presidents are limited human beings with strengths and weaknesses. That is precisely why the Constitution located the office in an intricate system of checks and balances.

8 The President's Team: A Tour of the White House

When Herbert Hoover moved into the Oval Office in 1929, he presided over a presidential staff of four administrative assistants, plus thirty-six typists, clerks, and messengers. That was it. No speechwriter, no press secretary, no congressional liaison; no chief of staff, no drug czar, no budget director. Today, the presidency is more than a person or an idea or a party. It is a bureaucracy staffed by thousands of people.

The Political Solar System: Presidential Appointments

Every time a new president is elected, hopes spread across the country. University professors who have always dreamed of government service, college students who worked on the campaign, business executives looking for a plum position on their résumé, and supporters who believe the president-elect will make America a better place: all want to work for the new administration.

To get a job in the executive branch, do not start by being modest. You must campaign: One executive angling to be a senior Treasury Department official a few years back tasked four subordinates to do nothing but promote his name to the administration's transition team in charge of selecting top appointees (yes, he got the job).

This section highlights those officials working directly for the president. A crucial opening point: Power is always measured by proximity to the Oval Office. The executive branch is like the solar system, with the president as the sun and everyone else rotating around him. A trump card in any Washington, DC, conversation: "When I was talking to the president yesterday. . . ." Most people who work for the president are in an orbit somewhere past Pluto: They never get any face time. Let us look at some who do.

The Vice President

Traditionally, the vice president's primary job was to stand in the wings in case the president died. That awful transition has happened eight times in American history, four times by murder. There were at least four more close calls: Assassins fired point-blank at Andrew Jackson (the gun jammed), Franklin D. Roosevelt (the shooter missed the president and killed the mayor of Chicago), Gerald Ford (a bystander grabbed the gunwoman's arm, diverting the shot), and Ronald Reagan (the bullet lodged less than an inch from his heart).

Besides standing by in case of catastrophe, vice presidents preside over the Senate and cast a vote in case of a tie. There is not much power in presiding, and the vice president only appears in the Senate chamber on special occasions.

Otherwise, a vice president's responsibilities are entirely up to the president. For a long time, the role was

Vice President Mike Pence served as governor of Indiana prior to assuming office.

meager. Senator Daniel Webster rejected the vice presidential nomination in 1848 with an acid comment: "I do not choose to be buried until I am really dead."[23] Bad move: Webster would have become the thirteenth president when Zachary Taylor died in the White House. Franklin D. Roosevelt's first vice president, John Nance Garner, offered an infamous assessment of the post when he said the job was "not worth a pitcher of warm piss."[24]

The weak vice presidency continued well into the twentieth century. Harry Truman had barely met with President Roosevelt when FDR's death in 1945 catapulted him into the Oval Office. "Boys," he said when he met the press the next day, "if you ever pray, pray for me now." In 1960, reporters asked President Eisenhower what ideas Vice President Nixon had contributed. "If you give me a week," quipped the president nastily, "I might think of one."[25]

The vice presidency became an important office during the Carter administration (1977–1981). From Carter through Trump, six of eight presidents were Washington outsiders who had never held a federal job; every newcomer chose a longtime federal government insider as his vice president, relying on him as advisor, confidant, and envoy. Slowly but surely, vice presidents gathered the emblems of power: a seat at cabinet meetings (1950s), an office in the White House (1970s), a vice presidential jet (Air Force 2, in the 1970s), a growing staff, and—perhaps most important in status-obsessed Washington—regular meetings with the president.

The Cabinet

Members of the cabinet have two primary roles: They run executive branch departments, and they meet to discuss policy with the president in cabinet meetings. Once the cabinet served as a president's governing team. As we saw earlier, Washington's initial cabinet had four members. By Abraham Lincoln's time, there were seven. Today the cabinet has grown to fifteen members; add the vice president and other important officers on the president's staff and meetings are too large to serve as a real decision-making body. We discuss the cabinet, and the hundreds of thousands of federal bureaucrats who work under cabinet secretaries in the executive agencies, in Chapter 15.

In most administrations, a handful of cabinet officers rise above the rest and shape administration policy. Political scientists call them the "inner cabinet": the secretaries of state, defense, the treasury, and justice—precisely the quartet in Washington's original cabinet. Most other cabinet secretaries operate far from the centers of power. Departments such as Transportation and Energy have vital roles to play. But unless the "outer cabinet" secretaries have personal connections or unusual responsibilities, they are rarely part of a president's inner circle.

Cabinet secretaries often come to see issues from the perspective of their own bureaucracy rather than that of the administration or the party. After all, they are surrounded by tens of thousands of employees who do a lot of work with limited resources and look to the secretary to champion their causes. Richard Nixon's close

President Nixon worked closely with National Security Advisor and later Secretary of State Henry Kissinger.

adviser John Ehrlichman groused that the administration chose solid, budget-cutting conservatives to run the cabinet departments—and then watched their appointees run off and "marry the natives."[26]

Presidents must manage the tension between senior cabinet officials and the circle of presidential advisors in the White House. At one cabinet meeting during the Carter years, the secretary of housing and urban development summed up her frustration by blurting out: "We can move government forward by putting phones in the White House staff offices and then using them." Translation: No one in the White House even returns my phone calls. The president's inner circle (and the power of proximity) had shifted from the cabinet to the White House staff.[27]

The Executive Office of the President

In modern times, influence over the president has leaked steadily into the **Executive Office of the President** (**EOP**), made up of agencies that help a president manage his daily activities. These administrators and advisors surround the chief executive. President Franklin D. Roosevelt organized the EOP in 1939; it now has about 1,800 employees. Many are experts who stay on from one administration to the next. Presidents who have been most adamant about expanding the EOP are conservatives frustrated that the cabinet agencies did not pursue their values. Richard Nixon created or revamped four of the EOP offices; Ronald Reagan added three more. Today, every president—left, right, or center—relies on them.

Table 14.4 illustrates the offices in the Executive Office of the President. The list reflects the hats and helmets that the president wears. Organizing a new EOP office is one way for administrations to signal the things they consider most important. Nixon added the Council on Environmental Quality, George W. Bush an office for his faith-based initiatives, Barack Obama, reflecting the high-tech/information age, created an Office of Digital Strategy.

> **Executive Office of the President (EOP):** The agencies that help the president manage daily activities.

TABLE 14.4 Offices in the Executive Office of the President, 2016

OFFICE	EMPLOYEES	YEAR ORGANIZED	ORGANIZED BY
White House Office	450	1939	F. D. Roosevelt
Council of Economic Advisers	27	1946	Truman
National Security Staff	58	1947	Truman
Office of the U.S. Trade Representative	240	1963	Kennedy
Council on Environmental Quality	24	1969	Nixon
Office of Management and Budget	487	1921/1971	Harding/Nixon
Office of the Vice President	25	1972	Nixon
Office of Science and Technology Policy	32	1976	Ford
Office of Administration	234	1977	Carter
Domestic Policy Council	25	1985	Reagan
Office of National Drug Control Policy	84	1988	Reagan
Homeland Security Council	18	2001	G. W. Bush
Executive Residence	96 (full-time)	—	—

In the Executive Office of the President, a familiar clash gets especially intense. On one hand, most EOP employees are experts on specific issues—drug policy, healthcare, or the budget. On the other, they have to serve each president's political philosophy (not to mention furthering his re-election prospects). Slowly, the balance between these goals has tipped toward politics.[28] Let us visit the most important offices in the EOP.

The Office of Management and Budget (OMB).

This is the most powerful agency in the executive branch—known (not very fondly) as "the agency that says no." The OMB uses its authority over the federal budget to manage the entire executive branch. During the Reagan administration, the agency acquired its most powerful weapon—**central clearance**: the power to review and "clear" (or okay) anything a member of the administration says or does in public. All members, from the secretary of defense to an analyst in the Small Business Bureau, must submit every speech they make, opinion piece they write, congressional testimony they deliver, and policy they propose to the OMB for its approval. Until they get the OMB's nod, they may not say or publish a word.

The OMB vets every administration proposal. When Congress passes a bill, the OMB coordinates various White House officials' recommendations about signing or vetoing the legislation. Officials at the OMB often get the last word as well. Imagine how frustrating it must be for energetic new secretaries to take over their departments, only to learn they must clear all their formal statements and policy proposals with the budget office.

Before the Nixon administration organized the OMB in 1971, fiscal control was much looser. President Lyndon Johnson famously low-balled his economic estimates. One day, instructing a young senator from Massachusetts named Ted Kennedy, Johnson warned him not to let economic projections slow up his favorite bills and illustrated the point with Medicare. "The fools [at the Bureau of the Budget] had to go projecting [Medicare] down the road five or six years, and when you project it the first year it runs $900 million," Johnson told Kennedy.[29] Those anticipated costs, complained LBJ, cost him votes in Congress; he advised the new senator to stop economists from interfering with important proposals. Today, the OMB requires cost-benefit analyses for all White House policy moves. The era of simply suppressing cost estimates is long past. Today, the formal rules of governing tilt toward and empower an economic perspective. Still, the future is never certain, and every savvy political operator knows plenty of ways to massage the numbers.

Central clearance: The OMB's authority to review and "clear" (or approve) anything a member of the administration says or does in public.

The Council of Economic Advisers (CEA).

Meet another clutch of economists. The Council and its chair keep an eye on the whole economy, private as well as public. CEA staff performs economic analysis for the president: unemployment predictions, productivity measurements, economic forecasts, and all the rest.

The National Security Council (NSC).

The NSC brings together the powerful officers who make national security policy: secretaries of state, defense, energy, and the treasury (economists again); the chair of the Joint Chiefs of Staff; and others who the president selects. The national security advisor directs the council and must work for consensus across all the different perspectives and formidable personalities: diplomatic, military, and economic. In some administrations, the national security advisor is as influential as the secretaries of state or defense. Empowering the NSC has tightened White House control over foreign policy, as we will see in Chapter 18.

The Heart of Power: The White House Office (WHO)

Our tour ends at the heart of power. The White House Office is part of the Executive Office of the President, but it also stands apart. This group of four hundred or so advisors, aides, and associates works directly for the president, most of them in the West Wing. At the center sits the **Chief of Staff**, the president's gatekeeper, traffic cop, and coordinator. Other important offices include speechwriters, White House counsel (the president's official lawyer), and the legislative affairs team.

Until President Obama, the two parties organized their White House Office very differently from one another. Franklin D. Roosevelt set a mixed example for future Democrats: creative chaos. Roosevelt surrounded himself with gifted intellectuals, gave them overlapping tasks, and let them freelance from issue to issue. In theory, bold ideas would flow from an office full of talented, loosely organized thinkers. Many Democratic administrations tried to mimic Roosevelt. John Kennedy valued broad-minded intellectuals and encouraged them to weigh in on any subject. So did Bill Clinton; early in his administration, staffers would jump in and out of meetings and conversations regardless of their assigned tasks. The bull sessions went on deep into the night.

In contrast, Republicans like clearly defined organization and tasks. You'll find no vague or dotted lines on their personnel tables. Republican executives usually model their organization on the military or traditional business: crisp lines of authority flow from the president to the Chief of Staff. Everyone has a clearly defined role.

No matter the style, the Chief of Staff makes the White House run. He or she directs traffic through the president's office, oversees the schedule, sums up the decisions that are made, and follows up to see that those decisions are understood and implemented. The position requires a strong, talented, smooth, competent administrator familiar with the levers of power. Occasionally, a president will try to act as his own Chief of Staff (Jimmy Carter) or bring in a political neophyte (Bill Clinton chose his pal Mack McLarty, whom he'd known since kindergarten); when that happens, chaos generally follows. The other extreme is equally dangerous. If the Chief of Staff seems arrogant, aloof, or rude, the White House loses support and cooperation.

The White House staff is like a little village, full of odd folkways and habits that reflect the way the president wishes to run the country. For example, Ronald Reagan put special emphasis on his speechwriting team; they spent hours watching tapes of his past speeches to learn his rhythms and his way of thinking. The president reworked their draft speeches with great care. Reagan's successor, George H. W. Bush, thought the president should speak more plainly and rejected all the attention on crafting speeches. He demonstrated the new order by stripping the speechwriting team of its White House Mess (dining hall) privileges. The village recognized a major demotion.

When a new president comes to town, attention focuses on his cabinet selections. The wise observer knows to track more subtle appointments to the White House Office. After all, no matter how brilliant the secretary of labor or how experienced the secretary of health and human services, they will have to rely on unseen advisors in the White House to convey their ideas, programs, and problems to the president. The route to influence—the path to "yes" on any program—runs through the White House Office staff.

Unlike the high-ranking members of the cabinet agencies, most EOP staffers are not subject to Senate confirmation. They are elected by no one, overseen only by the Chief of Staff, and often have regular access to the president's ear. Should the

Chief of Staff: The individual responsible for managing the president's office.

SPEAK LIKE A WEST WING INSIDER

Want to learn to talk like a member of the White House staff? Start practicing now. Casually toss off something like: "I'm given to understand that WHO is the real force in the EOP." Those are two indecipherable acronyms (the more the better) and, of course, the passive voice: You don't want to risk revealing your sources!

Do Presidents Need Such a Large Staff?

The Executive Office of the President (EOP) now houses more than 1,800 staff members, from economic and foreign policy advisors to communications specialists. All answer directly to the president and his top aides; most do not even require Senate confirmation. By comparison, President Lincoln had four personal assistants, and when Franklin D. Roosevelt took office eighty-two years ago, he had a staff of thirty-six. Does the modern presidency require such a large staff?

Yes, absolutely. Given the office's immense range of responsibilities, presidents need reliable, trustworthy experts and assistants to analyze intelligence and economic data, to assess overseas threats, and to help manage public perceptions of the president. In fact, it's surprising there isn't more support (Congress, after all, has more than twenty-five thousand staffers).

No—start staff cuts immediately. Modern technology could make the presidency far more efficient. If CEOs can run major companies with far fewer staff reporting to their office, and other sectors are able to function with far fewer personnel, so could the White House.

Not sure. The huge array of presidential staff reportedly work incredibly hard, and the White House certainly has a plateful of duties. But if past presidents got by with far fewer staff, perhaps we've gone too far, and could reduce this EOP army?

president's advisors, rather than the experienced cabinet secretaries confirmed by the Senate, run the executive branch? Again, we confront the fundamental issue: power and control versus democracy and enhanced accountability. Perhaps granting authority to White House staff makes the whole federal leviathan more responsive to the will of the people. Most democracies are, ultimately, ruled by experts. American government is run in part by men and women with a sharp eye on winning the next election.

One final feature of the White House staff strikes most newcomers: Its members are young—much younger than the staff running other governments, large corporations, universities, or major nonprofit organizations. Cabinet secretaries with years of experience often complain that their access to the president is governed by young people in their twenties and thirties.

The First Spouse

One team in the White House Office does not fit any traditional political category: the office of the president's spouse. Traditionally, the "First Lady" role was simply that of hostess. Eleanor Roosevelt broke the traditional mold and pioneered a new role: the First Lady as activist. Eleanor was a powerful liberal activist, a popular symbol of the New Deal, and a forceful advocate for Franklin D. and his policies. In effect, she became a one-woman campaign for liberal social policy. A *New Yorker* cartoon captures the First Lady's spirit of tirelessly campaigning for social and labor reform. Deep underground, two sooty coal miners stop their labors as one remarks with surprise: "For gosh sakes, here comes Mrs. Roosevelt!"

Few First Spouses were as active or committed as Eleanor Roosevelt, but she set a pattern of policy engagement that her successors have followed. Lady Bird Johnson chose "beautification" of American cities and highways as her policy focus. Nancy Reagan became a spokesperson for the war on drugs. Mrs. Reagan was the first to achieve that mark of status, an office in the West Wing. Bill Clinton assigned his wife, Hillary, the signature policy initiative of his presidency, national health-care reform. In fall 1993, Hillary Clinton's virtuoso performance in a series of congressional hearings appeared to signal success for national health insurance. The legislation failed, but Mrs. Clinton went on to her own successful political career—and established a new ceiling for First Ladies' contributions to presidential action.

Political scientists—especially those interested in gender and power—have begun to pay particular attention to the role of the First Spouse.[30] Melania Trump was less visible during the campaign than many of her predecessors; researchers are already seeking to explore the degree of influence she has with her husband and top advisers.

THE BOTTOM LINE

» Each president directs a massive organization—the executive branch of the federal government.

» Cabinet secretaries manage the great executive-branch bureaucracies, but only a few have influence in the White House.

» Over time, executive branch policymaking has migrated from the cabinet to the Executive Office of the Presidency—the network of offices that help the president manage the government.

» The president's innermost circle is the White House Office. These close advisors—often relatively young—include the Chief of Staff, speechwriters, the legislative liaison, and the office of the First Spouse.

Conclusion: The Most Powerful Office on Earth?

President Obama took office in 2009 amid soaring hopes. He was a symbol of American aspiration: After centuries of racial struggle, the United States had elected an African American leader. As with all presidents, Obama put a new set of ideas, proposals, and priorities before the American people.

The incoming president shifted America's policymaking. The issues he cared about became those in the news and before Congress: healthcare reform, college loans, education, and clean energy sources. Obama removed American troops from Iraq and expanded the number in Afghanistan, while setting a definite withdrawal date—all controversial actions. The Oval Office reverberates with power and responsibility.

From another angle, it is full of limitations, checks, and balances. The economy remained weak—and sapped President Obama's popularity. Congress rejected some of his signature reforms. It blocked him from closing the military prison at Guantánamo. He won healthcare reform—an extraordinary achievement—but eight years later had still not persuaded the public of its merits, to the great advantage of the Republicans who had been united against "Obamacare." By 2014, Obama's Democratic Party had lost its majorities in both the House and Senate. The most powerful office on earth was hemmed in by checks and balances.

Now a new president arrives in office, bursting with ideas and campaign promises—and raising, once again, the fundamental question about the presidency.

● Presidents regularly make history-changing choices—but often must wait and see how events ratify or rebuke their decisions. Here, senior officials watch with President Obama and Vice President Biden as the Navy SEAL raid on Osama bin Laden's compound is carried out.

see for yourself 14.3

Go online to see President Trump's Election Night 2016 address.

It is a far more powerful office than it was a century ago. Has it grown too powerful for a republic? Or is it too hobbled to carry out the mandate of the public? Perhaps it is most accurate to say that the same president can be both too powerful and too weak, depending on the issue, the circumstances, and the incumbent. How will we view the powers of the presidency as Donald Trump moves through his term in office? Watch as the Trump administration deals with all the hats and helmets we described. As you watch the administration, ask yourself whether the president is too powerful—or not powerful enough.

Who are we? The president offers us an answer—actually, several different answers. Americans seek a powerful, confident figure at their government's center. At the same time, we fear strong executives and hem them in with a labyrinth of checks and balances. We want our collective democratic voice ringing in the ears of our national leaders but also want our security protected in ways that may require secrecy and fast, decisive choices. We are a people who demand small government—yet complain when every need is not speedily met by the executive branch. We are a complicated, diverse, paradoxical people, like the presidency that reflects and serves us.

CHAPTER SUMMARY

● *The president personifies America.* More than any individual, the president tells us who we are—and what we are becoming.

● *The president injects new ideas into American politics.* Our discussion of Congress emphasized the institution and the rules of the game; the presidency puts more focus on individuals and ideas.

● The president has three types of powers: Those expressed in the Constitution, those delegated by Congress, and those inherent in the role of chief executive.

● The executive branch has grown far more powerful over time, especially when it comes to foreign policy.

● The office of the president constantly raises the same fundamental question: *Is the president too powerful for a democratic republic? Or is the office too weak to accomplish what Americans demand of it?* We may also consider whether the president is both too strong and too weak at the same time.

● The president wears many hats and helmets. Presidential roles include commander in chief, top diplomat, first legislator, head bureaucrat, economist in chief, head of state, and party leader. The president's authority has grown in every one of these many roles. At the same time, it is difficult for one person to do so many different things effectively.

● Presidents try to manage public perceptions of the job they are doing by going public and getting feedback from polls. Individual presidents do not completely control their own destiny. They operate in the historical cycle of *political orders.*

● The presidency always has a personal dimension. Presidents are limited human beings with strengths and weaknesses. That is precisely why the Constitution located the office within an intricate system of checks and balances.

● Over time, executive branch policy has flowed from the cabinet secretaries to the Executive Office of the Presidency—the network of offices that help the president manage the government.

● The president's innermost circle is the White House Office. These close advisors—who are often relatively young—include the Chief of Staff, speechwriters, the legislative liaison, and the office of the First Spouse.

KEY TERMS

Central clearance, p. 442
Chief of Staff, p. 443
Civil servants, p. 425
Delegated powers, p. 415
Executive agreements, p. 415
Executive Office of the
    President (EOP), p. 441

Executive order, p. 425
Executive privilege, p. 415
Expressed powers, p. 415
Going public, p. 430
Imperial presidency, p. 417
Inherent powers of the
    presidency, p. 415

Override, p. 424
Political appointees, p. 425
Political order, p. 435
Signing statements, p. 425
Unitary executive theory, p. 417
Veto power, p. 424

STUDY QUESTIONS

1. Some people have suggested changing the president's term to one seven-year term without the possibility of re-election. How would that proposal shift the incentives that currently face a first-term president?

2. Why is the Constitution considerably more vague about presidential than congressional powers? What problems—and benefits—does that ambiguity create?

3. What do you think: Is the president too strong or too weak? Defend your opinion.

4. Name seven different roles the president plays. Which do you consider the most important right now? How well do you think the president is carrying out this role today?

5. How well do you think President Trump "goes public"—appealing to the American public to support his policies? Do *you* respond positively to his speeches and legislative requests?

6. Should presidents care about their approval ratings from the American public? Why or why not?

7. Explain how presidents help Americans understand (and define) who we are. What does the president tell the world about the kind of nation and people we are?

8. Explain the role of the OMB. What does this agency do? What perspective was it designed to bring to policy debates?

9. Describe the role of the First Spouse. Despite getting involved in policies, spouses are often more popular than their presidential partners. Why do you think that is so?

10. Describe the three stages of every political order. Where do you think we stand today in the great cycle of presidential political time?

 Go to www.oup.com/us/Morone to find quizzes, flash cards, simulations, tutorials, videos, and other study tools.

Bureaucracy

15

U.S. ASTRONAUTS ON MARS, in the film *The Martian*, are forced by a howling dust storm to retreat to their ascent ship and leave the planet. One crew member, Mark Watney (played by Matt Damon), is struck by debris during the storm, presumed dead, and left behind.

Realizing that his best chance of rescue is the arrival of another crew in four years, Watney improvises brilliantly, growing potatoes in the harsh Martian soil and creating a way to communicate with his National Aeronautics and Space Administration (NASA) colleagues back on Earth. Eventually—well, we won't spoil the ending if you haven't seen the movie.

Here's one surprise, though: NASA, a federal-government agency with more than 18,000 employees, is portrayed in this Oscar-winning film as performing amazing feats. The Jet Propulsion Laboratory, which devised ingenious rescue plans for the stranded astronaut, is also part of NASA. State Department officials—representing an agency with nineteen thousand employees staffing 305 embassies and consulates around the world—reached out to China for help. Do you find Hollywood's positive highlighting of government agencies' achievements surprising? Likely so. Most Americans hold a very low opinion of the federal bureaucracy. Today, less than half of the public "trust[s] the government to do what is right always or most of the time"[1] (see Figure 15.1). Politicians often campaign for office against faceless officials in Washington, portraying the executive bureaucracy as "armies of regulators descending like locusts," as Republican presidential candidate (and U.S. Senator) Ted Cruz thundered in 2016.[2] GOP candidates such as Cruz promise to cut whole agencies—although they rarely do so when they win office. Democrats join in and promise to shrink government programs "that do not work."[3] Indeed, it is easy to find examples of bureaucracies doing foolish things.

This chapter tells a different story about the federal bureaucracy—one closer to *The Martian*'s depiction than to the standard critique. Bureaucrats, despite their terrible reputation, perform valuable, even life-saving services. The bureaucracy is what makes government run.

The criticism of generic bureaucrats generally melts away when pollsters ask about specific agencies. For example, over 70 percent of the public gives high marks to the National Park Service, the Centers for Disease Control, and NASA.[4] Bureaucrats look a lot better when we focus on what they actually do.

In this chapter, you will:

- Learn how the bureaucracy developed, how it is meant to work, and why programs and processes sometimes fail.

- See how federal agencies do their job.

- Examine the different types of agencies that comprise the public service.

- Consider who—if anyone—controls the bureaucracy.

- Review possible reforms.

● *Matt Damon, as seen in the box-office smash* The Martian. *Contrary to familiar critiques, bureaucrats such as the NASA astronaut played by Damon are the heroes of this film.*

449

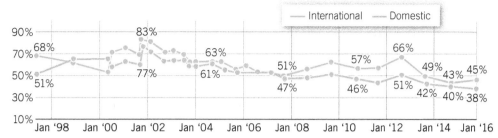

Trust in federal government to handle international and domestic problems

— International   — Domestic

FIGURE 15.1 *How much of the time do you think you can trust government in Washington to do what is right? Notice how trust peaked after the 9/11 attacks. Today, far fewer Americans take a positive view on this question. (Gallup)*

Who are we? In many ways, a country of bureaucrats: U.S. national departments and agencies employ 2.7 million civilians (and over 4 million men and women if you include active-duty military). State and local governments employ 19 million more Americans. These numbers add up to more than 23 million people on government payrolls—more than one in every ten American working-age adults. Moreover, compared to other branches of U.S. government, the federal bureaucracy most resembles the population it serves. Remember that Congress is overwhelmingly white, male, and middle-aged. But the U.S. civilian bureaucracy is as diverse as the nation itself (see Figure 15.2).

Does its diversity make the bureaucracy more representative? Not necessarily. One of the great challenges every national bureaucracy faces is how to synchronize its work with the people's will. The same question we raised in the last chapter—does presidential power threaten popular rule?—returns in this chapter in a slightly different

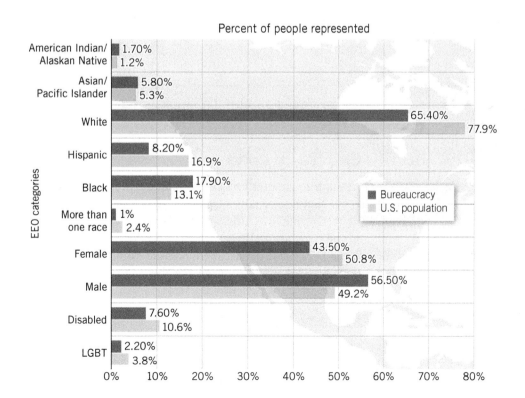

FIGURE 15.2 *U.S. civilian bureaucracy: demographic characteristics. (U.S. Census)*

The Bureaucracy

Number of cabinet departments, U.S. executive branch, 2017: **15**

Number of official independent agencies/commissions: **63**
Number of departments during the George Washington administration (1789): **4**
Number of departments during the Theodore Roosevelt administration (1905): **7**

Number of ministries (e.g., cabinet departments), Japanese government, 2001: **20**
Number of ministries in 2017, following extensive restructuring in recent years: **12**

Total federal bureaucracy workforce: **4.4 million**
Percentage of that total who work for the military: **39**
"Hidden workforce" of federal contractors and grantees: as many as **8 million**

Number of women, in U.S. history, who have headed cabinet-level departments: **31**
Number of those named since 1975: **29**
Total cabinet secretary positions filled since the end of World War II (1945): **259**

Miles of hallways in the largest U.S. federal building, the Pentagon: **17.5**
Maximum annual salary earned by a civil servant (GS-15, top of scale), 2016:
$133,433
Number of GS categories, which specify earnings ranges within each category: **15**

Average layers of upper management in large U.S. cabinet departments: **64**

---

form: Can a bureaucracy of 2.7 million unelected federal workers govern democratically? An efficient and effective federal bureaucracy is essential to good government. Can we make it fit with democratic governance?

How the Bureaucracy Grew

Predicting storms near Miami, keeping tabs on developments in the Middle East, and tracking terrorists in Nigeria or Syria take large, well-coordinated bureaucracies—as the National Oceanic and Atmospheric Administration (NOAA), the State Department, and the Central Intelligence Agency (CIA) are intended to be. In this section, we look at where the U.S. bureaucracy came from, how bureaucracies should be organized, and some of the problems that can hamper their success.

Birth of the Bureaucracy

In the nineteenth century, U.S. government jobs were political prizes. Men got their posts—as officers in the army, postmasters in rural towns, or tax collectors in the ports—because they helped politicians win elections. When George Washington

Plunkitt, a colorful New York politician, decided to enter politics, he went to the local party boss with what he called a marketable commodity: votes. He got his start in politics by delivering the votes of all his friends and neighbors.[5]

As you can imagine, this system was inefficient, unfair, and corrupt. Senator William Marcy, another New Yorker, gave the system its name when he declared, "To the victor belong the spoils." After he made his comment, giving jobs to political friends became known as the **spoils system**.

Spoils system: A system in which government jobs are given out as political favors.

Reformers fought for years to break this corruption. Jobs, they believed, should be distributed on the basis of merit, not political connections. These good-government advocates championed what we now call **universalistic politics**: a government of impartial rules that apply equally to everyone. That ideal was the basis for bureaucratic government in the United States. (No Nepotism)

Universalistic politics: A government run according to transparent rules, impartially applied.

A great political battle erupted between reformers and defenders of the spoils system. In 1883, a crazed office seeker assassinated President James Garfield. Suddenly, the reformers had a martyr for their cause. The spoils system, they said, had caused the president's assassination. Popular outcry pushed a reluctant Congress to pass the **Pendleton Civil Service Act**, which required the federal government to hire well-qualified individuals, who took demanding exams to qualify for their posts. It was the first step toward building the civil service—another name for the bureaucracy—that runs the government today.

Pendleton Civil Service Act: The law that shifted American government toward a merit-based public service.

Reformers fighting for a more efficient government had a big advantage: There were jobs that needed doing. As the society and economy grew more complex, the spoils system (which too often attracted the lazy and the incompetent) failed to answer the nation's needs. Five important national needs pushed the United States toward a more efficient—and more bureaucratic—government.

War. Each time the United States mobilized for war, the bureaucracy grew. Matters of life and death could not depend on political hacks; each military effort spurred a search for competent administrators and well-organized bureaus and offices. After each war, government maintained some of the new jobs. The number of civilian employees doubled during World War I and tripled during World War II. World War II, more than any other force in American history, created the large national bureaucracy we have today.[6]

● *James Garfield is assassinated in the Baltimore train station by a frustrated job seeker. Although it was the act of a madman, reformers blamed the spoils system and used the tragedy to introduce the civil service.*

Morality. Nineteenth-century observers often noted that the U.S. government was very active in regulating morality. Enforcing moral rules required the creation of increasingly sophisticated agencies. For example, the effort to outlaw all liquor (under Prohibition, which lasted from 1920 to 1933) created a powerful new law enforcement agency in the Department of the Treasury.[7]

Economics. Over time, the federal government took over responsibility for economic performance. This created many new government offices—commissions designed to regulate business (starting in 1887 with efforts to manage the giant railroads); the Federal Reserve, intended to stabilize banking (created in 1913 after a series of financial panics); and a host of offices and agencies in response to the Great Depression (in the 1930s).

Geography. The United States spread rapidly across the continent. Keeping the far-flung nation together led to the creation of a more sophisticated postal service (including, briefly, the famous Pony Express), new forms of transportation, the distribution of public lands to homesteaders, and repeated military actions against Native Americans.

Race/Ethnicity. The issue of slavery and civil rights constantly engaged the federal government—leading, most dramatically, to the Civil War and the Reconstruction-era occupation of southern lands by the federal army. Likewise, shifting immigration policies, often based on ethnicity (the Chinese Exclusion Act of the 1880s, for example), required a huge network of federal officials deciding who was permitted to settle in the United States.

"Your Honor, this woman gave birth to a naked child!"

⬤ Late nineteenth-century moral reformer Anthony Comstock and his quest to stamp out any signs of smut. His effort helped build a sophisticated postal bureaucracy.

Each of these forces—war, morality, economics, geography, and race/ethnicity questions—pushed the United States toward more efficient national bureaus and agencies. The Pendleton Act of 1883 laid the cornerstone for the civil service that developed into a professional national bureaucracy by 1900 (after the Spanish-American War). By 1946 (after World War II) the country had developed many of the agencies that govern America to this day.

The Bureaucratic Model

What is a bureaucracy supposed to look like? The German sociologist and political economist Max Weber (1864–1920) reduced it to five characteristics that, in theory, mark all modern bureaucracies—including the American civil service. Let us consider these one at a time. And remember, this is the way the bureaucracy is *supposed* to operate, not the way it always does.[8]

Hierarchy. All bureaucracies have a clear chain of command. Each individual reports to the person above him or her all the way up to the president—or the queen, or the pope, or the university chancellor. Every individual along the chain has well-defined superiors and subordinates. Weber noted that the desire to move up the ladder makes most individuals sensitive to their superior's orders. In this way, the efforts of thousands of people can be coordinated.

Figure 15.3 shows the hierarchy of the U.S. Department of Energy (DOE), starting with the cabinet secretary and moving down through elaborate subsets of assistants, deputies, and associate administrators. This chart lists only the top forty-eight positions, but more than fifteen thousand men and women work in the agency (and another eighty thousand or more work under contracts with the DOE). The principle of hierarchy allows leaders to coordinate the work of all their subordinates.

DEPARTMENT OF ENERGY

Boards & Councils

Secretary of Energy
Advisory Board
National Laboratory
Policy Council
Energy Council
Credit Review Board
Cyber Cyber Council
Nuclear Security Council
Jobs Council
ESAAB

Office of the Secretary

Associate Deputy Secretary

Federal Energy Regulatory Commission

Inspector General

Ombudsman

Office of the Under Secretary for Nuclear Security and National Nuclear SecurityAdministration

Office of the Under Secretary for Science & Energy

Office of the Under Secretary for Management & Performance

Assistant Secretary for International Affairs

U.S. Energy Information Administration

Assistant Secretary for Congressional & Inter governmental Affairs

Advanced Research Projects Agency -Energy

National Laboratory Operations Board

General Counsel

Energy Policy & Systems Analysis

Deputy Administrator for Defense Nuclear Nonproliferation

Deputy Administrator for Defense Programs

Office of Science

Associate Under Secretary for Environment, Health,Safety & Security

Chief Financial Officer

Loan Programs Office

Deputy Administrator for Naval Reactors

Deputy Under Secretary for Counter-terrorism & Counter-proliferation

Assistant Secretary for Energy Efficiency and Renewable Energy

Assistant Secretary for Environmental Management

Intelligence & Counterintelligence

Bonneville Power Administration

Associate Administrator for Defense Nuclear Security

Associate Administrator for Emergency Operations

Assistant Secretary for Energy Efficiency and Renewable Energy

Economic Impact for Environmental Management

Enterprise Assessments

Southwestern Power Administration

Associate Administrator for External Affairs

Associate Administrator for Safety, Infrastructure & Operations

Assistant Secretary for Nuclear Energy

Management

Public Affairs

Southeastern Power Administration

Associate Administrator for Management & Budget

Associate Administrator for Acquisition & Project Management

Assistant Secretary for Electricity Delivery and Energy Reliability

Chief Human Capital Officer

Small and Disadvantaged Business Utilization

Western Area Power Administration

Office of General Counsel

Associate Administrator for Information Management & Chief Information Officer

Indian Energy Policy and Programs

Chief Information Officer1

Office of Technology Transitions2

Project Management Oversight & Assessments

Legacy Management

Hearings & Appeals

[1]The CIO reports directly to the Secretary for the purposes of carrying out responsibilities
[2]The director of the Office of Technology Transitions also serves as DOE's Technology Transfer Coordinator who reports to the Secretary of Energy under Subchapter 44 U.S.C.§3506(a)(2)(A).   15 May 2016

FIGURE 15.3 *Organizational chart for the Department of Energy. (Department of Energy)*

Division of Labor. Bureaucracies divide up complex programs and assign each piece to an individual or a group. Members of the agencies become experts at their own specialized tasks. The hierarchy coordinates all the specialists into a smoothly working operation. For example, the division of labor permits the State Department to have specialists in each region of the globe, each language, and each country.

Fixed Routines. Rather than making things up as they go along, bureaucrats are expected to follow well-specified codes of conduct called standard operating procedures (SOPs).

Have you ever applied for food stamps or unemployment compensation? If you do, you will face a sequence of forms, sometimes bewildering details, and multiple visits to different offices. This is bureaucratic routine in action, designed to treat everybody the same way. If you have been stopped for speeding, recall the ritual that police officers follow, from requesting your license and registration to checking your plates for outstanding warrants. That's a fixed routine, too, and each step in the SOP has a purpose.

Equal Rules for All. The ideal is always the same in a bureaucracy: The rules apply equally to everyone. In the spoils system, it was all about whom you knew. In contrast, the bureaucratic official is not supposed to care whose daughter you are or what special story you have to tell.

Technical Qualifications. Because bureaucracies operate on the basis of expertise, people get their jobs only on the basis of their qualifications. For example, take another look at Figure 15.3. On the right of the organizational chart, you will find an Advanced Research Projects Agency (ARPA, which among other things maintains accelerators for research into the origins of the universe). George Washington Plunkitt got his job by rounding up votes for the Democratic Party of New York; in contrast, the ARPA staff got their jobs thanks to their scientific expertise.

Bureaucratic Pathologies

These five characteristics look good on paper. However, the real world can work entirely differently.

Almost everyone has an annoying or alarming bureaucrat story. You may have experienced one in dealing with your university: for example, "You cannot take this course until you take that one"—even though you took one just like it at another school—or, "You can't register till you've paid your tuition"—even though you paid it last week. People who deal with the federal government constantly experience this kind of bureaucratic error and are familiar with the annoying chorus: You filed the wrong form, stood in the wrong line, or are forbidden to receive a benefit you actually are eligible for.

Starting in 2010, eight-year-old Mikey Hicks, an ordinary American boy with no ties to terrorism, was stopped, searched, and interrogated every time he and his family boarded a plane. The Transportation Security Authority (TSA) explained that his name was on the agency's no-fly list (because a real suspect had a similar name). Despite his family's complaints, it took the TSA months to remove Mikey from the list. And while the TSA agents were grilling Mikey, a *real* terrorist, Umar Farouk Abdulmutallab, boarded a Northwest Airlines flight and unsuccessfully tried to blow it up. No one asked him any questions, even though two months earlier, his father, a prominent businessperson, had reported that his son was training at an Al Qaeda camp for terrorists in Yemen.

> **Bureaucratic pathologies:** The problems that tend to develop in bureaucratic systems.

Why do these errors happen? Because every feature of the ideal bureaucracy has its potential downside. The problems that develop are known as **bureaucratic pathologies**. Familiar pathologies include the following:

- *Rote*. Rote involves slavishly following old standardized routines despite new developments. The failure to adjust (often accompanied by the excuse of "I'm just doing my job") can lead to problems, even tragedies. When members of an organization get

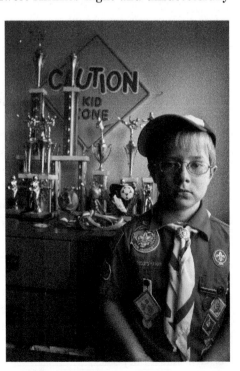

A threat to national security? Mikey Hicks was subjected to intense questioning every time he flew—thanks to a glitch in the no-fly list. Bureaucratic pathologies—such as an inability to break routines—are an exaggerated form of exactly what makes bureaucracies effective. Call it too much of a good thing.

too used to following SOPs, they avoid responsibility—and potential blame—by hiding behind their assigned routines.

- *Imperialism.* Bureaucracies compete just like private companies. They want bigger budgets and better staffs. This status seeking can lead them to grow too big and to engage in time-wasting turf wars.

- *Turf war.* Agencies often find that they are doing overlapping jobs. This replication leads to tensions about who is responsible for what. For example, there are at least nineteen intelligence agencies in the federal government. Agencies such as the FBI and CIA that view each other as competitors may fail to share information.

- *Lack of coordination.* Even agencies that are good at doing their own job often have few mechanisms for cooperating with other agencies. That is because their routines are internal to the agency and do not apply to other organizations. If the agencies are imperialistic or fighting a turf war, the problem can become acute.

- *Clientelism.* Sometimes an agency develops routines that favor some constituents over others. For example, if the Department of Agriculture sends out complicated forms to qualify for loans, they will favor agricultural corporations (which have bookkeepers and secretaries) over small family farms that have little time to complete fifty-page forms. The bias may not be explicit, but it is built into the SOPs. And because the favored clients—the big farms—don't complain, the routine continues.

What was the problem for Mikey? Primarily, the problem of *rote*. Once his name was on the watch list, the agency kept running through its routine and questioning him. Because the agency would be in serious trouble if it crossed a real terrorist off the list, the routine for removing names is slower, with more checkpoints and approvals, than the routine for adding a name. Why did the real terrorist slip through? Here, the problem was a *lack of coordination*, compounded by a *turf war*: different security agencies competing for resources failed to communicate. Umar Farouk Abdulmutallab's father contacted one agency, which neglected to pass the information to another. A tragic reminder of these bureaucratic pathologies came in summer 2016, with the terrorist attack at an Orlando nightclub. A gun shop owner reportedly called the FBI five days before the attack to warn them about the shooter, but—due to poor coordination—no follow-up took place.

In popular culture, the story of bureaucratic pathology often completely eclipses every other aspect of the subject. This is a mistake. We could not run the military, deliver the mail, operate an airport, process Social Security checks, or predict the weather without bureaucratic agencies. The key question for all governments—for all organizations,

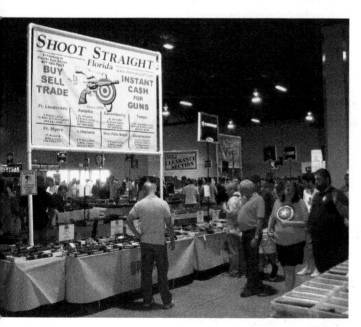

Browsers at a gun show. President Obama's 2016 executive order required more gun sellers to be licensed and expanded background checks on buyers—expanding the authority (and workload) of the FBI and Bureau of Alcohol, Tobacco, and Firearms (ATF). President Trump planned to reverse this order, as of early 2017.

including your college or university—is this: How do we produce the benefits of bureaucracy while minimizing the pathologies?

The Democratic Dilemma

Bureaucracies have an inherently difficult fit with democracy. Democracy works from the bottom up. Citizens express their opinions about what the government should do. Congress and the presidency are essentially democratic institutions because each claims to derive its authority directly from the people.

In contrast, bureaucracy runs on expertise. The deputy secretary of civilian radioactive waste management in the Energy Department relies on highly specialized knowledge. The security agencies handle classified information about potential terrorists. NOAA specialists monitor scientific weather data. None of these jobs involves public sentiment or popular votes about technical matters.

The difference between elected office and bureaucratic posts creates a clash of cultures. Democracy flows up from the people. Bureaucracy, when it runs properly, operates on the basis of specialized information, often organized top-down. An enduring challenge for American government is how to manage the tension between these two polarities.

Before we think about democratic controls on the bureaucracy, we turn to a more detailed look at what bureaucrats actually do.

THE BOTTOM LINE

» Before the rise of the bureaucracy, government jobs were distributed as spoils, or political rewards. Reformers challenged this system and eventually built a national bureaucracy.

» The ideal bureaucracy has five characteristics: hierarchy, division of labor, fixed routines, equal rules for all, and technical expertise.

» Bureaucracies are prone to pathologies, such as hewing too closely to a routine, fighting over turf, favoring some clients over others, and refusing to coordinate. These are all exaggerations of the very features that make bureaucracies efficient.

» Because they rely on specialized expertise and information, bureaucracies pose a dilemma for democratic governance.

What Bureaucracies Do

After Congress passes a law or the president issues an executive order, the bureaucracy puts it into effect. This immense task involves making many judgments because inevitably there are gaps in the law. Sometimes Congress sidesteps difficult questions to avoid a conflict or an unpopular decision, sometimes the laws are vague because they were written in a hurry or amended at the last minute, and sometimes legislation requires technical details that Congress simply leaves to the bureaucratic experts. There are two steps to the bureaucratic process of putting a law into practice: rule-making and implementation.

Rule-Making

Rule-making showcases classic bureaucratic principles in action: a fixed process with multiple steps always carried out in the same way (see Figure 15.4). First, the agency studies the law and proposes a "rule" that spells out how the new program will operate; the details must make clear to the thousands of businesses and individuals exactly what they are required to do. For example, in 2015–2016, a set of rules were issued requiring fast-food restaurants to list on their menu board the calories of an item, right next to its price.

Sounds simple, right? Generally the details are anything but. What restaurants must post calorie labels? Does the rule apply to hot-dog carts? Popcorn sold in movie theaters? Soup kitchens for people without homes? How large should the restaurant make its labels? (If the font size is not specified, some companies might list the calories in tiny numbers that no one will notice.) What about foods that can be prepared in many different ways? Can a restaurant just list the calories in a baked potato? Or does it have to include calorie counts when the diner adds sour cream, bacon bits, and cheese? It is the bureaucracy's job to spell out those kinds of details.

After the agency has devised the rule, it sends the rule to the Office of Management and Budget for approval. (You know from our tour of the White House in the last chapter that the OMB has the power of central clearance—it gets a chance to say "no" to almost anything.) After the OMB gives its okay, the agency publishes the **proposed rule** in a publication called the *Federal Register*, the daily journal of the federal government. Anybody who is interested can comment. Who reads the *Federal Register*? In theory, any citizen can read it online or at a library. In practice, most people do not know that it exists, while lobbyists and lawyers pore over it as if it were the latest hot novel. The day we wrote this chapter, for example, the *Federal Register* included proposed rules on air quality (from the Environmental Protection Agency) and a final rule regulating swordfish harvest limits off the North Atlantic coast of the United States (from NOAA). You can be sure that lawyers and lobbyists for manufacturing companies with high pollution emission rates and fishing fleets will be bombarding the agencies with comments and questions (also published in the *Federal Register*). Environmental and consumer groups also join the conversation. As you might guess, the actual details of the proposed rule and the comments are extremely technical.

The agency reviews all the public comments, makes changes, and proposes a **final rule**, along with an analysis of the likely impact of the new rule. Back it goes to the OMB, which has thirty days to review the final rule. Then the final rule is published in the *Federal Register*. Thirty days later, the regulation goes into effect. The final rule is not necessarily the end of the process, however. An individual citizen, group, or corporate firm that does not agree with the result can sue the agency for misinterpreting Congress's intent. Or it can appeal to its allies in

Proposed rule: A draft of administrative regulations published in the *Federal Register* for the purpose of gathering comments from interested parties.

Final rule: The rule that specifies how a program will actually operate.

FIGURE 15.4 *Rule-making in practice. Government rule-making showcases classic bureaucratic principles in action: a fixed process with multiple steps always carried out in the same way. (Office of Management and Budget)*

Agency employees draft proposed regulation

OMB approves

Proposed regulation published in Federal Register

Public comments

Agency prepares final rules and impact analysis

OMB approves

Final rules published in Federal Register and go into effect in 30 days

Affected interest can sue or go back to Congress and, if successful, agency starts back at step one

What goes on the label? Today, that's a controversial issue.

Congress and try to get the legislators to criticize the rule and push the agency to restart the process.

In practice, lobbyists for the industry negotiate with the agency as the proposed and final rules are being written. They offer advice or might threaten to sue. Experts in the agency push back and decide when to call the industry's bluff. Consumer groups often get in on the action as well, trying to balance the views of the industry. Once in a while, when a rule taps into a broader controversy, this debate spills over into the public eye. In 2015 the Environmental Protection Agency (EPA) issued a "Clean Power" rule directing states to curb carbon pollution from power plants. Coal producers and power-plant operators were furious, seeing it as a direct attack on their livelihood. Twenty-four states sued the EPA over the rule's legality, and the controversy continues today, with the Trump Administration set to weigh in.[9]

Apart from occasional flash points (like the EPA and carbon emissions), rule-making involves a very narrow slice of American life (like swordfish harvesting) that takes place every day, far from the public eye. Congress gets plenty of media coverage when it considers legislation. But negotiations over rules usually take place in the shadows, where only the most informed experts understand what is going on. This is the hidden debate that shapes every law, executive order, and public policy. It may be technical, but it involves all of us. Today's proposed rules are about countering climate change and ensuring a steady food supply; tomorrow's could affect student loans and affordable housing. Now you can see the importance of our central question about democracy: How can the public possibly control these battles that occur deep in the bureaucratic leviathan? We address that question in the final section of this chapter.

Implementation

After the rules are in place, bureaucracies have to implement the new policies. The swordfish have to be inspected and the power-plant emissions regulated.

Implementation is the last step in a long process. The president and/or members of Congress proposed the law; the House and Senate passed it; the courts upheld it; and the bureaucratic agency proposed draft rules, gathered comments, and published final rules in the *Federal Register*. Bureaucrats are active at every stage in the process. For example, they often are involved in shaping proposed programs, helping write the legislation (as experts on the topic), and testifying before congressional committees that are considering the law.

Sometimes executive bureaucrats develop close alliances with members of Congress as well as with interest-group lobbyists. A specialist in the EPA might spend years working with "green" members of Congress, along with the environmental groups and industries that are most affected by the regulations. As another

see for yourself 15.1

Go online to view a video about the history and operation of the *Federal Register*.

example, the Bureau of Alcohol, Tobacco, Firearms and Explosives connects frequently with gun makers and members of Congress who care about guns. Some criticize these arrangements as too cozy (recall the iron triangles discussed in Chapter 12). In any case, you should recognize that the bureaucracy is not walled off from other actors in government. It is part of the process all along the way.

The bureaucracy touches every aspect of our lives. It inspects the food you eat; monitors the air you breathe; negotiates the trade rules that governed the importation of your T-shirt; regulates seat belts, airbags, and the crash-resistant frame of your car; oversees your student loans; and awards your professors grants to study topics ranging from elections to Emily Dickinson's poems to nanotechnology. Almost everything you do today has been touched, one way or another, by bureaucracies implementing policies that were once proposed rules in the *Federal Register*.

THE BOTTOM LINE

» Once a law is passed or an executive order is signed, the program goes to the bureaucracy to be put into effect.

» Bureaucrats propose rules, publish them in the *Federal Register*, gather comments, rewrite the rules, and publish the final version. The law or executive order is now in effect.

» At every step of the process, lawyers and lobbyists interact with the bureaucracy; this interaction engages experts far from the political limelight.

» Bureaucratic officials take part in every step of the political process—from proposing legislation to putting it into effect.

How the Bureaucracy Is Organized

Each presidential administration names the heads of the government bureaucracy—about four thousand people known as political appointees. The Senate must approve these men and women, who include cabinet secretaries, their assistants and deputies, the ambassadors to countries around the world, and other top figures. Their role is to steer their agencies in the direction charted by the president and the voters.

Civil servants: Members of the permanent executive branch bureaucracy who are employed on the basis of competitive exams and keep their positions regardless of the presidential administration.

Under these four thousand appointees toil some 2.7 million **civil servants** who work at their jobs regardless of which party is in the White House. Imagine the tensions when a new political appointee (often a campaign official) arrives eagerly touting the new president's philosophy to an office of career officials. Those long-serving bureaucrats usually have more expertise than the political appointee who has just been named their boss. The civil servants know that before long (on average, a bit more than three years), the eager new appointee will move on, to be replaced by another. The civil servants are acutely aware of the rules, regulations, and SOPs that guide their agency. They literally tell their new bosses what they can do; how they should do it; and the many things that they might want to do but that could land them in trouble because they fall outside the rules, clash with another agency's mission, or raise a sore point with a powerful member of Congress.

Over the years, civil servants have built up a vocabulary of their own, often caricatured as "bureaucratese"—the cautious, cover-your-backside language of experts with lifetime positions who are tasked with providing three trillion dollars' worth of federal services every year. H. George Frederickson recently published a book of humorous "bureaucracy-speak" examples, and he has shared a few with us (see Talking Politics). Master these lines, and you will be ready for a summer internship in the executive branch!

The federal government's organizational chart includes four different types of agencies: cabinet departments, autonomous bureaus, independent regulatory agencies, and the bureaucracy's service organizations. Let us take a closer look at each type.

The Cabinet Departments

President George Washington's cabinet had just four departments: State, Treasury, War (now called Defense, which sounds a little less aggressive), and the Office of the Attorney General (later called the Justice Department). Over time, presidents added new departments until the cabinet reached its current size of fifteen. Table 15.1 lists each department, the year it was founded, and how large it is today. Notice how the military dominates the government's personnel count. The Department of Defense houses some 2.2 million employees, including the men and women in uniform, and manages facilities that take up thirty million acres around the world; no other organization in the United States comes close.

Because State and Treasury are the two oldest departments, the secretaries of state and the treasury always sit next to the president in cabinet meetings. The younger the agency, the farther away from the president the secretary sits. (Each position is indicated by a silver plaque on the back of the chair, with the department's founding date.) A similar protocol exists for any formal event—the leaders of the oldest departments enter first, with the secretary of the newest department (currently Homeland Security) bringing up the rear. In the event of a catastrophe, the secretary of state is fourth in line to take over the presidency, followed by each cabinet secretary—again in the order the agencies were founded.

The Challenge of Governing.   Unlike in nations with parliamentary systems, the U.S. president names each cabinet secretary (see Comparing Nations). It is part of the fanfare of a new administration. The event is full of optimism as the president sings the nominee's praises and the media speculates about fresh policy directions. Then the difficulties begin. Imagine that you are in the secretary's shoes: there are several hurdles you will face.

First, you must go before the Senate for confirmation. In the increasingly partisan Washington environment, any past indiscretion may surface and force you to withdraw. If all goes well, you take office when the president does, on a cold Washington day in late January.

Next, you have to select your staff—your team is not yet in place. The presidential transition group sends you boxes of résumés. You pick names for your deputies, your assistants, and the leaders of the dozens of offices in your agency; some you know, others the president's advisors recommend, and still others look especially impressive on paper. Next you send your selections over to the White House for a thumbs-up. Because White House staffers may have their own favorites, you will have to negotiate some of your choices. The FBI examines every nominee's background, which can sometimes take many months. After that, each nominee goes to the Senate for confirmation.

If you are lucky, the White House does not ask a thousand questions, nothing embarrassing turns up in the FBI's detailed check, and no senator objects to the appointment. You might then have your political appointees in place by August.

BUREAUCRACY BUZZWORDS

Bureaucrat: You need to be more proactive.

Meaning: You should have protected me from myself.

Bureaucrat: We want you to be the executive champion of this project.

Meaning: I want to be able to blame you for my mistakes.

Bureaucrat: We need to syndicate this decision.

Meaning: We need to spread the blame if it backfires.

Bureaucrat: I see you involved your peers in developing your proposal.

Meaning: One person couldn't possibly come up with something this stupid.

Bureaucrat: Our agency is going through a paradigm shift.

Meaning: We have no idea what we've been doing, but in the future we shall do something completely different.

Bureaucrat: Value-added.

Meaning: Expensive.

(Source: H. George Frederickson, Up the Bureaucracy, *2014).*

TABLE 15.1 **U.S. Executive Bureaucracies**

CABINET DEPARTMENT	YEAR OF FOUNDING	CURRENT EMPLOYEES
State	1789	69,000*
Treasury	1789	91,208
Defense	1789	729,060 civilians; 1.4 million uniformed military
Justice	1789	114,776
Interior	1849	69,757
Agriculture	1862	96,567
Commerce	1903	47,378
Labor	1913	15,889
Health and Human Services (originally "Health, Education, and Welfare")	1953	85,328
Housing and Urban Development	1965	8,209
Transportation	1966	54,769
Energy	1977	15,107
Education	1979	4,259
Veterans Affairs	1989	365,567
Homeland Security	2002	187,130
ADDITIONAL FEDERAL AGENCIES (NONCABINET)		
Social Security Administration		65,717
Environmental Protection Agency		15,445
National Aeronautics and Space Administration		17,260
General Services Administration		11,175
Other independent agencies		64,403
U.S. Postal Service (a semi-independent federal agency since 1971)		486,822
Executive Office of the President (detailed in Chapter 14)		1,852
Total Federal Service		**2,058,924 in the United States; Approximately 700,000 abroad**
Estimated number of federal contractors and grantees		**Between 7 million and 9 million (depending on who's counting and how)**

Source: U.S. Office of Personnel Management
*45,000 foreign service staff, 11,000 U.S. civil servants, and 13,000 foreign service officers

However, if you get caught in a bottleneck—at the White House, the FBI, or (most likely) in Congress—it can be a year or more before members of your team are in place and ready to go. Remember, there are fifteen cabinet departments—in addition to dozens of federal agencies—and all are scrambling to get their people through the neck of the bottle. In September 2001, President George W. Bush did not yet have most of his security team in office when the terrorists attacked the World Trade Center on September 11, eight months after Inauguration Day. As Washington has grown more partisan, the confirmation process has become more difficult. And remember that a single senator can put a hold on one of your appointments if you, your department, or your nominee has provoked him or her.

● A 2016 cabinet meeting in the White House. Each member has a plaque affixed to the back of his or her chair, specifying the agency he or she represents and the year it was founded.

Getting leaders into their offices is just the first challenge. New secretaries also face the more fundamental problem of managing a large bureaucracy that they know very little about. Cabinet secretaries are accomplished individuals, but they are unlikely to have much experience with the many facets of their department. For example, President Obama's first secretary of the Department of Homeland Security (DHS), Janet Napolitano, had previously been governor of Arizona. Although she was familiar with some homeland security issues, especially those surrounding immigration, Napolitano did not know much about the Office of Cybersecurity, the

---

COMPARING NATIONS 15.1   Parliamentary Systems

Parliamentary systems—such as those in England, Germany, Japan, or Israel—are different from the U.S. system when it comes to bureaucratic leadership. In all these nations, senior members of the legislature become ministers, the equivalent of cabinet secretaries in the United States. Notice the contrast: Legislative leaders from the majority party also lead the bureaucracy.

Each ministry has two heads. The elected minister drawn from parliament represents the public and sets the policy goals; the other leader is a career civil servant (often called the director general), who provides technical expertise and continuity across the years. Both these positions are highly prestigious—in England, an effective director general of an important ministry may very well earn a knighthood.

Some parliamentary systems result in coalition governments. Five parties together form the majority in the government of Israel. The different parties bargain for control of Israel's government

ministries—the defense ministry is in the hands of the Yisrael Beiteinu Party, the head of the Kulanu Party directs the ministry of finance, and so on.

Notice the many differences between these systems and the American system. In other nations, no one sends in a résumé—you have to win an election to parliament and work your way up the party hierarchy to become a minister. There is no long confirmation process, no hostile congressional committees overseeing the bureaucracy, no checks and balances between the executive and legislative branches. The civil service is extremely prestigious. Successful civil servants can climb to the top of the ministry—rather than always working for a new set of senior appointees rotating in after each presidential election.

If this system sounds like a better way to run things, you will have to amend the Constitution, which bars members of Congress from taking "any civil office"—they may not take posts in the bureaucracy or the judiciary. The founders, as always, insisted on checks and balances.

Coast Guard, or the Animal and Plant Inspection Service—all bureaus now under her direction. Almost all secretaries face the same problem. And with a new administration in town, a huge to-do list of policy goals awaits each new executive.

The Rotating Bureaucracy. The turnover at the top rung of the U.S. bureaucracy is unique. No other democracy works in this way—nor does any other major institution. No private company, nonprofit organization, or university routinely asks thousands of outsiders to take over for an average of three or so years and then expects them to step aside and make way for a new crop of leaders. Meanwhile, the political appointees scrambling to catch up are in charge of a huge bureaucratic leviathan. Thousands of civil servants toil away at the agency's tasks, working from one administration to the next.

Management consultants would run screaming from the room if you suggested setting up a business in this way. We cannot look to the Constitution for justification, because it does not mention cabinet departments, much less an entire bureaucracy. Many political scientists, however, think the bureaucracy does work. The civil service does its job, often quite well. And the political leadership, for all the problems facing a new administration, comes to the job with a definite philosophy, based on a president's central ideas.

Pairing a suitable philosophy with skilled political leadership can make a real difference in an agency's management. An example is the Federal Emergency Management Agency (FEMA), which responds to natural disasters. President Bill Clinton named a talented FEMA director, James Lee Witt, who had emergency management experience. With Clinton's support, Witt transformed the agency into a decentralized, authority-sharing, proactive outfit. When floods hit the Midwest in 1993, FEMA won widespread applause for its swift, well-organized assistance. People might despise federal bureaucrats, but Witt and his FEMA team drew high praise at the time.

When the George W. Bush administration came to office, FEMA was on its list of target agencies. From a conservative perspective, FEMA had become *too* proactive. The Bush administration restored the old FEMA policies and installed an inexperienced (but politically connected) campaign donor, Michael Brown, as director.

FEMA failure: Hurricane Katrina, 2005. FEMA success: Louisiana flood, 2016.

In this case, the changes led to political disaster. In part owing to the restoration of a rules-bound, elaborately hierarchical structure, and in part to Brown's inexperience as a leader, FEMA responded feebly to Hurricane Katrina, a massive storm that flooded New Orleans in 2005. The tragedy was broadcast live, as the media depicted widespread desperation: more than 1,800 people lost their lives in the storms and subsequent flooding—with no federal response in sight. Director Brown lost his job, and President Bush's popularity ratings tumbled.

President Obama, learning from his predecessors, appointed an experienced, well-regarded FEMA director, W. Craig Fugate, who had directed emergency services under Governor Jeb Bush in Florida. The agency received high marks when another devastating storm, Hurricane Sandy, hit the East Coast in 2012. "Officials and experts praising FEMA for its response to Hurricane Sandy," read a representative headline in the *Washington Post*.[10] Along with the value of savvy leadership, the FEMA example illustrates another important point about the federal bureaucracy. Calling for smaller government sounds promising on the campaign trail. However, each nook and cranny of the sprawling government establishment has a job to do; almost all deliver services that people rely on. That responsibility makes cutting government agencies difficult in practice.

The Cabinet and Diversity.   Recently, the cabinet has taken on another important role. Like the bureaucracy they lead, the fifteen secretaries reflect the American public. Table 15.2 shows the number of women and minority members in the cabinet over time. Until the mid-1960s, just two women had served in the cabinet in all of American history—and not a single African American, Latino, or Asian.

The dramatic change that began in the 1970s reflects the social revolution that swept the nation over one generation. During the first two hundred years of American history, only three women and two African Americans were appointed to the cabinet. Since the 1980s, every president (from both parties) has appointed a diverse cabinet that reflects the nation. These government executives are far more

TABLE 15.2 Demographic Makeup of Presidential Cabinets

PRESIDENT	WOMEN	MINORITIES	CABINET OFFICERS NAMED DURING ADMINISTRATION	YEARS
All presidents to 1963	2	0	—	1789–1963
Johnson	0	1	25	1963–1968
Nixon	0	0	31	1969–1974
Ford	1	1	22	1974–1976
Carter	4	1	22	1977–1980
Reagan	3	2	33	1981–1988
G. H. W. Bush	3	3	21	1989–1992
Clinton	5	10	30	1993–2000
G. W. Bush	6	8	34	2001–2008
Obama	8	9	33	2009–2016

representative of the U.S. population than their counterparts in finance, industry, or academia.

Other Agencies

Two-thirds of the federal bureaucracy—about 1.8 million civilians—works in the cabinet departments. There are three other categories of federal workers, and each offers a different twist on the life of the bureaucracy.

Executive Agencies.   Independent executive agencies have more specific assignments than do the cabinet departments. The Social Security Administration, for example, is responsible for running the Social Security program, which provides pensions for Americans over age sixty-six. The Environmental Protection Agency is entirely focused on the difficult job of overseeing the environment. In contrast, the Department of the Interior (a cabinet agency) has responsibilities that include—among many other things—supervising Indian affairs, national parks, geological surveys, oceans and energy, and surface mining.

The more than thirty independent executive agencies perform a wide range of jobs: They land astronauts on the moon (NASA), send Americans around the world to perform service projects (the Peace Corps), gather intelligence (CIA), manage the banking system (the Federal Reserve), monitor elections (the Federal Election Commission), and investigate violations of civil rights in the workplace (Equal Employment Opportunities Commission).

The U.S. Postal Service became a cabinet agency in 1792. Some 180 years later, in 1971, the post office became an independent agency of the U.S. federal government—operating without direct federal subsidy. The Postal Service has just under five hundred thousand employees (down from nearly eight hundred thousand in 1999) and 250,000 vehicles; it is the second-largest federal bureaucracy after the Defense Department.

Independent Regulatory Commissions.   Another type of bureau emerged to regulate business. The first one set the organizational template. In the 1880s, farmers and small business complained bitterly that they were at the mercy of the railroads, which could make or break them with their arbitrary freight rates. The farmers pleaded for government controls. However, reformers faced a problem. Railroad owners were so wealthy and powerful that they dominated the state legislatures and Congress. How could consumers be protected against these "robber barons"? Reformers organized a regulatory agency, the Interstate Commerce Commission (ICC), that would operate separately from Congress and the White House. Reformers hoped that the agency's independence would permit it to regulate industry—free from corrupting lobbyists and politics.

Independent regulatory commissions have the authority to issue regulations, enforce laws, and settle disputes—essentially combining legislative, executive, and judicial powers in one agency. A set of commissioners, nominated by the president and confirmed by the Senate, runs the agency for a fixed term that does not overlap with the president's term—still another way to minimize political influence. The hope, beginning with the ICC, was that modern management methods, rather than politics, would guide regulatory policy.

You likely recognize the reformers' naiveté: Independent agencies were no less political than any other branch of government. As we saw when we examined the rule-making process, regulating an industry inevitably involves plenty of

INFO/DATA: The Formation of Regulatory Commissions

Congress creates independent regulatory commissions in response to emerging needs within society, whether it is in response to a stock market failure, the rise of a new form of transportation, or a political demand to protect civil or consumer rights.

1. How do the types of regulatory agencies formed since 1887 reflect changes within American society and politics?

2. What new agencies might be formed in the future to address needs that are emerging today?

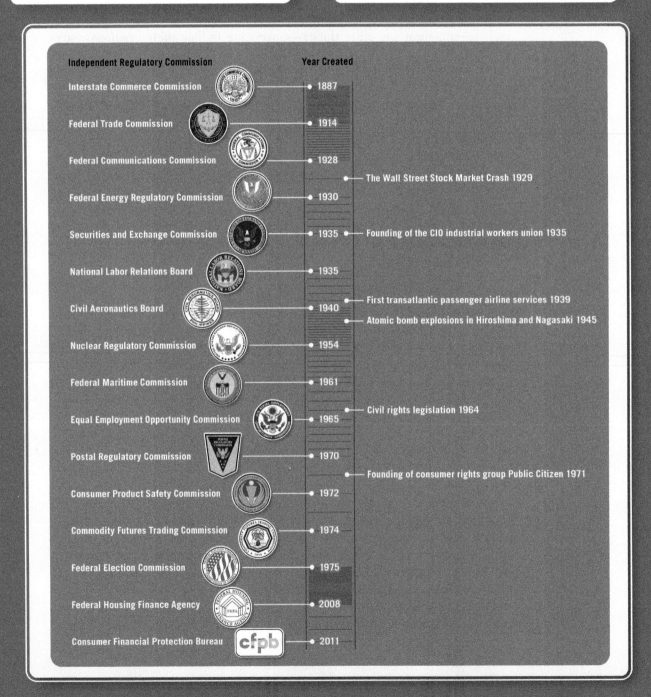

Independent Regulatory Commission	Year Created	
Interstate Commerce Commission	1887	
Federal Trade Commission	1914	
Federal Communications Commission	1928	
Federal Energy Regulatory Commission	1930	The Wall Street Stock Market Crash 1929
Securities and Exchange Commission	1935	Founding of the CIO industrial workers union 1935
National Labor Relations Board	1935	
Civil Aeronautics Board	1940	First transatlantic passenger airline services 1939
		Atomic bomb explosions in Hiroshima and Nagasaki 1945
Nuclear Regulatory Commission	1954	
Federal Maritime Commission	1961	
Equal Employment Opportunity Commission	1965	Civil rights legislation 1964
Postal Regulatory Commission	1970	
		Founding of consumer rights group Public Citizen 1971
Consumer Product Safety Commission	1972	
Commodity Futures Trading Commission	1974	
Federal Election Commission	1975	
Federal Housing Finance Agency	2008	
Consumer Financial Protection Bureau	2011	

HISTORY REPEATS ITSELF.— THE ROBBER BARONS OF THE MIDDLE AGES, AND THE ROBBER BARONS OF TO-DAY.

● *The nineteenth-century railroad owners were among the "robber barons"—mocked in this cartoon for squeezing farmers, workers, and businessmen as mercilessly as the barons of the Middle Ages.*

Regulatory capture: The theory that industries dominate the agencies that regulate them.

Central service agencies: The organizations that supply and staff the federal government.

back-and-forth negotiations between regulators and the industry. Moreover, to understand an industry well enough to monitor its activities, regulators generally need some relevant expertise. Commissioners therefore are frequently drawn from the ranks of the regulated industry. Ironically, the effort to keep the regulatory commissions independent of Congress and the White House has left them more susceptible to industry influence. For decades, critics have charged that the independent regulatory agencies are "captured" or "acquired" by the industry and simply do its bidding.

There is no escaping the politics that pervade the independent regulatory agencies. Still, the **"regulatory capture"** argument is often overstated. Consumer groups also lobby, provide information to, and sue the agencies. Moreover, agency civil servants often work hard to achieve their institution's goals—and express pride in its independent stance.

In the past thirty years, a new generation of reformers has promoted *deregulation*—that is, abolishing the agencies altogether and letting free-market competition protect consumers. The original ICC was dismantled in 1995. The Civil Aeronautics Board, another regulatory commission that protected the airline industry by limiting competition, was abolished in 1985, leading, directly or indirectly, to all kinds of consequences, good and bad—frequent-flier programs, fewer airlines, huge fluctuations in fares, and inedible food.

Deregulation brings us full circle. Once, farmers and small business pleaded for relief from predatory markets. Now, a new generation of reformers offers a solution to problems with the regulatory agencies: return to the markets.

An Army of Their Own. A small support army maintains and services the massive office buildings housing the executive branch. Imagine supplying 2.7 million workers; imagine the job of hiring, paying, reviewing, promoting, and sometimes firing all those workers. These details require still another type of institution in the American bureaucracy: independent **central service agencies**, most notably the Office of Personnel Management (OPM) and the General Services Administration (GSA).

Do you want to work for the U.S. government as a civil servant? The OPM manages the giant "USAJobs" website, which lists hundreds of thousands of federal bureaucracy job openings each year. Once you apply for a position, your application will be screened by OPM staff. If you are hired, your employment materials (pay level, vacation time details, and health benefits) will come from them. And when you are ready to leave government service, you will talk to the OPM about the government pension you may have accumulated.

While you are working for the government, the GSA manages all the details of maintenance and supply. Your building just got painted? The GSA did the work—or hired and supervised the company who did it under contract. Do you need a shipment of forest fire–fighting helicopters (for the National Park Service) or a more sophisticated smartphone (at the OMB)? The GSA is your one-stop shopping spot.

Private Contractors. The final category of government employees does not work directly for the government. They come from private companies that provide goods and services under contract to the government. **Private contractors** now perform many of the jobs that once were handled directly by government employees. For example, the military increasingly relies on private firms to provide meals, transportation, security services, and even commando teams. For the first time in American history, there were more private contractors (about 200,000) than uniformed military personnel (about 190,000) in the war zones in both Iraq (2003–2012) and Afghanistan. Besides war-related services, private companies provide a full range of government services, spreading to homeland security, international diplomacy, prison management, and garbage collection.

> **Private contractors:** Private companies that contract to provide goods and services for the government.

Why contract out government services? There are three main reasons: First, private companies, foundations, and nongovernmental organizations often have special skills and resources they can bring to a job. Second, they lobby hard for the business. And third, Americans critical of the bureaucracy often assert that private companies can do a better and cheaper job.

The truth is that sometimes private contractors can do a better job than the public sector, but at other times they charge more for inferior services. Recognizing that private contracting in government is here to stay, the key to making it work is ensuring that government officials maintain careful oversight of the work that is done for hire.[11]

● *Private contractors continue to provide security in war zones, including Iraq, as in this 2016 photo of a private guard protecting a U.S.–Iraqi diplomatic meeting.*

Executive branch agencies and commissions all face leadership challenges similar to those faced by the cabinet departments. The appointment process is cumbersome and complicated by politics. New appointees scramble to learn the bureaucratic ropes, even as the to-do list piles ever higher—and meanwhile the administrative team takes months or even years to get into place.

How can the nation's agencies operate effectively when their leaders are on the way in and just learning the ropes or are on the way out and operating as lame ducks? For an answer, we need to confront the complicated question of just who is in charge of the American bureaucracy.

THE BOTTOM LINE

» The federal bureaucracy includes five different types of agencies. The fifteen cabinet departments, forming the largest group, employ roughly 1.8 million civilians.

» The government includes four other types of bureaucracies: executive agencies focus on one type of issue, such as environmental quality; independent regulatory commissions oversee specific industries; central service agencies staff and supply the entire bureaucracy; and private contractors are licensed to provide goods and services for the government. Different types of agencies face different political problems and challenges.

» The president appoints a small number of executives; the rest are members of the permanent civil service. The cabinet has grown far more diverse in the past twenty-five years.

» The cabinet and other appointed executives provide political direction; the civil servants provide expertise and continuity.

» Among the many challenges to a smoothly functioning system is the time—often more than a year—that it takes a new administration to get its leadership team in place.

Who Controls the Federal Bureaucracy?

Controlling more than four million civilian bureaucrats and military personnel, and an unknown number of private contractors (one reliable estimate pegs it at 7.6 million),[12] is a daunting leadership responsibility—and a giant management headache. It is also crucial for democracy. Self-rule requires mastering the bureaucracy. But who is in charge?

The People

In a democracy, the federal government must ultimately respond to the people. Most executive departments trumpet something like *We Serve the People* on their websites. However, real popular control faces the problem we have discussed throughout this chapter: Much of what the bureaucracy does is too technical for direct public engagement.

Overhead democracy:
A system by which the people elect the president, who, through their appointees, controls the bureaucracy from the top.

How does the Internal Revenue Service (IRS) compute tax penalties for S corporations that wrongly elect to amortize anticipated losses with write-downs? What is the maximum engineering pendular sway ratio on truss-style bridges? Does the chemical compound bisphenol-A, widely used in plastics, leach into bottled drinking water—and if it does, how dangerous is it to public health? Few Americans have the time or the knowledge to develop opinions about such matters. We need someone else to act on our behalf.

The President

In theory, the president controls the bureaucracy. The Constitution is clear on this issue: "The executive Power shall be vested in a President of the United States of America." The president is the bureaucrat in chief. The form of bureaucratic control that follows from this declaration is known as **overhead democracy**: The people elect presidents who, through their appointees, control the bureaucracy from the top.

In practice, most presidents are frustrated in their efforts to manage the millions of men and women under their command. Harry Truman

● *Does the public control our federal bureaucracy? This cartoonist suggests otherwise.*

put it famously when he commented on his successor, General Dwight D. Eisenhower: "He'll sit here and he'll say 'Do this!' and 'Do that!' *And nothing will happen.* Poor Ike, it won't be a bit like the army. He'll find it very frustrating."[13]

When presidents appoint the directors of the executive branch, they quickly discover that the bureaucracy has its own preferences, processes, and routines. Before long, many executives begin to see the world through the eyes of their agencies—rather than from the perspective of the White House. When President Richard Nixon, a Republican, came to office, Democrats had run the government for twenty-eight of the previous thirty-six years, and Nixon believed that many of the career civil servants were simply Democrats waiting for the next liberal administration. "If we don't get rid of these people," Nixon wrote bluntly, "they will sit back on their well-paid asses and wait for the next election to bring back their old bosses."[14]

Congress

Although bureaucrats "belong" to the executive branch, the legislative branch wields a surprising amount of authority over them. Congress shapes the bureaucracy through four powers.

- *Funding.* Most important, Congress funds nearly all executive branch programs since it determines the federal budget. If Congress does not like a bureaucratic proposal, or if some agency head falls out of favor with a powerful subcommittee, that program or department may find its budget slashed by congressional appropriators.

- *Oversight.* Congress has formal power to supervise the executive branch, including both White House and federal bureaucratic operations. Policing department and agency actions is normally a routine operation—making sure that funds are properly expended or that programs achieve their stated goals. But Congress can extend its oversight authority into major investigations of executive branch actions. The mere mention of oversight hearings is a major threat to the bureaucracy.

- *Authorization.* Congress passes all laws and often has to reauthorize them after a specified number of years. Although we have seen that recent administrations have increasingly relied on executive orders, Congress wields the power to amend programs or even deny their reauthorization.

- *Reorganization.* Finally, Congress can change the structure and nature of executive branch organizations. Currently Congress is considering a White House proposal to merge various food-safety areas—within the Food and Drug Administration, Department of Agriculture, Department of Health and Human Services, and others—into one agency responsible for inspecting and protecting America's food supply.

These four sources of power add up to extensive congressional influence. Agency heads and cabinet secretaries are often more responsive to Congress—with its power of the purse and oversight authority—than to the president. Bureaucratic leaders regularly lobby Congress for additional funding or authority. They also frequently complain, however, about congressional "micromanagement."

Political scientists have recently focused on a theoretical way of looking at the relationship between Congress and the bureaucracy. **Principal-agent theory** analyzes problems that develop when a principal (in this case, Congress) hires an agent

Principal-agent theory: Details how policymakers (principals) control the actors who work for them (agents)—but who have far more information than they do.

(the bureaucracy) to do a job. The problem arises when the agent has much more information than the principal. How do you control a bureaucracy when there is "information asymmetry," that is, when "they" know a lot more than "you" do? The answer: Make sure their interests are the same as yours. Many scholars now suggest that although Congress cannot possibly oversee everything the bureaucracy does, the power of its weapons—especially funding and oversight—leads bureaucratic officials, by and large, to conform to congressional wishes. Put differently, the fear of being hauled before a congressional panel and threatened with a loss of funding is enough to make bureaucrats worry about congressional intent and desires.

Congressional power also is circumscribed, of course. The power to shape or influence the bureaucracy is still a far cry from the power to command or control it. Presidents and congressional leaders sometimes clash over who controls bureaucratic departments and agencies. Courts also weigh in, striking down regulatory-agency actions, as we saw in the rule-making discussion earlier. Meanwhile, another powerful set of players—interest groups—quietly exerts influence as well.

Interest Groups

Interest groups closely engage bureaucrats as they administer the laws. As we saw in Chapter 12, lobbying groups comment extensively on proposed rules. They offer information about the needs and capacity of the affected industry. As bureaucrats finalize the rules and implement the program, they often engage industry representatives, whose cooperation may be necessary to make the program work smoothly. Officials in the bureaucracy, trade groups, and consumer alliances often share expertise and interests. Over time, close relations often develop, making lobbyists influential in the day-to-day operations of the executive agencies. Interest groups—often fighting among themselves—also can publicly complain, report back to Congress, or sue about overzealous regulators. The result is another set of influences on bureaucrats in action.

Bureaucratic Autonomy

Partly because they have so many would-be masters, bureaucrats wind up with considerable autonomy in how they do their work. Many of these civil servants have strong views about their field, whether that is protecting the environment, enforcing civil rights laws, or keeping the homeland safe. They also have an interest in increasing their own autonomy—applying their best judgment to the problems they face.

Whistle-blower: A federal worker who reports corruption or fraud.

Some federal bureaucrats themselves call attention to abuses within their department or agency. These happen enough that there even is a term for a worker—public or private—who witnesses and reports corruption or fraud: **whistle-blower**. In many cases, permanent civil servants blow the whistle on fraudulent or misbehaving political appointees higher up in the department or agency. In 2014, for example, dozens of whistle-blowers in the Veterans Administration (VA), which provides healthcare to retired U.S. soldiers, reported fraudulent practices such as mistreatment of patients and falsified medical records to improve performance reviews. The ensuing scandal forced the VA secretary, Eric Shinseki (a former top Army general), to resign.

Street-level bureaucrats: Public officials who deal directly with the public.

This search for autonomy is especially true for government officials who deal directly with the public. These **street-level bureaucrats** are administrators at lower levels of an agency or department who interact directly with the public—welfare officers, police, teachers, poultry-plant inspectors, and so forth. General policies are formulated in the higher administration, but it is the street-level bureaucrats who actually run the programs, constantly using their own judgment. For example, the police officer may write you a speeding ticket—or let you off with a warning.[15]

Consider a more complicated case. The Women, Infants, and Children program (WIC) provides vouchers for meals to low-income families with children. On the national level, Congress debates WIC funding and the administration determines the rules for eligibility. On the local level, street-level bureaucrats constantly make judgment calls about how strictly to apply the rules. For example, one woman makes too much money on paper, but her ex-husband is not paying his child support—does she still qualify? Or another woman was ill and missed the application deadline—do you give her the benefit card allowing her to buy food anyway? Or still another family has broken the rules again and again, but if you cut them off from the program, the children will suffer. In all such cases, street-level bureaucrats decide what

● A street-level bureaucrat in action. A local official in the Modesto, California, Health Department measures the growth of a young client as part of the Women, Infants, and Children program.

to do—giving them enormous influence over how to apply the rules. Program beneficiaries quickly learn about the power of the bureaucrats they see again and again.

Moreover, at the street level, every program has its own tone. Some programs (e.g., Social Security) generally treat their beneficiaries with respect; others (like Temporary Assistance for Needy Families) reputedly take a more disciplinary stance.[16]

Democracy Revisited

Many agents—the president, Congress, courts, and interest groups—exert some control over the bureaucracy. Each does so on behalf of others: The White House tries to speak for the national public, Congress for voters in a state or district, courts to defend injured parties or protect the Constitution, and interest groups on behalf of clients who might range from a business sector to the environmental or civil rights community. Bureaucrats try to maximize their own discretion to do what they think is best. Do all these clashing forces add up to democratic control?

The answer is yes and no. At times, these different forms of democratic control offer a rough form of popular oversight. Administrations that focus on delivering services can have considerable success; presidents who seek to change the direction of federal policy can, if they stick to it, have some success; congressional oversight often improves responsiveness. But all the levers for democratic control are blunt instruments. Effectively using them takes hard work, constant attention, and considerable luck. In the next section, we examine three reform proposals that might improve the strength of popular control.

THE BOTTOM LINE

» In a democracy, the public must ultimately control the government bureaucracy. The question is how.

» Different actors exert some influence over the bureaucracy: the president (who names the leaders), Congress (through funding and oversight), and interest groups.

» Bureaucrats still operate with considerable autonomy, especially those at the "street level."

Reforming the Bureaucracy

Americans ask a great deal of the bureaucracy, but—as reported at the start of the chapter—we do not like it much. Next we review the classic criticisms of this institution, and then discuss some popular solutions.

Critiques

Three major sources of disapproval focus on cost, inertia, and public mistrust.

Cost. Critics complain about the high cost of the bureaucracy and its programs. The figures are certainly daunting (see Figure 15.5). As a proportion of America's gross national product (GNP), however, the cost of the bureaucracy—as well as the number of federal bureaucrats—has remained generally steady over the past forty years. And although every politician has a story to tell about waste or fraud, most bureaucratic programs have a substantial constituency who rely on the service they provide. The agencies of the bureaucracy meet real needs, which is one reason elected officials find them difficult to cut. The only president who significantly reduced the number of nonmilitary civil servants in the post–World War II period is Bill Clinton, who slashed the civil service by some 400,000 bureaucrats.

Inertia. American politics and culture are in constant motion. In our restless, innovative nation, the slow, rule-bound, hierarchical bureaucracy never seems to keep up. Many examples illustrate government organizations that are out of touch with a changing nation. Why do NASA flights, such as the space shuttle, always take off from Florida, despite uncertain weather and a growing population potentially endangered by crashes? Because an obscure 1950s rule prohibited the flight of test aircraft west of the Mississippi River. And, as we discussed previously, once bureaucratic routines are set, they are hard to change.

Inertia also comes from clashing political desires. For example, the government is prohibited—again by bureaucratic regulations—from purchasing knives, forks, and spoons from abroad. Employees on State Department business are prohibited from flying aboard non-American airlines. It is often less expensive, however, to buy foreign goods or to fly on international carriers. Why don't the

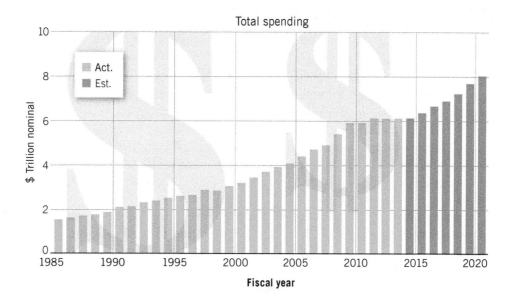

FIGURE 15.5 *Total spending on bureaucracy and its programs. (Christopher Chantrill)*

bureaucratic rules shift to accommodate this reality? Because multiple political constituencies demand different things. Congress, reflecting many voices, insists on both efficient purchasing policies *and* "buying American."

Clashing rules reflect different goals and values: We want to spread government contracts around the country, ensure social equity, stimulate new kinds of American products and services, and support American producers. These desires can clash with one another—and with the need for lower costs or faster services. Which priority deserves the most weight? The effort to choose among them is what democracy is all about. It is a debate that never ends.

Another, more troubling, problem is the increasing difficulty of recruiting the "best and the brightest" to government service. Individuals tapped for senior positions face the long process—and, often, hardball politics—we have described: Eager appointees linger in limbo for months waiting for a senator to lift their "hold." Then they must generate an extraordinary paper trail to pass security clearance; the media will unearth any indiscretion in their past; and, after all these impediments, appointees arrive on the job and discover that civil service pay scales have only inched up since 2010.

Public Mistrust.   Politicians from both parties bash the bureaucracy. Republican Ronald Reagan announced that "government is not the solution to our problem" and declared, "It is time to make [bureaucrats] stand by our side, not ride on our back." Democrat Bill Clinton declared, "The era of big government is over."[17]

Fueling public mistrust of bureaucrats are scandals and mistakes, many covered in detail by a 24/7 media mix of headlines, punditry, blogs, and tweets. In an institution as large as the federal bureaucracy, occasional examples of error, corruption, and fraud are inevitable. After all, government officials are human, just as prone to personal flaws and errors as anyone else. But in an environment of constant bureaucracy bashing, the bad news is far more prominently reported than are bureaucratic achievements, which only reinforces the general image of a corrupt, lazy bureaucracy riding "on our backs."

Reforming the Bureaucracy

The bureaucracy's reputation for being expensive, slow-moving, and scandal-ridden has attracted a long history of reform efforts. Let us consider three popular proposals.

Open Up the System.   The public's faith in government tumbled in the late 1960s and the early 1970s after an unpopular war in Vietnam, civil rights unrest, and President Nixon's shocking behavior during the Watergate scandal. One response was a concerted attempt to make the executive bureaucracy more transparent. Sunshine laws, which require public hearings and citizen input, open up bureaucratic debates to public view. The **Freedom of Information Act** (**FOIA**) extends citizen access to agency and department deliberations. Any individual or news organization may file a FOIA request to see an unreleased government document (the legislation created a new verb, "to FOIA" a document). Today, every federal agency has its own website that tries to explain just what it is doing.

Freedom of Information Act (FOIA): A 1966 law that facilitates full or partial disclosure of government information and documents.

Bureaucratic officials sometimes resist these efforts. Concerns have been raised about the potentially chilling effect on communication by politically motivated FOIA requests: as a recent *Forbes* headline asked, "Is the Freedom of Information Act Stifling Intellectual Freedom?"[18] Advocates of greater openness push for more access. Many government agencies drag their feet in response to a FOIA request.

Should We Privatize More Government Functions?

Although the benefits of privatization are still debated, research in this area suggests that competitive contracting can save money and boost quality. However, using private contractors poses its own problems, including the need for careful oversight. Do you think we should privatize more government functions?

Yes. Because private companies are driven by the profit motive, they will work hard to succeed. They bring expertise to the area and can adjust to changing conditions more quickly than can slow-moving government bureaucracies. And as long as public officials insist on competitive bids and monitor the job the company is doing, the result will be more efficient services.

No. The profit motive means that private companies are more interested in making money for investors than performing a public service well. Moreover, it is often difficult to monitor the work of private contractors; the public must pay for both the work and the monitoring. Finally, private companies go in and out of business all the time, while public services—from military support to school bus drivers—need to be reliable.

Not sure. Do you need more information? We'll return to this question in Chapters 17 and 18.

Some have genuine security concerns. Others resent the time and effort it takes to ensure transparency. And many simply want to protect themselves from criticism.

Reinventing Government. Efforts to enhance the bureaucracy are as old as the institution itself. During the Clinton administration, Vice President Al Gore ran a sweeping "Reinventing Government" project designed to cut bureaucratic delays, increase efficiency, reduce costs, decentralize management, and empower employees to make decisions.[19] Today, government innovators seek to work more efficiently through deploying technological advances; the OMB estimates that IT investments have saved some $2.7 billion over the past five years.

A call for efficiency works, however, only up to a point. Most businesses have a clear and simple goal: maximize returns for investors. In contrast, bureaucratic agencies have multiple constituencies with multiple goals. For example, if the Department of Agriculture focuses on farmers and helps to maintain price levels, complaints will arise from consumers (high prices), environmentalists (disappearing topsoil), and even foreign governments (protections may violate free trade). Efficiency *sounds* good. However, government officials are called on to meet other criteria, including fairness, responsiveness, objectivity, the national interest, and attention to international trade rules.

An employee of the Immigration and Customs Enforcement's Stewart Detention Center in Lumpkin, Georgia, waits for the front gate to be opened. The detention center is operated on contract by the Nashville-based Corrections Corporation of America.

Privatization. If the bureaucracy seems slow and inefficient, perhaps private companies can do the job better. As we explored earlier in this chapter, one powerful trend in government has been outsourcing public services to private firms. For-profit companies collect garbage, manage prisons, protect the homeland, cook for the troops, and launch commando raids abroad.

The movement for privatizing federal (and many state) programs took flight in the 1970s and received a boost from President Reagan in the 1980s. His administration turned some forty thousand government jobs over to private contractors, for reported savings of more than six hundred million dollars. As we noted previously, as many as seven or eight million private contractors—there is no accurate count available—are working for federal, state, and local governments today.

Private firms often can do a job for less. But the savings are at least partly offset by the need for government supervision. What happens when private managers— worrying, as they must, about the bottom line—cut corners or violate rules? Of the thirty-two federal programs listed in a 2015 Government Accounting Office study as at high risk for waste, fraud, or abuse, twenty-eight involved private contractors.[20]

The benefits of privatization are still debated, like the other reforms we discuss here. Research in this area suggests that *competitive contracting* (requiring more than one bid from outside contractors who want to provide government services) can save money and boost quality. However, the most important calculation, one often overlooked by reformers, is factoring in a way for government officials to supervise the private contractor. Careful oversight is a critical dimension of making privatization work.

THE BOTTOM LINE

» Critics of the bureaucracy focus on cost, inertia, and public mistrust.

» Solutions include sunshine reforms, reinventing government to make it more constituent friendly, and privatizing some of its functions.

🔘 Conclusion: The Real Solution Lies with You

President Kennedy came to office amid a burst of idealism and declared, "Ask not what your country can do for you— ask what you can do for your country." Inspired by the young president, the early civil rights movement, and the general optimism of the era, many college graduates streamed into public service. Today, fewer Americans are attracted to government service: just 6.6 percent of U.S. federal employees are under thirty, compared to more than 9 percent in 2010. Can this trend change? What would draw *you* into working for the government?

● *Wanted: a few good bureaucrats!*

The ultimate answer to the problems of bureaucracy, we believe, lies in the interest and commitment of a new generation. We are deeply concerned that men and women like you and your classmates—a well-educated group interested in political science—will bypass government altogether.

Indeed, politicians from both parties take shots at the bureaucracy. They freeze pay, downsize departments, and disparage millions of professionals. A closer look suggests that the bureaucracy performs many jobs we need and value, from predicting the weather to defending the United States. Ultimately, our government—our democracy—is only as good as the bureaucracy that puts public policy into effect. And this brings us back to your generation's commitment to public service, and what public officials can do to foster it.

CHAPTER SUMMARY

Within the executive branch, the U.S. federal bureaucracy does a vast amount of work in governing the country—and more closely resembles the nation's population than any other segment of our national government. However, Americans express deep ambivalence about our bureaucracy, generally rating it very low in opinion polls.

The American bureaucracy was established in reaction to the spoils system, which predominated between 1828 and 1901. A merit-based hiring system has been in place for more than a century since.

In theory, all bureaucracies share five characteristics: hierarchy, division of labor, fixed routines, equal rules for all, and technical qualifications.

Bureaucrats in the United States, as in other countries, perform a wide range of functions—from managing the nation's defense and national economy to organizing and providing food stamps and tax cuts. The bureaucracy is specifically charged with implementing the laws passed by Congress and signed by the president. This typically involves an administrative rule-making process, as well as actual delivery of services and carrying out of programs.

Since the 1930s, the federal bureaucracy has grown to more than four million employees—roughly two-thirds of whom are civilian and one-third military. This growth has occurred despite anti-"big government" sentiment among Americans; helping to overcome this sentiment have been the twin forces of war and enforcing morality. Organizing such a sprawling set of cabinet departments and agencies, populated by civil servants and political appointees, is an immense job.

It is not readily apparent who is in charge of managing the bureaucracy. Many different players have a role, including the public, the president, Congress, and interest groups. Even with—or perhaps because of—all those masters, bureaucrats have considerable discretion in how they carry out their work. This freedom can lead to serious tensions between Americans' democratic ideal of representative accountability and an unelected, often-*un*accountable workforce of civil servants.

Public disapproval of the bureaucracy arises from several different complaints. Our executive bureaucracy costs too much, say some critics; others argue that bureaucratic inertia makes it difficult to respond to policy crises. Moreover, a host of well-reported scandals influences Americans' perceptions of our bureaucracy, driving up mistrust. Reform efforts include enhancing the transparency of bureaucratic practices, reinventing government to improve responsiveness and reduce layers of management, and privatizing government services.

KEY TERMS

Bureaucratic pathologies, p. 455
Central service agencies, p. 468
Civil servants, p. 460
Final rule, p. 458
Freedom of Information Act
   (FOIA), p. 475

Overhead democracy, p. 470
Pendleton Civil Service
   Act, p. 452
Principal-agent theory, p. 471
Private contractors, p. 469
Proposed rule, p. 458

Regulatory capture, p. 468
Spoils system, p. 452
Street-level bureaucrats, p. 472
Universalistic politics, p. 452
Whistle-blower, p. 472

STUDY QUESTIONS

1. Look back at the Department of Energy's organizational chart on p. 454 of this chapter. If you were in charge of the DOE, how strict would you be about adhering to this chart? Would you allow wiggle room in the name of creativity and innovation? Or would you demand that reporting authority go up the proper channels to ensure that the rules are faithfully followed?

2. Is the U.S. federal bureaucracy too large? Do we need more than four million people working for the government—in addition to several million more hired under federal contracts? If you would like to see a smaller bureaucracy, where do you think we should start cutting workers?

3. Who *should* run the bureaucracy, in your informed view? Do bureaucrats have too much discretion in how they perform their duties? What

are the respective merits of a "street-level" or "top-down" management style? And should presidents (or Congress, or interest groups, etc.) have more authority than they currently wield to exert their will on the bureaucracy?

4. Let's say you have just learned about some unsavory doings in your bureaucratic agency or department. Do you blow the whistle—that is, report the problem? Or do you keep quiet, knowing your job could be in danger? What factors would affect your decision?

5. Based on what you now know about the U.S. bureaucracy, should we mount a major push for reform? What type(s) of reforms would be most useful? Or are the various parts of the bureaucracy working pretty well the way they are?

 Go to www.oup.com/us/Morone to find quizzes, flash cards, simulations, tutorials, videos, and other study tools.

The Judicial Branch

16

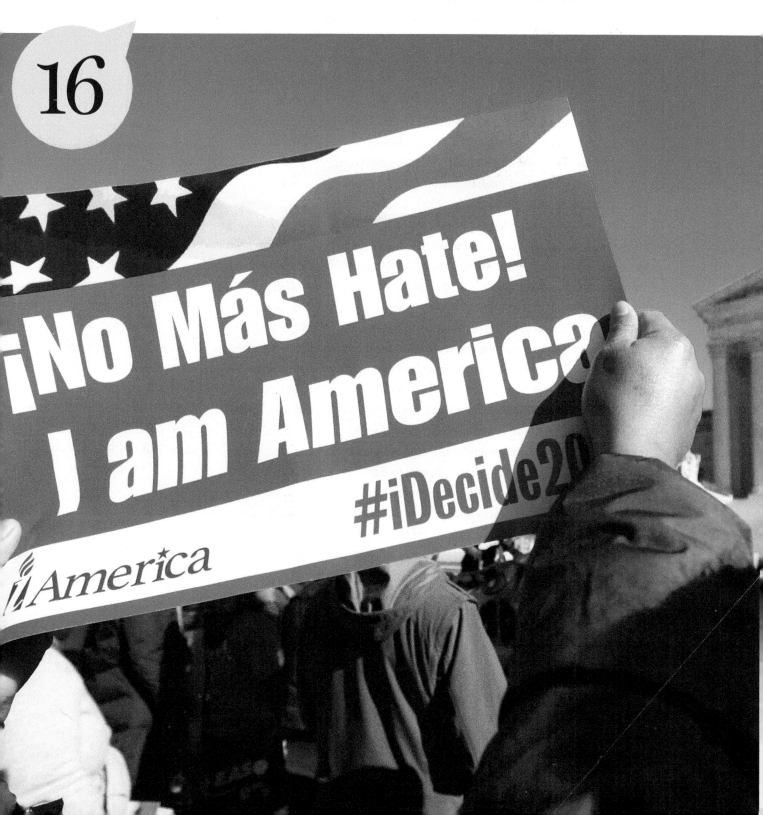

JUNE WEEKDAY MORNINGS are a good time to visit the Supreme Court's iconic marble steps. More judicial decisions are announced to the public in that month than any other, as the Court ends its annual term. June 23, 2016, was a landmark day even by usual standards: two major decisions were issued with sweeping implications. An executive order blocking deportation of illegal immigrants was denied by the Court in the case *United States v. Texas*, throwing immigration policy into turmoil. And, in the long-running case *Fisher v. University of Texas at Austin*, a surprise 4–3 majority upheld affirmative action as a factor in university admissions.

Both cases reshaped vital topics in American politics—exemplifying the continued central role of the judiciary. During the battle to ratify the Constitution, Alexander Hamilton predicted that the judiciary "will always be the least dangerous" and "the weakest" branch of government, for, he reasoned, it has "no influence" over "the sword" (the president controls the army) or "the purse" (Congress is in charge of the budget).[1] Yet since 1789, the U.S. judiciary has accumulated sweeping authority. It strikes down laws, rules, and regulations that violate the Constitution—as the courts interpret it.

We have seen the great reach and power of the Supreme Court throughout this book. For example, it struck down hard-won congressional compromises and protected slavery (in *Dred Scott*, 1857); it rejected segregation (*Brown v. Board of Education*, 1954); and it swept away a network of state laws prohibiting abortion (*Roe v. Wade*, 1973). More recently, the Supreme Court rejected bipartisan efforts to limit money flowing into American elections; upheld the Obama administration's Affordable Care Act; struck down sections of the Voting Rights Act that empowered the federal government to monitor election laws in places with a history of racial discrimination; and ruled that a privately held corporation could refuse to provide contraception under the Affordable Care Act.[2] These recent cases were all the more controversial because each was decided by a single vote—5–4. An even closer outcome came in the immigration case opening this chapter: the Supreme Court tied, 4–4, thereby upholding a lower federal court's ruling to deny the White House authority to grant amnesty to a select group of illegal immigrants.

In this chapter, you will:

- Consider how the law reflects the American people—and our national culture.

- Learn how the judicial system operates.

- Examine the courts' role in American politics.

- Explore the inner workings of the Supreme Court.

- Reflect on how judges decide cases.

- Review landmark judicial cases.

- Weigh proposals for reforming the court system.

United States v. Texas: *Supporters of a White House order to delay deportation of illegal immigrants anxiously await a Supreme Court decision in June 2016. Their hopes were dashed, though affirmative action advocates gathered nearby were encouraged by a positive Court decision the same day.*

481

The previous two chapters, on the presidency and on the bureaucracy, asked whether each still fit into a democratic framework. The question becomes even more pointed for the federal courts. Unelected officials with lifetime appointments wield the power to overrule the long, hard democratic process of forging legislation in both Washington and the states. The founders believed that the more political branches of government—the president and Congress—needed the courts to check them. Has that check now grown too powerful? And too politicized?

Who are we? A nation founded on the world's oldest constitution, which directly or indirectly governs almost every aspect of our collective life. The courts apply the Constitution to the problems we face. Small wonder that the United States long has been a nation of courts, lawyers, and people ready to sue.

We begin with the basics. What does the court system look like? How does it make decisions? How did it amass so much power over our politics, our government, and our daily lives? Throughout we will ask the same fundamental question: Does the American political system effectively balance the authority of elected officials and lifetime judges? The answer starts with the basic character of the American people: *Who we are.*

Who Are We? A Nation of Laws . . . and Lawyers

The United States relies on courts to resolve more matters than most nations. The result is a deeply legalistic political culture.

Embracing the Law—and Lawsuits

Litigation: The conduct of a lawsuit.

Lawsuits, or **litigation**, are a near-constant feature of American public life. The annual U.S. criminal caseload includes thirty-five to forty million cases filed in state courts. Traffic violations add another fifty-five million cases. Federal courts open about 400,000 new cases a year (notice that federal cases equal about 1% of the volume in state courts). And another 1.6 million cases enter bankruptcy courts. Add all of these up, and the United States approaches 100 million legal actions a year. And that is before we get to all the cases heard in specialized federal courts.

Courts are the primary sites for settling both private and public disputes. Advocacy groups, private citizens, and corporations go to court as a "first-strike" option. Litigation is an essential part of the rule-making process (discussed in Chapter 15). Business competition spills into the courts. Most other industrial nations rely more on **mediation** in noncriminal cases; citizens also are more likely to defer to civil servants. In contrast, Americans sue. Only a few other nations—most notably, Great Britain and Denmark—have as many suits per capita as the United States does.

Mediation: A way of resolving disputes without going to court, in which a third party (the mediator) helps two or more sides negotiate a settlement.

Americans are not only a people of litigation but also a people of lawyers, with roughly 1.1 million lawyers (782,200 in active practice). That number has risen fourfold since 1960, six times faster than population growth. The nation now has one lawyer for every 275 people—far outstripping Canada (one in every 450), India (one in every 1,200), France (one in 1,403), and every other nation (see Comparing

BY THE NUMBERS
The U.S. Judiciary

Original number of Supreme Court justices: **5**
Largest number of justices (1863–1866): **10**
Year in which the number of Supreme Court Justices was set at 9: **1869**

Number of Supreme Court justices appointed, 1882–1910: **18**
Number of Supreme Court justices appointed, 1982–2010: **9**

Average number of years a Supreme Court justice served before retiring from
    1790–1954: **16.5**
Average number of years a Supreme Court justice served before retiring from
    1970–2016: **25.4**

Number of Acts of Congress ruled unconstitutional per year from 1800–1900: **0.2**
Number of Acts of Congress ruled unconstitutional per year 1900–1999: **1.3**
Number of Acts of Congress ruled unconstitutional per year 2000–2016: **2.0**
Number of years John Marshall was chief justice of the United States: **34**
Number of chief justices in American history: **16**
Number since 1953: **4**

Total number of Catholic justices on Supreme Court, 1789–1910: **3**
Number of Catholic justices serving on Supreme Court in 2016, until Justice Scalia's
    death: **6**

Total number of cases heard by Supreme Court, 1987–1988 term: **155**
Total number of cases heard by Supreme Court, 2015–2016 term: **76**

Vacancies on the Supreme Court during Eisenhower presidency (1953–1960): **5**
Vacancies on the Supreme Court during Carter presidency (1977–1980): **0**

Charge for filing a civil case in federal district court: **$400**
Estimated number of Americans who served on federal juries in 2016: **58,000**
Estimated number who served on juries in state or local courts: **1.4 million**

Nations 16.1). As early as 1835, Alexis de Tocqueville could comment, "There is hardly any political question in the United States which does not, sooner or later, turn into a judicial one."[3]

Declining Trust

Traditionally, lawyers and courts enjoyed high prestige. Tocqueville described early nineteenth century lawyers as democracy's natural aristocrats and noted that the American people trusted them. Not anymore.

Today, law, lawyers, and the legal system all face shrinking reputations. During 2015, the Supreme Court's approval ratings dipped to their lowest level ever recorded, and have remained low since (see Figure 16.1). Individual cases have affected the American public's perception of the courts. The Court stopped the recount of Florida's ballots after the 2000 presidential election in what appeared to

Do you approve or disapprove of the way the Supreme Court is handling its job?

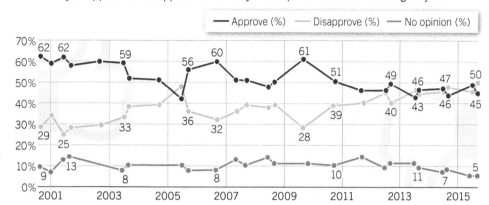

FIGURE 16.1 *The Supreme Court declines in public esteem. Recent polls put the Court's approval rate below 50 percent. (Gallup)*

be a partisan (5–4) vote. In his dissent to *Bush v. Gore*, Justice Stevens wrote, "Although we may never know with complete certainty the identity of the winner of this year's presidential election, the identity of the loser is perfectly clear. It is the nation's confidence in the judge as an impartial guardian of the rule of law."[4] That was certainly true for Democrats who accused the judiciary of usurping democracy. Republicans leveled the same charge after the Court refused to strike down the Affordable Care Act (in 2012) and protected same-sex marriage (in 2015). As a result, the Court's approval ratings plummeted to a record low (18%) among Republicans and surged to a record high (76%) among Democrats.[5]

However, even when the judiciary's prestige ebbs, it still generally ranks roughly the same as that of the president and towers over Congress. In June 2016, one Gallup poll pegged confidence in both presidency and Supreme Court at 36 percent, compared to just 9 percent for Congress.

Courts in American Culture

Images of law and lawyers run through American culture, with the image alternating between heroism and cynicism. On one side, in *To Kill a Mockingbird*, Gregory Peck's Atticus Finch wins the African American community's respect when he

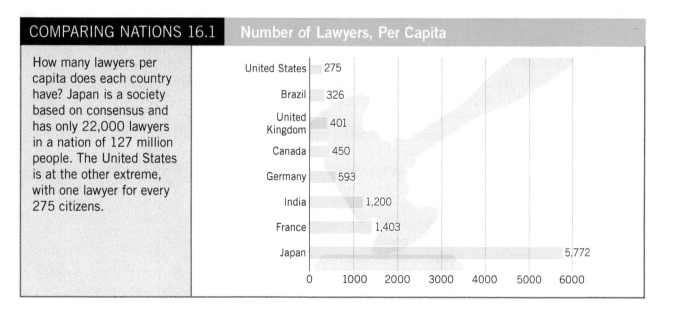

COMPARING NATIONS 16.1   Number of Lawyers, Per Capita

How many lawyers per capita does each country have? Japan is a society based on consensus and has only 22,000 lawyers in a nation of 127 million people. The United States is at the other extreme, with one lawyer for every 275 citizens.

passionately defends a black man unjustly accused of rape: "In our courts all men are created equal," he proclaims at the film's climax. "That's no ideal to me. That is a living, working reality." The book and movie's racial idealism reflected the optimism of the early 1960s. Julia Roberts played another legal heroine, the real-life Erin Brockovich, a clerk without any legal training whose indefatigable work led to a major environmental lawsuit against Pacific Gas and Electric for contaminating the water supply of Hinkley, California. A more recent example of movie heroes before the bar: Tom Hanks in *Bridge of Spies* playing real-life lawyer James

● *Images of law are everywhere in popular culture. Here, Tom Hanks defends an accused Russian spy in* Bridge of Spies.

Donovan, who defended an accused Communist spy then risked his life by arranging a spy exchange with East Germany and Soviet Russia during the Cold War. Images of law as a kind of crusade—for racial justice, environmental protection, or national security—reflect and reinforce images of political idealism.

In American culture, as in politics, the courts are a place where our highest ideals are on display—and where we simultaneously fear that corruption runs rampant. We will return at chapter's end to proposed reforms of the legal system. First, let us explore how that system works in practice.

THE BOTTOM LINE

» The United States relies on courts and litigation more than most other nations—a political reality reflected in both its number of lawsuits and its number of lawyers.

» Trust in the Supreme Court has declined in recent years.

» Law continues to play an important role in American popular culture, which portrays it in both idealistic and cynical terms.

Organizing the Judicial Branch

The Constitution offers detailed instruction for Congress (Article 1) and vague rules for the executive branch (Article 2). The judiciary gets the least attention of all. The Constitution vests judicial power in the Supreme Court without specifying the number of justices it should include and empowers Congress to design the rest of our federal court system. This section examines how the courts are organized. As usual, there's a distinctive look to how Americans run this branch of government.

Divided We Rule

By now you know the story: When Americans see government power, they divide it. Two chambers of Congress, with layers of committees and subcommittees; an executive branch split into departments, agencies, commissions, and White House offices; and a federalist system of national, state, and city officials all cooperating, competing, and overlapping. Court powers also are divided.

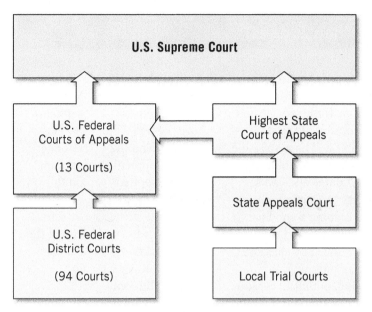

FIGURE 16.2 *Organization of the U.S. federal courts system.*

Most other nations feature a single unitary system of courts. In contrast, the United States exhibits *judicial federalism*. Both federal and state court systems are further divided into layers; the federal system has three layers as do most states (see Figure 16.2). Lower courts conduct trials, appellate courts hear appeals, and a supreme court in both state and federal systems renders a final verdict. The national Supreme Court is the ultimate arbiter for all cases. However, from the millions of cases filed each year, around ten thousand appeals reach the Supreme Court, which, in recent years, only accepts and hears eighty or fewer. That leaves a great deal of authority to the lower ranks of the judiciary.

State and Local Courts

Local trial and state appeals courts are the workhorses of the judiciary, handling most of the nontraffic cases in the United States each year. State courts are responsible for all cases that arise under state law; they rule on everything from antitrust disputes to murder cases, from medical malpractice to marijuana possession. Every state organizes its judicial system in its own way—so there is considerable variation around the nation.

The first stop in most cases is a state trial court. Appeals usually are handled in state appellate courts, which typically consist of an appellate court and then a court of final appeal, generally known as the state supreme court. Appeals from the top state courts may be heard by the U.S. Supreme Court. Many landmark cases originate—and sometimes reach settlement—in state courts. The 2012 decision to uphold the Obamacare health reform law began as a state decision, as did *Roe v. Wade* (which struck down a Texas law banning abortion), and *Bush v. Gore* (settling the disputed presidential ballots in Florida). However, very few of the millions of state cases ever reach a federal judge, as these cases did.

Judicial Selection

Do you think you might like to become a state judge? There are surprisingly few formal criteria for selection. You may not even need a law degree: twenty-two states and the federal courts require no formal training before judges start hearing cases. Most judges first make their name as lawyers, though many come from government or academic positions. If you plan to lobby a governor to ensure your judicial appointment, make sure you pick the right state: Only seventeen states authorize their governor to select judges, and two leave selection to the state legislature. Most states (thirty-one) *elect* judges. Judges' terms range across the states, from two to fourteen years, and are usually renewable.

The idea of electing judges is controversial. After all, the courts are meant to be above partisan politics, protecting rights and weighing evidence without political pressures. Elections, say the critics, undermine the courts' ability to stand up for the rights of unpopular minorities. Moreover, campaign contributions and campaign promises could lead to bias and even corruption on the state benches. Former Supreme Court justice Sandra Day O'Connor has been an especially vocal critic of

How Should States Select Their Judges?

Which of these three approaches to judicial selection in the states seems most persuasive to you?

Let the people vote. The people are the best guardians of their own welfare. Let them decide who their justices should be. No matter how courts are organized, it is naive to think that politics can be kept out of the equation. Today, 75 percent of the public thinks that justices sometimes let their own political views influence their rulings. Because politics is inevitable, the public should have a direct voice in judicial selection.

Appointment by a governor. A state governor (with the advice and consent of the state senate) will have valuable information about the candidates and can keep better track of which justice is doing a good job. It also avoids the problems introduced by elections: campaigning, fundraising, potential corruption, and the temptation to win votes by making promises that could later compromise the court.

Establish merit committees. Courts must be above politics. They must defend the rights of minorities and unpopular views. The only way to ensure such fairness is to let impartial merit commissions select judges. The commission's nominees can then be voted up or down by the legislature.

Unsure. You will probably develop a stronger opinion on this question by the end of the chapter.

electing judges; she calls judicial campaigns "tawdry and embarrassing."[6] Still, the United States is the land of five hundred thousand elected officials. The American ideal—government by the people—leads many states to insist that judges stand directly accountable to the public.

Federal Courts

Federal courts hear three types of cases. First, they handle crimes that violate federal laws, issues that involve federal treaties, and cases touching on the Constitution. Examples range from the dramatic to the mundane: terrorism, immigration, organized crime, civil rights, patents, insider trading, and flag burning. Second, they decide disputes that spill across state lines—for example, interstate drug trafficking and conflicts between parties in different states (when at least seventy-five thousand dollars is involved in the dispute). Finally, after state courts have ruled on a case, the parties can appeal to the federal courts.

Most federal cases begin in one of the ninety-four **district courts**, which together house just under seven hundred judges. Every state has at least one district court, and the larger states (like California and Texas) have as many as four. District courts determine the facts of the case (did John Smith try to blow up a federal building?), build a record detailing the evidence, and then apply the law to reach a ruling. Cases at this level are heard by a single district judge.

District court judges, like all federal judges, are appointed by the president, subject to the

District courts: The first level of federal courts, which actually try the cases. Each decision is based not on a statute but on previous judicial decisions.

● *Judicial elections: emblem of democracy—or path to corruption?*

"advice and consent" of the Senate, and hold their office for life. Until recently, the Senate routinely approved nearly all judicial appointments, sometimes with very little scrutiny. In today's hyperpartisan Congress, however, the opposition party generally challenges judicial nominations—slowing them down in the hope that their party will take the presidency and fill the empty seats. By the Obama administration's fourth year, a full 9 percent of the federal bench was vacant, creating an alarming backlog of cases. The Democratic majority in the Senate broke the logjam in 2013 by forbidding filibusters for lower court nominations (though not for Supreme Court nominations). When the Republicans took back the Senate in 2014, they applied the brakes again—over 11 percent of the federal bench remained vacant in at the end of 2016.

Circuit courts: The second stage of federal courts, which review the trial record of cases decided in district court to ensure they were settled properly.

Above the ninety-four district courts are thirteen federal appellate courts, known as **circuit courts**. A party that loses in district court can appeal to this next level. Three circuit court judges hear each case, usually to determine whether the district court made the correct ruling. They rule on the basis of the record established on the lower level; there is no jury and no cross-examination. Some 180 judges serve these circuit courts, collectively ruling on nearly seventy thousand cases in a typical year. As with the district courts, the circuit courts are organized geographically and referred to by their number (Figure 16.3 displays the current organization). Appeals from Ohio, for example, go to the Sixth Circuit Court of Appeals in Cincinnati. Some types of cases (like those involving patents or international trade) go directly to a court known as the U.S. Court of Appeals for the Federal Circuit. And also like district-court judges, those on circuit courts are nominated by the White House and subject to Senate confirmation.

Sometimes multiple versions of a case reach different district and circuit courts. Cases challenging the Affordable Care Act as unconstitutional were filed in forty

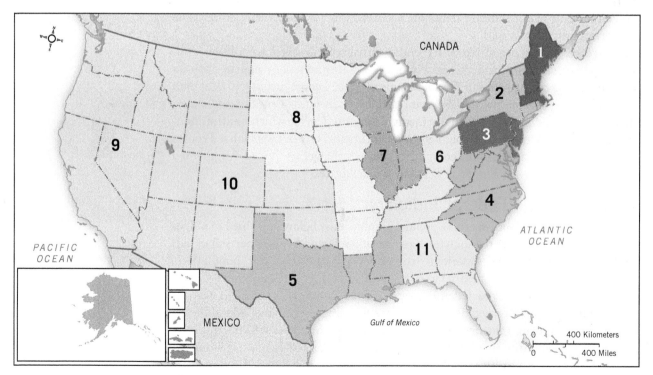

● **FIGURE 16.3** *A map of the federal circuit courts. (Federal Judicial Center)*

state courts across the United States. Nineteen different district courts considered the matter. On the next level, seven circuit courts eventually accepted appeals. Of these cases, one—the Eleventh Circuit's ruling that the individual mandate to buy insurance was unconstitutional—was ultimately heard by the Supreme Court, which issued the definitive ruling, overturning the Eleventh Circuit's ruling on the mandate. Other cases never make it into federal court, which means the state courts have the final say.

Specialized Courts

The federal judiciary also includes a set of specialized courts, each covering a specific subject such as military justice, tax disputes, and bankruptcy. These courts' workload rises and falls with larger societal changes: bankruptcy claims, for example, have dropped from more than 1.5 million (during the Great Recession) to about 800,000 in 2015. After 9/11, the federal government established a new secret court, the Foreign Intelligence Surveillance Court (FISC), to rule on federal government requests to conduct electronic surveillance.

The president appoints (and the Senate confirms) judges to all these courts. Unlike other federal judges, however, they do not serve for life. Bankruptcy judges, for example, serve renewable fourteen-year terms; federal magistrates, who handle certain types of civil trials, are appointed to renewable eight-year terms.

The U.S. military runs its own separate court system, which addresses breaches of justice by members of the armed forces. These courts became a source of controversy in recent years after President George W. Bush called for military tribunals to try defendants charged with terrorism against the United States, many of whom were being held as enemy combatants in Guantánamo Bay, Abu Ghraib, and other detention centers around the globe. The Obama administration at first suspended the military trials, but after Congress resisted moving the trials to civilian courts, the administration reinstated the tribunals with some changes in their rules. In rare cases, tribunals are permitted under the Constitution. The last large-scale use of military tribunals occurred after World War II, to try Nazi war criminals.

Together, these specialized courts, ranging from bankruptcy to military, constitute something of a "third judiciary" alongside state and federal courts. Periodically, critics advance proposals for a new type of special court, usually to deal with some technical area of law they believe regular citizen juries cannot handle adequately. The latest proposals focus on medical malpractice, for which multimillion-dollar damage suits turn on ambiguous "medical errors." Overall, specialized courts provide a further example of the complexity characterizing the divided, fragmented U.S. judicial branch—as Figure 16.4 vividly demonstrates.

Diversity in the Federal Judiciary

Do federal judges reflect America's population? No. Just below one-third of judges are women, and nearly three-quarters are white. Twelve-and-a-half percent of federal judges are African American (compared to 12.2% of the population), 9.7 percent are Hispanic (compared to 16.3%), 2.9 percent are Asian American (compared to 4.7%) and only one federal judge is Native American.[7] The eight years of Barack Obama's presidency did see improvement in diversifying the federal bench, as more non-white male justices were appointed than in any prior administration.

Does it make a difference if the judge presiding over a federal case is female or Latino? Supreme Court Justice Sonia Sotomayor suggested that it did, ten years before she was appointed to the court. "I would hope that a wise Latina woman,"

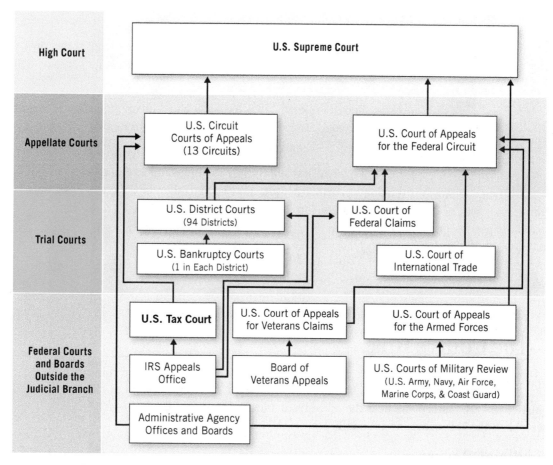

● **FIGURE 16.4** *Special courts within the federal system. A more detailed snapshot of the federal system illustrates that it is, in reality, far more complicated than the simple tripartite system of district, circuit, and supreme courts.*

Sotomayor said, "with the richness of her experience would more often than not reach a better conclusion than a white male who hasn't lived that life." In other words, personal experience does inform judicial decisions. The comment provided cause for reflection—and also raised controversy. Former House Speaker Newt Gingrich claimed that a white male judge making a similar claim on behalf of white men would be forced to resign.[8]

What Do You Think?

Identity on the Bench

Do you agree with Justice Sotomayor's comment that a person's life experience can deeply inform his or her judgment about politics, culture, and other matters?

Agree. Every person inevitably brings his or her life experience to bear in making important decisions, and justices are no different. That's why diversity on the bench is so important.

Disagree. Judges should rule on the basis of law. Their background is irrelevant and should not cloud sound legal judgment based on the laws and the facts of a case.

» State courts handle the vast majority of cases. Nearly all states divide their judiciary into three levels: trial courts, appeals courts, and a state supreme court. A majority of U.S. states elect their judges.

» Federal courts rule on cases involving constitutional questions, federal laws, and federal treaties. They are divided into ninety-four district courts, eleven appeals courts, and the Supreme Court.

» Federal justices are selected by the president and confirmed by the Senate, and they hold their position for life. Party polarization in Congress has created a serious problem of unfilled judgeships.

» Numerous additional federal courts handle everything from bankruptcy to military matters.

The Court's Role

Alexander Hamilton's assurance that the judiciary would play a minor role in American government did not last long. John Marshall, the longest-serving chief justice in U.S. history—he held the office from January 1801 to July 1835—helped establish the U.S. courts as unusually powerful. How did Marshall do it?

Judicial Review

The breakthrough came in the landmark case of *Marbury v. Madison*, in which Marshall asserted that the Supreme Court has the authority to overrule any act of Congress that violates the Constitution.

The case arose after John Adams lost the 1800 election and, during his final hours as president, made "midnight appointments" that installed his supporters in judicial positions. The new president, Thomas Jefferson, came to office with very different political views and vehemently opposed the last-minute appointments. Jefferson directed his secretary of state, James Madison, to destroy the appointment letters—including one naming William Marbury as justice of the peace for the District of Columbia. The Judiciary Act of 1789, which had established the position, referred some cases (those involving writs of mandamus, or direct orders to government officials) directly to the Supreme Court. Marbury duly petitioned the Court to order Madison to deliver his commission. This action constituted a high-stakes early test of the Court's authority.

Marshall and his fellow justices faced a trap. On the one hand, if the Court ruled in favor of Marbury, the recently elected President Jefferson might very well ignore the Court—and diminish its importance in the new federal government. In fact, neither Jefferson nor Madison, the party being sued, even bothered to show up at the Court for the case. They assumed the Court would rule against them and planned to ignore the decision. Marshall, however, did not wish to simply accept President Jefferson's defiance. Marshall found an ingenious way around the dilemma and vastly expanded the Court's role in American governance.

Led by Marshall, a unanimous Court ruled that Congress, in drafting the Judiciary Act of 1789, had erred in granting the Supreme Court the direct authority (or "original jurisdiction") to decide the question. The Constitution implied that the Supreme Court should rule on such cases only on appeal from the lower courts. However, the Constitution was silent on what would happen if Congress passed a law that clashed with the Constitution. Marshall filled in the blank with a dramatic move: "It is emphatically the province and duty" of the Court, wrote Marshall, to judge "if a law be in opposition to the Constitution." With that, Marshall established the court system's mighty power of **judicial review**—even though that authority is never mentioned in the Constitution itself.

● *John Marshall denied Marbury's suit and, in the process, asserted the power of the Supreme Court to strike down acts of Congress when they violated the Constitution.*

Judicial review: The Court's authority to strike down acts that violate the Constitution and to interpret what the Constitution means.

The Court decided the case by striking down Section 13 of the Judiciary Act of 1789—the section that referred writs of mandamus directly to the Supreme Court. Since Section 13 was the basis of Marbury's petition, the Court ruled that it had no constitutional authority to force the administration to deliver the petition. President Jefferson opposed Marshall's clever move, vigorously denouncing the "despotism" and "oligarchy" by which unelected officials "usurp[ed]" control of the Constitution from elected ones. But what could Jefferson do? In asserting the Court's power, Marshall had sided with the president and denied Marbury his petition. Jefferson had no way to defy a Court case that he had won. By apparently relinquishing power, Marshall permanently strengthened the federal judiciary.[9]

Marshall deftly addressed a basic issue in American government, with profound implications that reverberate to the present day. When there is doubt about what the Constitution holds or implies, the Supreme Court continues to claim that it is the one that makes the call.[10]

Activism Versus Restraint

The Supreme Court was slow to wield the power it had asserted. It did not overrule another act of Congress for fifty-four years, until the *Dred Scott* decision struck down the Missouri Compromise and declared that black people were "so far inferior that they had no rights which the white man was bound to respect."[11] That decision brought the issue of slavery to a boil in 1857 and established a pattern: Many of the most intense disputes in American politics wind up decided in court.

As Figure 16.5 shows, the judiciary has stepped up the pace at which it overrules Congress (see Figure 16.5). In the 150 years following *Marbury*, it struck down just twenty-two federal laws; in the twenty-five years between 1990 and 2015, it struck down fifty-three, including laws designed to limit flag burning, guns near schoolyards, child pornography, violence against women, barriers to voting, and same-sex marriage.

Today, the Supreme Court is embroiled in many intense debates. In addition to the immigration and affirmative action decisions described earlier, a few of the leading current issues: May Congress limit campaign contributions? Can the White House regulate emissions from power plants to combat global warming? Are there any limits to the right to bear arms? Does the right of privacy forbid states from banning or curtailing abortions? Each of these questions was removed from the court of public opinion, or the jurisdiction of elected officials, and settled by the Supreme Court—generally by a 5–4 (or, for many months following Justice Scalia's death in 2016, 4–4 vote).

The Supreme Court also reviews state and local statutes. This power required far less subtle maneuvering to establish. The Constitution's "supremacy clause" declares that "this Constitution and the laws of the United States . . . shall be the supreme Law of the Land" (Article 6). The Judiciary Act of 1789, which established the federal court system (yes, the same act that created William Marbury's position) granted the Court authority to enforce the supremacy clause and to strike down state laws

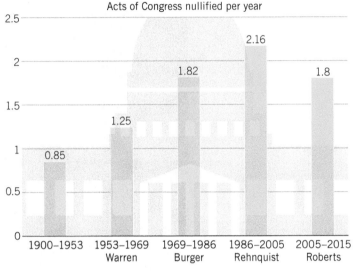

Acts of Congress nullified per year

● **FIGURE 16.5**: *Acts of Congress Nullified by the Supreme Court. (Journal of Legal Metrics)*

that clash with the Constitution or with federal statutes. The judiciary has been more active on this level, striking down state actions at about six times the rate it overturns federal laws. Over time, federal courts have declared almost 1,100 state and local laws unconstitutional and ruled that more than another 200 state and local laws were preempted by federal law. Landmark cases overruled state laws that established segregation, outlawed abortion, established school prayer, limited private property rights, or forbade same-sex marriage.

The growing number of rulings that strike down legislation raises an enduring question: How energetic should courts be in reviewing cases? Judicial activists take a vigorous approach to reviewing the other branches of government and believe that the courts must be vigilant in protecting rights. Between the 1950s and the 1970s, liberal activists were in the Supreme Court majority. During this period, the Court struck down segregation, forbade school prayer, and found a right to privacy in the penumbra (or shadow) of the Constitution (see Chapters 5 and 6 for a discussion of these cases).

Judicial restraint holds, on the contrary, that the courts should overturn the elected branches of government reluctantly and as a last resort. The terms *activism* and *restraint* are easily politicized. Conservatives bitterly attacked liberal **judicial activism** during the civil-rights era of the 1950s–early 1970s; as the courts turned conservative, however, liberals began to criticize activist judges for being eager to overrule the will of the people's representatives.

The idea of activism recalls our discussion in Chapter 3 about how to read the Constitution. Is it a living and evolving document, as the pragmatists believe? Or should we insist on faithfully reconstructing the original meaning, as originalists think we should do? As we noted

Judicial restraint:
Reluctance to interfere with elected branches, only doing so as a last resort.

Judicial activism:
A vigorous or active approach to reviewing the other branches of government.

● *Lethal injection chamber in Florida. In 2016, the Supreme Court declared unconstitutional Florida's entire death-penalty system, potentially ending death sentences in the state.*

in Chapter 3, the difference between these positions is less stark than it might appear. The Constitution can be ambiguous, and a nimble analysis is often required to apply it to a contemporary case—as Marshall illustrated when he first asserted the right of judicial review. Even staunch originalists regularly disagree with one another about the Constitution's meaning and how it applies in any individual case.

The Judicial Process

The judiciary's role goes far beyond weighing constitutionality. Legal cases constantly raise the question of how a law should be applied in a specific dispute. The court's job is to determine legislative intent. We saw this in Chapter 15, in the case of the bureaucratic rule-making process. If lobbyists do not like new regulations for inspecting poultry slaughterhouses, they can go to court and claim that the regulatory agency has mistaken what Congress intended when it authorized those inspections. Ultimately, the court has to rule on what Congress meant to do—perhaps in the distant past. Because lawsuits are a regular feature of policymaking, federal courts stay very busy interpreting the intent of the other branches.

Common law: A system of law developed by judges in deciding cases over the centuries.

Often there is no legislative record or executive action to settle a case. The American colonists introduced an English system known as **common law**. Common law (also known as *case law*) is a system of law developed by judges in deciding cases over the centuries. Because legal judgments should be consistent from case to case, each time a court settles a case it sets a **precedent** that will guide similar cases in the future. Over the years, the common law offers a rich legal heritage to guide judges in settling disputes. In countries without a common law tradition, such as France, judges may not rule unless there is a statute or regulation to guide them.

Precedent: Judicial decisions that offer a guide to similar cases in the future.

Civil law: Cases that involve disputes between two parties.

American courts handle two different kinds of cases. **Civil law** handles cases between two parties. William Marbury sues James Madison for his commission; a young man sues his Catholic diocese because a priest molested him; a major corporation sues a local pizza chain for borrowing its corporate logo. **Criminal law** involves cases in which someone is charged with doing something prohibited by the government, such as stealing private property or secretly arranging with a competitor business to set higher prices (an "antitrust" violation).

Criminal law: Cases in which someone is charged with breaking the law.

Plaintiff: The party who brings the action in a lawsuit.

The party who complains—Marbury, the man who was molested, or the government coming down on an alleged criminal—is called the **plaintiff**; the party who is being sued is the **defendant**. In court cases, the plaintiff is listed first and the defendant second; thus, the case is called *Marbury* (the plaintiff) *versus Madison* (the secretary of state who did not deliver the commission). When an administration loses in a lower court, it becomes the plaintiff on appeal; that is why you see case titles such as *United States v. Texas* (the 2016 immigration case) or, in attempts to constrain Obamacare, *Burwell* (the Secretary of Health and Human Services, which administers the Affordable Care Act) *v. Hobby Lobby* (the company that won a religious exemption from the Act's requirement that firms provide insurance coverage for female contraceptives).

Defendant: The party who is sued in a court case.

Too Much Power?

Keep in mind this key question about the Court: Should nine unelected, lifetime appointees wield this much power in a twenty-first-century democracy? Add to that the more than one-hundred circuit- and district-court federal judges, also all appointed to their posts: How can we say "the people" rule over the judicial branch?

Both our litigious society and the range of judicial authority—from judicial review to common law—give the courts the power to shape American policy.

Judges in other advanced democracies rarely exercise anything like the influence that American courts have over government and politics. In Japan, for example, the judiciary is widely viewed as a rubber stamp for executive and legislative decisions, almost never questioning (much less reversing) decisions of the other branches. The United Kingdom goes even further: The doctrine of "parliamentary sovereignty" holds that when Parliament passes a statute, it cannot be overturned in court. Canada abandoned parliamentary sovereignty in 1982 and granted the federal courts fuller judicial review powers; those are only rarely used, however. In Germany, the Supreme Constitutional Court has the power to review all legislation for adherence with the Constitution; it even has the authority to ban a political party (like the Nazi Party) if it moves to deny the rights of others. Yet the German high court does not take cases from lower courts on appeal—its role is solely as a constitutional court. Finally, less democratic nations generally place their power in the executive—their courts do not have the authority to challenge executive decisions. In its extensive authority to reshape public policies and other acts of the executive and legislative branches, the U.S. judiciary stands alone.

In other nations, the elected branches make vital decisions about environmental protection, gun rights, immigration rules, and other urgent questions. In the United States, unlike many other nations (see Comparing Nations 16.2), courts are major players in resolving these issues . . . and other issues in almost every policy realm.

American courts profoundly shape our politics. Are they the guarantors of American constitutional rights? Or are they an outmoded throwback to an earlier, more elitist, age? You can get a better sense in the following sections when we look behind the scenes at the inner workings of the Supreme Court.

. . . Or Still the "Least Dangerous" Branch?

Although the courts are undeniably powerful, every institution faces limits. The courts operate with four different types of restraints.

First, the federal courts have *no electoral base*. Their prestige and mystique are balanced by a lack of democratic authority. This has made some past courts careful about confronting elected officials. For example, the Supreme Court delayed its ruling in *Brown v. Board of Education* (striking down segregated schools) for almost two years while the justices struggled to reach unanimity. Chief Justice Earl Warren felt that such an important case should have the backing of all nine members because a major decision that went against popular opinion could harm the Court's authority and prestige.

Second, courts have relatively *limited resources* compared to other units of government. Senators generally command more than fifty staff members and can call on the Congressional Research Service and the Government Accountability Office: each has hundreds of experts who can study any question a member might raise. In contrast, most federal judges have only two or three clerks—young staffers, usually fresh from law school, with little judicial experience—who serve them for less than a year. Supreme Court justices, whose decisions can shape the course of government for generations, have at most four clerks, who serve for a year or occasionally two.

The courts also command small budgets. The Supreme Court operates on an annual budget of around ninety million dollars a year. The entire federal judiciary—thirteen circuit courts, ninety-four district courts, and the Supreme Court—receives less than six billion dollars annually. That is about the same budget as that of NOAA, the federal weather service. (Another $1 billion is allocated to the federal defender service, which provides lawyers to indigent clients, $565 million for security at federal court facilities, and $50 million to cover jurors' fees.)

Third, courts are by definition *reactive decision makers*. Executive branch agencies or legislators can tackle problems and devise solutions. Courts await disputes; cases must come to them. True, most major issues eventually do wind up before the courts—but, unlike the other branches, the courts do not define the problem or shape the question that is being disputed.

Finally, the courts must rely on other branches for *enforcement*. The Court rules. Other actors—in and out of government—implement the decisions. The Supreme Court could strike down school desegregation; it could not, however, enforce that decision by sending troops to Little Rock or cutting the budgets of schools that refused to comply. In fact, the *Brown* decision was blocked for years by intransigent state and local officials (until civil rights protests finally moved Congress to pass the Civil Rights Act). President Andrew Jackson made this point dramatically. When the Supreme Court struck down a Georgia law governing relations with the Cherokees, he reputedly said, of the chief justice: "John Marshall has made his decision, now let him enforce it."[12]

THE BOTTOM LINE

» Chief Justice John Marshall asserted the court's authority to review acts of Congress to ensure that they fit with the Constitution in *Marbury v. Madison*. The Judiciary Act of 1789 authorized the Court to review state laws.

» At first, the Court rarely struck down acts of Congress, but it began to do so at a quicker pace beginning in the 1990s.

» There are two general approaches to defining the courts' role in government: *activists* believe in a vigorous judiciary that scrutinizes the other branches; judicial *restraint* holds that courts should intervene rarely and reluctantly.

» The vital overarching question regarding the judiciary remains the same one that Chief Justice Marshall and President Jefferson crossed swords over more than two centuries ago: Is the Court acting in ways that are indispensable to democracy? Or is it acting in ways that threaten it?

The Supreme Court and How It Operates

Tucked away at the top of the majestic marble Supreme Court building on East Capitol Street, among all the justices' offices and conference rooms and libraries lined with leather law books, is . . . a small basketball court. Known as the "highest court in the land," the facility is used exclusively by Supreme Court insiders: the justices' clerks, both current and former; a few staff members; and occasionally even one of the justices. We can imagine the basketball court as symbolic of the Supreme Court itself: exclusive, little known, and open to a tiny membership for a lifetime.

Hearing Cases

The Supreme Court is in session for approximately nine months each year, traditionally opening on the first Monday in October. The justices are generally out of public view, except when the Court meets to hear *oral arguments*—the presentation of a case that the Court has agreed to review. Arguments are usually scheduled on Monday, Tuesday, and Wednesday mornings. If you are visiting Washington, DC, on a day when oral arguments are occurring, do attend. These fascinating sessions are free and open to the public, on a first-come, first-served basis. (We recommend that you get to the Court early to wait in line and bring something to read—perhaps this book!)

Supreme Court oral arguments do not resemble the courtroom scenes on TV. Rather than lawyers making dramatic arguments or cross-examining witnesses, the Supreme Court features justices as the sole audience: no jury, no witnesses. Any case that the Supreme Court agrees to hear has usually been thoroughly aired by at least one lower court. Normally, cases are heard in one hour, and each side's lawyer—called the "counsel" in Court-speak, regardless of whether it is one lawyer or many—is granted thirty minutes to make his or her best argument. When the Court took up the *Obergefell v. Hodges* same-sex marriage case in 2015, it signaled the importance of the case by scheduling two and a half hours of oral argument.

The justices usually interrupt the presenting lawyer almost immediately with questions, some supportive and others combative. They may also deliver mini-speeches of their own; no lawyer ever dares interrupt a Supreme Court justice, even if the lawyer's thirty minutes is slipping away. No photos are allowed, so sketches are the most accurate depiction available.

Before the hearing, both sides submit written briefs spelling out the details of their argument. Other interested parties may submit their own briefs endorsing the side they favor. The outside contributions are known as ***amicus curiae*** (Latin for "friend of the court") briefs. A creative, well-written amicus curiae brief, researchers have found, may well wind up being included in a justice's written opinion on the case.[13]

> **Amicus curiae:** A brief submitted by a person or group who is not a direct party to the case.

Are oral arguments important? Perhaps not. Justice Clarence Thomas told one interviewer that they influence his colleagues "in five or ten percent of the cases, maybe, and I'm being generous there." Chief Justice John Roberts once added, "The judges are debating among themselves and just using the lawyers as a blackboard."[14] What matters far more are the written briefs that the counsel submit.

Selecting Cases: Formal Requirements

How do the justices decide which cases to hear? Losing parties in lower courts are permitted, depending on the nature of the case, to file a petition with the Supreme Court stating the facts of the case and setting out detailed arguments as to why the Court should hear it. The petitions are split up among the justices and their clerks; on selected Fridays, the justices meet to choose the cases they will hear. At least four judges

● *Obama administration solicitor general Donald Verrilli, standing, defends the healthcare law before the Court. The chief justice sits at the center of the dais, and the seats closest to his are occupied by those justices with the most seniority. From left, Sotomayor, Breyer, Thomas, the late Scalia, Chief Justice Roberts, Kennedy, Ginsburg, Alito, and Kagan. Only sketches such as this one are permitted in the Supreme Court; no photographs or TV coverage.*

Rule of four: The requirement that at least four Supreme Court judges must agree to hear a case before it comes before the Court.

see for yourself 16.1

Go online to listen to oral arguments on the *Fisher v. University of Texas at Austin* affirmative action case.

see for yourself 16.2

Go online to listen to oral arguments on the *United States v. Texas* immigration case.

have to vote to hear a case for it to make it to the Supreme Court; that requirement is known as the **rule of four.**

When the justices agree to hear a case, the Supreme Court issues a *writ of certiorari* (legal-speak for "to be informed") demanding the official record from the lower court that heard the case. Roughly ten thousand petitions are filed with the Supreme Court each year, and some seventy or eighty are accepted—less than 1 percent. How do cases make it into that elite group? That remains one of the great mysteries of American government. The Court never gives any formal explanation for why it decides to grant certiorari to this case and not that one.

Formally, a case must meet three conditions before it is even eligible for the Supreme Court—or any other court, for these requirements apply at all judicial levels. The case must involve a *legitimate controversy*, that is, an actual dispute between two parties. Supreme Court justices do not deal with hypothetical matters; no court offers "advisory opinions" based on something that might someday happen.

Second, the parties bringing a case must have *standing*: They must prove an actual harm (or imminent harm) to receive a hearing. Merely being distressed or concerned about a far-off environmental disaster's effect is not enough to bring a lawsuit, for example; you must prove that the oil spill or pollutant is directly affecting your livelihood (or your health or your property).

Finally, if the Court's proceedings will no longer affect the issue at hand, it is considered *moot*—irrelevant—and the case is thrown out. A famous example comes from *Roe v. Wade*, in which a federal district court dismissed the case as moot because the plaintiff, "Jane Roe" (real name: Norma McCorvey), had already delivered her child. The Supreme Court rejected this view, noting that the typical length of legal appeals processes meant that pregnancies would usually conclude too soon for a court decision to be reached.

Selecting Cases: Informal Factors

Thousands of cases each year meet the standards—controversy, standing, and mootness. Informally, we can identify four additional factors that help predict whether a case is more or less likely to be accepted by the Court.

First, the Supreme Court is more inclined to hear a case when two lower courts decide the legal question differently (usually two federal courts, but sometimes federal and state). Different rulings in similar cases require a resolution; hence the Court considered during its 2016–2017 term whether the North Carolina Supreme Court or federal district court was right about allegedly racially biased redistricting practices in the state.

Second, justices are inclined to grant certiorari to cases in which a lower court decision conflicts with an existing Supreme Court ruling. In 1989, the Court ruled in *Penry v. Lynaugh* that a death sentence was sometimes permissible for criminals under the age of eighteen. More than a decade later, the Missouri Supreme Court declared that the death penalty for non-adults was "cruel and unusual punishment," citing a recent Supreme Court ruling that struck down capital punishment for mentally disabled people. The Supreme Court agreed and, in *Roper v. Simmons*, reversed its 1989 decision.

Third, the Supreme Court is more likely to look favorably on cases that have significance beyond the two parties involved. Rarely does a sexual harassment case reach the Supreme Court because this area of law is relatively settled. But when Paula Jones brought such a suit against President Bill Clinton, the Court agreed to hear *Clinton v. Jones* because the case tested the larger question of whether a sitting U.S. president is required to defend himself against a lawsuit while in office.

Seventeen-year-old Christopher Simmons and a younger friend tied up Shirley Crook while burglarizing her home, then drove her to a bridge and threw her off. Simmons received the death penalty. On appeal, the Supreme Court ruled that sentencing a minor to death is unconstitutional.

(*Yes*, the Court ruled; it allowed Jones's lawsuit to proceed—and set off a cascade of events that rocked the Clinton presidency and led the House of Representatives to impeach him—although the Senate voted against removing him from office.)

Fourth, the Supreme Court is especially likely to hear a case when the U.S. government is a party. Almost half of the Court's caseload involves the solicitor general, the attorney who represents the Department of Justice before the Supreme Court.

These criteria increase the odds of making it to the Supreme Court—but even a case that meets all four may be passed over. Again, the Court's decision on whether to grant certiorari to any particular case remains shrouded in mystery.

For the cases that the Court agrees to hear, oral arguments are scheduled (primarily on Monday, Tuesday, and Wednesday mornings) from early October through late April. The Court then issues decisions in all cases that it heard during the session, usually on weekday mornings in May and June. Those days are very exciting—and, for those involved in a case's outcome, very anxious—occasions, as we saw with the affirmative action and immigration decisions in June 2016. No one knows when the Court will hand down a decision in a given case, nor is there a set time period in which the justices must reach a decision. However, the Court generally decides all the cases it has heard during the term before the summer recess begins.

Conference Sessions and Written Decisions

What do the justices do when they are not on the bench hearing oral arguments? There is plenty of work to occupy them. Justices keep busy writing opinions (usually with substantial assistance from their clerks, who prepare drafts and discuss details with their boss), deciding which cases to hear in the future, and reading briefs for upcoming oral arguments. And, most intriguing of all, the justices meet in conference.

Supreme Court conferences, which typically take place on Thursday or Friday afternoons, are closed to everyone except the justices—even their clerks are not allowed in. Justices sit around a conference table; by tradition, the most junior justice sits nearest the door, opening it only to allow a staff member to wheel in carts piled with materials for the next case under consideration. The Supreme Court's most significant collective decisions take place in conference.

Justices discuss the cases recently heard in oral argument, indicating their voting preferences, and the chief justice assigns the job of writing the **majority opinion** in each decided case. This is the official statement of the Court. Any justice who wishes to can issue a **concurrent opinion** explaining why he or she voted in favor of the majority outcome—different justices come to the same conclusion for different reasons. Justices who disagree about the outcome write a **dissent** indicating why they voted against the majority. Some dissents become celebrated after the fact or form the basis for a future judicial rethinking of the issues at hand.

Though justices are much more publicity averse than a president or member of Congress, they do make public appearances. These are typically addresses to specific audiences: sometimes at law schools, or an organized panel on legal matters. Some justices speak at less formal events, especially after the year's session ends in June. Justice Stephen Breyer, for example, has a passion for literature and often delivers talks on Shakespeare; he also appeared on "Late Night With Stephen Colbert" in 2015. A website called SCOTUS Map tries to track all such appearances, although they are not formally announced by the Court or the individual justices. Whatever the topic, however, all justices maintain a strict norm of not publicly discussing cases currently before the Court.

Majority opinion: The official statement of the Supreme Court (or a district court, since they also have multiple justices).

Concurrent opinion: A statement that agrees with the majority opinion.

Dissent: A statement on behalf of the justices who voted in the minority.

Supreme Court Clerks

Supreme Court clerks, usually recent law school graduates, exercise a remarkable amount of influence. They help the justices write opinions and reach decisions, as well as performing initial screening of the thousands of certiorari petitions that reach the Court each year.

Though the process is kept strictly private, it is clear that clerks reject many of the petitions, choosing a smaller set of a few hundred potential cases for the justices' consideration. Remember: These cases can shape American government in powerful ways. And a small group of unelected people in their twenties often influence whether a case will reach the Court.

Are you interested in serving as a Supreme Court clerk? It is a tough position to attain: Of the more than one thousand applicants each year, only a tiny handful—less than three dozen—will achieve this post. After completing your law degree (JD), you would generally serve one year in a lower court clerkship for a district court judge or in a state supreme court. During that year, you would apply to a specific Supreme Court justice's chambers, although many aspirants apply to all nine to maximize their chances of being selected. As with other jobs, if you make it through the initial screening, you'll be invited in for an interview, first with the clerks, then with one of the justices. Those interviews are reputedly among the toughest going: Justice Scalia, for example, subjected his clerkship candidates to a "Scalia grilling" that covered, as one said afterward, "the law: all of it."[15]

Should you receive the congratulatory call, prepare to join one of the most exclusive clubs in American government. Supreme Court clerks who elect to stay in public service often go on to important posts or become professors at top law schools. If you decide instead to go into private practice, you will be a hot commodity: "Court clerk bonuses" to sign with a law firm competing for your talents can be as high as $250,000.

Confirmation Battles

On a Sunday morning in 2016, Supreme Court Justice Antonin Scalia did not show up for breakfast in a remote West Texas hunting lodge. As the hours passed, the owner of the lodge grew concerned and finally ventured into the justice's room—where Scalia lay dead at age seventy-nine. Although the judge suffered from chronic health issues, his death caught the nation by surprise.

Along with comments honoring the long-serving Scalia, public officials quickly began jousting about his successor. A confirmation battle, among the most visible political transitions in the American system, was underway. To the surprise of many, the Republican Senate broke with tradition and refused even to consider Merrick Garland, a moderate appeals-court chief justice nominated by President Obama to replace Scalia, a staunch conservative.

Given the lifetime tenure and the immense influence often wielded by the Supreme Court justices, one of the most significant moments on the American political calendar is the appointment of a new justice. Confirmation hearings have

Supreme Court nominee Robert Bork testifying at his confirmation hearing. His nomination was a watershed in the politicization of the Court. Before Judge Bork, the major focus was competence; now, the focus is on political perspectives.

become partisan debates engaging a wide range of interest groups and national campaigns—all designed to influence the Senate Judiciary Committee that holds hearings on a nominee and issues a recommendation to the full Senate.

Until recent decades, confirmations were usually uncontroversial. The most senior member of the Court, Justice Anthony Kennedy was unanimously confirmed. Nomination politics changed dramatically in 1987, when President Ronald Reagan nominated Robert Bork to the Court. Bork certainly seemed qualified: He was a national authority on antitrust law; he had served under President Nixon as solicitor general, representing the U.S. government in cases before the Supreme Court; and he had been acting attorney general and a circuit court judge.

However, Bork was also a no-apologies conservative who would replace Justice Lewis Powell, a moderate "swing vote." Liberal groups mobilized to oppose the nomination; Democratic senators, led by Ted Kennedy, criticized what they called "Robert Bork's America." After twelve days of hearings, the Senate defeated the nomination, 58 to 42. What surprised observers was the swift rise of organized opposition based not on the candidate's qualifications, but on his judicial philosophy. Conservatives coined a new word to describe the phenomenon: *Borking*. They have returned the favor. Every judicial appointment now faces a partisan nomination fight: packed hearings, demonstrations (pro and con), intense media coverage, and public opinion polls serving up regular updates on how the nominee fares in the public view (see Table 16.1).

President Obama proposed a prominent legal expert, Elena Kagan, when ninety-year-old justice John Paul Stevens retired after thirty-five years on the Court. During Kagan's confirmation hearings, Republican members of the Senate Judiciary Committee pushed her to take a strong stand on controversial issues. Kagan had criticized previous Court nominees for ducking substantive questions; now she discovered the wisdom of that strategy for herself. She was confirmed by a comfortable margin, 63 to 37, but Republicans voted 36–5 against her.

The party battles over each nominee reflect the new stakes that surround the Supreme Court. For years, the Court has been closely divided, lining up 5–4 on a wide range of social and political issues—and 4–4 after Scalia died. A single vote makes the difference on a host of issues: the right to privacy and abortion, gun control, the rights of criminals, campaign finance, immigration, healthcare reform, the rights of terrorism suspects—and the list goes on. Small wonder that the

● The Senate Judiciary Committee grills Elena Kagan before a packed hearing room—and a national audience.

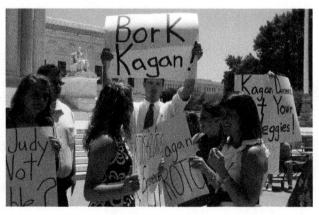

● Bork: to turn down a competent nominee for political reasons.

TABLE 16.1 Supreme Court Nominations and Confirmations

Nomination votes have gotten closer over the years. Before the Bork appointment, qualified justices were easily confirmed. Notice that Kennedy, like many justices before him, won confirmation unanimously. After Bork, unanimous votes disappeared and the hearings have gotten more contentious. Debates become especially heated when a swing vote is up for replacement. It is much easier to replace a liberal with a liberal or a conservative with a conservative.

JUDGE	APPOINTED BY (PRESIDENT)	SELECTED FROM	YEAR	SENATE VOTE		PUBLIC OPINION		
				YES	NO	YES	NO	NO OPINION
Elena Kagan	Obama	U.S. Solicitor General	2010	63	37	44	34	22
Sonia Sotomayor	Obama	U.S. Court of Appeals	2009	68	31	56	36	9
Samuel Alito	G. W. Bush	U.S. Court of Appeals	2006	58	42	54	30	16
John Roberts	G. W. Bush	U.S. Court of Appeals	2005	78	22	60	26	14
Stephen Breyer	Clinton	U.S. Court of Appeals	1994	87	9	—	—	—
Ruth Bader Ginsburg	Clinton	U.S. Court of Appeals	1993	96	3	53	14	33
Clarence Thomas	G. H. W. Bush	U.S. Court of Appeals	1991	52	48	58	30	12
Robert Bork	Reagan	U.S. Court of Appeals	1987	42	58	38	35	26
Anthony Kennedy	Reagan	U.S. Court of Appeals	1988	97	0	—	—	—

debates over each new justice get so heated, especially when a nominee's political philosophy differs from his or her predecessor, as when President Obama proposed the moderate Garland to replace the conservative Scalia. Donald Trump's surprise presidential victory owed in part to his promise to nominate a conservative to the Court. "The least dangerous branch" was not designed to be in the eye of the political hurricane.

THE BOTTOM LINE

» The Supreme Court generally hears cases on the basis of petitions requesting a review of lower court decisions. Four justices have to vote to hear a case before it becomes part of the 1 percent that comes before the Court.

» To be heard in federal court, a case must meet criteria involving controversy, standing, and mootness. Other factors that make it more likely that the case will be heard include the scope of the question: a clash between lower courts, the justices' own interests, and requests from the solicitor general.

» Cases involve oral arguments, written briefs, and conferences with only the justices present. The chief justice assigns a majority opinion; others write concurring or dissenting opinions for the record.

» Confirmation to the federal bench—and especially to the Supreme Court—was once a polite affair that largely involved questions of competence. Today, confirmations are some of the most politically charged events on the political calendar. This discord raises an important question: How does the charged politics that surrounds the Court affect its own workings—and its standing with the public?

Judicial Decision Making and Reform

How do judges reach their decisions in a case? Social scientists emphasize four different perspectives.

The Role of Law

In theory, justices decide cases on the basis of the legal facts, as laid out in the documents submitted. They read the law, consider the intent of those who framed the law, and place the case in the context of the Constitution.

According to long-established principle, justices generally abide by the precedents set in previously decided cases. This is known as **stare decisis** (literally, "stand by the things decided"). Occasionally (but rarely), the Supreme Court concludes that the precedents were wrongly decided and overrules a past decision. In general, however, legal theory suggests that the Supreme Court rules on the facts, guided by precedent. As Chief Justice John Roberts put it at his confirmation hearing, "Judges are like umpires. Umpires don't make the rules; they apply them. . . . My job is to call balls and strikes."[16]

Stare decisis: Deciding cases on the basis of previous rulings or precedents.

The umpire metaphor is appealing. However, legal cases are very often ambiguous. Applying the Constitution more than two centuries after its passage is rarely simple or straightforward. Political scientists who study Supreme Court decisions have found another perspective with a good deal of analytic power.

Ideology and Partisanship

Ideology provides another guide to the judicial mind. Political scientists have generally found that the justices' beliefs are the most powerful predictor of how they will vote, especially on difficult cases. Some studies look at the party identification of the justices, others at their ideology prior to confirmation, and still others at the views of the presidents who appointed them. No matter how ideology is measured, one study after another suggests a very strong relationship between the justices' beliefs and their votes (see Figure 16.6). In brief, we can predict the justices' votes over time with considerable accuracy, based on their political orientation.[17]

Ideology lines up with the judicial philosophy we discussed earlier. *Pragmatists* (who see the Constitution as a living, changing document) will approach cases differently from *originalists* (who believe we must interpret the document's text literally). Likewise, activists may be quicker to strike down acts of Congress, state laws, and court precedents. Conservatives charged liberal justices with being overly

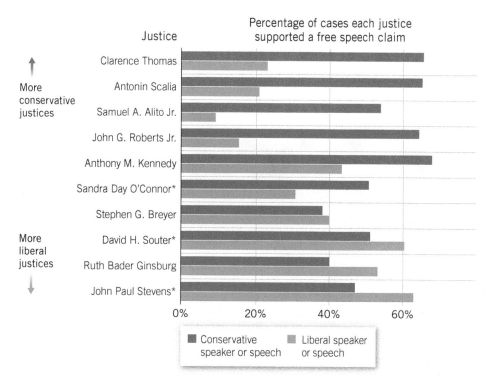

More conservative justices →

More liberal justices ↓

Justice

Percentage of cases each justice supported a free speech claim

Clarence Thomas
Antonin Scalia
Samuel A. Alito Jr.
John G. Roberts Jr.
Anthony M. Kennedy
Sandra Day O'Connor*
Stephen G. Breyer
David H. Souter*
Ruth Bader Ginsburg
John Paul Stevens*

0%   20%   40%   60%

■ Conservative speaker or speech   ■ Liberal speaker or speech

FIGURE 16.6 *Ideology and voting on the Supreme Court. (Epstein, Parker, Segal)*

activist during the Warren Court (1953–1969); today, liberals repeat the complaint about conservative justices. Ultimately, simple political perspective—liberal versus conservative—is one of the most effective ways of explaining how justices rule.

The general public has come to share the scholarly view about how justices decide. In recent polls a full 75 percent of the public suggested that Supreme Court justices "sometimes let their ideological views influence their decision."

The current Court breaks relatively evenly along the partisan divide: Three members are conservative—and, according to one study, rank among the seven most consistently conservative voters in the past fifty years. They are Chief Justice Roberts and associate justices Thomas and Alito, all of whom vote conservative more than 70 percent of the time. Justice Anthony Kennedy tends to vote conservative but provides a swing vote for liberals about one-third of the time. Four justices (Ginsburg, Breyer, Sotomayor, and Kagan) vote liberal between 60 and 70 percent of the time. In recent years, justices have begun to read their dissenting opinions aloud, a striking step designed to attract public attention to their dissatisfaction, which they often express in strong terms.[18]

To be sure, the ideological model has its limits and by no means explains all votes. In the 2015–2016 term, 44 percent of the cases were decided unanimously—down from a record 65 percent in 2013–2014. Ideology does not play a role in many technical cases.

Even so, the idea that the Court often rules on the basis of politics poses a dilemma for our democratic system. The Court is designed to stand above politics and, as Chief Justice Roberts said at his confirmation hearing, to interpret and explain the rules beyond any partisan consideration. That is the reason justices are selected for life. When they rule on the basis of political ideology—and are widely

INFO/DATA: How Americans View the Supreme Court: Liberal or Conservative?

Americans are relatively evenly divided about the Court's ideological outlook. In 2016, 36 percent called the Court "liberal" and just half that many saw it as "conservative" (down from 36 percent in 2007). The largest plurality, nearly 40 percent, believes that the Supreme Court is middle of the road.

1. Do you think that the public's shifting view of the Court is based on specific rulings? Why or why not?

2. Does the conviction that judges rule on the basis of ideology require us to rethink the way we appoint the justices or how the Court operates? Or is it desirable in our party-polarized age that justices exhibit strong viewpoints as so many politicians and ordinary citizens do today, thereby better representing the public?

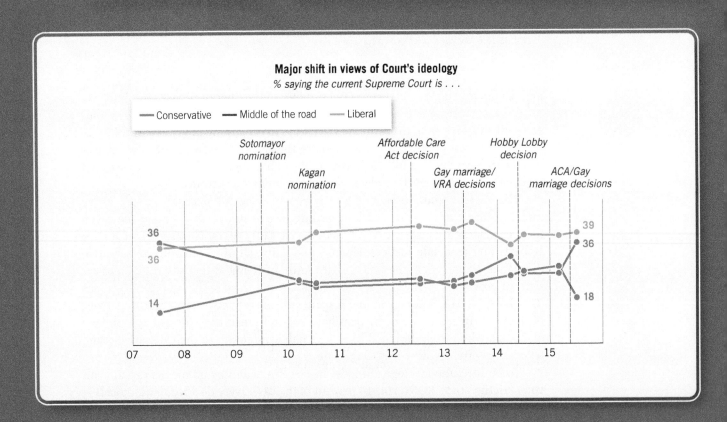

Major shift in views of Court's ideology
% saying the current Supreme Court is . . .

— Conservative   — Middle of the road   — Liberal

Sotomayor nomination

Kagan nomination

Affordable Care Act decision

Gay marriage/ VRA decisions

Hobby Lobby decision

ACA/Gay marriage decisions

36
36
14

39
36
18

07 08 09 10 11 12 13 14 15

Source: Pew Research Center

seen as doing so—they raise a problem for the legitimacy of this powerful institution, precisely as Justice John Paul Stevens warned when the Court stopped the recount in Florida with its *Bush v. Gore* decision (decided 5–4, along partisan lines).

Collegiality and Peer Pressure

A third factor shaping Court decisions is *collegiality*, or to put it more bluntly, *peer pressure*. Justices spend a lot of time together, hearing cases and discussing their decisions. They exert some influence on one another. Persuasion is a regular feature of Court discussions; according to the few insider reports available, as well as academic analysis, justices appear to change positions in many cases based on legal arguments and personal appeals of colleagues. They also may change their votes for strategic reasons—trading votes in different cases.[19] The evidence does suggest that past generations engaged in more give-and-take—in the 1950s and 1960s, at least one justice would switch his vote in about half of all cases.[20] Today, justices appear to be more settled in their convictions.

Another angle on the idea of "peer pressure" arises from the larger legal community. A few hundred people—law professors, law students, legal bloggers, congressional members, committee staff for the House and Senate Judiciary Committees, and interest-group activists—make up the attentive audience for most judicial decisions. The audience's judgment about a specific judicial opinion can be laudatory or scathing. Harvard Law professor Frederick Schauer demonstrated that judges—especially Supreme Court justices, the most scrutinized of all judicial figures—seem to notice. Analyzing a large dataset of Court decisions, Schauer found that "judicial reputation" played an important role in explaining why justices moved left or right on an ideological scale during their service on the Court.[21]

Institutional Concerns

Finally, justices sometimes appear to think about the interests of the Court as an institution. They spend many years on the bench and are aware of the outside forces that might affect the standing of the Court—public opinion, a hostile Congress, or a skeptical executive. We saw a prime example of this kind of thinking in the Court's early years with *Marbury v. Madison*. Marshall was considering the role and standing of his institution as he crafted his complicated opinion. Some recent studies underscore the importance of this perspective.[22]

During much of 2016, with the Court down to eight justices, four members—two liberals and two conservatives—came together and tried to forge a consensus in as many cases as possible. They argued that constant deadlock would diminish the reputation of the Court. Four others (two liberals and two conservatives) responded that it would not help the cause of justice by compromising their judicial philosophies. Which side would you agree with?

THE BOTTOM LINE

» Four different perspectives help explain how justices make their decisions.

» First, we should pay attention to their own explanation: They follow precedent and the facts of the case.

» Political scientists are more likely to find that ideology is the best predictor of justices' decisions in the long run. Recently, the public also has taken this view, which poses a dilemma for American governance: An institution designed to be above politics is increasingly seen as essentially political. That perception has helped turn confirmation hearings into volatile battles.

» Two final factors also play a role in judicial decision making: collegiality and institutional protection.

❶ Nineteen Cases You Should Know

The history of American Court cases includes a long list of famous—and occasionally infamous—decisions. You have already encountered some in our discussion of civil liberties (Chapter 5) and civil rights (Chapter 6). If you take a course in constitutional law (or decide to attend law school), you will study cases by the hundreds. All are part of American *jurisprudence*, or the study of law. Here we list nineteen cases that every student of American government ought to be familiar with, organized chronologically. The ones we have covered elsewhere in this book are briefly described here only to refresh your memory. We have left one place blank in the top twenty. Think about the other cases you have encountered in this and other chapters and join the conversation: Which case would *you* add to our "A list"? Are there any you would subtract?

1. *Marbury v. Madison* (1803)

Without Marshall's momentous decision, we might not have judicial review—or courts so deeply engaged in U.S. government and policymaking. You read about this case earlier in this chapter.

2. *McCulloch v. Maryland* (1819)

James William McCulloch was a clerk at the Baltimore branch of the National Bank of the United States. The state of Maryland levied an annual tax on all banks "not chartered by the state" of Maryland; at the time, the National Bank was the only one. On behalf of the bank, McCulloch refused to pay the Maryland tax and sued. The Maryland Supreme Court ruled against McCulloch, arguing that the Constitution said nothing about establishing a bank—the national bank was unconstitutional in the first place.

Taking a loose interpretation of the Constitution (rather than a strict construction that would have limited Congress to doing only what was explicitly allowed), Chief Justice Marshall upheld the constitutionality of the bank. Marshall argued that Congress had every right to establish a national bank under the Constitution's necessary and proper clause (which authorizes Congress to do anything that is "necessary and proper" for "carrying into execution" the powers it is granted).

Furthermore, declared the Court, Maryland was forbidden to tax the national bank. "The power to tax," declared Marshall for the unanimous majority, "involves the power to destroy."[23] The states had no such power over federal institutions, because the collective American citizenry had established a national government with the Constitution's ratification. The Court's action affirmed the federal government's superiority to state governments in all specific instances named by the Constitution; this decision marked a significant advance toward American nationhood.

3. *Dartmouth College v. Woodward* (1819)

In one of the classic speeches before the Supreme Court, future Senate leader Daniel Webster delivered a ringing address on behalf of his alma mater, Dartmouth College. New Hampshire's legislature had sought to extend control over the college, effectively converting it from a private to a public institution. The Court's decision—again written by Marshall, who was deeply impressed by Webster's oration—reaffirmed Dartmouth's private charter. King George had originally issued the charter, but the Court now ruled that it had to be respected as a private contract. Along the way, Marshall defined contracts as transactions involving private property rights (rather than "political relations between the government and its citizens"). The Court extended contract rights to private corporations, providing a foundation for free enterprise as we know it today.

4. *Dred Scott v. Sandford* (1857)

As tensions mounted over the spread of slavery into the West, Chief Justice Roger Taney inserted the Supreme Court squarely into the middle of the debate. Writing for a 7–2 Court majority, Taney ruled that Dred Scott, a Missouri slave who was taken to a free state and later back to Missouri, was still a slave. He might have stopped there. Remember, one cannot sue without *standing*, and slaves, by definition, did not have standing.

The Court, however, went on to rule that Congress did not have the power to prohibit slavery in the territories. Taney continued, in passages that are shocking to read today: blacks, he insisted, were "beings of an inferior order and altogether unfit to associate with the white race." They were not and could never become U.S. citizens. The bottom line: Slavery could not be restricted in any western territory.[24]

Chief Justice Roger Taney, who served on the Court from 1836 to 1864, authored the Dred Scott decision—often described as the worst decision in Court history.

Dred Scott, a slave, sued for his own freedom and that of his two daughters, arguing that he had been taken to Illinois and the Wisconsin Territory, both free areas. The Court rejected his bid for freedom, 7–2.

Many constitutional historians choose *Dred Scott* as the worst Supreme Court decision in American history (for more details, see Chapter 6).

5. *Santa Clara Co. v. Southern Pacific Railroad* (1886)

Santa Clara Co. v. Southern Pacific Railroad was a complex tax case, decided unanimously without much notice—but it reverberates through our politics today. California forbade corporations from deducting their debts from their taxable property. The Court ruled that California had acted improperly because corporations should be treated as persons and afforded the Fourteenth Amendment right of equal protection. The case established a precedent—later expanded—that enhanced the power of corporations. By 1938 Justice Hugo Black would complain that the Fourteenth Amendment had been written "to protect weak and helpless human beings," and not to "remove corporations in any fashion from the control of state governments." A decade later, Justice William O. Douglas added: "The *Santa Clara* case becomes one of the most momentous of all our decisions. . . . Corporations were now armed with constitutional prerogatives." The bottom line: *Santa Clara* set a precedent that, with time, gave corporations all the legal benefits of individual citizens. The legal theory in *Santa Clara* helped inform the Court when it struck down campaign finance laws (in *Citizens United* and other recent cases).[25]

see for yourself 16.3

Go online to see a discussion of the *Plessy* case.

6. *Plessy v. Ferguson* (1896)

The Civil War resulted in freedoms for black Americans, codified in three constitutional amendments (the Thirteenth, Fourteenth, and Fifteenth). After the turbulent period of Reconstruction, the South (followed, if less blatantly, by other sections of the United States) set about reasserting second-class status for African Americans. Across the region, state legislatures passed explicit laws mandating segregated facilities.

One 1890 Louisiana statute, "Law 111," required (among other restrictions) that railroads maintain separate cars for black and white ticketholders. Homer Plessy deliberately challenged the law by refusing to move to the "colored car" on an East Louisiana Railroad train. The case eventually reached the Supreme Court, where Plessy's lawyers argued that the segregation violated his Fourteenth Amendment rights. (Remember that the Fourteenth Amendment guaranteed to all Americans "equal protection under the law.") The Court rejected Plessy's argument and upheld Louisiana's law, cementing the infamous doctrine of "separate but equal" for nearly sixty years (until *Brown v. Board of Education* in 1954). The decision permitted racial segregation, and in the next ten years, the Jim Crow system was put firmly into place with the Supreme Court's blessing.

The sole dissenting justice, John Marshall Harlan (note his first and middle names), wrote a blistering critique of the decision, predicting accurately that *Plessy* "will prove as infamous" as the *Dred Scott* case and insisting that the Constitution was "color blind." After the decision was handed down, Homer Plessy pled guilty to the violation and paid a twenty-five dollar fine (for more details, see Chapter 6).

● *Keith Plessy and Phoebe Ferguson, descendants of the two men named in the famous case, have become friends and formed a foundation to promote innovative ways of studying civil rights. The battle for civil rights is passed on from generation to generation. Now it is in your hands.*

7. *Lochner v. New York* (1905)

The rise of mass industry and manufacturing in the late nineteenth century bred strong demands for worker protection. Several states passed laws limiting working hours and banning child labor. New York State's worker protections, passed in 1897, included a "Bakeshop Act" that prohibited anyone from working more than ten hours a day, or sixty hours a week, in a bakery.

Joseph Lochner, a bakery owner in Utica, was fined for requiring employees to exceed the sixty-hour weekly limit. He took his case to court, insisting that the Fourteenth Amendment protected his right to establish free contracts with his workers, independent of state influence.

Two New York courts denied Lochner's appeals. In a 7–2 ruling, the Supreme Court reversed the New York decisions, holding that the Bakeshop Act was an invalid exercise of the state's power. The decision ushered in a thirty-year **Lochner era**, during which courts repeatedly struck down state economic and labor regulations, including minimum wage laws, in the name of individual economic liberty. Governments could not interfere with the private right to contract by introducing worker protections.

In dissent, Justice Oliver Wendell Holmes wrote: "The Fourteenth Amendment does not enact Mr. Herbert Spencer's Social Statistics"—that is, society should not operate by survival of the fittest.

Lochner era: A period from 1905 to 1937, during which the Supreme Court struck down laws (e.g., worker protection or minimum wage laws) that were thought to infringe on economic liberty or the right to contract.

8. *Muller v. Oregon* (1908)

Oregon limited the number of hours women could work. Whereas *Lochner* ruled that the state could not regulate men's hours, the Court chose to treat women differently. The Court ruled that "the difference between the sexes does . . . justify a different rule respecting a restriction of the hours of labor." The concern about "healthy mothers" justified state intervention.

Louis Brandeis defended the law with an innovative strategy. He disposed of the legal arguments in two pages and then compiled page after page of data—health statistics, medical evidence, the experience of other nations. From that time forward, this kind of statistical brief, brimming with data, would be known as a "Brandeis brief."

The case is particularly important for gender readings of the law. Yes, women won labor protections, but notice how: The case supported the idea that a woman was different from a man and, more to the point, that her role as child bearer and mother was more important than her role as worker.

● *Lawyer Louis Brandeis, later a Supreme Court justice, relied on social science data to win* Muller v. Oregon. *To this day, we call an argument that emphasizes social science research rather than legal argument a "Brandeis brief."*

9. *Schenck v. United States* (1919)

Charles Schenck, the secretary of the U.S. Socialist Party, printed and distributed leaflets expressing opposition to a U.S. military draft during World War I. Schenck was convicted under the Espionage Act of aiding the enemy during wartime. Insisting that he was exercising his First Amendment free speech rights, Schenck took his appeal to the Supreme Court.

One of the Court's most prolific (and quotable) justices, Oliver Wendell Holmes, Jr., wrote the decision for a 9–0 majority that upheld Schenck's conviction. For the first time, the Court formally marked out boundaries around protected speech: As Holmes wrote, words presenting a "clear and present danger" were legitimate subjects of legislative prohibitions. The **clear and present danger** test guided the court for fifty years, until it was rewritten in 1969. Recall that a "test" is a general principle designed to guide future court decisions on a topic (for more details, see Chapter 5).

Clear and present danger: Court doctrine that permits restrictions of free speech if officials believe that the speech will lead to prohibited action like violence or terrorism.

10. *National Labor Relations Board v. Jones and Laughlin Steel Corporation* (1937)

Jones and Laughlin was the nation's fourth-largest manufacturer of steel—an industry that had very aggressively opposed unionization. The company fired ten workers who tried to launch a union, and was sued by the National Labor Relations

Board for violating the Wagner Act of 1935, which protected the right to unionize. The company responded that the Wagner Act violated the Constitution. The lower courts both agreed that precedent was on the company's side.

In a 5–4 decision, Chief Justice Charles Evans Hughes reversed the lower court decisions and held that Congress had the power, under the interstate commerce clause, to regulate the company's treatment of its workers. This decision broadly expanded congressional power to regulate economic matters. It meant that the Court—by a one-vote margin—would accept New Deal legislation. We can understand the enormous scope of this ruling when, three decades later Congress used its authority over interstate commerce to outlaw segregation in hotels and restaurants (with the Civil Rights Act of 1964, discussed in Chapter 6).

Along with another case, *West Coast Hotel Company v. Parrish* (also decided 5–4 in 1937), the courts now permitted legislatures to regulate relations between business and workers. The cases meant the end of the Lochner era. Today, conservative judicial activists are eager to roll back congressional use of the interstate commerce power. Some even call for a return of the Lochner era.

● *Fred Korematsu refused to enter a Japanese internment camp. Today, his lifelong fight on behalf of civil liberties is commemorated by the "Fred Korematsu Day of Civil Liberties and the Constitution."*

11. *Korematsu v. U.S.* (1944)

During World War II, an executive order by President Roosevelt forced Japanese Americans out of their homes and into hastily constructed internment camps. Fred Korematsu, a California native, was arrested for defying the order. The Court ruled 6–3 that the need to defend against espionage during wartime justified the order—and its violation of equal protection. The case was one of the first to adopt strict scrutiny of government actions: The Court is primed to strike down any law that singles out a race or ethnicity unless there is a very strong reason for doing so (see Chapter 6 for discussion). In this case, the Court ruled, the government's action met the standards of **strict scrutiny**.

Strict scrutiny: The tendency to strike down as unconstitutional any legislation that singles out race or ethnicity unless the government has a compelling interest in such legislation.

The case was always infamous for its mistreatment of Japanese Americans. It became even more so when legal historian Peter Irons, researching a book about the internment, discovered that the solicitor general had suppressed crucial information. A report from the Office of Naval Intelligence had concluded that there was no evidence that Japanese Americans were disloyal or acting as spies. In 1983, a federal district court in California used the new information to vacate (or void) Korematsu's conviction. To many people, including Fred Korematsu himself, the case stands as an enduring warning. War breeds fear that can threaten civil liberties. Korematsu drew on his own experience to file an amicus brief in a case involving the legal rights of enemy combatants held in Guantánamo Bay.

12. *Brown v. Board of Education* (1954)

This landmark decision, decided unanimously, declared that segregating schools for black and white children violated the equal protection clause of the Fourteenth Amendment. As Supreme Court Justice Earl Warren put it, "separate schools are inherently unequal." The decision boosted the civil rights movement and paved the way to an end to legal segregation. It overturned *Plessy v. Ferguson*, described previously (for more details, see Chapter 6).

13. *Mapp v. Ohio* (1961)

Cleveland police received a tip in 1959 that local resident Dollree Mapp was harboring a suspected bombing fugitive, and they swarmed her house without a search warrant. The police found no fugitive—but they did find obscene material, at the time legally forbidden in Ohio. Mapp was arrested and convicted. She appealed.

The Supreme Court reversed her conviction and, drawing on the Fourth Amendment (prohibiting unreasonable searches and seizures), devised the "exclusionary rule," stating that illegally obtained evidence cannot be admitted in a criminal trial. The Court extended this federal rule to cover state cases (incorporating part of the Fourth Amendment) and ruled that since the evidence against Mapp was obtained without a search warrant, she could go free. The conservative majority on the Roberts Court recently rolled back the exclusionary rule, and there is some speculation that it may be abolished altogether (for more detail, see Chapter 5).

14. *Gideon v. Wainwright* (1963)

Clarence Gideon, was accused (unjustly, as it eventually was proved) of a minor theft from a Florida pool hall. Lacking funds to hire a defense attorney, Gideon represented himself at his trial—a relatively common practice into the early 1960s. He was swiftly convicted, but he appealed his sentence based on the state's failure to provide him with a competent defense lawyer.

The Supreme Court held that Gideon was wrongly convicted and ordered a new trial. The *Gideon* legacy: Anyone charged with a serious criminal offense has the right to an attorney. Moreover, the state must provide a lawyer to any defendant unable to afford legal counsel. *Gideon* was the first in a series of landmark judicial decisions upholding the rights of defendants in criminal proceedings, including the so-called *Miranda rights* to counsel during police questioning. Recently, the Court has strengthened the right to counsel, holding that it applies to plea bargain cases in which a defendant is offered a deal: plead guilty, avoid a trial, and receive a lighter sentence (for more details, see Chapter 5).

15. *Lemon v. Kurtzman* (1971)

Religion is another constitutionally guaranteed freedom attracting frequent judicial attention. Recall from Chapter 5 that the First Amendment both guarantees the *free exercise* of religion to every person and forbids the *establishment* of religion. It erects what Thomas Jefferson termed a "wall of separation" between church and state.

In *Lemon v. Kurtzman*, described in Chapter 5, the Court created a three-pronged test for judging whether government action violated the first amendment by "establishing" a religion. The law could not create "excessive government entanglement" in religious affairs; it must not inhibit religious practice; and it must have a secular purpose. Any law that violates any of these tests is unconstitutional.

The Lemon test has come in for a great deal of criticism—especially from more conservative justices—and the Court has been growing more permissive about allowing religious practices. For example, in *Town of Greece v. Galloway* (2014), the court ruled (5–4) that the town's practice of starting its monthly meetings with a prayer did not violate the establishment clause. Despite the new, more permissive orientation, the Court has repeatedly refused to strike down the Lemon test (for more detail, see Chapter 5).

16. *Roe v. Wade* (1973)

The *Roe v. Wade* decision, written by Justice Harry Blackmun, struck down a Texas statute outlawing abortion—and expanded the personal right to privacy under the Constitution. The right to privacy, wrote Blackmun, is "fundamental" and "broad enough to encompass a woman's decision whether or not to terminate her pregnancy." The *Roe* decision—since qualified by other cases discussed in

● *The politics of abortion inflame passions, mobilize demonstrations, and shape American politics. For over forty years, the judiciary has been the central arena for this conflict.*

Chapter 5—remains one of the great dividing lines in American politics and a "litmus test" for most federal judicial nominations. Today, the Court appears to be divided, with three justices ready to overturn *Roe*, four eager to defend it, and one—Justice Kennedy—in the middle, balancing a woman's right to privacy with a state's interest in limiting abortions. The furor over the Bork appointment can be partially attributed to the intense feelings about this case: Retiring Justice Lewis Powell had supported the majority, and Robert Bork bluntly called the decision a mistake. After Bork was defeated, Justice Kennedy, the man in the middle today, won confirmation (for more detail, see Chapter 5).

17. *U.S. v. Nixon* (1974)

This case revolved around the Watergate break-in and the historic political debate that ensued. President Nixon refused to turn over audiotapes of White House conversations, along with other requested materials, to the special prosecutor investigating Watergate, on the grounds of "executive privilege," a sweeping claim of presidential immunity. In a unanimous 8–0 decision, Chief Justice Warren Burger (appointed by Nixon five years earlier) upheld the doctrine of executive privilege but concluded that presidents could not invoke it in criminal cases to withhold evidence. Nixon acquiesced—and resigned as president a month later.

18. *Bush v. Gore* (2000)

High drama surrounded a recount of some of Florida's disputed ballots in the 2000 presidential election, stretching well past the November 7 Election Day. On December 8, Florida's Supreme Court ordered a manual recount of ballots; George W. Bush's lawyers, fearing this would result in an advantage for Vice President Gore, appealed the decision to the U.S. Supreme Court. The Court, acting with unusual

see for yourself 16.4

Go online to listen to the Supreme Court's oral arguments in *Bush v. Gore* **(2000).**

speed because of the urgency of the issue—a presidential election hung in the balance—halted the recount the very next day. Two days later, on December 11, the Court scheduled time to hear from both sides' lawyers. Less than twenty-four hours later, Chief Justice Rehnquist handed down a 5–4 ruling that no constitutionally valid recount could be completed by Florida's December 12 deadline for certifying election results. The long presidential contest of 2000 was over. George Bush won Florida's twenty-five electoral votes and, with them, the presidential election.

19. *National Federation of Independent Business v. Sebelius* (2012)

This blockbuster decision took on two controversial features of the Obama administration health reform law (the Affordable Care Act, or ACA). The ACA required all Americans to buy health insurance or face a fine (paid with their income taxes); it also expanded Medicaid, a joint federal and state program, to cover all Americans under sixty-five who were poor or near poor (the federal government would pay 90 percent of the costs).

Can the federal government require individuals to carry health insurance? Proponents said yes: Congress has the power to regulate interstate commerce (see case number 10, above, *National Labor Relations Board v. Jones and Laughlin Steel Corporation*). Chief Justice Roberts and the four conservative justices ruled that Congress does *not* have the power under interstate commerce to require that people buy health insurance. Then, very dramatically, the chief justice broke with the conservatives and ruled that Congress does have the power to tax—and that the ACA constitutes a tax. The Obama reform was upheld. However, Roberts got Supreme Court–watchers buzzing. Remember, conservatives have long wanted to curtail the congressional use of interstate commerce. Was Roberts handing conservative jurisprudence a victory, perhaps a return to the Lochner era that conservatives have been calling for even while upholding the Obama healthcare law? Time will tell.

In the other part of the case, the Court ruled 7–2 that Congress could not change the rules of the Medicaid program and require states to expand their program. It could only offer the funds and encourage the states to participate. Was this, wondered analysts, a new rollback of the federal government's power over federalism? Again, time will tell. The true scope of a case like this often takes years to reveal itself.

What Do You Think?

Name Another Landmark Case

Why didn't we take our list to a nice round number? To leave room for your choice. Think about the many cases we have already discussed in this book. Then pick one that you would add to the list: What would it be?

Hint: Some cases that are frequently seen as landmark cases include *Obergefell v. Hodges* (which struck down bans on same-sex marriage, discussed above); the *Fisher* (affirmative action) and *U.S. v. Texas* (immigration) cases that opened this chapter; *Citizens United* (striking down campaign finance legislation, discussed in Chapter 10); *Miranda* (the right to remain silent; see Chapter 5); *Tinker* (student free speech; see Chapter 5); and *Bakke* (affirmative action; see Chapter 6); Now it is your turn. Choose a case, add it to the list, and explain why you consider it a landmark.

The Nineteen Cases—and the Power of the Court

This list illustrates the wide range of questions addressed in U.S. federal courts. There are issues affecting civil rights and liberties (*Dred Scott, Plessy, Korematsu*), federalism and nationhood (*McCulloch, National Federation of Independent Business*), criminal charges (*Mapp, Gideon*), First Amendment freedoms (*Schenck*), business regulation (*Dartmouth, Lochner, National Labor Relations Board, National Federation of Independent Business*), elections (*Bush v. Gore*), religion (*Lemon*), gender (*Muller, Roe*), and separated powers (*Nixon*). These cases also illustrate the formidable reach of the judiciary in American politics and government.

Many of these cases were very controversial when decided—and some remain disputed today. Such controversy repeatedly raises the question we have asked throughout the chapter: Does the Supreme Court (and do courts in general) overstep democratic boundaries when ruling on such momentous political matters? How deferential should they be to the people's representatives? Each case introduces a different type of judgment call—not just on the substance of the case but on the scope of the Court's authority.

THE BOTTOM LINE

» A few judicial decisions become landmark decisions, significantly reshaping American politics and society.

» We have listed nineteen of the most important Supreme Court decisions across more than two centuries. Any you would add—or subtract?

Criticizing the Judiciary

Americans hold a decidedly mixed view of the judicial branch. We go to court more frequently than citizens of most nations. But we are dubious about the legal system in general and give poor reviews to its main actors: lawyers, juries, and (increasingly criticized) justices.

Critiquing the Judiciary

An independent judiciary has deep roots in both our colonial English heritage and the classical liberal tradition (as you saw in Chapter 2). Yet despite its appetite for litigation, the public also expresses deep concerns about our legal system.[26] Four common critiques include the high cost of litigation, perceived bias, judicial power, and the possibility of corruption.

First, the costs associated with America's litigious society have become a source of widespread discontent, especially among conservatives. Critics estimate that more than five hundred billion dollars is spent annually responding to and adjudicating lawsuits.

Second, the U.S. legal system is sometimes perceived as biased. For example, many minorities, particularly African Americans, have for generations experienced the sting of *racial profiling*, or the use of race by police officers in deciding whom to stop or arrest. Others criticize ideological bias. Declining confidence in our criminal justice system is illustrated in Table 16.2.

TABLE 16.2: Americans' Ranking of Various Public Institutions

Percentage with "a great deal" or "quite a lot" of confidence in the institution.		
	2006	2016
Military	73%	73%
Police	58%	56%
Church or organized religion	52%	41%
Medical system	38%	39%
Presidency	33%	36%
U.S. Supreme Court	40%	36%
Public schools	37%	30%
Banks	49%	27%
Organized labor	24%	23%
Criminal justice system	25%	23%
Source: Gallup		

The power of the legal system is a third cause of concern. This concern partly owes to our fear of winding up in court, especially as a defendant. The legendary U.S. federal judge Learned Hand wrote in 1926, "As a litigant, I should dread a lawsuit beyond almost anything short of sickness and death."[27] If Judge Hand, after forty-three years as a federal judge, was made anxious by the law's power, imagine how most non-lawyers feel!

Finally, disgust with the perceived corruption of lawyers drives criticism. As we saw in Chapter 12 (Interest Groups), lawyers rank near the bottom of Gallup's annual survey of the honesty and ethical standards of various U.S. professions. As a nation, we have a low opinion of juries as well.

Ideas for Reform: More Resources

One of the most prominent reform proposals would grant the courts more resources. The American judiciary faces a "quiet crisis" in attracting talented judges. One reason is a long-term decline in judges' pay, which has fallen dramatically relative to that of other professionals. In 1969, district court judges earned a substantially higher salary than their academic counterparts at Harvard, the highest-paying law school. Today they make half as much as senior professors—and barely a third as much as law-school deans.

We also have seen that the U.S. court system runs on a very small budget, relative to that of other governing institutions. State courts stagger under the volume of cases—and cope by using strategies like pushing through plea bargains in the vast majority of criminal cases. Public defenders have impossible caseloads. The tensions of underfunding run throughout the court system. Perhaps courts should receive more resources. On the federal level, it may even be worth thinking about developing a research capacity to evaluate the potential impact of court rulings.

Term Limits

Judicial term limits (often proposed as eighteen years) would help address the fear of "unelected judges" overruling the elected branches.[28] Judicial term limits also may reduce the battles that surround judicial appointments, especially to the Supreme Court. Forty-year-old justices would no longer sit on the bench for three decades or more. It would still keep the Court insulated from political tumult—eighteen years is a long time—while providing for a regular circulation of new judges with fresh perspectives. One version of this proposal would permit the president to nominate a Supreme Court justice every two years so that the Court would always balance new ideas and experienced hands.

Should we limit the terms of Supreme Court justices? One proposal suggests limiting each justice to eighteen years on the Court (after that they would go to the appellate bench). The president would appoint (and the Senate confirm) a new appointee every two years. Would you support or oppose such an innovation? What do you think?

THE BOTTOM LINE

» The courts face four popular criticisms: cost, bias, power, and corruption.

» One reform proposal: Direct more resources to the judicial branch—in both the state and the federal courts.

» A second oft-proposed reform: Introduce term limits to the federal bench. Supreme Court justices would serve eighteen years, a time frame permitting each president a judicial nomination every two years.

Conclusion: Democracy and the Courts

Courts wield an unusual amount of influence in the United States—far more than courts in most other nations, and perhaps too much in a modern democratic society. At the same time, there are clear limits to judicial power—from the reactive nature of the judicial process to the courts' reliance on others to implement decisions. Expanding resources and imposing term limits could modernize the courts and enhance their ability to serve American government by doing what they do at their best: faithfully reflecting—and consistently enforcing—the constitutional rules that guide our public life.

Reforms can only go so far. The powerful role of the courts in a democracy will always be vexing for a simple reason: The courts are designed to serve as a check, ultimately, on "we, the people." The courts, when they are acting properly, stop the people and their representatives from violating the Constitution or from harming minority rights. However, as the steady parade of 5–4 decisions discussed in this chapter indicates, what exactly the Constitution means is often a highly controversial matter. As a result, the courts always face a delicate balance between enforcing the Constitution (as a majority on the Court sees it) and deferring to democracy (and the majority of the country).

CHAPTER SUMMARY

● The judiciary has a central place in U.S. government and politics—as well as in our legalistic national culture.

● Americans express uneasiness about their judicial system, despite their faith in the rule of law.

● Compared to other advanced democratic nations, U.S. courts possess a great deal of influence over our politics and government. This owes primarily to the power of judicial review, asserted long ago by Chief Justice John Marshall. Once again, Americans found a way to separate and fragment power—continuing the work begun in the Constitution.

● Alongside their uncommon influence, courts are hemmed in by restrictions such as limited resources, stare decisis requirements, and their lack of an electoral base (at the federal level).

● The judiciary has affected a vast range of areas through its authority to interpret the Constitution, from religion and race to economic regulations and even presidential election outcomes. This impact is evident in a set of landmark cases—each of which has aroused great controversy, leading to renewed calls for limits on judicial activism. The originalist and pragmatist schools of thought have very different views of what constitutes such "activism."

● The Supreme Court marks the pinnacle of judicial—and constitutional—authority in the United States. Its operations, often carried out behind closed doors, are the subject of fascinated speculation: How do nine justices decide? The leading theories: They follow the rule of law, they are guided by their ideology, they are moved by peer pressure, and they are concerned about the institution of the courts.

● Given the combination of the power of the courts and Americans' uncertainty about how that power should be wielded, a set of reforms is put forth each year. Two in particular deserve careful attention: the limitation of federal judges' current life terms, and the possibility of rewarding the judiciary's expansive responsibilities with more resources.

● KEY TERMS

Amicus curiae, p. 497	Defendant, p. 494	Majority opinion, p. 499
Circuit courts, p. 488	Dissent, p. 499	Mediation, p. 482
Civil law, p. 494	District courts, p. 487	Plaintiff, p. 494
Clear and present danger, p. 510	Judicial activism, p. 493	Precedent, p. 494
	Judicial restraint, p. 493	Rule of four, p. 498
Common law, p. 494	Judicial review, p. 492	*Stare decisis*, p. 503
Concurrent opinion, p. 499	Litigation, p. 482	Strict scrutiny, p. 511
Criminal law, p. 494	Lochner era, p. 510	

STUDY QUESTIONS

1. Should the judiciary have less power in American government and politics? If so, how would you propose restraining judicial authority in practice?

2. The Supreme Court, prior to Justice Scalia's death, for several years had been 33 percent female, around the same proportion as in other federal courts (district and circuit). Does that seem unjustly low to you, given that women make up nearly 52 percent of the U.S. population? What about the fact that none of the nine justices is Protestant in a country that is around 51 percent Protestant? Should we care about the religious preferences of Supreme Court justices?

3. Do Supreme Court clerks—and other federal judges' clerks—have too much influence, given their relatively young ages? Should they serve for longer than one year, given the importance of the work they do?

4. Should we mandate more transparency for judicial operations—televise Supreme Court oral arguments, for example, or require that Court conferences be transcribed and publicized? Are there any benefits to the secrecy that characterizes the federal judiciary?

5. Do either of the reforms raised at the end of this chapter appeal to you? Why or why not? Might they be most successful if offered as a package? (Combining term limits, which appeal to critics of judicial activism, with higher judicial pay and more resources for the courts might make term limits palatable to current and future judges.)

6. Should the federal judiciary be the last line of defense in protecting Americans' constitutional rights and liberties? Why or why not? And if not, what other institution or group of people should have this responsibility? Be specific: How would another actor or group protect rights and liberties better than federal judges, and ultimately the Supreme Court, do today?

 Go to www.oup.com/us/Morone to find quizzes, flash cards, simulations, tutorials, videos, and other study tools.

Public Policymaking and Budgeting

17

HOW MUCH MONEY should American workers make? Although specific wage and salary levels are left to employees and employers to negotiate, public policymakers weigh in on many details. In 2016, for example, California legislated a hike in the minimum wage—which sets a floor on hourly wages that employers are legally obligated to honor—to $15/hour, the highest in the United States. And as the year drew to a close, a U.S. Department of Labor (DOL) rule set minimum annual salaries for all "non-exempt" employees (those who are eligible for overtime pay, typically hourly workers) at $47,476—more than doubling the previous minimum, which had not changed since the 1970s.

Although many employees celebrated a sudden salary increase, other voices expressed concern. At colleges and universities, for example, some recent graduates have traditionally been hired into entry-level positions, such as admissions counselors (interviewing prospective students, reading applications, and the like) or athletics assistants (reviewing video of opponents). They earn a comparatively low salary but gain valuable experience, and often move into higher-level jobs or on to graduate school after a few years. Schools are still sorting out what will happen to these apprentice-style positions under the new DOL requirement. Congress stepped in to review the change, with some members sharply criticizing the administration for meddling with private economic decisions, but took no action.

The White House, Congress, and California lawmakers were debating not just pay levels, but *what government should do*. In other words, they were debating public policy. Exchanges like these about policy decisions have far-reaching implications, affecting tens of millions of Americans and many more millions around the world. Policy debates also return to this book's familiar chapter-opening question: *Who are we?*

Perhaps Americans are best described in terms of the policies we enact—and those that we reject or abandon. Why do we control privately owned land to protect spotted owls and flying squirrels? Why do we provide hefty government subsidies to farmers growing corn, dairy, and beef but virtually none to growers of fruits and vegetables? Why do we imprison one in nine young black men? Why do we closely regulate sex but not violence in movies? These and thousands of other policy decisions contribute to the kaleidoscopic portrait of who we are.

● *California's governor signs a $15/hour minimum wage bill into law after a spirited public debate. Policymakers can wield great authority at national, state, and local levels alike—though the complex U.S. policy system makes change difficult to achieve.*

In this chapter, you will:

● Trace the five stages of public policymaking.

● Review the history of U.S. social policy, with special attention to "entitlement" programs.

● Assess what counts as good policy, including claims for both fairness and economic efficiency.

● Discuss the privatization of public services and programs.

● Learn how the federal budget process drives much of our domestic policymaking.

● Consider how U.S. policymaking could be reformed.

521

All the actors introduced in this book—interest groups, Congress, the media, executive branch officials, the courts, and more—come together to make public policy. Here we will look at domestic policymaking, rather than foreign policy, which is the subject of Chapter 18. We will see how government officials craft public policies, with special emphasis on budgeting. In an age of shrinking monetary resources, it is impossible to discuss a policy proposal without attention to its costs.

Public Policymaking in Five (Not-So-Easy) Stages

Policies often take the form of laws, but they can also be regulations, presidential executive orders, funding formulas (determining who gets how much), established norms, or action plans. Think of an issue you care about: clean drinking water, infant mortality, or protection against terrorist acts. All of these, as with every political issue addressed by government officials, play out through public policymaking—whether in controlling waterborne pollutants, encouraging prenatal care and mandating safe infant delivery rooms, or devising effective anti-terrorism efforts.

Recall the seven basic American political ideas we explored in Chapter 2. For example, consider *limited government* or *self-rule*: both are at stake whenever we launch new domestic programs that expand federal government authority. At the same time, Americans' sense of *equality* is embedded in a whole range of policies, from affirmative action to welfare rules requiring recipients to find work within a certain time period.

Making domestic policy is an elaborate process, involving five stages. Figure 17.1 displays these stages graphically. We organize our trip through the public policy system by exploring each of these in turn.

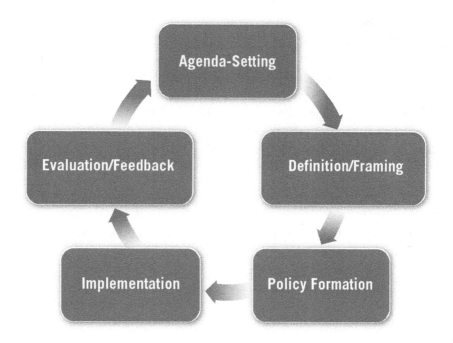

● **FIGURE 17.1** *The five stages of domestic policymaking.*

U.S. Public Policy

Number of policy proposals (congressional bills and resolutions) introduced,
114th Congress (January 2015–October 2016): **10,637**
Number of laws passed, 114th Congress (through November 2016): **244**
Number of laws passed, 110th Congress (January 2007–January 2009): **460**
Number of laws passed, 80th Congress (January 1947–January 1949) labeled the
"Do-Nothing Congress" by President Truman: **906**

Average number of new federal regulations introduced each year, 2010–2016: **3,550**
Total number of federal agencies, departments, and boards engaged in rule-making,
2016: **271**
Percentage of proposed federal rules required by the OMB to include a cost-benefit
analysis, 2012–2015: **94**

Number of the last thirteen U.S. presidents who gave their policy program a name
(e.g., "New Deal," "Fair Deal," or "Great Society"): **11**
Initial election year of the two presidents who did not (George W. Bush, Barack
Obama): **2000, 2008**
Fiscal year 2017 U.S. federal budget deficit (estimated): **$550 billion**
Spending on Social Security, Medicare, and Medicaid in FY 2016: **$2.049 trillion**
Percentage reduction in the national debt if Congress cut all nondefense discretionary
spending: **3.1**

Number of U.S. schools offering a master's degree in public policy and administration,
1990: **97**
Number offering this degree in 2017: **309**

1. Agenda Setting

Policymaking does not begin in earnest until public officials recognize that something is a problem worthy of government attention. President Obama, arriving in office in 2009, identified nuclear power as a promising "clean" alternative to coal and oil—two finite energy sources that pollute the air when burned. Nuclear power developers began to plan new construction across the United States; they won early encouragement in the form of tax incentives and relaxed regulatory restrictions. Then, in Spring 2011, a **focusing event** changed Americans' minds about nuclear power. A massive tidal wave, the result of an earthquake off the Japanese coast, hit a nuclear plant in Fukushima, Japan. Safety mechanisms failed, part of the plant melted down, and a radioactive leak affected water, land, and air for miles around. The disaster quickly made nuclear plant safety a high-level agenda item for American policymakers. Government support for new nuclear construction disappeared, and regulators' scrutiny sharpened, halting expansion plans.

Focusing events, such as the Fukushima nuclear meltdown, are critical to shaping **policy agendas**. Those agendas are typically the source of fierce competition, because the policy system can emphasize only a few priorities at any given time. As Table 17.1 shows, the policy agenda changes across the years.

Focusing event: A major happening, often of crisis or disaster proportions, that attracts widespread media attention to an issue.

Policy agenda: The issues that the media covers, the public considers important, and politicians address. Setting the agenda is the first step in political action.

TABLE 17.1 Comparison of Top National Agenda Items, Two Years Apart

MOST IMPORTANT PROBLEM FACING THE COUNTRY, SUMMER 2016	PERCENTAGE MENTIONING IN 2016	MOST IMPORTANT PROBLEM FACING THE COUNTRY, SUMMER 2014	PERCENTAGE MENTIONING IN 2014
Economy in general	18	Immigration/illegal aliens	17
Dissatisfaction with government	13	Dissatisfaction with government	16
Unemployment/jobs	8	Economy in general	15
Immigration/illegal aliens	7	Unemployment/jobs	14
Election reform	6	Poor healthcare/high cost of healthcare	8
Race relations/racism	5	Federal budget deficit	6
National security	5	Education	5
Education	5	Ethical/moral decline	4
Ethical/moral decline	5	Poverty/hunger/homelessness	3
Budget deficit	5	Judicial system/courts/laws	3
Terrorism	4	Foreign aid/focus overseas	3
Source: Gallup			

Policy agendas are difficult to pin down with any precision at a particular moment, as issues surge suddenly into Americans' collective consciousness . . . and often fade away just as swiftly. This process has only sped up in our social media age. Fueled by millions of tweets and posts on Facebook and Instagram, panic over the mosquito-borne Zika virus reached a peak in 2016. Athletes including the world's top-ranked golfer, Jason Day, even skipped the Rio Olympics, citing Zika fears. Policymakers leapt into action, commissioning studies and debating the proper government response. Once an issue hits the agenda, debates erupt about how to describe the topic—moving us to the next stage.

2. Framing

In translating agenda items into proposed policy solutions, questions arise. What are the root causes of the problem? How bad a problem *is* this? How should public officials respond, if at all? Most agenda issues involve framing questions like these (which we discussed in Chapter 9); the answers are far from obvious, and they can differ greatly depending on who is making the argument.

Let us consider an example from education policy. Every three years, a representative sample of 15-year-olds from around the world sits for exams in reading, math, and science. When the latest results were released, in winter 2016–2017, American secondary school students finished well behind their counterparts from many other advanced countries. Poor school performance dominated local and national conversations. Parents, teachers, and businesses anxious to hire well-trained employees in a globally competitive market all agreed: Scores had to improve.

That goal merely placed the issue on the agenda. Then disputes about defining, or framing, the problem began. Was it that American kids were poorly prepared for the tests, compared to children in other countries? Or that many U.S. classrooms were overcrowded, with too few teachers to provide pupils with personalized instruction? Were officials in the Department of Education better positioned to address the problem of mediocre test scores, or should solutions come from the local level, where children attend school?

On and on the discussion rages—retracing familiar paths. Federal officials had no formal say in education policy until the mid-1960s, when Congress established an extensive program of national funding through the Elementary and Secondary Education Act. The U.S. Department of Education was created later still, in 1979. Champions of local control of education have fought to limit federal activity ever since. In the 2016 presidential primary, several Republican candidates insisted that the Department of Education was a big part of the problem. To them, it had to be

● *Focusing event: a tragic accident in Japan. The nuclear plant in Fukushima, Japan, burns after a partial meltdown following a giant tsunami. The tragedy caused U.S. public approval for nuclear power to plummet, affecting plans to expand American nuclear energy production.*

restructured—or shut down altogether. Progressives and moderate Democrats instead insisted that national education officials had to step in to reduce inequities in school financing, so that the richest districts in a state, which are able to provide more resources, do not leave schoolchildren in lower-income areas far behind.

Should education—or, for that matter, any public problem—be addressed on a national or local level? Would progressive solutions reduce inequity or merely amount to federal government "meddling"? Do conservative solutions address inadequate instruction due, some insist, to unionized teachers allowed to remain in classrooms despite poor results or are they an unjustified assault on public schools? These different ways of "framing" issues, also called problem definition, have big consequences: They help determine which policy responses the government considers. As issues are framed and reframed, policy actors translate their preferred solutions into law, propelling policymaking to a third stage.

3. Policy Formation

After a problem reaches the policy agenda and the framing debate settles into one or two primary definitions, proposed solutions must be evaluated—and adopted or discarded. This process of policy formation is again a sprawling, complicated one. Members of Congress and often state and local legislators engage in the myriad activities you studied in Chapter 13: drafting bills, holding hearings, and hammering out compromises in committee meetings and floor debates. Executive branch experts weigh in, all the way up to the president if the issue is sufficiently high profile. Advocacy groups and industry lobbyists swarm around lawmakers; judicial rulings reshape the policy debate; and media experts opine through print, broadcast, the blogosphere, and Twitter.

Analyzing Policy, Ex Ante. Competing ideas, rhetorical displays, deft procedural moves, power plays: These features underpin policy formation in every society, as they have for hundreds of years. Recently, more technical work also has become vital to policy success. Policy analysis involves constructing scientific measures of a proposed policy's costs and benefits *ex ante*—before it passes and goes into effect.

STAHLER.
1997

AND THE LITTLE PIG WITH THE HIGHER MATH & VERBAL LIVED HAPPILY EVER AFTER. THE OTHER TWO WERE SWALLOWED UP BY THE WOLF.

● *Educational reform: the lighter side. Programs such as Head Start, No Child Left Behind, and Race to the Top respond to education policymakers' worries about U.S. students' performance, which can be exaggerated, as captured in this humorous cartoon.*

Cost effectiveness: The projected costs of a proposed policy, as revealed by a relatively simple study.

Cost-benefit analysis: A more complex study of the projected costs and benefits associated with a proposed policy.

Such assessment efforts are a central feature of contemporary policymaking in the United States and other advanced industrial nations.

A relatively straightforward approach to analyzing a proposed policy involves studies of **cost effectiveness**. In such studies, analysts compare several policy alternatives that deliver the same overall benefit to determine which one does so at the *lowest cost*. Imagine that a local government decides to repaint the town hall. Different painting companies bid for the job. Presumably they all provide the same basic service, perhaps with minor differences in paint color or warranty. City officials can compare these similar vendors based on proposed costs and ask which provides the most cost-effective service.

Not many policy decisions are that straightforward, however, especially when they reach the national agenda. In 2016, with gas prices at historic lows, President Obama and some Democratic members of Congress recommended a hike in the federal gasoline tax, both to pay for highway maintenance and to reduce Americans' oil consumption. For a quarter-century, the national gas tax has remained at 18.4 cents per gallon, after slowly rising over the preceding sixty years from a penny per gallon. To illuminate the likely effects of this policy shift—and to help estimate the range of an ideal tax increase—experts performed a **cost-benefit analysis**. This elaborate form of *ex ante* evaluation is carried out by trained analysts, some of them working in government and others in academia, lobbying firms, or think tanks.

The first step in a cost-benefit analysis is to list all the expected costs of a policy proposal, as well as all the expected benefits. For the gas tax, researchers identified two primary categories of cost and five main areas of benefit. The results are summarized in Table 17.2.

Researchers then "monetize," or assign dollar values to, these costs and benefits, using elaborate mathematical formulas. In the gas tax example, combining several policy analysis models for simplicity's sake, estimates were that the *costs* of a higher tax would average seventy-five cents per gallon: fifty-two cents for the increased price of services (such as higher costs of goods transported by truck) and twenty-three cents in direct costs to drivers. That is a pretty steep cost for each gallon of gas, but the predicted *benefits* were considerably higher. Adding together the estimated savings yielded a $1.76 benefit per gallon, as Table 17.3 shows.

TABLE 17.2 **Gas Tax Costs/Benefits**

GAS TAX COSTS
Direct cost of the tax to drivers (those in rural areas, and with lower incomes, would be hardest hit).
Higher price of services dependent on transportation, such as shipping goods by truck.
GAS TAX BENEFITS
Reduced urban air pollution (thereby improving public health).
Reduced CO_2 emissions (slowing the pace of climate change).
Reduced U.S. dependence on imported oil.
Diminished traffic congestion (saving drivers time).
Reduced traffic accidents (because people drive less or switch to mass transit).

TABLE 17.3 **Cost-Benefit Valuation of a Proposed Gas Tax**

COSTS OF GAS TAX	VALUE*	BENEFITS OF GAS TAX	VALUE*
Direct cost to drivers	$0.23	Public health (reduced air pollution)	$0.40
Transportation services	$0.52	Climate (reduced CO_2 emissions)	$0.11
		Reduced oil imports	$0.12
		Time saved (less traffic)	$0.58
		Reduced accidents	$0.55
TOTAL	**$0.75**		**$1.76**

*Values are estimated per gallon of gas.
Source: Authors' calculation, combining several existing models.

Thus, according to the cost-benefit analysis, national gas taxes could be raised by just over a dollar per gallon ($1.76 in benefits, minus the 75-cent cost). From the perspective of economic effectiveness, society would be better off as a whole. One more beneficiary, if the tax passed, would be the federal treasury, which could apply new tax dollars to transportation funding or reducing the national budget deficit.

From Cost-Benefit Analysis to Politics.   Cost-benefit and other ex ante evaluations are widely used in policymaking, with significant impacts on both legislative votes and judicial decisions. These analyses alone, however, do not determine policy.

The Obama Administration's 2016 proposal to impose a $10 tax on every barrel of oil, which would have raised the gas tax by an estimated twenty to twenty-two cents per gallon, was greeted with headlines such as "Republicans Savage Obama's Oil Tax Plan."[1] Turning more cautious in response, some congressional Democrats proposed a phased-in gas tax increase, rising incrementally from 18.4 cents to thirty-two cents per gallon by 2020. As the national election approached, however, Democrats, fearing the electoral penalty of any tax increase they advocated, quietly abandoned the plan. Political considerations can trump even a clearly positive policy analysis.

Policy window: A figurative description of the opportunity—often brief, measured in days or weeks rather than years—to pass a bill in Congress or a state legislature.

If the swirling legislative and executive branch preferences align just right, and the cost-benefit analysis comes out positive, a figurative **policy window** opens.[2] Might a new policy be launched? There is no guarantee of success, especially at the national level. Of the several thousand bills and measures introduced in Congress each year, only two hundred or so make it into the statute books. Policy windows rarely stay open for long. But determined advocates who are organized and savvy about the rules of the policy game can navigate this formation stage and achieve success.

4. Policy Implementation

When a new law does make it onto the books, policymaking passes to the implementation stage. As you read in Chapter 15's discussion of the bureaucracy in action, this process is not as visible or as well understood. During policy formation, televised congressional hearings, White House speeches urging action, and cliffhanger House and Senate floor votes keep the attentive public engaged. Afterward, however, the glare of media attention dims. The implementation of national policies is primarily handled by the executive bureaucracy, which labors mostly out of public view. Does this shift in visibility mean that the work of policy implementation is less politicized? Many American political thinkers and actors have thought so, dating back at least to Woodrow Wilson, who as a political scientist in 1887 described bureaucratic activity as "a technical science." Wilson insisted that "administrative questions are not political questions."[3]

As Wilson learned on becoming president thirty years later, implementing public policy is in fact a highly political event. Implementation involves two main steps: working out the specifics of the law, primarily through the rule-making process introduced in Chapter 15, and then delivering the government services or enforcing the new regulations. Both these steps attract intense interest—and, inevitably, political fighting—from the communities most affected by the policy change.

Rule-Making Revisited.   Once a law passes and the bureaucracy gets to work, politics is still front and center in this more obscure rule-making phase. As you will recall from Chapter 15, each aspect of a new law requires a separate rule, and each rule is spelled out in painstaking detail. For example, one part of the Affordable Care Act mandates that dependents up to age twenty-six remain eligible for health insurance through their parents; the previous cutoff age was eighteen or twenty-one for students enrolled in college. In the ACA as written by Congress, this requirement was spelled out in only a couple of sentences. However, the Department of Health and Human Services rule specifying details—who was eligible, under what circumstances, penalties for violation, and so forth—ran to more than twenty-five single-spaced, tiny-print pages in the *Federal Register*.[4] Each of these rules can impact the cost-benefit analysis of the policy in the long run (see Figure 17.2).

With such room for maneuvering, complaints abound about politicization by the bureaucracy. Agencies hurry rules along too quickly to permit proper review by interested parties, some critics charge. These critics include Supreme Court Chief Justice John Roberts, who expressed concern in a 2012 case about a rule that was completed in twenty-two days—warp speed in a rule-making process that can take more than a year to finish.[5] Others take exception to what they term "politicized

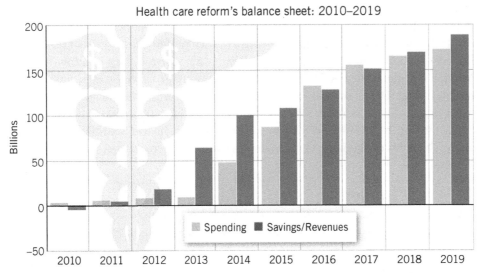

Health care reform's balance sheet: 2010–2019

● **FIGURE 17.2** *Cost-benefit (spending/revenues) calculation for "Obamacare." (Congressional Budget Office)*

science." In 2014, House Republicans introduced a bill criticizing the Environmental Protection Agency for "crippling" the rule-making process by using "secret science" to promote robust environmental regulations. The bill would require the EPA to hire independent scientists to reproduce results from peer-reviewed academic articles before citing research for rule-making—an expensive and time-consuming process. The bill passed the House in March 2015, but languished throughout 2016 in the Senate, partly given the threat of a presidential veto.[6]

Remember this key lesson from our discussion of public policy implementation. As with all steps in the policy process, rule-making involves politics alongside the technical details.

Top-Down Delivery.   Once the final rule setting out a policy's details has been reviewed and published, it is time to provide the benefits or regulations that the law was designed to produce. As the American national government stepped up its level of domestic policy activity following World War II, delivery of public services was established as a "top-down" process. Confident in the wake of victory, American and British architects of the new science of public policy proclaimed that the executive branch, working from clear goals and strategies, could deliver government services in a coherent, transparent manner. They saw cabinet secretaries and agency heads as firmly in charge of the process. Lower-level bureaucrats and "policy clients" (the people government was serving) were mainly concerned with *compliance*, or doing what they were told to do.

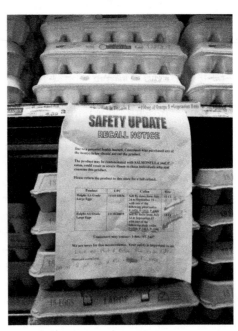

● *Tainted food and top-down policy response. When the Food and Drug Administration receives reports about possible dangerous tainted food products, the agency, along with the Department of Agriculture, spearheads a national top-down response.*

Many policy planners still promote this top-down model of delivering government benefits and services. It can work when a policy is relatively simple, with clear, well-specified goals that are not difficult to meet. Imagine a national ban on sales of a food product found to be tainted by potentially fatal bacteria, for example. A high-ranking figure, such as the secretary of agriculture or the head of the Food and Drug Administration, issues a public warning. Government inspectors then ensure that the dangerous product is removed from grocery shelves, law enforcement officials investigate the cause of the outbreak, and prosecutions may follow. The public's role is simple: avoid the tainted product. The policy aim is clear, as are the lines of authority.

As you know well by now, the world of politics and policymaking is rarely so predictable or straightforward. Most issues involve many interested actors, leading to struggles over jurisdiction. Five different House and Senate committees, in addition to a proposed conference committee, worked to get the Affordable Care Act passed. Policy goals can be ambiguous or confusing, slowing executive bureaucrats' ability to enact new regulations or hand out services. Our federalist system, described in Chapter 4, does not help matters by creating multiple levels of jurisdiction. Authorities are frequently stymied in their attempts to police pot growers, for example, given all the conflicting local, state, and federal regulations governing medicinal marijuana—especially with several states and Washington, DC, now permitting limited legal marijuana sales (see Figure 17.3).[7]

Bottom-Up Delivery. For complicated policies, "bottom-up" provisions of public services or regulations can be more effective than top-down efforts to command and control outcomes. Bottom-up service delivery starts with street-level bureaucrats, a group introduced in Chapter 15; recall that these officials work directly with recipients of government benefits. Examples include the social worker who calls on needy families to make sure their food stamps have arrived, the IRS agent who checks to confirm that your charitable claims are all legitimate donations, and the air-traffic controller who brings your flight in for a safe landing.

All these policy providers and regulators work directly with the public, and they can exercise discretion in making decisions. Certainly a hierarchy is still in place, with cabinet secretaries and agency heads at the top. But when street-level officials are allowed a measure of autonomy, or at least some input into decision making, government services are often delivered more efficiently and regulations are put in place with less disruption. Sometimes, these street-level actors may even ignore superiors' orders and do what they consider best, based on their experience.

Should we consider this autonomy to be democracy in action—or bureaucracy run amok? Think of residence advisors (RAs) in college and university dormitories. Although administrators like vice presidents and deans set official policies for dorm residents, RAs—who are usually students themselves—are directly aware of the needs and concerns of residents on their hall or floor. Academic studies have chronicled how these "street-level" RAs bring their personal experience and knowledge of individual students to improving the implementation of residence-hall rules and benefits.[8] Sometimes this may mean bending university regulations to make sure the residents' needs are served; occasionally, those rules are later revised as a result of an RA's timely suggestion. The same thing happens across the federal bureaucracy: Street-level employees who are directly aware of a policy's effects may change their practices to make sure a program performs effectively.

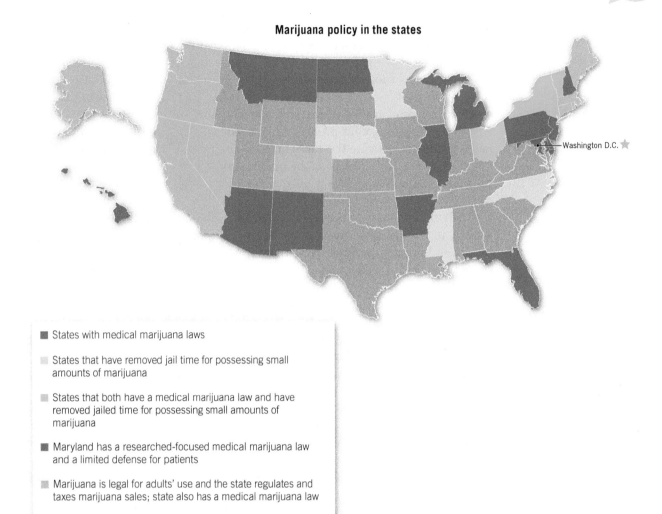

Marijuana policy in the states

■ States with medical marijuana laws

▨ States that have removed jail time for possessing small amounts of marijuana

▨ States that both have a medical marijuana law and have removed jailed time for possessing small amounts of marijuana

■ Maryland has a researched-focused medical marijuana law and a limited defense for patients

▨ Marijuana is legal for adults' use and the state regulates and taxes marijuana sales; state also has a medical marijuana law

● **FIGURE 17.3** *Marijuana policy in the states. A series of conflicting legal and legislative decisions on medicinal marijuana illustrate the complexity of policy implementation. (attn)*

5. Policy Evaluation and Feedback

Let us imagine that a policy problem has made it onto the agenda and been framed successfully. A solution has been formulated, passed into law, and implemented: The new service is being delivered or the new regulation put in place. Do these accomplishments mean our policymaking story has ended? Not at all. It is still essential to confirm whether a new benefit or regulation actually works.

This is the stage of policy evaluation. Does a school-lunch program need tweaking in practice because its benefits are not reaching many kids? Should we abandon an ineffective government effort to reduce tax fraud and try something else? Nearly every policy of significance, once adopted, "feeds back" into the policy process, shaping future public agendas. Sometimes that feedback process creates new policy problems in turn. In short, policymaking never really ends.

Policymaking proceeds in a context of uncertainty: even armed with *ex ante* analyses, no one can be sure how a policy will play out in practice. Therefore, it is essential to evaluate programs after implementation, or *ex post*, to determine how well they are working and make adjustments. The outcome may include devising yet another new policy to address changes rippling out from one recently put in place.

***Ex Post* Policy Evaluations.**   Ideally, evaluators would check every new government benefit or regulation, once in place, to see how well it works. Because of resource constraints, that usually does not happen, but many policies are subjected to at least occasional *ex post* evaluations. These tend to follow a prescribed sequence. An evaluator compares a policy program to the original goals that Congress and executive branch rule-makers had in mind, according to an established set of criteria. The evaluator could be a government agency, an academic or think tank analyst, an interest group, a court-appointed independent authority, or sometimes all of these, as prominent programs often attract multiple evaluations. The evaluator collects and assesses relevant information, using data if available; makes a judgment about program effectiveness; and issues recommendations.[9]

Do these steps add up to a reasonably objective effort, in your view? If a policy is performing more or less in line with its designers' goals, it should be left alone. If not, a good *ex post* evaluation will point out places where the policy could be tweaked to improve performance. But rarely is policymaking that straightforward.

When a law is initially introduced, advocates fight hard to frame the policy change positively, advance it through Congress, and win the president's signature. Many of them remain engaged during the rule-making process to make sure it is rolled out as they expected. Now imagine an *ex post* evaluation that suggests the policy is not working well. These supporters probably will not agree that all their energy was misspent. Instead, they may criticize the evaluation for flawed methodology and commission a competing evaluation. Likewise, in the face of a positive evaluation, the opposition—which fought against the new policy all the way from framing to rule-making—rarely gives up and admits that its criticisms were wrong.

A Case in Point: Gang Violence.   The apparently simple evaluator's question—Does the policy work?—is not often answered in a clear, unambiguous way. Take the issue of reducing youth gang violence. Some policymakers have argued for years that a "fight fire with fire" approach is the only sound one: boost police presence, including intrusive stop-and-frisk policies; toughen the penalties for youthful gang involvement; and treat even a first conviction with a long sentence, in harsh prison conditions.

A few years ago, a different idea surfaced in the form of a program called Ceasefire (since renamed "Cure Violence"). The brainchild of David Kennedy, a criminal justice professor, Cure Violence organized "call-ins"—meetings that brought together suspected young gang members with community leaders, ex-gang offenders, religious figures, prosecutors, and police. Organizers offered the youth in attendance counseling, job leads, and an opportunity to talk frankly without fear of reprisal. At the same time, the youth were warned that any hint of violent activity in the future would result in widespread arrests. Not only the offenders but their network of associates would be hauled into court as well.[10]

Cure Violence has been implemented in dozens of cities, both large ones such as Boston,

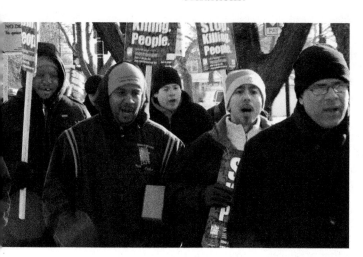

● *One approach to gang violence: Cure Violence, initially a controversial policy that was widely adopted after ex post evaluations demonstrated some success. Scientific evaluations of the program continue.*

Massachusetts, and Chicago, Illinois, and smaller places like High Point, North Carolina, and Erie, Pennsylvania. Evaluators have reached mixed conclusions about how well Cure Violence works. By some measures, such as incidents of violent crime during the first few weeks after implementation, Cure Violence appears preferable to tough police tactics. By other measurements, however, the program seems to have made little difference. Rates of youth unemployment in some neighborhoods have hardly changed, nor have longer-term trends in violent crime. Faced with mixed messages, should a mayor invest in Cure Violence in response to the spread of youth gangs? Policy evaluation, like much else in U.S. policymaking, is as much an art as a science.

Policy Feedback.   New policies, once implemented, do not just play out in a vacuum. They in turn shape and constrain future policymaking, as a growing body of political science research shows. Scholars term this process "policy feedback."

A program that distributes benefits will attract loyal supporters who will push for its extension. Lawmakers seeking to reform or cancel the program (perhaps based on an ex post evaluation) can find their efforts thwarted by these grateful recipients. More subtly, as a policy is rolled out, actors of various types will adapt to the policy, making it difficult to change. Bureaucrats get organized to administer a benefit; businesses rework their economic forecasts to account for a new regulatory framework. Political scientist Paul Pierson described these tendencies as **path dependence**: Once a policy is established, possibilities for reform or change are constrained by the "path" it has followed through implementation and service delivery.[11]

Path dependence: The tendency of policymakers to follow established routines in thinking about or acting on a specific topic.

A classic example of a policy with powerful feedback effects is Social Security, passed in 1935. By introducing a language of "entitlement," the designers of Social Security achieved far-reaching effects. Senior citizens feel that they have earned their right to receive old-age government benefits. Millions of Americans to this day organize their investment decisions and retirement planning around the path created by Social Security. This view makes it virtually untouchable by policymakers.

THE BOTTOM LINE

» U.S. policymaking may be described in terms of five stages. Policies do not proceed neatly from one to the next, but the "stages" idea is a useful way of distinguishing among different actions carried out by policy officials.

» The first of these stages is agenda setting, whereby concerns receiving widespread attention become policy issues.

» A second stage is problem definition and framing, featuring debates about how to describe an issue and which solutions are most viable.

» A third stage is policy formation, a process of legislative and executive activity to develop the policy idea in concrete terms.

» A fourth stage is policy implementation, marked by rule-making and service delivery.

» A fifth stage includes evaluation and policy feedback, steps that help determine whether a policy works—and that often start the debate all over again.

🔋 U.S. Social Policy

Public policy comes in many forms, as the various examples earlier in this chapter attest. *Fiscal policy* has to do with matters of finance, such as monetary supply and taxes; we address fiscal matters later in this chapter when we look at federal budgeting. *Foreign policy* covers topics including wars, defense, diplomacy, and trade agreements; we devote Chapter 18 to those. Most other issues are grouped together as *social policy*, or matters having to do with people's individual or group well-being. Health, housing, education, employment, criminal justice, child welfare, and old-age security: all these vital areas make up social policy. Also under this heading are controversial topics such as abortion, same-sex marriage, and recreational drug use.

Compared to industrialized Western European countries, the United States was slow to adopt modern social policies at a national level. Old-age insurance, for example, was provided in Germany as far back as 1883 and in Great Britain in 1911. Yet not until the mid-1930s and Franklin Roosevelt's New Deal was a similar policy (Social Security) established here. Many advanced democracies enacted universal health insurance starting in the 1880s; the United States still does not guarantee healthcare to all its citizens. Americans' embrace of self-help individualist doctrines and its long-standing resistance to "big government," along with a federalist structure that provides a patchwork of benefits through state and local officials, helps explain the distinctive (and slow) growth of social policymaking in the United States.

From colonial days onward, "poor relief" offered support for needy Americans, inspired by both religious tenets and laws inherited from Elizabethan England. Benefits were limited, however—and came with a price. People on relief sometimes faced the loss of their personal property and the right to vote. The able-bodied unemployed were often forced to work or were jailed, although laws varied from state to state. Even with all these conditions, until the Civil War, poor relief was the largest single budget item in most American towns and cities.[12] And the term was still used well into the twentieth century, especially during the Great Depression.

Wars and Social Policy

Wars and their aftermath were the source of most major social policy advances during the first century and a half after the Constitution was ratified. The Revolutionary War gave rise to the earliest state-level efforts to administer organized benefits. In New York, for example, a "Committee on Superintendence of the Poor" was created to aid people who lost their homes during the fighting. After the Civil War, national government benefits flowed at unprecedented levels to soldiers and their families. The first old-age pensions were provided to Union Army veterans during the late nineteenth century. Their mothers, widows, and children later received some state support, including monthly welfare payments and regulations on child labor—the sons and daughters of soldiers who died in combat should not be forced to work, the argument went.

A more recent instance of a policy that grew out of wartime is the GI Bill, passed in 1944 to reward American troops returning from World War II with a heavily subsidized college education. The bill's designers expected that soldiers would benefit personally from attending college; a secondary hope was that U.S. labor markets would be able to adjust slowly to millions of newly returned soldiers as universities absorbed many of the veterans.

What policymakers did not expect is that American higher education would be transformed by the GI Bill, as colleges and universities expanded to meet the needs of 4.4 million soldiers turned students—many of them with fewer family resources than the traditionally better-off young men and women who attended U.S. colleges before 1945. Moreover, many GI Bill beneficiaries, political scientist Suzanne Mettler demonstrated, went on to become unusually civic-minded Americans.[13] College attendance continued to grow in subsequent years, aided by a host of new government programs (policy feedback again!) stretching from Pell Grants and low-interest student loans, both established in the 1960s, to the American Opportunity Tax Credit, passed in 2010 and recently extended to 2018.

War's domestic equivalent is grave economic hardship, and the Great Depression, starting in 1929, helped lead to more extensive federal social policies, many arising from Franklin Roosevelt's New Deal. Among the numerous social programs run or financed by the U.S. government today, three of the longest lived and most extensive deserve attention here.

● During the Great Depression new federal social policies were created at a rapid clip. Traditional policies, such as "poor relief," were expanded as well in response to social need.

Old-Age Insurance: Social Security

Since its enactment in 1935, Social Security has provided Americans aged sixty-five and older—provided they have lived in the United States at least five years—with a monthly living stipend. The minimum age was recently raised to sixty-six, and Congress has discussed increasing it by another year or two. Social Security payments vary with income: A worker who retires making $65,000 a year would currently receive around $1,630 per month. The original act also created an unemployment insurance program (more on that later), paid benefits to disabled workers and their families, and offered financial assistance to low-income families with children. Today, as in the original act, financing comes from a payroll tax on all eligible workers.

The Social Security Act initially excluded a wide range of occupations from the program, primarily limiting benefits (and payroll-tax contributions) to white males. In subsequent years, such jobs as teachers, nurses, domestic helpers, librarians, and agricultural laborers were added to the act's coverage, effectively creating the first universal social policy in American history. Although the program began small—with only fifty-three thousand beneficiaries in 1937, the first full year of implementation, who together received a little over $1.2 million in benefits—it grew rapidly. In 2016, Social Security paid some $891 billion to more than sixty-five million workers, supported by payroll taxes from more than 143 million employees. At nearly 5 percent of the nation's **gross domestic product (GDP)**, Social Security is the largest single federal government program.

Gross domestic product (GDP): The value of all the goods and services produced in a nation over a year.

Although the old-age benefits provided by Social Security have helped lift many seniors out of poverty, for decades alarms have been sounded about financially supporting the program. Those concerns grow more urgent today, as the huge baby boomer generation increasingly receives benefits. A major debate turns on the gravity of the problem. Many moderates and conservatives argue that Social Security poses a dangerous economic risk as it moves inexorably toward a one trillion dollar annual cost. Many liberals accuse conservatives of exaggerating the threat

Ida May Fuller, the first recipient (in 1940) of a monthly Social Security check for $22.54.

and argue that relatively small adjustments (increasing the retirement age, raising taxes, limiting benefits) will fix the problem. Once again: a debate over problem definition. However serious the problem, the system is extremely difficult to reform and changes are routinely rejected. Social Security's sacrosanct status has given rise to a colorful metaphor borrowed from electrified train lines: Touch the "third rail" surging with electricity, say railroad workers, and you will receive a fatal shock. Likewise, politicians refer to Social Security as the "third rail of American politics": Propose major changes, and electoral penalties will swiftly follow.

Unemployment Benefits

As the Great Depression stretched into the 1930s, some thirty-four million Americans (more than a quarter of the 122 million population) lived in households with no full-time wage earner. Across the United States, unemployment rates reached shocking levels, topping out at 80 percent of able-bodied adults in Toledo, Ohio. In 1932, Wisconsin became the first state to provide cash assistance to temporarily jobless residents. Three years later, the Social Security Act included a provision for joint federal–state unemployment benefits, funded like old-age insurance through a payroll tax on employees. States administer the program, with federal oversight and funding assistance.

During the recent major recession, unemployment levels rose from less than 4 percent in 2008 to above 10 percent in 2009. A federal supplement to laid-off workers extended eligibility for unemployment benefits to ninety-nine weeks, up from the twenty-six weeks that most states provide. Costs soared accordingly, and Republicans sought to scale back the extra federal assistance. With unemployment rates dropping only slowly, job creation—and the cost of benefits for unemployed workers—was a central issue in the 2010 and 2012 elections. By 2016, unemployment had dropped below 5 percent, and issues such as the minimum wage and salary debates (as you saw at this chapter's opening) moved up the policy agenda.

Health and Disability: Medicare/Medicaid

In the early 1960s, America ranked as the wealthiest nation in the world, but barely half of the nation's seniors had health insurance. Even with Social Security, an estimated third of those over sixty-five lived in poverty, in significant part because of the cost of healthcare.

Lyndon Johnson, fresh from a landslide election victory in 1964, promoted health insurance coverage for all Americans over sixty-five as part of his Great Society plan. Critics fought hard against the proposed new social benefit. Johnson's Republican opponent in that election, Arizona senator Barry Goldwater, tapped into a long-lived American vein of disapproval for handouts: "Having given our pensioners their medical care in kind, why not food baskets, why not public housing

Should We Reform Social Security and Medicare?

Social Security and Medicare are perhaps the two most fiercely defended U.S. government programs. Any hint of a cut in either and senior citizens respond vehemently, as do the House and Senate members who represent them. Are you braver than most American elected officials? Are you willing to tackle cutting Social Security and Medicare (and, while you are at it, Medicaid)?

Yes, reform the Social Security and Medicare programs. The budget savings of even minor adjustments—such as raising the eligibility age—would be immense.

No, leave Social Security and Medicare intact. The political fallout would certainly be enormous, but so would the impact on the lives of seniors. Suggesting such reforms could also have long-term political consequences because the opposing party would sound the alarm immediately.

Unsure. To better understand the situation, think through the reasons that seniors (e.g., your grandparents or other people aged sixty-five and older you may know) would be upset to have the rules of the game changed, given that they have come to expect health coverage and an old-age pension. Can you think of any ways to salvage these programs with fewer consequences for older Americans?

accommodations, why not vacation resorts, why not a ration of cigarettes for those who smoke and of beer for those who drink?"[14]

After some fancy footwork in Congress, Medicare was passed in 1965 as an amendment to the Social Security Act. As with old-age and unemployment benefits, Medicare was financed through a payroll tax on all employees. And as with Social Security, the program grew rapidly after it was implemented in 1966. Today, some fifty-three million Americans receive Medicare benefits; by the late 2020s, the program is expected to serve nearly eighty million people, as the last of the baby boomer generation (born between 1945 and 1964) retire. The program's costs currently exceed $550 billion each year and are projected to grow to more than $1 trillion over the next decade.

Paying this giant tab became more difficult after 2006, when a new congressionally authorized prescription-drug benefit for seniors went into effect. Rising healthcare costs put constant pressure on this popular program.

As the battle over Medicare raged in 1965, a companion measure to provide health insurance to disabled and low-income people, dubbed "Medicaid," was quietly passed. Each state was encouraged (but not required) to establish a Medicaid program of its own; Arizona was the last state to sign on, in 1982. Over time, a variety of additional benefits were added to Medicaid, including dental and nursing home coverage.

Distinctive among these large American entitlement programs, Medicaid was established as a "means-tested" program, with benefits provided only to those below a certain income level—which varies by state. In Texas, the ceiling in 2016 was $4,374 for a family of four while in Connecticut it was $47,628. The Affordable Care Act initially included a requirement that all states provide Medicaid funding to everyone whose income is below 133 percent of the **federal poverty line** (around $32,000 for a family of four). The Supreme Court's historic 2012 decision to uphold the ACA as constitutional, described in Chapter 16, also repudiated the universal

Federal poverty line: The annually specified level of income (separately calculated for individuals and families) below which people are considered to live in poverty, becoming eligible for certain federal benefits. In 2016, the poverty line was set at $24,300 for a family of four.

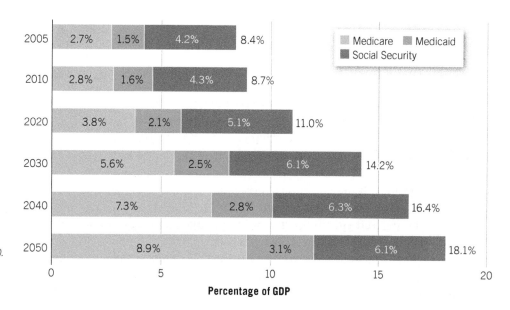

FIGURE 17.4 *Spending on the three big entitlement programs totals a little under 9 percent of U.S. gross domestic product (GDP). That figure is projected to double over the next thirty-plus years. (Congressional Budget Office)*

Medicaid funding requirement. Instead, each state is allowed to decide whether it will adopt the 133 percent standard.

Like Social Security and Medicare, Medicaid has grown rapidly, both in the number of people it serves and the associated expense. During its early years, only a few thousand beneficiaries sought Medicaid assistance for their healthcare. By 2016, more than fifty-six million people were enrolled in Medicaid, covering approximately five million people who were without coverage before the Affordable Care Act passed.

Figure 17.4 displays projected costs for Social Security, Medicaid, and Medicare in the years ahead, measured as a percentage of the expected U.S. GDP. Taken together, these **entitlement programs** will require some very tough choices about spending on other programs and about increasing tax rates to raise the revenue required to fund them.

Policymakers throughout Washington and the nation's universities and think tanks devote years of study to these giant social programs, raising various possibilities for "bending the cost curve"—in other words, reducing their drain on the federal budget. On the plus side, the growth of American social policies has greatly reduced the number of people—especially seniors and children, arguably our most vulnerable citizens—living in dire need. Balancing those needs against the budget-busting consequences of continued program growth is among the most important policy challenges facing the country in coming years.

Entitlement program:
A government benefit program whose recipients are *entitled* by law to receive payments. Social Security, Medicare, and Medicaid are the three largest.

THE BOTTOM LINE

» Social policymaking in the United States is typically more controversial, and features less expansive coverage, than social policymaking in other advanced industrial nations.

» Wars, along with severe economic downturns, have been major sources of expansions in American social policies across U.S. history.

» Three large social programs—old-age insurance, or Social Security; unemployment insurance; and health/disability benefits, or Medicare and Medicaid—are especially significant in U.S. politics and government.

Economic Policymaking: Fiscal and Monetary Policy

People judge their governments first and foremost on their economic performance. Despite scandalous affairs as well as domestic and foreign-policy disappointments, Bill Clinton's presidency is widely considered a success: economy roared ahead during his time in office. On the other hand, Clinton's predecessor, George H. W. Bush, enjoyed the highest popularity rating in modern history after the Gulf War (1990–1991). Barely a year later, a severe economic downturn battered Bush's public opinion ratings and left him a one-term president.

Economic policy is carried out in two primary ways. Government decisions about taxing and spending—generally managed through the budget process described in the following sections—is termed **fiscal policy**. Managing the economy through central banks' control of the money supply, directly affecting unemployment and inflation rates, is known as **monetary policy**. Let us look at each in turn.

Fiscal policy: Taxing and spending policies carried out by government, generally in an effort to affect national economic development.

Fiscal Policy

Well into the twentieth century, the U.S. government's fiscal policy can best be described as "laissez-faire," a French term meaning "leave it alone." Most presidents and congressional leaders sought to balance the (relatively small) federal budget, with limited tax or spending authority. That approach changed during wartime, when military needs drove tax collections and spending (mostly for defense) temporarily much higher.

Monetary policy: Actions of central banks, which in the United States culminate in the Federal Reserve, designed primarily to maximize employment and moderate inflation.

During the Great Depression, national economic devastation led Franklin Roosevelt and his "brain trust" of policy advisors to more actively manage the levers of fiscal policy. Immense New Deal programs were funded through government spending on an unprecedented scale. The resulting budget deficits—federal funds flowing out much faster than tax revenues coming in—reflected a Keynesian approach to national economic policy, named for the influential early twentieth-century British and later American economist John Maynard Keynes. Keynes recommended "pump-priming" during economic downturns: pouring government funds into a faltering economy and cutting taxes, giving consumers and businesses enough confidence (and cash) to start spending and hiring again.

Following close on the Depression came World War II, which resulted in a great spike in government spending. At the height of the war in 1943, the federal deficit reached an all-time high of 30 percent of GDP. After the war, American policymakers, brimming with confidence about their ability to manage the economy, adopted active taxing and spending policies as a routine national practice. Since then, through conservative and liberal presidents and across Democratic and Republican control of Congress, fiscal policy has continued to serve as a means of securing the general welfare of the American public.

The parties do differ on which fiscal levers to pull. Facing an economic downturn, Democrats are more likely to favor expanded spending—hence the large stimulus package passed early in the Obama presidency, designed to rescue the national economy from the brink of disaster. Republicans generally prefer tax cuts, on the argument that the economy benefits as consumers spend more of the windfall.[15]

Though fiscal policymaking may sound straightforward—or even boring, given what can seem like minor technical tweaks to tax or spending levels—few policy

Though rarely recognized in public, Federal Reserve chair Janet Yellen has been a key figure in managing the nation's money supply—a central feature of U.S. fiscal policy.

areas are more controversial in practice. Late in 2015, for example, the nation was riveted by the spectacle of an approaching "fiscal cliff," a failure by Congress and the White House to agree on specific tax cuts and spending reductions that would prevent the United States from paying its debt. The threat of a global economic meltdown loomed as a budget deadline approached. The crisis was averted through congressional compromise, but marked another dramatic political showdown in the realm of fiscal policy.

Monetary Policy

Following the collapse of the venerable Lehman Brothers investment bank in fall 2008, with other giant financial institutions tottering, the U.S. government leapt into action. Surprisingly, the main actors were not presidents or congressional leaders, but more obscure figures: the Federal Reserve chairman, the treasury secretary, and the chair of the Federal Reserve Bank of New York. And the economic tools they applied had nothing to do with increasing (or cutting) taxes or spending: Instead, the conversation was about liquidity and the national money supply.[16]

These experts were deploying monetary policy in response to the gravest financial crisis in seventy-five years. By manipulating the national money supply and interest rates, they aimed to increase employment while holding inflation (the rate at which the price of goods and services rises) in check. Such efforts also can impact expectations about economic performance. Although the White House and Congress are the chief institutional architects of fiscal policy, monetary shifts are carried out by central bankers: In the United States, the main actor is the Federal Reserve System, comprising a headquarters in Washington, DC, along with twelve bank branches around the country. The current Federal Reserve (or "Fed," in Washington-speak) director is Janet Yellen.

Put simply, the Federal Reserve has several tools—such as buying Treasury securities and setting required dollar reserve levels that banks are required to hold. These tools allow the Fed to influence interest rates. The Fed reduces interest rates to stimulate economic growth, making it easier for businesses to borrow money to expand production and hiring or invest in research and development; similarly, individuals can borrow at lower interest rates to buy new homes or consumer goods. If, however, economic demand is growing too fast, the Fed raises interest rates to reduce inflationary pressures that raise prices and result in an economic slowdown.

Think of the Federal Reserve as performing an essential balancing act—enabling growth when the economy balks, but slowing things down to ease inflation as the economy heats up. And during crisis times, the Fed and its monetary policy is often the strongest means of sustaining our national economy.

🜨 Economic Policymaking: The Federal Budget Process

"It's a good policy idea, but we don't have the budget to pursue it." Variations on that phrase have been repeated countless times in Washington in recent years, as American policymaking has become more oriented around the budget. This bottom-line focus owes primarily to the U.S. **federal budget deficit**—the gap between how much our national government spends and how much we take in through taxes and fees. The deficit for fiscal year 2017, which began October 1, 2016, is projected at $503 billion, around 2.5 percent of GDP; compare 2009's record high deficit of $1.3 trillion (or 9.8 percent of GDP).

Federal deficits have shrunk considerably but remain persistent. This is primarily because our most expensive trio of entitlement programs—Social Security, Medicare, and Medicaid—continue to grow rapidly. Together, they now cost an annual $1.7 trillion, nearly half the entire U.S. budget.

Can the historic deficits of recent years be reversed, and is such an effort even desirable? To tackle budget reform, it is essential first to grasp the basics of how national government budgeting works. As we will see, much of American domestic policymaking is organized around our budget process.

Budget politics, as with U.S. policymaking more generally, progresses more or less in stages. Formally, three primary stages are established by a pair of laws: the Budget and Accounting Act of 1921, passed in an age of much smaller American national government; and the Congressional Budget and Impoundment Control Act, passed in 1974 during a time of political turmoil and economic recession. The process begins with the White House (see Figure 17.5).

> **Federal budget deficit:** The gap between revenues received by the national government (primarily through individual income and corporate taxes) and spending on all public programs.

President's Budget Proposal

Since the 1921 Budget and Accounting Act, presidents have been the first movers in the elaborate dance that makes up federal budgeting. The United States starts its **fiscal year (FY)** each October 1, so FY 2017 began October 1, 2016. For each approaching fiscal year, the White House submits to Congress in early February a proposed budget. This document details projected federal spending for thousands of different government programs. The process of assembling that February proposal begins many months earlier in the executive branch, with each cabinet department and federal agency compiling its expected spending totals. The Office of

> **Fiscal year (FY):** In budget calculations, the "new year" beginning October 1 and ending the following September 30. Organized many decades ago for accounting purposes.

Feb.	President's budget submitted to Congress
May	House Budget Committee formulates budget resolution ⟷ Senate Budget Committee formulates budget resolution
	House floor votes — Senate floor votes
June	Budget Conference Committee reports out the concurrent resolution on the budget
	House floor votes ⟷ Senate floor votes
July	Concurrent Resolution is not signed by the President but is an agreement between the House and Senate on how much money will be spent this budget year. Funds are then allocated to each appropriations subcommittee and reconciliation instructions (optional) are sent to relevant authorizing committees

House authorizing committees report changes in law to comply with budget resolution (budget reconciliation)

House Appropriations Committee reports appropriations measures to comply with budget resolution (allocations)

Senate Appropriations Committee reports appropriations measures to comply with budget resolution (allocations)

Senate authorizing committees report changes in law to comply with budget resolution (budget reconciliation)

House authorizing committees' recommendations submitted to the House Budget Committee

House: 13 separate appropriations bills

Senate: 13 separate appropriations bills

Senate authorizing committees' recommendations submitted to the Senate Budget Committee

House vote on reconciliation

13 House votes

13 Senate votes

Senate vote on reconciliation

13 Conference Committees

House vote on each conference report

Senate vote on each conference report

Sept.

The president may sign or veto the 13 bills

Budget Reconciliation Conference Committee subconferences are held by authorizing committees

House vote on Omnibus Budget Reconciliation Act ⟷ Senate vote on Omnibus Budget Reconciliation Act

The president may sign or veto Omnibus Budget Reconciliation Act

Source: Heritage Foundation

Source: Congressional Budget Office

● **FIGURE 17.5** *The U.S. federal budget process. (House Budget Committee)*

INFO/DATA: The Federal Budget in Context

Comprehending the federal budget is made easier by understanding the per family expenditure, as well as the proportional cost of various programs and items, from Social Security (over $14,640 per family) to the Supreme Court's salaries and operation (barely one dollar per family).

1. Scan the various per family proportional costs on the top chart. Are there any surprises? Would you have predicted, for example, that we pay about as much in interest on the debt as we spend on every item in our budget except for mandatory spending (Social Security, Medicare, Medicaid, and income-security programs and defense?

2. The two left-hand columns in the budget reflect mandatory spending. Fully 70 percent of the budget goes to these programs. Does this information change your view of "entitlements" spending?

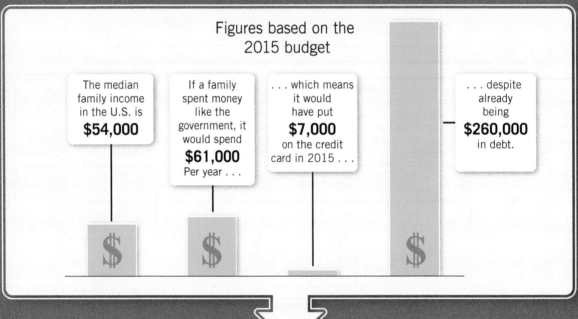

Figures based on the 2015 budget

The median family income in the U.S. is **$54,000**

If a family spent money like the government, it would spend **$61,000** Per year . . .

. . . which means it would have put **$7,000** on the credit card in 2015 . . .

. . . despite already being **$260,000** in debt.

Source: Heritage Foundation

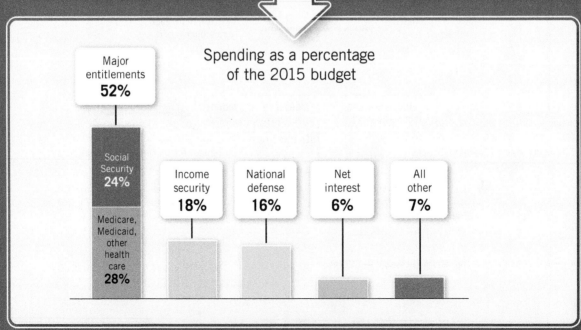

Spending as a percentage of the 2015 budget

Major entitlements **52%**

Social Security **24%**

Medicare, Medicaid, other health care **28%**

Income security **18%**

National defense **16%**

Net interest **6%**

All other **7%**

Source: Congressional Budget Office

543

Management and Budget has the massive task of coordinating all these estimates; the Treasury Department chimes in with its calculation of expected revenue figures. New presidential priorities are included as well, although the OMB pushes these groups to keep costs down so that the projected budget deficit is not too large.

Unlike most other countries, the president's budget proposal lacks any statutory authority; Congress is free to ignore it completely, as it chose to do with President Obama's 2017 budget proposal (Comparing Nations 17.1 shows how unusual this is). Its release by the White House is still a major event. Advocacy groups howl when funding for their pet projects is cut (or not increased enough to suit supporters), and businesses jockey to minimize the costs of new regulations or taxes. Congressional committees with budget responsibilities schedule hearings to question cabinet heads and senior presidential aides, and media organizations compile helpful charts.

Congressional Budget Resolution

Budget resolution: A joint House–Senate creation that outlines targets for federal spending, revenue levels, and the resultant budget deficit (or surplus) for the coming fiscal year.

While executive branch analysts compile figures to feed into the White House budget proposal, congressional budget experts are similarly working toward their own blueprint for spending and revenues, known as a **budget resolution**. As with the president's proposal, congressional budget resolutions are not binding laws, and they do not require a presidential signature. Instead, they provide a general "sense of Congress" about budgetary expectations and are meant to guide the committees responsible for finishing the budget during summer and fall.

Budget resolutions are less detailed than the president's several-hundred-page proposal. They set out overarching spending expectations in nineteen broad categories, known as "budget functions." Budget committees in both the House and the Senate, created by the 1974 Congressional Budget and Impoundment Control Act, carry out the bulk of this work. Each committee spends several months assembling a budget resolution, which must pass the full chamber. Senate and House versions are inevitably different, and they must be reconciled in a conference committee. The joint outcome, formally known as a "concurrent budget resolution," is supposed to be approved by April 15 of each year. Owing to partisan differences and other political battles, these resolutions are almost always late. Over the past forty years, Congress has only six times approved a budget resolution on schedule.

COMPARING NATIONS 17.1 — Budget Policymaking

Nearly all countries grant their chief executive the power to introduce spending bills. As we have seen, however, the U.S. president merely prepares a budget proposal, which Congress is free to ignore (and usually does). The national legislatures of most other countries hold a single, up-or-down binding vote on the executive's budget, with no amendments allowed. None has anything like the elaborate American tangle of budget resolutions, subcommittees, and reconciliation. Chief executives in other countries also have "line-item veto" authority, allowing them to eliminate individual budget items they do not like. Every recent U.S. president has called for line-item power, with only Bill Clinton managing to persuade Congress to pass it; the Supreme Court struck it down soon afterward, however. Partly as a result of more centralized and streamlined procedures, few other countries feature a budget deficit as large as America's; however, the U.S. deficit is a smaller portion of all economic activity (a smaller percentage of gross domestic product) than the deficit in many other advanced nations. Many factors feed into the large U.S. deficit, but the size of the deficit provides food for thought about how we organize budget policymaking.

Reign of the Cardinals: Appropriations Committee Action

The two budget committees were created in 1974 to simplify the unwieldy process of creating a budget and funding government programs. Unfortunately, Congress at the time left the old rules in place. As a result, the budget process got more complicated, not less.

A separate step in this process involves the Appropriations Committees in the House and the Senate, which are charged with specifying which departments and programs will get how much money. Recall from Chapter 13 that, because of their central role in spending decisions, members of Appropriations are informally known on Capitol Hill as "cardinals," after the high-ranking Vatican officials. The cardinals split up budget authority into thirteen separate jurisdictions (see Table 17.4). Critics complain that these divisions—which date back to 1921, with occasional revisions—make little sense. Some areas are far smaller than others: the District of Columbia appropriation is around $645 million yearly, around 1/100th of the $600 billion for national defense. Others reflect outmoded decisions: Military construction is handled separately from defense, for example.

Each of these thirteen areas is assigned to a separate Appropriations subcommittee in the House and Senate. Each subcommittee handles budget planning for all policy areas under its jurisdiction. Some, such as Labor, Health and Human Services, and Education (known informally on the Hill as "Labor-H"), supervise thousands of individual programs. Appropriations' cardinals must remain attentive to the budget resolution blueprint. If spending on all the programs in their jurisdiction exceeds the total specified in the resolution, they have to go back and make changes to bring it into line.

After a subcommittee approves its bill with program-by-program spending authorization, the measure must pass the full Appropriations Committee in that

TABLE 17.4 **Appropriations Subcommittees: Areas of Jurisdiction**

Agriculture; Food and Drug Administration
Departments of Commerce, Justice, and State
Department of Defense
District of Columbia
Energy and Water Development
Foreign Operations
Department of Interior
Departments of Labor, Health and Human Services, and Education
Legislative Branch
Military Construction
Department of Transportation
Department of Treasury; U.S. Postal Service
Department of Housing and Urban Development; Veterans Administration

chamber. If successful, it heads to the House or Senate floor. Each of the appropriations bills attracts intense attention from House and Senate members, who strive to add amendments funding their favorite programs. If an appropriations bill survives the floor vote in its chamber, a House–Senate conference committee is all but inevitable. This step provides another opportunity for members seeking financial benefits for their district—or lobbyists pushing a client's pet provision—to weigh in. Once the two sides agree in conference, the identical version is voted on in both House and Senate and sent to the president for consideration.

Discretionary programs: Non-entitlement program spending, subject to the decision ("discretion") of Congress each year.

Because they only deal with **discretionary programs**, which require legislative action to explicitly authorize spending, the thirteen appropriations bills cover only about a third of all U.S. government spending. Compare the large entitlement programs we read about earlier: Social Security, Medicare, and Medicaid. These are considered mandatory spending because they are funded annually, based on a formula, without requiring Congress's reauthorization each year. Thus, a giant chunk of the U.S. federal budget, nearly two trillion dollars, is essentially untouchable. Unless Congress elects to change the spending formula for a program such as Social Security, which would arouse anger from beneficiaries, those funds—with guaranteed annual increases—flow automatically.

Appropriations bills are supposed to be signed by September 1. With the start of the fiscal year looming on October 1, federal agencies and departments have a month to finalize their plans for spending funds and delivering services. As with other deadlines in the budget process, this September 1 marker is far more often missed than hit: 1995 was the last time that all thirteen appropriations bills were passed before the new fiscal year. What happens when one or more bills are not approved? As the new fiscal year approaches, with spending decisions necessary before federal funds can begin flowing, Congress may combine all the outstanding appropriations measures into a single "omnibus" spending bill. This can be thousands of pages long, listing funding for as many as twelve thousand separate programs. It is unlikely that anyone will read every line, especially as this legislation is typically cobbled together with only days or even hours to spare before the September 30 end to the fiscal year.

Continuing resolution (CR): A congressionally approved act required when no national budget has been passed before the start of a new fiscal year. This extends spending at current levels for a prescribed period of time.

More often than not in recent years, Congress fails even to pass an omnibus bill, leaving some areas unfunded as the new fiscal year opens. In that case, the president asks Congress to pass a **continuing resolution (CR)**, which keeps the dollars flowing—usually at the just-ended fiscal year's rate—for a specified period, usually two weeks or a month. In some years, Congress is forced to pass CR after CR. Otherwise, the government officially runs out of spending authority for discretionary programs and shuts down—as last happened in 2013.

All big decisions are affected by the budget because every government action has significant financial implications. And because most budget decisions have winners and losers—more money for my program means less for yours—this is one of the most politically charged aspects of policymaking. Who gets what, when, and how? In the United States, we make those decisions in significant part through our budget process.

Budgeting also underscores many of this book's basic lessons about politics and government. Separated powers slow the process by encouraging bargaining, battling, and compromise. The central place of economic efficiency in policymaking is reinforced by a politics organized around budgeting. Cost-benefit calculations are made in monetary terms, after all. Ultimately, budgeting involves the fundamental choices that help define how we Americans see ourselves.

Making Good Policy

You now have a handle on how policymaking works, as well as an introduction to economic policies and our largest social programs. Does this system produce desirable outcomes? That is a thorny question; it is by no means clear what counts as a "good" policy, or even how we would decide. But underpinning the heated discussions over U.S. policy—especially social policies—are three basic questions:

- *Is the proposed policy feasible?* Can it attract enough votes in Congress to pass, and will the president sign? And will it stand up to judicial scrutiny, if it winds up in the courts?

- *Is the proposed policy fair?* Is it the right thing to do? Does it correspond to widely held values such as equality and fairness (these concepts are, of course, contested, but most of us have an intuitive sense of them)? Or does it benefit one group, perhaps already in a favored position, at the expense of others?

- *Is the proposed policy effective?* Do the expected benefits of the policy outweigh its estimated costs? Are there more efficient—faster and cheaper—ways to achieve the desired aims?

Each of these questions leads to heated debates; these issues are not usually resolved before a policy goes into effect. But most high-profile policy proposals inspire sustained attention to these three dimensions: political (feasibility), moral (fairness/equity), and economic (effectiveness, usually measured in cost-benefit terms). The first dimension is almost self-evident: A policy counts as politically feasible if it passes Congress and unfeasible if it fails to attract sufficient support. Of course, the next legislative session might result in a different decision. The moral and economic dimensions are where the real contests over good domestic policy play out. Let us look at each.

Moral Policies: Justice or Democracy?

Some people—philosophers, regular citizens, politicians—say that the focus of public policy should be creating a *more just society*. In this view, the most important considerations in judging a policy's performance are equality, individual or group rights, and "distributive justice"—attention to a policy's beneficiaries and those who are negatively affected. If millions of Americans lack health insurance, some advocates argue that policymakers must provide it. Policy proposals to reform the healthcare system must keep the uninsured front and center—or so insist those who view public policy through the lens of justice.

Others might agree about the importance of emphasizing justice but throw up their hands at any president's or philosopher's ability to decide what is truly egalitarian or fair. These analysts see the work of policymakers as ensuring democratic outcomes: give a majority of the people what they want. That goal sounds great in principle, but recall from Chapter 8 that it is difficult to know what any group of Americans, much less the entire populace, wants to achieve. Even if we could measure public opinion more accurately, another vital question arises: Which people should we pay attention to? Yes, there may be too many uninsured in the United States—but 84 percent of the voting public, a large majority, do have health insurance. Many of them are dubious about paying more taxes or changing the healthcare system to help others. The question—what is the right thing to do—quickly comes down to that fundamental question we have asked in every chapter: Who are we—as a nation and as a people?

Economically Efficient Policies

Faced with the difficulty of determining the most just policy or the majority opinion, other policy thinkers favor a different approach to judging public policies. Relying on neoclassical economic theory, this view recommends the most efficient system of delivering government services. Utilize an objective assessment, such as a cost-benefit analysis, to identify one policy option as preferable to another: Which provides public goods at the lowest cost? If there is a clear answer, go with that policy.

Better still, these economic theorists say, use our free-enterprise system to maximize efficiency in our slow-moving, polarized policy system. Many Americans see markets as the most efficient way of organizing just about anything, and they are eager to apply that perspective to policymaking. Citizens should be given choices about the public programs and services they "consume."

To illustrate, again consider the topic of health insurance. Instead of government support for uninsured people, how about creating a big market for health insurance and letting Americans' economic preferences drive their decisions? If some want to be cautious about health risks and pay high premiums each month that is their business. If others figure their chances of getting sick are minimal, there is no need to make them pay for insurance. Recent college graduates, for example, often prefer a regular cash flow to spending funds on the unlikely chance (as they see it) that they will become ill. Why not let them choose for themselves?

Many advocates of economic efficiency believe in *rational-choice theory*, which considers individual rationality to be the basis for determining what counts as good public policy. People acting rationally will choose to maximize their self-interest, and the majority—the largest group sharing an interest—will determine more and less desirable policy choices. Through market-style competitive pressures, as different companies or nonprofit organizations compete to provide services, their cost will come down, saving taxpayers money.

Although in practice Americans combine moral, majoritarian, and economic-efficiency preferences, a belief in markets' guidance has been the dominant view

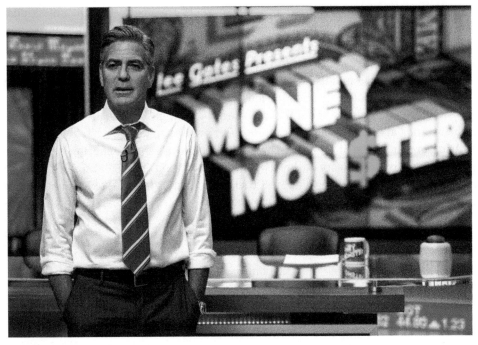

● *Many of the biggest-selling cultural icons onscreen in recent years express a clear concern about market dominance, such as* Money Monster, *in which George Clooney and Julia Roberts take on Wall Street and high finance.*

among policymakers, especially those who lean to the conservative side, in recent years. One result is the privatization of public services, discussed in Chapter 15.

Yet the "contracting out" of government functions—turning them over to private firms—is increasingly controversial. Critics of this system have multiplied, even as privatized services have spread across national, state, and local governments. Economic efficiency may be an appealing notion, but its dominance leaves many Americans uneasy. How do we know? Just head to the movies.

Capitalism Goes to the Movies

We know from opinion polls that Americans tend to prefer market-style decisions to "big-government" regulation. You might imagine that those preferences would show up in our most popular movies and books—those drawing the biggest audiences.

Instead, American popular culture displays a deep suspicion of the free-enterprise system. *Avatar*, for example—the largest-grossing film ever—is at heart a morality fable about the dangers of corporate greed, as Earth-based mining companies relentlessly pursue the not-so-subtly named mineral "unobtanium." One blockbuster film of 2016, *Captain America: Civil War*, centers on a team of superheroes refusing to work for the "restrictive capitalist system," as one character dismissively says. Another, *Money Monster*, depicts a deeply compromised financial and political system. Even animated films, aimed primarily at children, tell a similar story. The huge-grossing *Lego Movie* features an ordinary working man turned hero who defeats the evil Lord Business.

What does popular culture have to do with policymaking? The evident appeal of these works testifies to the different values Americans hold simultaneously. Yes, we are suspicious of big government, but we also question the benefits of big, unregulated markets.

THE BOTTOM LINE

» Although everyone wants "good" public policies passed, Americans have a hard time agreeing on what constitutes those.

» Moral arguments about equality and fairness in policymaking have declined in recent years, as attention to economic efficiency as a measure of a policy's worthiness has grown.

» One article of faith among efficiency advocates is that privatizing government programs enables more cost-effective and higher-quality services. But concerns about markets sorting out public policies also are evident: Just take a look at many popular American movies.

Reforming U.S. Policymaking

Most would-be reformers of U.S. domestic policymaking and budgeting address specific policies, from protecting against disastrous accidents at nuclear plants to reducing youth violence. Some reformers also work at the *system* level, seeking to alter the procedures or institutions that underlie policymaking.

Systemic Reform

Occasionally critics propose scrapping the U.S. separated powers arrangement in favor of a parliamentary model, one that would allow for swifter and more decisive policy changes. But given Americans' veneration of the Constitution, as well as most people's acceptance of the principle of checks and balances, a massive overhaul is unlikely to happen here. More than 225 years of operation creates very strong path dependence!

In between full-scale revision and tweaks to individual policies, a few prominent reform proposals have surfaced. Term limits for members of Congress (and perhaps other federal officials) would rotate representatives and senators every six years or so, bringing a regular infusion of new blood to Washington. Perhaps the resultant sense of urgency—or the reduced need for campaign funds to run for multiple terms—would improve policymaking. From the contrary point of view, a Congress made up mostly of new and soon-departing members would lack institutional memory and legislative skills. Interest-group lobbyists likely would gain even more sway over policymaking than they already have.

Other calls to streamline the slow-moving process of policy formation range from revising the Senate filibuster rules, which effectively require sixty votes to advance any policy idea, to requiring Congress to spend several five-day workweeks on legislative labors in Washington. As we saw in Chapter 13, most members of the House and Senate fly back home to their district or state every Thursday afternoon, returning to the Capitol the following Tuesday—creating a "workweek" in Washington of less than three days.[17]

Political scientist Paul Light, echoing Alexander Hamilton in the *Federalist Papers*, notes the importance to good policymaking of a "government well executed." He warns that today's federal service, bogged down by lengthy hiring delays and difficulty motivating its workers, is too often a government *ill* executed. Light and fellow executive branch reformers call for a greatly streamlined hiring process, along with financial and other incentives designed to attract the "best and brightest" young Americans to work for the national government.[18]

Ambitious but manageable reforms like these seem more achievable than a full-system overhaul. In the past decade, Congress has initiated internal reforms, such as an extensive gift ban and other ethics changes. Likewise, the executive branch has recently undergone a long process of reinventing government, as we saw in Chapter 14.

Policy Entrepreneurs

In recent years, the term "policy entrepreneur" has been applied to those who generate new ideas, help move them up policy agendas, translate them into workable proposals, and often help implement them as well. Not infrequently, these entrepreneurs are young, often just out of college. They have not been part of the regular policymaking system long enough to be subject to "groupthink," the tendency to recycle familiar (and sometimes stale) ideas.

What do we know about these innovative individuals? A few common characteristics have emerged. For one, policy entrepreneurs are willing to invest time and resources to achieve their aims, often at the risk of their own comfort and financial well-being, hoping for future return in the form of policy change. These innovators also tend to be talented storytellers, able to convey complex policy information through simplified stories and scenarios. Recall from Chapter 8 the importance of powerful narratives in successful policy framing. Third, policy entrepreneurs tend to be connected across the policy system. Though some policy entrepreneurs may engage in a lonely struggle for change, most successful efforts involve a network of entrepreneurs, diffusing policy ideas across towns, cities, and states.[19]

Over the years, American government has proved resistant to large-scale changes in individual policy areas—in part because the existing ways of carrying out policy have become institutionalized, reinforcing the status quo. Although this trend can be discouraging to would-be reformers, remember from our discussion of interest groups in Chapter 12 that a great virtue of the U.S. policy system is its remarkable stability. Those who can pursue policies within a context of predictable rules may achieve the most long-lasting reforms. That flexible combination also may help explain how America's system of policymaking has endured for so long.

Eight Steps to Successful Policy Reform

Imagine that you want to change an existing policy or advance a bill in Congress to address a problem you care about. Put on your policy entrepreneur's hat and begin connecting to fellow innovators. Here are eight lessons—distilling much of what you have learned in this book—about how to best achieve reform and advance your policy goals.

Have Passion.   To gain supporters across the decision-making community, it is essential both to have passion and to inspire it in others. Democratic presidential candidate Bernie Sanders's surprisingly strong showing owed much to his passionate advocacy of policy changes including free public college, higher taxes on the wealthy, and campaign finance reform.

Act with Speed.   As we emphasized earlier, policy windows are typically open only briefly. With the financial system potentially on the brink of failure in 2008, a handful of policymakers swiftly organized a bailout plan that may well have averted a global economic meltdown. Most advocates do not face decisions of that

Students influencing policy: University of California student regent assigns each student to a specific legislator to lobby against tuition hikes.

magnitude, but the ability to move quickly to take advantage of favorable contexts is still essential.

Bring a Plan.   James Madison is known as the "Father of the Constitution" not because he was the most effective orator or backslapper at the Constitutional Convention. Madison was a shy, quiet man, but he had one vital asset: the Virginia Plan, which he had painstakingly worked out in advance of the convention. He traveled early to Philadelphia and strategically approached other members as they arrived in town. Once the convention opened, it adopted the Virginia Plan as its working document.

Mind the Symbols.   Simple, stark words and compelling visual depictions—the American flag, a hungry child, government "death panels"—are essential to successful policy framing. Efforts to reform criminal justice policies in 2015–2017 turned in part on advocates chanting "Hands Up; Don't Shoot," in homage to the slain Michael Brown—although evidence is unclear whether Brown actually uttered those words before his fatal shooting.

Have a Philosophy.   Symbols and stories help convey ideas, but reform must connect to an underlying philosophy to survive the policy process. Franklin Roosevelt articulated his guiding perspective at the height of the Great Depression in 1933, in his first inaugural address as president: "These dark days will be worth all they cost us if they teach us that our true destiny is not to be ministered unto but to minister to ourselves and to our fellow-men."[20] This idea—that government is a source of collective support, helping those down on their luck—was woven through all FDR's subsequent New Deal programs.

Go Public.   We saw in Chapter 14 that Ronald Reagan, faced with a Democratic Congress's opposition to his tax reform proposal, successfully took his case to the American public. Few of us have as prominent a "bully pulpit" as President Reagan did (or his communication skills). But policy reformers who can connect with a wider audience are more likely to see an advance toward law.

Know the Rules.   When Lyndon Johnson was inaugurated as a new senator in 1949, he spent his first several weeks quietly at his desk on the Senate floor, following the action but never seeking recognition to speak. This behavior seemed strange, given Johnson's previous years as a famously energetic House member. Johnson's aides worried that he had become depressed. Eventually Johnson explained brusquely, "I'm learning the rules."[21] LBJ went on to be perhaps the most effective Senate majority leader ever, in part because he knew the rulebook down to every loophole, variation, and exception.

Learn How to Lose.   The U.S. system is organized around fragmented power, rather than a unified system that promotes sweeping policy changes. Thus even the most talented advocate will rack up far more losses than wins in policy battles. To survive to fight another day, it is essential to accept defeat graciously and bounce back.

> » System-wide policy change is frequently pursued by reformers, but it is very difficult to achieve in a United States that organizes its policymaking around separated powers.
>
> » Policy entrepreneurs, drawn from all walks of life, seek innovative solutions for public policies. The most successful among them tend to develop compelling narratives about their preferred issue, are willing to risk creature comforts to pursue policy change, and develop networks to diffuse and test their ideas.
>
> » Although novel policies are hard to push through to completion, the contest over agenda setting and problem definition is relatively open. As in the business or the nonprofit sector, a persistent entrepreneur can realize rewards.

Conclusion: Policy Matters

As you go about your day today, on campus or off, take a moment to notice all the different ways you encounter the policy system. Notice the "USDA Organic" label on your breakfast cereal or yogurt container, along with all those government-mandated nutrition facts. Hopping in your car or on your bike? The cost of any gas you buy, the condition of the roads you travel on, the street signs you navigate by: All those are the result of policy decisions, often hard-fought ones. Federal agencies license and manage the electromagnetic spectrum that you use to communicate by smartphone or watch TV, regulate the safety of the gym where you work out, and inspect (plus, moving to the state and local levels, charge tax on) the food you buy. Headed to class? Policy decisions determined the subsidy supporting you and the rates you pay on any student loans you hold—and if you attend a public university, they may have some say over the curriculum you study.

These are just a few of the ways in which public policy helps shape your daily experience. We return once more to a theme throughout this book: As a member of this vast but often surprisingly accessible democracy, you have the ability (and now, we hope the enhanced knowledge) to shape those policy decisions in turn. May you find a fulfilling role in the great continuing American experiment: government by the people.

CHAPTER SUMMARY

● Public policymaking inevitably involves choices: Should we reduce the interest rate on student-loan repayments? Launch a manned mission to Mars? Ban automatic weapons in the wake of a tragic shooting? Understanding those choices is the essence of politics and government in America.

● Five stages mark the process of devising domestic policies. These are not a recipe or blueprint for action, but most policy achievements pass through all these.

- *Agenda setting* describes the transformation of an idea into a policy issue as public attention expands.

- Once a topic is on the agenda, it must be *defined*—What is this issue about?—and *framed*: How lawmakers and the public talk about an agenda item often determines whether it will move forward or gather dust.

- A third stage, *policy formation*, involves the legislative and executive activities that translate talk into concrete statutory language.

- Once a policy has been passed into law, it must be *implemented*, involving rule-making and then delivery of public services.

- Finally, policies are *evaluated*; once implemented, they create a *feedback* process that affects future policymaking in that area.

● The largest U.S. policy programs, in terms of spending and numbers of people served, are social policies such as Social Security, Medicare, Medicaid, and unemployment insurance. The longtime American resistance to big government helps to explain the slow growth of these and other social policies. That same resistance has encouraged a turn toward privatization—shifting public services to the private sector.

● Heightened attention to fiscal and monetary policy, combined with harder economic times, has elevated the importance of budgeting in American politics and government. The federal budget process is a complicated, slow-moving machine, which rarely meets its key deadlines—largely because the financial stakes are so high.

● Every stakeholder agrees on the importance of passing good public policies—but controversies will never end about what these are. Some measure "good" policy in moral terms of right and wrong; others prefer clearer metrics like economic efficiency, utilizing cost-benefit and related analyses.

● As you have seen throughout this book, reform-minded groups and individuals seek change, both in the rules of the game (systemic changes) and in specific policy areas. Entrepreneurs who succeed tend to tell memorable stories, sacrifice comfort and resources to advance their policy efforts, and work collaboratively with like-minded reformers. Engaging in the policy process, though it moves slowly and incrementally, can be immensely fulfilling.

KEY TERMS

Budget resolution, p. 544	Entitlement program, p. 538	Gross domestic product
Continuing resolution	Federal budget deficit, p. 541	(GDP), p. 535
(CR), p. 546	Federal poverty line, p. 537	Monetary policy, p. 539
Cost-benefit analysis, p. 526	Fiscal policy, p. 539	Path dependence, p. 533
Cost effectiveness, p. 526	Fiscal year (FY), p. 541	Policy agenda, p. 523
Discretionary programs, p. 546	Focusing event, p. 523	Policy window, p. 528

STUDY QUESTIONS

1. What is "public policy"? Why is it so important to the work of government?

2. How do items get on the policy agenda?

3. Think of an issue you care about. How is it currently *framed* in national discussions about the issue? Would you frame it differently—and if so, how?

4. Why does policy formation—translating a topic from "good idea" into a bill ready for a congressional vote—typically take so long?

5. What is the difference between an *ex ante* and *ex post* policy evaluation? How are both useful in helping shape a government program?

6. Why are our largest entitlement programs—Social Security, Medicare, and Medicaid—so expensive?

7. Given a choice, would you emphasize managing the economy through fiscal policy (taxing and spending) or monetary policy (managed by banks, especially the Federal Reserve)? Defend your choice.

8. Why does Congress have to pass continuing resolutions at the end of most budget years?

9. How important, in your view, is balancing the U.S. budget?

10. What are at least two ways to determine whether a policy idea is worth pursuing (in other words, whether it is a good idea)? Do you prefer one approach to others?

11. If you could adopt a major reform to the American policymaking process, what would it be? (You may choose from among options in the last section of this chapter, or propose your own.)

12. What qualities characterize successful policy entrepreneurs?

 Go to www.oup.com/us/Morone to find quizzes, flash cards, simulations, tutorials, videos, and other study tools.

Foreign Policy

A POWERFUL CYBERATTACK penetrated the U.S. government. The attackers seized social security numbers, mental health records, financial data, and fingerprints of over twenty-two million Americans. Who was behind the attack? American officials immediately fingered the Chinese government. "They'll find a million ways to use this," said one cyber expert, "and none of them are good for the U.S." The Chinese might be able to blackmail American officials, unmask agents, and manipulate citizens.[1]

The U.S. government responded in subtle fashion. The administration prepared a series of economic sanctions against Chinese firms that could profit from security breaches. That seemed to get results. Just before Chinese President Xi Jinping visited the United States, the Chinese government surprised security experts by announcing the arrest of five hackers. Were they really responsible for the breach? Washington officials cannot say for sure, but the threat of sanctions clearly provoked a strong response. President Xi went on to promise that the Chinese government would not condone hacking.

American officials worked quietly behind the scenes in part because they also employ cyberattacks. For example, a sophisticated malware program was unleashed on an Iranian nuclear power plant, destroying over 1,000 centrifuges and reportedly setting back Iran's arms program two years. Who launched that attack? State Department officials appeared to take credit: They reported the breach and noted that the United States and its allies were doing everything they could to make life difficult for Iran's nuclear program. Cybersecurity involves attacks, defense, economic sanctions, quiet negotiations, veiled threats, public statements and high stakes—all essential features of American foreign policy.

International policies define American relations with external nations, groups, and problems. Foreign policy involves countless small decisions, such as negotiating trade rules with Korea or Brazil, as well as major moves, like deploying special forces to fight terrorism. American foreign policies have changed the world. They also boomerang back home and change the United States.

Who are we? Foreign policy always offers an answer. What we do around the world broadcasts our values and our interests. Our international policies

● *Former Secretary of State John Kerry and Chinese President Xi Jinping discuss hacking and cybersecurity at a 2016 summit meeting.*

557

announce what we stand for as a nation. They also trigger intense arguments. Foreign-policy debates raise a host of important questions: What are America's most fundamental interests? How should the nation pursue them? Should we act alone? Or rely on the web of alliances, partnerships, and relations with nations around the globe?

Foreign policy differs from everything you have read so far. The American political process is usually slow and full of checks and balances. In contrast, foreign policy moves fast, the stakes are high, and the results—triumphs or disasters—are often immediately clear.

American Foreign-Policy Goal No. 1: Security

Three primary goals guide foreign policy—security, prosperity, and the spread of American values. These goals often clash with one another; pursuing one sometimes means sacrificing another. As we describe each goal, think about which seems most important to you.

First, the United States must defend itself. *Security means protecting important national values from external threats.* But American policymakers must decide what constitutes an external threat. Should they focus on terrorists? China's rising military power? Economic decline? Or perhaps the greatest danger comes from global warming, or limits on natural resources. Different threats require different strategies.

Military Primacy

Every administration, whether Democratic or Republican, seeks security through a powerful military. The United States spends as much on its armed forces as the other top seven nations combined (see Comparing Nations 18.1). Even these numbers understate total military spending, however. The Department of

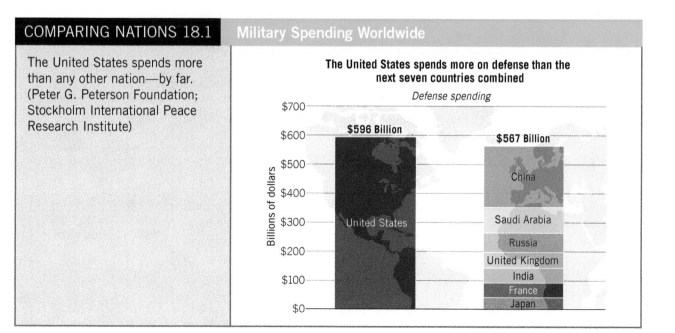

COMPARING NATIONS 18.1 | **Military Spending Worldwide**

The United States spends more than any other nation—by far. (Peter G. Peterson Foundation; Stockholm International Peace Research Institute)

The United States spends more on defense than the next seven countries combined

Defense spending

Billions of dollars

United States — $596 Billion

$567 Billion:
China
Saudi Arabia
Russia
United Kingdom
India
France
Japan

BY THE NUMBERS
Foreign Policy

Number of new international treaties the U.S. entered into, January to June 2016: **26**
Number of refugees/forcibly displaced people worldwide, 2016: **86.6 million**
(the most ever)
Proportion of those refugees/displaced people now housed in the Americas
(U.S., Canada, Latin America): **12 percent**
U.S. military spending as a percentage of all global military spending, 2015: **36**
Percentage spent by China: **12.8**
Percentage spent by Russia: **3.9**

Percentage of U.S. federal budget spent on defense, 1960: **52**
Percentage spent on defense, 2016: **16**

Rank of the U.S. economy in the world, 2016: **1**
Rank of the Chinese, Japanese, and German economies, respectively: **2, 3, 4**

Total U.S. economic activity, 2016: **$18.6 trillion**
Total combined economic activity of Japan, China, and Germany: **$19.3 trillion**
Rank of the United States, among the top fifteen economies, in economic growth
in the last five years: **10**

Rank of the United States and Russia, respectively, as global arms merchants: **1, 2**

Number of times the U.S. military was deployed on foreign soil, 1776–1941: **165**
Number of times deployed since 1941: **131**
Percentage increase in annual deaths from terrorism, 2000 to 2014: **900 percent**
Groups responsible for over half of all terrorism deaths, 2014–2015:
Boko Haram, ISIS

Homeland Security, intelligence agencies, and the Veterans Administration add more than $200 billion to the total.

A large military comes with a very high price tag (see Figure 18.1). Why spend so much more than other nations? Because U.S. military strategy is based on the theory of **primacy**: The United States can best protect its security by maintaining an unrivaled military force.

Primacy: The doctrine asserting that the United States should maintain an unrivaled military.

Basis for Primacy: Realism

Two main views of the U.S. role in the world have colored American foreign-policy debates since the 1950s. **Realism** holds that the world is an inherently dangerous, risk-filled place characterized by nations' constantly seeking to improve their competitive position. If the way to ensure national survival is to maximize military and economic power, as realists suggest, then the American officials must place a high priority on maintaining supremacy in both areas.

Realism. A doctrine holding that nation–states seek to amass power to ensure their self-preservation.

Realists in American foreign-policy debates sound the alarm about rising international security threats, particularly from organized terrorist groups such as ISIS and Al Qaeda, over the past two decades. They also warn of rising military

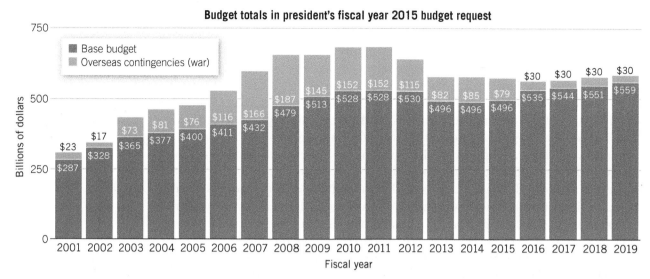

Budget totals in president's fiscal year 2015 budget request

○ **FIGURE 18.1** *Military spending rises—even as the wars in Iraq and Afghanistan wind down. (U.S. Department of Defense)*

and economic threats from China, Russia, and the Middle East. Given such an unstable world, realists recommend increased military spending—and deployment of U.S. troops wherever our self-interest appears threatened.

Realism has long been the dominant view in foreign policy, both American and elsewhere. No surprise that the military enjoys higher public approval than any other national institution. It ranks number one, outpolling business, churches, and doctors. Yes, it is large and expensive, but no other military has the same reach, and none can move as swiftly to respond to trouble around the globe. Many Americans believe the United States must pay the price of national security.

A Different View: Liberalism

Liberalism: A doctrine that views nation–states as benefiting most from mutual cooperation, aided by international organizations.

Dissenting voices about military primacy offer a different worldview. **Liberalism** provides a contrast to realism, emphasizing instead international cooperation. The U.S., in this view, should promote cultural exchanges and other forms of "soft power," rather than the "hard power" of military force and economic sanctions. Nation–states, working in concert toward mutual benefits alongside international organizations such as the United Nations, can create a far more desirable world than one dominated by military force and self-interest.

Liberal critics of the realist strain in U.S. foreign policy raise an alarming question: Could building such a large military make the United States *less* secure? Liberals identify three potential problems with military primacy.

Security trap: The idea that using military force creates multiple, often unforeseen, problems.

First, they warn of a **security trap**: Using military force often produces a backlash. It humiliates other nations and leaves them more susceptible to anti-American sentiments. Great power, in this view, must be used cautiously.[2] When the United States deploys its military, civilians are inevitably killed. Some one hundred thousand civilians died in Iraq and over one million in the air raids over Japanese cities during World War II. Civilian casualties are not America's responsibility alone— but they are sobering.

Second, military primacy costs more than half a trillion dollars a year (see Figure 18.1). This is a high economic burden. It means less spending on needs like infrastructure and education. Critics worry that it distorts national priorities and the economy as a whole. Liberal thinkers also point out that an emphasis on mutual engagement can lead to exports of American culture (movies, music, etc.), as well as goods and financial services: These enhance the nation's bottom line, rather than swelling already high military costs.

Finally, liberal thinkers are joined by conservatives in warning that too much emphasis on military power undermines liberty. As we saw in Chapter 2, Americans long feared that a large army would turn a republic into an empire. That critique evaporated during the cold war. Facing communists armed with atomic bombs, America could not afford to worry about the problems posed by a standing army. Once communism fell, the critics argued that the military and its suppliers wield what President Dwight Eisenhower called "unwarranted influence" over American government. Each side insists that the nation can remain a democratic superpower only *its* way—by maintaining military primacy or downsizing the military.

Those promoting cuts in military spending face the same problem we have seen in almost every chapter: entrenched institutions. Many local economies depend on military bases, military contractors, or military suppliers.

Soft Power

Political scientist Joseph Nye first coined "soft power" to refer to ways of persuading, rather than coercing, other states to pursue a desired outcome. In line with liberal foreign-policy doctrines, **soft power** promotes the sharing of culture and political values that people find appealing. Roughly a million foreign students attend American universities, with the largest numbers coming from China, India, South Korea, Canada, and Japan.[3] Along with France, the United States is one of the world's two leading tourist destinations, attracting some 80 million visitors in 2016. Packed stadiums from Barcelona, Spain, to Shanghai, China, shout out the words at Beyoncé concerts. American music, movies, and television are everywhere—indeed, some foreign critics accuse the U.S. of "cultural imperialism." For better or for worse, you can find McDonald's, Coke, Starbucks, and Apple stores in every corner of the world. Sharing these cultural experiences forms bonds among people, which create a different type of security. Soft power, wrote Nye, is "the means to success in world politics."[4]

President Obama, like most leaders, balanced "hard" and "soft" elements, continuing the policy of drone strikes while avidly promoting multilateral engagement. For example, while President George W. Bush unilaterally intervened in Iraq and Afghanistan, the United States under Obama took a back seat in the coalition of democratic countries intervening to aid Syrian rebels against the Assad regime.

One prominent voice in Obama's cabinet was then-Secretary of State Hillary Clinton. Rejecting the strong distinction between hard and soft power, Clinton describes her approach as "smart power," deploying U.S. assets where they both protect American interests and lead to more international cooperation. Clinton exhibits elements of both realism and liberalism in foreign policy.

see for yourself 18.1

Go online to see then-Secretary of State Hillary Clinton discuss "smart power."

Soft power: The influence a nation exerts through culture and commerce; a contrast to attempted influence through force.

● *Soft power: American lattes are welcome where the army is not. Here, Starbucks in the heart of the Forbidden City, the imperial palace in Beijing, China.*

Foreign Aid and National Security

The United States is the largest foreign aid donor in the world. Many Americans believe we spend too much on such aid. The reality is that we devote less than 1 percent (less than half of 1 percent if we take out military aid) of our gross national income (see Comparing Nations 18.2). Is this too little—or too much?

Those with a more liberal view of America's role in the world believe that assisting other nations is an important path to security. It builds goodwill and helps lift nations out of the poverty that breeds extremism. Others counter that financial

---

COMPARING NATIONS 18.2 — Official Development Assistance (ODA) Expenditures

Top: The United States pays more in foreign aid than any other nation. Bottom: Now, look at ODA as a percentage of the gross national income (GNI), or total economy: The United States is low relative to other wealthy nations. (globalissues.org/OECD)

Official development assistance, net

(Billions of dollars: United States, United Kingdom, Germany, EU Institutions, France, Japan, Sweden, Netherlands, Norway, Australia)

Oversees aid as percentage of national income

Agreed target: 0.7% of GNI

(% of GNI: United States, Sweden, Luxembourg, Norway, Denmark, United Kingdom, Netherlands, Finland, Switzerland, Belgium, Germany)

assistance only makes other nations reliant. Moreover, foreign aid often flies straight into the pockets of the rich and the powerful. The argument goes on, but the reality is that foreign aid forms a tiny part of the U.S. budget.

THE BOTTOM LINE

» The first goal of American foreign policy is security.

» Two leading foreign-policy views, realism and liberalism, differ sharply on how best to ensure security for Americans and allied countries.

» To pursue security, the United States deploys a large military and maintains a policy of primacy—the idea that no military power should rival ours.

» Liberal thinkers prefer diplomacy and other forms of multinational cooperation, soft (or cultural) power, and foreign aid.

❽ American Foreign-Policy Goal No. 2: Prosperity

The second goal of foreign policy is to ensure prosperity. A nation's power ultimately rests not on its armies but on its economic engine. Although the United States continues to lead the world by a significant margin in military spending, Americans are fast losing the economic lead they have long enjoyed over other countries. In the 1990s, the combined U.S. economic and military might led political scientists to describe global relations as *unipolar*: led by one nation, the United States. Today, most experts view the international economy as a multipolar system, with large and growing centers of economic power in Asia, Europe, and elsewhere challenging U.S. supremacy.

Economic Superpower or Nation in Decline?

Today, the U.S. economy is the largest in the world—it makes up more than a fifth of the entire global economy. Will the United States retain its economic power? Or is that power indeed declining, as many informed observers claim?

At first glance, the United States certainly does not look like a country on the skids. It accounts for more than 50 percent greater economic production than China, more than three and a half times as much as Japan, and over four times as much as Germany—and more than 163 other nations *combined* (see Figure 18.2). Every nation uses American dollars for trade, and English has become the language of international affairs.

Although the U.S. economy remains by far the largest in the world, China is rapidly catching up. Look at economic performance in recent years, and the winners and losers look very different. Saudi Arabia, China, and India have faster growing economies than the United States. In little more than a decade, China vaulted ahead of Japan and now has an economy more than half the size of America's. Another rival for economic power is the European Union—although the EU's future was cast into doubt after "Brexit"—British voters electing to leave the Union—in 2016. If growth trends in China and/or the EU continue (a very big if), the United States will soon have one or more genuine economic rivals.

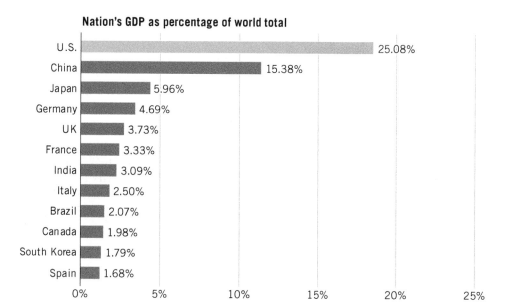

Nation's GDP as percentage of world total

U.S. 25.08%
China 15.38%
Japan 5.96%
Germany 4.69%
UK 3.73%
France 3.33%
India 3.09%
Italy 2.50%
Brazil 2.07%
Canada 1.98%
South Korea 1.79%
Spain 1.68%

0%   5%   10%   15%   20%   25%

● **FIGURE 18.2** *The nation's GDP as percentage of world total. Note that the United States is still the largest economy by far—though China has been catching up. (International Monetary Fund)*

Trade deficit: The deficit arising when a nation imports (or buys) more goods from foreign nations than it exports (or sells) to them.

Another possible risk: The United States buys more from other nations than it sells to them. This imbalance, known as a **trade deficit**, has existed every year since 1975. Is it a problem that Americans import more than they export? Economists differ. Most believe that the United States cannot continue buying more from other nations than it sells to them without eventual economic consequences.

Some critics also worry that the United States is failing to invest in its *infrastructure*—its roads, train tracks, air terminals, and public transportation. Travelers to Asia marvel at the sleek airports and railroads. Does the Chinese growth of the past decade mean that authoritarian governments are more efficient at organizing the economy than America's democracy is? President Trump made his fortune through ambitious private infrastructure projects—even some of his critics hope he can be as innovative in the public sector.

How do all of these concerns add up? Pessimists worry that other nations, especially China, or economic blocs such as the EU will overtake the United States economically. The heavy American military burden will only make things more difficult. Optimists disagree. The world's biggest economy can afford to buy more goods and services from around the world. It has been running both trade and budget deficits for forty years, and the financial sky has not fallen. Yes, politicians bicker, but they do not diminish the energy of American inventors. American entrepreneurial genius has powered the information age through Microsoft, Apple, Google, Facebook, Amazon, and the Internet itself. The United States remains an economic powerhouse.

Which is it? A nation in decline? Or an entrepreneurial dynamo setting the pace for the world? You can keep your own score in the years ahead by tracking just one measure of world power: the size of the American economy relative to the rest of the world.

Free Trade

Free trade: Goods and services moving across international boundaries without government interference.

American economic policy champions **free trade**—*the idea that goods and services should move across international boundaries without government interference.* Until the twentieth century, most governments tried to protect their own industries. They slapped tariffs on foreign goods—special taxes that made imports more expensive than local products. Governments also boosted local business with subsidies and tax breaks. This favoritism is called **protectionism** because it is designed to protect local business from foreign competition.

For the past fifty years, U.S. policymakers have worked to eliminate the protectionist policies that have kept American goods and services out of other countries. A quarter of all our economic activity involves imports or exports. In theory, free trade helps businesses and consumers in every country, because it offers more choices and lower prices. If Detroit can make better cars at a lower price, consumers from Kansas to Kazakhstan should be able to buy them.

After World War II, the international community established a new framework for international trade through the **General Agreement on Tariffs and Trade** (known as **GATT**). The agreement created procedures by which nations would negotiate agreements designed to reduce the barriers to free trade. Eight different negotiations have resulted in treaties; each is known as a *round* and is named after the place where the discussions were held. In 1994, the negotiations produced the **World Trade Organization** (**WTO**), which now oversees the negotiations and the rules that result.

Nations also negotiate bilateral or multilateral trade agreements among themselves. These agreements reduce barriers to trading between their member countries. For example, the United States, Canada, and Mexico established the North Atlantic Free Trade Agreement (NAFTA) in 1994. NAFTA phased out taxes on imports and exports between the three countries and increased trade. Although economists agree that NAFTA has boosted economic growth in all three countries, many U.S. companies relocated to Mexico in the wake of NAFTA, leaving hundreds of thousands of workers at least temporarily without jobs. Partly as a result, somboth presidential candidates opposed the Trans-Pacific Partnership (TPP), ratified in 2016 by twelve countries including the United States, Japan, Australia, and Mexico.

Trade agreements such as the TPP can be controversial. The last round of WTO trade talks, held in Doha (the capital of Qatar), stretched on for more than fifteen years and involved 141 nations. Ultimately, no agreement was reached.[5] Why? We will see in the next section.

Challenges to Free Trade

Every administration and almost every policy textbook agree: Free trade makes everyone better off. However, many Americans disagree, and this sentiment helped secure President's Trump 2016 election. Free trade faces four main challenges.

First, critics of free trade charge that it is cheaper to produce goods in nations that pollute, outlaw unions, and reject safety standards. Jobs will move to those nations. The critics suggest an alternative to free trade: **fair trade**, which reduces trade barriers but also negotiates worker protections and environmental regulations into trade agreements. In these ways, say proponents, the workers of all nations can compete with the same rules.

Second, free markets cause social displacement, at least in the short run. Free trade in agriculture, for example, pushes small farmers in poor nations such as Nigeria off their farms and into the slums of megacities like Lagos. What happens to the Nigerian farmer and his family when they lose their land? What happens to software engineers in Boston, Massachusetts, who find their jobs migrating to Bangalore, India? Most nations have not put policies in place to help workers who are displaced by international competition. Even if everyone is better off in the long run, as free trade advocates argue, politics—and individuals—focus on troubles in the short run.

Protectionism: Efforts to protect local business from foreign competition.

General Agreement on Tariffs and Trade (GATT): A framework for negotiating reductions in trade barriers between nations.

World Trade Organization (WTO): An international organization that oversees efforts to open markets and promote free trade.

see for yourself 18.2

Watch 2016 presidential candidates Bernie Sanders and Donald Trump, although on opposite sides of most issues, both criticize the TPP.

Fair trade: Trade that emphasizes the inclusion of environmental and labor protections in agreements so that nations do not receive unfair advantages by exploiting workers or harming the environment.

Third, as international markets have expanded to facilitate the huge sums involved in free trade, they have grown volatile. The Greek debt crisis, a Chinese stock market crash, and Russia's financial troubles all reverberate through the global economy. Liberal economists such as Paul Krugman warn that free markets create a wild ride full of booms, bubbles, and busts.[6]

Fourth, American leaders champion free trade only until they run into powerful interests. When government helps American farmers, it violates the rules of free trade that the government itself is championing. However, because few politicians are willing to take on the farm lobby or the rural states, American farm subsidies stay in place despite the different administrations' commitment to free trade.

Almost all experts and most political leaders reject a return to protectionism. At the same time, opposition to free trade has grown. In the 2016 election, every successful candidate in both parties criticized free trade for its effects on American workers. Public polls, likely as a result of this hostility from national political leaders, showed a dip in support. Yet on balance, American public opinion about free trade has improved in recent years (see Figure 18.3).

Energy

Foreign policymakers keep a close eye on energy supplies. The United States consumes over twenty million barrels of oil a day, a quarter of the world total. In the last twenty years, the United States has fought three major wars in the Middle East—which has an estimated 60 percent of the world's oil reserves. However, the energy story is changing rapidly and today the United States and Canada produce almost 60 percent of the nation's supply. Although reliance on foreign energy has diminished, the recent plummeting of energy prices has pushed many U.S. energy companies to the brink of bankruptcy.

Economic Weapons

As we saw in the cybersecurity case, American officials use economic relations as carrots to reward other nations or as sticks to punish them—for attacking another country, trying to build nuclear weapons, or hacking American firms. Economic sanctions include the following:

- A boycott, or refusing to buy goods or services from a country.

- An economic embargo, or restricting the flow of trade into a country. Sometimes the Navy or the Air Force enforces the embargo.

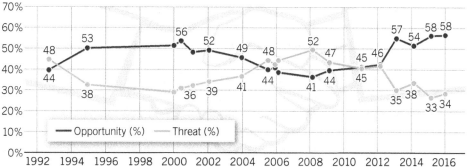

FIGURE 18.3 *American views of international trade: Public opinion about free trade agreements. Despite criticisms of free trade from almost every presidential candidate in 2016, a significant majority of Americans—the most since polling began on this question in 1992—see trade as an opportunity, outweighing the threat. (Gallup)*

- Divestment, or refusing to invest in another country. Even local governments and private actors can use this strategy.

- Freezing assets, or seizing the bank accounts and other financial assets that foreign nationals have invested here. This strategy targets elites in particular by stripping them of their foreign bank accounts.

- Finally, withholding foreign aid—if the country is receiving any.

Applying these economic sanctions is never easy, because it requires building an international coalition. If other countries refuse to go along, the United States simply loses a market for its own goods without applying any real pressure. Economic weapons also can hurt ordinary people long before they touch the rich and powerful.

THE BOTTOM LINE

» A second primary goal of foreign policy is to protect prosperity. Economic strength is the ultimate source of power on the world stage.

» Today, the U.S. economy is the largest in the world—but many Americans and allies around the globe wonder: Will the United States maintain its economic strength relative to other nations?

» American economic policy has been guided by the pursuit of free trade—the removal of barriers to international commerce. Resistance has grown to free trade, especially among congressional Democrats. Many support *fair* trade.

» International economic policy also focuses on protecting energy sources and using economic sticks and carrots to influence the behavior of other nations.

Foreign-Policy Goal No. 3: Spreading American Ideals

Most people believe that every nation's foreign-policy goal can be described simply: blunt self-interest. However, explaining American action only in terms of power or prosperity misses something important.

In the very first inaugural address, delivered in 1789, President George Washington declared that the new nation had a special mission: "The sacred fire of liberty and the destiny of the republican model of government are . . . entrusted to the hands of the American people." This, he told his countrymen, might even be liberty's best and final chance.[7] From the very start, American leaders believed that the United States had a special role in the world—to champion liberty.

American leaders often justify foreign-policy action in terms of promoting values such as liberty and democracy. The United States entered World War I, said President Woodrow Wilson, because "the world must be made safe for democracy." America is "privileged to spend its blood," he continued, for "a universal dominion of right." A century later, Secretary of State Hilliary Clinton, described her foreign policy in these terms: "upholding universal values and human rights is at

● *Nineteenth-century artists imagined a spirit of providential destiny that guided America. Here, America flies forward, the star of empire on her forehead and learning and technology in either hand, as Native Americans and wild beasts flee before the irresistible civilization. This painting, by John Gast, was widely copied and reprinted.*

American exceptionalism:
The view that the United States is unique, marked by a distinct set of ideas such as equality, self-rule, and limited government.

Theory of democratic peace:
Theory that strongly democratic nations are less to engage in wars with one another.

the core of what it means to be American. If we sacrifice those values or let our policies diverge too far from our ideals, our influence will wane."[8]

American Exceptionalism

Again and again, American leaders return to the idea that the United States has a unique duty to spread freedom, democracy, and peace to other nations. The belief that the United States plays a special role in world affairs is known as **American exceptionalism**. This does not mean that Americans ignore their own interests. America's deepest interest, according to this view, lies in promoting the peace, freedom, and democracy that will benefit all people.[9]

Is the United States exceptional? Some observers warn that American exceptionalism is a dangerous myth. It can lead Americans to reduce complicated reality into a simple clash between good and evil. A faith in America's special destiny, whether it is truth or a myth, makes foreign policy more controversial. Political science research has suggested that the pursuit of peace, through support for nongovernmental or international institutions and by advancing democratic values and economic growth in underdeveloped countries (a goal to which the U.S. government has devoted an estimated $30 billion annually[10]), has a beneficial payoff. According to the **theory of democratic peace**, nations with legitimate democratic governments do not go to war with each other.[11] While Republicans have traditionally emphasized a faith in American exceptionalism, President Trump is skeptical of the idea, deeming it insulting to the rest of the world.

The View from Abroad

How do others see the United States? As Donald Trump took office, the United States was viewed more favorably by most nations than in the recent past. U.S. efforts to contain the global threat posed by the Islamic State (ISIS), end the civil war in

What Do You Think? Is America Exceptional?

Every nation is unique in many ways. But is the United States exceptional in the way that George Washington and many others have claimed?

Yes. The United States is exceptional in that it makes sacrifices to spread values such as freedom and democracy around the world. It does not ignore self-interest but equates it with the spread of liberty and democracy.

No. Americans may like to think that they are acting purely on principle. But, like every other nation, the United States pursues its own self-interest. It is dangerous and misleading to insist that we are helping others when in reality we are helping ourselves.

It depends. Americans pursue their self-interest. They also pursue values like democracy and rights. Some leaders get the balance right and are cheered around the world. Others are less effective. It depends on the leader and the situation.

Syria and accompanying refugee crisis, keep nuclear weapons out of Iran's hands, and contain Russian military expansion all spurred America's rise in global public opinion. In addition, memories of the fiercely unpopular War in Iraq are fading. From Germany (57 percent favorable opinion of the U.S. in 2016, up from 30 percent in 2007), and France (63 percent favorable, up from 29) to Indonesia (62 percent favorable, up from 29) and China (50 percent, up from 34), people around the world are more likely today to have a favorable view of the United States.[12] Will those high approval ratings last as President Trump reverses Obama's popular policies? Time will tell.

The debate continues about American values and their meaning for other nations. Even supporters, at home and overseas, fear American society is increasingly unequal, marked by less opportunity and a growing gulf between rich and poor. The United States seems, to many observers, more fixed on hard-knuckle economic competition and amassing great wealth than on a genuine belief that all people are equal.

Nevertheless, more immigrants still crowd into the United States than into any other nation. Even in countries that are skeptical of America's intentions, people stand in long lines to sign up for the lottery that will grant a few of them a visa. People even risk their lives to pursue the American Dream. If the United States is a nation in decline, then why are so many people fighting to move here?

In short, American values play a crucial role in guiding American foreign policy. The key question is whether these values are still vital or are beginning to fade—and whether they can inspire people around the world, or seem like simple rhetorical cover for American self-interest.

THE
BOTTOM
LINE

» The United States tries to spread its own values of democracy and freedom— sometimes creating goodwill, at other times a backlash. This is a rare goal for a nation's foreign policy.

» After a decline in popularity in the 2000s, many nations now see the United States in a more positive light.

» Critics argue that the United States simply uses the language of values to pursue its self-interest. They see even the nation's talk of liberty as little more than a cover for unbridled capitalism and inequality.

Foreign-Policy Perspectives

Every administration develops a foreign-policy strategy by answering three key questions. Should the United States engage the world or withdraw from it? Do we go it alone or work with others? Which foreign-policy goals and values are most important?

Engage the World? Isolationism Versus Intervention

George Washington warned his countrymen to stay clear of foreign politics: "The great rule of conduct for us, in regard to foreign nations, is . . . to have . . . as little *political* connection as possible." In other words, the United States should limit itself to commerce. We can promote our values simply by building an ideal society that other nations will admire and want to imitate.[13]

Americans wary of global involvement

% saying each …

U.S. should …

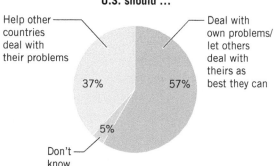

Help other countries deal with their problems — 37%

Deal with own problems/ let others deal with theirs as best they can — 57%

Don't know — 5%

FIGURE 18.4 *American views on global involvement.* (Pew Research Center)

Strategic disengagement:
The doctrine that a nation should not interfere in other nations' affairs unless such involvement clearly advances its own interests.

Many Americans hold a version of this view, now known as **strategic disengagement**.[14] Senator Rand Paul (R-KY), a long-shot presidential candidate in 2016, drew cheers when he declared in speeches "I see an America strong enough to deter foreign aggression, but wise enough to avoid unnecessary intervention."[15] Though few politicians today embrace all-out **isolationsim**—avoiding any involvement in other nations' affairs—there is a long-standing strain of belief holding that the United States will remain strong and secure by limiting its involvement overseas, especially military activity (see Figure 18.4).

In contrast, most contemporary foreign-policy analysts practice **internationalism.** They believe that America's interests are best protected by actively engaging the world. Both the United States and the world would be worse off, they argue, if the United States withdrew into its own borders. Americans must combat terrorism, confront Russian meddling in Syria, fight radical jihadists, protect Asia from an unpredictable North Korea—and the list goes on. This perspective insists that withdrawing from world affairs will allow problems to fester, enemies to multiply, and people to suffer.

One especially pressing issue is the spread of nuclear weapons. Five nations openly possess them (the United States, England, France, Russia, and China). Four others are thought to have developed them (India, Pakistan, North Korea, and Israel). A small number of foreign-policy experts argue that the spread of these weapons makes wars less likely, because either side can annihilate the other.[16] Most observers believe the opposite: As nuclear weapons spread to less stable nations, they are more likely to be used and to fall into the hands of extremist groups. In the words of a past U.S. Secretary of Defense, "Today, the danger of . . . a nuclear catastrophe is greater than it was during the Cold War and most people are blissfully unaware of this fact."[17] American foreign policy must work around the globe to avoid this nightmare scenario.

Many people believe that the United States traditionally practiced isolationism. This is a myth. Right from the start, the United States exerted its muscle around the world. It battled

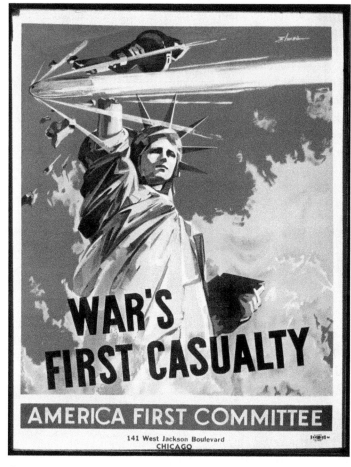

An isolationist poster from just before World War II. The view is blunt: Going to war threatens American liberty. The attitude vanished when the United States was attacked at Pearl Harbor. Although full-blown isolationism remains rare, many Americans are skeptical of military intervention today.

the French navy in 1798, just ten years after the Constitution went into effect. It fought the Barbary Wars on the north coast of Africa beginning in 1801. (If you are familiar with the Marine Corps anthem, its "shores of Tripoli" refers to the Barbary Wars.) American forces entered Mexico ("the halls of Montezuma") five times between 1836 and 1848 before declaring all-out war. By one count, the military deployed overseas 165 times before World War II.

For all the action, however, the United States maintained only a small standing army until the end of World War II. Then, locked in a Cold War with the Soviet Union, the country built an army ready to deploy anywhere around the globe at a moment's notice. The sheer size and sophistication of its military pushes the United States away from isolationism.

> **Isolationsim:** The doctrine that a nation should avoid all foreign policy commitments and alliances and withdraw from world affairs.

> **Internationalism:** The belief that national interests are best served by actively engaging and working with other nations around the world.

Go It Alone or Act with Others?

Although the United States was rarely isolationist, through most of its history it acted alone. President Washington broke the alliance with France that had helped win the Revolutionary War, and America did not enter another peacetime alliance for the next 150 years. This perspective is known as **unilateralism**—American foreign policy should be independent and self-sufficient. Unilateralists oppose treaties with foreign nations or international organizations, because they perceive such agreements as tying America down. Those supporting strategic disengagement, given their caution about U.S. intervention or even involvement in most foreign disputes, insist that it should lead the way and avoid what Thomas Jefferson, in his first inaugural address, dismissed as "entangling alliances."

> **Unilateralism:** A doctrine that holds that the United States should act independently of other nations. It should decide what is best for itself—not in coordination with partners and allies.

After World War II, American policy changed. **Multilateralism** means acting together with other nations to pursue common goals. In an increasingly interdependent world, argue multilateralists, no nation can succeed by going it alone. We cannot solve modern problems by ourselves. Fighting communism during the Cold War required concerted action. Today, only international cooperation can defeat terrorism, reverse climate change, secure prosperity, win energy security, end starvation, stop ethnic killing, resist global pandemics, reduce the international traffic in drugs and sex, and end violence against women. Foreign-policy officials who take an internationalist view are, as you would expect, strong supporters of multilateralism.

> **Multilateralism:** A doctrine that emphasizes operating together with other nations to pursue common goals.

Millennial Americans tend to express a clear preference for multilateralism, owing in part to their relatively high level of global engagement: More than three times as many millennials study abroad than did members of "Generation X" twenty-five years ago.[18] That preference shows up in support for foreign-policy approaches such as the U.S.-brokered complicated deal to block Iran from obtaining nuclear weapons, negotiated among six nations.

Four Approaches

As you can see, Americans have a lot to balance in making foreign policy—three overarching goals, isolation versus action, and unilateralism versus multilateralism. How do we bring together these goals? Over time, Americans have generally supported four different camps. Each

● *Institutions tilt politics: The sheer size and sophistication of the American military pushes the nation away from isolationism. Here, the new F-35 Joint Strike Fighter plane on a test run.*

Foreign-Policy Perspectives

It is time for you to pick a perspective that ties foreign policy together. Where do your values lie? With which of the following do you most identify?

I am a Wilsonian.	I believe that American foreign policy must rest on American values and work with other nations to secure them.
I am a Hamiltonian.	I believe that the business of America is business.
I am a Jeffersonian.	I prefer to worry about democracy on the home front.
I am a Jacksonian.	I believe that the only criteria for foreign action are American security and American prosperity.
None of these choices seem right.	Feel free to develop a different perspective. You can emphasize some other goal of American foreign policy. Or, simply mix and match from these.

(Source: Adapted from Walter Russell Mead)

approach emphasizes different foreign-policy goals. Each is named after a famous statesman who helped define it.[19]

Wilsonians believe that American values ought to be the number one consideration guiding foreign policy. Fighting a war to make the world safe for democracy, as Woodrow Wilson urged America to do during World War I, is the classic Wilsonian move.

Hamiltonians believe that American foreign policy should focus on protecting American prosperity. Named after Alexander Hamilton, the first secretary of the treasury, this approach emphasizes making economic deals that benefit the United States. Hamiltonians favor big business and accept big government. To them, military intervention should always be weighed not against vague values such as freedom or morality, but against hard-headed analysis. Is the action in America's economic interest?

Jeffersonians focus on freedom and democracy at home. Building up a large military and deploying it around the world threatens the American ideals of local and democratic government. Jeffersonians are nervous about the military-industrial complex and its corrosive effect on American freedom. President Thomas Jefferson warned that international alliances would "entangle" the nation in foreign wars and power politics.

Jacksonians believe that the United States should simply focus on its own security and well-being. It should worry about itself and let other nations do the same. Jacksonians are skeptical of foreign aid, indifferent to international diplomacy, and slow to support foreign action. However, they put special emphasis on honor. Once the military is deployed, they insist on total victory. Of the four traditions, the Jacksonians are most likely to be chanting, *"USA! USA!"*

» Three decisions guide foreign policy: First, policymakers must choose between strategic engagement (only get involved in a global conflict or alliance when it clearly advances the U.S. national interest) or internationalism (engagement with the world).

» Second, policymakers must choose whether to act unilaterally (go it alone) or multilaterally (in alliance with other nations).

» Third, policymakers put it all together with an overall perspective: Wilsonians focus on values, Hamiltonians on economics, Jeffersonians on democracy at home, and Jacksonians on defending American security and well-being.

Who Makes Foreign Policy?

What is misleading about the following newspaper headlines?

- "United States Warns Syria About Attacks on Protesters"
- "South Korea Seeks to Balance Relations with China, United States"
- "Iran Threatens Saudi Arabia"

They all describe nations as if they were *unitary actors,* or individuals with minds of their own. Every chapter in this book has told another story. The United States constructs politics out of many perspectives, interests, institutions, and arguments. So does every other nation. Foreign policy emerges out of negotiation. Several major players have a seat at the table when American foreign policy is made.

Congress

The Constitution carefully balances responsibility for foreign policy between Congress and the president. Congress has the power to declare war, to set the military's budget, and to ratify treaties. These responsibilities worked fine in a slower world. In the early nineteenth century, the Americans defeated the English in the Battle of New Orleans because word had not filtered back across the Atlantic that a peace treaty had already ended the War of 1812.

Today, response time can be measured in minutes rather than weeks or months. As the decision clock sped up, defense—and, more generally, foreign policy—shifted away from Congress to the White House. Congress has not declared war since 1941 despite major wars in Korea (where thirty-six thousand Americans died), Vietnam (another fifty-eight thousand), the Persian Gulf, the Balkans, Afghanistan, and Iraq. Congress is divided, slow to act, uneasy about taking risks, focused on domestic issues, and always running for reelection. For all these reasons, it has let control of foreign policy slip to the executive branch.

In 1973 Congress tried to reassert some control by passing the **War Powers Act**, which requires presidents to get congressional permission for military action after troops are in the field for no more than sixty days. Presidents generally ask Congress for support before they commit troops (see Chapter 14 for details). And when wars drag on and grow unpopular, Congress asserts itself: It holds hearings, rallies opposition, and squeezes the budget.

War Powers Act: Legislation passed in 1973 to increase congressional involvement in undeclared wars. It requires Congress to approve military action undertaken by the president in no more than sixty days.

The Constitution requires the Senate to ratify international treaties with a two-thirds vote—a very high bar in our partisan era. To get around the requirement, presidents sign *executive agreements* with other nations; these have the same legal effect as formal treaties but do not require the two-thirds vote. *Legislative-executive agreements* pass with a simple majority, as any other legislation. A *sole executive agreement* is simply signed by the president without any congressional approval at all.

The Constitution also makes Congress responsible for confirming top foreign-policy appointments. Again, partisan politics has slowed this process in recent years.

In short, Congress has evolved from a partner to a type of check on executive foreign policymaking. The executive branch crafts the policies. It then must win over Congress for funding, legislation, confirmations, and cooperation. In effect, Congress pushes back when presidential policies become unpopular.

The President

The president commands the military, negotiates treaties, rallies Americans during crises, and oversees relations with more than two hundred nations. Each administration defines America's stance toward the world. Presidents and their team decide whether, when, where, and how to intervene around the globe. They balance foreign policy with domestic priorities and political calculations.

Recent administrations have demonstrated the enormous power inherent in the president's foreign-policy role. Ironically, modern presidents have more authority and less experience. Early presidents all had a rich foreign-policy background. Most recent presidents have arrived in the White House with no foreign-policy experience at all (see Table 18.1). Trump's victory came, in part, from a great wave of distrust towards Washington insiders—like candidate Hillary Clinton.

Although presidents take the lead, they have many partners in conducting international affairs. One key to presidential success is wisely managing the enormous foreign-policy bureaucracy. Each office in the pyramid does a different job and sees the world in its own way.

The State Department

The State Department, the very first cabinet agency established under the Constitution, is responsible for managing diplomatic relations with more than two hundred nations. State is responsible for negotiating treaties, distributing foreign assistance, and managing daily contact with other nations.

State Department officers are interested in understanding other nations and cultures. They learn foreign languages, live abroad, and favor diplomatic solutions—usually multilateral. The department is sometimes accused of being out of step with majority American opinion, which can favor skeptical disengagement. Critics often have a bit of sarcastic fun with the location of the State Department's headquarters—an area of Washington, DC, known as Foggy Bottom.

This skepticism leads to a serious problem: The State Department is chronically underfunded. Its offices around the world lack key personnel. Many observers (as well as foreign-policy officers talking off the record) worry that the United States is shortchanging its diplomatic efforts by underfunding the State Department.

TABLE 18.1	Presidents' Foreign-Policy Experience

The first six presidents had extensive foreign policy experience. Of the six most recent presidents, only one, George H. W. Bush, had any foreign policy experience at all.

	SECRETARY OF STATE	OTHER DIPLOMATIC OR CABINET POST	CHIEF U.S. REPRESENTATIVE TO GREAT BRITAIN	CHIEF U.S. REPRESENTATIVE TO OTHER MAJOR POWER	COMMANDED U.S. FORCES IN WAR
FIRST SIX PRESIDENTS					
George Washington					X
John Adams		X	X	X	
Thomas Jefferson	X	X		X	
James Madison	X				
James Monroe	X	X	X	X	
John Quincy Adams	X	X	X	X	
MOST RECENT PRESIDENTS					
Jimmy Carter					
Ronald Reagan					
George H. W. Bush		X		X	
Bill Clinton					
George W. Bush					
Barack Obama					
Donald Trump					

The Department of Defense

The Department of Defense (DOD) manages the military. It is the largest organization in government and the biggest employer in the United States. The DOD is responsible for over two million military personnel and seven hundred thousand civilian employees—all led by the secretary of defense, who is always a civilian. The department is housed in a huge five-sided office building known as the Pentagon.

Not surprisingly, Defense Department officials see the world very differently than the State Department. The DOD makes military calculations, toting up risks and threats, assets, and strategy. As you can see, when you were talking "government-speak" about the Pentagon and Foggy Bottom, you were sounding a familiar Washington lament about the failure of these two important cabinet offices to coordinate with one another.

Two problems haunt the Defense Department. First, the massive bureaucracy is bound up in red tape and very slow to change. Today, more than thirty-seven thousand American troops are stationed in Germany—roughly four times the number as in Afghanistan. They were originally deployed there because Germany

Talking POLITICS

SOUND LIKE A FOREIGN-POLICY PRO

Do you want to sound like an experienced foreign-policy hand? Repeat after us: "If only the Pentagon and Foggy Bottom could get on the same page." What did you just say? Read on.

was on the front line in the standoff with the Soviet Union. But the Soviet threat disappeared more than twenty years ago, and today Germany is surrounded by peaceful democracies. However, Pentagon leaders have found it difficult to reorient American military strategy away from a land battle in Europe.

Second, the military is divided by rivalry between the services. The Army, Navy, Air Force, and Marine Corps are all eager to deploy their own tactical assets during military operations. These tensions can create such confusion that, in one notorious case, a Marine involved in the invasion of Grenada had to use a pay phone to report details back to Washington. The Chairman of the Joint Chiefs of Staff, a military figure, is charged on behalf of the president and secretary of defense with coordinating the branches—a tall order, given rivalries among them.

Intelligence

The United States has a large and complicated intelligence community. More than fifteen different agencies and offices gather information from around the world. The best known is the Central Intelligence Agency, which is responsible for foreign intelligence. However, the Departments of State, Defense, Energy, and the Treasury all have their own foreign intelligence operations, as do the military branches. The Federal Bureau of Investigation is responsible for domestic intelligence, which often has to be coordinated with information from abroad.

In theory, each intelligence office and agency monitors a different spectrum of threats. In reality, they have overlapping jurisdictions and act as rivals (a familiar theme in the foreign-policy bureaucracy). They are slow to share information or communicate. There is a standard answer to turf wars like the one in the spy community: Create a new agency and charge it with coordinating all the others. In 2004, after hearings into the 9/11 terrorist attacks exposed the chaos, Congress created a director of national intelligence charged with bringing order to American intelligence. Did this mandate impose coordination or simply inject one more voice into the contest? Answer: Both.

The National Security Council

The National Security Council is part of the Executive Office of the President. It brings the most important foreign-policy officers together to advise the president. The council includes the president and the vice president, along with the secretaries of state, defense, and homeland security. It also includes the director of national intelligence, the head of the Joint Chiefs of Staff (the top military officer), and others who the president may name. This is one of the most high-powered groups in a city of high-powered groups. Very different perspectives and personalities come together to hammer out major foreign-policy decisions.

Other Executive Agencies

A great many other bureaus and agencies engage in foreign policy. The president's economic team plays an important role. The Office of the U.S. Trade Representative negotiates trade deals. The Labor Department leads business groups abroad. The Department of

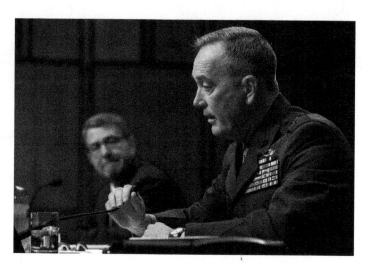

● Secretary of Defense Ash Carter refers a Senate committee question to the Chairman of the Joint Chiefs of Staff. Several different federal bureaucratic departments must coordinate U.S. foreign policy—not always a smooth process.

INFO/DATA: Are You a Global Citizen?

The age-old U.S. debate between skeptical disengagement and internationalism plays out in every country: Should we be more or less involved in world affairs? One key factor: How international minded are a country's citizens? This info-graphic shows selected nations' public polling in 2016, in response to the question "Are you a global citizen?"

1. ■ Answer the poll question yourself: Do you consider yourself a citizen of the globe? (Along with, of course, a citizen of your home country; the question does not require choosing one or the other.) Why or why not?

2. ■ Should public opinion play a major role in foreign policy? Or should it be left to the experts? On the one hand, the public knows little about events abroad. On the other, it will have to pay (in blood and taxes) for every mistake its leaders might make. The extent to which any nation's people view themselves as globally minded can help shape leaders' decisions to get involved around the world.

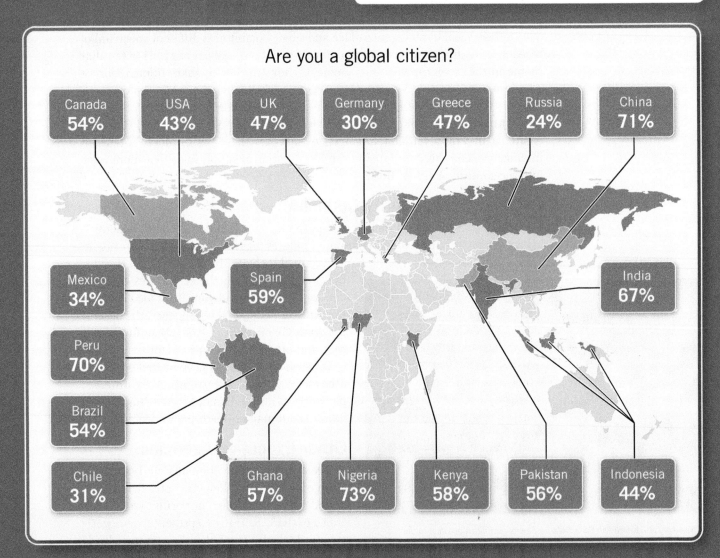

Are you a global citizen?

Country	%
Canada	54%
USA	43%
UK	47%
Germany	30%
Greece	47%
Russia	24%
China	71%
Mexico	34%
Spain	59%
India	67%
Peru	70%
Brazil	54%
Chile	31%
Ghana	57%
Nigeria	73%
Kenya	58%
Pakistan	56%
Indonesia	44%

Source: GlobeScan/BBC

Homeland Security brings together a host of agencies ranging from the Coast Guard to the Immigration Service. Each agency and office pushes to define foreign-policy problems. Each seeks to put its own spin on America's approach to the world.

Interest Groups and the Public

Organized groups play an active role in foreign policymaking—far more so than in most other nations. On high-profile issues such as trade agreements, every side mobilizes and lobbies. Some groups focus support for specific countries (see Figure 18.5), while others lobby for specific causes: Human rights groups and Christian organizations that are concerned about religious persecution in other nations are among the most familiar interest groups on Capitol Hill.

Groups are most effective at exerting influence on low-profile issues; cherry growers or health insurance companies can often persuade policymakers to slip favors into a law or regulation. It is much harder to affect high-profile issues because policymakers are usually committed to their positions. In these cases, interest groups assist officials who are already on their side by arming them with information, arguments, and elegant PowerPoint presentations (see Chapter 12).

Public opinion and the media can also have a powerful impact. The public generally does not pay much attention to foreign policy. Even major events, such as Russian-backed hackers meddling in the 2016 U.S. presidential election, fade quickly from public attention. Once in a while, however, a foreign-policy issue moves to the forefront of American politics. The media plays it up and the public leaps in with its opinions.

Wars are the most common major events, and they often follow a cycle. At first, the American majority rallies around the flag and throws its support to the president and the troops. The inevitable antiwar demonstrations get scant media attention. Over time, especially if the war bogs down or its purpose grows murky, as in Vietnam or Iraq, the public turns against the action. It becomes a major story. Even small antiwar protests make the news. Congress begins to stir, holding hearings and scrutinizing appropriations. Public outcry, fanned by media coverage, makes unpopular wars difficult to prosecute.

Success or Fragmentation?

The policies produced by these many agencies, offices, legislators, and groups—all pulling and hauling and scrambling for influence—are typical of American government. It is chaotic, messy, unpredictable, open—and often democratic. Yet there is always the foreign-policy difference: At the end of the process, the president can make a decision and break the stalemate—deploy the Navy, issue a warning, embrace a foreign leader. And despite the messy process, U.S. foreign policy has been relatively successful through much of the nation's history. The United States emerged victorious and more powerful than ever from World War I, World War II, and the Cold War.

The great question about the foreign-policy process today is one that we have raised in many other contexts. Does the fragmented, wide-open American policy scramble capture a democratic energy that forces policymakers to see things from many different perspectives? Or has it grown too chaotic to meet the challenges of the twenty-first century?

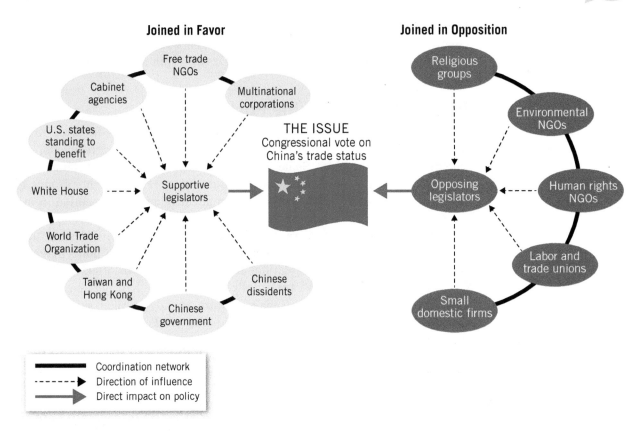

Joined in Favor

Free trade NGOs

Cabinet agencies

Multinational corporations

U.S. states standing to benefit

White House

Supportive legislators

World Trade Organization

Taiwan and Hong Kong

Chinese government

Chinese dissidents

THE ISSUE
Congressional vote on China's trade status

Joined in Opposition

Religious groups

Environmental NGOs

Opposing legislators

Human rights NGOs

Labor and trade unions

Small domestic firms

——— Coordination network
------▶ Direction of influence
——▶ Direct impact on policy

● **FIGURE 18.5** *Lobbying the vote on China's trade status as a most favorable nation (MFN). A big vote in Congress brings out the full range of policy influences. Along with the many interest groups fighting for and against legislation to grant favorable trade status to China, the most important actors trying to influence Congress in this case were the government agencies themselves. The Office of the Trade Representative, the State Department, and the White House all effectively rounded up votes. The proposal passed. (Hook)*

THE BOTTOM LINE

» Although we often talk about nations as if they had a single interest, many different individuals and institutions shape foreign policy.

» Congress and the presidents were originally foreign-policy partners. During the Cold War, the checks and balances diminished. Today, the president takes the lead and Congress offers a check.

» The most important executive agencies in foreign policymaking are the State Department, the Defense Department, and the National Security Council.

» Other important foreign-policy influences include intelligence agencies such as the CIA, economic bureaus like the Office of the U.S. Trade Representative, interest groups, corporations, foreign governments, the media, and the public.

» The key question about American foreign policy: Is the messy, fragmented system swirling around the president an effective way to generate new ideas? Or is it too chaotic for the twenty-first century? Or both?

Adding All of It Up: Grand Strategies in U.S. History

Grand strategy: An overarching vision that defines and guides a nation's foreign policy.

American leaders create an overall framework to meet the challenges of the time. Their **grand strategy** includes everything from a military doctrine to ways of seeing and interpreting the world. The United States has adopted four different grand strategies over the past century. Once a strategy is in place it can be very difficult to change—until a dramatic event breaks up the old order.

Standing Alone (1918–1939)

World War I was horrific. The fighting bogged down in trenches in eastern France, and hundreds of thousands of men died moving the battle line back and forth a few miles. After Europeans on both sides had bled their armies for three years, the United States entered the war and quickly tipped the balance. In a little more than a year, the United States led England and France to victory over Germany and Austria.

President Woodrow Wilson championed a new international order after the war. The United States would spread democracy to every nation and join with other countries in a collective security organization called the League of Nations. Wilson's dreams were, he said, "to correct the evil" and to "purify . . . every process of our common life."[20]

Wilson's highly moral and multilateral vision met with furious opposition. Many Americans were scornful of the European leaders who had blundered into the terrible war. Some became isolationists and wanted nothing more to do with international affairs. Many others became unilateralists. They were willing to act abroad, but only on American terms. They would not permit the League of Nations—or any other international organization—to make decisions for the United States. In November 1918, the Republicans won both houses of Congress and, when President Wilson refused to compromise on his multilateral approach. Congress voted down his peace treaty and refused to join the League of Nations.

In the years following World War I, the American grand strategy was simple: The United States would intervene, unilaterally, only when its own interests were threatened. The U.S. sent ships and troops around the world—to Russia (during and after the Bolshevik Revolution), Mexico, Panama, Turkey, China, and many other places. It almost always acted independently and minded its own interests.

The Cold War (1945–1991)

When World War II began in 1939, many Americans wanted nothing to do with another foreign war. "America first," they said. On December 7, 1941, Japan attacked the naval base at Pearl Harbor, sank eleven ships, and killed 2,400 men. On that day, the era of standing alone ended.

Less than four years later, large swaths of Europe and Asia lay in rubble. A mind-numbing number of people were dead (the chilling estimates vary from thirty-eight to seventy million). When the war ended, in September 1945, the only rival to the United States was the Soviet Union, whose armies occupied the nations of Central Europe. Many observers warned that the Soviets were poised to extend their control. If anyone was going to lead the free world against the Soviet Union, it had to be the United States.

The Truman administration decided to accept the Soviets' current sphere of influence but to oppose every effort to expand it, a policy known as **containment**

Containment: American Cold War strategy designed to stop the spread of communism.

● **FIGURE 18.6** *Europe during the Cold War. For fifty years, American foreign policy, operating with its allies (through the North Atlantic Treaty Organization, or NATO) focused on containing the Soviet Union in its sphere. The U.S. military prepared itself for a land war in Europe.*

(see Figure 18.6). The crucial test came in February 1947. The Democratic administration asked a Republican Congress to pour funds into Greece and Turkey to stop them from turning to communism. Legend has it that the chair of the Foreign Relations Committee, Senator Arthur Vandenberg (R-MI), promised to support Truman but gave him a word of advice about rallying the nation: "You are going to have to scare the hell out of the American people."[21] Truman proceeded to do just this in a famous speech before Congress.

Although the United States retained economic and military primacy, it joined with other nations in **multilateral organizations** dedicated to opposing communism and spreading democracy and capitalism. It broke with its own past to help establish multiple organizations: the United Nations (formed in 1945), the Organization of American States (OAS, 1948), the North Atlantic Treaty Organization (NATO, 1949), and the Southeast Asia Treaty Organization (SEATO, 1954). Senator Vandenberg gave the era its famous slogan when he quipped that American party politics "stopped at the water's edge." In other words, Democrats and Republicans would no longer disagree (at least, not too loudly) about international affairs.[22]

All the same, the era posed new and difficult questions for American leaders. Should the United States support brutal dictators if they joined us in fighting communists? Should it resist popular democratic movements if they seemed to tilt

Multilateral organization: An international organization of three or more nations organized around a common goal.

585

toward communism? Where and when should we send troops? Each of these questions eventually escalated into an angry debate. Conservatives defended the fight against "the Evil Empire," as some of them dubbed the Soviet Union. Liberals began to charge that an increasingly knee-jerk fight against the fading threat of communism was leading the United States to repress democratic movements around the world.

The debate grew heated. However, with thousands of American and Soviet missiles still threatening a nuclear holocaust, the Cold War framework remained in place—until Soviet communism suddenly collapsed.

The New World Order (1989–2001)

see for yourself 18.3

Go online to see footage of the joyous destruction of the Berlin Wall in 1989.

Around the world, people gaped at the incredible television footage in November 1989. Germans were clambering onto the Berlin Wall and ripping it apart. For almost thirty years, the wall—running through Berlin and separating communist Germany from democratic Germany—had been the symbol of the Cold War. Communist guards had shot people trying to leap to freedom. President John Kennedy had looked out at the wall and declared, "All free [people], wherever they may live, are citizens of Berlin." Ronald Reagan had stood on the same spot and challenged the Soviet leader, "Mr. Gorbachev, tear down this wall." Now the East German guards stood awkwardly by, uncertain what to do, as the delirious mob hammered the wall to pieces. Within two years, the entire Soviet empire collapsed. The framework that had guided American foreign policy for more than fifty years was suddenly irrelevant. What next?

President George H. W. Bush proclaimed "a new world order." He touted an active, multilateral march toward free markets and democracy. On his right, the neoconservatives began to press for a more muscular foreign policy. The United States should use its unchallenged military strength to make the world more peaceful, democratic, and secure, this group argued. If allies did not want to get on board, they should just get out of our way.

One of history's turning points: Jubilant Berliners climb the Berlin Wall as communism collapses. Suddenly, American foreign policymakers needed an entirely new grand strategy.

The War on Terror (2001–Present)

The 9/11 attacks killed almost three thousand people. The attacks shut down American institutions from coast to coast—financial markets in New York, Disney World in Florida, the great arch in St. Louis, and air travel across American airspace (for five days). In the stunned aftermath, the George W. Bush administration constructed a formidable new foreign-policy framework. To define the attacks as a crime would have brought in the American justice system. Instead, the administration declared them an act of war and responded with a "war on terror." That choice changed America's role in the world.

The war on terror targeted terrorists, nations that harbored terrorists, and any organizations that assisted terrorists. The war's architects took firm action to protect the homeland. They focused energy and resources on security. Opponents soon rose up and charged that a war on terror would become an endless conflict against an amorphous foe and would, in the long run, weaken the United States by undermining its bedrock values—liberty and the rule of law (we discussed this debate in Chapter 5, on civil liberties).

During the Cold War, the United States operated on the theory of *deterrence*: build a military so overpowering—including nuclear weapons—that other nations will be afraid to attack. Deterrence is aimed at other governments. However, the strategy does not work with extremists who are willing to sacrifice their lives for a cause.

What can be done against such fanatics? President George W. Bush defined the Bush Doctrine—the strategy of **preemptive war**. As the president explained it at West Point, "deterrence—the promise of massive retaliation against nations— means nothing against shadowy terrorist networks with no nation or citizens to defend." The United States, he continued, had to eliminate threats "before they emerge." Our military "must be ready to strike in any dark corner of the globe"— before a nation or group directly threatens us.[23] We must attack them before they can strike at us. In responding to terrorist threats, the United States launched long and costly wars in Afghanistan and Iraq; it launched air strikes or sent special forces into Libya, Syria, Yemen, Cameroon, and many other hot spots. However, in tackling terrorist threats, conventional means of warfare, such as invading another country, prove less effective than policing measures such as gathering intelligence and punishing criminal behavior.

The United States has struggled to implement such methods. As we have seen, intelligence agencies within the United States do not always cooperate. Preventing terrorist attacks often requires teamwork with foreign intelligence services—a

Preemptive war: The effort to attack hostile powers before they launch attacks. Highly controversial because it sanctions striking first.

What Do You Think?
Terrorists and the Rule of Law

From the start of this chapter, we described the debate between two foreign-policy goals: bolstering security and projecting American values. That tension has taken a new form in recent times. Which of the following policies would you choose in pursuing the war on terror in the future?

Hunt down terrorists. The United States has no choice but to chase after terrorists with every weapon at its disposal. Terrorists are evil and kill innocent people. We must interrogate terrorism suspects using any method that can elicit information, hunt down those who plan to do us harm, and attack nations that harbor terrorists before they can attack civilian populations around the world. A strong emphasis on national security is the only way to keep the United States—and the world—safe.

Let the law prevail. America has always stood for the rule of law. Permanent security lies not in killing terrorists but in inspiring people around the world with the power of our ideas—democracy, equality, and equal protection under the law. We proclaim our view of justice to the world when we give even our worst enemies a fair trial. The war on terror undermines our Constitution, subverts our values, and makes us weaker.

Not sure. Maybe the truth lies in between these choices. Perhaps you can design your own policy somewhere between these positions.

further complication. Because the United States cannot extradite terrorists from areas where they have proliferated, the government has resorted to dramatic policies that have raised humanitarian concerns. Controversial actions include *extraordinary rendition*, or snatching suspects off the street and whisking them away to a foreign prison. Some of these "ghost prisoners" have later reappeared in public and proclaimed their innocence. Although the Obama administration scaled back the secret programs and outlawed "harsh interrogation techniques" such as waterboarding, it never formally rejected the practice of extraordinary rendition.

The Obama administration tried to pivot toward a more cooperative and multilateral approach. However, it proved difficult to do so. Terrorist attacks horrified citizens around the world. The summer of 2016 saw attacks In Nice, France; multiple locations in Iraq; Bosso, Niger; Dhaka, Bangladesh; and Orlando, Florida. The mounting casualties rattled Western nations. Counter attacks by American drones killed terrorist leaders—and kindled an intense argument about whether they were slowly reducing terrorism or simply perpetuating the cycle of violence (illustrating the backlash or security trap introduced earlier).

As with many foreign-policy issues, the war on terror has major implications for domestic American policy. The USA Patriot Act gave police and security personnel far more latitude to monitor, search, and detain suspects both abroad and at home. The war on terror also injected new divisions into American politics. Each side emphasizes a different foreign-policy goal described at the start of the chapter—security versus American principles of justice. Each side blames the other for imperiling America's greatest strength.

As we have seen so often, institutions—once established—are hard to undo. The vital matter confronting Americans remains: What sort of grand strategy should the nation now pursue?

THE BOTTOM LINE

» The United States forged four grand strategies in the twentieth century: It stood alone and acted unilaterally (1918–1939), it led the democratic nations in multilateral coalitions during the Cold War (1945–1991), it debated a new world order after the Cold War (1991–2001), and it launched a war on terror (2001–present).

» The Obama administration called for a move away from the war on terror but found that difficult to do. Obama's White House had scaled back many of the Bush administration policies (forbidding torture, overseeing extraordinary rendition, quietly dropping the phrase "war on terror" itself); nevertheless, it has kept the basic institutional framework of the war on terror in place.

Conclusion: The Next Grand Strategy

The Obama administration came to office with a clear goal: pivot away from the Bush administration's war on terror and reestablish a multilateral foreign policy. Obama attempted to engage with allies to solve common international problems:

the overthrow of a dictator in Lybia, peacefully ending Iraq's nuclear program; isoalating threatening states such as Iran and North Korea, restraining Russia in Ukraine, piecing together an international response to the civil war in Syria. Foreign policy under Obama paid more attention to Asia and Latin America, tried to foster international cooperation in financial regulation, and worked with other nations when committing military forces to a conflict.

In short, the emerging grand strategy keeps the United States active in the world but downplays military response, reduces unilateral action, moves foreign policy through law and diplomacy, and emphasizes—above all—cooperation with other nations.[24]

Arlington National Cemetery holds the remains of soldiers from every American war. It reminds us that foreign policy reflects America's deepest values and convictions—and often calls for the nation's greatest sacrifices.

Now a new administration ponders its own grand strategy. As a candidate Donald Trump surprised security experts with offhand comments that sent shock waves through international diplomacy—mentioning, for example, a need for the United States to reassess its relations with NATO. His positions largely reflected a realist view, signaling a desire to strengthen the armed forces, to renegotiate international trade deals to favor the U.S. economy, to pull out of climate change protocols, and to work with allies to crush ISIS. In the meantime, Americans will continue to debate their foreign policy. They can choose among the following options.

- *Emphasize strategic disengagement.* Withdraw from very active—and especially military—participation in world affairs. Many liberals and conservatives believe that the United States is too involved around the world. Some would even return to the strategy that Americans adopted before World War II: Stand alone. Worry about our domestic issues.

- Return to the neoconservative grand strategy of the Bush years, with an emphasis on unilateral action. But Donald Trump appeared ambivalent about it.

- *Extend internationalism.* Continue to build a new order that works with other nations to solve the common problems of our shrinking world. Proponents of this view believe that nations must work together, in alliances, to restore peace, foster democracy, increase economic cooperation, and address environmental concerns.

Which path would you take? As you reflect on the options, go back to the goals of American foreign policy. Any grand strategy must successfully protect national security, enhance our economic well-being, and reflect American values. As you can see, the national discussion about how best to accomplish these goals suggests completely different directions—from going it alone to engaging the world and collaborating with others.

No matter what you would choose, remember the basic truth: The next American foreign-policy strategy will—like all the past ones—reflect American ideals and values. It will answer the same question raised in every chapter of this book, the deepest question of American politics: *Who are we?*

CHAPTER SUMMARY

● Foreign policy explores how the United States engages the world. Ultimately, it raises the deepest question about the nation: Is the United States the richest and most powerful country, ready to lead the world, or is it a declining superpower?

● The three goals of American foreign policy are security, prosperity, and spreading American values. These three goals sometimes conflict.

● The United States spends as much on its military as do other leading powers combined. Primacy suggests that it should act with unparalleled power. The security trap suggests that an effort to achieve and maintain primacy builds resentments and resistance. Soft power leads instead through culture and values.

● The United States is responsible for almost a quarter of the world economy and more than two and half times as much as its nearest rival, China. However, China's economic growth rate in recent years has been more than eight times higher than that of the United States.

● U.S. economic policy has generally revolved around free trade—reducing barriers to trade between nations. Lately, free trade has met resistance.

● American policymakers have to choose between isolationism and active engagement with the world. Americans also have to choose between unilateralism (going it alone) and multilateralism (working with other nations in organizations and associations).

● Congress originally shared foreign policy with the executive branch, but today prime responsibility has shifted to the executive. However, foreign policy is best understood in light of domestic policy, as the outcome of many agencies and groups pushing for their own interests and advantage.

● Twentieth-century grand strategies included standing alone (1918–1939), primacy in a coalition of anticommunist nations (1946–1989), the search for a new world order (1991–2001), and the war on terror (since 2001).

● The key question of contemporary foreign policy is whether war makes the United States more secure or whether pursuing security has compromised American values and harmed America's stance in the world.

KEY TERMS

American exceptionalism, p. 568
Containment, p. 580
Fair trade, p. 565
Free trade, p. 564
General Agreement on Tariffs and Trade (GATT), p. 565
Grand strategy, p. 580
Internationalism, p. 571

Isolationism, p. 570
Liberalism, p. 560
Multilateralism, p. 571
Multilateral organization, p. 581
Preemptive war, p. 583
Primacy, p. 559
Protectionism, p. 565
Realism, p. 559
Security trap, p. 560

Soft power, p. 561
Strategic disengagement, p. 570
Theory of democratic peace, p. 568
Trade deficit, p. 564
Unilateralism, p. 571
War Powers Act, p. 573
World Trade Organization, (WTO) p. 565

STUDY QUESTIONS

1. Name the three foreign-policy goals that the United States pursues. Discuss the relative importance of each goal. If you had to stress one, which would it be?

2. What do you consider the most important threat to American security? Would it be a traditional threat like foreign enemies, or a more common problem such as global warming? Explain your thinking.

3. What is free trade? Describe the difference between free trade and fair trade.

4. Describe "American exceptionalism." Do you consider it a truth, a myth, or something in between? Defend your answer.

5. Define strategic disengagement and internationalism. Pick one perspective and defend it.

6. Define unilateralism and multilateralism. Which position makes more sense to you? Explain why.

7. What do neoconservatives believe? Do you agree or disagree with this perspective?

8. We described four approaches to foreign policy: Wilsonian, Hamiltonian, Jeffersonian, and Jacksonian. Defend the one that most appeals to you.

9. What four grand strategies did the United States pursue in the twentieth century? Describe each.

10. If you had to design a grand strategy for today, what would you emphasize?

 Go to www.oup.com/us/Morone to find quizzes, flash cards, simulations, tutorials, videos, and other study tools.

THE DECLARATION OF INDEPENDENCE

When in the course of human events, it becomes necessary for one people to dissolve the political bands which have connected them with another, and to assume, among the powers of the earth, the separate and equal station to which the Laws of Nature and of Nature's God entitle them, a decent respect to the opinions of mankind requires that they should declare the causes which impel them to the separation.

We hold these truths to be self-evident, that all men are created equal, that they are endowed by their Creator with certain unalienable Rights, that among these are life, liberty and the pursuit of happiness. That to secure these rights, governments are instituted among men, deriving their just powers from the consent of the governed; that whenever any form of government becomes destructive of these ends, it is the right of the people to alter or to abolish it, and to institute new Government, laying its foundation on such principles and organizing its powers in such form, as to them shall seem most likely to effect their safety and happiness. Prudence, indeed, will dictate that Governments long established should not be changed for light and transient causes; and, accordingly, all experience hath shown, that mankind are more disposed to suffer, while evils are sufferable, than to right themselves by abolishing the forms to which they are accustomed. But when a long train of abuses and usurpations, pursuing invariably the same object evinces a design to reduce them under absolute despotism, it is their right, it is their duty, to throw off such government, and to provide new guards for their future security. Such has been the patient sufferance of these colonies; and such is now the necessity which constrains them to alter their former systems of government. The history of the present King of Great Britain is a history of repeated injuries and usurpations, all having in direct object the establishment of an absolute tyranny over these States. To prove this, let facts be submitted to a candid world:

He has refused his assent to laws, the most wholesome and necessary for the public good.

He has forbidden his governors to pass laws of immediate and pressing importance, unless suspended in their operation till his assent should be obtained; and, when so suspended, he has utterly neglected to attend to them.

He has refused to pass other laws for the accommodation of large districts of people, unless those people would relinquish the right of representation in the legislature, a right inestimable to them and formidable to tyrants only.

He has called together legislative bodies at places unusual, uncomfortable, and distant from the depository of their public records, for the sole purpose of fatiguing them into compliance with his measures.

He has dissolved representative houses repeatedly, for opposing with manly firmness his invasions on the rights of the people.

He has refused for a long time, after such dissolutions, to cause others to be elected; whereby the legislative powers, incapable of annihilation, have returned to the People at large for their exercise; the State remaining in the mean time exposed to all the dangers of invasion from without, and convulsions within.

He has endeavored to prevent the population of these States; for that purpose obstructing the laws for naturalization of foreigners; refusing to pass others to encourage their migrations hither, and raising the conditions of new appropriations of lands.

He has obstructed the administration of justice, by refusing his assent to laws for establishing judiciary powers.

He has made judges dependent on his will alone, for the tenure of their offices, and the amount and payment of their salaries.

He has erected a multitude of new offices, and sent hither swarms of officers to harass our people, and eat out their substance.

He has kept among us, in times of peace, standing armies without the consent of our legislatures.

He has affected to render the Military independent of, and superior to, the civil power.

A-1

He has combined with others to subject us to a jurisdiction foreign to our constitution and unacknowledged by our laws; giving his assent to their acts of pretended legislation:

For quartering large bodies of armed troops among us;

For protecting them, by a mock trial, from punishment for any murders which they should commit on the inhabitants of these States;

For cutting off our trade with all parts of the world;

For imposing taxes on us without our Consent;

For depriving us, in many cases, of the benefits of Trial by Jury;

For transporting us beyond Seas to be tried for pretended offences;

For abolishing the free System of English Laws in a neighbouring Province, establishing therein an Arbitrary government, and enlarging its Boundaries so as to render it at once an example and fit instrument for introducing the same absolute rule into these colonies;

For taking away our charters, abolishing our most valuable laws, and altering fundamentally the forms of our governments;

For suspending our own legislatures, and declaring themselves invested with power to legislate for us in all cases whatsoever.

He has abdicated government here, by declaring us out of his protection and waging war against us.

He has plundered our seas, ravaged our coasts, burnt our towns, and destroyed the lives of our people.

He is at this time transporting large armies of foreign mercenaries to complete the works of death, desolation and tyranny, already begun with circumstances of cruelty and perfidy scarcely paralleled in the most barbarous ages, and totally unworthy the head of a civilized nation.

He has constrained our fellow citizens taken captive on the high seas to bear arms against their country, to become the executioners of their friends and brethren, or to fall themselves by their hands.

He has excited domestic insurrections amongst us, and has endeavored to bring on the inhabitants of our frontiers, the merciless Indian savages, whose known rule of warfare, is an undistinguished destruction of all ages, sexes and conditions.

In every stage of these oppressions we have petitioned for redress in the most humble terms; our repeated petitions have been answered only by repeated injury. A prince whose character is thus marked by every act which may define a tyrant, is unfit to be the ruler of a free people.

Nor have we been wanting in attentions to our British brethren. We have warned them from time to time of attempts by their legislature to extend an unwarrantable jurisdiction over us. We have reminded them of the circumstances of our emigration and settlement here. We have appealed to their native justice and magnanimity, and we have conjured them by the ties of our common kindred to disavow these usurpations, which, would inevitably interrupt our connections and correspondence. They, too, have been deaf to the voice of justice and of consanguinity. We must, therefore, acquiesce in the necessity, which denounces our separation, and hold them, as we hold the rest of mankind, enemies in war, in peace friends.

We, therefore, the representatives of the United States of America, in general Congress, assembled, appealing to the Supreme Judge of the world for the rectitude of our intentions, do, in the name, and by the authority of the good people of these colonies, solemnly publish and declare, that these united colonies are, and of right ought to be free and independent states; that they are absolved from all allegiance to the British Crown, and that all political connection between them and the state of Great Britain, is and ought to be totally dissolved; and that, as free and independent states, they have full power to levy war, conclude peace, contract alliances, establish commerce, and to do all other acts and things which independent states may of right do. And for the support of this declaration, with a firm reliance on the protection of Divine Providence, we mutually pledge to each other our lives, our fortunes and our sacred honor.

THE CONSTITUTION OF THE UNITED STATES OF AMERICA

We the People of the United States, in Order to form a more perfect Union, establish Justice, insure domestic Tranquility, provide for the common defence, promote the general Welfare, and secure the Blessings of Liberty to ourselves and our Posterity, do ordain and establish this Constitution for the United States of America.

Article I

Section 1

All legislative Powers herein granted shall be vested in a Congress of the United States, which shall consist of a Senate and House of Representatives.

Section 2

The House of Representatives shall be composed of Members chosen every second Year by the People of the several States, and the Electors in each State shall have the Qualifications requisite for Electors of the most numerous Branch of the State Legislature.

No Person shall be a Representative who shall not have attained to the Age of twenty five Years, and been seven Years a Citizen of the United States, and who shall not, when elected, be an Inhabitant of that State in which he shall be chosen.

Representatives [and direct Taxes]* shall be apportioned among the several States [which may be included within this Union, according to their respective Numbers, which shall be determined by adding to the whole Number of free Persons, including those bound to Service for a Term of Years, and excluding Indians not taxed, three fifths of all other Persons].** The actual Enumeration shall be made within three Years after the first Meeting of the Congress of the United States, and within every subsequent Term of ten Years, in such Manner as they shall by Law direct. The Number of Representatives shall not exceed one for every thirty Thousand, but each State shall have at Least one Representative; and until such enumeration shall be made, the State of New Hampshire shall be entitled to choose three, Massachusetts eight, Rhode-Island and Providence Plantations one, Connecticut five, New York six, New Jersey four, Pennsylvania eight, Delaware one, Maryland six, Virginia ten, North Carolina five, South Carolina five, and Georgia three.

When vacancies happen in the Representation from any State, the Executive Authority thereof shall issue Writs of Election to fill such Vacancies.

The House of Representatives shall choose their Speaker and other Officers; and shall have the sole Power of Impeachment.

Section 3

The Senate of the United States shall be composed of two Senators from each State, chosen [by the Legislature thereof]*** for six Years; and each Senator shall have one Vote.

---

*Modified by the Sixteenth Amendment.
**Negated by the Fourteenth Amendment.
***Changed by the Seventeenth Amendment.

Immediately after they shall be assembled in Consequence of the first Election, they shall be divided as equally as may be into three Classes. The Seats of the Senators of the first Class shall be vacated at the Expiration of the second Year, of the second Class at the Expiration of the fourth Year, and of the third Class at the Expiration of the sixth Year, so that one third may be chosen every second Year, [and if Vacancies happen by Resignation, or otherwise, during the Recess of the Legislature of any State, the Executive thereof may make temporary Appointments until the next Meeting of the Legislature, which shall then fill such Vacancies].*

No Person shall be a Senator who shall not have attained to the Age of thirty Years, and been nine Years a Citizen of the United States, and who shall not, when elected, be an Inhabitant of that State for which he shall be chosen.

The Vice President of the United States shall be President of the Senate, but shall have no Vote, unless they be equally divided.

The Senate shall choose their other Officers, and also a President pro tempore, in the Absence of the Vice President, or when he shall exercise the Office of President of the United States.

The Senate shall have the sole Power to try all Impeachments. When sitting for that Purpose, they shall be on Oath or Affirmation. When the President of the United States is tried, the Chief Justice shall preside: And no Person shall be convicted without the Concurrence of two thirds of the Members present.

Judgment in Cases of Impeachment shall not extend further than to removal from Office, and disqualification to hold and enjoy any Office of honor, Trust or Profit under the United States: but the Party convicted shall nevertheless be liable and subject to Indictment, Trial, Judgment and Punishment, according to Law.

Section 4

The Times, Places and Manner of holding Elections for Senators and Representatives, shall be prescribed in each State by the Legislature thereof; but the Congress may at any time by Law make or alter such Regulations, except as to the Places of chusing Senators.

[The Congress shall assemble at least once in every Year, and such Meeting shall be on the first Monday in December, unless they shall by Law appoint a different Day.]**

Section 5

Each House shall be the Judge of the Elections, Returns and Qualifications of its own Members, and a Majority of each shall constitute a Quorum to do Business; but a smaller Number may adjourn from day to day, and may be authorized to compel the Attendance of absent Members, in such Manner, and under such Penalties as each House may provide.

Each House may determine the Rules of its Proceedings, punish its Members for disorderly Behaviour, and, with the Concurrence of two thirds, expel a Member.

Each House shall keep a Journal of its Proceedings, and from time to time publish the same, excepting such Parts as may in their Judgment require Secrecy; and the Yeas and Nays of the Members of either House on any question shall, at the Desire of one fifth of those Present, be entered on the Journal.

Neither House, during the Session of Congress, shall, without the Consent of the other, adjourn for more than three days, nor to any other Place than that in which the two Houses shall be sitting.

---

*Modified by the Seventeenth Amendment.
**Changed to January 3 by the Twentieth Amendment.

Section 6

The Senators and Representatives shall receive a Compensation for their Services, to be ascertained by Law, and paid out of the Treasury of the United States. They shall in all Cases, except Treason, Felony and Breach of the Peace, be privileged from Arrest during their Attendance at the Session of their respective Houses, and in going to and returning from the same; and for any Speech or Debate in either House, they shall not be questioned in any other Place.

No Senator or Representative shall, during the Time for which he was elected, be appointed to any civil Office under the Authority of the United States, which shall have been created, or the Emoluments whereof shall have been increased during such time; and no Person holding any Office under the United States, shall be a Member of either House during his Continuance in Office.

Section 7

All Bills for raising Revenue shall originate in the House of Representatives; but the Senate may propose or concur with Amendments as on other Bills.

Every Bill which shall have passed the House of Representatives and the Senate, shall, before it become a Law, be presented to the President of the United States: If he approve he shall sign it, but if not he shall return it, with his Objections to that House in which it shall have originated, who shall enter the Objections at large on their Journal, and proceed to reconsider it. If after such Reconsideration two thirds of that House shall agree to pass the Bill, it shall be sent, together with the Objections, to the other House, by which it shall likewise be reconsidered, and if approved by two thirds of that House, it shall become a Law. But in all such Cases the Votes of both Houses shall be determined by yeas and Nays, and the Names of the Persons voting for and against the Bill shall be entered on the Journal of each House respectively. If any Bill shall not be returned by the President within ten Days (Sundays excepted) after it shall have been presented to him, the Same shall be a Law, in like Manner as if he had signed it, unless the Congress by their Adjournment prevent its Return, in which Case it shall not be a Law.

Every Order, Resolution, or Vote to which the Concurrence of the Senate and House of Representatives may be necessary (except on a question of Adjournment) shall be presented to the President of the United States; and before the Same shall take Effect, shall be approved by him, or being disapproved by him, shall be re-passed by two thirds of the Senate and House of Representatives, according to the Rules and Limitations prescribed in the Case of a Bill.

Section 8

The Congress shall have Power

To lay and collect Taxes, Duties, Imposts and Excises, to pay the Debts and provide for the common Defence and general Welfare of the United States; but all Duties, Imposts and Excises shall be uniform throughout the United States;

To borrow Money on the credit of the United States;

To regulate Commerce with foreign Nations, and among the several States, and with the Indian Tribes;

To establish an uniform Rule of Naturalization, and uniform Laws on the subject of Bankruptcies throughout the United States;

To coin Money, regulate the Value thereof, and of foreign Coin, and fix the Standard of Weights and Measures;

To provide for the Punishment of counterfeiting the Securities and current Coin of the United States;

To establish Post Offices and post Roads;

To promote the Progress of Science and useful Arts, by securing for limited Times to Authors and Inventors the exclusive Right to their respective Writings and Discoveries;

To constitute Tribunals inferior to the supreme Court;

To define and punish Piracies and Felonies committed on the high Seas, and Offences against the Law of Nations;

To declare War, grant Letters of Marque and Reprisal, and make Rules concerning Captures on Land and Water;

To raise and support Armies, but no Appropriation of Money to that Use shall be for a longer Term than two Years;

To provide and maintain a Navy;

To make Rules for the Government and Regulation of the land and naval Forces;

To provide for calling forth the Militia to execute the Laws of the Union, suppress Insurrections and repel Invasions;

To provide for organizing, arming, and disciplining the Militia, and for governing such Part of them as may be employed in the Service of the United States, reserving to the States respectively, the Appointment of the Officers, and the Authority of training the Militia according to the discipline prescribed by Congress;

To exercise exclusive Legislation in all Cases whatsoever, over such District (not exceeding ten Miles square) as may, by Cession of particular States, and the Acceptance of Congress, become the Seat of the Government of the United States, and to exercise like Authority over all Places purchased by the Consent of the Legislature of the State in which the Same shall be, for the Erection of Forts, Magazines, Arsenals, dock-Yards, and other needful Buildings;—And

To make all Laws which shall be necessary and proper for carrying into Execution the foregoing Powers, and all other Powers vested by this Constitution in the Government of the United States, or in any Department or Officer thereof.

Section 9

The Migration or Importation of such Persons as any of the States now existing shall think proper to admit, shall not be prohibited by the Congress prior to the Year one thousand eight hundred and eight, but a Tax or duty may be imposed on such Importation, not exceeding ten dollars for each Person.

The Privilege of the Writ of Habeas Corpus shall not be suspended, unless when in Cases of Rebellion or Invasion the public Safety may require it.

No Bill of Attainder or ex post facto Law shall be passed.

[No Capitation, or other direct, Tax shall be laid, unless in Proportion to the Census or enumeration herein before directed to be taken.]*

No Tax or Duty shall be laid on Articles exported from any State.

No Preference shall be given by any Regulation of Commerce or Revenue to the Ports of one State over those of another; nor shall Vessels bound to, or from, one State, be obliged to enter, clear, or pay Duties in another.

No Money shall be drawn from the Treasury, but in Consequence of Appropriations made by Law; and a regular Statement and Account of the Receipts and Expenditures of all public Money shall be published from time to time.

No Title of Nobility shall be granted by the United States: And no Person holding any Office of Profit or Trust under them, shall, without the Consent of the Congress, accept of any present, Emolument, Office, or Title, of any kind whatever, from any King, Prince, or foreign State.

---

*Modified by the Sixteenth Amendment.

Section 10

No State shall enter into any Treaty, Alliance, or Confederation; grant Letters of Marque and Reprisal; coin Money; emit Bills of Credit; make any Thing but gold and silver Coin a Tender in Payment of Debts; pass any Bill of Attainder, ex post facto Law, or Law impairing the Obligation of Contracts, or grant any Title of Nobility.

No State shall, without the Consent of the Congress, lay any Imposts or Duties on Imports or Exports, except what may be absolutely necessary for executing it's inspection Laws: and the net Produce of all Duties and Imposts, laid by any State on Imports or Exports, shall be for the Use of the Treasury of the United States; and all such Laws shall be subject to the Revision and Control of the Congress.

No State shall, without the Consent of Congress, lay any Duty of Tonnage, keep Troops, or Ships of War in time of Peace, enter into any Agreement or Compact with another State, or with a foreign Power, or engage in War, unless actually invaded, or in such imminent Danger as will not admit of delay.

Article II

Section 1

The executive Power shall be vested in a President of the United States of America. He shall hold his Office during the Term of four Years, and, together with the Vice President, chosen for the same Term, be elected, as follows:

Each State shall appoint, in such Manner as the Legislature thereof may direct, a Number of Electors, equal to the whole Number of Senators and Representatives to which the State may be entitled in the Congress: but no Senator or Representative, or Person holding an Office of Trust or Profit under the United States, shall be appointed an Elector.

[The Electors shall meet in their respective States, and vote by Ballot for two Persons, of whom one at least shall not be an Inhabitant of the same State with themselves. And they shall make a List of all the Persons voted for, and of the Number of Votes for each; which List they shall sign and certify, and transmit sealed to the Seat of the Government of the United States, directed to the President of the Senate. The President of the Senate shall, in the Presence of the Senate and House of Representatives, open all the Certificates, and the Votes shall then be counted. The Person having the greatest Number of Votes shall be the President, if such Number be a Majority of the whole Number of Electors appointed; and if there be more than one who have such Majority, and have an equal Number of Votes, then the House of Representatives shall immediately choose by Ballot one of them for President; and if no Person have a Majority, then from the five highest on the List the said House shall in like Manner choose the President. But in choosing the President, the Votes shall be taken by States, the Representation from each State having one Vote; a quorum for this purpose shall consist of a Member or Members from two thirds of the States, and a Majority of all the States shall be necessary to a Choice. In every Case, after the Choice of the President, the Person having the greatest Number of Votes of the Electors shall be the Vice President. But if there should remain two or more who have equal Votes, the Senate shall choose from them by Ballot the Vice President.]*

The Congress may determine the Time of choosing the Electors, and the Day on which they shall give their Votes; which Day shall be the same throughout the United States.

No Person except a natural born Citizen, or a Citizen of the United States, at the time of the Adoption of this Constitution, shall be eligible to the Office of

---

*Changed by the Twelfth and Twentieth Amendments.

President; neither shall any Person be eligible to that Office who shall not have attained to the Age of thirty five Years, and been fourteen Years a Resident within the United States.

In Case of the Removal of the President from Office, or of his Death, Resignation, or Inability to discharge the Powers and Duties of the said Office, the Same shall devolve on the Vice President, and the Congress may by Law provide for the Case of Removal, Death, Resignation or Inability, both of the President and Vice President, declaring what Officer shall then act as President, and such Officer shall act accordingly, until the Disability be removed, or a President shall be elected.

The President shall, at stated Times, receive for his Services, a Compensation, which shall neither be increased nor diminished during the Period for which he shall have been elected, and he shall not receive within that Period any other Emolument from the United States, or any of them.

Before he enter on the Execution of his Office, he shall take the following Oath or Affirmation:—"I do solemnly swear (or affirm) that I will faithfully execute the Office of President of the United States, and will to the best of my Ability, preserve, protect and defend the Constitution of the United States."

Section 2

The President shall be Commander in Chief of the Army and Navy of the United States, and of the Militia of the several States, when called into the actual Service of the United States; he may require the Opinion, in writing, of the principal Officer in each of the executive Departments, upon any Subject relating to the Duties of their respective Offices, and he shall have Power to grant Reprieves and Pardons for Offences against the United States, except in Cases of Impeachment.

He shall have Power, by and with the Advice and Consent of the Senate, to make Treaties, provided two thirds of the Senators present concur; and he shall nominate, and by and with the Advice and Consent of the Senate, shall appoint Ambassadors, other public Ministers and Consuls, Judges of the supreme Court, and all other Officers of the United States, whose Appointments are not herein otherwise provided for, and which shall be established by Law: but the Congress may by Law vest the Appointment of such inferior Officers, as they think proper, in the President alone, in the Courts of Law, or in the Heads of Departments.

The President shall have Power to fill up all Vacancies that may happen during the Recess of the Senate, by granting Commissions which shall expire at the End of their next Session.

Section 3

He shall from time to time give to the Congress Information of the State of the Union, and recommend to their Consideration such Measures as he shall judge necessary and expedient; he may, on extraordinary Occasions, convene both Houses, or either of them, and in Case of Disagreement between them, with Respect to the Time of Adjournment, he may adjourn them to such Time as he shall think proper; he shall receive Ambassadors and other public Ministers; he shall take Care that the Laws be faithfully executed, and shall Commission all the Officers of the United States.

Section 4

The President, Vice President and all civil Officers of the United States, shall be removed from Office on Impeachment for, and Conviction of, Treason, Bribery, or other high Crimes and Misdemeanors.

Article III

Section 1

The judicial Power of the United States shall be vested in one supreme Court, and in such inferior Courts as the Congress may from time to time ordain and establish. The Judges, both of the supreme and inferior Courts, shall hold their Offices during good Behaviour, and shall, at stated Times, receive for their Services a Compensation, which shall not be diminished during their Continuance in Office.

Section 2

The judicial Power shall extend to all Cases, in Law and Equity, arising under this Constitution, the Laws of the United States, and Treaties made, or which shall be made, under their Authority;—to all Cases affecting Ambassadors, other public Ministers and Consuls;—to all Cases of admiralty and maritime Jurisdiction;—to Controversies to which the United States shall be a Party;—to Controversies between two or more States;—[between a State and Citizens of another State];—between Citizens of different States;—between Citizens of the same State claiming Lands under Grants of different States, [and between a State,] or the Citizens thereof, [and foreign States, Citizens or Subjects].*

In all Cases affecting Ambassadors, other public Ministers and Consuls, and those in which a State shall be Party, the supreme Court shall have original Jurisdiction. In all the other Cases before mentioned, the supreme Court shall have appellate Jurisdiction, both as to Law and Fact, with such Exceptions, and under such Regulations as the Congress shall make.

The Trial of all Crimes, except in Cases of Impeachment, shall be by Jury; and such Trial shall be held in the State where the said Crimes shall have been committed; but when not committed within any State, the Trial shall be at such Place or Places as the Congress may by Law have directed.

Section 3

Treason against the United States, shall consist only in levying War against them, or in adhering to their Enemies, giving them Aid and Comfort. No Person shall be convicted of Treason unless on the Testimony of two Witnesses to the same overt Act, or on Confession in open Court.

The Congress shall have Power to declare the Punishment of Treason, but no Attainder of Treason shall work Corruption of Blood, or Forfeiture except during the Life of the Person attainted.

Article IV

Section 1

Full Faith and Credit shall be given in each State to the public Acts, Records, and judicial Proceedings of every other State. And the Congress may by general Laws prescribe the Manner in which such Acts, Records and Proceedings shall be proved, and the Effect thereof.

Section 2

The Citizens of each State shall be entitled to all Privileges and Immunities of Citizens in the several States.

---

*Altered by the Twelfth Amendment.

A Person charged in any State with Treason, Felony, or other Crime, who shall flee from Justice, and be found in another State, shall on Demand of the executive Authority of the State from which he fled, be delivered up, to be removed to the State having Jurisdiction of the Crime.

[No Person held to Service or Labour in one State, under the Laws thereof, escaping into another, shall, in Consequence of any Law or Regulation therein, be discharged from such Service or Labour, but shall be delivered up on Claim of the Party to whom such Service or Labour may be due.]*

Section 3

New States may be admitted by the Congress into this Union; but no new State shall be formed or erected within the Jurisdiction of any other State; nor any State be formed by the Junction of two or more States, or Parts of States, without the Consent of the Legislatures of the States concerned as well as of the Congress.

The Congress shall have Power to dispose of and make all needful Rules and Regulations respecting the Territory or other Property belonging to the United States; and nothing in this Constitution shall be so construed as to Prejudice any Claims of the United States, or of any particular State.

Section 4

The United States shall guarantee to every State in this Union a Republican Form of Government, and shall protect each of them against Invasion; and on Application of the Legislature, or of the Executive (when the Legislature cannot be convened), against domestic Violence.

Article V

The Congress, whenever two thirds of both Houses shall deem it necessary, shall propose Amendments to this Constitution, or, on the Application of the Legislatures of two thirds of the several States, shall call a Convention for proposing Amendments, which, in either Case, shall be valid to all Intents and Purposes, as Part of this Constitution, when ratified by the Legislatures of three fourths of the several States, or by Conventions in three fourths thereof, as the one or the other Mode of Ratification may be proposed by the Congress; Provided that no Amendment which may be made prior to the Year One thousand eight hundred and eight shall in any Manner affect the first and fourth Clauses in the Ninth Section of the first Article; and that no State, without its Consent, shall be deprived of its equal Suffrage in the Senate.

Article VI

All Debts contracted and Engagements entered into, before the Adoption of this Constitution, shall be as valid against the United States under this Constitution, as under the Confederation.

This Constitution, and the Laws of the United States which shall be made in Pursuance thereof; and all Treaties made, or which shall be made, under the Authority of the United States, shall be the supreme Law of the Land; and the Judges in every State shall be bound thereby, any Thing in the Constitution or Laws of any State to the Contrary notwithstanding.

The Senators and Representatives before mentioned, and the Members of the several State Legislatures, and all executive and judicial Officers, both of the United

*Repealed by the Thirteenth Amendment.

States and of the several States, shall be bound by Oath or Affirmation, to support this Constitution; but no religious Test shall ever be required as a Qualification to any Office or public Trust under the United States.

Article VII

The Ratification of the Conventions of nine States, shall be sufficient for the Establishment of this Constitution between the States so ratifying the Same.

The Word, "the," being interlined between the seventh and eighth Lines of the first Page, the Word "Thirty" being partly written on an Erazure in the fifteenth Line of the first Page, The Words "is tried" being interlined between the thirty second and thirty third Lines of the first Page and the Word "the" being interlined between the forty third and forty fourth Lines of the second Page.

Attest William Jackson Secretary

Done in Convention by the Unanimous Consent of the States present the Seventeenth Day of September in the Year of our Lord one thousand seven hundred and Eighty seven and of the Independence of the United States of America the Twelfth In witness whereof We have hereunto subscribed our Names,

G°. WASHINGTON

Presidt and deputy from Virginia

Delaware
Geo: Read
Gunning Bedford
    jun
John Dickinson
Richard Bassett
Jaco: Broom

Maryland
James McHenry
Dan of St Thos. Jenifer
Danl. Carroll

Virginia
John Blair
James Madison Jr.

North Carolina
Wm. Blount
Richd. Dobbs
    Spaight
Hu Williamson

South Carolina
J. Rutledge
Charles Cotesworth
    Pinckney
Charles Pinckney
Pierce Butler

Georgia
William Few
Abr Baldwin

New Hampshire
John Langdon
Nicholas Gilman

Massachusetts
Nathaniel Gorham
Rufus King

Connecticut
Wm. Saml. Johnson
Roger Sherman

New York
Alexander Hamilton

New Jersey
Wil: Livingston
David Brearley
Wm. Paterson
Jona: Dayton

Pennsylvania
B Franklin
Thomas Mifflin
Robt. Morris
Geo. Clymer
Thos. FitzSimons
Jared Ingersoll
James Wilson
Gouv Morris

Articles

In addition to, and Amendment of the Constitution of the United States of America, proposed by Congress, and ratified by the Legislatures of the several States, pursuant to the fifth Article of the original Constitution.

(The first ten amendments to the U.S. Constitution were ratified December 15, 1791, and form what is known as the "Bill of Rights.")

Amendment I

Congress shall make no law respecting an establishment of religion, or prohibiting the free exercise thereof; or abridging the freedom of speech, or of the press; or the right of the people peaceably to assemble, and to petition the Government for a redress of grievances.

Amendment II

A well regulated Militia, being necessary to the security of a free State, the right of the people to keep and bear Arms, shall not be infringed.

Amendment III

No Soldier shall, in time of peace be quartered in any house, without the consent of the Owner, nor in time of war, but in a manner to be prescribed by law.

Amendment IV

The right of the people to be secure in their persons, houses, papers, and effects, against unreasonable searches and seizures, shall not be violated, and no Warrants shall issue, but upon probable cause, supported by Oath or affirmation, and particularly describing the place to be searched, and the persons or things to be seized.

Amendment V

No person shall be held to answer for a capital, or otherwise infamous crime, unless on a presentment or indictment of a Grand Jury, except in cases arising in the land or naval forces, or in the Militia, when in actual service in time of War or public danger; nor shall any person be subject for the same offence to be twice put in jeopardy of life or limb; nor shall be compelled in any criminal case to be a witness against himself, nor be deprived of life, liberty, or property, without due process of law; nor shall private property be taken for public use, without just compensation.

Amendment VI

In all criminal prosecutions, the accused shall enjoy the right to a speedy and public trial, by an impartial jury of the State and district wherein the crime shall have been committed, which district shall have been previously ascertained by law, and to be informed of the nature and cause of the accusation; to be confronted with the witnesses against him; to have compulsory process for obtaining witnesses in his favor, and to have the Assistance of Counsel for his defence.

Amendment VII

In Suits at common law, where the value in controversy shall exceed twenty dollars, the right of trial by jury shall be preserved, and no fact tried by a jury, shall be otherwise re-examined in any Court of the United States, than according to the rules of the common law.

Amendment VIII

Excessive bail shall not be required, nor excessive fines imposed, nor cruel and unusual punishments inflicted.

Amendment IX

The enumeration in the Constitution, of certain rights, shall not be construed to deny or disparage others retained by the people.

Amendment X

The powers not delegated to the United States by the Constitution, nor prohibited by it to the States, are reserved to the States respectively, or to the people.

Amendment XI

Passed by Congress March 4, 1794. Ratified February 7, 1795.

Note: Article III, Section 2, of the Constitution was modified by Amendment XI.

The Judicial power of the United States shall not be construed to extend to any suit in law or equity, commenced or prosecuted against one of the United States by Citizens of another State, or by Citizens or Subjects of any Foreign State.

Amendment XII

Passed by Congress December 9, 1803. Ratified June 15, 1804.

Note: A portion of Article II, Section 1, of the Constitution was superseded by the Twelfth Amendment.

The Electors shall meet in their respective states and vote by ballot for President and Vice-President, one of whom, at least, shall not be an inhabitant of the same state with themselves; they shall name in their ballots the person voted for as President, and in distinct ballots the person voted for as Vice-President, and they shall make distinct lists of all persons voted for as President, and of all persons voted for as Vice-President, and of the number of votes for each, which lists they shall sign and certify, and transmit sealed to the seat of the government of the United States, directed to the President of the Senate;—the President of the Senate shall, in the presence of the Senate and House of Representatives, open all the certificates and the votes shall then be counted;—The person having the greatest number of votes for President, shall be the President, if such number be a majority of the whole number of Electors appointed; and if no person have such majority, then from the persons having the highest numbers not exceeding three on the list of those voted for as President, the House of Representatives shall choose immediately, by ballot, the President. But in choosing the President, the votes shall be taken by states, the representation from each state having one vote; a quorum for this purpose shall consist of a member or members from two-thirds of the states, and a majority of all the states shall be necessary to a choice. [And if the House of Representatives shall not choose a President whenever the right of choice shall devolve upon them, before the fourth day of March next following, then the Vice-President shall act as President, as in case of the death or other constitutional disability of the President.—]* The person having the greatest number of votes as Vice-President, shall be the Vice-President, if such number be a majority of the whole number of Electors appointed, and if no person have a majority, then from the two highest numbers on the list, the Senate shall choose the Vice-President; a quorum for the purpose shall consist of two-thirds of the whole number of Senators, and a majority of the whole number shall be necessary to a choice. But no person constitutionally ineligible to the office of President shall be eligible to that of Vice-President of the United States.

---

*Superseded by Section 3 of the Twentieth Amendment.

Amendment XIII

Passed by Congress January 31, 1865. Ratified December 6, 1865.

Note: A portion of Article IV, Section 2, of the Constitution was superseded by the Thirteenth Amendment.

Section 1

Neither slavery nor involuntary servitude, except as a punishment for crime whereof the party shall have been duly convicted, shall exist within the United States, or any place subject to their jurisdiction.

Section 2

Congress shall have power to enforce this article by appropriate legislation.

Amendment XIV

Passed by Congress June 13, 1866. Ratified July 9, 1868.

Note: Article I, Section 2, of the Constitution was modified by Section 2 of the Fourteenth Amendment.

Section 1

All persons born or naturalized in the United States, and subject to the jurisdiction thereof, are citizens of the United States and of the State wherein they reside. No State shall make or enforce any law which shall abridge the privileges or immunities of citizens of the United States; nor shall any State deprive any person of life, liberty, or property, without due process of law; nor deny to any person within its jurisdiction the equal protection of the laws.

Section 2

Representatives shall be apportioned among the several States according to their respective numbers, counting the whole number of persons in each State, excluding Indians not taxed. But when the right to vote at any election for the choice of electors for President and Vice-President of the United States, Representatives in Congress, the Executive and Judicial officers of a State, or the members of the Legislature thereof, is denied to any of the male inhabitants of such State, being twenty-one years of age,* and citizens of the United States, or in any way abridged, except for participation in rebellion, or other crime, the basis of representation therein shall be reduced in the proportion which the number of such male citizens shall bear to the whole number of male citizens twenty-one years of age in such State.

Section 3

No person shall be a Senator or Representative in Congress, or elector of President and Vice-President, or hold any office, civil or military, under the United States, or under any State, who, having previously taken an oath, as a member of Congress, or as an officer of the United States, or as a member of any State legislature, or as an executive or judicial officer of any State, to support the Constitution of the United States, shall have engaged in insurrection or rebellion against the same, or given aid or comfort to the enemies thereof. But Congress may by a vote of two-thirds of each House, remove such disability.

---

*Changed by Section 1 of the Twenty-sixth Amendment.

Section 4

The validity of the public debt of the United States, authorized by law, including debts incurred for payment of pensions and bounties for services in suppressing insurrection or rebellion, shall not be questioned. But neither the United States nor any State shall assume or pay any debt or obligation incurred in aid of insurrection or rebellion against the United States, or any claim for the loss or emancipation of any slave; but all such debts, obligations and claims shall be held illegal and void.

Section 5

The Congress shall have the power to enforce, by appropriate legislation, the provisions of this article.

Amendment XV

Passed by Congress February 26, 1869. Ratified February 3, 1870.

Section 1

The right of citizens of the United States to vote shall not be denied or abridged by the United States or by any State on account of race, color, or previous condition of servitude.

Section 2

The Congress shall have the power to enforce this article by appropriate legislation.

Amendment XVI

Passed by Congress July 2, 1909. Ratified February 3, 1913.

Note: Article I, Section 9, of the Constitution was modified by Amendment XVI.

The Congress shall have power to lay and collect taxes on incomes, from whatever source derived, without apportionment among the several States, and without regard to any census or enumeration.

Amendment XVII

Passed by Congress May 13, 1912. Ratified April 8, 1913.

Note: Article I, Section 3, of the Constitution was modified by the Seventeenth Amendment.

The Senate of the United States shall be composed of two Senators from each State, elected by the people thereof, for six years; and each Senator shall have one vote. The electors in each State shall have the qualifications requisite for electors of the most numerous branch of the State legislatures.

When vacancies happen in the representation of any State in the Senate, the executive authority of such State shall issue writs of election to fill such vacancies: Provided, That the legislature of any State may empower the executive thereof to make temporary appointments until the people fill the vacancies by election as the legislature may direct.

This amendment shall not be so construed as to affect the election or term of any Senator chosen before it becomes valid as part of the Constitution.

Amendment XVIII

Passed by Congress December 18, 1917. Ratified January 16, 1919. Repealed by Amendment XXI.

Section 1

After one year from the ratification of this article the manufacture, sale, or transportation of intoxicating liquors within, the importation thereof into, or the exportation thereof from the United States and all territory subject to the jurisdiction thereof for beverage purposes is hereby prohibited.

Section 2

The Congress and the several States shall have concurrent power to enforce this article by appropriate legislation.

Section 3

This article shall be inoperative unless it shall have been ratified as an amendment to the Constitution by the legislatures of the several States, as provided in the Constitution, within seven years from the date of the submission hereof to the States by the Congress.

Amendment XIX

Passed by Congress June 4, 1919. Ratified August 18, 1920.

The right of citizens of the United States to vote shall not be denied or abridged by the United States or by any State on account of sex.

Congress shall have power to enforce this article by appropriate legislation.

Amendment XX

Passed by Congress March 2, 1932. Ratified January 23, 1933.

Note: Article I, Section 4, of the Constitution was modified by Section 2 of this amendment. In addition, a portion of the Twelfth Amendment was superseded by Section 3.

Section 1

The terms of the President and the Vice President shall end at noon on the 20th day of January, and the terms of Senators and Representatives at noon on the 3d day of January, of the years in which such terms would have ended if this article had not been ratified; and the terms of their successors shall then begin.

Section 2

The Congress shall assemble at least once in every year, and such meeting shall begin at noon on the 3d day of January, unless they shall by law appoint a different day.

Section 3

If, at the time fixed for the beginning of the term of the President, the President elect shall have died, the Vice President elect shall become President. If a President shall not have been chosen before the time fixed for the beginning of his term, or if the President elect shall have failed to qualify, then the Vice President elect shall act as President until a President shall have qualified; and the Congress may by law provide for the case wherein neither a President elect nor a Vice President shall have qualified, declaring who shall then act as President, or the manner in which one who is to act shall be selected, and such person shall act accordingly until a President or Vice President shall have qualified.

Section 4

The Congress may by law provide for the case of the death of any of the persons from whom the House of Representatives may choose a President whenever the right of choice shall have devolved upon them, and for the case of the death of any of the persons from whom the Senate may choose a Vice President whenever the right of choice shall have devolved upon them.

Section 5

Sections 1 and 2 shall take effect on the 15th day of October following the ratification of this article.

Section 6

This article shall be inoperative unless it shall have been ratified as an amendment to the Constitution by the legislatures of three-fourths of the several States within seven years from the date of its submission.

Amendment XXI

Passed by Congress February 20, 1933. Ratified December 5, 1933.

Section 1

The eighteenth article of amendment to the Constitution of the United States is hereby repealed.

Section 2

The transportation or importation into any State, Territory, or Possession of the United States for delivery or use therein of intoxicating liquors, in violation of the laws thereof, is hereby prohibited.

Section 3

This article shall be inoperative unless it shall have been ratified as an amendment to the Constitution by conventions in the several States, as provided in the Constitution, within seven years from the date of the submission hereof to the States by the Congress.

Amendment XXII

Passed by Congress March 21, 1947. Ratified February 27, 1951.

Section 1

No person shall be elected to the office of the President more than twice, and no person who has held the office of President, or acted as President, for more than two years of a term to which some other person was elected President shall be elected to the office of President more than once. But this Article shall not apply to any person holding the office of President when this Article was proposed by Congress, and shall not prevent any person who may be holding the office of President, or acting as President, during the term within which this Article becomes operative from holding the office of President or acting as President during the remainder of such term.

Section 2

This article shall be inoperative unless it shall have been ratified as an amendment to the Constitution by the legislatures of three-fourths of the several States within seven years from the date of its submission to the States by the Congress.

Amendment XXIII

Passed by Congress June 16, 1960. Ratified March 29, 1961.

Section 1

The District constituting the seat of Government of the United States shall appoint in such manner as Congress may direct:

A number of electors of President and Vice President equal to the whole number of Senators and Representatives in Congress to which the District would be entitled if it were a State, but in no event more than the least populous State; they shall be in addition to those appointed by the States, but they shall be considered, for the purposes of the election of President and Vice President, to be electors appointed by a State; and they shall meet in the District and perform such duties as provided by the twelfth article of amendment.

Section 2

The Congress shall have power to enforce this article by appropriate legislation.

Amendment XXIV

Passed by Congress August 27, 1962. Ratified January 23, 1964.

Section 1

The right of citizens of the United States to vote in any primary or other election for President or Vice President, for electors for President or Vice President, or for Senator or Representative in Congress, shall not be denied or abridged by the United States or any State by reason of failure to pay poll tax or other tax.

Section 2

The Congress shall have power to enforce this article by appropriate legislation.

Amendment XXV

Passed by Congress July 6, 1965. Ratified February 10, 1967.

Note: Article II, Section 1, of the Constitution was affected by the Twenty-Fifth Amendment.

Section 1

In case of the removal of the President from office or of his death or resignation, the Vice President shall become President.

Section 2

Whenever there is a vacancy in the office of the Vice President, the President shall nominate a Vice President who shall take office upon confirmation by a majority vote of both Houses of Congress.

Section 3

Whenever the President transmits to the President pro tempore of the Senate and the Speaker of the House of Representatives his written declaration that he is unable to discharge the powers and duties of his office, and until he transmits to them a written declaration to the contrary, such powers and duties shall be discharged by the Vice President as Acting President.

Section 4

Whenever the Vice President and a majority of either the principal officers of the executive departments or of such other body as Congress may by law provide, transmit to the President pro tempore of the Senate and the Speaker of the House of Representatives their written declaration that the President is unable to discharge the powers and duties of his office, the Vice President shall immediately assume the powers and duties of the office as Acting President.

Thereafter, when the President transmits to the President pro tempore of the Senate and the Speaker of the House of Representatives his written declaration that no inability exists, he shall resume the powers and duties of his office unless the Vice President and a majority of either the principal officers of the executive department or of such other body as Congress may by law provide, transmit within four days to the President pro tempore of the Senate and the Speaker of the House of Representatives their written declaration that the President is unable to discharge the powers and duties of his office. Thereupon Congress shall decide the issue, assembling within forty-eight hours for that purpose if not in session. If the Congress, within twenty-one days after receipt of the latter written declaration, or, if Congress is not in session, within twenty-one days after Congress is required to assemble, determines by two-thirds vote of both Houses that the President is unable to discharge the powers and duties of his office, the Vice President shall continue to discharge the same as Acting President; otherwise, the President shall resume the powers and duties of his office.

Amendment XXVI

Passed by Congress March 23, 1971. Ratified July 1, 1971.

Note: Amendment XIV, Section 2, of the Constitution was modified by Section 1 of the Twenty-Sixth Amendment.

Section 1

The right of citizens of the United States, who are eighteen years of age or older, to vote shall not be denied or abridged by the United States or by any State on account of age.

Section 2

The Congress shall have power to enforce this article by appropriate legislation.

Amendment XXVII

Originally proposed Sept. 25, 1789. Ratified May 7, 1992.

No law, varying the compensation for the services of the Senators and Representatives, shall take effect, until an election of representatives shall have intervened.

APPENDIX III

THE FEDERALIST PAPERS

By Alexander Hamilton, James Madison, John Jay

The debate over ratifying the Constitution in 1787-8 was very close, especially in New York. To persuade the people of the state, Hamilton, Madison, and Jay wrote eighty-five newspaper essays arguing for ratification. Three of the most influential, reproduced here, are Federalist Papers 1, 10, and 51.

FEDERALIST No. 1
General Introduction
For the Independent Journal. Saturday, October 27, 1787

HAMILTON
To the People of the State of New York:

AFTER an unequivocal experience of the inefficacy of the subsisting federal government, you are called upon to deliberate on a new Constitution for the United States of America. The subject speaks its own importance; comprehending in its consequences nothing less than the existence of the UNION, the safety and welfare of the parts of which it is composed, the fate of an empire in many respects the most interesting in the world. It has been frequently remarked that it seems to have been reserved to the people of this country, by their conduct and example, to decide the important question, whether societies of men are really capable or not of establishing good government from reflection and choice, or whether they are forever destined to depend for their political constitutions on accident and force. If there be any truth in the remark, the crisis at which we are arrived may with propriety be regarded as the era in which that decision is to be made; and a wrong election of the part we shall act may, in this view, deserve to be considered as the general misfortune of mankind.

This idea will add the inducements of philanthropy to those of patriotism, to heighten the solicitude which all considerate and good men must feel for the event. Happy will it be if our choice should be directed by a judicious estimate of our true interests, unperplexed and unbiased by considerations not connected with the public good. But this is a thing more ardently to be wished than seriously to be expected. The plan offered to our deliberations affects too many particular interests, innovates upon too many local institutions, not to involve in its discussion a variety of objects foreign to its merits, and of views, passions and prejudices little favorable to the discovery of truth.

Among the most formidable of the obstacles which the new Constitution will have to encounter may readily be distinguished the obvious interest of a certain class of men in every State to resist all changes which may hazard a diminution of the power, emolument, and consequence of the offices they hold under the State establishments; and the perverted ambition of another class of men, who will either hope to aggrandize themselves by the confusions of their country, or will flatter themselves with fairer prospects of elevation from the subdivision of the empire into several partial confederacies than from its union under one government.

It is not, however, my design to dwell upon observations of this nature. I am well aware that it would be disingenuous to resolve indiscriminately the opposition of any set of men (merely because their situations might subject them to suspicion) into interested or ambitious views. Candor will oblige us to admit that even such men may be actuated by upright intentions; and it cannot be doubted that much of the opposition which has made its appearance, or may hereafter make its appearance, will spring from sources, blameless at least, if not respectable—the honest errors of minds led astray by preconceived jealousies and fears. So numerous indeed and so powerful are the causes which serve to give a false bias to the judgment, that we, upon many occasions, see wise and good men on the wrong as well as on the right side of questions of the first magnitude to society. This circumstance, if duly attended to, would furnish a lesson of moderation to those who are ever so much persuaded of their being in the right in any controversy. And a further reason for caution, in this

A-20

respect, might be drawn from the reflection that we are not always sure that those who advocate the truth are influenced by purer principles than their antagonists. Ambition, avarice, personal animosity, party opposition, and many other motives not more laudable than these, are apt to operate as well upon those who support as those who oppose the right side of a question. Were there not even these inducements to moderation, nothing could be more ill-judged than that intolerant spirit which has, at all times, characterized political parties. For in politics, as in religion, it is equally absurd to aim at making proselytes by fire and sword. Heresies in either can rarely be cured by persecution.

And yet, however just these sentiments will be allowed to be, we have already sufficient indications that it will happen in this as in all former cases of great national discussion. A torrent of angry and malignant passions will be let loose. To judge from the conduct of the opposite parties, we shall be led to conclude that they will mutually hope to evince the justness of their opinions, and to increase the number of their converts by the loudness of their declamations and the bitterness of their invectives. An enlightened zeal for the energy and efficiency of government will be stigmatized as the offspring of a temper fond of despotic power and hostile to the principles of liberty. An over-scrupulous jealousy of danger to the rights of the people, which is more commonly the fault of the head than of the heart, will be represented as mere pretense and artifice, the stale bait for popularity at the expense of the public good. It will be forgotten, on the one hand, that jealousy is the usual concomitant of love, and that the noble enthusiasm of liberty is apt to be infected with a spirit of narrow and illiberal distrust. On the other hand, it will be equally forgotten that the vigor of government is essential to the security of liberty; that, in the contemplation of a sound and well-informed judgment, their interest can never be separated; and that a dangerous ambition more often lurks behind the specious mask of zeal for the rights of the people than under the forbidden appearance of zeal for the firmness and efficiency of government. History will teach us that the former has been found a much more certain road to the introduction of despotism than the latter, and that of those men who have overturned the liberties of republics, the greatest number have

begun their career by paying an obsequious court to the people; commencing demagogues, and ending tyrants.

In the course of the preceding observations, I have had an eye, my fellow-citizens, to putting you upon your guard against all attempts, from whatever quarter, to influence your decision in a matter of the utmost moment to your welfare, by any impressions other than those which may result from the evidence of truth. You will, no doubt, at the same time, have collected from the general scope of them, that they proceed from a source not unfriendly to the new Constitution. Yes, my countrymen, I own to you that, after having given it an attentive consideration, I am clearly of opinion it is your interest to adopt it. I am convinced that this is the safest course for your liberty, your dignity, and your happiness. I affect not reserves which I do not feel. I will not amuse you with an appearance of deliberation when I have decided. I frankly acknowledge to you my convictions, and I will freely lay before you the reasons on which they are founded. The consciousness of good intentions disdains ambiguity. I shall not, however, multiply professions on this head. My motives must remain in the depository of my own breast. My arguments will be open to all, and may be judged of by all. They shall at least be offered in a spirit which will not disgrace the cause of truth.

I propose, in a series of papers, to discuss the following interesting particulars:

THE UTILITY OF THE UNION TO YOUR POLITICAL PROSPERITY—THE INSUFFICIENCY OF THE PRESENT CONFEDERATION TO PRESERVE THAT UNION—THE NECESSITY OF A GOVERNMENT AT LEAST EQUALLY ENERGETIC WITH THE ONE PROPOSED, TO THE ATTAINMENT OF THIS OBJECT—THE CONFORMITY OF THE PROPOSED CONSTITUTION TO THE TRUE PRINCIPLES OF REPUBLICAN GOVERNMENT—ITS ANALOGY TO YOUR OWN STATE CONSTITUTION—and lastly, THE ADDITIONAL SECURITY WHICH ITS ADOPTION WILL AFFORD TO THE PRESERVATION OF THAT SPECIES OF GOVERNMENT, TO LIBERTY, AND TO PROPERTY.

In the progress of this discussion I shall endeavor to give a satisfactory answer to all the objections which shall have made their appearance, that may seem to have any claim to your attention.

It may perhaps be thought superfluous to offer arguments to prove the utility of the UNION, a point, no doubt, deeply engraved on the hearts of the great body of the people in every State, and one, which it may be imagined, has no adversaries. But the fact is, that we already hear it whispered in the private circles of those who oppose the new Constitution, that the thirteen States are of too great extent for any general system, and that we must of necessity resort to separate confederacies of distinct portions of the whole. This doctrine will, in all probability, be gradually propagated, till it has votaries enough to countenance an open avowal of it. For nothing can be more evident, to those who are able to take an enlarged view of the subject, than the alternative of an adoption of the new Constitution or a dismemberment of the Union. It will therefore be of use to begin by examining the advantages of that Union, the certain evils, and the probable dangers, to which every State will be exposed from its dissolution. This shall accordingly constitute the subject of my next address.

PUBLIUS

FEDERALIST No. 10

The Same Subject Continued (The Union as a Safeguard Against Domestic Faction and Insurrection)
From the Daily Advertiser. Thursday, November 22, 1787.

MADISON
To the People of the State of New York:

AMONG the numerous advantages promised by a well constructed Union, none deserves to be more accurately developed than its tendency to break and control the violence of faction. The friend of popular governments never finds himself so much alarmed for their character and fate, as when he contemplates their propensity to this dangerous vice. He will not fail, therefore, to set a due value on any plan which, without violating the principles to which he is attached, provides a proper cure for it. The instability, injustice, and confusion introduced into the public councils, have, in truth, been the mortal diseases under which popular governments have everywhere perished; as they continue to be the favorite and fruitful topics from which the adversaries to liberty derive their most specious declamations. The valuable improvements made by the American constitutions on the popular models, both ancient and modern, cannot certainly be too much admired; but it would be an unwarrantable partiality, to contend that they have as effectually obviated the danger on this side, as was wished and expected. Complaints are everywhere heard from our most considerate and virtuous citizens, equally the friends of public and private faith, and of public and personal liberty, that our governments are too unstable, that the public good is disregarded in the conflicts of rival parties, and that measures are too often decided, not according to the rules of justice and the rights of the minor party, but by the superior force of an interested and overbearing majority. However anxiously we may wish that these complaints had no foundation, the evidence, of known facts will not permit us to deny that they are in some degree true. It will be found, indeed, on a candid review of our situation, that some of the distresses under which we labor have been erroneously charged on the operation of our governments; but it will be found, at the same time, that other causes will not alone account for many of our heaviest misfortunes; and, particularly, for that prevailing and increasing distrust of public engagements, and alarm for private rights, which are echoed from one end of the continent to the other. These must be chiefly, if not wholly, effects of the unsteadiness and injustice with which a factious spirit has tainted our public administrations.

By a faction, I understand a number of citizens, whether amounting to a majority or a minority of the whole, who are united and actuated by some common impulse of passion, or of interest, adversed to the rights of other citizens, or to the permanent and aggregate interests of the community.

There are two methods of curing the mischiefs of faction: the one, by removing its causes; the other, by controlling its effects.

There are again two methods of removing the causes of faction: the one, by destroying the liberty which is essential to its existence; the other, by giving to every citizen the same opinions, the same passions, and the same interests.

It could never be more truly said than of the first remedy, that it was worse than the disease.

Liberty is to faction what air is to fire, an aliment without which it instantly expires. But it could not be less folly to abolish liberty, which is essential to political life, because it nourishes faction, than it would be to wish the annihilation of air, which is essential to animal life, because it imparts to fire its destructive agency.

The second expedient is as impracticable as the first would be unwise. As long as the reason of man continues fallible, and he is at liberty to exercise it, different opinions will be formed. As long as the connection subsists between his reason and his self-love, his opinions and his passions will have a reciprocal influence on each other; and the former will be objects to which the latter will attach themselves. The diversity in the faculties of men, from which the rights of property originate, is not less an insuperable obstacle to a uniformity of interests. The protection of these faculties is the first object of government. From the protection of different and unequal faculties of acquiring property, the possession of different degrees and kinds of property immediately results; and from the influence of these on the sentiments and views of the respective proprietors, ensues a division of the society into different interests and parties.

The latent causes of faction are thus sown in the nature of man; and we see them everywhere brought into different degrees of activity, according to the different circumstances of civil society. A zeal for different opinions concerning religion, concerning government, and many other points, as well of speculation as of practice; an attachment to different leaders ambitiously contending for pre-eminence and power; or to persons of other descriptions whose fortunes have been interesting to the human passions, have, in turn, divided mankind into parties, inflamed them with mutual animosity, and rendered them much more disposed to vex and oppress each other than to co-operate for their common good. So strong is this propensity of mankind to fall into mutual animosities, that where no substantial occasion presents itself, the most frivolous and fanciful distinctions have been sufficient to kindle their unfriendly passions and excite their most violent conflicts. But the most common and durable source of factions has been the various and unequal distribution of property. Those who hold and those who are without property have

ever formed distinct interests in society. Those who are creditors, and those who are debtors, fall under a like discrimination. A landed interest, a manufacturing interest, a mercantile interest, a moneyed interest, with many lesser interests, grow up of necessity in civilized nations, and divide them into different classes, actuated by different sentiments and views. The regulation of these various and interfering interests forms the principal task of modern legislation, and involves the spirit of party and faction in the necessary and ordinary operations of the government.

No man is allowed to be a judge in his own cause, because his interest would certainly bias his judgment, and, not improbably, corrupt his integrity. With equal, nay with greater reason, a body of men are unfit to be both judges and parties at the same time; yet what are many of the most important acts of legislation, but so many judicial determinations, not indeed concerning the rights of single persons, but concerning the rights of large bodies of citizens? And what are the different classes of legislators but advocates and parties to the causes which they determine? Is a law proposed concerning private debts? It is a question to which the creditors are parties on one side and the debtors on the other. Justice ought to hold the balance between them. Yet the parties are, and must be, themselves the judges; and the most numerous party, or, in other words, the most powerful faction must be expected to prevail. Shall domestic manufactures be encouraged, and in what degree, by restrictions on foreign manufactures? are questions which would be differently decided by the landed and the manufacturing classes, and probably by neither with a sole regard to justice and the public good. The apportionment of taxes on the various descriptions of property is an act which seems to require the most exact impartiality; yet there is, perhaps, no legislative act in which greater opportunity and temptation are given to a predominant party to trample on the rules of justice. Every shilling with which they overburden the inferior number, is a shilling saved to their own pockets.

It is in vain to say that enlightened statesmen will be able to adjust these clashing interests, and render them all subservient to the public good. Enlightened statesmen will not always be at the helm. Nor, in many cases, can such an adjustment be made at all without taking into view indirect and remote considerations, which will rarely prevail over the immediate interest which one party may find in disregarding the rights of another or the good of the whole.

The inference to which we are brought is, that the CAUSES of faction cannot be removed, and that relief is only to be sought in the means of controlling its EFFECTS.

If a faction consists of less than a majority, relief is supplied by the republican principle, which enables the majority to defeat its sinister views by regular vote. It may clog the administration, it may convulse the society; but it will be unable to execute and mask its violence under the forms of the Constitution. When a majority is included in a faction, the form of popular government, on the other hand, enables it to sacrifice to its ruling passion or interest both the public good and the rights of other citizens. To secure the public good and private rights against the danger of such a faction, and at the same time to preserve the spirit and the form of popular government, is then the great object to which our inquiries are directed. Let me add that it is the great desideratum by which this form of government can be rescued from the opprobrium under which it has so long labored, and be recommended to the esteem and adoption of mankind.

By what means is this object attainable? Evidently by one of two only. Either the existence of the same passion or interest in a majority at the same time must be prevented, or the majority, having such coexistent passion or interest, must be rendered, by their number and local situation, unable to concert and carry into effect schemes of oppression. If the impulse and the opportunity be suffered to coincide, we well know that neither moral nor religious motives can be relied on as an adequate control. They are not found to be such on the injustice and violence of individuals, and lose their efficacy in proportion to the number combined together, that is, in proportion as their efficacy becomes needful.

From this view of the subject it may be concluded that a pure democracy, by which I mean a society consisting of a small number of citizens, who assemble and administer the government in person, can admit of no cure for the mischiefs of faction. A common passion or interest will, in almost every case, be felt by a majority of the whole; a communication and concert result from

the form of government itself; and there is nothing to check the inducements to sacrifice the weaker party or an obnoxious individual. Hence it is that such democracies have ever been spectacles of turbulence and contention; have ever been found incompatible with personal security or the rights of property; and have in general been as short in their lives as they have been violent in their deaths. Theoretic politicians, who have patronized this species of government, have erroneously supposed that by reducing mankind to a perfect equality in their political rights, they would, at the same time, be perfectly equalized and assimilated in their possessions, their opinions, and their passions.

A republic, by which I mean a government in which the scheme of representation takes place, opens a different prospect, and promises the cure for which we are seeking. Let us examine the points in which it varies from pure democracy, and we shall comprehend both the nature of the cure and the efficacy which it must derive from the Union.

The two great points of difference between a democracy and a republic are: first, the delegation of the government, in the latter, to a small number of citizens elected by the rest; secondly, the greater number of citizens, and greater sphere of country, over which the latter may be extended.

The effect of the first difference is, on the one hand, to refine and enlarge the public views, by passing them through the medium of a chosen body of citizens, whose wisdom may best discern the true interest of their country, and whose patriotism and love of justice will be least likely to sacrifice it to temporary or partial considerations. Under such a regulation, it may well happen that the public voice, pronounced by the representatives of the people, will be more consonant to the public good than if pronounced by the people themselves, convened for the purpose. On the other hand, the effect may be inverted. Men of factious tempers, of local prejudices, or of sinister designs, may, by intrigue, by corruption, or by other means, first obtain the suffrages, and then betray the interests, of the people. The question resulting is, whether small or extensive republics are more favorable to the election of proper guardians of the public weal; and it is clearly decided in favor of the latter by two obvious considerations:

In the first place, it is to be remarked that, however small the republic may be, the representatives must be raised to a certain number, in order to guard against the cabals of a few; and that, however large it may be, they must be limited to a certain number, in order to guard against the confusion of a multitude. Hence, the number of representatives in the two cases not being in proportion to that of the two constituents, and being proportionally greater in the small republic, it follows that, if the proportion of fit characters be not less in the large than in the small republic, the former will present a greater option, and consequently a greater probability of a fit choice.

In the next place, as each representative will be chosen by a greater number of citizens in the large than in the small republic, it will be more difficult for unworthy candidates to practice with success the vicious arts by which elections are too often carried; and the suffrages of the people being more free, will be more likely to centre in men who possess the most attractive merit and the most diffusive and established characters.

It must be confessed that in this, as in most other cases, there is a mean, on both sides of which inconveniences will be found to lie. By enlarging too much the number of electors, you render the representatives too little acquainted with all their local circumstances and lesser interests; as by reducing it too much, you render him unduly attached to these, and too little fit to comprehend and pursue great and national objects. The federal Constitution forms a happy combination in this respect; the great and aggregate interests being referred to the national, the local and particular to the State legislatures.

The other point of difference is, the greater number of citizens and extent of territory which may be brought within the compass of republican than of democratic government; and it is this circumstance principally which renders factious combinations less to be dreaded in the former than in the latter. The smaller the society, the fewer probably will be the distinct parties and interests composing it; the fewer the distinct parties and interests, the more frequently will a majority be found of the same party; and the smaller the number of individuals composing a majority, and the smaller the compass within which they are placed, the more easily will they concert and execute their plans of oppression. Extend the sphere, and you take in a greater variety of parties and interests; you make it less probable that a majority of the whole will have a common motive to invade the rights of other citizens; or if such a common motive exists, it will be more difficult for all who feel it to discover their own strength, and to act in unison with each other. Besides other impediments, it may be remarked that, where there is a consciousness of unjust or dishonorable purposes, communication is always checked by distrust in proportion to the number whose concurrence is necessary.

Hence, it clearly appears, that the same advantage which a republic has over a democracy, in controlling the effects of faction, is enjoyed by a large over a small republic,—is enjoyed by the Union over the States composing it. Does the advantage consist in the substitution of representatives whose enlightened views and virtuous sentiments render them superior to local prejudices and schemes of injustice? It will not be denied that the representation of the Union will be most likely to possess these requisite endowments. Does it consist in the greater security afforded by a greater variety of parties, against the event of any one party being able to outnumber and oppress the rest? In an equal degree does the increased variety of parties comprised within the Union, increase this security. Does it, in fine, consist in the greater obstacles opposed to the concert and accomplishment of the secret wishes of an unjust and interested majority? Here, again, the extent of the Union gives it the most palpable advantage.

The influence of factious leaders may kindle a flame within their particular States, but will be unable to spread a general conflagration through the other States. A religious sect may degenerate into a political faction in a part of the Confederacy; but the variety of sects dispersed over the entire face of it must secure the national councils against any danger from that source. A rage for paper money, for an abolition of debts, for an equal division of property, or for any other improper or wicked project, will be less apt to pervade the whole body of the Union than a particular member of it; in the same proportion as such a malady is more likely to taint a particular county or district, than an entire State.

In the extent and proper structure of the Union, therefore, we behold a republican remedy for the diseases most incident to republican government. And according to the degree of pleasure and pride we feel in being republicans, ought to be our zeal in cherishing the spirit and supporting the character of Federalists.

PUBLIUS

FEDERALIST No. 51
The Structure of the Government Must Furnish the Proper Checks and Balances Between the Different Departments.
For the Independent Journal. Wednesday, February 6, 1788.

MADISON
To the People of the State of New York:

TO WHAT expedient, then, shall we finally resort, for maintaining in practice the necessary partition of power among the several departments, as laid down in the Constitution? The only answer that can be given is, that as all these exterior provisions are found to be inadequate, the defect must be supplied, by so contriving the interior structure of the government as that its several constituent parts may, by their mutual relations, be the means of keeping each other in their proper places. Without presuming to undertake a full development of this important idea, I will hazard a few general observations, which may perhaps place it in a clearer light, and enable us to form a more correct judgment of the principles and structure of the government planned by the convention.

In order to lay a due foundation for that separate and distinct exercise of the different powers of government, which to a certain extent is admitted on all hands to be essential to the preservation of liberty, it is evident that each department should have a will of its own; and consequently should be so constituted that the members of each should have as little agency as possible in the appointment of the members of the others. Were this principle rigorously adhered to, it would require that all the appointments for the supreme executive, legislative, and judiciary magistracies should be drawn from the same fountain of authority, the people, through channels having no communication whatever with one another. Perhaps such a plan of constructing the several departments would be less difficult in practice than it may in contemplation appear. Some difficulties, however, and some additional expense would attend the execution of it. Some deviations, therefore, from the principle must be admitted. In the constitution of the judiciary department in particular, it might be inexpedient to insist rigorously on the principle: first, because peculiar qualifications being essential in the members, the primary consideration ought to be to select that mode of choice which best secures these qualifications; secondly, because the permanent tenure by which the appointments are held in that department, must soon destroy all sense of dependence on the authority conferring them.

It is equally evident, that the members of each department should be as little dependent as possible on those of the others, for the emoluments annexed to their offices. Were the executive magistrate, or the judges, not independent of the legislature in this particular, their independence in every other would be merely nominal.

But the great security against a gradual concentration of the several powers in the same department, consists in giving to those who administer each department the necessary constitutional means and personal motives to resist encroachments of the others. The provision for defense must in this, as in all other cases, be made commensurate to the danger of attack. Ambition must be made to counteract ambition. The interest of the man must be connected with the constitutional rights of the place. It may be a reflection on human nature, that such devices should be necessary to control the abuses of government. But what is government itself, but the greatest of all reflections on human nature? If men were angels, no government would be necessary. If angels were to govern men, neither external nor internal controls on government would be necessary. In framing a government which is to be administered by men over men, the great difficulty lies in this: you must first enable the government to control the governed; and in the next place oblige it to control itself. A dependence on the people is, no doubt, the primary control on the government; but experience has taught mankind the necessity of auxiliary precautions.

This policy of supplying, by opposite and rival interests, the defect of better motives, might be traced through the whole system of human affairs, private as well as public. We see it particularly displayed in all the subordinate distributions of power, where the constant aim is to divide and arrange the several offices in such a manner as that each may be a check on the other—that the private interest of every individual may be a sentinel over the public rights. These inventions of prudence cannot be less requisite in the distribution of the supreme powers of the State.

But it is not possible to give to each department an equal power of self-defense. In republican government, the legislative authority necessarily predominates. The remedy for this inconveniency is to divide the legislature into different branches; and to render them, by different modes of election and different principles of action, as little connected with each other as the nature of their common functions and their common dependence on the society will admit. It may even be necessary to guard against dangerous encroachments by still further precautions. As the weight of the legislative authority requires that it should be thus divided, the weakness of the executive may require, on the other hand, that it should be fortified. An absolute negative on the legislature appears, at first view, to be the natural defense with which the executive magistrate should be armed. But perhaps it would be neither altogether safe nor alone sufficient. On ordinary occasions it might not be exerted with the requisite firmness, and on extraordinary occasions it might be perfidiously abused. May not this defect of an absolute negative be supplied by some qualified connection between this weaker department and the weaker branch of the stronger department, by which the latter may be led to support the constitutional rights of the former, without being too much detached from the rights of its own department?

If the principles on which these observations are founded be just, as I persuade myself they are, and they be applied as a criterion to the several State constitutions, and to the federal Constitution it will be found that if the latter does not perfectly correspond with them, the former are infinitely less able to bear such a test.

There are, moreover, two considerations particularly applicable to the federal system of America, which place that system in a very interesting point of view.

First. In a single republic, all the power surrendered by the people is submitted to the administration of a single government; and the usurpations are guarded against by a division of the government into distinct and separate departments. In the compound republic of America, the power surrendered by the people is first divided between two distinct governments, and then the portion allotted to each subdivided among distinct and separate departments. Hence a double security arises to the rights of the people. The different governments will control each other, at the same time that each will be controlled by itself.

Second. It is of great importance in a republic not only to guard the society against the oppression of its rulers, but to guard one part of the society against the injustice of the other part. Different interests necessarily exist in different classes of citizens. If a majority be united by a common interest, the rights of the minority will be insecure. There are but two methods of providing against this evil: the one by creating a will in the community independent of the majority—that is, of the society itself; the other, by comprehending in the society so many separate descriptions of citizens as will render an unjust combination of a majority of the whole very improbable, if not impracticable. The first method prevails in all governments possessing an hereditary or self-appointed authority. This, at best, is but a precarious security; because a power independent of the society may as well espouse the unjust views of the major, as the rightful interests of the minor party, and may possibly be turned against both parties. The second method will be exemplified in the federal republic of the United States. Whilst all authority in it will be derived from and dependent on the society, the society itself will be broken into so many parts, interests, and classes of citizens, that the rights of individuals, or of the minority, will be in little danger from interested combinations of the majority. In a free government the security for civil rights must be the same as that for religious rights. It consists in the one case in the multiplicity of interests, and in the other in the multiplicity of sects. The degree of security in both cases will depend on the number of interests and sects; and this may be presumed to depend on the extent of country and number of people comprehended under the same government. This view of the subject must particularly recommend a proper federal system to all the sincere and considerate friends of republican government, since it shows that in exact proportion as the territory of the Union may be formed into more circumscribed Confederacies, or States, oppressive combinations of a majority will be facilitated: the best security, under the republican forms, for the rights of every class of citizens, will be diminished: and consequently the stability and independence of some member of the government, the only other security, must be proportionately increased. Justice is the end of government. It is the end of civil society. It ever has been and ever will be pursued until it be obtained, or until liberty be lost in the pursuit. In a society under the forms of which the stronger faction can readily unite and oppress the weaker, anarchy may as truly be said to reign as in a state of nature, where the weaker individual is not secured against the violence of the stronger; and as, in the latter state, even the stronger individuals are prompted, by the uncertainty of their condition, to submit to a government which may protect the weak as well as themselves; so, in the former state, will the more powerful factions or parties be gradually induced, by a like motive, to wish for a government which will protect all parties, the weaker as well as the more powerful. It can be little doubted that if the State of Rhode Island was separated from the Confederacy and left to itself, the insecurity of rights under the popular form of government within such narrow limits would be displayed by such reiterated oppressions of factious majorities that some power altogether independent of the people would soon be called for by the voice of the very factions whose misrule had proved the necessity of it. In the extended republic of the United States, and among the great variety of interests, parties, and sects which it embraces, a coalition of a majority of the whole society could seldom take place on any other principles than those of justice and the general good; whilst there being thus less danger to a minor from the will of a major party, there must be less pretext, also, to provide for the security of the former, by introducing into the government a will not dependent on the latter, or, in other words, a will independent of the society itself. It is no less certain than it is important, notwithstanding the contrary opinions which have been entertained, that the larger the society, provided it lie within a practical sphere, the more duly capable it will be of self-government. And happily for the REPUBLICAN CAUSE, the practicable sphere may be carried to a very great extent, by a judicious modification and mixture of the FEDERAL PRINCIPLE.

PUBLIUS

Glossary

115th Congress: The Congress elected in November 2016, meeting in 2017–2018. The first Congress met in 1789–1790. Each Congress is elected for a two-year session and numbered consecutively.

1963 March on Washington: A massive rally for civil rights that included Martin Luther King's "I Have a Dream" speech.

527 groups: Organizations governed by Section 527 of the federal tax code; they are allowed to raise and spend unlimited amounts for "issue advocacy" but are forbidden to coordinate their efforts with any candidate or campaign.

Abolition: A nineteenth-century movement demanding an immediate and unconditional end to slavery.

Accommodation: The principle that government does not violate the establishment clause as long as it does not confer an advantage to some religions over others. (See "strict separation.")

Advocacy explosion: A vast and relatively swift increase in interest groups active in Washington, DC, beginning in the mid-1960s.

Affirmative action: Direct steps to recruit members of previously underrepresented groups into schools and jobs.

American exceptionalism: The view that the United States is uniquely characterized by a distinct set of ideas such as equality, self-rule, and limited government.

Amicus curiae: A brief submitted by a person or group who is not a direct party to the case.

Approval rating: A measure of public support for a political figure or institution.

Astroturf lobbying: An attempt by interest groups to simulate widespread public engagement on an issue.

Bandwagon effect: When people join a cause because it seems popular or support a candidate who is leading in the polls.

Base voters: Party members who tend to vote loyally for their party's candidates in most elections.

Bicameral: Having two legislative houses or chambers—such as the House and the Senate.

Bill of Rights: The first ten amendments to the Constitution, listing the rights guaranteed to every citizen.

Black power: A slogan that emphasized pride in black heritage and the construction of black institutions to nurture black interests. It often implied racial separation in reaction to white racism.

Block grants: National government funding provided to state and local governments with relatively few restrictions or requirements on spending.

Boomerang effect: The discrepancy between candidates' high poll ratings and election performance, caused by supporters' assumption that an easy win means they need not turn out.

Brown v. Board of Education: The landmark Supreme Court case that struck down segregated schools as unconstitutional.

Budget resolution: A joint House–Senate creation that outlines targets for federal spending, revenue levels, and the resultant budget deficit (or surplus) for the coming fiscal year.

Bundling: A form of fundraising in which an individual persuades others to donate large amounts that are then delivered together to a candidate or campaign.

Bureaucratic pathologies: The problems that tend to develop in bureaucratic systems.

Call list: A long list of potential donors who candidates must phone.

Candidate-centered elections: A political system in which individual candidates decide to run, raise their own money, and design their own strategy—as opposed to party systems, in which political parties play these roles.

Central clearance: The OMB's authority to review and "clear" (or approve) anything a member of the administration says or does in public.

Central service agencies: The organizations that supply and staff the federal government.

Checks and balances: The principle that each branch of government has the authority to block the other branches, making it more difficult for any one branch or individual to exercise too much power. This system makes passing legislation far more difficult in the United States than in most other democracies.

Chicanismo: A defiant movement expressing pride in Latino origins and culture in the face of discrimination.

Chief of Staff: The individual responsible for managing the president's office.

Circle of nonparticipation: Resistance by political parties to mobilizing disengaged Americans to vote—because their lack of involvement makes their allegiance to one or the other party suspect.

Circuit courts: The second stage of federal courts, which review the trial record of cases decided in district court to ensure they were settled properly.

Civic voluntarism: Citizen participation in public life without government incentives or coercion (speaking at a town meeting vs. paying taxes, for example).

Civil law: Cases that involve disputes between two parties.

Civil liberties: The limits on government that allow people to freely exercise their rights.

Civil rights: The freedom to participate in the full life of the community—to vote, use public facilities, and exercise equal economic opportunity.

Civil Rights Act of 1964: Landmark legislation that forbade discrimination on the basis of race, sex, religion, or national origin.

Civil servants: Members of the permanent executive branch bureaucracy who are employed on the basis of competitive exams and keep their positions regardless of the presidential administration.

Class action: A lawsuit filed on behalf of an entire category of individuals, such as all people in public housing in a state or all the female managers of a large company.

Classical republicanism: A democratic ideal, rooted in ancient Greece and Rome, that calls on citizens to participate in public affairs, seek the public interest, shun private gain, and defer to natural leaders.

Clear and present danger: Court doctrine that permits restrictions of free speech if officials believe that the speech will lead to prohibited action such as violence or terrorism.

Clicktivism: Democratic engagement in an online age: point your mouse or scan a QR code, click, and you have donated funds, "liked" a candidate, or (in some states) even cast your vote.

Cloture vote: The Senate's only approved method for halting a filibuster or lifting a legislative hold. If sixty senators—three-fifths of the body, changed in 1975 from the original two-thirds—vote for cloture, the measure can proceed to a vote.

Commerce clause: The Constitutional declaration (in Article 1, Section 8) empowering Congress to regulate commerce with foreign nations, between states, and with Indian tribes.

Committee hearing: A way for committees to gather information as legislative policymaking gets underway. Hearings usually feature witnesses who submit testimony, make an oral presentation, and answer questions from members of Congress.

Committee markup session: A gathering of a full committee to draft the final version of a bill before the committee votes on it.

Common law: A system of law developed by judges in deciding cases over the centuries.

Compact: A mutual agreement that provides for joint action to achieve defined goals.

Compromise of 1850: A complicated compromise over slavery that permitted territories to vote on whether they would be slave or free. It also included a strict fugitive slave law forcing Northerners to return black men and women into bondage and permitted California to enter the Union as a free state.

Concurrent opinion: A statement that agrees with the majority opinion.

Concurrent powers: Governmental authority shared by national and state governments, such as the power to tax residents.

Confederation: A group of independent states or nations that yield some of their powers to a national government, although each state retains a degree of sovereign authority.

Conference committee: A temporary collection of House and Senate members appointed to work out a compromise version of legislation that passed both chambers in different forms.

Conservatives: Americans who believe in reduced government spending, personal responsibility, traditional moral values, and a strong national defense. Also known as *right* or *right-wing.*

Consolidation: The process whereby a media company grows, acquires other companies, and threatens to dominate the market.

Containment: American Cold War strategy designed to stop the spread of communism.

Continuing resolution (CR): A congressionally approved act required when no national budget has been passed before the start of a new fiscal year. This extends spending at current levels for a prescribed period of time.

Cooperative federalism: Also called marble cake federalism, a system of mingled governing authority, with functions overlapping across national and state governments.

Cost effectiveness: The projected costs of a proposed policy, as revealed by a relatively simple study.

Cost-benefit analysis: A more complex study of the projected costs and benefits associated with a proposed policy.

Covenant: A compact invoking religious or moral authority.

Criminal law: Cases in which someone is charged with breaking the law.

De facto discrimination: More subtle forms of discrimination that exist without a legal basis.

De jure discrimination: Discrimination established by laws.

Defendant: The party who is sued in a court case.

Delegate representation: Representatives follow the expressed wishes of the voters.

Delegated powers: Powers that Congress passes on to the president.

Democracy: A form of government involving power held by the people, who may rule directly or through elected representatives.

Demographic group: People sharing specific characteristics such as age, ethnicity/race, religion, or country of origin.

Demosclerosis: The collective effect of the vast number of Washington lobbyists in slowing the process of American democratic policymaking.

Devolution: The transfer of authority from the national to the state or local government level.

Diffusion: The spreading of policy ideas from one city or state to others; a process typical of U.S. federalism.

Din: Shorthand for the sheer volume of information and noise generated by online sources; can be a disincentive to participate politically.

Direct action: Participating outside of normal political and social channels through civil disobedience, demonstrations, and even riots.

Discretionary programs: Non-entitlement program spending, subject to the decision ("discretion") of Congress each year.

Disproportionate impact: The effect some policies have of discriminating, even if discrimination is not consciously intended.

Dissent: A statement on behalf of the justices who voted in the minority.

District courts: The first level of federal courts, which actually try the cases. Each decision is based not on a statute but on previous judicial decisions.

Divided government: Periods during which at least one house of Congress is controlled by a party different from the one occupying the White House.

Domestic dependent nation: Special status that grants local sovereignty to tribal nations but does not grant them full sovereignty equivalent to that enjoyed by independent nations.

Double jeopardy: The principle that an individual cannot be tried twice for the same offense.

***Dred Scott v. Sandford*:** A landmark Supreme Court decision holding that black men could not be citizens under the Constitution of the United States. It created a national uproar.

Dual federalism: Also called layer cake federalism, the clear division of governing authority between national and state governments.

Earmark: A legislative item, usually included in spending ("appropriations") bills, that directs Congress to fund a particular item in one House member's district or a senator's state.

Economic equality: A situation in which there are only small differences in wealth among citizens.

Electoral activities: Public engagement in the form of voting, running for office, volunteering in a campaign, or otherwise participating in elections.

Electoral bounce: The spike in the polls that follows an event such as a party's national convention.

Electoral College: The system established by the Constitution to elect the president; each state has a group of electors (equal in size to that of its congressional delegation in the House and the Senate); the public in each state votes for electors, who then vote for the president.

Emancipation Proclamation: An executive order issued by President Abraham Lincoln that declared the slaves in all rebel states to be free.

Entitlement program: A government benefit program whose recipients are *entitled* by law to receive payments. Social Security, Medicare, and Medicaid are the three largest.

Equal Employment Opportunity Commission (EEOC): Federal law enforcement agency charged with monitoring compliance with the Civil Rights Act.

Equal opportunity: The idea that every American has the same chance to influence politics and achieve economic success.

Equal outcome: The idea that citizens should have roughly equal economic circumstances.

Equal protection of the laws: The landmark phrase in the Fourteenth Amendment that requires equal treatment for all citizens.

Equal Rights Amendment: An amendment, originally drafted by Alice Paul in 1923, passed by Congress in 1972, and ratified by thirty-five states, that declared: "Equality of rights . . . shall not be denied or abridged . . . on account of sex."

Equality: All citizens enjoy the same privileges, status, and rights before the laws.

Establishment clause: In the First Amendment, the principle that government may not establish an official religion.

Exclusionary rule: The ruling that evidence obtained in an illegal search may not be introduced in a trial.

Executive agreements: An international agreement made by the president that does not require the approval of the Senate.

Executive Office of the President (EOP): The agencies that help the president manage daily activities.

Executive order: A presidential declaration, with the force of law, that issues instructions to the executive branch without any requirement for congressional action or approval.

Executive privilege: Power claimed by the president to resist requests for authority by Congress, the courts, or the public. Not mentioned in the Constitution but based on the separation of powers.

Expressed powers: Powers the Constitution explicitly grants to the president.

Fair trade: Trade that emphasizes the inclusion of environmental and labor protections in agreements so that nations do not receive unfair advantages by exploiting workers or harming the environment.

Fairness doctrine: Regulation that required media outlets to devote equal time to opposite perspectives.

Federal budget deficit: The gap between revenues received by the national government (primarily through individual income and corporate taxes) and spending on all public programs.

Federal poverty line: The annually specified level of income (separately calculated for individuals and families) below which people are considered to live in poverty, becoming eligible for certain federal benefits. In 2016, the poverty line was set at $24,300 for a family of four.

Federal Regulation of Lobbying Act: The initial U.S. statute spelling out requirements on lobbyists active in Congress, which was passed in 1946.

Federalism: Power divided between national and state government. Each has its own sovereignty (independent authority) and its own duties.

Fighting words: Expressions inherently likely to provoke violent reactions and not necessarily protected by the First Amendment.

Filibuster: Rule unique to the U.S. Senate that allows any senator to hold the floor indefinitely and thereby delay a vote on a bill to which he or she objects. Ended only when sixty senators vote for cloture.

Final rule: The rule that specifies how a program will actually operate.

First Continental Congress: A convention of delegates from twelve of the thirteen colonies that met in 1774.

Fiscal policy: Taxing and spending policies carried out by government, generally in an effort to affect national economic development.

Fiscal year (FY): In budget calculations, the "new year" beginning October 1 and ending the following September 30. Organized many decades ago for accounting purposes.

Floor: The full chamber, either in the House of Representatives or the Senate. A bill "goes to the floor" for the final debate and vote.

Focusing event: A major happening, often of crisis or disaster proportions, that attracts widespread media attention to an issue.

Framing: The way an issue is defined; every issue has many possible frames, each with a slightly different tilt in describing the problem and highlighting solutions.

Framing effects: The influence, on the respondent, of how a polling question is asked; changes in wording can significantly alter many people's answers.

Free exercise clause: In the First Amendment, the principle that government may not interfere in religious practice.

Free rider problem: A barrier to group or collective action arising because people who do not participate still reap the benefits.

Free trade: Goods and services moving across international boundaries without government interference.

Freedom: The ability to pursue one's own desires without interference from others.

Freedom of Information Act (FOIA): A 1966 law that facilitates full or partial disclosure of government information and documents.

Full faith and credit clause: The constitutional requirement (in Article 4, Section 1) that each state recognize and uphold laws passed by any other state.

General Agreement on Tariffs and Trade (GATT): A framework for negotiating reductions in trade barriers between nations.

Gerrymander: Redrawing an election district in a way that gives the advantage to one party.

Gift ban: A regulation that eliminates (or sharply reduces the permitted dollar amount of) gifts from interest groups to lawmakers.

Going public: Directly addressing the public to win support for oneself or one's ideas.

Grand jury: A jury that does not decide on guilt or innocence but only on whether there is enough evidence for the case to go to trial.

Grand Old Party (GOP): Long-standing nickname for the Republican Party; ironically, bestowed early in the party's history, in the 1870s.

Grand strategy: An overarching vision that defines and guides a nation's foreign policy.

Granted powers: National government powers listed explicitly in the Constitution.

Grants-in-aid: National government funding provided to state and local governments, along with specific instructions about how the funds may be used.

Great Migration: The vast movement of African Americans from the rural South to the urban North between 1910 and the 1960s.

Gross domestic product (GDP): The value of all the goods and services produced in a nation over a year.

Groupthink: The tendency among a small group of decision makers to converge on a shared set of views; can limit creative thinking or solutions to policy problems.

Hate speech: Hostile statements based on someone's personal characteristics, such as race, ethnicity, religion, or sexual orientation.

Imperial presidency: A characterization of the American presidency that suggests it is demonstrating imperial traits, and that the republic is morphing into an empire.

Incorporation: The process by which the Supreme Court declares that a right in the Bill of Rights also applies to state governments.

Incumbency advantage: The tendency for members of Congress to win reelection in overwhelming numbers.

Indentured servant: A colonial American settler contracted to work for a fixed period (usually three to seven years) in exchange for food, shelter, and transportation to the New World.

Individualism: The idea that individuals, not the society, are responsible for their own well-being.

Information shortcuts: Cues about candidates and policies drawn from everyday life.

Infotainment: The blurred line between news and entertainment.

Inherent powers: National government powers implied by, but not specifically named in, the Constitution.

Inherent powers of the presidency: Powers assumed by presidents, often during a crisis, on the basis of the constitutional phrase "The executive power shall be vested in the president."

Initiative: A process in which citizens propose new laws or amendments to the state constitution.

Institutions: The organizations, norms, and rules that structure government and public action.

Interest group: An organization whose goal is to influence government.

Intergovernmental lobbying: Attempts by officials in one part of the government to influence their counterparts in another branch, or at a different (state or local) level.

Internationalism: The belief that national interests are best served by actively engaging and working with other nations around the world.

Iron triangle: The cozy relationship in one issue area between interest-group lobbyists, congressional staffers, and executive branch agencies.

Isolationsim: The doctrine that a nation should avoid all foreign policy commitments and alliances and withdraw from world affairs.

Issue advocacy: Organized effort to advance (or block) a proposed public policy change.

Issue campaign: A concerted effort by interest groups to arouse popular support or opposition for a policy issue.

Issue network: Shifting alliances of public and private interest groups, lawmakers, and other stakeholders all focused on the same policy area.

Jim Crow: The system of racial segregation in the U.S. South that lasted from 1890 to 1965, and that was often violently enforced.

Judicial activism: A vigorous or active approach to reviewing the other branches of government.

Judicial restraint: Reluctance to interfere with elected branches, only doing so as a last resort.

Judicial review: The Court's authority to strike down acts that violate the Constitution and to interpret what the Constitution means.

Judicial rules: Hard-and-fast boundaries between what is lawful and what is not.

Judicial standards: Guiding principles that help governments make judgment calls.

K Street: A major street in downtown Washington, DC, that is home to the headquarters for many lobbying firms and advocacy groups—and thus synonymous with interest-group lobbying.

Legislative hold: An informal way for a senator to object to a bill or other measure reaching the Senate floor. The action effectively halts Senate proceedings on that issue, sometimes for weeks or longer.

Liberalism: A doctrine that views nation-states as benefiting most from mutual cooperation, aided by international organizations.

Liberals: Americans who value cultural diversity, government programs for the needy, public intervention in the economy, and individuals' right to a lifestyle based on their own social and moral positions. Also known as *left* or *left-wing*.

Libertarians: People who believe in minimal government—specifically, that public officials' only role should be defending borders, prosecuting crime, and protecting private property.

Likely voters: Persons identified as probable voters in an upcoming election. Often preferred by polling organizations, but difficult to specify with great accuracy.

Literacy test: A requirement that voters be literate; in reality, a way to restrict black suffrage.

Litigation: The conduct of a lawsuit.

Lobbying coalition: A collection of lobbyists working on related topics or a specific legislative proposal.

Lobbyist: A person who contacts government officials on behalf of a particular cause or issue.

Lochner era: A period from 1905 to 1937, during which the Supreme Court struck down laws (e.g., worker protection or minimum wage laws) that were thought to infringe on economic liberty or the right to contract.

Loud signal: Media stories with very broad coverage and an unambiguous message.

Majority opinion: The official statement of the Supreme Court (or a district court, since they also have multiple justices).

Mandate: Political authority claimed by an election winner as reflecting the approval of the people.

Margin of sampling error: The degree of inaccuracy in any poll, arising from the fact that surveys involve a *sample* of respondents from a population, rather than every member.

Mass media: Information and entertainment for broad popular audiences including newspapers, magazines, radio, and television.

Material benefits: Items distributed by public interest groups as incentives to sign up or remain a member.

Median: A statistical term for the number in the middle or the case that has an equal number of examples above and below it.

Mediation: A way of resolving disputes without going to court, in which a third party (the mediator) helps two or more sides negotiate a settlement.

Midterm elections: National elections held between presidential elections, involving all seats in the House of Representatives, one-third of those in the Senate, thirty-six governorships, and other positions.

Midterm loss: When the party of the president loses seats in Congress during the midterm elections. This has occurred in almost all midterm elections.

Millennials: Americans born between 1983–2001. Though very large (some 80 million people) and diverse, many millennials tend to share certain characteristics, including political outlook.

Miranda warnings: A set of rights that police officers are required to inform suspects of, including the right to remain silent.

Missouri Compromise: An agreement to open southern territories west of the Mississippi to slavery while closing northern territories to slavery.

Monetary policy: Actions of central banks, which in the United States culminate in the Federal Reserve, designed primarily to maximize employment and moderate inflation.

Motor voter law: Passed in 1993, this act enables prospective voters to register when they receive their driver's license.

Multilateral organization: An international organization of three or more nations organized around a common goal.

Multilateralism: A doctrine that emphasizes operating together with other nations to pursue common goals.

Name recognition: An advantage possessed by a well-known political figure, a political celebrity.

National Association for the Advancement of Colored People (NAACP): A civil rights organization formed in 1906 and dedicated to racial equality.

National Organization for Women (NOW): An organization formed in 1966 to take action for women's equality.

Necessary and proper clause: The constitutional declaration (in Article 1, Section 8) that defines Congress's constitutional authority to exercise the "necessary and proper" powers to carry out its designated functions.

Negative campaigning: Running for office by attacking the opponent. An unpopular tactic that is nevertheless very effective.

Negative liberty: Freedom from constraints or the interference of others.

New Deal: Broad series of economic programs and reforms introduced between 1933 and 1936 and associated with the Franklin Roosevelt administration.

New federalism: A version of cooperative federalism, but with stronger emphasis on state and local government activity versus national government.

New Jersey Plan: Put forward at the Constitutional Convention by the small states, this plan left most government authority with the state governments.

New media: On-demand access to information and entertainment through digital devices that also features interactive participation with content.

Nonattitudes: The lack of a stable perspective in response to opinion surveys; answers to questions may be self-contradictory or may display no ideological consistency.

Nonpartisan election: An election in which candidates run as individuals, without any party affiliation. Many towns and cities feature nonpartisan elections.

Open seat: A seat in Congress without an incumbent running for reelection.

Originalism: A principle of legal interpretation that relies on the original meaning of those who wrote the Constitution.

Overhead democracy: A system by which the people elect the president, who, through their appointees, controls the bureaucracy from the top.

Override: The process by which Congress can overcome a presidential veto with a two-thirds vote in both chambers.

Partisanship: Taking the side of a party or espousing a viewpoint that reflects a political party's principles or position on an issue. Often decried by those who wish the parties would work together.

Party boss: The senior figure in a party machine.

Party caucus: A meeting of all House or Senate members of one or the other main party, usually to discuss political and policy strategies.

Party identification: Strong attachment to one political party, often established at an early age.

Party in government: The portion of a political party's organization that comprises elected officials and candidates for office.

Party in the electorate: The largest (and least organized) component of a political party, drawn from the public at large: registered members and regular supporters.

Party machine: A hierarchical arrangement of party workers, often organized in an urban area to help integrate immigrants and minority groups into the political system. Most active in the late nineteenth and early twentieth centuries.

Party organization: The portion of a political party that includes activists, state/local leaders, and affiliated professionals such as fundraisers and public relations experts.

Party platform: The written statement of a party's core convictions and issue priorities. Generally revised every four years, in time for the national party convention.

Party system: The broad organization of U.S. politics comprising the two main parties, the coalition of supporters backing each, the positions they take on major issues, and each party's electoral achievements.

Path dependence: The tendency of policymakers to follow established routines in thinking about or acting on a specific topic.

Pendleton Civil Service Act: The law that shifted American government toward a merit-based public service.

Personal presidency: The idea that the president has a personal link to the public. Made initially possible by twentieth-century media.

Plaintiff: The party who brings the action in a lawsuit.

Plessy v. Ferguson: An 1896 Supreme Court case that permitted racial segregation.

Pluralism: An open, participatory style of government in which many different interests are represented.

Policy agenda: The issues that the media covers, the public considers important, and politicians address. Setting the agenda is the first step in political action.

Policy window: A figurative description of the opportunity—often brief, measured in days or weeks rather than years—to pass a bill in Congress or a state legislature.

Political action committee (PAC): An organization of at least fifty people, affiliated with an interest group that is permitted to make contributions to candidates for federal office.

Political appointees: Top officials in the executive agencies, appointed by the president.

Political culture: The orientation of citizens of a state toward politics.

Political elites: Individuals who control significant wealth, status, power, or visibility and consequently have significant influence over public debates.

Political equality: All citizens have the same political rights and opportunities.

Political mobilization: Efforts to encourage people to engage in the public sphere: to vote for a particular candidate (or donate money, work on the campaign, etc.) or to get involved in specific issues.

Political order: The set of institutions, interests, and ideas that shape a political era. Great presidents reconstruct the framework, launching a new order.

Political socialization: Education about how the government works and which policies one should support; provided by parents, peers, schools, parties, and other national institutions.

Political voice: Exercising one's public rights, often through speaking out in protest or in favor of some policy change.

Positive liberty: The ability—and provision of basic necessities—to pursue one's goals.

Power elite theory: The view that a small handful of wealthy, influential Americans exercises extensive control over government decisions.

Pragmatism: A principle of legal interpretation based on the idea that the Constitution evolves and that interpretations of the Constitution must be put in the context of contemporary realities.

Precedent: Judicial decisions that offer a guide to similar cases in the future.

Preemption: The invalidation of a U.S. state law that conflicts with Federal law.

Preemptive war: The effort to attack hostile powers before they launch attacks. Highly controversial because it sanctions striking first.

President pro tempore: Majority party senator with the longest Senate service.

Primacy: The doctrine asserting that the United States should maintain an unrivaled military.

Priming: Affecting voters' or poll respondents' perception of candidates or public officials by raising issues that are perceived to enhance or diminish the candidates.

Principal-agent theory: Details how policymakers (principals) control the actors who work for them (agents)—but who have far more information than they do.

Prior restraint: Legal effort to stop speech before it occurs—in effect, censorship.

Private contractors: Private companies that contract to provide goods and services for the government.

Progressive federalism: Approach that gives state officials considerable leeway in achieving national programs and goals.

Proportional representation: The allocation of votes or delegates on the basis of the percentage of the vote received; contrasts with the winner-take-all system.

Proposed rule: A draft of administrative regulations published in the *Federal Register* for the purpose of gathering comments from interested parties.

Protectionism: Efforts to protect local business from foreign competition.

Public ownership: A situation in which media outlets are run by the government and paid for by tax dollars.

Public watchdog: Media coverage that alerts the public when a problem arises in politics or society.

Public–private partnership: A government program or service provided through the joint efforts of private sector actors (usually businesses) and public officials.

Push poll: A form of negative campaigning that masquerades as a regular opinion survey. Usually conducted by a campaign or allied group; features strongly critical or unflattering information about an opponent.

Quasi-suspect category: A legal standard that requires governments to have an important state purpose for any legislation that singles out sex or gender. This is not as strong as the *suspect category*, which requires strict scrutiny.

Racial profiling: A law enforcement practice of singling out people on the basis of physical features such as race or ethnicity.

Random sample: A sample in which everyone in the population (sampling frame) has an equal probability of being selected.

Rational-choice theory: An approach to political behavior that views individuals as rational, decisive actors who know their political interests and seek to act on them.

Realism: A doctrine holding that nation-states seek to amass power to ensure their self-preservation.

Reapportionment: Reorganization of the boundaries of House districts, a process that follows the results of the U.S. census, taken every ten years. District lines are redrawn to ensure rough equality in the number of constituents represented by each House member.

Reconstruction: The failed effort, pursued by Northerners and Southerners, to rebuild the South and establish racial equality after the Civil War.

Referendum: An election in which citizens vote directly on an issue.

Reframe the issue: To redefine the popular perception of an issue; to show it in a new light with a new set of costs or benefits.

Regulatory capture: The theory that industries dominate the agencies that regulate them.

Republic: A government in which citizens rule indirectly and make government decisions through their elected representatives.

Reserved powers: The constitutional guarantee (in the Tenth Amendment) that the states retain government authority not explicitly granted to the national government.

Response bias: The tendency of poll respondents to misstate their views, frequently to avoid "shameful" opinions such as sexism or racism.

Reverse lobbying: Attempts by government officials to influence interest groups on behalf of their preferred policies.

Revolving door: The tendency of Washington's most seasoned lobbyists to move from government work (e.g., as a presidential advisor) to lobbying and back again.

Roll-call vote: A congressional vote in which all members' votes are recorded, either by roll call (Senate) or electronically (House).

Rule of four: The requirement that at least four Supreme Court judges must agree to hear a case before it comes before the Court.

Sampling frame: A designated group of people from whom a set of poll respondents is randomly selected.

School busing: An effort to integrate public schools by mixing students from different neighborhoods.

Second Continental Congress: A convention of delegates from the thirteen colonies that became the acting national government for the duration of the Revolutionary War.

Section 504: An obscure provision in an obscure rehabilitation act that required all institutions that received federal funds to accommodate people with disabilities.

Security trap: The idea that using military force creates multiple, often unforeseen, problems.

Selective incorporation: The extension of protections from the Bill of Rights to the state governments, one right at a time.

Self-rule: The idea that legitimate government flows from the people.

Seneca Falls Convention: The first convention dedicated to women's rights, held in July 1848 in Seneca Falls, NY.

Signing statements: Written presidential declarations commenting on the bill that is being signed into law—often including criticism of one or more provisions.

Social capital: Relations between people that build closer ties of trust and civic engagement, yielding productive benefits for the larger society.

Social democracy: A government in which citizens are responsible for one another's well-being and use government policy to ensure that all are comfortably cared for.

Social equality: All individuals enjoy the same status in society.

Soft power: The influence a nation exerts through culture and commerce; a contrast to attempted influence through force.

Solidarity benefits: The feeling of shared commitment and purpose experienced by individuals who join a public interest group.

Sound bite: A short clip of speech taken from a longer piece of audio. Often refers to a brief excerpt from a speech by a candidate or politician.

Speaker of the House: The chief administrative officer in the House of Representatives.

Special interest: A pejorative term, often used to designate an interest group whose aims or issue preferences one does not share.

Split-ticket voter: Votes for at least one candidate from each party, dividing his or her ballot between the two (or more) parties.

Spoils system: A system in which government jobs are given out as political favors.

Stare decisis: Deciding cases on the basis of previous rulings or precedents.

Straight-ticket voter: Votes for the same party for all offices on a ballot.

Strategic disengagement: The doctrine that a nation should not interfere in other nations' affairs unless such involvement clearly advances its own interests.

Street-level bureaucrats: Public officials who deal directly with the public.

Strict scrutiny: The tendency to strike down as unconstitutional any legislation that singles out race or ethnicity unless the government has a compelling interest in such legislation.

Strict separation: The strict principles articulated in the Lemon test for judging whether a law establishes a religion. (See "accommodation.")

Sunshine laws: Laws that permit the public to watch policymakers in action and to access the records of the proceedings.

Super PACs: Organizations that are permitted to raise and spend unlimited amounts of money to promote a candidate or publicize a cause. However, they may not directly contribute to a candidate or coordinate with a campaign.

Super Tuesday: The date on the presidential primary calendar when multiple states hold primaries and caucuses.

Supermajority: An amount higher than a simple majority (50 percent plus one)—typically, three-fifths or two-thirds of the voters.

Supremacy clause: The constitutional declaration (in Article 6, Section 2) that the national government's authority prevails over any conflicting state or local government's claims, provided the power is granted to the federal government.

Survey research: Systematic study of a defined population, analyzing a representative sample's views to draw inferences about the larger public's views. Also termed *opinion poll.*

Symbolic expression: An act, rather than actual speech, used to demonstrate a point of view.

Telecommunications Act of 1996: A major overhaul of communications law that opened the door to far more competition by permitting companies to own outlets in multiple media markets such as radio, television, and magazines.

The Paradox of Voting: For most individuals, the cost of voting (acquiring necessary information, traveling to polling site, and waiting in line) outweighs the apparent benefits. Economic theory would predict very low voter turnout, given this analysis.

The New Jim Crow: The idea that mass incarceration of African Americans has the sweeping effects of Jim Crow discrimination laws. The term was the title of a book by Michelle Alexander.

Theory of democratic peace: Theory that strongly democratic nations are less likely to engage in wars with one another.

Time, place, and manner clause: The constitutional clause that delegates control of elections to the state governments.

Trade association: An organized group representing individuals and businesses that belong to the same industry.

Trade deficit: The deficit arising when a nation imports (or buys) more goods from foreign nations than it exports (or sells) to them.

Traditional participation: Engaging in political activities through the formal channels of government and society.

Trustee representation: Representatives do what they regard as being in the best interest of their constituents—even if constituents do not agree.

Unanimous consent: A Senate requirement, applied to most of that body's business that all senators agree before an action can proceed.

Underdog effect: Sympathy for a candidate behind in the polls, contributing to a higher-than-predicted vote total—and sometimes a surprise election victory.

Unfunded mandate: An obligation imposed on state or local government officials by federal legislation without sufficient federal funding support to cover the costs.

Unicameral: Having a single legislative house or chamber.

Unilateralism: A doctrine that holds that the United States should act independently of other nations. It should decide what is best for itself—not in coordination with partners and allies.

Unitary executive theory: The idea that the Constitution puts the president in charge of executing the laws and that therefore no other branch may limit presidential discretion over executive matters.

Unitary government: A national polity governed as a single unit, with the central government exercising all or most political authority.

Universalistic politics: A government run according to transparent rules, impartially applied.

USA Patriot Act: Legislation that sought to enhance national security, passed in the aftermath of the September 11, 2001, terrorist attacks.

Veto: The constitutional procedure by which a president can prevent enactment of legislation passed by Congress.

Veto power: The presidential power to block an act of Congress by refusing to sign it.

Virginia Plan: Madison's plan, embraced by the Constitutional Convention delegates from larger states; this plan strengthened the national government relative to state governments.

Voice vote: A congressional vote in which the presiding officer asks those for and against to say "yea" or "nay," respectively, and announces the result. No record is kept of House or Senate members voting on each side.

Voter turnout: A measure of what proportion of eligible voters actually cast a legitimate ballot in a given election.

War Powers Act: Legislation passed in 1973 to increase congressional involvement in undeclared wars. It requires Congress to approve military action undertaken by the president in no more than sixty days.

Watergate scandal: A failed effort in 1972 by Republican operatives to break into Democratic Party headquarters in the Watergate office complex in Washington, DC. President Nixon tried to cover up the event—eventually causing him to resign from the presidency.

Whistle-blower: A federal worker who reports corruption or fraud.

Winner-take-all: The candidate receiving a simple majority (or, among multiple candidates, a plurality) receives all electoral votes or primary delegates. Sometimes called "first-past-the-post."

World Trade Organization (WTO): An international organization that oversees efforts to open markets and promote free trade.

Notes

Chapter 1 The Spirit of American Politics

1. Andrew Dugan, "Majority of Americans See Congress as Out of Touch, Corrupt," *Gallup Politics*, September 28, 2015, http://www.gallup.com/poll/185918/majority-americans-congress-touch-corrupt.aspx?utm_source=alert&utm_medium=email&utm_content=heading&utm_campaign=syndication.

2. *Dred Scott v. Sandford*, 60 U.S. (19 How) 393 (1857).

3. Mitch Potter, "Stephen Colbert and Herman Cain Hold Rally in South Carolina," *Toronto Star*, January 20, 2012, A11.

4. Harold D. Lasswell, *Politics: Who Gets What, When, and How*, rev. ed. (New York: Smith Books, 1990).

5. Roger Sherman, quoted in James Madison, *Notes of Debates in the Federal Convention*, ed. Adrienne Koch (New York: Norton, 1987), p. 39.

6. Philip Tetlock, *Expert Political Judgment: How Good Is It? How Can We Know?* (Princeton, NJ: Princeton University Press, 2005).

7. Some historians question whether Henry actually uttered these words—he spoke without notes, and the story was first written years later, on the basis of what those present remembered. See Jim Cox, "The Speech: It May Not Be the One That Patrick Henry So Famously Made," *CW Journal* 11:1 (Winter 2002–2003), https://www.history.org/Foundation/journal/Winter02-03/speech.cfm.

8. Alexis de Tocqueville, a young French aristocrat, spent nine months traveling around the United States in 1831–1832 and published a book on his observations, *Democracy in America*. It is one of our favorite books on America and on democracy. Many of his observations remain fresh today; no matter where you are on the political spectrum, you will find insights to challenge your views. For a vital book on civic engagement, see Robert Putnam, *Bowling Alone* (New York: Simon & Schuster, 2000).

9. Pew Research Center, "Americans' Views on Open Government Data," April, 21, 2015, http://www.pewinternet.org/files/2014/10/PI_OpenData_072815.pdf.

10. Michael Lind, *Land of Promise: An Economic History of the United States* (New York: HarperCollins, 2012), 205.

11. Pew Research Center, "Beyond Distrust: How Americans View Their Government," November 23, 2015, accessed June 21, 2016, http://pewrsr.ch/1IaB4tp.

12. Organisation for Economic Co-operation and Development, OECD.STAT, "Revenue Statistics—Comparative Tables," https://stats.oecd.org/Index.aspx?DataSetCode=REV.

13. Suzanne Mettler, *The Submerged State* (Chicago: University of Chicago Press, 2011); Christopher Howard, *The Hidden Welfare State* (Princeton, NJ: Princeton University Press, 1997); Jacob Hacker, *The Divided Welfare State* (New York: Cambridge University Press, 2002).

14. Jonathan Gruber, "The Tax Exclusion for Employer-Sponsored Health Insurance," https://ideas.repec.org/p/nbr/nberwo/15766.html; Matthew Rae, Gary Claxton, Nirmita Panchal, and Larry Levitt, "Tax Subsidies for Private Health Insurance," October 27, 2014, http://kff.org/private-insurance/issue-brief/tax-subsidies-for-private-health-insurance/.

15. David Blumenthal and James Morone, *The Heart of Power: Health and Politics in the Oval Office* (Berkeley: University of California Press, 2009), chap. 3.

16. For more details, including screenshots of the improved form, see Jessica Schafer and Chuck Werner, "Student Loan Repayment Tool Revamp," May 14, 2015, http://cfpb.github.io/articles/repay-student-debt-feature-revamp/.

17. Paul Taylor, "Next America," April 10, 2014, http://www.pewresearch.org/next-america/#Liberal-Youth-Conservative-Elders.

Chapter 2 The Ideas That Shape America

1. Simon Schama, *Rough Crossings: Britain, the Slaves, and the American Revolution* (New York: Harper-Collins, 2006).

2. The classic statement comes from Isaiah Berlin, "Two Concepts of Liberty," reprinted in *Liberty*, ed. Henry Hardy (Oxford: Oxford University Press, 2002), 166–217.

3. Samuel Huntington, *American Politics: The Promise of Disharmony* (Cambridge, MA: Harvard University Press, 1983); Rogers Smith, *Civic Ideals: Conflicting Visions of Citizenship in U.S. History* (New Haven, CT: Yale University Press, 1997).

4. Quoted in James A. Morone, *The Democratic Wish: Popular Participation and the Limits of American Government* (New Haven, CT: Yale University Press, 1998), 54.

5. Thomas Jefferson, "Response to the Citizens of Albemarle," February 12, 1790; First Inaugural Address, March 4, 1801. Jefferson's first inaugural address offers the best summary of what we now call Jeffersonian democracy.

6. James Madison, *Federalist* no. 10. The quote is from Roger Sherman, recorded in "Madison's Notes of Debates," in *The Federal Convention and the Formation of the Union*, ed. Winston Solberg (Indianapolis, IN: Bobbs Merrill, 1958), 84–85.

7. Michael Kammen, *People of Paradox* (New York: Knopf, 1972), 31.

8. Alexis de Tocqueville, *Democracy in America*, trans. George Lawrence (Garden City, NY: Doubleday, 1969), 1:60, 89; James Bryce, *The American Commonwealth* (London: Macmillan, 1888), 3:267.

9. Thomas Jefferson, "Response to the Citizens of Albemarle," February 12, 1790. In Jefferson, *Writings*, ed. Merrill D. Peterson (New York: Library of America, 2011), 451.

10. John Kingdon, *America the Unusual* (New York: St. Martin's Press, 1999), 1.

11. Martin Luther King Jr., Speech given at Ohio Northern University, January 11, 1968, http://www.onu.edu/node/28513.

12. Milton Friedman, *Capitalism and Freedom* (Chicago: University of Chicago Press, 1962).

13. Pew Research Center, "The American-Western European Values Gap" (February 29, 2012), http://pewrsr.ch/V7cHun.

14. The original statement of this theory is by Louis Hartz, *The Liberal Tradition in America* (New York: Harcourt, Brace, and World, 1955).

15. See Noel Ignatiev, *How the Irish Became White*, 2nd ed. (New York: Routledge, 2009).

N-1

16. Franklin quotes taken from *Poor Richard's Almanac*, see http://www.ushistory.org/franklin/quotable/.

17. James Truslow Adams, *The Epic of America* (New York: Taylor and Francis, 1938).

18. Quoted in Jennifer Hochschild, *Facing Up to the American Dream* (Princeton, NJ: Princeton University Press, 1995), vi, 18.

19. Gordon Wood, *The Radicalism of the American Revolution* (New York: Knopf, 1992), 369.

20. Bureau of Labor Statistics, "Measuring Wage Inequality in and Across U.S. Metropolitan Areas, 2003–13," *Monthly Labor Review* (September 2015): 1.

21. Timothy Noah, *The Great Divergence: America's Growing Inequality Crisis and What We Can Do About It* (New York: Bloomsbury, 2012).

22. Roosevelt quoted in James Morone, *Hellfire Nation* (New Haven, CT: Yale University Press, 2004), 347.

23. Johnson quoted in Morone, *Hellfire Nation*, 427.

24. Robert Sattelmeyer, "'When He Became My Enemy': Emerson and Thoreau, 1848–49," *New England Quarterly* 62, no. 2 (1989): 188–89.

25. Nick Gass, "Poll: Half of Millennials Say the American Dream is Dead," *Politico*, December 10, 2015, http://politi.co/1ZZ49jL.

26. Tocqueville, *Democracy in America*, 1:9.

27. Hugh Brogan, *Alexis de Tocqueville: A Life* (New Haven, CT: Yale University Press, 2007), 352.

28. Tocqueville, *Democracy in America*, 2:558.

29. George Gao, "15 Striking Findings from 2015," December 22, 2015, http://www.pewresearch.org/fact-tank/2015/12/22/15-striking-findings-from-2015/.

30. John Winthrop, "A Model of Christian Charity" (Sermon delivered aboard the *Arbella*, 1630). Collections of the Massachusetts Historical Society, Boston, 1838, 3rd series, 7:31–48.

31. Gallup.com, "Religion," http://www.gallup.com/poll/1690/religion.aspx.

32. See Robert Putnam and David Campbell, *American Grace: How Religion Divides and Unites Us* (New York: Simon & Schuster, 2010) and David Masci, "Why Millennials Are Less Religious than Older Americans," Pew Research Center, January 8, 2016, http://pewrsr.ch/1Rymao7.

33. Eileen W. Lindner, ed., *Yearbook of American & Canadian Churches* (Washington, DC: National Council of Churches, 2013).

34. Pew Research Center, Religion and Public Life Project, "Religious Landscape Study," http://religions.pewforum.org/.

35. Pew Research Center, "Millennials in Adulthood," (March 2014): 13.

36. Thomas Jefferson, "Letter to the Danbury (Connecticut) Baptists," Library of Congress collection, http://www.loc.gov/loc/lcib/9806/danpost.html.

37. Clifford Geertz, *The Interpretation of Cultures* (New York: Basic Books, 1973).

38. Madison, *Federalist* no. 10.

Chapter 3 The Constitution

1. Edmund Burke, "Speech to the Bristol Electors," in *Representation*, ed. Hannah Pitkin (New York: Atherton Press, 1969), 175–76.

2. Robert Middlekauff, *The Glorious Cause* (New York: Oxford University Press, 1982), 74.

3. Bernard Bailyn, David Brion Davis, David Herbert Donald, John Thomas, Robert Wiebe, and Gordon Wood, *The Great Republic: A History of the American People* (Boston: Little, Brown, 1977), 256.

4. Middlekauff, *Glorious Cause*, 223–28, quotation on 226.

5. David Hackett Fischer, *Liberty and Freedom: A Visual History of America's Founding Ideas* (New York: Oxford University Press, 2005), 95–96.

6. See David Hackett Fischer, *Washington's Crossing* (New York: Oxford University Press, 2004), 384–85.

7. Gordon Wood, *The Creation of the American Republic* (Chapel Hill: University of North Carolina Press, 1969), 404.

8. Rogan Kersh, *Dreams of a More Perfect Union* (Ithaca, NY: Cornell University Press, 2001), 60–67.

9. Quoted in Gordon Wood, *Empire of Liberty* (New York: Oxford University Press, 2009), 14.

10. Richard Beeman, *Plain, Honest Men: The Making of the American Constitution* (New York: Random House, 2009), 3–7.

11. Beeman, *Plain, Honest Men*, 12.

12. Leonard Richards, *Shays's Rebellion: The American Revolution's Final Battle* (Philadelphia: University of Pennsylvania Press, 2002).

13. Beeman, *Plain, Honest Men*, 84.

14. James Madison, "Madison's Notes of Debates," in *The Federal Convention and the Formation of the Union*, ed. Winston Solberg (Indianapolis: Bobbs Merrill, 1958), 84–85.

15. Madison, "Madison's Notes," 81.

16. Madison, "Madison's Notes," 81.

17. Madison, "Madison's Notes," 122 (quotes); also see David Brian Robertson, *The Constitution and America's Destiny* (New York: Cambridge University Press, 2005), 139.

18. Luther Martin, "Letter on the Federal Convention of 1787," American Constitution Society, http://www.constitution.org/je/lumarltr.htm.

19. Robertson, *Constitution and America's Destiny*, 140.

20. Max Farrand, ed., *The Records of the Federal Convention of 1787*, rev. ed. (New Haven: Yale University Press, 1966), 3:179.

21. Beeman, *Plain, Honest Men*, 335. On slavery in early America, see also Wendy Warren, *New England Bound* (New York: Norton, 2016).

22. Beeman, *Plain, Honest Men*, 333.

23. Madison, "Madison's Notes," 344.

24. Beeman, *Plain, Honest Men*, 349.

25. Herbert Storing, *What the Anti-Federalists Were For: The Political Writings of the Opponents of the Constitution* (Chicago: University of Chicago Press, 1981).

26. Gordon Wood, *Radicalism of the American Revolution*.

27. Thomas Jefferson, "Letter to Samuel Kercheval, July 12, 1816," in *The Works of Thomas Jefferson*, ed. Paul Leicester Ford (New York: Putnam's Sons, 1905), 12:13–14.

28. Robert Dahl, *How Democratic Is the American Constitution?*, 2nd ed. (New Haven, CT: Yale University Press, 2003).

Chapter 4 Federalism and Nationalism

1. Christina Littlefield, "Sanctuary Cities: How Kathryn Steinle's Death Intensified the Immigration Debate," *Los Angeles Times*, July 24, 2015, http://www.latimes.com/local/california/la-me-immigration-sanctuary-kathryn-steinle-20150723-htmlstory.html.

2. Dolores Story (name changed) from Tiffany Joseph, "The Growing Citizen-Noncitizen Divide: Life Along the Documentation Status Continuum," Working Paper, February 2015; Michael Barajas, "Stop Calling Houston a Sanctuary City," *Houston Press*, March 18, 2015, http://www.houstonpress.com/news/stop-calling-houston-a-sanctuary-city-6729418.

3. David Brian Robertson, *Federalism and the Making of America* (New York: Routledge, 2012).

4. From Justice Brandeis's dissenting opinion in *New State Ice Co. v. Liebmann*, 285 U.S. 262, 311 (1932).

5. William Berry, Richard Fording, and Russell Hanson, "Reassessing the Race to the Bottom in State Welfare

Policy," *Journal of Politics* 65, no. 2 (2003): 327–49. A study that reviews both diffusion and "race to the bottom" ideas is Martino Maggetti and Fabrizio Gilardi, "Problems (and Solutions) in the Measurement of Policy Diffusion Mechanisms," *Journal of Public Policy* 36, no. 1 (2016): 87–107, http://dx.doi.org/10.1017/S0143814X1400035X.

6. James Morone, *Hellfire Nation: The Politics of Sin in American History* (New Haven, CT: Yale University Press, 2003): part 3.

7. Dirksen quoted in Richard P. Nathan, "Updating Theories of American Federalism," in *Intergovernmental Management for the Twenty-First Century*, ed. Timothy Conlan and Paul Posner (Washington, DC: Brookings Institution Press, 2008), 15.

8. Quoted in Robert Dreyfuss, "Grover Norquist: 'Field Marshal' of the Bush Plan," *The Nation*, May 14, 2001.

9. Max Ehrenfreund, "Bernie Sanders is Right: Bill Clinton's Welfare Law Doubled Extreme Poverty," *The Washington Post*, Saturday February 27, 2016, https://www.washingtonpost.com/news/wonk/wp/2016/02/27/bernie-sanders-is-right-bill-clintons-welfare-law-doubled-extreme-poverty/.

10. *McCulloch v. Maryland*, 17 U.S. 316 (1819).

11. Robert Taylor, Mary-Jo Kline, and Greg L. Lint, eds., *Papers of John Adams* (Cambridge, MA: Harvard University Press, 1980), 3:141.

12. David Waldstreicher, *"In the Midst of Perpetual Fetes": The Making of American Nationalism, 1776–1820* (Chapel Hill: University of North Carolina Press, 1997).

13. John R. Hibbing and Elizabeth Theiss-Morse, *Stealth Democracy: Americans' Beliefs About How Government Should Work* (New York: Cambridge University Press, 2002).

14. Tocqueville, *Democracy in America*, 1:115n (see chap. 2, n. 8). For a modern perspective, see Anthony M. Pellegrino, Kristen Zenkov, Melissa A. Gallagher, and Liz Long, "Picturing New Notions of Civic Engagement in the U.S.: Youth-Facilitated, Visually-Based Explorations of the Prospections of Our Least Franchised and Most Diverse Citizens," in *Youth Voices, Public Spaces, and Civic Engagement*, ed. Stuart Greene, Kevin J. Burke, and Maria K. McKenna (New York: Routledge, 2016), 25–49.

Chapter 5 Civil Liberties

1. Samuel Smith, "Christian Pizza Shop Owners' In Hiding' Amid Death Threats" *The Christian Post*, April 2, 2015, http://bit.ly/29UXmpr.

2. Tom Coyne, "After Anti-Gay Controversy, Indiana's Memories Pizza Reopens to a Packed House," *Huffington Post*, April 10, 2015, http://www.huffingtonpost.com/2015/04/10/indiana-memories-pizza-reopens_n_7039644.html.

3. Melissa Hudson, "High School Coach Suspended After Tweet About Pizzeria," *ABC 57 News*, April 1, 2015, http://www.abc57.com/story/28696535/high-school-coach-suspended-after-tweet-about-pizzeria.

4. Shawn Francis Peters, *Judging Jehovah's Witnesses: Religious Persecution and the Dawn of the Rights Revolution* (Lawrence: University Press of Kansas, 2000).

5. The two cases are *Minersville School District v. Gobitis*, 310 U.S. 586 (1940), and *West Virginia State Board of Education v. Barnette*, 319 U.S. 624 (1943). Not only did Walter Gobitas lose the case, but a clerk for the court misspelled his name, and the case is always referred to by the misspelled name, Gobitis.

6. Tocqueville, *Democracy in America*, 252 (see chap. 2, note 9).

7. *Barron v. Baltimore*, 32 U.S. 243 (1833).

8. The *Slaughter-House Cases*, 83 U.S. 36 (1873).

9. *Palko v. Connecticut*, 302 U.S. 319 (1937).

10. If you're interested in reading more on any of the cases we discuss, see Corey Brettschneider, ed., *Constitutional Law and American Democracy: Cases and Readings* (New York: Wolters Kluwer, 2012).

11. Thomas Jefferson, "Letter to the Danbury Baptist Association," January 1, 1802, https://www.loc.gov/loc/lcib/9806/danpre.html.

12. *Everson v. Board of Education*, 330 U.S. 1 (1947).

13. *Engel v. Vitale*, 370 U.S. 421 (1962).

14. In *Good News Club v. Milford Central School*, 533 U.S. 98 (2001), the Court ruled 6–3 in favor of the club.

15. *Employment Division, Department of Human Resources of Oregon v. Smith*, 494 U.S. 872 (1990).

16. The decision that explicitly adopted a preferred position for free speech was *Brandenburg v. Ohio*, 395 U.S. 444 (1969), discussed later in this section.

17. John Stuart Mill, *On Liberty* (New York: Penguin Classics, 1982), 103. Oliver Wendell Holmes expressed a powerful faith in the marketplace of ideas in his dissent in *Abrams v. United States*, 250 U.S 616 (1919).

18. Cornell Law School's "Death Penalty Worldwide" project, at www.deathpenaltyworldwide.org.

19. *Gitlow v. New York*, 268 U.S. 652 (1925). Gitlow, the socialist author of a left-wing manifesto, was convicted, but in the process the courts incorporated free speech.

20. *Brandenburg v. Ohio*, 395 U.S. 444 (1969). For a fine discussion, see Harold Sullivan, *Civil Rights and Liberties* (Upper Saddle River, NJ: Pearson Prentice Hall, 2005), chap. 2.

21. Cass R. Sunstein, "Beyond Cheneyism and Snowdenism," *University of Chicago Law Review* 83, no. 1 (2016): 271–93, https://lawreview.uchicago.edu/sites/lawreview.uchicago.edu/files/uploads/83_1/12%20Sunstein_SYMP_Final.pdf; Posner cited in Patricia J. Williams, "ISIS Is Changing Our Attitude Toward Free Speech," *The Nation*, February 4, 2016, http://bit.ly/29VHnYd.

22. *Virginia v. Black*, 538 U.S. 343 (2003).

23. *Texas v. Johnson*, 109 S. Ct. 2544 (1989).

24. *Chaplinsky v. New Hampshire*, 315 U.S. 568 (1942).

25. *Tinker v. Des Moines Independent Community School District*, 393 U.S. 503 (1969).

26. *Bethel School District No. 403 v. Fraser*, 478 U.S. 675 (1986); *Hazelwood School District v. Kuhlmeier*, 484 U.S 260 (1988).

27. *Morse v. Frederick*, 551 U.S. 393 (2007).

28. *New York Times Company v. United States*, 403 U.S. 713 (1971).

29. Bob Egelko, "S.F. Judge Dissolves His Wikileaks Injunction," *San Francisco Chronicle*, March 1, 2008, http://www.sfgate.com/bayarea/article/S-F-judge-dissolves-his-Wikileaks-injunction-3226168.php.

30. *United States v. Stevens*, 130 U.S.C. 1577 (2010).

31. Catharine MacKinnon, "Pornography, Civil Rights, and Speech," in *Constitutional Law and American Democracy*, ed. Corey Brettschneider (New York: Wolters Kluwer), see note 10, 661–70.

32. *United States v. Williams*, 553 U.S. 285 (2008).

33. Seth Lipsky, *The Citizen's Constitution: An Animated Guide* (New York: Basic Books, 2009), 222.

34. Joseph Story, *Commentaries on the Constitution of the United States* (Boston: Hilliard, Gray, 1833), 3:746; Charlton Heston quoted in "Charlton Heston Rips Media," *Chicago Tribune*, September 12, 1997.

35. *District of Columbia v. Heller*, 554 U.S. 570 (2008).

36. Bruce A. Arrigo and Austin Acheson, "Concealed Carry Bans and the

American College Campus: A Law, Social Sciences, and Policy Perspective," *Contemporary Justice Review* 19 no. 1 (2016): 120–41, http://dx.doi .org/10.1080/10282580.2015.1101688.

37. Adam Nagourney and Erik Eckholm, "2nd Amendment Does Not Guarantee Right to Carry Concealed Weapons, Court Rules," *New York Times,* June 9, 2016, http://www .nytimes.com/2016/06/10/us/second -amendment-concealed-carry .html?_r=0.

38. *Olmstead v. United States,* 277 U.S. 438 (1928).

39. *United States v. Leon,* 468 U.S. 897 (1984).

40. *Herring v. United States,* 555 U.S. 135 (2009).

41. *Kentucky v. King,* 131 U.S. 865 (2011).

42. Linda Monk, *The Words We Live By: Your Annotated Guide to the Constitution* (New York: Hyperion, 2003), 165.

43. *Dickerson v. United States,* 530 U.S. 428 (2000).

44. *Illinois v. Perkins,* 496 U.S. 292 (1990); *New York v. Quarles,* 467 U.S. 649 (1984); *Harris v. New York,* 401 U.S. 222 (1970).

45. Anthony Lewis, *Gideon's Trumpet* (New York: Vintage, 1989).

46. *Missouri v. Frye,* 132 U.S. 55 (2012).

47. U.S. Department of Justice, "Access to Justice," http://www.justice .gov/atj/file/788166/download.

48. For an updated list of inmates whose crimes have been exonerated by Innocence Project efforts, see http:// www.innocenceproject.org/free -innocent/improve-the-law/fact -sheets/dna-exonerations-nationwide.

49. *Kennedy v. Louisiana,* 554 U.S. 407 (2008); *Atkins v. Virginia,* 536 U.S. 304 (2002); *Roper v. Simmons,* 543 U.S. 551 (2005); *Baez v. Rees,* 271 S. W. 3d. 207 affirmed (2007).

50. Adam Goldman, Jia Lynn Yang, and John Muyskens, "The Islamic State's Suspected Inroads into America," *Washington Post,* June 23, 2016, https://www.washingtonpost.com /graphics/national/isis-suspects/.

51. Senator Dianne Feinstein quoted in Tom Curry, "Congressional Intelligence Chairmen Applaud Obama for Backing Surveillance," *NBC Politics,* January 19, 2014, http://nbcpolitics .nbcnews.com/_news/2014/01/19/ 22358363-congressional-intelligence- chairmen-applaud-obama-for-backing- surveillance.

52. Erik Lichtblau and Katie Brenner, "Apple Fights Order to Unlock San Bernardino Gunman's iPhone," *New York Times,* February 17, 2016, 1.

Chapter 6 The Struggle for Civil Rights

1. Samuel Huntington, *American Politics: The Promise of Disharmony* (Cambridge, MA: Harvard University Press, 1981).

2. Smith, *Civic Ideals* (see chap. 2, note 3).

3. *Pierce v. Society of Sisters,* 268 U.S. 510 (1925); *Romer v. Evans,* 517 U.S. 620 (1996).

4. W. E. B. DuBois, *The Souls of Black Folk* (New York: New American Library, 1982), 220.

5. Garry Wills, *Lincoln at Gettysburg* (New York: Simon & Schuster, 1992).

6. C. Vann Woodward, *The Burden of Southern History,* 3rd ed. (Baton Rouge: University of Louisiana Press, 1993), 72.

7. The Civil Rights Cases, 109 U.S. 3 (1883).

8. Richard Valelly, *The Two Reconstructions* (Chicago: University of Chicago Press, 2004), 2.

9. *Plessy v. Ferguson,* 163 U.S. 537 (1896).

10. Jessie Parkhurst Guzman, *The Negro Yearbook* (Tuskegee, AL: Tuskegee Institute, 1947).

11. Peggy Pascoe, *What Comes Naturally: Miscegenation Law and the Making of Race in America* (New York: Oxford University Press, 2008).

12. Daniel P. Franklin, *Politics and Film: The Political Culture of Film in the United States* (Lanham, MD: Rowman and Littlefield, 2006).

13. *Smith v. Allright,* 21 U.S. 649 (1944).

14. *Morgan v. Virginia,* 328 U.S. 373 (1946); *Sweatt v. Painter,* 339 U.S. 629 (1950); *McLaurin v. Oklahoma,* 339 U.S. 637 (1950).

15. *Brown v. Board of Education,* 347 U.S. 483 (1954).

16. Taylor Branch, *Parting the Waters* (New York: Simon & Schuster, 1988), 203.

17. *Heart of Atlanta Motel Inc. v. United States,* 379 U.S. 241 (1964); *Katzenbach v. McClung,* 379 U.S. 294 (1964).

18. *Griggs v. Duke Power Co.,* 401 U.S. 424 (1971).

19. *Sheet Metal Workers v. EEOC,* 478 U.S. 421 (1986).

20. *Adarand Construction v. Peña,* 515 U.S. 299 (1995).

21. *University of California v. Bakke,* 438 U.S. 265 (1978); *Fisher v. University of Texas* at Austin et al., 579 U.S. 14–981 (2016).

22. Abby Kelly Foster, quoted in Morone, *Hellfire Nation,* 166 (see chap. 2, note 22).

23. Cecilia Hyunjung Mo, "The Consequences of Explicit and Implicit Gender Attitudes and Candidate Quality in the Calculation of Voters," *Political Behavior* 37, no. 2 (2015): 357–95.

24. Donald Critchlow, *Phyllis Schlafly and Grassroots Conservatism* (Princeton, NJ: Princeton University Press, 2005), chap. 9.

25. Francine D. Blau and Lawrence M. Kahn, "The Gender Wage Gap: Extent, Trends, and Explanations," *IZA Discussion Paper* 9656 (January 2016), http://ftp.iza.org/dp9656.pdf.

26. Sheryl Gay Stolberg, "Obama Signs Equal Pay Legislation," *New York Times,* January 1, 2009.

27. *Wal-Mart Stores Inc. v. Dukes,* 603 F. 3d 571, reversed (2011).

28. "Contraception: Freedom from Fear," *Time,* April 6, 1967, 79.

29. Department of Homeland Security, Office of Immigration Statistics, "2015 Annual Update" (August 31, 2015), https://www.dhs.gov/immigration -data-statistics.

30. Dayana Morales Gomez, "Undocumented Immigrants Urge Others to 'Come Out' in Push for Reform," *Huffington Post,* July 2, 2015, http:// www.huffingtonpost.com/2015/07/02 /jose-antonio-vargas-undocumented _n_7715162.html.

31. For updates on Hispanic inequality, see David Grusky, Tomás Jiménez, Doug Massey, and Beth Mattingly, "Hispanic Poverty and Inequality," Stanford Center on Poverty & Inequality, http:// inequality.stanford.edu/cpi-research/ area/hispanic-trends.

32. Heather Silber Mohamed, "Immigration, Protests, and the Politics of Latino/a Identity" (PhD dissertation, Brown University, 2012).

33. US Census Bureau data, released June 23, 2016, at http://www.census .gov/newsroom/press-releases/2016 /cb16-107.html.

34. Smith, *Civic Ideals,* 361 (see chap. 2, note 3).

35. Charlotte Brooks, *Alien Neighbors, Foreign Friends: Asian Americans, Housing and the Transformation of Urban California* (Chicago: University of Chicago Press, 2009), 194; Cindy I-Fen Cheng, *Citizens of Asian America: Democracy and Race during the Cold War* (New York: New York University Press, 2013).

36. Kristina Campbell, "The 'New Selma' and the Old Selma: Arizona, Alabama, and the Immigration Civil

Rights Movement in the Twenty-First Century," *Journal of American Ethnic History* 35, no. 3 (Spring 2016), 76–81, http://www.jstor.org/stable/10.5406/jamerethnhist.35.3.0076.

37. Tocqueville, *Democracy in America*, 1:323–24 (see chap. 2, note 3).

38. Pekka Hämäläinen, *The Comanche Empire* (New Haven, CT: Yale University Press, 2008).

39. *Dollar General v. Mississippi Band of Choctaw Indians*, 579 U.S. 13–1496 (2016).

40. *California v. Cabazon Band of Mission Indians*, 480 U.S. 202 (1987).

41. *Bowers v. Hardwick*, 478 U.S. 186 (1986); *Lawrence v. Texas*, 539 U.S. 558 (2003).

42. See Jaime M. Grant, et al., *Injustice at Every Turn: A Report of the National Transgender Discrimination Survey* (Washington, DC: National Center for Transgender Equality and National Gay and Lesbian Task Force, 2011), 2.

43. "CA Governor Brown Signs Historic Transgender Students Bill into Law," n.d., Transgender Law Center, http://transgenderlawcenter.org/archives/8756.

44. *Shelby County v. Holder*, 557 U.S. 193 (2013).

45. Marina Sheriff, "Testimony: Public Hearings on the Rockefeller Drug Laws, Special Housing Units, and Transitional Services for Inmates," n.d., New York Civil Liberties Union, http://www.nyclu.org/node/728.

Chapter 7 Public Opinion

1. Hannah Fingerhut, "Support Steady for Same-Sex Marriage and Acceptance of Homosexuality," Pew Research Center, May 12, 2016, http://pewrsr.ch/2ajmvN7; a 2016 update from Gallup: "In Depth: Topics A to Z: Marriage," http://bit.ly/1iiDKeI.

2. Michael Jackman, ed., *Crown's Book of Political Quotations* (New York: Crown Books, 1982), 181.

3. Mark Losey, "Why I Am a Democrat," DemocraticUnderground.com, accessed July 24, 2011, http://bit.ly/oHsB2C.

4. Orrin Hatch, "Why I Am a Republican," *Ripon Forum* 41, no. 6 (2008): 8.

5. Christopher Ingraham, "The Dramatic Shift Among College Professors That's Hurting Students' Education," *Washington Post*, January 11, 2016, https://www.washingtonpost.com/news/wonk/wp/2016/01/11/the-dramatic-shift-among-college-professors-thats-hurting-students-education/.

6. Drew DeSilver, "Partisan Polarization, in Congress and Among Public, Is

Greater than Ever," Pew Research Center, July 17, 2013, http://www.pewresearch.org/fact-tank/2013/07/17/partisan-polarization-in-congress-and-among-public-is-greater-than-ever/.

7. John Zaller, *The Nature and Origins of Mass Opinion* (New York: Cambridge University Press, 1992).

8. Bruce Drake, "More Americans Say U.S. Failed to Achieve Its Goals in Iraq," Pew Research Center, June 12, 2014, http://pewrsr.ch/1lsN29q.

9. Peter Stevenson, "The Fix: The South Carolina Push Poll Controversy Explained," *Washington Post*, February 12, 2016, https://www.washingtonpost.com/news/the-fix/wp/2016/02/12/the-south-carolina-push-poll-controversy-explained-video/.

10. Scott Keeter and Kyley McGeeney, "Pew Research Will Call More Cellphones in 2015," Pew Research Center, January 7, 2015, http://www.pewresearch.org/fact-tank/2015/01/07/pew-research-will-call-more-cellphones-in-2015/.

11. See, e.g., Laura Reston, "Trump and the Bandwagon Effect," *New Republic*, April 26, 2016, http://bit.ly/2aOONgP.

12. Walter Lippmann, *Public Opinion* (New York: Harcourt, Brace, 1922). On the movement to govern through technical expertise, see Morone, *The Democratic Wish*, chap. 3 (see chap 2, note 4).

13. Russell Hardin, "Ignorant Democracy," *Critical Review* 18, nos. 1–3 (2006): 179–95.

14. Angus Campbell, Philip E. Converse, Warren E. Miller, and Donald E. Stokes, *The American Voter* (New York: Wiley, 1960).

15. Michael S. Lewis-Beck, William G. Jacoby, Helmut Norpoth, and Herbert F. Weisberg, *The American Voter Revisited* (Ann Arbor: University of Michigan Press, 2008); Rick Shenkman, *Just How Stupid Are We? Facing the Truth About the American Voter* (New York: Basic Books, 2008).

16. Milton Lodge and Charles Taber, *The Rationalizing Voter* (Cambridge: Cambridge University Press, 2013).

17. Benjamin I. Page and Robert Y. Shapiro, *The Rational Public: Fifty Years of Trends in Americans' Policy Preferences* (Chicago: University of Chicago Press, 1992).

18. James Surowiecki, *The Wisdom of Crowds* (New York: Doubleday, 2004), xii.

19. Jon Marino, "The US Is Still Angry at Wall Street, and It May Be Hurting Recruiting," *CNBC News, Finance*, June 9, 2016, http://cnb.cx/1tel2h4.

20. John F. Harris, *The Survivor: Bill Clinton in the White House* (New York: Random House, 2005), 331.

21. Lawrence R. Jacobs and Robert Y. Shapiro, *Politicians Don't Pander: Political Manipulation and the Loss of Democratic Responsiveness* (Chicago: University of Chicago Press, 2000).

22. Barry Schwartz, *The Paradox of Choice: Why More Is Less* (New York: Harper Perennial, 2004).

Chapter 8 Political Participation

1. Bruce Schneier, "By November, Russian Hackers Could Target Voting Machines," *Washington Post*, July 27, 2016, http://wapo.st/2a0fhi7.

2. Tocqueville, *Democracy in America*, 1:189–95 (see chap. 2, note 3).

3. Peter Augustine Lawler, "Days of Apathy," *American Enterprise Review* (November 1, 1997): 22–24.

4. Pew Research Center, U.S. Politics & Policy, "Political Engagement" (June 12, 2014), http://www.people-press.org/2014/06/12/political-engagement-table/; Hansard Society, "Audit of Political Engagement 12: The 2015 Report," (2015), http://www.auditofpoliticalengagement.org/media/reports/Audit-of-Political-Engagement-12-2015.pdf; Statistics Canada, "Description for Chart 10 Participation in Political Activities in the Past 10 Months, 2003, 2008, and 2013," (November 30, 2015), http://www.statcan.gc.ca/pub/89-652-x/2015006/c-g/desc/desc10-eng.htm.

5. Larry M. Bartels, *Unequal Democracy: The Political Economy of the New Gilded Age* (Princeton, NJ: Princeton University Press, 2008).

6. See, e.g., Gustavo López and Renee Stepler, "Latinos in the 2016 Election: California," Pew Research Center, January 19, 2016, http://pewrsr.ch/1VKfSVx; Jennifer C. Lee and Samuel Kye, "Racialized Assimilation of Asian Americans," *Annual Review of Sociology* 42 (July 2016): 253–73, 10.1146/annurev-soc-081715-074310.

7. Donald P. Green and Alan S. Gerber, *Get Out the Vote: How to Increase Voter Turnout*, 2nd ed. (Washington, DC: Brookings Institution Press, 2008).

8. Mark Guarino, "How Organic Farming and YouTube Are Taming the Wilds of Detroit," *The Washington Post*, November 14, 2015. https://www.washingtonpost.com/national/how-organic-farming-and-youtube-are-taming-the-wilds-of-detroit/2015/11/14/c8f8df26-71da-11e5-8d93-0af317ed58c9_story.html.

9. James H. Fowler, Laura A. Baker, and Christopher T. Dawes, "Genetic Variation in Political Participation," *American Political Science Review* 102, no. 2 (2008): 233–48; Sven Oskarsson, et. al., "Linking Genes and Political Orientations," *Political Psychology* 36, no. 6 (December 2015): 649–65, 10.1111/pops.12230.

10. Doug McAdam and Karina Kloos, *Deeply Divided: Racial Politics and Social Movements in Post War America* (New York: Oxford University Press, 2014).

11. Joe Soss, *Unwanted Claims* (Ann Arbor: University of Michigan, 2002).

12. Doug McAdam, *Political Process and the Development of Black Insurgency, 1930–1970*, 2nd ed. (Chicago: University of Chicago Press, 1999).

13. Sidney Verba and Norman Nie, *Voice and Equality* (Chicago: University of Chicago, 1972).

14. John D. Griffin and Michael Keane, "Descriptive Representation and the Composition of African American Turnout," *American Journal of Political Science* 50, no. 4 (2006): 998–1012.

15. E. J. Dionne, *Why Americans Hate Politics: The Death of the Democratic Process* (New York: Simon & Schuster, 1991).

16. John Kenneth Galbraith, *The Culture of Contentment* (New York: Mariner Books, 1993).

17. Theda Skocpol, "Voice and Inequality: The Transformation of American Civic Democracy," *Perspectives on Politics* 2, no. 1 (2004): 14.

18. Clay Shirky, "The Political Power of Social Media: Technology, the Public Sphere, and Political Change," *Foreign Affairs* 90, no. 1 (January/February 2011).

19. See Matthew Hindman, *The Myth of Digital Democracy* (Princeton, NJ: Princeton University Press, 2009).

20. Trevor Timm, "The Most Concerning Element of Facebook's Potential New Power," *CJR.org* (April 13, 2015), http://www.cjr.org/criticism/facebook_news_censorship.php.

21. U.S. Department of Defense, *Cybersecurity Compliance and Culture Initiative* (Washington, DC, 2015), *http://www.defense.gov/Portals/1/Documents/pubs/OSD011517-15-RES*.

22. See Saul Levmore and Martha C. Nussbaum, eds., *The Offensive Internet* (Cambridge, MA: Harvard University Press, 2010). See, for falsehoods, Rhodri Marsden, "Websites Can Create Outrageous Lies Just for Clicks," *Independent*, July 9, 2015, http://www.independent.co.uk/news/science/websites-can-create-outrageous-lies -just-for-clicks-but-why-and-how-is -this-legal-10379088.html.

23. Michael Grunwald, "How Obama Is Using the Science of Change," *Time*, April 2, 2009.

24. Ron Fournier, "The Outsiders: How Can Millennials Change Washington If They Hate It?" *Atlantic*, August 2013.

25. Pew Charitable Trusts, *Millennials in Adulthood: Detached from Institutions, Networked with Friends* (Washington, DC: Pew Research Center, 2014): 7.

26. Tom Spengler, "Civic Engagement: Why Millennials Have Outpaced Seniors," *Huffington Post* (blog), June 13, 2013, August 13, 2014, http://www.huffingtonpost.com/tom-spengler/civic-engagement-why-mill_b_5492478.html; Tracy McVeigh, "Baby Boomers Leave Unpaid Voluntary Work to the Young," *The Guardian*, November 21, 2015, https://www.theguardian.com/society/2015/nov/21/baby-boomers-leave-voluntary-work-to-young-charities; "More Millennials Value Volunteering than Previous Generation Did," *Philanthropy News Digest*, January 5, 2015, http://bit.ly/1Axp5E9.

Chapter 9 Media, Technology, and Government

1. Properly speaking, *media* is the plural of *medium*—usually defined as the way we convey something. We use the term *media*—meaning mass communication—as a singular noun in keeping with the way the language is evolving.

2. Shanto Iyengar and Donald R. Kinder, *News that Matters: Television and Public Opinion*, 2nd ed. (Chicago: University of Chicago Press, 2010).

3. David Bach and Daniel J. Blake, "Frame or Get Framed," *California Management Review* 58:3 (2016).

4. Reliable counts of U.S. newspapers appears in the Inter-University Consortium for Political and Social Research's "United States Newspaper Panel." At http://bit.ly/29IGdmh (accessed July 19, 2016).

5. American Society of Newspaper Editors, "2015 Census" (Columbia, MO, 2015), accessed May 20, 2016, http://asne.org/content.asp?contentid=415.

6. Julie Bacon, "The *Rush Limbaugh Show* and the Expanding Culture War," in *Systemic Crises of Global Climate Change: Intersections of Race, Class, and Gender*, ed., Phoebe Godfrey and Denise Torres (New York: Routledge, 2016).

7. Jeff Bercovici, "Science Settles It: NPR's Liberal, But Not Very," *Forbes*, March 22, 2011, http://www.forbes.com/sites/jeffbercovici/2011/03/22/science-settles-it-nprs-liberal-but-not-very/#ce7d7d799e8c.

8. Doris A. Graber and Johanna L. Dunaway, *Mass Media and American Politics*, 9th ed. (Washington, DC: CQ Press, 2015), chap. 4.

9. Eric Alterman, *What Liberal Bias? The Truth About Bias and the News* (New York: Basic, 2003).

10. See, for example, Isaac Chotiner, "Did the Press Create Donald Trump?" *Slate*, March 22, 2016, at http://slate.me/22u0KjM.

11. Justin Wolfers, "Perceptions Haven't Caught Up to Decline in Crime," *New York Times*, September 16, 2014, http://nyti.ms/1THsJnH.

12. Graber, *Mass Media and American Politics*, 8th ed. (2010), 266.

13. Broadcasters' Audience Research Board, "Share by Channel," n.d., accessed June 22, 2016, http://www.barb.co.uk/trendspotting/analysis/share-by-channel-2/.

14. The media in European countries is increasingly overseen by the European Union, which creates different rules for three different sectors: public media, which is run by national governments (often the largest sector); commercial media; and fledgling community media. See Stefanie Walter, "A Network Perspective on European Union News," *Mass Communication and Society* (March 2016), http://bit.ly/1s4lwpD.

15. Andrei Markovits, *Uncouth Nation: Why Europeans Dislike America* (Princeton, NJ: Princeton University Press, 2007).

16. Michael Wines and Sharon LaFraniere, "In Baring Facts of Train Crash, Blogs Erode China Censorship," *New York Times*, July 29, 2011.

17. Charles Clover, "China's Strict New Internet Rules Send Chill into Foreign Media," *Financial Times*, March 22, 2016, 1.

18. Michael Jetter, "Terrorism and the Media," IZA Discussion Paper, Social Science Research Network (2015), http://papers.ssrn.com/sol3/papers.cfm?abstract_id=2505359.

19. Ivengar, *News that Matters: Television and Public Opinion*, 1st ed. (1989).

Chapter 10 Campaigns and Elections

1. John Cassidy, "How Donald Trump Won the G.O.P. Nomination," *The New Yorker*, May 4, 2016, http://bit.ly/1rnbJKQ; Ali Breland, "Romney: Trump Will Cause 'Trickle-Down Racism,'" *Politico*, June 10, 2016, http://politi.co/1XNRZy9.

2. On the Trump and Sanders voters, see, J. Eric Oliver and Wendy M. Rahn, "Rise of the *Trumpenvolk*: Populism in the 2016 American Election," *Annals of the American Academy of Political and Social Science* 667, no. 1 (2016): 189–206, 10.1177/0002716216662639.

3. William J. Feltus, Kenneth M. Goldstein, and Matthew Dallek, *Inside Campaigns: Elections Through the Eyes of Political Professionals* (New York: Sage, 2017), esp. chap. 2 ["Political Math: How Campaigns Matter"]; John Sides and Lynn Vavreck, *The Gamble: Choice and Chance in the 2012 Presidential Election* (Princeton, NJ: Princeton University Press, 2013).

4. David Shribman, "In Canada, the Lean Season," *Boston Globe*, May 23, 1997, A3.

5. Open Secrets: Center for Responsive Government, "Influence & Lobbying/Interest Groups/Finance/Insurance/Real Estate/Summary," http://www.opensecrets.org/industries/indus.php?Ind=F.

6. Open Secrets: Center for Responsive Government and includes all donations reported by July 27, 2016, http://www.opensecrets.org.

7. Benjy Sarlin, "United States of Trump: An Inside Look at the Voters Who Took Over the Republican Party," *NBC News*, June 20, 2016, http://www.nbcnews.com/specials/donald-trump-republican-party?cid=eml_onsite.

8. Adrienne LaFrance, "Three Decades of Donald Trump Film and TV Cameos," *The Atlantic*, December 21, 2015, http://www.theatlantic.com/entertainment/archive/2015/12/three-decades-of-donald-trump-film-and-tv-cameos/421257/.

9. Ashley Parker and David E. Sanger, "Donald Trump Calls on Russia to Find Hillary Clinton's Missing Emails," *New York Times*, July 27, 2016, http://www.nytimes.com/2016/07/28/us/politics/donald-trump-russia-clinton-emails.html?_r=0.

10. Halpern, *Double Down*, 177–96.

11. Samuel L. Popkin, *The Candidate: What It Takes to Win—and Hold—the White House* (New York: Oxford University Press, 2012).

12. On campaigns' use of increasingly sophisticated models, see Feltus, *Inside Campaigns*, 62–83.

13. Nathan Burroughs, "The 'Money Primary' and Political Inequality in Congressional Elections," SSRN Working Paper, 2013, http://dx.doi.org/10.2139/ssrn.2251978.

14. On the Frelinghuysen family and other American "dynasties," see Stephen Hess, *America's Political Dynasties: From Adams to Clinton*, 2nd ed. (Washington, DC: Brookings Institution Press, 2016).

15. Jennifer L. Lawless and Richard L. Fox, *It Takes a Candidate: Why Women Don't Run for Office* (New York: Cambridge University Press, 2005).

16. Richard F. Fenno, Jr., *Homestyle: House Members in Their Districts* (New York: Longman Classics, 2002).

17. *Shaw v. Reno*, 509 U.S. 630 (1993).

18. For the classic account of candidate-centered politics, see Martin P. Wattenberg, *The Rise of Candidate-Centered Politics: Presidential Elections of the 1980s* (Cambridge, MA: Harvard University Press, 1991).

19. Gerald M. Pomper, *Voters, Elections and Parties: The Practice of Democratic Theory* (Piscataway, NJ: Transaction, 1988), 104. See also Sean J. Miller, "Why Technology Can't Replace Old-Fashioned Politicking," *Campaigns & Elections*, April 19, 2012, https://www.campaignsandelections.com/campaign-insider/why-technology-can-t-replace-old-fashioned-politicking.

20. Clayton D. Peoples, "Campaign Finance and Policymaking: PACs, Campaign Contributions, and Interest Group Influence in Congress," *Sociology Compass* 7, no. 11 (2013): 900–13, doi:10.1111/soc4.12079.

Chapter 11 Political Parties

1. Pew Research Center, "Think Environmental Laws and Regulations Should Be Stricter," April 18, 2007, http://pewrsr.ch/2bCNp4U.

2. Pew Research Center, "Political Partisanship and Animosity in 2016," June 22, 2016, http://pewrsr.ch/28WYkmr; Coral Davenport, "Climate Change Divide Bursts to Forefront of Presidential Campaign," *New York Times*, August 1, 2016, http://nyti.ms/2af8L2W.

3. Thomas Jefferson to Francis Hopkinson, Paris, March 13, 1789, http://founders.archives.gov/documents/Jefferson/01-14-02-0402. For Washington's text and an informed commentary, see Matthew Spalding and Patrick J. Garrity, *A Sacred Union of Citizens: George Washington's Farewell Address and the American Character* (Lanham, MD: Rowman & Littlefield, 1998).

4. John H. Aldrich, *Why Parties? The Origin and Transformation of Political Parties in America* (Chicago: University of Chicago Press, 1995).

5. See especially Teresa Amato, *Grand Illusion: The Myth of Voter Choice in a Two-Party Tyranny* (New York: New Press, 2009).

6. J. David Gillespie, *Challengers to Duopoly: Why Third Parties Matter in Two-Party American Politics* (Columbia: University of South Carolina Press, 2012).

7. R. Kent Newmyer, *Supreme Court Justice Joseph Story: Statesman of the Old Republic* (Chapel Hill: University of North Carolina Press, 1985), 158.

8. Daniel Walker Howe, *What Hath God Wrought: The Transformation of America, 1815–1848* (New York: Oxford University Press, 2007).

9. A good summary of this and related views is in Mark E. Neely, Jr., *The Union Divided: Party Conflict in the Civil War North* (Cambridge, MA: Harvard University Press, 2002).

10. You can read all about Prohibition in Morone, *Hellfire Nation*, chapters 9 and 10 (see chap. 2, note 22).

11. President William Jefferson Clinton, State of the Union Address, January 23, 1996, Washington DC, https://clinton2.nara.gov/WH/New/other/sotu.html; President Barack Hussein Obama, Inaugural Address, January 20, 2009, Washington DC, http://bit.ly/1VG1k9q.

12. See Katherine Tate, *Concordance: Black Lawmaking in the U.S. Congress from Carter to Obama* (Ann Arbor: University of Michigan Press, 2014).

13. Alan S. Gerber, Gregory A. Huber, David Doherty, Conor M. Dowling, and Shang E. Ha, "Personality and Political Attitudes: Relationships Across Issue Domains and Political Contexts," *American Political Science Review* 104, no. 1 (2010): 111–33, http://dx.doi.org/10.1017/S0003055410000031.

14. Frank D. Bean, "Changing Ethnic and Racial Diversity in the United States," *Population and Development Review* 42, no. 1 (2016): 135–42, 10.1111/j.1728-4457.2016.00113.x.

15. Marjorie Randon Hershey, *Party Politics in America*, 16th ed. (New York: Routledge, 2016), 108.

16. Pew Research Center, U.S. Politics & Policy, "Partisan Polarization Surges in Bush and Obama Years: Trends in American Values: 1987–2012," June 4, 2012, http://www.people-press.org/2012/06/04/partisan-polarization-surges-in-bush-obama-years/.

17. Joseph Lowndes, "White Populism and the Transformation of the Silent Majority," *The Forum* 14, no. 1 (April 2016): 25–37, 10.1515/for-2016-0004.

18. David S. Broder, *The Party's Over: The Failure of Politics in America* (New York: Harper & Row, 1972); Martin P. Wattenberg, *The Decline of American Political Parties, 1952–1980*

(Cambridge, MA: Harvard University Press, 1985).

19. On rising party polarization and possible responses, see the essays in Nathaniel Persily, ed., *Solutions to Political Polarization in America* (New York: Cambridge University Press, 2015).

20. Nancy Roman, "Bitter Fruits of Partisanship," *Baltimore Sun*, October 19, 2005.

21. David R. Mayhew, *Divided We Govern: Party Control, Investigations, and Lawmaking, 1946–2002*, 2nd ed. (New Haven, CT: Yale University Press, 2005).

22. See Thomas E. Mann and Norman J. Ornstein, *It's Even Worse than It Was: How the American Constitutional System Collided with the New Politics of Extremism*, 2nd ed. (New York: Basic Books, 2016); Alan I. Abramowitz, *The Disappearing Center: Engaged Citizens, Polarization and American Democracy* (New Haven, CT: Yale University Press, 2010).

23. On the benefits that proportional representation could bring to the United States, see generally Douglas J. Amy, *Real Choices/New Voices: How Proportional Representation Elections Could Revitalize American Democracy* (New York: Columbia University Press, 2002).

24. The term *core commitments* and an extended argument on behalf of stronger parties is in Russell Muirhead, *The Promise of Party in a Polarized Age* (Cambridge, MA: Harvard University Press, 2014).

Chapter 12 Interest Groups

1. Jeffrey Berry and Clyde Wilcox, *The Interest Group Society*, 5th ed. (New York: Routledge, 2008).

2. For more on how AARP (and other membership groups) wield influence, see Peter Murray, "The Secret of Scale," *Stanford Social Innovation Review* (Fall 2013), http://ssir.org/articles/entry/the_secret_of_scale.

3. Jonathan Rauch, *Demosclerosis: The Silent Killer of American Government* (New York: Crown, 1994).

4. Kay Lehman Schlozman, Sidney Verba, and Henry Brady, *The Unheavenly Chorus: Unequal Political Voice and the Broken Promise of American Democracy* (Princeton, NJ: Princeton University Press, 2012), chap. 1; E. E. Schattschneider, *The Semi-Sovereign People: A Realist View of Democracy in America* (New York: Holt, Rinehart and Wilson, 1960), 35.

5. Professional Association of Therapeutic Horsemanship: professionals who provide equine therapy to children and adults.

6. Elise Viebeck, "Insurers Tire of 'Frenemy' White House," *The Hill*, March 27, 2014.

7. Jeffrey H. Birnbaum, *The Lobbyists: How Influence Peddlers Work Their Way in Washington* (New York: Times Books, 1993), 8.

8. Rogan Kersh, "Ten Myths About Health Lobbyists," in *Health Politics and Policy*, 5th ed., ed. James A. Morone and Daniel C. Ehlke (Stamford, CT: Cengage, 2014).

9. Cindy Skrzycki, "GOP's Young Lions Are Now in the Lobbying Catbird Seat," *Washington Post*, December 23, 1994.

10. Sheryl Gay Stolberg, "Pugnacious Builder of the Business Lobby," *New York Times*, June 1, 2013.

11. Fraser Nelson, David W. Brady, and Alana Conner Snibbe, "Learn to Love Lobbying," *Stanford Social Innovation Review* 5, no. 2 (Spring 2007): 57.

12. Mark Peterson, "Congress in the 1990s: From Iron Triangles to Policy Networks," in *The Politics of Health Care Reform*, ed. James Morone and Gary Belkin (Durham, NC: Duke University Press, 1994), 108, 127.

13. Paul F. Boller, Jr., *Congressional Anecdotes* (New York: Oxford University Press, 1991), 122.

14. James Thurber quoted in Marcus E. Howard, "Penalty Against Lobbying Firm Sends Message," *Los Angeles Times*, November 30, 2015.

15. On the shift to lobbying states, see Dante Chinni, "With Gridlock in Washington, Lobbyists Turn to Statehouses," *Wall Street Journal*, January 16, 2016.

16. Eric R. Hansen and Virginia Gray, "Interest Group Density and Policy Change in the States" (Paper, Southern Political Science Convention, San Juan, Puerto Rico, January 2016).

17. See Lee Fang, "Where Have All the Lobbyists Gone?" *The Nation*, March 17, 2014.

18. Energy groups' activity is summarized in Karam Kang, "Policy Influence and Private Returns from Lobbying in the Energy Sector," *Review of Economic Studies* 83, no. 1 (2016).

19. One book-length study of interest groups concludes that "the connection between money and influence is subtle." Thomas Holyoke, *Interest Groups and Lobbying: Pursuing Political Interests in America* (Boulder, CO: Westview Press, 2014), 251.

20. Paul S. Herrnson, Ronald G. Shaiko, and Clyde Wilcox, *The Interest Group Connection* (Chatham, NJ: Chatham House, 1998), 389.

21. Bok quoted in Ronald J. Hrebenar and Clive S. Thomas, "American Interest Group Politics in the 21st Century" (Paper, Western Political Science Association, Vancouver, Canada, March 20, 2009).

22. Ronnie Greene, "Bush Blasts 'Swarms of Lobbyists' But Once Registered as One," *Associated Press*, July 23, 2015, http://apne.ws/1VUcMhZ.

23. See Lee Drutman, *The Business of America is Lobbying* (New York: Oxford University Press, 2015).

24. Theda Skocpol and Vanessa Williamson, *The Tea Party and the Remaking of Republican Conservatism* (New York: Oxford University Press, 2012), 100–101.

25. For a good recent study of citizen groups' influence, in this case on behalf of uninsured Americans, see Timothy Callaghan and Lawrence W. Jacobs, "Interest Group Conflict Over Medicaid Expansion," *American Journal of Public Health* 106, no. 2 (2016).

26. Daniel E. Bergan, Alan S. Gerber, Donald P. Green, and Costas Panagopoulos, "Grassroots Mobilization and Voter Turnout in 2004," *Public Opinion Quarterly* 69, no. 5 (2005): 760–77.

Chapter 13 Congress

1. Ed O'Keefe, "The House Has Voted 54 Times in Four Years on Obamacare," *Washington Post*, March 21, 2014, A18.

2. Lee Hamilton, "Those Who Know Congress Best Are Shaking Their Heads," *Syndicated Op Ed*, May 12, 2016, http://howeypolitics.com/Content/Columns/Columns/Article/Lee-Hamilton-Those-who-know-Congress-best-are-shaking-their-heads/10/20/13866.

3. Thomas E. Mann and Norman J. Ornstein, *The Broken Branch: How Congress Is Failing America and How to Get It Back On Track* (New York: Oxford University Press, 2006).

4. Robert A. Caro, *Master of the Senate: The Years of Lyndon Johnson* (New York: Knopf, 2002), 52.

5. For more along this line, see Mark Twain and Charles Dudley Warner, *The Gilded Age* (New York: Oxford University Press, 1996).

6. Frank Bruni, "An Obama Nominee's Crushed Hopes," *New York Times*, June 6, 2016, http://nyti.ms/2aC1OIG. On the rising use of filibusters and holds more generally, see Gregory Koger, "Partisanship, Filibustering, and Reform in the Senate," in *Party and Procedure in the*

United States Congress, 2nd ed., ed. Jacob R. Straus and Matthew E. Glassman (Lanham, MD: Rowman & Littlefield, 2016), chap. 10.

7. Caro, *Master of the Senate,* 9.

8. Sean Theriault, *The Gingrich Senators: The Roots of Partisan Warfare in Congress* (New York: Oxford University Press, 2013).

9. Jane Mansbridge, "Rethinking Representation," *American Political Science Review* 97, no. 4 (2003): 515–28.

10. Paul F. Boller, *Congressional Anecdotes* (New York: Oxford University Press, 1992).

11. Lawrence R. Jacobs and Robert Y. Shapiro, *Politicians Don't Pander: Political Manipulation and the Loss of Democratic Responsiveness* (Chicago: University of Chicago Press, 2000).

12. Nora Kelly, "Are Members of Congress Overpaid?" *The Atlantic,* June 2, 2016, http://theatln.tc/28NLSaE.

13. David E. Price, "Congressional-Executive Balance in an Era of Congressional Dysfunction," *PS: Political Science & Politics* 49, no. 3 (2016): 485–86, http://dx.doi.org/10.1017/S1049096516000755.

14. Carl Bernstein, *A Woman in Charge: The Life of Hillary Rodham Clinton* (New York: Knopf, 2007), 546–47.

15. Linda Greenhouse, "David E. Price; Professor in Congress Is Doing Homework on Theory and Reality," *New York Times,* February 11, 1988.

16. Public Policy Polling, "Congress Losing Out to Zombies, Wall Street, and . . . Hipsters," October 8, 2013, accessed August 1, 2014, http://www.publicpolicypolling.com/main/2013/10/congress-losing-out-to-zombies-wall-street-andhipsters.html.

17. Juliet Eilperin, *Fight Club Politics: How Partisanship Is Poisoning the House of Representatives* (Lanham, MD: Rowman & Littlefield, 2007), 13.

18. Barbara Sinclair, *Unorthodox Lawmaking: New Legislative Processes in the U.S. Congress,* 3rd ed. (Washington, DC: CQ Press, 2007), 71.

19. Eilperin, *Fight Club;* Mann and Ornstein, *Broken Branch;* Lawrence Lessig, *Republic Lost: How Money Corrupts Congress—And a Plan to Stop It* (New York: Twelve Books, 2011); Peter Hanson, *Too Weak to Govern: Majority Party Power and Appropriations in the U.S. Senate* (New York: Cambridge University Press, 2014); Thomas E. Mann and Norman J. Ornstein, *It's Even Worse Than It Looks: How the American Constitutional System Collided with the New Politics of Extremism* (New York: Basic Books, 2012).

20. Jacob S. Hacker and Paul Pierson, *Off Center: The Republican Revolution and the Erosion of American Democracy* (New Haven, CT: Yale University Press, 2006).

21. David R. Mayhew, *Divided We Govern: Party Control, Lawmaking, and Investigations, 1946–2002,* 2nd ed. (New Haven, CT: Yale University Press, 2005); Keith Krehbiel, *Pivotal Politics: A Theory of U.S. Lawmaking* (Chicago: University of Chicago Press, 1998).

22. Sarah Binder, *Stalemate: Causes and Consequences of Legislative Gridlock* (Washington, DC: Brookings Institution Press, 2003); Mann and Ornstein, *It's Even Worse Than It Looks,* 110.

23. John R. Hibbing and Elizabeth Theiss-Morse, *Stealth Democracy: Americans' Beliefs About How Government Should Work* (New York: Cambridge University Press, 2002).

Chapter 14 The Presidency

1. Joseph Ellis, *His Excellency: George Washington* (New York: Random House, 2004), 194–95.

2. On a new president's complex decisions, concerning drones and other foreign-policy decisions, see Colin Dueck, "Strategic Planning for the Next President," *Orbis* 60, no. 3 (2016): 331–52.

3. Paul Harris, Kamal Ahmed, and Martin Bright, "Seeing Eye to Eye," *Observer,* November 16, 2003, 1; David Nakamura and Carol D. Leonnig, "Five Myths About Presidential Travel," *Washington Post,* January 23, 2015, http://wapo.st/1SxP5qa.

4. Ashley Parker, "'Imperial Presidency' Becomes a Rallying Cry for Republicans," *New York Times,* March 31, 2014.

5. Kirk Scharfenberg, "Now It Can Be Told: The Story Behind Campaign '82's Favorite Insult," *Boston Globe,* November 6, 1982.

6. Francis Biddle, *In Brief Authority* (New York: Doubleday, 1962), 219.

7. See, e.g., Tim Dowling, "So What Will David Cameron See on Air Force One?" *The Guardian,* March 12, 2012, 3.

8. For a description of this episode, taken from White House telephone tapes, see David Blumenthal and James Morone, *The Heart of Power: Health and Politics in the Oval Office* (Berkeley: University of California Press, 2009), 142.

9. Leonard White, *The Federalists* (New York: Macmillan, 1942).

10. For a description of Roosevelt's approach, see James Morone, *The Democratic Wish* (New Haven, CT: Yale University Press, 1998), 131.

11. Memo from Pat Caddell to "Governor Carter," December 21, 1976, Carter Library; see also Blumenthal, *Heart of Power,* 249.

12. Richard Neustadt, *Presidential Power and the Modern Presidents,* rev. ed. (New York: Free Press, 1991).

13. Samuel Kernell, *Going Public* (Washington, DC: CQ Press, 2007).

14. Lawrence R. Jacobs and Robert Y. Shapiro, *Politicians Don't Pander: Political Manipulation and the Loss of Democratic Responsiveness* (Chicago: University of Chicago Press, 2000).

15. Barbara Hinckley, *Follow the Leader: Opinion Polls and the Modern President* (New York: Basic Books, 1992).

16. Marc Landy and Sidney Milkis, *Presidential Greatness* (Lawrence: University Press of Kansas, 2001).

17. Stephen Skowronek, *The Politics Presidents Make: Leadership from John Adams to Bill Clinton* (Cambridge, MA: Harvard University Press, 1997).

18. Peggy Noonan, *When Character Was King* (New York: Penguin Books, 2001), 242–43, 245–49.

19. Blumenthal, *Heart of Power,* 293.

20. On personality theories, see Michael Nelson, "The Psychological Presidency," in *The Presidency and the Political System,* 10th ed. (Washington, DC: CQ Press, 2013), 167–90.

21. Mortality data from Robert E. Gilbert, *The Mortal Presidency: Illness and Anguish in the White House* (New York: Fordham University Press, 1998), 4–5.

22. Rose McDermott, *Presidential Leadership, Illness, and Decision Making* (New York: Cambridge University Press, 2008).

23. Quoted in Jody C. Baumgartner, "The Second Best Choice? Vice-Presidential Candidates in the Modern Era," in *White House Studies Compendium,* ed. Anthony J. Eksterowicz and Glenn P. Hastedt (New York: Nova Science Publishers, 2008), 158.

24. Quoted in Elliot A. Rosen, "'Not Worth a Pitcher of Warm Piss': John Nance Garner as Vice President," in *At the President's Side: The Vice Presidency in the Twentieth Century* ed. Timothy Walch (Columbia: University of Missouri Press, 2007), 45.

25. David McCullough, *Truman* (New York: Simon & Schuster, 1992), 436; Stephen E. Ambrose, *Eisenhower: Soldier and President* (New York: Simon & Schuster, 1990), 564.

26. Richard J. Ellis, *The Development of the American Presidency* (New York: Routledge, 2012), 284.

27. Joseph Califano, *Governing America: An Insider's Report from the White House and the Cabinet* (New York: Simon & Schuster, 1981), 431; personal interview with the authors, June 15, 2006.

28. For a fine description, see Matthew Dickinson, "The Executive Office of the President: The Paradox of Politicization," in *The Executive Branch*, ed. Joel Aberbach and Mark Peterson (New York: Oxford University Press, 2005), 135–73.

29. Johnson, quoted in Blumenthal, *Heart of Power*, 8.

30. See the excellent treatment in Lauren A. Wright, *On Behalf of the President: Presidential Spouses and White House Communications Strategy Today* (Santa Barbara, CA: Praeger, 2016).

Chapter 15 Bureaucracy

1. Pew Research Center, "Trust in Government: 1958–2015," November 23, 2015, http://www.people-press.org /2015/11/23/1-trust-in-government -1958-2015/.

2. Stuart Shapiro, "Government Bureaucrats Are People Too," *The Hill*, November 12, 2015, http://thehill.com/ blogs/pundits-blog/labor/259907 -government-bureaucrats-are-people -too.

3. President Barack Obama, First Inaugural Address (see chap. 11, note 11).

4. Pew Research Center, "Ratings of Federal Agencies, Congress and the Supreme Court," November 23, 2015, http://pewrsr.ch/1P5Zmgc.

5. William Riordan, *Plunkitt of Tammany Hall: A Series of Very Plain Talks on Very Practical Politics* (New York: Penguin, 1995).

6. James Sparrow, *Warfare State: World War II Americans and the Age of Big Government* (New York: Oxford University Press, 2012).

7. See Daniel Carpenter, *The Forging of Bureaucratic Autonomy: Reputations, Networks, and Policy Innovation in Executive Agencies* (Princeton, NJ: Princeton University Press, 2001); Morone, *Hellfire Nation* (see chap. 2, note 22).

8. Max Weber, "Bureaucracy," in *From Max Weber: Essays in Sociology*, ed. H. H. Gerth and C. Wright Mills (New York: Oxford University Press, 1946), 196–98.

9. Timothy Cama, "Two Dozen States Sue Obama Over Coal Plant Emissions Rule," *The Hill*, October 23, 2015, http:// thehill.com/policy/energy-environment/ 257856-24-states-coal-company-sue -obama-over-climate-rule.

10. Steve Vogel, "Officials and Experts Praising FEMA for Its Response to Hurricane Sandy," *Washington Post*, November 1, 2012, A1.

11. Allison Stanger, *One Nation Under Contract: The Outsourcing of American Power and the Future of Foreign Policy* (New Haven, CT: Yale University Press, 2011).

12. Paul Light, "Creating High-Performance Government: A Once-in-a-Generation Opportunity" (Report, New York: Global Center on Public Service, NYU Wagner School, 2011), 4.

13. Truman quoted in Richard Neustadt, *Presidential Power* (New York: Free Press, 1990), 10.

14. Richard Nixon, *RN: Memoirs of Richard Nixon* (New York: Simon & Schuster, 1990), 352.

15. Michael Lipsky, *Street-Level Bureaucracy: Dilemmas of the Individual in Public Services* (New York: Russell Sage Foundation, 1980).

16. Joe Soss, *Unwanted Claims: The Politics of Participation in the U.S. Welfare System* (Ann Arbor: University of Michigan Press, 2000).

17. President Ronald Reagan, First Inaugural Address, January 20, 1981, http://www.presidency.ucsb.edu/ws /?pid=43130; President William J. Clinton, State of the Union Message, January 23, 1996, http://www .presidency.ucsb.edu/ws/index .php?pid=53091.

18. Emily Willingham, "Is the Freedom of Information Act Stifling Intellectual Freedom?" *Forbes*, November 21, 2015, http://www.forbes.com/sites /emilywillingham/2015/11/21/is-the -freedom-of-information-act-stifling -intellectual-freedom/#513b72a655b6.

19. Al Gore, *Common Sense Government: Works Better and Costs Less* (New York: Random House, 1995).

20. Donald F. Kettl, *Escaping Jurassic Government* (Washington, DC: Brookings Institution Press, 2016).

Chapter 16 The Judicial Branch

1. Alexander Hamilton, *Federalist* no. 78.

2. The cases are, respectively: *Citizens United* followed by *McCutcheon v. Federal Election Commission* (on money in elections); *National Federation of Independent Business v. Sebelius* (on Obamacare); *Shelby County v. Holder* (striking down key sections of the voting rights act); and *Burwell v. Hobby Lobby* (limiting contraception).

3. Tocqueville, *Democracy in America*, 1:270 (see chap. 2, note 3).

4. *Bush v. Gore*, 531 U.S. 98 (2000).

5. Jeffrey M. Jones, "Republicans' Approval of the Supreme Court Sinks to 18%," *Gallup Politics*, July 16, 2015, http://www.gallup.com/poll/184160 /republicans-approval-supreme-court -sinks.aspx?g_source=Supreme %20Court&g_medium=search&g _campaign=tiles.

6. John Schwartz, "Effort Begun to End Voting for Judges," *New York Times*, December 23, 2009.

7. Barry J. McMillion, "U.S. Circuit and District Court Judges: Profile of Select Characteristics," *Congressional Research Service*, March 19, 2014, https://www.fas.org/sgp/crs/misc /R43426.pdf.

8. Charlie Savage, "A Judge's View of Judging Is on the Record," *New York Times*, May 14, 2009.

9. Thomas Jefferson, "Letter to Justice Spencer Roane on the Limits of Judicial Review," in Thomas Jefferson, *Writings* (New York: Library of America, 1984), 1425–28.

10. See, e.g., Robert G. McCloskey and Sanford Levinson, *The American Supreme Court*, 6th ed. (Chicago: University of Chicago Press, 2016), esp. 302–12.

11. *Dred Scott v. Sandford*, 60 U.S. 393 (1857).

12. The case was *Worcester v. Georgia*, 31 U.S. (6 Pet.) 515 (1832).

13. Paul M. Collins Jr., Pamela C. Corley, and Jesse Hamner, "The Influence of Amicus Curiae Briefs on U.S. Supreme Court Opinion Content," *Law and Society Review* 49, no. 4 (December 2015), 917–44, 10.1111/lasr.12166.

14. Adam Liptak, "Are Oral Arguments Worth Arguing About?" *New York Times: Sunday Review*, May 6, 2012.

15. Randee Fenner, "Clerking at the Supreme Court," *Stanford Lawyer* 77 (Fall 2007): 7–9.

16. Senate Hrg. 109–158, Hearing Before the Committee on the Judiciary, United States Senate One Hundred Ninth Congress (September 12, 2005), http://bit.ly/2aLRGSW.

17. See, e.g., Kevin Buckler and Elizabeth L. Gilmore, "Originalism, Pragmatic Conservatism, and Living Document Judicial Philosophies: Explaining Variation in U.S. Supreme Court Votes in Criminal Procedure Cases for the 1994–2004 Terms of Court," *American Journal of Criminal Justice* 42, published electronically July 28, 2016, http://bit.ly/2aUoirR.

18. Adam Liptak, "In a Polarized Court, Getting the Last Word," *New York Times*, March 8, 2010. For data on justices' voting patterns and other details, see Lee Epstein, Jeffrey A. Segal, Harold J. Spaeth, and Thomas G. Walker, *Supreme Court Compendium*, 6th ed. (Washington, DC: CQ Press, 2015).

19. Jeffrey R. Lax and Kelly Rader, "Bargaining Power in the Supreme Court: Evidence From Opinion Assignment and Vote Switching," *Journal of Politics* 77:3 (2015), 648–63.

20. Saul Brenner, "Fluidity on the Supreme Court, 1956–1967," *American Journal of Political Science* 90, no. 56 (1996): 90–107.

21. Frederick Schauer, "Incentives, Reputation, and the Inglorious Determinants of Judicial Behavior," *University of Cincinnati Law Review* 68, no. 3 (2000): 615–36.

22. Thomas Keck, "Party, Policy, or Duty: Why Does the Supreme Court Invalidate Federal Statutes?" *American Political Science Review* 101, no. 2 (May 2007): 321ff.

23. *McCulloch v. Maryland*, 17 U.S. (4 Wheat.) 316 (1819).

24. *Dred Scott v. Sandford*, 60 U.S. 393 (1857).

25. Justice Black in *Connecticut General Life Insurance Co. v. Johnson*, 303 U.S. 77 (1938); William O. Douglas, "Stare Decisis," *Columbia Law Review* 49, no. 6 (1949): 735–58.

26. A good political science survey of the Supreme Court's declining public approval is in James L. Gibson and Michael J. Nelson, "Changes in Institutional Support for the U.S. Supreme Court," *Public Opinion Quarterly* 80, no. 3 (2016).

27. Learned Hand, "The Deficiencies of Trials to Reach the Heart of the Matter," *Lectures on Legal Topics* 3 (1926): 89, 105.

28. Steven G. Calabresi and James Lindgren, "Term Limits for the Supreme Court: Life Tenure Reconsidered," *Harvard Journal of Law & Public Policy* 29, no. 3 (2009): 769–877.

Chapter 17 Public Policymaking and Budgeting

1. Elana Schor, "Republicans Savage Obama's Oil Tax Plan," *Politico*, February 2, 2016, http://politi.co/1P9Rxnc.

2. Deborah Stone, *Policy Paradox: The Art of Political Decision Making*, 3rd ed. (New York: Norton, 2011).

3. Woodrow Wilson, "The Study of Administration," *Political Science Quarterly* 2, no. 2 (1887): 197–222.

4. Rogan Kersh, "Health Reform: The Politics of Implementation," *Journal of Health Politics, Policy, and Law* 36, no. 3 (2011): 613–23.

5. Lawrence Hurley and John McArdle, "Supreme Court Puts Spotlight on Speed of Rulemaking," *Environment & Energy News*, December 4, 2012, http://www.eenews.net/stories /1059973307.

6. Secret Science Reform Act of 2014 (H.R. 4012).

7. "Confusing State, National Pot Policies Must Be Reconciled," Editorial, *Los Angeles Daily News*, October 23, 2011; Ramla Benmaamar, "Colorado: A First in the USA for Legal Sale of Marijuana," *Lancet Oncology* 15, no. 2 (2014): e55.

8. Emil Robert Mackey, *Street-Level Bureaucrats and the Shaping of University Housing Policy* (Fayetteville: University of Arkansas Press, 2008).

9. On this sequence, see Mark Bovens, Paul 't Hart, and Sanneke Kuipers, "The Politics of Policy Evaluation," in *Oxford Handbook of Public Policy*, ed. Michael Moran, Martin Rein, and Robert E. Goodin (New York: Oxford University Press, 2008), 320.

10. Anthony A. Braga, David M. Kennedy, Elin J. Waring, and Anne Morrison Piehl, "Problem-Oriented Policing, Deterrence, and Youth Violence: An Evaluation of Boston's Operation Ceasefire," *Journal of Research in Crime and Delinquency* 38, no. 3 (2001): 195–225.

11. Paul Pierson, "When Effect Becomes Cause: Policy Feedback and Political Change," *World Politics* 45, no. 4 (1993): 595–628; for a recent overview of policy feedback and path dependence, see Joe Soss and Donald P. Moynihan, "Policy Feedback and the Politics of Administration," *Public Administration Review* 74, no. 3 (May/June 2014): 320–32.

12. Walter I. Trattner, *From Poor Law to Welfare State: A History of Social Welfare in America*, 6th ed. (New York: Free Press, 1998).

13. Suzanne Mettler, *Soldiers to Citizens: The G.I. Bill and the Making of the Greatest Generation* (New York: Oxford University Press, 2005).

14. American Medical Association, "Goldwater–Johnson: Remarks," *Washington News* 189, no. 3 (July 20, 1964): 3.

15. A good contrast of Republican and Democratic views of fiscal policy, especially of tax cuts, is in Alexander Hertel-Fernandez and Theda Skocpol, "Congress Makes Tax Policy," in Jeffrey A. Jenkins and Eric M. Patashnik, *Congress and Policy Making in the 21st Century* (New York: Cambridge University Press, 2016).

16. For a good insider's recap of the crisis and monetary policy responses, see Timothy F. Geithner, *Stress Test: Reflections on Financial Crises* (New York: Random House, 2014), 258–387.

17. Mann, *The Broken Branch*, 2006 (see chap. 13, note 3).

18. Paul Light, *A Government Ill Executed: The Decline of the Federal Service and How to Reverse It* (Cambridge, MA: Harvard University Press, 2008).

19. On policy entrepreneurship, see Lynn Ross. *Policy Entrepreneurship: A Guide to Shaping and Understanding Policy* (Washington, DC: Brookings Institution Press, 2016).

20. President Franklin Delano Roosevelt, First Inaugural Address, March 4, 1933, http://avalon.law.yale .edu/20th_century/froos1.asp.

21. Robert Caro, *Master of the Senate* (New York: Knopf, 2002), 151–53.

Chapter 18 Foreign Policy

1. Ellen Nakashima, "Chinese Government Has Arrested Hackers It Says Breached OPM Database," *Washington Post*, December 2, 2015, http://wapo .st/1PwmNiO.

2. John Ikenberry, "America's Security Trap," *Democracy: A Journal of Ideas* 1, no. 2 (Fall 2006), http://www .democracyjournal.org/2/6481 .php?page=all.

3. Cory Turner, "U.S. Colleges See a Big Bump in International Students," *NPR News*, November 18, 2015, http://n.pr/1PPznrV.

4. Joseph Nye, *Soft Power: The Means to Success in World Politics* (New York: Public Affairs Books, 2004).

5. On the "failed" Doha Round of international trade negotiations, see Richard Baldwin, "The World Trade Organization and the Future of Multilateralism," *Journal of Economic Perspectives* 30, no. 1 (2016): 95–116, 10.1257/jep.30.1.95.

6. Paul Krugman, "How Did Economists Get It So Wrong?," *New York Times Magazine*, September 2, 2009.

7. George Washington, "First Inaugural Address, in the City of New York," April 30, 1789, http:// www.bartleby.com/124/pres13.html.

8. President Woodrow Wilson, "Joint Address to Congress Leading to Declaration of War Against Germany (1917)," April 2, 1917, https://www .ourdocuments.gov/doc_large_image .php?doc=61; Hillary Clinton, *Hard Choices* (New York: Simon & Schuster, 2014), p. 566.

9. On foreign policy and American exceptionalism, see Kalevi Holsti, *Kalevi Holsti: A Pioneer in International Relations Theory, Foreign Policy, Analysis, History of International Order, and Security Studies* (New York: Springer, 2016), chap. 8.

10. As measured by the Organisation for Economic Co-Operation and Development (OECD), see annual reports "overseas democracy assistance," OECD Development Co-operation Directorate,

"The Global Picture of Official Development Assistance," http://bit.ly/2a3lIOW.

11. For a recent summary of "democratic peace" debates in political science, see Alex Weisiger and Erik Gartzke, "Debating the Democratic Peace in the International System," *International Organization* 60 (2016), http://dx.doi.org/10.1093/isq/sqw022.

12. Pew Research Center, "Global Indicators Database: Opinion of the United States: Do You Have a Favorable or Unfavorable View of the U.S.," http://www.pewglobal.org/database/indicator/1/survey/all/.

13. George Washington, Farewell Address: To the People of the United States, September 19, 1796, http://avalon.law.yale.edu/18th_century/washing.asp.

14. A thoughtful summary appears in Richard Falk, "An Unlikely AMEXIT: Pivoting Away from the Middle East: The Case for Disengagement," *Global Justice in the 21st Century* (blog), July 14, 2016, http://bit.ly/2a8JoEz.

15. Quoted in Spencer Ackerman, "Rand Paul's Foreign Policy Speech Raises More Questions than It Answers," *The Guardian*, April 9, 2015, http://bit.ly/29NhWsE.

16. Ken Waltz, "Why Iran Should Get the Bomb," *Foreign Affairs*, July/August 2012; John Mearsheimer, "Here We Go Again," *New York Times*, May 17, 1998 [Opinion], http://www.nytimes.com/1998/05/17/opinion/here-we-go-again.html.

17. Secretary William Perry quoted in Jerry Brown, "A Stark Nuclear Warning," *New York Review of Books*, July 14, 2016, p. 11.

18. Philip Lohaus, "The Foreign Policy Message Millennials Need," *U.S. News & World Report*, April 13, 2016, http://bit.ly/29nm2Wn.

19. These categories are adopted from Walter Russell Mead, *Special Providence: American Foreign Policy and How It Changed the World* (New York: Routledge, 2001).

20. Woodrow Wilson, "First Inaugural Address," March 4, 1913, http://www.pbs.org/wgbh/americanexperience/features/primary-resources/tr-woodrow/.

21. Robert Mann, *A Grand Delusion: America's Descent into Vietnam* (New York: Basic Books, 2002), 24.

22. Arthur Vandenberg, *American Foreign Policy, January 10, 1945 (In the Senate)*, http://www.senate.gov/artandhistory/history/resources/pdf/VandenbergSpeech.pdf.

23. President George W. Bush, Graduation Address, United States Military Academy, June 1, 2002, https://georgewbush-whitehouse.archives.gov/news/releases/2002/06/20020601-3.html.

24. President Barack Obama, Graduation Address, United States Military Academy, May 28, 2014, https://www.whitehouse.gov/the-press-office/2014/05/28/remarks-president-united-states-military-academy-commencement-ceremony.

Credits

Photos

About the Authors

p. xv: Gabby Salazar; p. xiv: WFU/Ken Bennett

Preface

p. xvi: Joe Amon, The Denver Post

Chapter 1

p. 2: AP Photo/Mary Altaffer; p. 4: © Bettmann/CORBIS; p. 4: Kyodo via AP Images; p. 6: AP Photo/Alex Brandon, Pool; p. 8: Getty/Mark Wilson; p. 9: © Bettmann/CORBIS; p. 10: AP Photo/Suzanne Plunket; p. 11: Andy Katz/Pacific Press; p. 11: Rex Features via AP Images; p. 11: Huntington Beach Police Department via AP; p. 13: Gary Varvel; p. 17: Library of Congress Prints and Photographs Division Washington D.C. 20540 USA

Chapter 2

p. 22: Courtesy of the U.S. Air Force. Photo by Sgt Aaron D. Allmon II; p. 25: © Bettmann/CORBIS; p. 26: Philip Dawe (attributed), The Bostonians Paying the Excise-man, or Tarring and Feathering (31 October 1774) p. 28: Jim Morin, *The Miami Herald*; p. 31: AP Photo/Nick Ut, File; p. 33: Mark Seliger, TIME; p. 35: AP Photo/The Star-Ledger, David Gard, POOL; p. 37: Gary Cosby Jr.,/The Tuscaloosa News via AP; p. 39: Photo by MPI/Getty Images; p. 46: AP Photo Rick Bowmer; p. 46: JustASC/Shutterstock.com Copyright © 2003–2012, Shutterstock Images LLC; p. 51: DOONESBURY © 2011 G.B. Trudeau. Reprinted with permission of UNIVERSAL UCLICK. All rights reserved; p. 52: a katz/Shutterstock.com

Chapter 3

p. 56: Time & Life Pictures/Getty Images; p. 60: Signing of the Mayflower Compact Edward Percy Moran (1862–1935 American) © SuperStock/SuperStock; p. 62: Jackson Walker Orlando Florida Artist © 2010 All rights reserved; p. 64: Image copyright © The Metropolitan Museum of Art. Image source: Art Resource, NY; p. 68: The Art Archive at Art Resource, NY; p. 69: The Granger Collection, NYC—All rights reserved.; p. 71: Image copyright © The Metropolitan Museum of Art. Image source: Art Resource, NY; p. 71: © Corbis; p. 73: Courtesy of the Saint Louis Art Museum/The County Election; Saint Louis Art Museum, Gift of Bank of America 45:2001; p. 75: Commissioned by Delaware, Pennsylvania, and New Jersey State Societies Daughters of the American Revolution Independence National Historical Park Collection, 1987; p. 81: Original Photographers: McPherson and Oliver. Part of the Blakeslee Collection, apparently collected by John Taylor of Hartford, Connecticut, USA–Archive national des

États-Unis-National Archives and Records Administration; p. 88: Superstock; p. 90: Sara Krulwich/The New York Times/Redux; p. 93: Christopher Futcher/Getty Images

Chapter 4

p. 98: Dean J. Koepfler/The News Tribune; p. 100: POOL/REUTERS/Michael Macor; p. 103: AP Photo/Jim Urquhart; p. 108: Boston Globe/Getty Images; p. 110: Widening the Augusta Canal 1875, by Bernard Willington. Oil on Canvas. Painted in 2006; p. 110: Copyright Bettmann/Corbis/AP Images; Brooks Kraft/Corbis/AP Images; p. 111: "In Two Words, Yes and No." A 1949 Herblock Cartoon, copyright by The Herb Block Foundation; p. 112: Jason Reed/Reuters; p. 114: Rob Kerr/Getty Images; p. 115: Nick Anderson; p. 119: Andrew Harrer/Bloomberg via Getty Images; p. 121: The First American Macadam Road by Carl Rakeman (1823). Federal Highway Administration, United States Department of Transportation; p. 122: REUTERS/Mary Schwalm

Chapter 5

p. 124: AP Photo/Doug McSchooler; p. 127: Confederate Til Death/English Wikipedia; p. 128: © Bettmann/CORBIS; p. 131: AP Photo/Alan Mothner, File; p. 133: AP Photo/David J. Phillip; p. 135: AP Photo/Harry Cabluck; p. 135: AP Photo/Roger Alford; p. 136: AP Photo/Javier Galeano; p. 139: AP Photo/Alaric Lambert; p. 140: Photo by Dylan Slagle, Carroll County Times; p. 141: Mark Peterson/Redux/eyevine; p. 141: Mark Peterson/Redux/eyevine; p. 142: Clay Good/ZUMA Press; p. 143: © REUTERS/Svein Ove Ekornesvaag/NTB Scanpix/Files; p. 145: Rex Features via AP Images; p. 146: AP Photo/Tony Gutierrez, File; p. 151: Copyright Bettmann/Corbis/AP Images; p. 154: Gina Ferazzi/Getty Images

Chapter 6

p. 158: Melissa Renwick, Toronto Star; p. 162: © Bettmann/CORBIS; p. 163: AFP PHOTO/Ramzi HAIDAR; p. 165: Library of Congress Prints and Photographs Division Washington, D.C. 20540 USA http://hdl.loc.gov/loc.pnp/pp.print; p. 167: photography by Lawrence Beitler; August 7, 1930; p. 169: Copyright Bettmann/Corbis/AP Images; p. 169: Copyright Bettmann/Corbis/AP Images; p. 170: Copyright Bettmann/Corbis/AP Images; p. 171: AP Photo/File; p. 174: Stanley Forman for The Boston Herald American; p. 175: AP Photo/Jacquelyn Martin; p. 177: Photo by Larry Radloff/ICON Sportswire via AP Images; p. 181: Adam Jones, PhD; p. 182: Courtesy of the Department of Special Collections, Stanford University Libraries; p. 184: AP Photo/Matt Rourke; p. 187: U.S. National Archives and Records Administration; p. 188: Frontier Forts; p. 189: Hannah Foslien/Getty Images

Chapter 7

p. 198: The Washington Post; p. 202: AP Photo/Julio Cortez; p. 204: Rex Features via AP Images; p. 208: Jake Fuller; p. 215: mamado/istock; p. 216: AP Photo/ Charlotte Observer, Diedra Laird; p. 217: Douglas Graham/Getty Images

Chapter 8

p. 220: Congressional Quarterly/Getty Images; p. 222: David Howells/Getty Images; p. 224: AP Photo/J. Pat Carter; p. 225: AP Photo/The Brownsville Herald, Brad Doherty; p. 230: AP Photo/Files; p. 231: Salwan Georges/Washington Post; p. 233: REUTERS/Jeff Haynes; p. 235: Getty/Chip Somodevilla; p. 237: Dave Granlund/Cagle Cartoons; p. 237: CartoonStock.com–Rob Rogers/Pittsburgh Post Gazette; p. 241: ZUMA Press/Alamy

Chapter 9

p. 248: Bill Clark/CQ Roll Call via AP Images; p. 250: Ronald Reagan Speaks Out Against Socialized Medicine LP Cover (1961). http://www.huffingtonpost .com/rj-eskow/operation-coffeecup-reaga_b_45444 .html; p. 250: Twitter/Donald J. Trump; p. 252: Twitter/Donald J. Trump; p. 253: Joe Heller/Cagle Cartoons; p. 256: The Granger Collection, NYC–All Rights Reserved; p. 257: AP Photo; p. 258: Photo by Paul Schutzer/Time & Life Pictures/Getty Images; p. 263: iStock/welcomia; p. 263: Kevin Mazur; p. 266: AP Photo/Matt Rourke; p. 271: AP Photo/Nick Ut; p. 272: AP Photo/Chris O'Meara

Chapter 10

p. 278: Tasos Katopodis/Stringer/Getty Images; p. 280: Source: Senate Office of Public Records lobbying database; p. 289: AP Photo/Cheryl Senter; p. 293: © Bettmann/CORBIS; p. 294: Time Life Pictures/ National Archives/Time Life Pictures/ Getty Images; p. 295: Alex Wong; p. 298: AP Photo/Rogelio V. Solis; p. 299: Hulton Archive/Getty Images; p. 299: Photo By Douglas Graham/Roll Call via Getty Images Copyright © Roll Call Group; p. 302: U.S. Senate Collection, Center for Legislative Archives, National Archives; p. 303: © Bettmann/CORBIS; p. 310: The Granger Collection, NYC–All rights reserved; p. 310: John Darkow

Chapter 11

p. 314: Photo by Tom Williams/CQ Roll Call/Getty Images; p. 319: National Archives/MCT/Newscom; p. 319: Mario Tama/Getty Images; p. 320: AP Photo/ Michael Sohn; p. 322: © CORBIS; p. 322: AP Photo/ Tom Olmscheid; p. 324: duncan1890/iStock; p. 325: © CORBIS; p. 326: © CORBIS; p. 326: The Granger Collection, NYC–All rights reserved; p. 327: History. com Photo Galleries (Prohibition); p. 329: Kevin KAL Kallaugher, The Economist, Kaltoons.com; p. 333: REUTERS/Chris Keane/TPX IMAGES OF THE DAY; p. 335: AP Photo/Matt Rourke; p. 335: Photo by Zach D. Rogers/NurPhoto/SipA via AP Images; p. 341: Scott Stantis/USA Today

Chapter 12

p. 344: Joe Amon/Contributor; p. 347: Alex Wong/ Getty Images; p. 348: Cagle Cartoons–Archive for Brian Fairrington; p. 348: AP Photo/Mickey Krakowski; p. 350: AP Photo/Brennan Linsley; p. 350: AP Photo/John Hanna; p. 353: AP Photo/Alex Brandon; p. 356: AP Photo/Al Goldis; p. 357: AP Photo/Charles Dharapak; p. 360: REUTERS/Joshua Roberts; p. 367: Hannibal Pictures/Rollercoaster Entertainment/Art Takes Over Films; p. 368: Jonathan McIntosh

Chapter 13

p. 372: Tom Williams/CQ Roll Call/Getty Images; p. 376: AP Photo/J. Scott Applewhite; p. 380: FPG Getty Images; p. 386: AP Photo/J. Scott Applewhite; p. 387: AP Photo/Charles Dharapak; p. 394: AP Photo/ Giles Communications, Ron Thomas; p. 396: Chip Somodevilla/Getty Images; p. 398: Tom Williams/ Getty Images; p. 399: Tom Williams/CQ Roll Call; p. 403: Copyright Bettmann/Corbis/AP Images; p. 406: John Darkow politicalcartoons.com

Chapter 14

p. 410: Ida Mae Astute/Contributor/Getty Images; p. 414: Corbis ©; p. 414: Mario Tama/Staff; p. 415: Joseph Parrish, Chicago Tribune; p. 417: AP Photo/ Ringo H.W. Chiu; p. 418: John Cole/Cagle Cartoons; p. 420: AP Photo/Ron Edwards; p. 421: © Reuters; p. 422: AP Photo/Scott Stewart; p. 425: AP Photo/ Evan Vucci; p. 428: AP Photo/Greg Gibson; p. 429: © Bettmann/CORBIS; p. 430: LBJ Library Photo by Yoichi R. Okamoto; p. 432: AP Photo/Doug Mills; p. 437: Rich Lipski/Copyright Bettmann/Corbis/AP Images; p. 438: Charles Ommanney/Contributor; p. 438: Pool/Pool; p. 439: Aaron P. Bernstein/Stringer/ Getty Images; p. 440: REX/Shutterstock; p. 446: AP Photo/The White House, Pete Souza

Chapter 15

p. 448: Scott Free Productions/Kinberg Genre/TSG Entertainment/20th Century Fox; p. 452: The Granger Collection, NYC—All rights reserved; p. 453: The Granger Collection, NYC—All rights reserved; p. 455: FRED R. CONRAD/© The New York Times; p. 456: Greg Allen/NPR; p. 459: AP Photo; p. 463: SAUL LOEB/AFP/Getty Images; p. 464: David J. Phillip/AFP/Getty Images; p. 464: Photo by Joe Raedle/Getty Images; p. 468: The Granger Collection, NYC–All rights reserved; p. 469: DAVID FURST/ Stringer/Getty Images; p. 470: Jeff Parker/Florida Today; p. 473: © Debbie Noda/Modesto Bee; p. 476: AP Photo/Kate Brumback; p. 477: The Granger Collection, NYC–All rights reserved

Chapter 16

p. 480: REUTERS/Kevin Lamarque; p. 485: Jaap Buitendijk, DreamWorks; p. 487: AP Photo/Andy Manis; p. 492: The Granger Collection, NYC–All rights reserved; p. 493: Florida Politics; p. 497: AP Photo/Dana Verkouteren; p. 498: Missouri Department of Corrections; p. 500: Photo by CNP/Getty Images; p. 501: AP Photo/Pablo Martinez Monsivais, Pool; p. 501: CD1 WENN Photos/Newscom; p. 508: Library of Congress Prints and Photographs Division Washington, D.C. 20540 USA; p. 508: Copyright Bettmann/Corbis/AP Images; p. 510: AP Photo/Bill Haber; p. 510: Photo by Fotosearch/Getty Images;

p. 511: © Chris Stewart/San Francisco Chronicle/Corbis; p. 513: Greg Gibson/AFP/Getty Images

Chapter 17

p. 520: Lucy Nicholson/Reuters; p. 525: STR/EPA/Newscom; p. 526: STAHLER © 1999 Jeff Stahler. Reprinted by Permission of Universal Uclick for UFS. All rights reserved; p. 529: AP Photo/Reed Saxon; p. 532: HO/REUTERS/Newscom; p. 535: Walter P. Reuther Library, Wayne State University; p. 536: AP Photo; p. 540: Sandy Huffaker/Bloomberg via Getty Images; p. 549: TriStar Pictures/The Allegiance Theater/IM Global/Smoke House Pictures; p. 552: AP Photo/Steve Yeater

Chapter 18

p. 556: AP Photo/Andy Wong, Pool; p. 561: © Macduff Everton/CORBIS; p. 568: The Granger Collection, NYC–All rights reserved; p. 570: "War's First Casualty," America First Committee, propaganda poster from World War I (litho), American School, (20th century)/Private Collection/Topham Picturepoint/The Bridgeman Art Library; p. 571: U.S. Navy photo by Mass Communication Specialist 2nd Class James R. Evans/Released; p. 576: Jonathan Ernst/Reuters; p. 582: © STR/epa/Corbis; p. 585: KAREN BLEIER/AFP/Getty Images

Figures

Chapter 1

p. 12: Created by OUP based on data from Gallup. Copyright © 2016 Gallup, Inc. All rights reserved. The content is used with permission; however, Gallup retains all rights of republication; p. 13: Created by OUP based on data from usgovernmentspending.com; p. 15: Created by OUP based on data from the OECD; p. 15: Created by OUP based on data from the Cornell Chronicle/Cornell Survey Research Institute; p. 18: Created by OUP based on data from the Pew Research Center

Chapter 2

p. 28: Created by OUP based on data from Gallup; p. 30: Created by OUP using data from http://nyconstitution.org/issue/Referendum; p. 33: Gallup; p. 38: Created by OUP using data from the Pew Research Center Global Attitudes Project. American Exceptionalism Subsides: The American-Western European Values Gap, November 17, 2011; updated February 29, 2012; p. 42: Created by OUP based on data from Robert Frank, Falling Behind. University of California Press, 2007; p. 42: Created by OUP based on data from Elizabeth Sawhill and John Morton, Economic Mobility: Is the American Dream Alive and Well? Economic Mobility Project, Pew Charitable Trusts; Larry Bartells, Unequal Democracy (Princeton, NJ: Princeton University Press/ Russell Sage Foundation, 2008), Chap. 1; p. 43: Created by OUP based on data from the OECD © 2014. OECD calculations based on the World Top Income Database; p. 45: Created by OUP based on data from the 1952 polling based on University of Michigan National Election Survey. Copyright © 2014 Gallup, Inc. All rights reserved; p. 45: Created by OUP

based on data from MacArthur Foundation; p. 48: Created by OUP based on data from the Pew Research Center; p. 49: Created by OUP based on data from the Pew Research Center; p. 49: Created by OUP based on data from the Pew Research Center. Source: The Future of World Religions: Population Growth Projections, 2010–2050

Chapter 3

p. 62: Helen Hornbeck Tanner, Atlas of Great Lakes Indian History (Norman, Univ. of OK Press, 1987); p. 77: Source: http://uselectionatlas.org/FORUM/index.php?action=profile;u=256); p. 95: Created by OUP based on data from the Spring 2015 Global Attitudes Survey; p. 95: Created by OUP based on data from the General Social Survey; The Washington Post

Chapter 4

p. 102: Created by OUP based on data from Gallup; p. 104: Created by OUP based on data from the Kaiser Family Foundation; p. 108: Created by OUP; p. 111: Created by OUP; p. 116: Center for Internet and Society, 'Automated Driving' Policy Tracker (2016); p. 111: Haeyoun Park, Jeremy Ashkenas, and Mike Bostock, "Taking the Battle to the States," New York Times, January 11, 2014 © 2014 The New York Times Company; p. 120: Created by OUP based on data from the OECD National Account Statistics

Chapter 5

p. 147: National Conference of State Legislatures; p. 149: Created by OUP; p. 153: Created by OUP based on data from the Death Penalty Information Center

Chapter 6

p. 164: Created by OUP; p. 172: Created by OUP; p. 176: Created by OUP; p. 177: Created by authors; p. 185: Created by OUP based on data from the U.S. Census Bureau; p. 186: Created by OUP based on data from the U.S. Census Bureau; p. 191: Created by OUP based on data from the CDC; p. 194: Created by OUP based on data from the U.S. Census Bureau and the Pew Research Center; p. 195: Created by OUP Based on data from the U.S. Census Bureau

Chapter 7

p. 200: Created by OUP based on data from the Pew Research Center; p. 201: Created by OUP based on data from the Pew Research Center; p. 203: Created by OUP based on data from the Pew Research Center; p. 205: Created by OUP based on data from Gallup; p. 207: Created by OUP based on data from the Pew Research Center; p. 209: Created by OUP based on data from the Pew Research Center; p. 210: Created by OUP based on data from the Pew Research Center

Chapter 8

p. 225: Created by OUP based on data from the Brookings Institution; p. 228: Created by OUP based on data from the U.S. Census Bureau, Current Population Survey; p. 229: Created by OUP based on data from the U.S. Census Bureau, Current Population

Survey; p. 230: Created by OUP based on data from the Pew Research Center; p. 234: Pew Research Center; p. 236: Edleman; p. 239: Created by OUP based on data from the Pew Research Center; p. 242: Created by OUP based on data from the Pew Research Center; p. 244: Created by OUP based on data from the Pew Research Center

Chapter 9

p. 255: Pew Research Center, June 2015; p. 259: PRRI/Brookings, Religion, Values and Immigration Reform Survey Panel Call Back, June 2014; p. 261: Gallup; p. 262: Lars Willnat and David H. Weaver, The American Journalist in the Digital Age (Indiana University, 2014), p. 11; p. 268: Created by OUP based from data by © FrugalDad

Chapter 10

p. 284: Source: https://www.opensecrets.org/overview/; p. 286: Created by OUP based on data from the Center for Responsive Politics; p. 287: Sources: Washington Post Information Graphics, April 2, 2014, © 1996–2014, The Washington Post; Federal Election Commission, http://www.fec.gov/info/contriblimitschart1516.pdf; Open Secrets, http://www.opensecrets.org/pacs/; p. 292: Created by OUP based on data from Real Clear Politics Republican Nomination Average; p. 300: Created by Authors; p. 303: Created by OUP; p. 308: Created by OUP based on data from Steve Benen, Maddowblog

Chapter 11

p. 316: Created by OUP based on data from the Pew Research Center 2012 Values Survey; p. 330: Created by OUP based on data from the Pew Research Center; p. 338: Created by OUP based on data from National Conference of State Legislatures (Copyright 2016)

Chapter 12

p. 359: Created by OUP; p. 360: Created by OUP; p. 362: Created by OUP based on data from the Center for Responsive Politics; p. 364: Created by OUP based on data from Center for Responsive Politics http://www.opensecrets.org/industries/

Chapter 13

p. 379: Created by OUP based on data from the Pew Research Center; Source: CQ Roll Call, Congressional Research Service, Brookings Institution; p. 392: Created by OUP based on data by GovTrack from Civic Impulse, LLC; p. 398: Created by OUP based on data from the U.S. Senate; p. 400: Created by OUP based on data from WVUSAdvocacy; p. 402: Created by OUP based on data from "Political Polarization in the American Public" Pew Research Center, 2014; p. 403: Created by OUP based on data from Gallup (2012)

Chapter 14

p. 419: Created by OUP based on data from Historical Statistics, Statistical Abstracts; p. 426: Created by OUP based on data from Gallup's Presidential Job Approval Center; p. 433: Created by OUP based on data from Gallup's Presidential Job Approval Center

Chapter 15

p. 450: Created by OUP based on data from Gallup. Copyright © 2012 Gallup, Inc. All rights reserved. The content is used with permission; however, Gallup retains all rights of republication; p. 450: Created by OUP based on data from the U.S. Census; p. 454: U.S. Department of Energy; p. 458: Created by OUP based on data from the Office of Management and Budget; p. 467: Provided by Authors and Created by OUP; p. 474: Created by OUP based on data from usgovernmentspending.com

Chapter 16

p. 484: Created by OUP based on data from Gallup; p. 486: Created by OUP; p. 488: Created by OUP; p. 490: Created by OUP; p. 493: Ryan Emenaker "Constitutional Interpretation and Congressional Overrides: Changing Trends in Court-Congress Relations," Journal of Legal Metrics 2 (2013): 197–236; p. 504: Created by OUP based on data from Lee Epstein, Christopher M. Parker, and Jeffrey A. Segal, "Do Justices Defend the Speech They Hate?"; p. 505: Created by OUP based on data from Pew Research Center

Chapter 17

p. 522: Created by OUP; p. 529: Created by OUP based on data from the Congressional Budget Office; p. 531: Created by OUP based on data from ATTN:, Inc. All rights reserved; p. 538: Created by OUP based on data from the Congressional Budget Office; p. 542: Created by OUP based on data from The Heritage Foundation. All Rights Reserved, p. 543: Adapted from the House of Representative Committee on the Budget

Chapter 18

p. 558: Created by OUP based on data from the Stockholm International Peace Research Institute; p. 560: Created by OUP based on data from the Defense Industry Daily, LLC; p. 562: Created by OUP based on data from www.globalissues.org and the OECD; p. 564: Created by OUP based on data from The World Bank Group; p. 566: Created by OUP based on data from PSRA and the Pew Research Center; p. 570: Created by OUP based on data from Pew Research Center; p. 577: Created by OUP based on data from the GlobeScan Poll for the BBC; p. 579: Adapted from Steven Hook, U.S. Foreign Policy: The Paradox of World Power (Washington, D.C.: CQ Press, 2010), 83–84; p. 581: Created by OUP. Office of Management and Budget; p. 626: Created by OUP based on data from www.globalissues.org and the OECD; p. 629: Created by OUP based on data from PSRA and the Pew Research Center; p. 643: Created by OUP based on data from The World Bank Group; p. 645: Adapted from Steven Hook, U.S. Foreign Policy: The Paradox of World Power (Washington, D.C.: CQ Press, 2010), 83–84.; p. 647: Created by OUP based on data from the Pew Research Center

Index

Note: Page numbers followed by *f* and *t* indicate a figure or table on the indicated page. Page numbers in italics refer to photographs or illustrations.

I-1